International Security Studies

This new textbook provides students with a comprehensive and accessible introduction to the subject of Security Studies, with a strong emphasis on the use of case studies.

In addition to presenting the major theoretical perspectives, the book examines a range of important and controversial topics in modern debates, covering both traditional military and non-military security issues such as proliferation, humanitarian intervention, food security and environmental security. Unlike most standard textbooks, the volume also offers a wide range of case studies – including chapters on the US, China, the Middle East, Russia, Africa, the Arctic, Europe and Latin America – providing detailed analyses of important global security issues.

The thirty-four chapters contain pedagogical features such as textboxes, summary points and recommended further reading, and are divided into five thematic sections:

– **Conceptual and Theoretical**
– **Military Security**
– **Non-Military Security**
– **Institutions and Security**
– **Case Studies**

This textbook will be essential reading for all students of Security Studies and highly recommended for students of Critical Security Studies, Human Security, peace and conflict studies, foreign policy and International Relations in general.

Peter Hough is Associate Professor in International Politics at Middlesex University, and author of *Understanding Global Security* (3rd edn, Routledge 2013) and *Environmental Security* (Routledge 2014).

Shahin Malik is Senior Lecturer in International Relations at London Metropolitan University and co-author of *World Politics* (2011).

Andrew Moran is Associate Professor of International Relations and a University Teaching Fellow at London Metropolitan University.

Bruce Pilbeam is Senior Lecturer in Politics and International Relations at London Metropolitan University and author of *Conservatism in Crisis?* (2003).

International Security Studies
Theory and practice

Peter Hough, Shahin Malik, Andrew Moran and Bruce Pilbeam

Routledge
Taylor & Francis Group

LONDON AND NEW YORK

First published 2015
by Routledge
2 Park Square, Milton Park, Abingdon, Oxon OX14 4RN

and by Routledge
711 Third Avenue, New York, NY 10017

Routledge is an imprint of the Taylor & Francis Group, an informa business

British Library Cataloguing-in-Publication Data
A catalogue record for this book is available from the British Library

Library of Congress Cataloging-in-Publication Data
International security studies : theory and practice / [edited by] Peter
Hough, Shahin Malik, Andrew Moran, Bruce Pilbeam.
pages cm
Includes bibliographical references and index.
ISBN 978-0-415-73435-6 (hardback) – ISBN 978-0-415-73437-0 (paperback)
– ISBN 978-1-315-81681-4 (ebook) 1. Security, International. 2. Food
security. I. Hough, Peter, 1967-
JZ5588.I585 2015
355′.033–dc23
2014036439

ISBN: 978-0-415-73435-6 (hbk)
ISBN: 978-0-415-73437-0 (pbk)
ISBN: 978-1-315-81681-4 (ebk)

Typeset in Baskerville
by Saxon Graphics Ltd, Derby

Contents

Figures

Tables

Boxes

Contributors

Felix Abt is a Swiss entrepreneur. In 2002 the Swedish engineering group ABB appointed Felix its country director for North Korea. He lived and worked in North Korea for seven years, one of the few foreign businessmen there. After the experience Abt felt compelled to write *A Capitalist in North Korea* to describe the multifaceted society he had encountered. North Korea at that time (as now) was heavily sanctioned by the UN, which made it extremely difficult to do business. However, he discovered that it was a place where plastic surgery and South Korean TV dramas were wildly popular, and where he rarely needed to walk more than a block to grab a quick hamburger. He was closely monitored, and once faced accusations of spying, but he learned that young North Koreans are hopeful – signing up for business courses in anticipation of a brighter, more open future. In *A Capitalist in North Korea*, Abt shares these and many other unusual facts and insights about one of the world's most secretive nations.

Tunç Aybak is currently the Director of the International Politics Programme in the School of Law at Middlesex University. He graduated in International Relations and Diplomacy from the University of Ankara in Turkey and completed his PhD at the University of Hull in International Law and Politics. He teaches on the BA International Politics and MA International Relations programmes at Middlesex University, specialising in geopolitics, diplomacy, foreign policy analysis, international political economy and the politics of Europe. His main research areas and field work include Turkish and Russian foreign policy, citizenship and identity issues in Europe, the enlargement of the EU, energy geopolitics and pipelines with particular reference to human security issues in the Black Sea and the Middle East area. He is currently working on research projects to be published on *Europe's Final Frontier* and *Critical Geopolitics of Pipelines*.

Jeffrey Haynes is Associate Dean (Research), Head of the School of Social Sciences, and Director of the Centre for the Study of Religion, Conflict and Cooperation in the Faculty of Social Sciences and Humanities at London Metropolitan University. He has research interests in the following areas: religion and international relations; religion and politics; democracy and democratisation; development studies; and comparative politics and globalisation. He has written many books, journal articles and book chapters, totalling around two hundred such publications since 1986. His most recent and forthcoming books are: *Religion and Political Change in the Modern World* (editor), London, Routledge, 2014; *Religion, Secularism and Politics* (co-edited with Guy Ben-Porat), London, Routledge, 2014; *Faith-based Organisations at the United Nations*, New York, Palgrave Macmillan, 2014; and *Handbook of Religion and Politics* (editor), 2nd ed., London, Routledge, 2015.

Peter Hough lectures in International Relations and is based at Middlesex University, London. He graduated from the London School of Economics and Political Science. His chief areas of research interest are human security and global environmental politics. Among his most prominent publications are the following single-authored books: *Understanding Global Security* (Routledge, 3rd ed. 2013), *The Arctic in International Politics: Coming in From the Cold* (Routledge, 2013), and *Environmental Security: an Introduction* (Routledge, 2014).

Neil Hughes is the Director of Modern Language Teaching at the University of Nottingham. He is a Hispanist with research interests in both Spanish and Latin American political economics and the uses of technology in language and area studies teaching.

Shahin Malik is a Senior Lecturer in International Relations and Security Studies at London Metropolitan University, where he has taught since 2000. He completed his PhD at the University of Birmingham and has previously taught at the University of Wales Swansea. He is Course Leader for the MA in Security Studies, is closely involved with delivering and managing the MA in International Relations, and teaches core modules on the BA in International Relations. His previous publications include *Peacekeeping and the United Nations* (Dartmouth, 1996), *Deconstructing and Reconstructing the Cold War* (Ashgate, 1999) and, most recently, a co-authored book entitled *World Politics* (Pearson, 2011).

Dermot McCann undertook his graduate studies at the European University Institute in Florence. His teaching and research are focused on European and European Union politics. His most recent book is entitled *The Political Economy of the European Union: An institutionalist perspective*, Polity, 2010.

Andrew Moran has a PhD in American Political Economy and has taught at London Metropolitan University since 1993, where he is Course Leader for the BA International Relations and BA International Development programmes. He has contributed to scholarly journals such as *Presidential Studies Quarterly*, *White House Studies*, *Political Studies*, *Party Politics*, *The Amicus Journal*, and *Democratization* (for which he was also the Book Reviews Editor) and has appeared on *BBC News 24*, *CNN* and *Bloomberg TV*. Andrew's research interests include the foreign policy, history and politics of the United States of America, the death penalty, cyberspace, and International Relations.

Lloyd Pettiford is based at Nottingham Trent University, and he has published numerous books across a range of topics in International Relations, from environmental politics, democratisation and security to IR theory, foreign policy analysis and area studies. He is currently Associate Dean of the School of Arts and Humanities and is teaching and researching on Holocaust and Genocide and Latin American Studies.

Bruce Pilbeam has a PhD from the University of Sheffield and is a Senior Lecturer in Politics and International Relations at London Metropolitan University. His main teaching and research interests are in the areas of International Relations, International Conflict Resolution and US politics. His previous publications include the book *Conservatism in Crisis?* (Palgrave Macmillan, 2003), as well as articles in journals such as *Political Studies* and the *Journal of Political Ideologies*.

Ronald Ranta is a lecturer in Politics and the Arab–Israeli conflict at University College of London. He has also taught the Arab–Israeli conflict at SOAS, Kingston University and the University of Bath. He is the author of *Non Decision Making: Israel and the Occupied Territories 1967–1977* (Palgrave Macmillan, 2014). He is currently writing on the place of Palestinians in the construction of Israeli identity, *Palestinian Culture, Israeli Identity: Contesting Food and Language in the Middle East* (Ashgate, forthcoming).

Ian Shields spent thirty-two years in the Royal Air Force as a navigator, operating both the Vulcan Bomber in a strategic strike role and later the Hercules transport aircraft. Having commanded a squadron and undertaken a variety of staff appointments he ended his career in a very academic stream, gaining an MA in War Studies from King's College, London and an MPhil in International Relations from Queen's College, Cambridge. He is now an Associate Lecturer at London Metropolitan University where he lectures in International Relations, particularly from a security perspective.

Edward Smith is a PhD student at the University of London. His thesis deals with the behaviour of the US Senate Foreign Relations Committee towards key foreign policy issues in comparison to the wider Senate Floor. He has a MSc in US Foreign Policy from the University of London and a MA in International Relations from the University of Essex. Edward has taught various modules at London Metropolitan University including International Relations Theory and International Security Studies. His wider research interests are realism in International Relations, the ideas of Nicholas Spykman, and the domestic pressures on US Foreign Policy.

Wendy Stokes is Academic Leader in Politics and International Relations at London Metropolitan University. She was a graduate student at St Antony's College, Oxford and London Guildhall University. Her research interests include gender and politics, women in politics and theories of democracy and representation. She has published in these areas, including *Women in Contemporary Politics* (Polity, 2005) and is currently researching women's political movements in the UK.

Section 1

Conceptual and theoretical

1 Framing a discipline

Shahin Malik

Box 1.1: Twenty-four-hour news

Since the end of the Cold War we have witnessed a dramatic development, often referred to as the 'CNN Effect' or 'Twenty-Four-Hour News'. We no longer have to wait for the 'News at Ten' to get the latest on what is happening around us, since we can access one of the many news networks which broadcast constantly throughout the day. Among the countless news reports there will sometimes be references to earthquakes, tsunamis and other natural disasters. In addition, correspondents will appear 'live from the battlefield' to report on conflicts in various parts of the world. Others will refer to the plight of refugees, the impact of poverty or diseases such as AIDS, and even the dangers presented by a long overdue strain of influenza which could wipe out millions of people. Closer to home, there may be references to the murder or rape of a person or persons, the state of the economy, the number of jobless people, instances of domestic violence, or the state of the climate. We cannot foresee with any certainty what the main news items will be on a particular day, but we can guarantee that some of the topics listed above will feature.

Introduction

Understanding the nature of a discipline requires us to begin by considering its central concepts. International Security Studies is no different. Much of the literature in this field has been and remains preoccupied with the meaning of 'security', but despite everything that has been written over the past two decades, consensus regarding a definition of this term has remained elusive. It is with this in mind that we have established three key objectives for this book. The first is to frame the intellectual debates within the discipline of International Security Studies by investigating a range of concepts and theories central to the field. The second is to provide an overview of the contemporary security environment, and in doing so the book intends to cover a wide variety of topics, ranging from a consideration of armed conflict to subjects such as the environment, human rights, the impact of terrorism, the role of international institutions, and food security. In the final section we present a number of key regional and thematic case studies with the intention of building upon the most important aspects of the earlier sections.

Before turning to the more detailed sections of this book, this introductory chapter provides a brief overview. It begins by tracing the evolution of the discipline of Security Studies and then considers the purpose of each of the sections and how they are linked. In order to achieve this, we refer to a number of key chapters and provide brief overviews of these in the hope that this will make it easier to use the book.

The state of the discipline – early developments

At its most basic level, 'security' refers to the protection of values we hold dear. It is for this reason that we are all interested in achieving it. We search for it, we constantly pursue it, we deny it to others, and when we achieve it for ourselves we relish it. Undoubtedly, feeling secure and well protected is one of humankind's most cherished goals. However, our incessant search for security remains one of our most fiercely debated topics, and to this day we remain unconvinced regarding the best way of achieving what is, for many, an elusive commodity. This is compounded by a number of problems facing thinkers in the field. As a concept, 'security' refers simply to the safety or protection of some entity. Traditionally, the first problem relates to whether it is the state, the individual or some other unit that ought to be prioritised and made secure. To use the correct terminology, academics debate over what the '*referent object*' should be. This debate continues today as it has over the past two decades, and it takes place primarily between those who advocate the 'state' and those who argue that the basic unit has to be the individual. This is not the end of the matter, however, since a second, related problem faces us – namely, what is the nature of the threats that face us? Again, the academic world is divided, with a variety of opinions, a significant number of which insist that military force is central to world politics and that the primary actors are states. Because of this, it becomes necessary for states to continuously guard themselves from possible attack by other states. However, an increasingly influential viewpoint is that the focus on states and military force is far too narrow and does not consider a wider range of threats that both states and individuals have to face.

We begin by asking one important question – from where did this emphasis on the state and the military come? One possible answer lies in another discipline – International Relations (IR) – with which Security Studies shares considerable common ground. The first university department dedicated to the study of international events was established at Aberystwyth in 1919, and among the many topics worthy of consideration were the causes of war. Since then the subject matter of IR has grown massively, with the terrorist attacks on 11 September 2001 coming at the end of a century which had seen key events influencing the human condition in unprecedented ways. Not only did the twentieth century see two massive world wars, it also saw humans develop (and use) weapons of immense destructive capabilities. The first half of the twentieth century was dominated by the First World War (1914–1918) which centred on Europe and involved all of the world's great powers. Twenty years later the Second World War (1939–1945) broke out when Germany invaded Poland, and eventually this too involved all of the great powers, including most other nations. Germany surrendered to the Allied forces on 7 May 1945, but the war in Asia against Japan continued until the US felt compelled to use atomic bombs on Nagasaki and Hiroshima. This attack on the two Japanese cities in August 1945 hastened the end of the Second World War in Asia, but it also ushered in an era dominated by superpower competition, the arms race, technological rivalry, and conflict short of full-scale war. The term 'Cold War' is often used to describe the period between 1945 and 1989, and although the mutual hostility between the United States and the Soviet Union varied in intensity, a number of key features are worthy of analysis.

The Cold War was characterised by intense political and economic rivalry between the two superpowers. Importantly, this competition also extended to the military sector, which led to both states engaging in an arms race which resulted in the production of huge stockpiles of nuclear weapons. During this period, Realist theory provided a powerful basis for explaining state behaviour and the pursuit of security through military and other means. On the strength of the evidence provided by the Cold War, many analysts concluded that war and conflict were indeed a central feature of the international system. In this type of system states were the key actors, and they existed under a condition of anarchy where there was no global authority capable of managing world affairs. Consequently states were compelled to search for their own security, and to achieve this they continuously sought to enhance their power by building up their armed forces, securing access to resources and balancing against other states. According to this view, trust or friendship did not feature between states, and the belief that conflict was a distinct possibility created an environment where ensuring state survival became the overriding concern.

Realist theory provided the intellectual support for the fledgling discipline which came to be known as *National Security Studies* in the United States and *Strategic Studies* in British universities. The field dominated security thinking between the 1940s and the 1980s, and its analysts set about considering how politics, geography, economic processes and military power interlinked with state concerns over their security. Ultimately the field became narrowly focused on the military security of states. Alongside this, the dominance of Realism, the nuclear revolution and the perceptions of an increasingly hostile Soviet Union provided ample justification for this narrowing. Therefore, academics within the field naturally turned to topics such as deterrence theories, arms control, disarmament, preventive war, the nuclear taboo and the impact of technology on warfare. However, given that its prime objective was to analyse the possibility of a clash between the superpowers, Strategic Studies soon came under intense criticism for its narrow focus and its dismissal of wider security concerns and other referent objects.

This narrow focus and a tendency to ignore non-military issues soon led to calls by many academics for a realignment of the discipline. Among the most notable early advocates of this were Richard Ullman and Jessica Mathews. In the 1980s Ullman argued that during the entire Cold War period 'every administration in Washington ha[d] defined American national security in excessively military terms', and that this had resulted in the relegation of the many non-military threats facing states. He went on to compare natural disasters (such as earthquakes) with nuclear conflict and stressed that the former could be equally devastating. In an article entitled 'Redefining Security' published in 1983, Ullman defined a threat to national security as 'an action or sequence of events that threatens drastically and over a relatively brief span of time to degrade the quality of life for the inhabitants of a state' (Ullman, 1983). Later, in 1989 Mathews argued along similar lines when she stressed that the concept of security had to be rethought 'so as to include awareness of mounting threats to the global environment' (Mathews, 1989). She stated that:

> The 1990s will demand a redefinition of what constitutes national security. In the 1970s the concept was expanded to include international economics as it became clear that the US economy was no longer the independent force it had once been, but was powerfully affected by economic policies in dozens of other

countries. Global developments now suggest the need for another analogous, broadening definition of national security to include resource, environmental and demographic issues.

(Mathews, 1989: 162)

However, few texts have been as influential as *People, States and Fear*. Published by Barry Buzan in 1983, the book succeeded in encouraging many to recognise the existence of specific non-military components of state security. He argued that the military security of a state was only one feature, and that states would do well to be mindful of threats to their political system, their economic resources, their society and the environment. The development of the field along these broader lines stalled, however, because of a number of key events, including the Soviet invasion of Afghanistan in 1979 and the end of détente. At this stage it appeared as if the discipline was destined to remain committed to the narrow, traditionalist views of security, defined as the 'study of the threat, use and control of military force' (Walt, 1991: 212). Although new non-military insights emerged during the 1980s, topics such as deterrence, nuclear and conventional military balances and the power projection capabilities of the superpowers remained central.

The Cold War undoubtedly had a major impact in that it not only influenced the US, causing it to view its security policy in narrow military terms, but also militarised the academic study of security. It wasn't until the Cold War ended in 1989, with the corresponding decline in tensions between the two superpowers, that the field successfully realigned itself away from the narrow preoccupations of Strategic Studies to the broader, more eclectic essence of Security Studies. This realignment was based on the increasingly influential premise that Strategic Studies was no longer adequate for dealing with post-Cold War security concerns. Suddenly the earlier work of academics such as Buzan, Mathews and Ullman began to attract increasing attention. Indeed, it was Buzan's second, and much expanded, edition of *People, States and Fear*, published in 1991, which decisively shifted the field's attention away from its preoccupation with military force.

The post-Cold War era

What has happened to Security Studies since the end of the Cold War and Buzan's publication? There is no simple answer to this question, and that is one of the reasons why we have written this book. However, one thing is certain, namely, that the field has expanded to such an extent that some have even called for it to become independent from the discipline of International Relations. Primarily we need to be concerned with three broad areas:

• Defining security
• The role of theories in the discipline
• The nature of the subject matter of Security Studies.

This book is arranged in such a way as to address these issues, with the chapters in Section 1 dealing with the definitions of security as well as the role that theories can play in illuminating the field. Section 2 acknowledges the important ongoing connections between Security Studies and the use of military force, and the various chapters in Section 3 deal with the broader non-military components of the discipline.

Defining security and using this book

As this book will show, defining security is no longer a simple task. The Cold War may have succeeded in simplifying the concept by concentrating purely on the military component of state security, but the post-Cold War era has revealed major divisions among academics. The variations are in large part dependent upon the rich array of theoretical traditions competing for centre stage within the field. Box 1.2 shows a range of views, and even a cursory glance shows significant differences.

Box 1.2: Security: multiple visions

Traditional: 'The main focus of Security Studies is easy to identify ... it is the phenomenon of war. Security Studies assumes that conflict between states is always a possibility and ... [a]ccordingly, Security Studies may be defined as the study of the threat, use, and control of military force' (Walt, 1991: 212).

'Security itself is a relative freedom from war, coupled with a relatively high expectation that defeat will not be a consequence of any war that should occur' (Bellamy, 1981: 102).

Critical Security Studies: 'Emancipation is the freeing of people ... from the physical and human constraints which stop them carrying out what they would freely choose to do ... Security and emancipation are two sides of the same coin. Emancipation, not power or order, produces true security. Emancipation, theoretically, is security' (Booth, 1991: 319).

Human Security: '... to protect the vital core of all human lives in ways that enhance human freedoms and human fulfilment. Human security means protecting fundamental freedoms – freedoms that are the essence of life. It means protecting people from critical (severe) and pervasive (widespread) threats and situations. It means using processes that build on people's strengths and aspirations. It means creating political, social, environmental, economic, military and cultural systems that together give people the building blocks of survival, livelihood and dignity' (CHS, 2003: 4).

Feminism: 'The feminist perspective is highly critical of the masculinist underpinnings of a state-centric approach and offers theoretical insights as well as practical mechanisms on how a fusion of masculine and feminine values may serve the goals of human security over and above those of the state' (Hudson, 1998).

This multi-dimensional nature of the concept has caused great confusion among those who concern themselves with the field of Security Studies, and perhaps the only way to simplify our trip through the minefield of opinions is to recognise the value of the various theoretical traditions – all of which have made valuable contributions. It is with this in mind and in order to provide coverage of security which is as broad as possible that we have arranged the chapters in this book in the following way. Section 1 of the book identifies the key theoretical traditions within Security Studies. Given the impact of the traditional approaches on the field, the first substantial chapter looks at how Liberalism, and particularly Realism, influenced the development of Strategic Studies during the Cold War. This is then followed by Chapter 3, which provides a detailed account of one of the most crucial developments in Security Studies – the debates over the key referent object. An influential book published by Keith Krause and Michael Williams in 1997 had an impact on the whole approach known as Critical Security Studies. They did not intend to develop a single unified critical theory; rather, their purpose was to create opposition to the narrowness of the traditional concepts of security. They succeeded in this endeavour and since 1997 the boundaries of the discipline have expanded considerably. Today the field is no longer tied to the state as the key referent object, and a variety of approaches highlighting the centrality of individuals, societies, and the environment (among others) have emerged.

This chapter also introduces the reader to more recent developments in the field, including Post-Structuralism and Post-Colonial views. Although very diverse in nature, the former generally takes issue with the traditionalist goals of achieving fixed and unshakeable knowledge about the concept of security. For instance, Realism rests entirely on notions of state sovereignty, military power and the anarchic international system, and supporters of this tradition unquestioningly accept these assumptions. Post-Structuralists make the crucial point that theories such as Realism fail to recognise that their central concepts have been conditioned by specific cultural positions and are therefore subject to important misinterpretations and biases. This gives rise to the possibility that a Realist understanding of the concepts is based on erroneous assumptions. Therefore, this chapter will highlight how Post-Structuralists refuse to accept any definitions which are outside linguistic and discursive practices.

Remaining with the theme of Critical Security, this section of the book also considers the impact of a growing amount of Post-Colonial literature on security which criticises the discipline for its largely Euro-centric emphasis since the Second World War. Authors within this tradition have increasingly voiced their concern over the premise that the discipline as it stands represents only a partial account of global security in its failure to seriously consider the non-European world in any analysis of the concept of security. Similarly, Chapter 4 on gender demonstrates how Feminist approaches to security have remained on the periphery of the discipline in the face of powerful traditionalist explanations. The framework highlighted by Realism is that the anarchic international system compels states to be mindful of military threats from other states. This gives the impression that the international system is dominated by conflict and populated by soldiers, diplomats, generals and their political masters. Feminist perspectives oppose this masculinist view which, in its drive to secure the state, marginalises groups such as women, thereby diminishing their value as independent agents. As this chapter will show, Feminist perspectives therefore seek to draw attention to this shortcoming in the Security Studies literature by highlighting what the discipline might look like if the concerns of marginalised groups such as women were made more central.

Other chapters in this section include a consideration of the theme of Human Security and the impact of Social Constructivism on the field of Security Studies. First coined by the United Nations in the mid-1990s, advocates of the concept of Human Security argued that it was necessary to go beyond the statist and military-centric views of traditional approaches. Consequently, the chapter on Human Security will seek to show that this perspective sees security as multi-dimensional, comprising (among other things) developmental, economic, environmental and health components in addition to military factors. The final chapter in this section deals with the importance of the arrival of Social Constructivism. This approach has been instrumental in encouraging academics to resist the rigidity imposed by traditionalist approaches to the concept of security. Also referred to as the Copenhagen School and headed by the likes of Barry Buzan and Ole Weaver, this tradition has introduced us to the notion of *Securitization*. This can be defined as the process which takes an issue out of the realm of normal everyday politics and gives it an elevated, special status. The process is dependent upon what is referred to as the *speech act*, which involves attempts by influential players in society – such as politicians – to persuade the wider community that a particular issue deserves special media, political and societal attention. Constant reference to a new issue leads to citizens becoming conditioned into accepting the seriousness of the newly constructed threat – it is at this stage that the issue becomes *securitized*.

It is in recognition of the importance and persistence of traditional approaches to security that the chapters in Section 2 are largely concerned with military issues. The list in this section is by no means exhaustive, but we are convinced that these chapters will provide an excellent overview of many of the traditional military issues which the international community still faces. The topics covered range from a consideration of the role of nuclear deterrence during the Cold War to post-Cold War periods, proliferation, the international arms trade, terrorism, the impact of religion on conflict, intelligence, the causes of war, the impact of the privatisation of security, and the security problems posed by failing or failed states. Many strategists agree that nuclear deterrence provided the basis for Cold War stability between the two superpowers, but now question whether it will continue to be as successful in the post-9/11 era given that the nuclear landscape is much more complicated. States such as North Korea, India and Pakistan have crossed the nuclear threshold in recent years, and the question emerges as to whether they will recognise the deterrent capabilities of these weapons of mass destruction in the same way as was acknowledged by the older nuclear weapon states. Pakistan's status as a nuclear power is of particular concern given that it is in the midst of a violent militant insurgency. The nightmare scenario of a nuclear warhead falling into the hands of terrorists should not be discounted. These and the other chapters in this section will, therefore, show that traditional concerns remain central to the international security mindset.

Many of the chapters in Section 1 are dedicated to showing that the state-centric military focus of traditional approaches such as Realism is now seen as inadequate by many academics. It is for this reason that the chapters in Section 3 adopt a much broader understanding of security. Indeed, many of the topics covered here cannot be analysed adequately from within a traditionalist framework, and subject areas such as the environment, food and health security, Human Security and the security implications of natural disasters must be considered as broad components of the concept of security. In Section 4 we shift our attention to the few security institutions with a global outlook, including the United Nations (UN) and the North Atlantic Treaty Organization (NATO). The fortunes of these and regional institutions have been rather mixed, and these chapters concern themselves with their ethos and purpose as well as the problems they face.

Finally, while many of the textbooks on Security Studies use examples to highlight the conceptual and theoretical features of the discipline, none of those we have reviewed brings together a large number of detailed case studies in one volume. In our long-standing experience as lecturers, we have often encountered students who, while recognising the importance of the conceptual and theoretical basis of the discipline, struggle to make connections at the practical level. In the section devoted to Regional Case Studies, our intention is to build upon some of the concepts and ideas highlighted in the earlier core chapters by relating them to key contemporary concerns. We believe that students will gain further understanding of the concepts discussed when they are given practical examples in the form of case studies. Therefore these shorter chapters will consider a wide range of issues, ranging from the objectives of great powers in the post-Cold War era to an analysis of the security dynamics of various regions, as well as a number of Human Security concerns.

Conclusion

Apart from demonstrating the ambiguous nature of the concept of security, this chapter has highlighted the kinds of topics considered by the discipline of Security Studies. This book provides an introduction to a wide variety of these topics while at the same time continuously questioning the definition of security, which is still an important source of disagreement. Some academics advocate retaining the traditionalist narrow focus, whereas others are in favour of further expansion. Traditionalist academics such as Stephen Walt have pleaded for the focus of the discipline to be restricted to 'the study of the threat, use and control of military force' (Walt, 1991: 212). They are fearful that both the concept of security and the discipline of Security Studies will lose intellectual coherence if they are expanded excessively. However, we must remain mindful that all of the topics covered in this book are essentially important components of security, and there must be a forum within which they can be considered.

Summary points

1   Some of the key debates within Security Studies have been about which entity ought to be prioritised as the key *referent object.*
2   The military, political and economic rivalry between the two superpowers during the Cold War gave rise to an intense narrowing of the field – so much so that many analysts concluded that war and conflict were a central feature of the international system.
3   The end of the Cold War encouraged the emergence of a range of perspectives which highlighted the problems with the narrow state/military-centric nature of the discipline.
4   These new perspectives have broadened the boundaries of the discipline and it is now widely recognised that there are both military as well as non-military components of security.

Recommended reading

Booth, K. 'Security and Emancipation', *Review of International Studies*, vol. 17, no. 4, 1991, 313–326.
Buzan, B. *People, States and Fear: An Agenda for International Security Studies in the Post-Cold War Era*, 2nd edition, London: Harvester Wheatsheaf, 1991.
Buzan, B., Weaver, O. and de Wilde, J. *Security: A New Framework for Analysis*, Boulder: Lynne Rienner Publishers, 1997.
Commission on Human Security (CHS), *Human Security Now: Final Report*, New York: CHS, 2003.
Krause, K. and Williams, M. *Critical Security Studies: Concepts and Cases*, London: UCL Press Ltd, 1997.

Mathews, J. 'Redefining Security', *Foreign Affairs*, vol. 68, no. 2, Spring 1989, 162–177.
Ullman, R. 'Redefining Security', *International Security*, vol. 8, no. 1, Summer 1983, 129–153.
Walt, S.M. 'The Renaissance of Security Studies', *International Studies Quarterly*, vol. 35, no. 2, June 1991, 211–239.

2 The traditional routes to security

Realism and Liberalism

Edward Smith

Box 2.1: Understanding traditionalism

One of the most enduring difficulties for students of contemporary International Security Studies is how to perceive what are deemed to be 'traditional approaches' to the field. Seemingly validated by the Cold War in their core assertions, Neorealist scholars, and to a large extent their Neoliberal counterparts, sought to build the discipline around the referent object of the state. This chapter offers an overview of the traditionalist approaches to International Security and their accompanying intellectual lineage. It provides some explanation as to the persistence of state-based approaches within International Security Studies. It attempts to justify how those who are wedded to the concept of the nation state can remain relevant when discussing the concept of security in a world that is increasingly moving towards alternative forms of political community.

Introduction

Since its inception as a distinct academic discipline, the field of Security Studies has been based on three fundamental questions that have driven debate – namely, what is the referent object of security, what are the threats it may face, and how should we provide security against such threats? For the traditionalist scholars in International Security Studies (ISS), those who draw their inspiration largely from Realist or Liberal theories in mainstream International Relations, the answer to the first of these questions is simply *states*. For these scholars, the process of globalisation, powerful as it may be, has failed to alter the most fundamental characteristic of the international system, namely, the world of sovereign state entities that was established by the Treaty of Westphalia in 1648. In light of this largely static concept of the international system, advocates of traditional security approaches insist that their continued focus on inter-state conflict is entirely justified in a world where many ISS scholars have prioritised new referent objects and defined new causes of insecurity.

However, the use of 'traditionalism' as an umbrella term, primarily employed by those who embrace a more critical interpretation of Security Studies (see Chapters 3 to 6), masks a number of important debates between Realist and Liberal security theorists. These debates revolve primarily around *what* threats are faced by states, and *how* the security of the state can be ensured in the face of such threats. This chapter will explore this debate further, and draw on the intellectual lineage of both theoretical traditions to highlight their particular approaches to defining security as a concept. This will enable students to identify the contours of traditionalist thinking within ISS, to outline the commonalities and distinctions within traditionalist approaches to ISS, and to locate the broad traditionalist school in opposition to the critical revolution within the ISS landscape.

The traditionalist preoccupation with the state

As already stated, the term 'traditionalism' within Security Studies encompasses both the Realist and Liberal perspectives on security, including the vast array of theoretical variants that are included under each of these banners, such as Classical Realism, Neorealism, Liberal Idealism, and Neoliberal Institutionalism. What makes the term 'traditionalism' viable is that all these approaches share one defining characteristic, thereby enabling critical security theorists to present the idea of a traditionalist monolith within Security Studies, namely the unwavering commitment to the state as the sole referent object of analysis. This is sometimes confusing for students who are new to ISS or International Relations, many of whom refer to the central role of *individual* agency within various classical Liberal literature sources, or the fundamental emphasis on the *international system* within Neorealist theory. However, it is important to remember that, despite their respective emphases on these 'top-down' or 'bottom-up' pressures that influence the actions of states, it is nonetheless this behaviour of *states* that remains the fundamental issue within all of the traditionalist ISS perspectives.

So why has the state as an entity dominated traditionalist concepts of security since the Second World War? This period has seen a number of important security concerns – such as guerrilla warfare in Colombia, domestic terrorism in the United Kingdom and the global AIDS epidemic – that cannot be explained simply as part of an inter-state conflict, and yet traditionalist approaches remain committed to placing the state as the primary referent object of analysis within ISS. There are theoretical and historical reasons for this. In theoretical terms, traditionalists argue that sovereign nation-states continue to be the 'building blocks' of what remains in essence a Westphalian international system. They claim that states are the primary entities through which people define their (national) identity; they are the most sophisticated units of human communal organisation within world politics; and most importantly, they are the only legitimate and significant possessors of organised violence – and hence *power* – in the international system. Such propositions were reinforced by the historical context of the Cold War, since the nuclear stand-off between the United States and the Soviet Union became the primary focus of interest for those within the realm of Strategic Studies, the forerunner of ISS.

However, a broad distinction should be drawn between precisely how Realist and Liberal practitioners of ISS perceive their referent object of analysis. For Realists, the nation-state is a rational unitary actor with a fixed and pre-determined national interest, namely the accumulation of power defined in terms of military capabilities. The sub-state level has therefore been largely ignored by Realist theorists, who assume a behavioural uniformity of self-interest among states, originating either from the flawed nature of man (classical Realists) or the pressures of an anarchic international system (Neorealists). In contrast, Liberals are not comfortable with the conceptualisation of states as unitary actors, although, as noted by their post-positivist critics, they remain largely committed to the idea of states as rational actors. Rather, Liberals are keen to explore a number of issues at the sub-state level, such as determining exactly which domestic groups governments (and hence states) are seeking to represent, or how non-governmental actors can assist in fostering inter-state cooperation. As will be discussed later in the chapter, the *Liberal Peace Theorists* have been particularly important in opening up the 'black boxes' of state actors and adopting a Kantian posture to argue that the domestic political system of a particular state may relate directly to its behaviour vis-à-vis other states.

The traditionalist approaches in ISS are therefore intrinsically linked through their adherence to a state-centric conceptualisation of international security. While this was a particularly attractive and popular lens of analysis during the era of the Cold War, affording Realist and Liberal approaches a position of primacy within the discipline, it has sparked criticism in the post-Cold War era from those keen to incorporate newer, more relevant referent objects such as the individual or society itself. It is this fierce debate over the use of the state as the primary referent object that most clearly delineates the traditional (positivist) from the newer critical (post-positivist) approaches to international security, with the former group linked primarily by their adherence to state-centrism, and the latter group united *only* by their criticism of this state-centrism. However, a number of newer perspectives concerning international security do not reject the state specifically as a referent object of analysis, but rather reject the traditionalist refusal to accept the relevance of alternative referent objects within the boundaries of ISS.

Realism and Security Studies

Let us begin by examining the Realist approach to the concept of security. Regarded by most as the dominant paradigmatic approach to ISS even today, Realism offers a crude but powerful interpretation of security, defining the term in a deliberately narrow manner, with the state as the sole referent object of analysis, and with security threats described solely in terms of military power. The Realist tradition understands that states are seeking to survive in an anarchic international system in which the primary source of insecurity stems from inter-state conflict, and therefore that the only method of achieving security is for states to maximise their own military capabilities. Yet it is important for students of ISS to understand the Realist tradition not in terms of a single, unified explanatory theory, but rather as an evolving theoretical tradition that houses a number of important conceptual strands. All Realist theories may indeed adopt a state-centric definition of security that stresses the conflictual nature of world politics, but each strand of Realism differs somewhat as to the reasons *why* this situation inevitably occurs.

If Realism remains unmatched in terms of its longevity and influence within the subfield of ISS, it is also unmatched in the degree of criticism that it has attracted, particularly during the post-Cold War era. Critics perennially accuse the Realist tradition of being irrelevant to the study of world politics today, a theoretical anachronism whose dogged emphasis on inter-state conflict undermines its explanatory power in the contemporary era. Yet the Realist tradition has proven itself to be a remarkably resilient approach when dealing with issues of international security, and continues in a position of pre-eminence within ISS that its critics have been unable to assail.

The 'classical Realist' tradition in International Relations

With an enviable intellectual ancestry that dates back to Thucydides' *History of the Peloponnesian War*, Political Realism has often been labelled the dominant theoretical tradition in the study of world politics. In addition to Thucydides, works such as Machiavelli's *The Prince* or Hobbes' *Leviathan* are also central to the Realist tradition, since they emphasise the self-interested, conflictual nature of world politics. To these, one may add the writings of military strategists such as Sun Tzu and Von Clausewitz, who presented war as an inevitable continuation of state politics, establishing a clear military dimension to the politics of Realism. Such ideas were also fundamental to the foreign policies of Europe's dynastic states between the seventeenth and early twentieth centuries, with the principles of *realpolitik* practised by a succession of renowned statesmen including Richelieu, Mazarin, Metternich and Bismarck (Lynn-Jones, 1999: 57).

When International Relations developed as an academic field of study in the aftermath of the First World War, it was figures such as these who would inspire a generation of 'classical Realists' – the likes of E.H. Carr, Reinhold Niebuhr, and Nicholas Spykman – to articulate a largely pessimistic interpretation of the international system during the inter-war period. Such authors criticised what they perceived to be a naive and 'utopian' analysis of world politics by Liberal scholars of International Relations, arguing that the flawed – or even evil – nature of the human individual would inevitably manifest itself in the aggressive behaviour of states. Within this 'First Image' interpretation of inter-state conflict, Realists were particularly critical of the League of Nations, arguing that it would ultimately fall victim to the self-interest of its member states. The failure of the League and the outbreak of the Second World War in 1939 seemed to validate much of the classical Realist pessimism with respect to world politics, particularly concerning the inevitable occurrence of inter-state conflict in an international system based on self-help.

The Cold War and the primacy of Realism in Strategic Studies

It was the onset of the Cold War in 1945, however, that firmly established the primacy of Realist thinking in the newly recognised academic discipline of *Strategic Studies*, the precursor to contemporary *International Security Studies*, thus allowing a generation of Realist thinkers to dictate the contours of 'security' for the next four decades. The key Realist literature of this era emerged in 1948 with the publication of Hans Morgenthau's *Politics among Nations: the Struggle for Power and Peace*, the most developed articulation of the classical Realist world view through its emphasis on a national interest defined in terms of maximising power. Morgenthau re-emphasised his central arguments in 1951 with the release of *In Defense of National Interest*, again highlighting the importance of national interest as the sole foundation of US foreign policy in the post-Second World War era. His argument resonated within the work of several other key scholars of Strategic Studies – the likes of Robert Osgood, Arnold Wolfers, and Henry Kissinger – all of whom contributed to defining security in fundamentally Realist terms, as a state-centric concept in which the key currency for addressing threats remained the maximisation of military power.

Box 2.2: Morgenthau's six principles of political Realism

1   Politics is governed by objective laws.
2   International politics is to be understood through the concept of interest defined in terms of power.
3   Power can change but interests remain.
4   Universal moral principles cannot be applied to the actions of states.
5   No universally agreed moral framework.
6   The realm of politics is autonomous.

Although Morgenthau's work provided an important articulation of the Realist world view, it was the simultaneous emergence of a bipolar international system and the development of nuclear weapons which allowed Realism to establish itself as the dominant theoretical approach to defining the concept of security. Indeed, the nuclear standoff between the superpower rivals served to explicitly link ideas of national security, geopolitics, territorial sovereignty and military power into a new concept of security that was espoused by the likes of George Kennan and Paul Nitze. This was soon institutionalised within the Truman administration with the assistance of the National Security Act (1947) which established the Department of Defense, the National Security Council, and the Central Intelligence Agency. This was followed three years later by Nitze's infamous NSC-68 document that became the blueprint for US foreign policy throughout the remainder of the Cold War, framing US security interests solely in the context of combating the threat of the Soviet Union through a containment strategy based on its conventional and nuclear military capabilities.

The early years of the Cold War therefore saw classical Realism emerge as the dominant theoretical paradigm within Strategic Studies, dictating not simply *what* were the key issues of international politics (the superpower rivalry), but also *how* such problems (containment, nuclear deterrence etc.) should be addressed by the policy-makers of the day. The dual emergent pressures of systemic bipolarity and advanced nuclear delivery systems shaped the international system in a manner that could be easily accommodated within the classical Realist tradition, and that had come to dominate the field of Strategic Studies by the close of the 1950s since other aspects of security had become firmly marginalised within this state-centric, military focused paradigm (Buzan and Hansen, 2009: 27). This process served to merge the concepts of 'security' and 'strategy' within Strategic Studies, a fusion that would ultimately remain intact until the critical revolution within ISS during the 1990s.

The emergence of Neorealism

By the 1970s, the Cold War had begun to thaw somewhat as the United States and the Soviet Union entered into a number of significant arms control agreements that included the ABM Treaty, START I, and START II. Ironically, the non-ideological *realpolitik* strategy pursued by the Nixon administration and the resulting era of détente with the Soviet Union provided evidence to many scholars that the international system was neither as inflexible nor as pessimistic as classical Realists continued to claim. This led many Liberals to question the Realist world view at the heart of Strategic Studies and seek alternative interpretations of world politics, thereby precipitating a 'Liberal Age' within International Relations and its various sub-disciplines. The explanatory power of Realism suffered further as events such as the Oil Crisis of 1973 and the Second Oil Crisis of 1979 highlighted the vulnerability of states to 'security' threats that could not be framed within the traditional perspective of inter-state military conflicts.

However, in 1979 Kenneth Waltz precipitated a resurgence in the Realist tradition with the release of his *Theory of International Politics*, in which he moved the Realist tradition away from its emphasis on human nature as the underpinning element of the inherently conflictual international system. Instead, Waltz offered a systemic-level interpretation of international politics that, while reaffirming the Realist perception of a conflictual international system, suggested that the inevitability of inter-state conflict lay within the ordering principle of 'structural anarchy' as opposed to the ills of human nature. Waltz argued that states, while subject to variations in their individual capabilities, are fundamentally similar units who lack any central authority within the international system they inhabit. It is this 'ordering principle' of anarchy that fosters the self-help, conflictual environment in which survival can – and must – be the only goal of states (Waltz, 1979: 93).

In terms of ISS, the emergence of Neorealism proved significant for a number of reasons. First, despite its emphasis on the power of structural anarchy, Neorealism reiterated the traditionalist desire to define the concept of security in terms of power-maximising states operating in a self-help system that would inevitably witness regular inter-state conflict. Second, it abandoned the classical Realist emphasis on the flawed nature of individuals as the root cause of the conflictual nature of world politics, and ensured that the next generation of debates *within* the traditionalist wing of ISS would centre largely on the consequences of international anarchy as opposed to the character of human nature. Third, Waltz argued that it provided Realism with a clear and testable conceptual framework that harnessed the methodological rigour of the natural sciences, something which had previously been missing from the Realist analysis of international politics. Finally, it forced traditionalist scholars to better analyse how the distribution of capabilities between various states impacted upon the stability of the international system, particularly whether it was polarity of the system or the existence of nuclear weapons that better explained the events of the Cold War, thus reviving a question first posed by Waltz fifteen years previously (Buzan and Hansen, 2009: 68). Waltz famously argued that bipolar systems were preferable to multipolar (or indeed unipolar) systems given their tendency towards stability, an argument that opened a number of new research avenues within ISS, particularly on the subject of nuclear deterrence, where Waltz and Mearsheimer wrote extensively on what they perceived to be the stabilising influence of nuclear weapons (see, for example, Mearsheimer, 1993).

Debates within the Realist tradition

Particularly important within the Realist tradition with respect to ISS are the differing approaches of *Defensive Realism* and *Offensive Realism* to state behaviour and the international system. *Defensive Realism* refers to the likes of Kenneth Waltz, Stephen Walt, and Robert Jervis, all of whom accept that the security concerns of a particular state can be satisfied – although possibly only temporarily – through a series of favourable relative gains. In contrast, *Offensive Realists* such as John Mearsheimer posit that a state can never be assured of its security in an anarchic world of competing power-maximising states and must therefore take every opportunity to aggressively expand its power, rather than relying on incremental gains.

Articulated originally within Mearsheimer's *The Tragedy of Great Power Politics*, *Offensive Realism* is based on the premise that the security needs of states can never be sufficiently satisfied. States are therefore forced to aggressively maximise their power at every opportunity. The goal, therefore, is to achieve the status of a hegemonic power, thereby providing the only effective protection against a challenge from a rival power-seeking state (Mearsheimer, 2001). Total security is therefore almost impossible for states to achieve, and inter-state conflict is essentially a certainty for *Offensive Realists*. *Defensive Realists*, on the other hand, shun the overt pessimism of the *Offensive Realists*, and instead place greater faith in balance-of-power mechanisms to assure the security concerns of states seeking only to survive. Their argument is that nuclear weapons, and the possession of a second-strike capability in particular, have tipped the offence–defence balance overwhelmingly in favour of the defender, thus providing a degree of security for those in possession of such weapons, regardless of the unknown intentions of their rival states.

But what are the consequences of such a division for ISS? The mutual emphasis on structural anarchy and its power to determine the behaviour of states is undisputed within the Neorealist camp, as is the need to maintain the state as the sole referent object of analysis. Likewise, the conceptualisation of international security is fundamentally the same, the key question being how states can survive in an anarchic international system. The two are therefore fundamentally cut from the same cloth in theoretical terms, with the only significant difference emerging around their perceptions of the *frequency* and *degree* of inter-state conflict within the international system. A useful contrast is provided by John Mearsheimer when interpreting the threat posed by a rising China. *Offensive Realists*, with their insistence on the insatiable desire of states to maximise their power, will argue that China's strategy is based upon rapidly becoming the sole regional hegemon in Asia, in the process undermining the power base of neighbours such as Japan and Russia. Such a strategy is likely to draw an assertive counter-action from the USA and possibly even generate a new 'Cold War' of sorts. In contrast, *Defensive Realists*, while admitting that security competition between China and the USA is inevitable to some extent, suggest that China will more likely pursue a strategy of pre-eminence rather than hegemony. They argue that China will pursue only incremental increases in its regional power so to prevent any counter-balancing from its rivals, a particularly unattractive scenario for the Chinese given the number of its competitors who currently possess or who have the potential to possess a nuclear deterrent. The *Defensive Realists*, therefore, argue that it is the prospect of an immovable nuclear blockade to its expansion that will act as a check on Chinese aspirations for regional hegemony (Mearsheimer, 2006: 83–86).

Summary: the Realist tradition in Security Studies

The Realist tradition in ISS is therefore best understood as the study of *insecurity* among sovereign states, an immovable and permanent feature of an international system that is brought about by the anarchy of the international system. The move from classical Realism to Neorealism (and its variants) may have altered the Realist perceptions concerning the causes of war from a 'first image' (human nature) to a 'third image' analysis (the international system), but it failed to disentangle the concept of security from the state-centric, military-defined notion of national security that had become dominant in Strategic Studies during the early years of the Cold War (Waltz, 1959). The Cold War era saw Realism reach the apex of its explanatory power, with the bipolar nuclear rivalry between the two superpowers seemingly confirming the Realist perception of world politics in which inter-state conflict should be accepted as a permanent feature of the international system, and the concept of security should be defined solely in terms of narrow, militarist threats to state sovereignty.

As has been emphasised previously, *all* Realist scholars within ISS are advocates of placing the sovereign state as the primary referent object of analysis, and focusing their attention on what they understand to be an inevitable cycle of (military) conflict between these power-seeking entities. Even today, Realist scholars in ISS continue to offer steadfast resistance to the dual processes of 'broadening' and 'deepening' the concept of security, arguing, as in the case of Stephen Walt, that ISS is in danger of losing its theoretical coherence in the face of attempts to redefine the concept of security to include non-state actors and non-military threats such as environmental disasters, disease, famine, and societal problems. They maintain that the international system has changed little over time, even in the post-Cold War era, with the continued presence of international anarchy serving to ensure the permanence of inter-state conflict within world politics. Hence, Realists argue that their narrow state-centric notion of security, with power defined solely in terms of military capabilities, continues to explain world politics as it is, not as it should be.

The Liberal tradition and Security Studies

The other important wing of traditionalism in ISS is the Liberal perspective. Liberal ideas regarding the concept of security, like those of Realism, are also able to draw inspiration from a rich and diverse intellectual tradition that dates back to the likes of Adam Smith, Jeremy Bentham, and perhaps most importantly, Immanuel Kant. Akin to the Realists, Liberal scholars generally accept that the international system is characterised by a degree of anarchy, and that, left unchecked, world politics would often degenerate into the cycles of inter-state conflict predicted by the Realists. What is important for Liberals, however, is that the occurrence of inter-state conflict, while a possibility, is not an *inevitability* as suggested by the Realist tradition, and the Liberal strands to security are therefore dominated by interpretations of how to reduce the likelihood of inter-state conflict.

While this is in no way a comprehensive analysis of the multiple Liberal strands, there are three dominant Liberal approaches with which students of ISS must be familiar, each of which has a different perspective on the question of how states can best address the threats to their security. *Liberal Idealism* focuses on the use of legally-defined collective security as an instrument of international peace; *Liberal Peace Theory* highlights the spread of democratic state systems as the most effective mechanism of preventing inter-state conflict; and *Neoliberal Institutionalism* emphasises utilising international institutions to promote inter-state cooperation and offset the pressures of structural anarchy.

Liberal Idealism

Derisively referred to as 'utopianism' by its Realist critics, Liberal Idealism is most commonly associated with the inter-war period and the views of the twenty-eighth

President of the United States, Woodrow Wilson. In what has sometimes been labelled the 'First Great Debate' of International Relations, the Liberal Idealism espoused by Wilson, which emphasised the fundamental good at the core of human nature, offered a drastically different view of the world from that of Wilson's Realist contemporaries. Wilson accepted – as do his theoretical descendants – that conflict between states would continue to be a feature of world politics unless it was mitigated by mechanisms designed to provide the same degree of law and order to the international system as had been possible in the domestic realm. In perhaps the earliest example of institutionalised collective security, he therefore proposed a *League of Nations* that would be guided by a universal legal charter and would utilise the collective force of its members as a tool of enforcement if so required. While the League was ultimately a failure in preventing the outbreak of the Second World War, it is this dual focus on international law and collective security that continues, eighty years later, to underpin Liberal idealist thought concerning the prevention of inter-state conflict.

Contemporary manifestations of Liberal Idealism stress the importance of collective security, democratic governance, self-determination, and other such mechanisms that allow the fundamentally positive nature of human beings to foster peaceful collaboration and coexistence between states. While Liberal Idealism in its purest form has largely been consigned to the annals of history, it has nevertheless left a significant imprint within ISS and its sister field of Peace Research, with proponents keen to identify and reform those institutional structures which fail to harness the positive nature of the human individual. In 1993, for example, Charles Kegley argued that Wilsonian ideals had perhaps assumed a renewed relevance in the post-Cold War era – a period in which traditional Realist notions of *realpolitik* were severely constrained in terms of explanatory power, and one where the renewed emphasis on collective security and international regimes was in clear parallel with the Wilsonian perception of world politics outlined eight decades previously (Kegley, 1993: 134).

Liberal Peace Theory

Increasingly ascendant in the contemporary era, Liberal Peace Theory draws its inspiration from the ideas articulated by Immanuel Kant within his essay on *Perpetual Peace*. Kant put forward the simple yet powerful proposition that states with constitutional republican systems of government were less likely to engage in inter-state conflict. Kant reasoned that the civilian population were those most adversely affected by the occurrence of military conflict, and that, given the opportunity to actively participate in the political process, they would serve as a constraining element on the actions of their country's decision-makers. For Kant, republican government served to make leaders accountable to a conflict-averse electorate, and thus those states that guaranteed popular representation through constitutional law were likely to be more pacific in the international system than those with an absolute monarchy or an autocratic system of government.

Kant's rationale has been accepted by contemporary Liberal Peace Theorists who have themselves produced a clear and unambiguous proposition, namely that liberal democracies do not go to war with other liberal democracies. While there is no empirical evidence to justify the claim that liberal democracies are the most peaceful in an absolute sense, the concept of the 'separate peace of democracies' has attracted widespread support, with several scholars referring to it as the closest thing to an 'empirical law' within contemporary International Relations (Layne, 1994: 8). While the precise reasons behind the democratic peace phenomenon are still contested by its advocates, the implications for ISS are resoundingly clear: the occurrence of inter-state conflict is best mitigated by the spread of liberal democracy wherever and whenever possible.

Neoliberal Institutionalism

Recognised as the dominant strand of Liberal theory within contemporary International Relations, Neoliberal Institutionalism has also contributed significantly to developing Liberal ideas within the subfield of ISS, particularly in terms of repudiating the Neorealist focus on deterministic structural anarchy. For most Neoliberals, international anarchy exists insofar as there is no overarching authority, although they refuse to accept that it shapes state behaviour to the extent claimed by Neorealists such as Kenneth Waltz. Indeed, Neoliberals assert that the use of the term 'anarchy' is so poorly defined by Neorealists, who themselves offer a number of simplistic and contrary conceptual interpretations, that it cannot – and should not – be accepted as evidence that the international system is forever destined to be consumed by inter-state conflict (Milner, 1993: 68).

For Neoliberal Institutionalists, the aim is therefore to challenge the fundamental Neorealist notion that the structural anarchy of the international system imprisons states within a permanent cycle of inter-state conflict. Neoliberals accept that, in an anarchic system, any co-operative interaction between states is threatened by the absence of external enforcement that would mitigate states' uncertainty regarding the intentions of other states and prevent them 'cheating' on their agreements. However, they reject Neorealist claims concerning the minimal chances for inter-state co-operation under conditions of international anarchy, and refer to the power of international institutions as an effective mechanism for overcoming the pressures on state behaviour that arise from misperceptions and confusion regarding the behaviour of other state entities. Such institutions can assist states in increasing communication and transparency by a host of different means that include brokering multilateral agreements, arranging mutual military inspections, facilitating arms control programmes, and establishing international regimes, all of which allow states to circumvent the ill-effects of structural anarchy on their own security needs.

Finally, Neoliberalism is particularly important within ISS given that its focus on the economic dimensions of co-operation represents the clearest example within the traditionalist approaches of attempting to 'broaden' the concept of security. Inspired by the arguments of Robert Keohane and Joseph Nye in *Power and Interdependence*, Neoliberals suggest that military force is declining as a tool of foreign policy as states seek the greater economic interaction necessary to prosper in a globalised world (Keohane and Nye, 2001). While 'hard power' capabilities remain important to Neoliberals, they argue that states are increasingly developing transnational economic connections at all levels, thus reducing the likelihood of inter-state conflict given the adverse economic consequences for all parties in such a scenario. Keohane and Nye's approach therefore incorporates the economic dimension that Buzan would describe as essential to redefining the concept of security away from the narrow Realist notion (Buzan, 1991), and it provides evidence that Liberals have at least a limited desire to 'broaden' our interpretation of international security.

Summary: the Liberal tradition in Security Studies

It should therefore be apparent to students of ISS that to speak of a single unified Liberal 'theory' regarding security is highly misleading given the variety of strands discussed within this chapter. As in the case of Realism, it is perhaps best characterised as an approach, or even a philosophy, to the study of international security, one that encompasses a number of competing theoretical thrusts when addressing the question of international security, with each contributing a different solution to the problem of reducing inter-state conflict within the international system. As has been discussed, these range from the institutional solutions forwarded by Neoliberals to the collective security ideas of Liberal Idealists.

However, there are a number of important elements that form a common link within the Liberal tradition. In philosophical terms, the Liberal tradition is fundamentally optimistic, with all Liberal approaches to security stressing the possibility of change and progress within the international system. All Liberal approaches – and those of Realism – identify the state as the primary referent object of analysis, and highlight inter-state military conflict as the primary source of insecurity within the international system. Yet, in contrast to Realism, Liberal approaches refuse to accept that the anarchy of the international system inevitably translates to an international system consumed by mistrust and conflict. Of course, Liberals recognise that a certain degree of inter-state conflict will always be present within world politics, but nonetheless they remain optimistic that such conflict can be largely mitigated by developing pluralistic security communities in which states realise their common security interests through cooperation.

The key fault line in traditionalist perspectives: the 'security dilemma'

It is therefore apparent that, despite the tendency to view traditionalist approaches within ISS as a theoretical monolith, the Realist and Liberal traditions have their own distinct features, and they focus somewhat differently on the issue of international security. Both advocate a state-centric approach to defining the concept of security, and both utilise a positivist epistemology in their analysis of international politics, focusing on material rather than ideational structures of power. Nevertheless, some important distinctions can be drawn between the Realist and Liberal traditions regarding their respective definitions of key concepts relating to the study of both International Relations and ISS. For instance, we have seen that *anarchy* is a term used with great frequency by Realists and Liberals alike, albeit with markedly different connotations, with the deterministic driver of inter-state conflict envisaged by Realists providing a stark contrast to the definition preferred by Liberal scholars, where authority is more literally absent. It is also worth noting the current methodological disputes within the traditionalist wing of ISS, where the formalised, quantitative methods associated with contemporary Liberal research on peace studies are rejected by Realists such as Stephen Walt, who favour a greater reliance on historicism and the 'classical method' when examining world politics.

However, the most important division within the traditionalist wing of ISS concerns the question of the 'security dilemma'. Coined in 1950 by scholar John Herz, the 'security dilemma' quickly became one of the most important pieces of terminology connected with the discipline of Strategic Studies, and today it remains pivotal to the Realist school within ISS. The term refers to the structural problem that arises when the attempts of one state to satisfy its security needs, however peaceful in intent, lead to rising insecurity for other states, all of whom interpret their own actions as defensive in character (Herz, 1950: 157). In other words, in an anarchic international system where *relative* gains are more salient than *absolute* gains, a state will often find that increases in its own security capabilities prompt a counter-response from rival states who interpret their measures as offensive. Such a dilemma is more likely in circumstances where there are difficulties in distinguishing between the offensive and defensive behaviour of states or between the defensive and offensive applications of certain military technology. The 'security dilemma' is seen by Realists as an intractable and immovable feature of the international system, and it has become one of the foundations on which they have constructed their approach to ISS.

The Liberal tradition within ISS rejects the inevitable occurrence and permanence of Herz's 'security dilemma', arguing that states are not prisoners of anarchy as suggested by their Realist counterparts. For Liberals, the 'security dilemma' is an issue of perception rather than reality, which occurs because states often misperceive the intentions of rival states, mistaking the defensive intentions of a rival for offensive behaviour (Buzan and Hansen, 2009: 33). This product of international anarchy can therefore be readily circumvented by introducing mechanisms designed to facilitate greater communication and transparency between states, particularly in terms of distinguishing offensive and defensive military capabilities. For Neoliberals, the answer is the use of international institutions and agreements to assist in minimising the occurrence of the misperceptions that can so rapidly escalate into inter-state conflict. Liberal Idealists also reject the inevitability of this Realist 'security dilemma', arguing that the mechanism of collective security – as discussed above – is able to establish networks of trust and cooperation between potential rivals, thereby reducing the likelihood of inter-state conflict; this is the same prediction, albeit with a different prescription, as in other Liberal strands of ISS.

Box 2.3: John Herz

John Herz (1908–2005) was one of the most significant contributors to thinking about the concept of security in the twentieth century. Through the introduction of what he labelled the 'security dilemma', Herz elaborated on the fragile nature of the international order and the difficulties of establishing stability. Although often described as a Realist, Herz actually rejected the contemporary Realist–Liberal debate over the fundamental character of human nature. Instead he argued that the true divisions in International Security were between those who saw a way of managing the inevitable egoism of state actors and those who saw this as an immovable aspect of international politics. In other words, the question central to International Security was whether or not the 'security dilemma' could be overcome. Such an issue would be central to the debate between Neorealists and Neoliberals that took place during the 1980s.

Surviving the critical revolution: traditionalism in the 1990s

The collapse of the Soviet Union and the end of the Cold War provided the first significant redistribution of power within the international system since the Second

World War, and sent a seismic shock wave through the discipline of International Relations and its associated subfields. Critics immediately began questioning the relevance of the traditionalist approaches to ISS, reserving particular criticism for the Realist tradition whose so-called explanatory theory of world politics had not simply failed to predict the end of the Cold War, but had actually asserted the longevity and stability of this bipolar system. Seizing upon the dissatisfaction with traditional concepts of security in the post-Cold War era, a number of newer approaches were introduced by those academics who sought to move away from the state-centric, military focus of the Cold War years (see Chapters 3 to 6) and explore security threats that had previously been marginalised by the traditionalist fixation on the nuclear rivalry between the two superpowers. For the first time within the discipline of ISS, the dominant traditionalist approaches were therefore the victims of a conceptual challenge external to their own theoretical traditions, as the likes of Critical Security Studies and Human Security attempted to establish a foothold within a field now subject to a dual process of 'broadening' and 'deepening' of the concept of security.

There is certainly no denying that traditionalism in ISS, particularly the Realist element, underwent a serious challenge during the 1990s. Indeed, attempts by the dwindling Neorealist community to rearticulate their position in the post-Cold War era were largely ineffective in halting this decline, with the likes of Mearsheimer, Waltz, and Walt all attempting, with little success, to reinvigorate the Realist security agenda. Waltz's attempts to underplay the previous Neorealist confidence in the longevity and stability of the bipolar era, and to argue that the fundamental principles of world politics were not altered by the end of the Cold War, have enjoyed little support from the ISS community (Waltz, 2000; 39). Likewise, Mearsheimer's predictions that post-Cold War Europe was likely to experience significant instability from a belligerent unified Germany (Mearsheimer, 1990), and that international institutions would prove of little value to the new world order (Mearsheimer, 1994) both drew widespread criticism from Liberal and Critical Security scholars alike. Released in the closing stages of the Cold War, Walt's attempt to shift the Realist tradition from a balance-of-power interpretation of state behaviour towards a 'balance-of-threat' model was perhaps the most creative addition within the Realist tradition, offering an admission of sorts that the perceptions of security were as important as the realities of power distribution, if not more so. However, Buzan noted the limitations of this shift, arguing that it introduced a subjective interpretation to the objective concept of security as opposed to rejecting the objective definition of security that was demanded by the newer critical approaches (Buzan and Hansen, 2009: 33).

As well as the end of the primacy of Realism within ISS, the 1990s also saw Realism usurped as the dominant theory *within* the traditionalist family, with the world entering what some labelled the 'Liberal Age'. The end of the Cold War had undoubtedly surprised Liberal scholars as well as their Realist adversaries, but they found themselves far better equipped than their Realist counterparts to adapt to life in the new 'unipolar' world. Their willingness to 'broaden' the scope of security, at least as regards an economic dimension, and their less deterministic definition of international anarchy allowed them to flourish in an environment where inter-state cooperation, self-determination and collective security were all gaining significant momentum, at least in Europe and the Americas. While they too had been forced to address questions posed by Critical Security scholars concerning their continued adherence to a state-centric focus and a positivist epistemology, the Liberal tradition found little difficulty in accommodating the events of the 1990s within their respective theories. The *Liberal Peace Theorists*, for example, were able to suggest that the wave of European democratisation which had brought the Cold War to an end had served to reduce the likelihood of future inter-state conflict (and hence international insecurity) through the spread of more pacific liberal democratic systems.

Despite the critical revolution in ISS during the 1990s, traditionalist approaches continued to generate a significant amount of research relating to areas such as inter-state cooperation, deterrence theory, and the nature of international anarchy. Realists and Liberals have continued to defend their research against post-positivist critics by noting the ability of traditionalism in ISS to address salient aspects of real-world politics. The rather contentious debate between Robert Keohane and the noted feminist scholar J. Ann Tickner highlighted the frustration of traditionalist scholars with the critical wing of ISS. Keohane challenged approaches such as feminism to move beyond a criticism of traditionalist theories and produce their own research agenda, with testable and quantifiable propositions relevant to the contemporary issues of international security (Keohane, 1998: 194). It was perhaps this failure on the part of feminists and critical theorists to develop a distinct research agenda relating to international security that afforded traditionalist approaches a degree of much needed 'breathing space' and allowed them to emerge from the 1990s with their intellectual pre-eminence largely intact within ISS.

Traditionalist approaches and 9/11

The co-ordinated attacks by the al-Qaeda terrorist network upon the United States on September 11th 2001 forced ISS scholars of all persuasions to thoroughly re-examine their field of study and question many of their most cherished assumptions regarding the concept of security. Indeed, the 9/11 suicide attacks were not simply the first attack upon the United States since Pearl Harbor fifty years previously, but also the first ever by a non-state entity. Did these events signal that a post-statist view of security was required to fully comprehend the threat posed by the al-Qaeda terrorist network? And what did the 9/11 attacks mean for those traditionalist approaches within ISS who defined security solely in terms of inter-state conflict?

The attacks of 9/11 and the subsequent American-led response were both problematic and oddly reassuring for the Realist community within the discipline of ISS. To some commentators, these events illustrated the permanence of conflict within world politics, shattering the false 'Liberal' illusions of the 1990s. Indeed, the al-Qaeda attacks on New York and Washington were evidence to Neorealists in particular that the international system had *not* fundamentally moved beyond its central ordering principle of structural anarchy. Yet the events of 9/11 were also highly problematic for Realists within ISS. As Barry Buzan notes: 'The prominence of globally networked non-state actors raised questions about state centrism and the rationality assumptions that underpinned traditionalist thought' (Buzan and Hansen, 2009: 229). Realists had largely sidestepped these questions prior to 9/11, but they were now forced to confront them with the emergence of a 'global war on terror'. Critics therefore referred to the obvious problems Realism faced in addressing an international conflict against a non-rational, non-state actor who failed to conform to the power-maximising rationale that underpinned the Realist concepts of security.

The events of 9/11 and the subsequent invasions of Afghanistan and Iraq proved just as challenging for scholars of a Liberal persuasion to interpret, with the questions surrounding the relevance of state centrism equally as applicable to exponents of this tradition as to their Realist counterparts. Furthermore, the Liberals had to deal with a number of important questions concerning the mechanisms of conflict resolution that they had previously championed in the context of reducing the occurrence of inter-state conflict. The casual willingness of the US (and indeed Iraq) to renege on their international legal obligations raised questions concerning the fundamentals of *Liberal Idealism* within ISS, while the seeming impotence of the UN to resolve the issue prior to military action was equally problematic for Neoliberals. While not violating the pure democratic peace thesis per se, the actions of the US and the United Kingdom, two of the world's most liberal democratic states, nevertheless raised some uncomfortable questions for *Liberal Peace Theorists* concerning their failure to more clearly define why the peaceful impulses of democratic states towards each other is not replicated in their behaviour towards non-democratic states.

The attacks of 9/11 and the resulting debate regarding the US grand strategy served to illustrate the important differences that remain *between* Realist and Liberal prescriptions for dealing with international insecurity. The ideological response of the Bush administration, often seen as neoconservative in nature, was an extreme manifestation both of Kantian ideals concerning the importance of spreading democracy as a response to international security, and of Wilsonian ideals concerning the fundamental good of people and thus Liberal democracies. In short, the Bush Doctrine added an element of force to long-standing Liberal prescriptions for addressing international insecurity, producing what John Mearsheimer has labelled 'Wilsonianism with teeth' (Mearsheimer, 2005). In this respect, it could be suggested that 9/11 served only to lengthen – and indeed re-militarise – the Liberal strand within ISS. In contrast, the Realist element in ISS remained sceptical regarding the Iraq invasion and the Liberal desire to forcibly build democracy within the region. They argued that both 'logic and historical experience' suggested that Iraq – like any other state actor – could be dealt with by means of a dual-track strategy of containment and deterrence akin to that applied against the Soviet Union. For Realists, the brutal nature of Saddam Hussein's regime was irrelevant and did not alter the fact that Iraq had behaved with a considerable degree of consistency within its regional theatre, as dictated by the pressure of ensuring survival in an anarchic international system.

However, perhaps the most important point is the remarkable continuity within the traditionalist wing of ISS; despite the US suffering an attack from a non-state enemy, both Realists and Liberals framed their preferred response to the attack in terms of a state-centric, (military) power-based action designed to deal with the alleged sponsors/hosts of global terrorism rather than the al-Qaeda terror network itself. For traditionalists, this highlighted the applicability of their approaches in the post-Cold War era in which the fundamental nature of the international system remained unchanged from the previous sixty years of state-based security threats. For the likes of Human Security or Critical Security theorists, the failure to address the root causes behind the growth of al-Qaeda, or to offer a prescription for incorporating such a sub-state entity into their rational actor model, was further evidence that the traditionalist movement in ISS had ended with the passing of the Cold War.

How relevant are traditionalist approaches today?

As the process of 'broadening' and 'deepening' the concept of security continues to gather momentum into the twenty-first century, can the traditionalist approaches of the Cold War era be of any relevance to the contemporary International Security Studies agenda? Critics have resoundingly rejected such approaches, particularly those inspired by Realist theory, as antiquated, obsolete, and ill-equipped to address the pressing security concerns of a globalised and post-statist world system. They question such an intractable adherence to the state as a referent object of study, asking how traditionalists can claim to offer explanatory theories of world politics and international security while at the same time marginalising a host of emergent threats such as failed states, global terrorism, economic recession, environmental disasters, pandemic disease, and global poverty, all of which have been placed at the heart of the newer, critical approaches to ISS.

Does traditionalism therefore have a future in the discipline of Security Studies? The answer is inevitably yes, but to what extent? Buzan and Hansen have suggested that traditionalist scholars have largely retreated into two distinct camps in the post-Cold War era, essentially abandoning the newly-populated ISS in favour of returning to their 'parent' fields of research – Strategic Studies in the case of Realists, and Peace Studies in the case of Liberals (Buzan and Hansen, 2009: 157). This is due largely to the fact that the collapse of the bipolar nuclear system removed the common concept of security that essentially linked the traditionalist approaches throughout the Cold War. However, it is also rooted in the methodological preferences of each tradition, with the Realists preferring to retain the use of historicism while the Liberals increasingly favour a formalised statistical approach to the study of international security. For Realists, the focus has now largely shifted towards the analysis of power politics, where existing Neorealist theory still has the potential to offer much insight into bilateral state relationships such as those between the US and China and between India and Pakistan. Liberal scholars, on the other hand, have largely immersed themselves in 'positivist peace research', drawing on the Liberal approaches discussed previously to promote new strategies and mechanisms of conflict resolution. Despite this divergence in their research agendas, the differences *between* traditionalist approaches nevertheless remain marginal by comparison with the divisions between traditionalist and critical approaches to security – a case in point being the famous Waltz–Sagan debate regarding nuclear deterrence in which the Realists and Liberals traded blows over an aspect of international security that remained framed within a militaristic, state-centric concept of security underpinned by a positivist methodology, with the sole point of contention being the efficacy of nuclear proliferation in negating the security dilemma of states (Sagan and Waltz, 2002).

In theoretical terms, the recent emergence of neoclassical Realism has possibly provided the most promising development in terms of ensuring that the Realist tradition remains relevant in contemporary ISS. By recognising the criticisms of the now dominant constructivist approach in International Relations, a generation of Realists has emerged who accept the need to incorporate an intersubjective element into their analysis of world politics. By moving beyond an analysis of material structures and accepting a role for ideational processes, these neoclassical Realists have been able to redress one of the major criticisms levelled at their Neorealist predecessors: the inability to account for sudden change in the international system, such as the changing Soviet–US perception of threats during the Gorbachev–Reagan era. By connecting structural factors to domestic political processes, the neoclassical approach essentially pairs Neorealist theory with a constructivist methodology to provide a theory of *foreign policy* as opposed to a theory solely of *international politics* as envisaged by Waltz, recognising that unit-level actors are not always held prisoner by systemic-level pressures.

However, this has largely failed to satisfy the critics of traditionalist approaches, with many arguing that the move to neoclassical Realism has failed to move the Realist tradition beyond the militaristic state-centrism which remains the fundamental source of friction between Realists and Human Security or Critical Security advocates. This should not come as a surprise, given that the Realist tradition has no fundamental interest in 'broadening' or 'deepening' the concept of security, with the likes of Stephen Walt continuing to stress that the study of international security should be deliberately restricted to the use and utility of military power by state actors, even in the post-Cold War era, for the sake of maintaining the intellectual boundaries of a discipline that is in danger of being overloaded with newer security 'threats' that cannot be accommodated within a cohesive theoretical framework.

Although certainly not experiencing the same degree of criticism as their Realist counterparts, the Liberal tradition in ISS has also been attacked for their failure to move beyond a Cold War concept of security, with critics arguing that this approach also retains a narrow state-centric approach fundamentally in keeping with that of the Realist tradition. Post-positivists have further attacked the Liberal project in ISS for its inherent Western-centrism, questioning whether an approach based on utilising Western concepts of democracy and international law is actually applicable in regions such as Africa where such ideals have only limited exposure. In short, critics of the Liberal approach posit that it too remains a positivist and universalist theory of inter-state conflict, which offers the same restrictive and narrow understanding of the concept of security as the Realists against whom they claim to have differentiated themselves.

Conclusion

There can be little doubt that despite the considerable criticism afforded to them by Critical Security scholars in particular, traditionalist approaches remain an integral part of the contemporary ISS landscape. Both Realist and Liberal perspectives on international security offer powerful explanatory theories that have persisted, with some degree of success, two decades after the end of the Cold War highlighted some of the most glaring deficiencies within ISS traditionalism, particularly Neorealism. As in mainstream International Relations, the predicted demise of Realism (and to a lesser extent, Liberalism) have been shown to be grossly premature, with both traditions showing a remarkable resilience to the post-positivist assault on their core assumptions.

It is perhaps the simplicity at the core of these approaches that is responsible for their longevity within ISS discourse. Critics may chastise traditionalist approaches for their resistance to 'deepening' the referent object of analysis, or for their failure to 'broaden' their definition of security to include societal or environmental dimensions, but the traditionalist response is that the study of inter-state conflict remains one of the most salient issues connected with the study of contemporary world politics. Traditionalists argue that the process of globalisation has failed to displace the state as the most basic and primary unit within the sphere of world politics, and therefore that their Westphalian concepts of international security remain valid in an international environment that continues to be defined by *state sovereignty*, *power*, and above all, *anarchy*. Traditionalists do not fail to recognise that important issues, such as environmental degradation, exist in world politics, but they reject their inclusion within the discipline of ISS. In short, traditionalists claim that their respective approaches continue to explain the most salient features of the international system; they do not explain – or seek to explain – those issues which they exclude from their narrow understanding of international security, which is focused exclusively on the study of conflict (or cooperation) between sovereign state entities in an anarchic international system.

Critics will inevitably continue to deride such approaches, particularly Realism, for ignoring a host of increasingly significant issues within the new post-positivist security agenda, as well as the various sub-state and transnational actors who feel the impact of threats such as poverty, disease, and natural disasters. Traditionalism within ISS has held its ground largely because none of the emerging critical approaches have been able to wrestle the impetus away from those who place 'high politics' at the centre of our efforts to define the concept of security, and in doing so, move the discipline away from the Cold War ideals that continue – even today – to provide the foundations for much of the contemporary thinking within ISS. As will be outlined in the following chapters, one of the major shortcomings of the critical security project is the failure of its various strands to develop explanatory theories that directly challenge the core assumptions and conclusions produced over sixty years of traditionalist research within ISS. Indeed, Lynn-Jones argued two decades ago that the most significant challenge to the primacy of Realism within International Relations and its associated subfields has actually originated from the *Liberal Peace Thesis* as opposed to the critical security project of the last decade.

Summary points

1   The traditionalist perspectives on International Security are united by their focus on the state as the primary form of political community and hence the key referent object in the study of security as a concept.
2   Traditional approaches tend to prioritise military interpretations of security above all else.
3   The key division within the traditionalist perspective concerns the question of the 'security dilemma'. Realists understand the security dilemma as a permanent feature of International Security, whereas Liberals are much more optimistic concerning the ability of states to mitigate the problem through cooperation.
4   The events of 9/11 and the subsequent response by the US-led coalition highlight the contemporary challenge for those who adhere to traditional ideas of security. How can transnational security concerns, such as terrorism, be incorporated into a definition of security that is so firmly wedded to the state as the key referent object?
5   Despite a significant 'critical revolution' within International Security Studies over the past two decades, traditional conceptions of security persist within the field as a result of the work of scholars such as Stephen Walt.

Recommended reading

Buzan, B. *People, States and Fears: An Agenda for International Security Studies in the Post-Cold War Era*, Boulder, CO: Lynne Rienner, 1991.

Kolodziej, E.A. *Security and International Relations*, Cambridge: Cambridge University Press, 2005.

Lynn-Jones, S.M. 'Realism and Security Studies', in C.A. Snyder (ed.), *Contemporary Security and Strategy*, New York: Routledge, 1999.

Mearsheimer, J.J. and Walt, S.M. 'An Unnecessary War', *Foreign Policy*, no. 134, January/February, 2003, 50–59.

Russett, B.M. and Oneal, J.R. *Triangulating Peace: Democracy, Interdependence, and International Organizations*, New York: W.W. Norton and Company, 2001.

Walt, S.M. 'The Renaissance of Security Studies', *International Studies Quarterly*, vol. 35, no. 2, June 1991, 211–239.

3　Challenging orthodoxy
Critical Security Studies

Shahin Malik

Box 3.1: The individual vs. the state

In a world so heavily dominated by sovereign states, one would imagine the security of the individual to be closely tied to that of the state. We do not dispute this premise – but we would like you to imagine scenarios which demonstrate the inability of states to protect their citizens, their territories and other state assets. Consider also times when states have deliberately diminished the security of individuals through the use of draconian laws, the persecution of specific groups and other measures.

Three events in recent history aptly illustrate the impotence of states in the face of natural disasters. The 2004 Indonesian tsunami killed more than 250,000 people and affected millions in over fourteen countries. Then in 2010, the floods in Pakistan destroyed over half a million homes, five thousand miles of road, seven thousand schools and covered 2.6 million acres of crop land with water. More recently in 2011, an earthquake off the coast of northern Japan caused a major tsunami which laid waste to entire communities, killed over 25,000 people and severely damaged the Fukushima nuclear power plant, with three reactors experiencing full meltdown. In light of these events the following quote by Lao Tzu (the Father of Taoism), writing in the sixth century BC, seems very appropriate.

> Nothing is more flexible
> more yielding or softer than water
> yet when it attacks none can withstand it
> (Lao Tzu)

Introduction

In Chapter 2 we demonstrated that during much of the Cold War, the discipline of Security Studies remained focused around the control, threat or use of force (Nye and Lynn-Jones, 1988: 5–27). States were seen both as the users of force and as the main targets. It was for this reason that the field of Security Studies was traditionally dominated by academics who sought to keep the discipline narrowly focused on military threats to the state. This state-centric view was reinforced by two theories, Realism and Liberalism, both of which played a crucial role in the discipline's arsenal since both have, for a long time, been at the forefront when offering solutions to the unremitting problem of international conflict. Central to their claim was the view that the prime recipient of security was the state, and a major proportion of societal resources needed to be devoted to safeguarding it. Realism in particular provided the backdrop for the discipline's initial focus on military concerns, and the events of the Cold War supplied academics and politicians with ample justification for narrowing the perspective in this way. As shown in Chapter 2, the perceptions of a hostile Soviet Union and the nuclear competition between the superpowers led to an increase in the importance of topics concerned with the military angle of security.

Realist explanations of security, however, faced intense criticism largely because of this narrow focus and its tendency to ignore non-military issues. This criticism highlighted that there was no universal acceptance over the definition of security, thereby heightening calls for a realignment of the discipline. It is in this context that the complex nature, but also the vibrancy, of this discipline becomes apparent. Perhaps the most vocal of dissenters are to be found within the subfield of Critical Security Studies (CSS), where a large collection of academics and views join forces to voice their opposition. Grasping the essence of critical approaches is challenging, particularly because these views do not constitute a single unified theory. Indeed, in the first book to carry the title *Critical Security Studies* (published in 1997), Keith Krause and Michael Williams declared that their intention was to bring together many different perspectives which were becoming associated with this term.

One of the greatest challenges here is to grasp what is meant by 'critical security', because there is no singular critical perspective. At its most basic level, to be critical refers to an 'ability to make judgements', and one can perhaps assume this to be an area of common ground between the different approaches. They all appear critical of certain restrictions placed upon the study of security by traditionalist approaches such as Realism, and therefore they expend considerable effort in bypassing them. Among the most important restraints is the view that only the state has legitimate control of its military forces and territory. This in turn has the effect of providing the state with a privileged position; it becomes the prime entity, the key referent object, thereby relegating all other entities and forms of security to a level below that of the state.

In the opening box of this chapter we highlighted instances where natural disasters have threatened the security of individuals and it is in this context that many Critical Theorists ask the question – what of the security of individuals? We acknowledge that often the security of the state is closely connected to that of its people, but history is replete with instances (see Box 3.2) where states have themselves actively diminished the security of their own citizens, or where they do not in fact have the ability to protect them – as in the case of major natural disasters. Chapter 2 showed that Realism has trouble in distinguishing between security for the state and security for the individual, and it is against this seeming lack of concern that Critical Theorists strive. Consequently, all critical approaches are constantly engaging with restrictive definitions of security and offering judgements regarding the subject matter of the discipline. This forces us to recognize that although the concept of security is constantly used in a variety of contexts, its meaning is far from settled. The Cold War succeeded in restricting its boundaries considerably, but at the same time individuals, academics, social groups, and global movements constantly reminded us of the existence of a large number of insecurities outside the US–Soviet military competition. Indeed, critical approaches take issue with traditionalist views that security could be singular in meaning. This multilayered view stems from an analysis of the nature of the referent object. States, especially powerful states, generally experience threats from the military forces of other states and therefore respond by buttressing their own military resources. The key for Critical Theorists is to recognise that other potential actors – such as individuals and groups – will be threatened in other ways. It is in this light, therefore, that Critical Theorists are only comfortable when they are constantly questioning the nature of the referent object and by extension the meaning of 'security'.

What is so different about being 'critical'?

Critical approaches do not constitute a single unified theory, and neither do all who desire a redefinition of the concept of security consider themselves Critical Theorists. There are even other perspectives which make room for alternative referent objects and yet do not share the same intellectual ground as critical approaches. One such approach is Human Security, to which Chapter 5 is devoted. Critical Security Studies, on the other hand, is a broad approach which incorporates a number of strands. The first has its roots in a conference organised by Keith Krause and Michael Williams in 1994. Based on ideas conceived at the York Centre for International and Strategic Studies (YCISS) in Toronto, their goal was not to develop a unified critical approach to security; rather, their project was based on the large number of concerns regarding the narrow focus imposed by traditional military and state-centric ideas of security. They sought to question why so much attention was given to the state, and to reveal how other entities had become marginalized in the face of state dominance. They succeeded in bringing together a large variety of critiques of the traditional approaches under the umbrella term '*critical*'. The proceedings of the conference were published in a book entitled *Critical Security Studies* (Krause and Williams, 1997) with the clear intention ***not*** of identifying a single framework, but rather of stimulating debate among those who opposed the dominant discourse. Their efforts succeeded in creating a platform, so that a variety of concerns that were marginalized in Security Studies could be voiced regarding the narrowness imposed by traditional approaches.

Among the numerous approaches represented in their 'Critical Security Studies' were those which not only questioned the referent object but also saw security as being more than just military security. These approaches also sought to question the methods which traditionalist approaches had adopted in studying security. Realism claimed that its methods were objective and scientific (positivist). However, this was increasingly seen as irrelevant to the analysis of human interactions, and therefore critical perspectives now advocated post-positivist forms of knowledge and understanding. Included in the mix of perspectives were Feminism and Social Constructivism, to which entire chapters are devoted later in this book. In this chapter we provide brief overviews of a number of critical viewpoints, including Robert Cox's distinction between problem-solving and Critical Theory, Ken Booth's Welsh School, Post-Structuralism and Post-Colonialism – all of which oppose the narrow, military and state-centric nature of so-called positivist approaches such as Realism.

Problem-solving and Critical Theory

In addition to seeking an understanding of the world, theories need to justify their existence by displaying purpose and usefulness. This causes confusion among students of Security Studies who often begin to highlight what have become common questions, such as – what is the purpose behind critical approaches, and why is there such an emphasis on theories in our discipline anyway? Both questions can be answered by referring to Robert Cox's famous dictum: 'theory is always for someone and for some purpose' (Cox, 1995: 85). This aptly highlights the central purpose behind critical approaches, but also hints at the importance of theory in Security Studies – namely, that theories exist for the purpose of creating processes that improve peoples' lives. This is generally referred to by Critical Theorists as 'emancipation'.

Cox went further and provided an important comparison within the field when he created a distinction between Critical Theory and traditional approaches to security, or 'problem-solving' theories, as he called them. He saw theories as a tool to understand our surroundings and, crucially, as a basis which could be used to change the world for the better – in line with the 'emancipatory processes' mentioned above. Consequently, Cox highlighted two distinct goals for theories; the first was the problem-solving purpose specified by approaches such as Liberalism or Realism. In this case theories can identify problems in the international system and provide a guide for correcting dysfunctional processes, thereby enabling the smooth running of the system. Importantly, Cox does not reject this aspect of problem-solving theories – indeed, he acknowledges that the strength of such theories lies in their use as a means of identifying problem areas within the existing political structures of the international system, so that inconsistencies that might destabilise that system can be isolated and addressed. So, for example, if military imbalance between states is deemed to be a problem leading to instability within a region, a problem-solving theory such as Neorealism would advocate the establishment of military equilibrium between the conflicting states as a step towards the possible re-establishment of stability.

However, critical thinkers remain dissatisfied with the limited goals expressed by problem-solving theories – especially since these theories are based on an acceptance of the prevailing order in the international system. It would appear, then, that the basis of problem-solving theories is merely to work alongside existing state institutions in order to identify solutions to the problems faced within the international system. The key consequence of this acceptance of 'the world as it is' is that it contributes to the perpetuation of the existing structures of the system, and if those structures are fundamentally unfair, then problem-solving theories fail to provide any emancipatory outcomes. It is particularly in this context that Critical Theory differs considerably from problem-solving approaches. A refusal to accept the world as it is forms the basis of its expression of dissatisfaction with traditional theories such as Realism and Liberalism. In these traditional approaches, the understanding of the international system is based on certain rigid, fixed assumptions which have to form the essence of any further understanding of the way states interact with one another. For instance, anarchy is one such assumption, and in both Realism and Liberalism (along with their more recent 'neo' versions) this is a fundamental and unshakeable condition of the international system.

It is this type of rigidity which is incompatible with Critical Theory, leading to assertions by Critical Theorists such as Cox that their form of theorising is far superior to traditional theories, given that it refuses to accept the prevailing order. This is bolstered by the key objective of questioning the nature and origins of that order in determining whether the established system is actually fair or not. It is this goal which enables Critical Theorists to claim that their theorising is based on emancipation. By questioning the very structural conditions that form the tacit assumptions for problem-solving theory, Critical Theorists have been instrumental in persuading theorists of all types to question their own approaches to understanding the international system. Critical Theory does not take state, regional or global institutions for granted, but rather brings into question their origins and whether or not they might be part of the process of change which brings about improvement in peoples' lives. Critical Theorists further argue that by accepting the system as it is, problem-solving theories merely succeed in perpetuating the status quo in the international system, including the unfair practices which exist within it. Critical Theory claims to be reflective, and if the purpose of social enquiry is to question established practices *and* bring about change for the better in human life, then critical theorising is best placed to act as the guide to enact such changes. Critical Theorists seek to remind us that the international system cannot spontaneously exist, but that it must have been brought into existence. If this is the case then its structures and processes can be 'created' in such a way as to be emancipatory to humans rather than oppressive or damaging.

A brief comparison between the Human Security approach and Cox's views provides a useful backdrop. The initial concept of Human Security stemmed from a report by the United Nations, published in 1994, which drew on a wide variety of subject areas including International Relations, Development Studies and Strategic Studies. This people-centred approach advocates both 'freedom from want' and 'freedom from fear' as hallmarks for international security. Following its inception, various components of the approach have been adopted by states such as Japan, Norway and Canada, and one of the central goals of Human Security is to ensure that states make a commitment to preserving and enhancing the security of individuals. This provides the approach with a **strong policy orientation**, and its adoption as a policy framework by some governments has led to accusations that it denotes an unwillingness to challenge the state. Conversely, Critical Theorists see the state as one of the key causes of insecurity for individuals and accuse Human Security of conceding to the 'reality' of state power (see Box 3.2). Although the Human Security approach appears to make the individual the referent object of security, it does not oppose traditional constructions such as 'state sovereignty', 'balance of power' or 'national security'. This means that the approach may not be as critical of the state as it appears to be, and this continues to be seen as a major failing among Critical Theorists inspired by Cox.

This brief account has highlighted the basic elements of the critical approach. One over-arching element shared by those calling themselves Critical Theorists is their often vocal opposition to the narrow state-centric emphasis on military security. This has had the effect of deepening the concept of security beyond the military realm, as well as strengthening the view that it is often actually the state which heightens the insecurity of individuals. Traditionalists view state security as being of paramount importance and claim that security for individuals is indivisible from that of the state. This emphasis on the state is further bolstered by the Realist insistence that the prevailing condition in the international system is one of anarchy, thereby making the state the ultimate arbiter of its own fortunes. No other institution is in a position to 'protect' the state, its interests or its physical wellbeing from aggressors. Consequently, states are left to their own devices, their own potential, their own military capabilities and their own diplomatic skills to safeguard themselves from the aggressive desires of other states within the international system. Clearly, then, this view leaves no room for referent objects other than the state and diminishes the importance of the individual to the level of a mere chattel belonging to the state. This does not sit well with those who seek to refocus the discipline of Security Studies away from the state to the individual, and they stress in response that states themselves often intentionally harm individuals. The examples in Box 3.2 further highlight this conflict between the state and the individual.

Box 3.2: Diminishing the security of individuals

There are countless examples where states have threatened their own citizens, and the following few stand out as particularly terrible instances.

Saloth Sar and the Killing Fields of Cambodia. One of the most horrific examples of mass violence by a state against its own citizens came in the form of Saloth Sar's regime in Cambodia during the 1970s. As Prime Minister (1976–1979) his policies included the massive collectivisation of farms, and the abolition of education, religion, private property and even money. Enforced labour on the farms, a lack of medical care and purges of those opposed to Sar's regime led to the deaths of up to two million people – nearly a third of the population.

Saddam Hussein and Halabja (1986–1989). One of the worst chemical attacks in history by a regime against its own civilian population occurred in March 1988 when, during the closing days of the Iran–Iraq War (1980–1988), the then President of Iraq Saddam Hussein dropped chemical weapons on the Kurdish town of Halabja. The attack immediately killed approximately five thousand people and injured up to ten thousand more. Many more have since died because of after-effects in the form of diseases and birth defects. Halabja formed part of a wider campaign conducted between 1986 and 1989 by the Saddam regime against the Kurdish population of northern Iraq. Known as *Anfal*, the onslaught by the Iraqi army included ground and air offensives to destroy civilian centres, mass deportations and summary executions, culminating in chemical warfare. The campaign resulted in the destruction of over four thousand Kurdish villages, estimates of more than two million deaths and the displacement of more than a third of Iraq's 3.5 million Kurdish population. The campaign has been recognised by the international community as a crime against humanity as well as an example of genocide.

Robert Mugabe's Zimbabwe. For many in Zimbabwe, Mugabe was and is still regarded as a liberator. It was his role in the liberation movement against white minority rule which swept him to power in 1980. After being Prime Minister between 1980 and 1987 he then became the first executive head of state in 1987, and he has remained in that position ever since. The violence in Zimbabwe in recent years has its roots in the era of colonial rule which resulted in inequitable land distribution, whereby a small number of white Zimbabweans owned much of the fertile farming land. It was supposedly to correct this inequity that Mugabe's government began a highly controversial programme aimed at redistributing land away from whites to the black population. Applauded by many for correcting colonial injustices, the manner in which the process has taken place has come under severe criticism by many states – such as Britain – who have accused Mugabe of seizing land in a violent manner. This violence has included the rape of women and the murder of opposition members and civilians opposed to his rule and policies.

These examples bring a number of issues into the limelight, of which possibly the most important is: whose responsibility is it to look after individuals when the state itself turns against them? It is far too simple to claim that the United Nations and the international community need to step in and take over the role of protecting vulnerable civilians. That is not to say that the international community has not intervened in cases where civilians are being threatened and killed. Indeed, a reading of the history of the UN since its inception in 1945 shows many interventions. However, one common feature of most of these interventions has been their rather mixed and often poor results, with the UN either failing to secure peace and security or contributing to a further deterioration of the prevailing conditions, thereby further diminishing the security of civilians. It is beyond the remit of this chapter to deal with these cases, but we highlight some key issues and cases in the Chapter on the United Nations. Therefore, history is replete with examples of states colluding in barbaric acts against their own citizens, and we are left in no doubt that this particular entity has often and actively worked towards diminishing the security of individuals. Consequently, Critical Theorists of all persuasions, including those of the Welsh School, have a particular view of the state – namely, that it should act as a means to achieving security for individuals, rather than the final recipient.

Ken Booth and the Welsh School

The emancipation of the individual and the state as a provider of security rather than the final recipient are further developed as themes by Ken Booth, who emphasises his position clearly when he argues that true security can only be achieved when emancipation is reserved for the individual human. Booth began expressing these ideas in his seminal article published in 1991 entitled *Security and Emancipation* and developed them further in two books – *Critical Security Studies and World Politics* (2005) and *Theory of World Security* (2007) – both of which provide a definitive attempt to strengthen Critical Theory. In these publications Booth begins by calling for a decisive redefinition of the concept of security and declares the emancipation of the individual human to be the new direction of the field. His association with the University of Wales – Aberystwyth provided his views with a label – *the Welsh School* – and its main notable difference from other critical approaches is its links to the post-Marxist inspired views associated with the Frankfurt School tradition of Critical Theory.

Among other ideas, Booth can be credited with highlighting two factors in particular: first, emancipation must be elevated to a position where it is the primary purpose of Security Studies; and second, all forms of research into security issues must be self-reflective and adopt a normative basis. Ultimately, this sits comfortably with the tradition's central objective, namely being concerned with human emancipation. Traditionalist views stress objectivity and thereby diminish the importance of the normative basis of the Welsh School, but as Steve Smith has argued, there remains 'no neutral place to stand to pronounce on the meanings of security [and] all definitions are theory-dependent, and [consequently] all definitions reflect normative commitments' (Smith, 2005: 28). Booth, therefore, portrays emancipation as a privilege and argues that 'true (stable) security can only be achieved by people and groups if they do not deprive others of it' (Booth, 1991: 319).

Indeed, for Booth security and emancipation are two sides of the same coin, and this approach stands in opposition to the military focused state-centric views of

Realism. Emancipation for Booth is achieved when humans are freed 'from those physical and human constraints which stop them carrying out what they would freely choose to do'. He goes on to stress that 'War and threat of war is one of those constraints, together with poverty, poor education, political oppression and so on' (Booth, 1991: 319). Adopting this emancipatory approach has provided Booth with a point of departure from the problem-solving nature of traditionalist approaches. Ultimately, his opposition to the state-centric view of Realism rests on its acceptance of the state as the primary recipient of security. Booth sees this as illogical and advocates the state as the means of achieving security for individuals rather than an end in itself. He aptly explains this point by drawing an analogy with a house and its inhabitants.

> A house requires upkeep, but it is illogical to spend excessive amounts of money and effort to protect the house against flood, dry rot and burglars if this is at the cost of the well-being of the inhabitants. There is obviously a relationship between the well-being of the sheltered and the state of the shelter, but can there be any question as to whose security is primary?
>
> (Booth, 1991: 320)

Finally, Booth does not dismiss the state, and nor does he disregard the Realist grasp of world politics. He does, however, insist that politics needed to evolve and be much more mindful of ethical and human-centric concerns – elements which traditionalist approaches such as Realism largely ignore. By elevating the state the Realists exact a heavy price – the exclusion of all other possible referent objects. It is this feature which Critical Theorists such as Booth and Cox find so objectionable. Booth in particular has been instrumental in expanding the boundaries of the discipline of Security Studies by stressing the importance of the individual. He further encourages us to resist traditionalist dominance by arguing that people everywhere are subjected to insecurity by a combination of a wide variety of threats including human rights abuses, civil conflict, political oppression, corruption, environmental degradation and a lack of good governance. This demonstrates that there is a strong practical element to emancipation and that it is not some unrealistic utopian goal. Booth stresses that the everyday struggles of groups, people and individuals the world over provide an important basis upon which notions of emancipation are built.

Alternative critical approaches

Clearly Critical Security Studies has succeeded in questioning a number of key elements that traditionalist approaches such as Realism take for granted. Realism's blind and unquestioning acceptance of the state as the pre-eminent actor in international life has particularly come under scrutiny by Critical Theorists, who have reminded us that often it is states themselves that threaten individuals. The arrival of Critical Security Studies has significantly expanded the boundaries of the discipline and this can only be a welcome development. However, an analysis of critical approaches would not be complete without some reference to two further traditions – Post-Structuralism and Post-Colonialism. Including these in a chapter on critical approaches makes sense given they also display an intense objection to many of the assumptions held by traditionalist theories such as Realism. Post-Structuralism holds that if we are to grasp any aspect of international life, then we must place greater importance on interpretation and reflection rather than accept pre-determined explanations characteristic of the scientific (positivist) methods adopted by traditionalist approaches such as Realism (or Liberalism). Post-Colonial approaches go even further in their critique when they point to the Western orientation of Security Studies and question whether the discipline contains adequate theoretical tools to analyse the peculiar problems facing the developing world – many of which are former colonies of European states. Indeed, we contend that the historical, political, social and cultural contexts of the developing world require their own set of theoretical criteria with which to analyse the security problems facing them.

Post-Structuralism

Post-Structuralism is undoubtedly a complicated notion, and to aid understanding a degree of simplification is necessary. One way of achieving this is to consider the term 'Structuralism', since Post-Structuralism aims to go beyond this approach and opposes its central premise. Structuralism developed during the first half of the twentieth century, and its impact continues to be felt within the social sciences. Structuralism sought to be deterministic and a-historical, emphasising the need to arrive at secure and objective knowledge. In Security Studies, theories such as Realism claim that secure, objective knowledge, created through adherence to positivism, forms the basis for an understanding of international life. Structuralists further claim that societies are organised in accordance with certain pre-determined structures and patterns, and that by analysing these structures, disciplines such as Politics, Sociology, International Relations, or indeed Security Studies can analyse their respective phenomena by employing the objective principles of positivist methodology – an approach perhaps better suited to the natural sciences than the social.

Initially, Structuralism began as a theory of language strongly influenced by Ferdinand de Saussure, who argued that languages contained definitive structures that needed to be followed if successful communication was to be achieved. Other disciplines have taken this notion further, applying it to their respective areas and stressing the importance of determinism, objectivity and a-historicism. Didier Bigo, for instance, argues that the knowledge embodied within the discipline of Security Studies has been heavily influenced by the rigidity imposed by political scientists:

> [They] displayed a preference for rational choice theory and general abstraction, as well as a "case study" approach, i.e., transforming historical and sociological trajectories into (dependent and independent) "variables". Consequently, the key concepts in these disciplines have been naturalized and essentialized – that is, they have lost their specific historicity. Theory has been associated with pure abstraction and minimalist statements in an attempt to mimic "scientific laws".
>
> (Bigo, 2013: 121)

The roots of Structuralism lie in both modernity and the Enlightenment – with the former stressing the transition from feudalism to capitalism and the arrival of industrialization, secularization, rationality and the ascendancy of the nation-state. The Enlightenment, on the other hand, stressed the ability of man to 'reason' and therefore cast aside the religious dogma and superstition characteristic of medievalism. This cultural movement dominated Europe during the eighteenth century, and apart from stressing man's innate capacity for reason, it highlighted the importance of knowledge gained through the scientific process. Consequently, superstition, intolerance, and abuses by church or state came to be seen as social evils that needed to be superseded by a resort to rational structures and institutions in society. The impact of this is still felt in Security Studies in the manner in which traditionalist approaches such as Realism rely on modernist and positivist bases to construct knowledge about how the world works. Furthermore, this knowledge is also described as being objective, value-free and scientific. Much of the theorising in Security Studies continues to rely heavily on Realist views of the world, and as we have stated elsewhere this book, Realist knowledge is largely based on a rationally acting state sharing space with similar entities in an anarchic environment where military primacy defines state behaviour. A prominent Post-Structuralist, Richard Ashley, sees such approaches as being trapped in a logic that 'treated the given order as the natural order' (Ashley, 1986: 259).

Post-Structuralism, then, seeks to go beyond what it sees as the rigidity imposed by Structuralist notions, and in this sense it shares a number of key factors with the other critical approaches highlighted in this chapter. Its rejection of positivist methodology in the construction of knowledge and its acceptance of the need for critique are central to the goals of other Critical Theorists. However, Post-Structuralism also stands far apart because of its radical agenda, which is dominated by a refusal to acknowledge claims made by objectivist and scientific grand narratives such as Realism. Indeed, Post-Structuralists remain much more open to the view that knowledge is never fixed and that it remains unstable, unpredictable and erratic. Not only does this view reject traditionalist approaches such as Realism, but it also rather unceremoniously brings into question the ideas of emancipation and human social progress that form the basis of the Welsh School of Critical Security Studies headed by Ken Booth. Its critique of the powerful narratives that claim to construct knowledge of the human condition (including those within Security Studies) is certainly a commendable goal, but its failure to offer alternative options to that condition is often seen as a serious shortcoming.

Post-Structuralism is a challenging approach to grasp, but a number of thinkers such as Jacques Derrida have highlighted some common themes. He uses the notion of 'logocentricism' to refer to the manner in which certain strands within texts prevail in importance over others. Logocentricism involves the construction of dualities (inclusion/exclusion or inside/outside) within texts, followed by the establishment of a hierarchy between the opposing themes. One of the most celebrated dichotomous relationships in Security Studies is that between anarchy and sovereignty. Traditionalist approaches such as Realism place the utmost importance on the concept of the state as a firmly established sovereign entity. The inside of the state is characterised by the rule of law, stability, and an environment safe from the anarchy which exists outside – which in turn is seen as a quasi-Hobbesian condition lacking in the rule of law and exemplified by the continuous possibility of deadly conflict between states. Therefore, for Realism, the state solidifies the boundary between inside and outside space, sovereignty/anarchy, us/them and duty/indifference. However, Ashley has questioned how the privileging of state-centric accounts of international relations has come to be seen as natural and inevitable. He reminds us, for instance, that the notion of sovereignty is problematic given that it relies heavily on a high degree of consensus within each state. He goes on to argue that the sovereignty narrative can only function when the variations within states are discarded, thus giving the impression of homogeneity (Ashley, 1989).

Michel Foucault, another important contributor to Post-Structuralist thought, uses Jeremy Bentham's notion of the panopticon to demonstrate how certain narratives become privileged over others. Bentham saw the panopticon as a prison which would function as a constant surveillance instrument. The panoptic construction of the prison ensured that none of the inmates was able to see the prison guard, who was located in a central, elevated position and therefore able to observe any of the prisoners at any time. The idea behind this was that no prisoner would ever know the moment when he was being observed – and the mental uncertainty that this created was deemed to be sufficient to condition the prisoners into disciplining themselves.

Of particular importance is Michel Foucault's use of Bentham's idea of the panopticon as a metaphor to explain how societies function on two levels. The first is the notion of inside/outside dualism, where whatever is inside is seen as fitting certain acceptable moral codes and is therefore considered to be good, while the outside functions according to unacceptable, dangerous and secondary codes. This closely relates to the anarchy/sovereignty dichotomy referred to earlier. The second component refers to the manner in which the panopticon functions as a symbol of power in contemporary societies. In *Discipline and Punish*, published in 1975, Foucault showed how modern institutions – such as the army, hospitals and schools – have acquired panoptic-like characteristics over time (Foucault, 1975). Those in charge of these hierarchical structures are able to achieve almost constant surveillance of subordinates, and this panoptic gaze has been enhanced considerably as technology has developed. Today, near invisible surveillance techniques provide a constant reminder to the general population that it is now possible to gaze into their daily lives. Foucault would argue that the disciplining of society is complete.

Post-Structuralism entered the discipline of International Relations in the 1980s and Security Studies soon after. In addition to Foucault, Derrida and Ashley, mentioned above, there have been a number of other influential Post-Structuralist thinkers, including James Der Derian and Michael Shapiro. Their early studies concentrated mainly on critiquing the claims to knowledge of traditionalist approaches such as Realism and Neorealism. Writing in the late 1980s, their intention was to show how these approaches placed significant restrictions on what could be claimed about world politics. Their restrictive and rigid assumptions about power, the state and anarchy, combined with their positivist stance and dominance of the field, not only defined the subject matter of the discipline, but also framed the kinds of questions which could be asked. Post-Structuralists rebelled against these restrictions and have criticised the traditional approaches not only for ignoring the role of new transnational actors, but also for marginalising the views of the poor, oppressed and excluded people of the world. The essence of Post-Structuralism is, therefore, clearly 'critical', and there also appears to be a strong ethical undertone in its engagement with mainstream approaches.

Post-Colonialism

A discussion of critical approaches to Security Studies would not be complete without a brief introduction to another important development in the field – namely Post-

Colonialism. The one component shared between Post-Colonialism and the other approaches highlighted in this chapter is their tendency to be critical of mainstream explanations of security. Indeed, Post-Colonial literature provides a damning indictment of the Western orientation of the discipline of Security Studies. Post-Colonialism also shares considerable ground with Post-Structuralism in that both have rebelled against the dominance of mainstream approaches such as Realism. For instance, both share the premise that globalisation and decolonisation have transformed world politics in significant ways, and that this factor should be sufficient to encourage traditional Realists to acknowledge that their approach is insufficient to explain the changes. However, Post-Colonial and Post-Structural thinkers have complained about the manner in which approaches such as Realism have succeeded in marginalising alternative views and actors while at the same time ignoring the pleas for recognition by those groups, individuals and ideas that have remained on the periphery of Security Studies.

The prime purpose of Post-Colonial literature, therefore, is to challenge the failure of the developing world to feature in the analysis of Western security considerations. Indeed, the strong Euro-centric character of Security Studies has been reflected in the manner in which the field has traditionally focused on struggles between sovereign states including, importantly, questions of war and peace. This feature became particularly entrenched during the Cold War, when superpower politics revolved around the need to protect state sovereignty by maintaining a balance of military power. This in turn meant that the discipline largely failed to develop the theoretical tools needed to reflect on the particular problems facing former colonies. Critical Security Studies has of course gone some way towards addressing the neglect of non-state/military components of security, but there are those who argue that even this development within the field has remained within the fold of Western-centrism. Claire Wilkinson, for instance, discredits the Copenhagen School's presumptions that Western understandings of security and the state are somehow universally applicable (Wilkinson, 2007).

Conclusion

Critical Security Studies is undoubtedly challenging. It is a broad field which incorporates many differing perspectives and it has now evolved to occupy a prominent position within the discipline. Although disagreement remains among the various proponents in the field, it has nevertheless been possible to draw out some central commitments. The rallying point for early thinkers was the intense dissatisfaction with the military/state-centric core of traditional security theories such as Realism. The critical approaches featured in this chapter have all highlighted serious shortcomings within the traditional core in that its emphasis on military security and state sovereignty is often at the expense of the security of the individual. To a large extent these views have also taken issue with the lack of an ethical dimension in traditional theorising. Ken Booth's preoccupation with emancipation, Robert Cox's concern as to whether international structures are fundamentally fair or not, and the Post-Colonial drive to steer towards a consideration of the problems facing individuals and societies in non-Western states have considerably expanded the normative boundaries of the discipline.

Summary points

1 Critical Security Studies is a broad subfield which incorporates a number of strands, all of which criticise the narrow focus imposed by traditional military and state-centric ideas of security.
2 Ken Booth seeks to shift attention away from the state to the individual. For him the emancipation of the individual is the only way to achieve true security.
3 Robert Cox makes the distinction between problem-solving theories and his Critical Theory, where the former takes the world as it is and fails to consider whether it is fundamentally fair or not, whereas the latter seeks to change unfair structures and practices.
4 Post-Structural studies critique the claims to knowledge of traditionalist approaches such as Realism and Neorealism. Their intention has been to show how traditional approaches place significant restrictions on what could be claimed about world politics.
5 Post-Colonial approaches criticise the whole field of Security Studies, including the Critical Theory subfield, for marginalising the particular problems facing the developing world.

Recommended reading

Ashley, R. 'Living on Borderlines: Man, Post Structuralism, and War', in J. Der Derian and M.J. Shapiro (eds), *International/Intertextual Relations: Postmodern Readings of World Politics*, Lexington, Mass: Lexington Books, 1989.

Booth, K. 'Security and Emancipation', *Review of International Studies*, vol. 17, no. 4, October 1991, 313–326.

Buzan, B. and Hansen, L. *The Evolution of International Security Studies*, Cambridge: Cambridge University Press, 2009.

Cox, R. 'Social forces, states and world orders: beyond international relations theory', *Millennium: Journal of International Studies*, vol. 10, no. 2, 1981, 126–155.

Foucault, M. *Discipline and Punish: The Birth of the Prison*, London: Penguin Books, first translation 1978.

Krause, K. and Williams, M. *Critical Security Studies: Concepts and Strategies*, London: Routledge, 1997.

4 Feminist Security Studies

Wendy Stokes

Box 4.1: Why Feminist Security Studies?

- 'Feminism is politics' (Phillips, 1998: 1).
- 'Nowhere is the silence towards gender more deafening than in the field of International Security' (Wadley, 2010: 39).
- 'The role of women with respect to national security has been ambiguous: defined as those whom the state and its men are protecting, women have had little control over the conditions of their protection' (Tickner, 1992: 28).
- 'There is a real danger that collapsing femininity or masculinity into the term "human" could conceal the gendered underpinnings of security practices' (Hudson, 2005: 157).
- 'In the name of universality, realists have constructed a worldview based on the experiences of a certain man: it is therefore a worldview that offers us only a partial view of reality' (Tickner, 1992: 30).
- 'A gender-sensitive concept of Human Security must therefore link women's everyday experiences with broader regional and global political processes and structures' (Hudson, 2005: 164).

Introduction

Feminist Security Studies is a critical approach to security. In common with other critical approaches, it argues for a broader definition of security that, at the least, includes consideration of women's experiences, roles, and perceptions of war and state security, and in its more developed forms demands the extension of 'security' to include a range of different criteria such as domestic violence, economic, food, and environmental security, as well as consideration of the gendered nature of the concept of 'state security'. In order to fully grasp how Feminism engages with Security Studies the following chapter gives a brief introduction to Feminism and then defines Feminist Political Theory and Feminist theories of International Relations, before addressing Feminist Security Studies. Under the heading of Feminist approaches to security it examines Feminist perspectives on war and peace, and its relation to Human Security.

Feminism

Feminism, more than any other political theory, is grounded in the practice of daily life. Its conception of inequality is grounded in the observation of difference and inequality between men and women in daily life; its conception of change is grounded in the practices of individuals and groups that create the practice of women's movements.

Women's movements are described in 'waves'. The first wave was the push for the vote and political inclusion in the nineteenth and early twentieth centuries; the second wave was the demand for full legal and social equality in the mid-twentieth century; and the third wave is more diffuse but is forcing societies to acknowledge a range of violent and exclusionary practices and put them right.

In between the waves, women's movements subside and Feminist theory dips below the horizon, living on in books, university departments and the occasional novel or play, but largely unseen – even scorned – in public life. After a period of quiescence in the late twentieth century, women are moving again: Femen, women's budget groups, the education of girls, opposition to FGM (female genital mutilation), and mobilising against sexual violence during armed conflict are just a few of the women's initiatives that make headline news.

The task here is not to describe or analyse Feminism in general, but to consider its role in the study of International Relations and Security Studies. However, before going into the particular, it is important to understand the general. Feminist theory is not a dry, academic construction; it is neither passive nor complete. It is a growing, adapting, learning theory of society and human relations that responds to the changing practices of gender in the world, just as it shapes how we react to such practices.

Texts like this book, which are aimed at young scholars acquiring the building blocks of theory, tend to start by describing different schools of Feminist theory. Yet thinking in terms of these 'schools' does not fairly reflect the realities of how we theorise the world, and fails to reflect the living, changing nature of Feminism. All versions of Feminist theory share the perception that gender inequality underpins both the practices of inequality across societies, and flawed beliefs about how the world works. Writers and activists engaged in Feminism and women's movements range across a wide spectrum in their perceptions of how inequality is expressed and caused, as well as how it should be addressed. They are interested in different fields where sex/gender inequality is to be found, and give priority to different instances of discrimination, exploitation, or ignorance.

Rather than separating Feminist theories into tidy boxes, each with a name on the lid, it is better to view the expanse of Feminist ideas across a spectrum. At one end, we would put the idea that men and women are essentially different – essentially feminine and masculine – while at the other would be the idea that all social life, including gender, is socially constructed and malleable. Along the continuum would be shades of opinion about the roles of men and women, gender and power in the world, as well as the various insights from politics, sociology, anthropology, psychology, psychoanalysis, evolution, and other approaches to learning. There would also be variations in how to address inequality, whether through equal opportunities strategies that enable women to make the same choices as men, or through more radical change to social structures that would alter the opportunities available to both men and women.

Feminism has a long history, although the name is relatively new, dating from the nineteenth century. Despite the early contributions of Christine de Pizan in fourteenth-century France and others, modern Feminist thinking is traceable to the late eighteenth century, where it emerged under the influence of the American and French revolutions and Enlightenment thought. French writers Olympe de Gouges,

Madelaine de Puisieux and Nicolas de Condorcet, along with American activists Abigail Adams, Sarah Moore Grimke and Lucretia Mott and writers Mary Wollstonecraft and Catherine Macaulay in England, set the tone of Western feminism for the next two hundred years. It was and is an essentially political and critical set of ideas and practices. It is descriptive, analytical and prescriptive: observing inequalities and gendered power; analysing the roots and expressions of these; and theorising means to overcome them and achieve a different future.

This chapter considers the role of Feminism in the development of theory in the interrelated fields of Politics, International Relations and Security Studies. In considering Feminist theories of security, we shall look at the growth of Feminist security theory, its position as a critical theory, its ambivalent focus on peace, and its identification with a Human Security approach.

Feminist Political Theory

The body of what we usually think of as Feminist Political Theory has grown up since the second wave women's movements of the 1960s. Deeply embedded in these movements, Feminist writers sought to understand gender – the social construction of male and female as different and unequal, and the unequal power of men and women – through the study of social structures and practices such as unequal pay, unequal status, domestic violence and sexual violence. They examined literature, films, theatre, and art as well as the professions, political office, the family, legislation and social mores in order to understand how gender difference and inequality persist across time and place. The guiding themes from this period were patriarchy and dominance: the idea that there was an overarching social structure that privileged masculine values and men over female values and women, and that this led to the domination of men over women. It was understood that this was an over-simplification and that class, race and other variables crosscut gender power, but the insistence that gender was a relation of power imbalance was a vital correction to a field of thought that assumed undifferentiated political actors. This was framed by the concepts of public and private spheres: a separation of human life and activity that had been vital to the development of political ideas. The public was the world of political life, accessible to all citizens as equals, where the decisions that constituted community life were made and executed. The private, on the other hand, was the world of domesticity and care, which was excluded from politics and collective decision-making. Historically, the public had been the domain of male citizens, who also had access to the private; this was the domain of women, children and slaves, who did not have access to the public.

Feminist Political Theory criticised the canon of Western political thought, pointing out that if you add women and the things that women do into the theories of Marx or Hobbes (to take just two of the more egregious proponents) you get some very different outcomes. For example, Susan Moller Okin famously asked who was shopping, cooking, cleaning and looking after the children while Marx's post-revolutionary man was hunting, fishing and philosophising, and one is forced to wonder how the human race perpetuated itself in the Hobbesian state of nature when everyone competed with and lived in fear of everyone else. Feminist Political Theory then went on to develop its own theories of (among other things) democracy and political representation, pointing out that including women and breaking down the public/private divide fundamentally altered the meanings of such terms as democracy, equality, liberty, consent and representation.

The trajectory of Feminist politics is well described by Joni Lovenduski in her Introduction to *Different Roles, Different Voices,* where she traces the development of the Feminist contribution to the study of politics from initially adding women in to the study of traditional political topics, through extending the purview of the discipline to include alternative political arenas outside of the formal politics of parliaments and parties, such as local government, pressure groups and social movements, in which women play larger roles, to a gendered critique of the assumptions and values underpinning political theories and institutions and the ways in which they are studied (Lovenduski, 1994: ix–xvi).

Feminist International Relations

The study of International Relations was slow to take on a Feminist dimension: much slower than most areas of life or the academy. Despite the synchronous development of IR and Feminism both as practices and as areas of academic study, the two did not really meet each other until the 1990s. For many years not only was the practice of International Relations overwhelmingly conducted by men; research into it was also conducted by men, who saw the world of IR as a fairly simple one of high-level interaction between nation states in conflict and the resolution of these conflicts. IR scholars might argue that since their focus was the nation state, individual people and the differences between them were irrelevant because considerations of sex, race and age were invisible in the sweep of large-scale politics. However, that would be to assume that a nation state was a homogenous entity, quite the reverse of everything that the twentieth century demonstrated, and a denial of the greatest causes of conflict in the past thirty years.

J. Anne Tickner elucidates the problem in a 2004 article in which she suggests that the very natures of IR theory and Feminist theory are such that bringing them together is a struggle. IR theory tends to follow the logic of the natural sciences: 'The goal of theory building for conventional IR, which includes most realists, has been to generate propositions that are testable and that can help explain the security-seeking behavior of states in the international system' (Tickner, 2004: 44). Feminist theory, on the other hand, 'is explicitly normative and often emancipatory. Believing that claims of objectivity and universality that rest on knowledge primarily about men must be questioned, feminists seek to develop what they call "practical knowledge" or knowledge developed out of the everyday practices of peoples' lives. Preferring bottom-up rather than top-down knowledge, feminists believe that theory cannot be separated from political practice' (Tickner, 2004: 45).

Nevertheless, Feminist approaches were introduced to the study of IR and there is now a growing literature analysing how women (and gender) have been considered and constructed in the research, theorising and writing in this newly-emerged subject area. Feminist International Relations is both a critical and a creative approach to understanding, and the study of Feminist International Relations goes beyond criticism of the mainstream discipline and what might be called the 'adding women in' approach, to create alternative perspectives (see Youngs, 2004). Rather like Feminist politics, Feminist International Relations has insisted that women are counted in, that the particular spaces and experiences of women are included in the field of study, and that a Feminist perspective is a critical approach to International Relations that articulates a critical agenda (see Steans, 2013). Despite the efforts of such eminent figures in the field of IR as Fred Halliday, Ralph Pettman and Barry Buzan, the discipline at large has been very slow to accept either a sex/gender disaggregated population or Feminist International Relations, and consideration of women, gender and IR has been very much the concern of female academics such as Cynthia Cockburn, Cynthia Enloe, Jan Jindy Pettman, Jill Steans, J. Anne Tickner, Gillian Youngs and Nira Yuval-Davis.

The emergence of a visible Feminist critique and the start of its impact are usually dated to the publication of the first edition of Cynthia Enloe's *Bananas, Beaches and Bases* in 1989. At around the same time the journal *Millennium* published the first of its issues dedicated to women/gender and IR, an initiative that was repeated in 1998 and 2008. In the study of IR the different strands of adding women in, examining different political spaces and evolving a Feminist perspective have run together rather more than in the earlier Feminist politics. Despite having the model of Feminist political critique, not to mention the Feminist development of most other academic disciplines, International Relations was surprisingly resistant. Perhaps because the origins of the discipline lay in the study of organisations and events with little reference to individuals or indeed people, consideration of the differentiation of human beings, differentiated impact of events and policies, and differentiated experiences seemed irrelevant. Only as the discipline matured and started to consider in more depth the nature of the nation states, the impact of the international organisations, and the effects of policies, did consideration of the people who underpinned the nations, organisations and policies acquire salience. Further, as scholars of IR sought greater theoretical rigour than that provided by Realism, they had to confront the gendering of social and political theory that had been taking place for some decades. Feminist International Relations has developed largely in parallel to the mainstream and is only now being absorbed rather than tagged on as a token (see Youngs, 2004 for a discussion of Feminist IR).

Feminist Security Studies

Following closely on the heels of Cynthia Enloe's revelation that 'relations between governments depend not only on capital and weaponry, but also on the control of women as symbols, consumers, workers and emotional comforters' (Enloe, 1989: xii), J. Anne Tickner wrote what was probably the first gender and IR textbook, *Gender in International Relations: Feminist Perspectives in Achieving Global Security*. Published in 1992, its five chapters inject Feminist insights into key areas of IR: national security, economic security, and ecological security (Tickner, 1992). While the first chapter sets up the problem of masculine IR and conceptions of security, the final chapter outlines a 'non-gendered' perspective on global security. A Feminist, or non-gendered, conception of security is defined as: 'the absence of violence whether it be military, economic or sexual' (Tickner, 1992: 66). Her summary of the development of IR theory from its initial liberal hopefulness, through Realism, Neorealism and the growth of critical perspectives leads to the conclusion that: 'among realism's critics, virtually no attention has been given to gender as a category of analysis' (Tickner, 1992: 14).

When it comes to Security Studies, this means that both the content of security and the means to achieve it have been defined in the absence of any consideration of the experiences and status of women (or indeed minorities of any sort), and of any reflection on whether the values adopted in either the practice or theory of security are partial rather than universal. The predominant criticism that Feminism poses to Security Studies is one that it shares with other critical perspectives: security requires more than just the absence of armed conflict between nation states. This is not a revelation. Other disciplines such as Psychology, Sociology and Anthropology, as well as Feminist analyses, have long been aware of this, but IR scholars are remarkably slow to pick up insights from other areas of research. Security for most people is a fact of daily life, entwined with the freedoms or capacities often associated with human rights. From this perspective security includes: protection from violence in the home and on the street; economic stability; access to shelter, food and water; freedom to choose whether, when and with whom to have sex, marry or cohabit, and whether or when to have children; as well as rather more remote considerations of national defence.

Consideration of women is key, but consideration of gender is not quite the same thing. Including gender as well as women means reflecting on the nature of social difference and its role in power relations. Importantly, True introduces consideration of masculinity into the mix, discussing work that has been done on identifying the formation of masculinity (as well as femininity) and in particular the dominant form of masculinity at any one time or place (hegemonic masculinity) (True, 2012: 36). This is important because in discussions of gender we often forget about the male half of the equation, or at least take it as a given that does not require investigation. Also, there is a tendency in denouncing patriarchy to associate it with all men and assume that all men benefit from it. Analysis of hegemonic masculinity shows us that there is hierarchy among men, and those men, and those characteristics, that conform to the current ideal-type of masculinity take precedence not only over women, but also over men whose masculinity is differently expressed. Right now, we may think that metrosexual men with toned muscles, elite education, highly-paid professional occupations and so on set the pace, but in the past and in other places it may have been the strongest, the oldest, or the most devout whose contours defined the mould of supremacy.

Although it shares much with other critical approaches, Feminism focuses on a gendered critique and the adoption of a female point of view, which other critical theories may or may not include. From a Feminist perspective, traditional Security Studies is doubly flawed: first, it adopts a stance which is 'gendered' insofar as it is assumed to be universal while it is in fact shaped by the privileges, values and experiences of the men making policies and analysing them, who are predominantly men from the dominant classes, groups and ethnicities; and second, it is 'gendered' because it does not take on the range of human experience, focusing instead on a generalised notion of a citizen, all of whose characteristics are those of a man.

The following sections will look at particular elements of Feminist Security Studies: the identification of women with peace; a gendered approach to understanding conflict; and the curious relationship between Feminism and Human Security.

The identification of women with peace

Feminist IR is largely indistinguishable from Feminist Security Studies, perhaps because from the outset – as suggested by the title of Tickner's 1992 book – the exclusion of women from consideration of conflict, conflict resolution, arms regulation and other key topics was seen as relevant to women's security. Women have been most easily encompassed by conventional Security Studies through an identification with peace: peace movements, peacemaking, peacetime. This has been coherent with one tendency in Feminism, which is to associate femininity with peace as opposed to the masculine quality of aggression and practice of making war. While this perspective has been popular, as well as quite useful for the rhetoric of peace groups such as Greenham Women, it is not the view of all Feminists, many of whom consider it problematic and reductive to generalise about women and men in order to create such an opposition. It is broadly in keeping with a Feminist approach referred to as a politics of care or maternal thinking, in which 'feminine' characteristics, including compassion, forgiveness and cooperation, are contrasted with 'masculine' characteristics such as aggression and dominance. Although writers in this tradition frequently deny that they assume gendered characteristics to be innate to men and women, the theories are often interpreted as such. Critics also claim that a politics of care idealises family and personal relationships, overlooking the tyranny and emotional blackmail that such connections can entail, and thus drawing a rather over-estimated distinction between the formal relations of the public sphere and the loving relations of the private. Nonetheless, these theories are broadly in keeping with an approach to peace studies that identifies peace with feminine characteristics, thus endowing women with a special access to peace and a rejection of conflict and war.

A Feminist commitment to approach security as peace studies is not necessarily the same as considering women to be inherently more peaceful than men, but Sylvester argues that a Feminist commitment to peace studies is challenged by women's participation in armed conflict (Sylvester, 2010: 609). In order to develop understanding of armed conflict, Feminist researchers have investigated how, when and where women are active participants. The goal is to get a more rounded picture of conflict and a bottom-up perspective on what drives participants. Miranda Alison sets out to counter the belief that women are 'naturally' peaceful by examining the roles of female combatants in anti-state or liberatory ('ethno-nationalist') forces (Alison, 2004: 453). Her research focused on two conflicts in Northern Ireland and Sri Lanka, where she found women active in a range of roles. She concluded that organisations included women as a demonstration of their progressive inclusionary politics, incorporated images of women into their iconography as freedom fighters (Alison, 2004: 453), and that 'In many cases, women involved in nationalist struggles, while themselves undertaking non-traditional gender roles, have utilized existing conservative gender constructions and stereotypes to pursue their objectives against the state or their perceived enemy' (Alison, 2004: 456). However, she introduces the proviso that fighting for the security of their communities just like the men alongside them does not guarantee women equality after the conflict. Their equality in combat is regarded as a temporary change to the status quo (Alison, 2004: 458). She concludes that: 'the figure of the female combatant remains riven with tension and ambivalence. The evidence presented in this article suggests that, even when women participate in military roles in nationalist mobilizations their presence and actions are experienced by some male members as threatening what we might call the psychological security of clear-cut, gender-differentiated roles' (Alison, 2004: 460).

In considering women as combatants, writers argue for the inclusion of women and their perspectives in peace negotiations and reconstruction. For example, it might be argued that the Northern Ireland conflict would have been settled more quickly if women from the Loyalist paramilitaries had been included in negotiations. Similarly, looking at Sierra Leone, it might be thought that discounting women's participation as combatants, and thus excluding them from post-conflict reconstruction processes, undermined those processes, while research among female militants in Kashmir and Sri Lanka suggests that 'understanding women's participation in militancy will improve scholarly understandings of gender and conflict' (Sjoberg, 2010: Introduction). Thus research into women's participation in conflict suggests that their relative absence is more likely to be a result of the societal construction of gender roles and public and private spheres than any innate aversion.

If women are not necessarily unwarlike, is there any other connection between gender and conflict? A rather different approach to linking women with peace was adopted by Hudson *et al.* in a piece of research that equates women's security to sex equality and thereby links gender inequality and the treatment/security of women to the security of the state. Using a range of methodologies garnered from Evolutionary Biology, Psychology, Political Psychology, social diffusion theory, and social learning theory, the writers demonstrate that the processes and structures of gender correlate to the predisposition of a state 'to become involved in militarized interstate disputes and in violent interstate disputes, to be the aggressors during interstate disputes and to rely on force when involved in an international dispute' (Hudson *et al.*, 2008: 30). The writers accumulate and synthesise an array of international data. Using standard statistical analysis they conclude that the physical security of women is strongly associated with the peacefulness of the state; further, the physical security of women is a stronger variable in the identification of peacefulness than the level of democracy, the level of wealth, or the prevalence of Islamic culture (Hudson *et al.*, 2008: 39).

Thus we see that women are and can be involved in conflict and war in a variety of roles. However, although there may be no simple correlation between women and peacefulness – that is, women are not necessarily innately more peaceful and peace-making than men – a peaceful and secure society is likely to be one in which there is greater equality of the sexes. Therefore, in the interest of security, as well as the interest of women, a society might do well to maximise sex/gender equality.

Feminist perspectives on war

Writers have made efforts to understand why women are more associated with peace and men with war. On the one hand, as Tickner points out, until recently, not only have all wars been fought by men, but it has been men who made all the decisions about whether, when and where to engage in conflict. More recently, it was male scholars who developed the discipline of IR in order to identify the causes of war, and men who continue to make up the bulk of researchers in the field. Thus, she claims, it is not surprising that the dominant theory in IR, Realism, focuses on power, autonomy, self-reliance and rationality – all characteristics associated with the '"socially constructed", "ideal-type" masculinity' (Tickner, 2004: 44). On the other hand, research into socialisation tends to show that girl-children are rewarded for gentle behaviours, while boy-children are more likely to get positive reinforcement for assertive, if not actually aggressive, behaviour (Tickner, 2004: 47).

Mainstream Security Studies, like mainstream IR, tends to assume that conflict and war are natural and unavoidable conditions for humanity. Moreover, conflict and war are conceptualised as events in the public sphere, primarily between nation states, although civil war and other conflicts within a state have assumed increasing significance since the end of the Cold War. Feminist analyses place armed conflict in the broader spectrum of violence and look for patterns that might link armed conflict, domestic violence, structures of power and inequality, and the socially determined forms of gender relations – not just femininity, but also hegemonic masculinity.

Box 4.2: Violence against women

According to UNIFEM, acts of violence cause more death and disability among women aged between fifteen and forty-four than cancer, malaria, traffic accidents and war combined.[1] Similarly, Hudson *et al.* marshal data to demonstrate that in the twentieth century more women have died owing to 'Societal Devaluation of Female Life' than people have died as a result of war/civil strife (Hudson *et al.*, 2008: 10). Alternatively, the World Bank estimated in 1993 that violence against women was as serious a cause of death and incapacity among women of reproductive age as cancer, and a greater cause of ill health than traffic accidents and malaria combined (World Bank, 1993).

According to a World Health Organization report published in 2013 that pulled together data from around the world, some 38% of all murdered women are killed by an intimate partner, compared with 6% of all murdered men (World Health Organization, 2013). Intimate femicide, as this has recently been named, is both the most acute, and the most measurable, expression of violence against women. Measures of other expressions of violence are less reliable, but the same report gives the global prevalence of intimate partner violence among those women who have ever had a partner as 30% (World Health Organization, 2013: 16). Non-partner sexual violence is considerably lower, pushing the global proportion of women who have ever experienced either non-partner sexual violence and/or intimate partner sexual and/or physical violence to 35.6% (World Health Organization, 2013; sources of the data are given on pages 10–11; data on murder on page 26).

Consideration of the experiences and perspectives of women and children causes Feminist critics to pose (at least two) alternative insights. First, conflict in the private sphere of the domestic or local cannot be separated from conflict in the public. Second, conflict affects a far wider range of people than just armed combatants, it affects them in a wide variety of ways, and the effects last much longer than the actual conflict. Hence, we are forced to consider domestic violence and crimes against women as well as inter- or intra-state violence, and investigate connections, and to look at the roles and conditions of civilians both during a conflict and subsequent to an agreed peace.

As we have seen above, Hudson *et al.* found correlations between gender equality and the peacefulness of a nation state. Similarly, Caprioli argues that since women are not secure in either the public or private spheres, the two are inextricably linked. Therefore, in order to secure women's safety in the public, it has to be secured in the private (Caprioli, 2004: 412). She claims that the definition of insecurity as state-perpetrated violence is inadequate and social violence must be included. Citing the 1999 UNDP *Human Development Report*, she claims that 'any type of discrimination that impedes the freedom and safety necessary to exercise social, political, and economic choices undermines human security', and that 'norms of violence, the antithesis of human security, are inherent in hierarchical social structures' (Caprioli, 2004: 412–413). 'Security in the private sphere' (by which is meant not just the home but all the places where daily life takes place) 'is crucial to women's security but is often excluded from prevailing measures of security that focus on public rights' (Caprioli, 2004: 413).

Box 4.3: Gender inequalities indices

In the ten years since Caprioli's research gender (in)equalities indices have been developed that illuminate a far broader range of inequality that she had access to, in far greater detail. Indices include the African Gender and Development Index introduced by the United Nations Economic Commission for Africa in 2004, the Global Gender Gap Index devised by the World Economic Forum in 2006, and the Social Institutions and Gender Index (SIGI) produced by the Organisation for Economic Co-operation and Development (OECD) in 2009.

The World Economic Forum *Global Gender Gap Report* uses economic participation and opportunity, educational attainment, health and survival, and political empowerment as its criteria for measurement. Each criterion is based on several different variables. For example, educational attainment is based on literacy, enrolment in primary education, enrolment in secondary education, and enrolment in tertiary education. The 2013 Report lists the Nordic countries as the most equal (Iceland, Finland, Norway, then Sweden) with Syria, Chad, Pakistan and Yemen as the least equal. The UK appears at number 18, and the USA at 23. While the UK is less equal than it was in 2009 (number 15), the USA is more equal (31 in 2009).

SIGI includes a range of social indicators: age at marriage, incidence of domestic violence, freedom of movement, and access to land and credit, alongside more common measures such as literacy, access to secondary and higher education, health, and proportions of men and women in professional occupations and elected office, in order to compare the life chances of men and women in and across countries.

Feminist writers from Susan Brownmiller to the present have argued that sexual violence is prevalent during armed conflict, and have presented data to prove it. Brownmiller gave a vast number of accounts in her path-breaking text which later researchers and writers have followed up, looking at conflicts in, for example, the Balkans, Asia, and Africa. Rape and other forms of sexual violence are now identified as prevalent in war zones, as well as the trafficking and prostitution of women to service the armed forces.

True discusses violence against women during conflict, pointing out that rape and sexual assault are not only perpetrated by militias, but also by national forces and by civilians. She emphasises that the conditions of conflict create a milieu in which violence against women is an option. She also points out that women and children make up 80% of people displaced into refugee camps and resettlement zones, and argues that despite an end of conflict, women continue to be subject to violence, exacerbated by their poor economic and political status (True, 2012: 135). Peacekeeping forces have been shown to increase the demand for commercial sex; True claims that 'Ironically, the creation of a thriving sex industry is one of the lasting legacies of the UN mission in Kosovo' (True, 2012: 140). Recent campaigns to raise awareness and combat sexual violence as an instrument of war back up UN measures

1820 and 1325 that classify sexual violence as a war crime and insist that women and women's perspectives are included in peace-making assemblies.

A Feminist perspective on war looks beyond armed forces and military strategy to ask what is happening to non-combatants, women and children in particular. Women pick up the slack when men go off to war – in Britain in the 1940s this meant working in armaments factories and agriculture, as well as becoming both wage-earner and homemaker for the family, and it is not so different anywhere in the world where there is a twenty-first century conflict. Non-combatants are not spared injury in modern warfare. From the Vietnam War to the present, civilians suspected of harbouring the enemy are likely to become victims. The use of drones and other forms of remote attack means that non-combatants are often vulnerable, resulting in high civilian casualties in most modern wars. Wars leave a legacy of damage. Some of this is human: the dead and the disabled; some is environmental: the impact of depleted uranium shells on soil, crops and DNA; some is economic: the destroyed infrastructure of production; and then there are the remnants of war: the landmines that continue to maim and kill for years after a conflict has ended.

Thus Feminist theorising about armed conflict does not see it in isolation, but rather as part of a continuum of violence, linking the private, domestic, local and global. Mainstream theories of conflict are criticised for the dominance of narrow, male-gendered perspectives, while the question is raised of whether conflict itself is an effect of gender power structures and the dominance of masculine values. Feminist approaches to conflict extend the field of study – from armed combatants to civilians, from the period of conflict to the years following, from the direct impact of war to the diverse, dispersed effects across populations and time. Feminist Security Studies questions the normality of conflict and war and asks whether these assumptions derive from the dominance of masculine perspectives and values, while linking violent conflict to violence in the private and domestic spheres.

The identification of Feminist security with Human Security

What does it mean to be secure, or, indeed, to be insecure? In matters of security, which are as much to do with perception as empirical reality, how are priorities decided and policies implemented? The dominant assumptions about international security were called into question by the articulation of a Human Security agenda that attempted to make national security debates more reflective of the lived-world by inserting human rights issues and perspectives: it shifts the focus from the state to the individual.

The term Human Security was first used in the 1994 UNDP *Human Development Report*. This report, supplemented by later statements, defined Human Security broadly as freedom from fear, freedom from want, and freedom to live with dignity. While there is agreement among theorists and activists that it is vital to consider the security of individual people, there is little consensus about the content of Human Security. This falls broadly into narrow and broad interpretations of the term. Narrow interpretations focus on violence but extend concern from the state to violence, and the fear of violence, against individuals. Broad interpretations, however, look beyond overt violence to safety from hunger, poverty, disease, pollution and other less overt threats. Both narrow and broad conceptions focus on non-coercive means to combat violence, such as diplomacy, conflict management, and the promotion of democracy and egalitarian economic development rather than military force.

Both Human Security per se and the broadening approach have been criticised for diverting Security Studies from its proper focus on the eradication of large-scale conflicts, and confusing the issue by introducing the interests of individual people and such issues as health, food, the environment and the economy, which are already addressed in other fields of study (such as development and public policy) (Hoogensen and Stuvøy, 2006: 210). Despite the suggestion that all the approaches are, in fact, complementary rather than in competition, Human Security has become a contested term and approach, questioned from both within and without, as some scholars and activists debate narrow and broad approaches while others defend a traditional definition of state security.

While both narrow and broad approaches are critical of orthodox Security Studies and the practice of state security, and are, arguably, more friendly towards the inclusion of women, broad approaches are more obviously conducive to Feminist interpretations. In common with Human Security theorists, Feminist security analysts focus on redefining security so that it reflects the lived-world and is able to include the perspectives of all people and the full range of insecurities. Both approaches also pay attention to the ways that the perception of security and insecurity varies according to the context, arguing that top-down definitions of security are inadequate to capture the realities on the ground. Further, Feminists and Human Security theorists are ambivalent towards the state. While it provides protection, the state can also be a threat to the individual or group (see Hoogensen and Stuvøy, 2006: 211). An orthodox approach that focuses on improving state security misses the possibility that the state itself puts people at risk. While this can take a wide range of forms, such as invasion of privacy or initiating armed conflict, Feminist writers have been quite clear in their ambivalence towards the state: on the one hand it has the means to protect and, through the welfare state, to increase equality via redistribution, but on the other hand it is the state that creates laws which entrench or even create inequalities and power imbalances. To take a recent example, changes to welfare and taxation in the UK in response to the 2008 financial crisis have had a far greater impact on women than men (True, 2012: 101–105). More traditional examples include marriage, divorce and property inheritance regulation, as well as the historical reliance on couverture – the practice by which women had no legal existence in their own right but were included within the citizenship of their fathers, husbands or brothers.

Thus, Feminist approaches to Security Studies share much common ground with Human Security. Both are critical approaches that question mainstream assumptions about the nature and content of security, extend their field of vision beyond state security to the security of individuals in daily life, and question the role of the state.

Conclusion

Feminist approaches to security provide an essential critical perspective on Security Studies. With its roots in women's movements, Feminist Political Theory, and Feminist International Relations, Feminist security provides a critical perspective that privileges the experiences of women and feminine values. A narrow Feminist window on security would add women into analyses of war and peace, while a broad view would extend to other forms of security/insecurity such as poverty, the environment and the economy, and in so doing create an alternative structure of security. This links Feminist security to other critical theories that focus on emancipation and liberation of the individual, while elaborating the feminist themes of gender inequality and patriarchal power.

Feminism is not a unified approach. While some theorists tend towards an essentialist view of gender, it is more common to argue for the social construction of gender roles. Thus, the assumed connection between women and peace/men and war is questioned. We have seen that women participate in conflict, also that they are affected by conflict in ways specific to their sex. Perhaps more importantly, Feminist researchers argue that the more gender-equal a society, the less likely that it will engage in conflict. Feminism has a particular affinity to Human Security since both focus on a bottom-up, critical approach to the content of security that is ambivalent towards the role of the state.

Summary points

1   Feminist theory is not a dry, academic construction; it is neither passive nor complete. It is a growing, adapting, learning theory of society and human relations that responds to the changing practices of gender in the world, just as it shapes how we react to such practices.
2   Feminist International Relations has insisted that women are counted in, that the particular spaces and experiences of women are included in the field of study, and that a Feminist perspective is a critical approach to International Relations that articulates a critical agenda.
3   Feminist, or non-gendered, conception of security is defined as the absence of violence, whether it be military, economic or sexual.
4   Throughout history, women have been more associated with peace than men, who are more associated with conflict and war. Feminist researchers have investigated women's roles in conflict to find that they are not just passive victims, but often active, although in different ways from men.
5   If we equate peace to security, we find the interesting insight that a more gender-equal society is also more secure.
6   Feminist Security Studies questions the normality of conflict and war, as well as the narrow focus on combatants and the duration of conflict.

Note

1   www.unifem.org/gender_issues/violence_against_women/facts_figures.html (accessed 20.4.14).

Recommended reading

Cohn, C., Kinsella, H. and Gibbings, S. 'Women, Peace and Security Resolution 1325', *International Feminist Journal of Politics*, vol. 6, no. 1, June 2010, 130–140.
Detraz, N. *International Security and Gender*, Cambridge: Polity Press, 2012.
Enloe, C. *Bananas, Beaches and Bases: Making feminist sense of international politics*, London: Rivers Oram Press, 1989.
Shepherd, L.J. (ed.) *Gender Matters in Global Politics*, London: Routledge, 2010.
—— 'The State of Feminist Security Studies: Continuing the Conversation', *International Studies Perspectives*, vol. 14, 2013, 436–439.
Sjoberg, L. (ed.) *Gender and International Security*, London: Routledge, 2010.
Steans, J. *Gender and International Relations*, Cambridge: Polity, 2013.
True, J. *The Political Economy of Violence Against Women*, Oxford: Oxford University Press, 2012.

5 Human Security

Shahin Malik

Box 5.1: United Nations Development Programme (UNDP) *Human Development Report, 1994*

For most people, a feeling of insecurity arises more from worries about daily life than from the dread of a cataclysmic world event. Will they and their families have enough to eat? Will they lose their jobs? Will their streets and neighbourhoods be safe from crime? Will they be tortured by a repressive state? Will they become a victim of violence because of their gender? Will their religion or ethnic origin target them for persecution?

(UNDP, 1994: 22)

Introduction

Each of the theoretical traditions discussed in this book engages with the concept of security from a different angle. Chapter 2, for instance, analysed Realism's dominance in the field since the beginning of the Second World War. Its views revolve around the premise that the anarchic condition which prevails in the international system compels states to seek survival either through the acquisition of their own military might or via alliances with more powerful states. Furthermore, foreign policy decisions are based on national security considerations rather than on the intangible principle of morality. Neorealism, for instance, presents a very rigid image of the international system, one based purely on anarchy, in which there is no overarching authority able to maintain security for states. In this type of international system, states become primarily interested in their own survival and view all other states as possible threats. Realism remains the primary theory when security affairs are addressed, and the evidence continues to support its primacy; conflict remains a significant feature of world politics, states such as North Korea, India, Israel and Pakistan continue to develop weapons, including weapons of mass destruction, and the old nuclear states continue to rely on them to enhance their own security. Therefore there is little doubt that the Realist tradition retains a leading position within the field.

However, despite its dominance, Realism has been criticised for rigidly adhering to a core which advocates a state-centric approach to international events. This framework fails to allow for emphasis on other referent objects such as the individual. Indeed, not only is the security of the state of prime importance, but the security of citizens is seen as being indivisible from that of the state. This therefore has the effect of marginalising the security concerns of individuals as well as those of specific groups. It was to highlight the intense dissatisfaction with Realist military and state-centric rigidity that Critical Theorists brought to our attention the premise that it is the states themselves which often threaten the security of individuals. As a result, theorists such as Ken Booth have advocated the emancipation of the individual as a necessary component of security, and others such as Robert Cox have called for scrutiny of the processes and structures of the existing international system which give rise to practices that diminish the security of humans (see Chapter 3). Such Critical Theorists insist that the state must be dislodged as the key recipient of security, and they put forward not only the individual but also a wide range of non-state actors as possible referent objects. Critical Theorists such as Booth have expanded the concept of security to the extent that they see individual security as being of far greater importance than that of the state. This opposition to Realist tenets is now widespread within the field, and it was further strengthened by the end of the Cold War in 1989, which removed one of the main sources of military conflict, namely, the ideological and military competition between the two superpowers. The fortunes of this powerful approach may not have diminished significantly in recent years, but the end of the Cold War has undoubtedly raised many dissenters including the critical traditions discussed elsewhere in this book.

This chapter will continue this theme and consider whether there is any value to one further approach which has sought to place the individual at the heart of its analysis – the so-called Human Security Paradigm. This approach has had a considerable impact on the field and has developed a strong following among academics, politicians and other groups since it was popularised by the United Nations Development Programme (UNDP) through its *Human Development Report* published in 1994. This report sought to encourage a conceptual shift in thinking about security, away from Cold War dynamics to a concern with human rights and development. Nearly two decades after the UN's report, however, early claims of paradigm shifts away from traditional security to a more human-centred approach remain largely unrealised, and its early success has stagnated due to a gradual loss of interest among its main supporters. The concept remains ill-defined and its association with the UN has had the effect of diminishing its value among some policy-makers tied to a state/military-centric vision of international affairs.

The UN has been the leading proponent of the concept, and so the chapter begins by looking at its broad vision for linking social, humanitarian and economic issues in order to enhance the security of humans wherever possible. However, after the initial optimism brought about by state support for the UN's vision, events had the effect of reasserting the logic of power politics and enhancing high political issues of war and peace. This has been particularly manifest in the US War on Terror, which has led to the invasion of two states – Afghanistan in 2001 and Iraq in 2003. This ongoing war has raised the prospect that the essence of Human Security is incompatible with the foreign policy objectives of those states pursuing the war. Despite this, however, Human Security has featured prominently in academic literature over the past two decades, and an analysis of the opinions of the leading proponents is necessary. The chapter therefore begins by looking at the early development of the concept, along with the controversies surrounding its definitions. Furthermore, given that the concept's heyday began at a time when much was being made of the impact of globalisation, it is only fitting that the connections between the two phenomena are briefly analysed. Finally, given the UN's association with the concept, a strong practical basis is implied, and the chapter ends with an analysis of the adoption of elements of Human Security as part of the foreign policy agendas of two states – Japan and Canada – both of whom have adhered to widely differing definitions and views. In a sense, the differences between the Japanese and Canadian approaches to Human Security represent some of the problems with the concept.

Defining Human Security

Early developments

Ken Booth's emphasis on the emancipation of the individual (see Chapter 3) began at the start of the 1990s when he advocated the elevation of humans above the state. This call for a decisive redefinition of the concept of security had the effect of providing a human-centric rather than state-centric focus for the discipline. Since then Critical Security Studies has become increasingly populated with approaches which have sought to diminish the value of the state as the ultimate referent object. This in turn has raised the question of whether Human Security as a separate field is even necessary, given the myriad other approaches opposed to the conventional core. The term Human Security has been used increasingly in the literature since the end of the Cold War, and this certainly gives the impression that it represents a point of departure from a past era dominated by nuclear weapons, armed forces and state-centric preoccupation.

The United Nations Development Programme and its *Human Development Report* of 1994 are credited with popularising the concept. The Report's departure from the Realist, state-centric concept of security has important implications in that it called attention to new issues and vulnerabilities that were not on the traditional agenda. Importantly, catering for individual security is not a new development and the ideas embodied within the concept are strongly implied in the work of the United Nations. Following the carnage of the Second World War states sought to protect individuals through the establishment of a number of international conventions, some of which are listed in Box 5.2. Such conventions have led to the establishment of new norms, and this has been important in that they provide a legal basis to challenge state practices that depart from the norms. In addition to this the UN Charter itself asserted links between peace, stability and development with a central concern for social progress.

However, despite these attempts at introducing an ethical basis to international politics, state interests, inter-state conflict, arms development and the maximisation of the ability to wage wars have dominated both the field of Security Studies and the behaviour of many key states in the international system. This can be explained largely in the context of a number of key events following the end of the Cold War. The decreased likelihood of nuclear confrontation between the superpowers created a framework for the inclusion of non-military threats into academic and policy-making circles. Democratisation in Eastern Europe and elsewhere provided an added impetus for an increased concern with human life and welfare. The slow erosion of Westphalian ideas of sovereignty, combined with the impact of globalisation, the shrinking of geographical distances and more porous state borders, contributed to

---

Box 5.2: Key conventions for the protection of humans

- *The Universal Declaration of Human Rights* was adopted by the UN General Assembly in 1948. This was the first global response to the carnage of the Second World War and an attempt to enshrine the rights to which all humans are entitled.
- *The Convention for the Prevention and Punishment of the Crime of Genocide* was adopted in January 1951. This convention attempted to provide a definition of genocide, and currently 145 states have ratified it.
- *The Geneva Conventions* were drawn up in 1949 and there are four in existence, dealing with armed forces on Land and Sea, Prisoners of War, and Civilians. The essence of the conventions is to set down the rules of what is and is not lawful during times of conflict. The purpose is to protect vulnerable and defenceless individuals.
- *The Declaration on the Protection of Women and Children in Emergency and Armed Conflict* was adopted by the UN in 1974. Its adoption was a recognition that during times of conflict it was often children and women who were deliberately targeted. The Declaration seeks to encourage states to end the persecution, violence, degrading treatment, collective punishment and criminal acts against such vulnerable groups.

---

the struggle against the narrow state-based core of the discipline. Alongside this, the liberalisation of the global economy heightened the economic insecurities of regions of the globe which were already poverty-stricken. One consequence of this, however, was the extension of international norms into areas such as human rights, development, poverty alleviation and the combating of disease.

Given the dynamics of the Cold War, it is easy to understand why the discipline came to rely so heavily on a narrow state/military-centric conceptualisation of the concept of security. However, calls for an alternative to traditional notions of security were intensified following the eruption of an increasing number of brutal civil wars in Europe (the former Yugoslavia), Africa and Asia. These led to unprecedented humanitarian disasters with millions of people being displaced from their communities, violent ethnic cleansing, genocide and other forms of violence. The end of the Cold War was also characterised by the end of the bipolar era which had been based on two superpowers, two Europes, an arms race and a security dilemma. New ideas challenged the traditionalist model that privileged state security and high politics and stressed the need to encompass threats beyond physical and inter-state violence. The response by advocates of Human Security, for instance, was to encapsulate as broad a range of threats to humans as possible. Box 5.3 provides examples of the types of threats faced by individuals and communities.

Rothschild encapsulates this broad vision very well when she states that Human Security applies downwards to

> "the security of groups and individuals;" upward, "to the security of international systems;" horizontally, from military security "to political, economic, social, environmental, or 'human security'" and in all directions "upwards to international institutions, downwards to regional or local government, sideways to nongovernmental organizations, to public opinion and the press, and to the abstract forces of nature or of the market."
>
> (Rothschild 1995: 55)

Box 5.3: The threats that face humans

Natural disasters

We humans have always had to contend with the impact of natural disasters, some of which have been truly devastating in terms of lives lost. Even in recent decades, states have been shown to be largely impotent when faced with some of the worst that Mother Nature has thrown at them. One of the deadliest tropical cyclones ever recorded occurred over East Pakistan (now Bangladesh) in November 1970. Known as the Bhola Cyclone, it killed over 500,000 people. Over 650,000 people are estimated to have been killed in Tangshan, China in July 1976 when the largest earthquake of the twentieth Century (in terms of numbers killed) struck the city. More recently, the 2010 earthquake in Haiti killed over 160,000 people and sparked a huge international aid operation. The 2004 Indonesian tsunami killed nearly 250,000 and affected millions of people in numerous countries with coastlines on the Indian Ocean. Even rich and powerful states are unable to prevent the devastating impact of natural disasters. The earthquake off the coast of northern Japan in 2011 and the resulting tsunami resulted in the death of 25,000 people and severely damaged the Fukushima nuclear power plant. The situation has still not been brought under control, with the Japanese government admitting as recently as August 2013 that water and radiation continue to leak all over the site of the original meltdown.

Poverty

Today there are nearly 1.3 billion people living on less than $1.25 per day. While this is considerably less than the 2 billion in 1981, nevertheless it is a significant portion of the world population and it represents a major challenge to the international system. Although these figures represent a global phenomenon, some regions, such as India, are more adversely affected, accounting for nearly 400 million experiencing abject poverty. In addition, states in sub-Saharan Africa continue to have the highest percentage (47%) of their populations living on less than $1.25 a day.

Contemporary slavery

There is little doubt that there are far more slaves in the world today than there ever were during the Atlantic Slave Trade. It is just that they are a smaller proportion of the total human race, and modern slavery is now quite different from the way it was practised historically. In the past slaves cost a considerable amount of money and formed a long term 'relationship' with their owners. Today, slavery is not simply a case of one person owning another, but also encompasses a considerable variety of forms and impacts, ranging from **bonded labour**, where a person's work is the security for a debt, to **serfdom** where a person is tied to another's land and has to work for them. Other forms of forced labour include situations where passports are seized and domestic servants are kept hidden away from the authorities. Brutal as these forms of slavery are, perhaps the most harrowing are the use of children as soldiers during wartime and the trafficking of women and children for the purpose of sexual exploitation. All world states may have outlawed slavery, but there can be little doubt that such practices exist because of official complicity.

In this broad context, therefore, it appears that Human Security incorporates both 'freedom from want' and 'freedom from fear'. This gives the impression that the approach seeks to encourage states to supplant the amoral basis of their national interests, rooted in Realism, with an ethical responsibility to the individual. Consequently the United Nations has continued with its broad vision in a variety of contexts, including its pledge to the 2001 Millennium Development Goals (MDGs). These goals closely complemented the UN's long-standing commitment to enhancing the development of societies through eradicating poverty, reducing child mortality, combating diseases and, among others, expanding environmental sustainability. The UN's vision for Human Security, therefore, is highly integrative, and incorporates the whole range of threats beyond militarism, embracing human rights and the development of societies. Given these objectives, proponents also highlight the strong policy orientation of the approach, stressing that state behaviour should be adapted for the purpose of improving the welfare of their citizens.

The impact of globalisation

Much of the initial work on globalisation concentrated on the emergence of key technological developments and the way in which they had contributed to a major shrinking of distances and the time required to traverse those distances. These intense levels of interconnectivity encouraged globalisation optimists to refer to the dramatic increase in global trade and other cultural, political and social exchanges. Undoubtedly, the end of the Cold War further accelerated the forces of globalisation by eliminating the ideological differences between the former Soviet Union and the West, which resulted in a convergence between the two in the belief of the value of capitalist markets as well as that of free trade. Liberal ideas seemed to confirm that trade fostered peace between the states that engaged in it, and mounting evidence identified increasing economic interdependence, democratic peace and interstate trade with a substantial reduction in conflicts. Many such studies stress not only that these new processes could no longer be considered under the state and military-centric assumptions of Realism, but also that globalisation was contributing to these developments (McMillan, 1997).

Conversely, an increasingly common belief since the end of the Cold War has been the view that although inequalities and poverty have always existed, they have increased significantly due to the impact of globalisation. At the forefront of research on the changing conditions in the post-Cold War period have been academics such as Mary Kaldor, who has written extensively on the connections between globalisation and the many civil conflicts raging in what have been increasingly viewed as 'failed states'. Her thesis refers to the premise that although globalisation has helped to raise the standard of living of countless people across the globe, it has also contributed to widespread poverty, given that there has been a rapid rise of unregulated and largely profit-driven capitalist markets. Vulnerable states in various stages of failure have been unable to compete with the wealthier parts of the world and have therefore been driven further into poverty and despair. The consequence for many such states has been insecurity for many millions in the developing world. Kaldor's analysis of globalisation goes further, however, when she stresses that failing states begin to lose control over their own territory as a result of the deterioration in the quality of the armed and police forces. The inevitable rise in the vulnerability of already weak states in the face of globalisation has other unfortunate consequences, especially with the emergence of criminal groups, warlords, mercenaries and, among other actors, insurgency groups. Such groups begin to compete with one another for the resources of the failing states and this competition has often taken a violent turn. There is substantial evidence in support of Kaldor's somewhat controversial thesis, as can be seen in the many civil wars that have erupted since the end of the Cold War (Kaldor, 2006).

The debates over the influence of globalisation are likely to continue – but there is little doubt that organisations such as the UNDP have considered its negative consequences when formulating their perceptions on Human Security. Indeed, numerous key individuals within the UN have at various stages sought to highlight the connections between globalisation and the new challenges in the post-Cold War era. For instance, Kofi Annan (Secretary-General of the UN from 1997 to 2007) saw Human Security to be far more than the absence of violent conflict. As he stated in 2005:

> Ask a New York investment banker who walks past Ground Zero every day on her way to work what today's biggest threat is. Then ask an illiterate twelve-year-old orphan in Malawi who lost his parents to AIDS. You will get two very different answers. Invite an Indonesian fisherman mourning the loss of his entire family and the destruction of his village from the recent, devastating tsunami to tell you what he fears most. Then ask a villager in Darfur, stalked by murderous militias and fearful of bombing raids. Their answers, too, are likely to diverge.
>
> (UNGA, 2005)

For the UN's Secretary General, therefore, Human Security encompassed a wide variety of threats to humans including concern over human rights, encouraging good governance, and access to education and health facilities. Central to these goals have been the attempts to reduce poverty, stimulate economic growth and ultimately prevent conflict (UN Press Release, SG/SM/7382, 8–10 May 2000). In fact, poverty alleviation has been central to the broad view and the UN has been at the forefront in encouraging states to enact policies that may reduce its impact not just in their own territories but elsewhere as well. A UN General Assembly Report entitled *In Larger Freedom*, published in 2005, reinforced this commitment through recognition that 'more than a billion people … live on less than a dollar a day [as well as warning that over] 11 million children die before their fifth birthday' (UNGA, 2005). The Report also stated that a world dominated by such processes could not be regarded as one in which individuals enjoyed freedom or had the facilities to realise their full potential.

Similarly, Sadako Ogata (UN High Commissioner for Refugees, from 1991 to 2000) saw globalisation as having magnified the threats facing individuals and communities the world over, and she also supported Kofi Annan's vision that Human Security was the way forward in providing the security that individuals sought. Her role as High Commissioner for Refugees placed her in an ideal position to witness the impact that the numerous post-Cold War conflicts were having on individuals and communities. However, her primary concern was that there needed to be a recognition that none of the crises that her office had dealt with could be solved 'without addressing the underlying political, social and economic causes'. This belief was clearly in line with her strong opinion that Human Security had necessarily to be broad and incorporate the whole range of threats that individuals experienced, and in this context, therefore, it is understandable why the UN does not distinguish between 'freedom from fear' and 'freedom from war' for individuals. In this respect, despite a lack of agreement over a precise definition, there appears to be some consensus on the need to deviate away from state-based security.

Problems with the UN's broad vision of Human Security

Conceptual problems: Many supporters of the UN's view of Human Security have gone so far as to claim that the concept represents a major shift in an intellectual as well as a practical sense. Indeed, its integration of security, human rights and development appears to represent a major departure from the rigidity of the Cold War imposed by the Realist state and military-centric world view. However, this broad vision has invited a great deal of criticism, with a significant number of academics and practitioners expressing concern over the feasibility of achieving these goals in practice. Consequently, the concept faces many challenges from dissenters and those who seek either to narrow the concept considerably or to disband it completely. One such critic, Roland Paris, has stressed that the concept of Human Security lacked a precise definition and that it was therefore too vague and ambiguous to be sufficiently meaningful. Furthermore, he saw its association with developmental issues as merely adding to the already high levels of ambiguity prevalent within the UN's view of the concept. This expansive, all-encompassing nature meant that for Paris Human Security failed to provide policy-makers with any guidance in what threats to prioritise, and academics with little sense of what, exactly, is to be studied (Paris, 2001: 88). Even the UN's attempt at clarifying the range of issues it saw as deserving of the label does little to help in identifying clear guidelines. For instance, it grouped the range of threats faced by humans under several categories including economic, food, health, environmental, personal, community and political. However, it is easy to see how expansive and all-inclusive this list is – and this problem has provided critics of the concept with ammunition with which to refute the UN's claims that it has succeeded in establishing a paradigm that challenges the dominant Realist discourse.

One of the declared aims of the 1994 *Human Development Report* was to influence states to accept the shift in the discourse from territorial security to a much greater emphasis on people. This was to be achieved by encouraging states to make use of the so-called 'peace dividend' at the end of the Cold War by ensuring that resources devoted to the military would now increasingly be diverted to more human-centred programmes. The consequence of this issue-led agenda was that throughout the 1990s a huge number of international actors, such as the UN High Commission for Refugees, the International Organization for Migration and the Global Partnership for the Prevention of Armed Conflict, began to incorporate the concept into their own discourses. Human Security therefore evolved as a result of the political, economic and security challenges of the post-Cold War era, and as a concept it was therefore influenced by a wide range of factors which were now seen as needing to be taken into account. These included the diminished risk of nuclear war, democratisation in various states of Europe and elsewhere, the increased marginalisation of the poor and disenfranchised, increases in economic divisions between the global north and south, and the emergence of brutal civil conflicts further fuelled by the spread of small arms and light weapons.

Human Security has therefore been heavily influenced by a large number of factors, and although there are variations within the broad conceptualisation of the concept, most definitions stress the key referent object to be the individual – even though some definitions seek to focus specifically on human communities. Other variations occur in a number of areas including the *values* which should be emphasised: survival, development, physical safety, dignity, or indeed personal freedom. Kanit Bajpai, for instance, places prime importance on physical safety, wellbeing and individual freedom (Bajpai, 2000: 38–39), whereas Prezelj lists the 'spectrum of threats' embodied within the broad view of Human Security as shown in Box 5.4.

Box 5.4: Prezelj's spectrum of threats

- economic threats
- food threats
- health threats
- environmental threats
- personal threats
- community threats
- political threats
- demographic threats
- crime in all forms, including terrorism
- natural disasters
- violent conflicts and wars
- genocide
- anti-personnel mines, SALW, etc.

Source: Prezelj (2008)

This list demonstrates that the threats facing individuals and human communities are greatly varied and difficult to categorise under one specific heading. It is this variation which has further heightened the confusion surrounding the concept (Prezelj, 2008: 8).

The post-9/11 world

In addition to the conceptual problems highlighted, one further issue has contributed to the disillusion with the concept, namely the impact of the terrorist attacks on the World Trade Center in New York on 11 September 2001. It was following these attacks that the United States made the fight against terrorism its main focus, and it was this event, along with the Taliban regime's refusal to hand over Osama Bin Laden, that persuaded George W. Bush (the US President at the time) to invade Afghanistan on 7 October 2001. Soon afterwards, Bush, under pressure from neoconservatives, was to launch another invasion – that of Iraq in 2003. Both invasions are often explained in the context of the Bush Doctrine, the essence of which was to pursue an aggressive unilateralist policy which saw the US reject the Kyoto Protocol, withdraw from the Anti-Ballistic Missile Treaty of 1972 and pursue preventive war against states that aid terrorist groups.

Conversely, the UN's vision of Human Security is undoubtedly a powerful critique of violence in all its forms, including of course the impact of the War on Terror. However, given that this particular war has been pursued largely through a traditionalist/Realist perspective, it has been the root cause of countless violations of civil and human rights. This leads to the inevitable conclusion that Human Security and the vision of security as expressed in the War on Terror are polar opposites. Ian Gibson supports this when he claims that security for liberal democracies in the post-9/11 era is 'largely based on achieving invulnerability at the expense of others'. He further argues that 'it is the state and not the citizenry for whom invulnerability is sought' (Gibson, 2004: 158). This quote encapsulates the contradiction between the two forms of security, but also hints at the growing number of opinions claiming that Human Security has faced increasing challenges in the post-9/11 era as many governments have turned to more traditional ways of achieving security.

Incorporating Human Security into foreign policy agendas

As this and other chapters of the book demonstrate, disillusion with the narrow state/military-centric nature of traditional security raised intense opposition to it, resulting in the emergence of a number of subfields such as Critical Security Studies, the Copenhagen School and Human Security – all of which have focused on referent objects other than the state. However, the latest offering seems to be considerably different given that there appears to be a strong underlying practical element to it. The tendency for Human Security to complement state security has made it easier for some states to incorporate elements of it into their foreign policy agendas. Combined with this is the wider acceptance that threats are increasingly varied and their resolution can only be managed through non-coercive mechanisms – especially through multilateral institutions. The need to deal with 'non-military' threats has therefore strengthened the practical essence of Human Security, and in turn this has compelled states to respond in policy terms.

The *Human Security Report* of 2005 entitled 'In Larger Freedom' is particularly important in that it built upon the UNDP Report of 1994 and exemplified the view that Human Security was increasingly important for foreign, security and development policy. Not only had the concept entered the lexicon of international politics, but there had also been notable successes such as the establishment of the Human Security Network and the Commission on Human Security, and the ideas behind the concept were also instrumental in leading to the 1997 Convention banning anti-personnel mines. Furthermore, the establishment of the International Criminal Court (ICC) cannot be understood without referring to Human Security. Indeed, elements of the concept have even begun to feature in the foreign policy-making process of many states, including Canada, Japan, Norway and Switzerland. However, it is important not to over-estimate its impact – especially when considering recent international events such as the US opposition to the ICC, its invasion of Iraq in 2003 and ample evidence of extra-judicial detainment and killings in the so-called War on Terror. Despite such events, there is now little doubt that Human Security has entered the foreign policy discourse of many states as well as that of numerous international institutions.

Although the practical basis of Human Security and its emphasis on non-military threats are easy to describe and understand, the conceptual basis of the concept is much more complicated, and even now, more than a decade after the 1994 UNDP Report, it continues to be surrounded by ambiguity, giving rise to confusion in the academic world and frustration in the context of policy-making. Variations in opinions regarding definitions and its practical value are often influenced in terms of regions, and also depend on the nature of the institutions for which Human Security is central. The UN framework, for instance, continues to be largely influenced by the UNDP Report of 1994 and is implemented in a variety of ways, particularly through peacekeeping, humanitarian operations and the management of refugees. The variations arise over how states view the concept, since it is in this context that the differences become apparent, further hampering efforts at achieving consensus regarding definitions.

Japan and the Asia Pacific region

The Japanese view of Human Security must be placed in the context of its history during the Second World War and the international role it has played globally and regionally since then. As one of the Axis powers between 1941 and 1945, Japan's lack of access to raw materials persuaded it to begin hostilities in Southeast Asia and establish control over Singapore, Malaya, Burma and elsewhere. Its attack on the US Naval Base at Pearl Harbor in 1941 had been instigated in order to weaken the only power capable of preventing its aggression in the region. Consequently, the war in the Pacific continued until August 1945 when the United States bombed two Japanese cities – Hiroshima and Nagasaki – in an act which soon led to the end of the war. Since then Japan's behaviour in the region has been largely decided by a constitution which is overwhelmingly pacifist in nature. Its aggression towards its neighbours during the war has meant that since then Japan has been keen to allay any fears they might harbour regarding its motives. Therefore, as Lam Peng Er states, it has avoided: 'a hard security approach towards the region'. Incorporating elements of Human Security into its international behaviour has allowed it to play a wide-ranging role in Southeast Asia, from providing development assistance to relief in times of natural disasters, and going so far as 'providing massive financial assistance and currency swap arrangements in the aftermath of the 1996–98 Asian financial crisis to stabilize regional economies'. Peng Er further states that Japan has in the recent past assumed a peacebuilding role in East Timor, Aceh and Mindanao, and 'deployed the largest contingent of Japanese troops since the end of World War II for humanitarian assistance' following the Indonesian tsunami in 2004 (Peng Er, 2006: 143).

Japan established the Commission on Human Security in 2001, thereby confirming its decidedly non-military and human-centred view. Developmental concerns were clearly central and the Commission's final report, presented to Koizumi Junichiro (Prime Minister of Japan at the time) in 2003, further confirmed that human life needed to be protected in times of violent conflict – thus confirming Japan's wish to maintain a wide adherence to Human Security which incorporated both freedom from want and freedom from fear. During a speech in Hanoi, made in 1998, Obuchi Keizo (Japanese Prime Minister from 1998 to 2000) declared that one of Japan's priorities was to encourage a human-centred approach to global politics during the twenty-first century. In order to facilitate this and to demonstrate its commitment, Japan, along with the UN Secretariat, launched a Trust Fund for Human Security in March 1999, which has since provided a basis for Japan's non-military and human-orientated approach to international conduct. Indeed, successive administrations have maintained strong support for the broad vision of Human Security, clearly expressed by Mori Yoshiro (Obuchi's successor) when he declared that Human Security had become one of the pillars of Japanese diplomacy.

Further financial contributions to the Human Security Trust Fund and the establishment of the Commission on Human Security in 2001 also demonstrate Japan's continuing commitment to the concept's broad vision. A particularly important indication of Japan's adherence to this broad view came soon after the terrorist attacks in the United States in September 2001. Mori's successor, Koizumi Junichirō, addressed the International Symposium on Human Security in December 2001 and stressed that, rather than adopting a traditional military response to the terrorist acts, the eradication of terrorism needed to be linked to the need to address 'other diverse threats to individuals because armed conflicts, poverty, and other socio-economic factors create[d] hotbeds for terrorism' (Koizumi, 2001).

The United Nations Millennium Summit in 2000 galvanised Japan to initiate the Commission on Human Security (CHS), the declared purpose of which was to:

> protect the vital core of all human lives in ways that enhance human freedoms and human fulfilment. Human Security means protecting fundamental freedoms – freedoms that are the essence of life … It means creating political, social, environmental, economic, military and cultural systems that together give people the building blocks of survival, livelihood, and dignity.
>
> (Commission on Human Security, 2003: 4)

It should be noted, however, that the CHS Report was issued just prior to the 9/11 attacks, and consequently its impact was diluted significantly. Japan is faced by a hostile and increasingly powerful China, a nuclear-armed North Korea and an ally which is actively pursuing the War on Terror. Consequently, one would expect a volte face in Japan's foreign policy and a retreat from concern with Human Security. However, this has not happened, and although Japan has fully supported the US in the War on Terror, it has continued to pursue multilateral Human Security objectives in co-operation with the United Nations and a number of UN agencies.

Obuchi placed Japan on a foreign policy path that incorporated a human-centred approach to security, and this has been the case ever since, as demonstrated by the many contributions made by the Japanese-sponsored Trust Fund for Human Security to development projects in numerous states. Since 2009, for instance, the Fund has carried out projects in locations such as the Congo, Ecuador, Bosnia Hercegovina, Tajikistan, Pakistan, Mexico, Nicaragua, Bolivia, Uzbekistan, the Philippines, Colombia, the Gabonese Republic, Thailand and Nepal (MOFA of Japan). Since Obuchi's time in government Japan has had numerous Prime Ministers and experienced changes in political direction and major policy shifts. However, despite major challenges and cuts in the development assistance budget, its attempts at mainstreaming Human Security have continued throughout the first decade of the new millennium.

Canada's response to the broad vision

Although Canada has also experimented by incorporating elements of Human Security into its foreign policy, the result has been quite different from that of Japan. The Canadian criticism of the broad UN view has stemmed, in some senses, from what Canada sees as a rather unrealistic set of overly broad objectives as outlined by the United Nations. Consequently, Canadian foreign policy rests on the view that the physical protection of human life in times of conflict and other physical disasters needs to take priority over other broader portions of the objectives outlined by the UNDP Report of 1994. There is little doubt that towards the end of the 1990s Canada was playing a significant role in pushing the UN agenda, as shown by Ottawa's involvement in notable successes such as the Anti-Personnel Mine Ban Convention. For instance, Lloyd Axworthy, Canada's Foreign Minister between 1996 and 2000, saw the discourse on Human Security beginning to be profoundly affected by the increasing levels of interconnectivity brought about by globalisation, and stated, 'In this interconnected world, our own security is increasingly indivisible from that of our neighbours – at home and abroad' (Axworthy, 2001). He also stressed that globalisation had not only magnified human suffering but made it a universal concern – not just for states but also for non-state actors.

Canada's early support for the Human Security Network (established in 1998) was a clear expression of its commitment to encourage a shift from focusing on the security of the state to the human. It was through this network that Canada influenced the adoption of the treaty banning mines (highlighted above), and also the establishment of the International Criminal Court, the main objective of which is to provide a forum for the prosecution of individuals who perpetrate crimes against humanity. Canada's approach to Human Security appears, therefore, to incorporate two key aspects – the safety of people and the prevention of physical harm to humans through international law and treaties. There is little doubt that Canadian enthusiasm for the UN's objectives was based on a change in its foreign policy stance following the end of the Cold War. Most specifically, as Neufeld suggests, there was a discernible attempt to identify alternatives to Cold War Realism. Foreign policy was now to be much more concerned with setting an example 'of social and environmental responsibility … take the initiative on debt relief and take a leadership role in efforts to forge a new, more just and sustainable international economic order' (Canadian Peace Alliance, 1992).

However, it is equally important to realise that the success of Canada's experiment with Human Security was entirely dependent upon the domestic as well as the international environment. The demise of the Soviet Union at the end of the Cold War, the democratisation across Eastern Europe, and the international community's success in the 1990–91 Gulf War against Saddam Hussein's Iraq led to a great deal of optimism that international politics was moving decisively away from the traditional ideas which had dominated the Cold War. However, since then there have been many conflicts in the international system, including the collapse of the Somali state in 1992, the UN indecisiveness in Rwanda in 1994 which resulted in the deaths of over 800,000 people, as well as NATO's attempts to pacify the protracted and brutal conflicts in former Yugoslavia. NATO's intervention in Kosovo in 1999 further compelled the Canadians to definitively shift away from the broad *freedom from want* vision of the UN, and the ambiguity of the concept has added to the problems of converting the UN's objectives into policy. Finally, among all the external pressures, perhaps the most notable is that of Canada's relationship with the United States. The latter's scepticism over Human Security is based on its links to 'soft power', and this departs significantly from Washington's view that it is hard military power which enhances security.

Bearing this in mind, we end with a brief account of the impact of 11 September 2001. As this chapter has demonstrated, the conceptual strength of Human Security began to diminish as soon as academics and politicians began to question its practical value. In Canada this occurred soon after Lloyd Axworthy left office in 2000, and the pressures to move away from incorporating Human Security into its foreign policy have undoubtedly intensified after 9/11. Many of the Human Security conventions that Canada has sponsored or has been an active member of – such as the International Criminal Court, Small Arms and Light Weapons Agreements and War-affected Children Conventions – have been actively opposed by the United States. Consequently, it faces immense challenges as its southern neighbour continues to pursue security in the traditional military-centric sense. Nevertheless, even though Canada has taken many decisions that have aligned it closely to the US in the War on Terror, it has nevertheless continued to pursue a foreign policy influenced by a liberal and multilateral approach.

Conclusion

The popularity of Human Security during the 1990s led to the establishment of the Human Security Network, to which states such as Canada, Japan and Norway (among others) have since contributed significantly. The UNDP's efforts also aimed to persuade states to begin seeing security more broadly in contrast to the traditional military/ state-centric views expressed by traditionalist approaches. Despite this, however, and as this chapter has shown, the concept remains underdeveloped and contentious, and even its strongest supporters have failed to achieve a consensus as regards its meaning. The UNDP's formulation was the broadest in the sense that it encompassed myriad threats to the human individual. The broad vision not only involves the physical protection of people during times of violent conflict, but also the empowerment of individuals in post-conflict scenarios where reconstruction and the stabilisation of society are of central concern. However, other elements such as economic security, access to health and education, social protection, other features of development and even the protection of human rights all form the basis of the *freedom from want* perspective. It was this all-encompassing vision that led many academics as well as states to claim that the UNDP's concept was of limited value, since it was near impossible for policy-makers to prioritise its wide range of choices. The overly expansive nature of the UN's view also led to states such as Canada losing their initial enthusiasm and moving towards a more restrictive definition based largely on the protection of human life during times of conflict – also referred to as the *freedom from fear* perspective. States such as Japan and Canada have come under pressure as a result of their close ally's pursuit of the War on Terror, and this has led to them having to identify with elements of Human Security which do not alienate their close relationship with the US.

Summary points

1   Human Security was popularised by the United Nations Development Programme in its *Human Development Report* published in 1994. This report sought to encourage a conceptual shift in thinking about security, away from Cold War dynamics to a concern with human rights and development.
2   Given its connections to the United Nations, there is a strong practical element to Human Security.
3   Definitional problems have arisen since the term came into usage, with academics, politicians and NGOs disagreeing over its meaning. This lack of consensus has led to

a disagreement over whether states should be concerned with human development (Freedom from Want) or the protection of human life (Freedom from Fear).

4 States such as Canada and Japan have incorporated elements of Human Security into their foreign policy agendas and are good examples of the differences in approach.

5 The War on Terror has enabled the Realist tradition to continue to claim success. This has thrown up a serious challenge to those who advocate Human Security.

Recommended reading

Bajpai, K. 'Human Security: Concept and Measurement', *Kroc Institute Occasional Paper (Number 19)*, Notre Dame, Indiana: University of Notre Dame, 2000.

Booth, K. 'Security and Emancipation', *Review of International Studies*, vol. 17, no. 4, October 1991, 313–326.

Gibson, I. 'Human Security Post 9-11: Gender Perspectives and Security Exclusion', *Ritsumeikan Annual Review of International Studies*, vol. 3, 2004, 157–175.

Kaldor, M. 'Wanted: Global Politics', *The Nation*, vol. 273, no. 14, 5 November 2001, 15–18.

Kaldor, M. *New and Old Wars: Organised Violence in a Global Era*, 2nd Edition, Oxford: Polity, 2006.

Paris, R. 'Human Security: Paradigm Shift or Hot Air?', *International Security*, vol. 26, no. 2, Autumn 2001, 87–102.

6 Constructing security

Shahin Malik

Box 6.1: Alexander Wendt: 'anarchy is what states make of it'

Alexander Wendt, who is generally considered to be the founder of Social Constructivism, took issue with the Neorealist view that self-help and power politics were an inevitable feature of anarchy. He argued that anarchy should be treated as something which is 'constructed' by the states themselves, and that it is therefore inseparable from the conduct of international politics and the way in which the states perceive it.

Realists assume anarchy to be an essential and rigid characteristic of the international system, with states therefore refraining from attaching any meaning to it and merely responding to its desires. However, once anarchy is treated as a social construct, this has the effect of ensuring that self-help and power politics are no longer essential features of state interaction. In this context anarchy is no longer a defining character of international relations, but rather a social construct whose identity can change.

In essence Alexander Wendt has introduced the notion of '*process*' into theorising about international politics and state behaviour (Wendt, 1992).

Introduction

The preceding chapters have shown that fundamental differences exist among scholars seeking to conceptualise 'security'. Among the many variations are groups who argue for a broadened concept which rejects the elevation of the sovereign state as the primary referent object. Previous chapters have highlighted Critical Theorists, Feminists and those who advocate Human Security as being primarily concerned with emphasising that it is often states that diminish the security of individuals, and that the focus of the discipline should shift away from the state to the individual human. At the other extreme are the *traditional* security scholars – primarily the Realists, the Neorealists and even the Liberals – who have continued to insist that it is the state which provides security to all groups residing within its territory, and therefore that its own security needs to be elevated. Their grounds for rejecting a broadened concept lie in the belief that such a step risks damaging the intellectual coherence of the discipline, and consequently many such academics have called for the field of Security Studies to be restricted to a 'study of the threat, use and control of military force' (Walt, 1991: 212).

However, the schism does not end there. Indeed, divisions exist even among those who have sought to broaden the concept beyond the narrow confines imposed by the traditionalists. Even those who unite in the criticism of approaches such as Realism often disagree on how to tackle the problems that they identify. Feminists, for instance, differ considerably over the methods for attaining equal rights for marginalised groups. Similarly, as highlighted in the respective chapters, even though Critical Theory and Human Security both seek to shift attention away from the state to the individual as the primary agent of security, their conceptualisation and methods differ. These variations aptly demonstrate that security is a contested concept and that it defies consensus as regards its meanings. This is further reinforced by another approach highlighted in this chapter, namely Constructivism, one of the most influential of the many theoretical approaches that reject the narrow state/military-centric nature of Realism. Therefore, this chapter will consider the relevance of Constructivism to the field of Security Studies and introduce the reader to 'Securitization Theory' as advocated by academics affiliated to the Copenhagen School. The crucial connection between Constructivism and Securitization Theory is that they both advocate *social process*. Constructivism is concerned with the manner in which identities are formed and meanings are attached to material objects. Securitization Theory is also concerned with the process that leads to certain issues becoming a matter of security. This essentially means that any issue can be elevated to a position of importance, and as a consequence Securitization Theory can only be comfortable with multiple referent objects. In analysing these elements, the chapter will contend that the Constructivist tradition, although a relatively recent addition to Security Studies, has nevertheless established itself as a strong contender among the approaches that dispute the narrow rigidity of traditional approaches such as Realism.

Constructivism

Any discussion of Constructivism must be placed in the context of the debate between the different methods of conducting social enquiry. Despite focusing directly on questions of epistemology, certain aspects of the debate between positivism and post-positivism are particularly relevant to an understanding of Constructivism. With its emphasis on the methodologies of the natural sciences to explain social behaviour, positivism has dominated the study of international politics throughout the twentieth century. Epistemological questions became sidelined in the headlong rush to adopt positivist assumptions, and this has had the effect of placing rigid boundaries around what could actually be analysed, in that if events could not be explained scientifically, then they could not be construed as legitimate knowledge. The Realist project has been rigidly coupled with positivism and therefore it claims to be a scientific approach that is capable of revealing the underlying reality of world politics.

Positivist approaches such as Realism, therefore, seek to explain reality by emphasising empirical observation, where the analyst is able to detach himself from the analytical process. On the other hand, post-positivism appears much more concerned with 'understanding', and the analyst is assumed to be part of the analytical process. In the case of post-positivist approaches such as Critical Theory or Post-Structuralism, there is no such thing as an objective reality that exists independent of human understanding. Another way to understand this notion is to use God as an example, since a religious person would claim that such a deity exists as a real entity independent of our knowledge of it. On the other hand, it is possible to argue that, given there is no objective scientific proof of the existence of God, he has been brought into existence through discursive processes embodied within the symbols and linguistic practices of humans throughout the ages. Therefore, he does not exist as a real objective entity 'out there', such as the Sun or Solar System, but as a social construct, and his continued existence is entirely dependent upon a need for religious humans to constantly 'think' him into existence, through discourses in which religious practices are an important component.

This debate between positivists and post-positivists has had a tremendous impact on the recent progress of social sciences such as International Relations and Security Studies, and the contribution made by the Constructivists needs to be considered in the context of this ongoing debate. Defining and identifying the core principles of Constructivism is not easy, however, since it is a broad approach which exhibits characteristics of both positivism and post-positivism. Its central premise, that 'ideas and discourse' are an important component of any explanation of world events, underpins research in a variety of traditions such as Post-Structuralism, Critical Theory and Feminism. As shown elsewhere in this book, these 'critical' approaches have all taken issue with the rigidity of the narrow traditional core of Security Studies, and the key debates since the 1980s have reflected this. On the other hand, the traditionalists have at times launched counter-attacks and have in turn accused post-positivists of engaging purely in meta-theoretic debate with little to say about the 'real world' of international politics.

Alexander Wendt's article (see Box 6.1) was published in 1992, after the Cold War had ended, and it signalled the arrival of the Constructivist project in theorising about world politics. The earlier debate between the positivists and the post-positivists evolved to incorporate a number of distinct positions: the debates between the Critical Theorists and Constructivists on the one hand, and between the Constructivists and the Positivists on the other. The common denominator here, Constructivism, sought to challenge the positivism of the traditionalists and at the same time attempted to push critical thinkers away from engaging purely in meta-theoretical criticism towards an empirical analysis of world politics. Therefore, despite roots in Critical Theory, Constructivism differs due to its increasing emphasis on empirical analysis, and it is this feature which has led to a realisation that it occupies a 'middle ground' between positivist and post-positivist approaches.

This notion of the middle ground needs further elaboration. Critical Theory and Post-Structuralism (see Chapter 3) have questioned positivist approaches to knowledge by throwing down a challenge against the scientific method. Critical Theorists, along with Post-Structuralists, have played an active role in undermining the foundations of dominant approaches such as Realism. Their criticism of 'objective, empirically verifiable truth statements ... rejection of a single scientific method ... [and] rationalist conceptions of human nature' dramatically oppose the views embodied within positivism (Price and Reus-Smit, 1998: 263). Indeed, Post-Structuralists have gone further by rejecting all meta-narratives such as Realism and criticising their all-encompassing explanations and world views. Post-Structuralists see the world as being highly complex, and as a result they reject all narratives which seek to acquire hegemonic status. Realism, with its emphasis on the state, sovereignty, power and anarchy, is one such narrative. It seeks to discover, through direct observation, causal factors for questions of world politics, but this process has limited value among post-positivist approaches. Where, therefore, does Constructivism stand in this epistemological and methodological debate?

Views differ regarding the essence of Constructivism, with some academics such as Peter Katzenstein stressing that the approach is broadly compatible with an empiricist epistemology (Katzenstein, 1996). Others such as Reus-Smit, however, raise a powerful counter-claim, arguing that Constructivism's core assumptions remain firmly embedded within Critical Theory. They make this claim despite accepting that Constructivism is less occupied with meta-theoretical issues and even though Constructivist analysis has engaged with the mainstream on issues of interpretation and evidence (Price and Reus-Smit, 1998: 260). Similarly, Wendt provides a useful connection between Critical Theory and Constructivism by referring to the former as a family of theories (as opposed to a single theory) which includes Post-Structuralism, Constructivism, and some Feminist theories. Their common denominator is their concern regarding 'how world politics is socially constructed'. Wendt goes on to argue that this premise involves two basic assumptions: first, that the fundamental structures of international politics are social rather than strictly material; and second, that structures shape actors' identities and interests rather than simply their behaviour.

The fundamental essence of Constructivism is that it sees international relations as being socially constructed by identity, meanings, the assumptions of actors themselves, and indeed by the analysts' linguistic interpretations of social phenomena. Ontologically, Social Constructivism embodies a number of core principles, beginning with the importance that it places on ideational as well as material structures. The assumption here is that structures in international relations are able to constrain or shape behaviour. Neorealists, for instance, emphasise systemic anarchy as shaping state behaviour, which is ultimately based on material structures such as the balance of power and military capabilities. Constructivists, on the other hand, argue that ideas, values and beliefs also exhibit structural characteristics and can therefore also influence social and political action. However, this is not to say that Constructivists dismiss material structures. Indeed, material and ideational structures both play a role in shaping behaviour, but for Constructivists it is the system of meanings which defines how actors interpret their material environment. As Wendt argues, 'material resources only acquire meaning for human action through the shared knowledge in which they are embedded', and this is in contrast to the de-socialised view held by Neorealists (Wendt, 1995: 73). For Constructivists, therefore, individuals are social beings whose interactions involve subjectivity and interpretations, and meaning is created through the process of human understanding of the material world.

Hopf provides an excellent analysis of the notion of ideational and material structures by adopting the notion of 'power' as a lens. He argues that although power is central to mainstream and constructivist theorising, their conceptualisation of it differs. Despite their differences, Neorealism and Neoliberalism see material power, whether military or economic, as 'the single most important source of influence and authority in global politics'. Constructivists, on the other hand, emphasise both material and discursive power as necessary for any understanding of world affairs. For example, Hopf defines 'discursive power' as the 'power of knowledge, ideas, culture, and language' (Hopf, 1998: 177). Ideas as important structures are central to constructivist thought, and Wendt goes so far as to claim that material capabilities in themselves explain very little, arguing that asking 'when do ideas as opposed to power and interest matter is to ask the wrong question. Ideas always matter, since power and interest do not have effects apart from the shared knowledge that constitutes them as such' (Wendt, 1995: 74).

Secondly, social interactions, subjective interpretations and human understanding of the international environment mean that for Constructivists the creation of identities is a necessary feature of international politics. Identities bring order and predictability to the anarchic structure. As Hopf writes, 'A world without identities is a world of chaos, a world of pervasive and irremediable uncertainty, a world much more dangerous than anarchy'. He goes on to qualify the importance of identities by highlighting the functions that they perform, namely: 'they tell you and others who you are and they tell you who others are. In telling you who you are, identities strongly imply a particular set of interests or preferences with respect to choices of action in particular domains, and with respect to particular actors' (Hopf, 1998: 175). In other words, identities inform interests, which in turn outline particular forms of action.

Clearly, therefore, Constructivists see identities and interests as being closely connected. When comparing this notion to the perceptions held by conventional theories such as Neorealism and Neoliberalism, the differences become even more apparent. Mainstream theories define interests and identities as exogenous and given, so that actors approach one another with interests and preferences already established. Such theorists are not interested in the mechanisms which gave rise to the preferences, being merely content with considering how the actors pursue those preferences strategically. In contrast to this de-socialised view, Constructivists claim that it is necessary to understand how actors develop these interests and identities, since this provides the ability to explain a wider range of international political phenomena that traditional approaches ignore.

Neorealism, for instance, conceptualises the structure of international relations in terms of self-help, which explains the competitive nature of anarchy and thus, as Wendt argues, 'occupies a privileged explanatory role ... setting the terms for and unaffected by interaction [and] states failing to conform to [this logic are likely to be] driven from the system' (Wendt, 1992: 393). This shows that such features are exogenous to the states and their interactions. The notion of self-help clearly exists independently of time, place and state interaction. However, Constructivists argue that this logic fails to explain why, for instance, some states are allies and others are enemies. Neorealism sees states as lacking the autonomy in their abilities to mitigate against the effects of anarchy, since this assumption remains rigid regardless of time and space. Similarly, Realism devotes much of its attention to the notion of national interest, arguing that the policies and actions of states emerge from their need for security in an international system based solely on anarchy and the distribution of power. Indeed, Realism tends to see international politics as a struggle for power, and when this is combined with their rigid view of anarchy, Realists insist that states always remain concerned with the possibility of conflict. However, basing the behaviour of states solely on the anarchy of the international system excludes the possibility that the states themselves may be in a position to alter the nature of that system.

Post-positivists have a tendency to regard the empiricist epistemology upon which traditional approaches rely as being highly questionable, especially since it ignores the importance of process and interpretation. Its assumption that there is an independent reality which outlines objectively and accurately the threats to a state, its national interests and policy options is seen as necessarily flawed, given that analysts are social beings prone to subjective values and incapable of the pure objectivity demanded by empiricism. This, therefore, is one important reason why ideas are central to Constructivist thought, which sees identity and state interests as able to be created and changed through intersubjective processes. The way in which actors behave towards objects is dependent upon the meanings that those objects have for them, and these meanings are intersubjectively constituted. As Wendt argues, 'states act differently towards enemies than they do towards friends because enemies are threatening and friends are not'. (In contrast, the de-socialised ethos of Neorealism is unable to distinguish between such social characteristics.) Despite accepting that the distribution of power and the anarchic structure of the international system affect state behaviour, Wendt also believes that how they do so 'depends on the intersubjective understandings and expectations, on the distribution of knowledge, that constitute [its] conceptions of self and other' (Wendt, 1992: 396–397).

Another key characteristic of Constructivism is that of mutual constitution, namely the perception that observer and observed cannot be separate entities. Reality for Constructivists is socially constructed, as the material and social worlds construct or constitute each other. Despite key Constructivists like Katzenstein (mentioned earlier) adopting positions which are compatible with positivist epistemology, certain positivist tenets regarding the methodological unity of science are rejected. As Dunne outlines, this rejection of the scientism of naturalism ensures that the interests of the observer cannot be separated from the subject being observed. This mutually constitutive nature means that subject matter and observer are part of a single process (Dunne, 1995: 373–374). The implications of this for Constructivist analysis are profound, since the analysts' own perceptions of reality take on added significance. It is also an acceptance that there may be multiple realities which are all equally valid. Undoubtedly this assumption has its roots in the post-positivist rejection of hegemonic claims by meta-narratives.

The notion of mutual constitution also extends to the structure–agency debate, with Constructivists claiming that actor behaviour is neither exclusively determined by social structures nor the result of individual agents. Instead, the relationship has a mutual orientation whereby agents and structure constitute one another. Normative and ideational structures may well influence the behaviour, interests and even identities of actors, but those structures would not have been brought into existence without the impact of the actors themselves. This is in clear contrast to the specifications established by traditional approaches, where agents are the dominant element whose practices are responsible for the formation of structures, or where structures have greater force than agents and are therefore able to set conditions and constraints upon their practices. The Constructivist alternative specifies that agents and structures remain inseparable, so that structures are able to impose constraints on agents, but can themselves only be explained by the practices of agents. This 'middle ground' adopted by Constructivism can once again be contrasted with the Neorealist position where states are seen to have no autonomy in their interactions in the face of the structural constraints imposed by anarchy. Under Neorealism the anarchic structure is a given, setting the terms for state interaction and existing independently of it. The Constructivist emphasis on social as well as material structures, its treatment of identities and interests as a consequence of social practices, and the importance it attaches to the mutual constitution of structure and agency show that anarchy is, ultimately, 'what states make of it' through their social interaction, namely their creation, and their cultural and linguistic practices (Wendt, 1992).

Box 6.2: Key academic: John Ruggie, *Constructing the World Polity: Essays on International Institutionalism*, **Routledge, London, 1998.**

Ruggie has claimed that it was the post-Second World War aversion to idealism and the resulting primacy of Realist theory which led to the relegation of ideational factors in international relations. The Neorealist and Neoliberal treatment of ideas in strictly neo-utilitarian terms reinforced this position, and it wasn't until the full-scale debates between positivist and post-positivist theories that the discipline began to emerge from its narrow confines. As Ruggie states, Neorealism and Neoliberalism 'share a view of the world … in utilitarian terms: an atomistic universe of self-regarding units whose identity is assured, given and fixed, and who are responsive largely … to material interests …' (p. 3). Social Constructivism, on the other hand, 'seeks to account for what neo-utilitarianism assumes: the identity and/or interests of actors … In addition, it attributes to ideational factors … social efficacy over and above any functional utility they may have, including a role in shaping the way in which actors define their identity and interests in the first place' (p. 4).

Connecting Constructivism to Security Studies and the Copenhagen School

Constructivism, therefore, can be differentiated from rationalist theories such as Neorealism in terms of its core assumptions. Whereas theories such as Neorealism and Neoliberalism treat material structures as exogenous and given in a de-socialised world, the essence of Constructivism is that it sees international relations as being socially constructed through the interplay of ideational as well as material structures. These systems of shared ideas, meanings, the assumptions of the actors themselves and linguistic interpretations also have structural characteristics which enable them to exert influence on political action. Material structures are not dismissed, but for Constructivists the interpretation of material objects depends upon the meanings that those objects have for individuals. Clearly this becomes a two-way relationship in which human perception and the material world are involved in a mutually constitutive process whereby they construct each other.

Closely linked to this is the importance that Constructivism attaches to the notion of identity. Identities define the self and others, but they carry with them significant implications as regards relationships and actions – hence, crucially, identities inform interests. This contrasts with mainstream theories such as Neorealism, which treat identities and interests in the same way as they treat material structures – as exogenous and given. In other words, actors approach international relations with preconceived notions irrespective of time and space. As this chapter demonstrates, Constructivists such as Wendt have shown that identities and interests are endogenous to international relations and can be created and changed through intersubjective processes.

For Constructivists, therefore, reality is socially constructed by individuals whose interactions involve subjectivity and interpretation. The epistemological foundations of positivism are not entirely rejected, but at the same time Constructivism can lay claim to the 'middle ground' with its emphasis on interpretation, reflection and the laying down of constitutive questions. It succeeds in claiming origins in Critical Theory, but it also steers away from meta-theoretic discussion towards asking questions about 'real world international relations'. Nevertheless, its rejection of the hegemony of rationalist meta-narratives crucially opens the door into the realm of interpretation and the resulting multiple explanations. Linked to this notion of interpretation is the view that the analyst and the subject matter are no longer separate but rather part of a single process. The perceptions, opinions, subjectivity and consciousness of the observer provide meaning to the subject matter, thus ensuring that there are no neutral and entirely objective facts. By conceiving international relations as the product of social practices, they become dynamic and can be changed or reconstituted by actors – in essence, international relations are dependent upon how actors interpret their environment and the meanings they attach to the material world.

Finally, we must recognise that Constructivism is a broad approach which has its roots in Critical Theory, and these origins have led to considerable variations among academics referring to themselves as Constructivists. For instance, they differ regarding which level to concentrate on when analysing the construction of world politics. For instance, Wendt largely sidelines the role of domestic culture in his analysis of state interaction, whereas others such as Finnemore seek to analyse the impact of international norms on state interests. In Katzenstein's edited volume it quickly becomes apparent that many Constructivists also include the notion of identity, in addition to culture and norms, when specifying threats to national security. The differences in approach also extend to the way world politics is analysed on different sides of the Atlantic, with Europe being much closer to a critical understanding where power and discourse are central to analysis. The Americans, on the other hand, promote what is often labelled 'conventional Constructivism', where identity and norms form the basis of the analysis. Ultimately, Hopf's use of the notion of the power of discourse can be interpreted as highlighting the premise that Constructivists are generally beholden to the perception that all relevant forms of human understanding of the material world are crucial to a realisation of how world politics is constructed.

The importance of process

One of the key contributions of Constructivism has been to highlight the need to analyse the *process* that leads to the establishment of state policy. To illustrate this, we can consider the widely accepted premise that the consolidated Liberal democracies of the West do not go to war with one another. This premise is now almost universally accepted, both among the academics who analyse international relations and among the politicians who establish the policies and then carry them out. As a traditional approach, reliant on the scientific method and prone to be reliant on law-like assumptions, Liberalism is likely to accept this development at face value, but in so doing, it fails to consider the mechanisms and processes that have led to such a condition becoming established. It is particularly in this context that Constructivism enables us to consider a far greater range of causal mechanisms, thereby demonstrating its potential for providing a much broader range of explanations for state behaviour than traditional approaches such as Realism or Liberalism.

Ultimately, it is the importance placed on the *process* which provides one crucial contextual element to the ideas advocated by the Copenhagen School of Security Studies. This school puts forward the notion of *Securitization*, which is based on earlier work developed by Barry Buzan in his 1983 book entitled *People, States and Fear*. Here Buzan argued that the traditional definition of security is too narrow, and his goal was to offer a much broader framework which included facets not previously considered to be part of the security landscape, such as *political, military, societal, economic* and *environmental* sectors. Importantly, despite providing a specific focal point in the security *problematique*, each of these sectors was closely linked to the others. He does, however, provide examples of the types of threats associated with each, with the state as the referent object in the case of the military sector and sovereignty experiencing threats in the case of the political sector. In the societal sector, on the other hand, 'the referent object is the large-scale collective identities that can function independently of the state, such as the nation or religions' (Buzan *et al.*, 1998: 17). A vital element in his analysis was the view that societies, individuals and states are able to construct or 'securitize' threats, and this Constructivist approach to defining security led to a significant broadening away from the narrow military-centric views expressed by traditionalists.

Influenced by the debates raging at the end of the Cold War, Buzan began to question whether traditionalist approaches could adequately explain the wide range of threats facing humans. Consequently, his increasing focus on societal security specified that it depended on the maintenance of national identity, language and other cultural symbols such as religion and customs. This shift towards acknowledging the importance of societal security stemmed from a realisation that factors such as migration into European states were also a security concern, and that such issues could not be fitted into traditional security perceptions. These ideas especially influenced another academic, Ole Waever (a colleague of Buzan's), and together they continued to argue in favour of expanding the concept of security. Their method was to advocate the manner in which certain threats came to be seen as sufficiently grave enough to devote resources to reducing their impact. It was in this context that Waever defined security as the outcome of a '*speech act*' and Securitization as the linguistic process which led a particular issue to be seen as an existential threat. For Waever, Securitization was dependent upon stages which included, first, a declaration by elites that an issue was a security problem, and second, an acceptance by the audience that the issue is indeed an important one. As Waever states, 'something is designated as an international security issue because it can be argued that this issue is more important than other issues and should take absolute priority' (Waever, 1998: 24).

In this sense, then, the key to understanding **Securitization** lies in the premise that security is a function of social construction. Its roots in the debates at the end of the Cold War are important given that they sought to question the value of traditionalist approaches in explaining wider threats to states, societies and other referent objects. Influenced by the easing of tensions brought about by the end of the Cold War and the ultimate collapse of the Soviet Union, the new assumptions centred on the belief that the security of the state was now assured, and attention could therefore be shifted to other referent objects. Various chapters in this book have referred to the wide range of objectors to traditionalist views, including Feminists, Critical Theorists and those who highlight Human Security as the key to achieving stability for societies and communities. These views stressed that privileging the state failed to acknowledge that humans experienced a wide range of threats at the level of the individual or at the sub-state level. The Copenhagen School also contributed to these debates throughout the 1990s, and its Constructivist roots are apparent in its criticism of the traditionalist approaches which regard security as being pre-determined. The Copenhagen School refuses to accept the Realist premise that threats and referent objects can be removed from the social context within which they are embedded. Consequently, the only way to understand security and threats is to analyse the *process*, which leads to threats being constructed through discursive practices.

The notion of Securitization was first introduced by Ole Waever during the mid-1990s, and it was in his 1998 book *Security: A New Framework for Analysis* that the concept was further developed. Securitization refers to the process that ultimately constructs a shared social understanding of what threats the relevant referent object faces. An issue is usually presented as an existential threat by elites, but the next stage is just as important in the construction of the threat. The audience must accept the existential nature of the threat, because it is only then that emergency procedures are put in place and the issue is removed from the boundaries of 'normal politics' and placed in a special, 'separate' area. For Buzan, security is a 'self-referential' practice because 'it is in this practice that the issue becomes a security issue – not necessarily because a real existential threat exists but because the issue is presented as such a threat' (Buzan *et al.*, 1998: 24) (and see Box 6.4). Security, therefore, is dependent upon the manner in which it is framed by the social actors, and it is through the process of securitization that actors move the issue from the realm of low politics to one defined as high politics. Differences between the two realms are apparent in the sense that rules and decision-making procedures dominate low politics, whereas a sense of urgency and priority dominate high politics.

In the case of state-to-state relations, Securitization would require the replacement of the norms, treaties and other rules which governed their relations during peace time. The state that feels threatened then claims the right to rely on its own resources in order to deal with the existential threat facing it.

Box 6.3: How to prevent 'everything' from becoming a security issue

According to Barry Buzan, Securitization is entirely dependent on a number of steps, including:

1 The identification of the existential threat.
2 Establishing the need for action in order to resolve the threat.
3 A rejection of the rules which govern the relationship between two units under normal conditions.

At the intersection between traditional and critical approaches

There is little doubt that Constructivism has become a significant force among the many approaches competing with each other as means of explaining world politics. Within the field of Security Studies, Securitization Theory has enjoyed similar success, and like Constructivism, it too presents itself as the middle ground between traditional and new theories of Security Studies. Indeed, its ability to consider traditional military threats as well as wider issues, such as gender or the environment, has placed the approach in a unique position within the field. The close connections between Constructivism and Securitization are important given that neither of them accept the premise that events in the international system always reflect material and objective circumstances. Constructivists have highlighted that although the material world exists, it needs to be defined and interpreted by humans, and it is in this context that identities and ideational structures acquire great importance. Similarly, Securitization Theory accepts that although security issues may at times be a reflection of the material conditions of the world, more often they are the result of attempts by individuals, groups or other collectives to understand their circumstances. Interpreting events and the conditions facing them often enables these individuals to construct their own environment and contribute to actually creating the threats that face them.

Elsewhere in the book we have highlighted a variety of critical approaches which stress the emancipation of the individual as the key to achieving security. For instance, the Welsh School and Feminism both see human emancipation as constrained by the narrow rigidity imposed by Realism and Neorealism. Since their arrival into the field of Security Studies much has been written on Critical Theory and Securitization, and yet they have had limited contact with each other. One could assume that since the objectives of both subfields vary considerably from each other, there is no need to highlight commonalities between them. However, an increasingly popular view is that not only are there analytical connections between the fields, but they also share normative values. For instance, the most important shared element is that they both seek to move beyond traditional frameworks of security, and although they do not ignore the military components, they stress that it cannot be privileged over other sectors. Furthermore, both the Welsh School and Securitization Theory highlight the existence of multiple referent objects at the individual level and also at the regional and global levels. More fundamentally, however, academics are increasingly beginning to engage with the notion of 'desecuritization', whereby the threat becomes deconstructed and is no longer considered to be a security issue. In the case of securitization, the speech act focuses the audience's attention on the existential nature of a threat, leading to the placing of said threat into a special area outside of 'normal politics'. In the case of desecuritization, however, it appears to be diametrically opposed to the securitizing act. In a sense, the conditions for Securitization appear to operate in reverse to the process of Desecuritization. If a speech act is involved, then the speaker stresses that the threat is not existential and that the issue can be resolved within normal politics.

Finally, this gives the impression that Desecuritization is preferable to Securitization. Indeed, it is possible to argue that normal everyday politics is much more democratic, for instance, than politics which comes to be viewed as exceptional. It is often assumed that Securitization is far too accepting of traditional security assumptions, given that in essence it involves identifying existential threats. Therefore, theorists within the critical mould argue that Securitization theory is not 'critical enough', and that while it may have extended security beyond the state as the key referent object, it continues to privilege the state – an approach which is, of course, heavily criticised by critical approaches. Interlinked with this is the view that Securitization fails to provide space for normative objectives. This is especially apparent given that it is possible to view Securitization as a failure of normal politics, namely the realm where democratic and other rule-based norms exist. Given that the Copenhagen School appears to provide a negative image of Securitization, analysts have turned to Desecuritization as the link to a more critical way of looking at security. However, this is made difficult by the fact that this approach still remains under-theorised.

Box 6.4: Securitizing threats as existential even when they are not

The US-led invasion of Iraq in 2003 was based on two original justifications:

1   That Iraq was linked to al-Qaeda and the attacks of 11 September 2001; and
2   That Iraq possessed weapons of mass destruction and was seeking to possess more.

Traditional theories such as Realism highlight material factors such as Iraq's capabilities, including the two factors mentioned above. However, Constructivists would see this explanation as too limited and consequently highlight the identity of Iraq or Saddam Hussein as a threat to the region and further afield. The issue is particularly complicated by subsequent revelations that the invasion was based on faulty intelligence. For instance, a BBC article published on 9 September 2006 reported that the US Senate Intelligence Committee had found no evidence of links between the regime of Saddam Hussein and al-Qaeda, and neither did it find any evidence concerning Iraq's weapons of mass destruction. We can conclude from this example that security is in fact socially constructed and that threats can be constructed/created even if they do not exist in a real/objective sense.

Conclusion

Constructivism has added an interesting and important angle to the debate regarding the notion of security. Its view that the international system is constructed on the basis of a set of ideas and a system of norms by groups of people is highly innovative. The nature of social reality, including threats, is dependent upon humans, who reproduce it on a daily basis. These human agents do not exist apart from the social environment within which they are embedded and with which they interact constantly. In addition, as highlighted in this chapter, Constructivism places immense importance on structures, but not purely of the material kind. Indeed, ideational structures are a crucial component and apply to the process through which humans actually interpret the material objects present in the international system. The material and rationalist assumptions that are central to theories such as Realism have been successfully challenged by Constructivists, and its promotion of the need to analyse social process in the construction of world politics is central to the notion of Securitization advocated by the Copenhagen School. This particular offshoot of Constructivism has presented security analysts with a means of considering the manner in which threats are subject to social construction. It has also allowed us to realise that it is not possible to understand the security dynamics of the international system without reference to actors' identities, their perceptions of each other, and how they perceive the material objects central to world politics.

Summary points

1   Key features of world politics are socially constructed rather than being determined by the nature of the international system or by human nature.
2   The focus of Constructivism is on human awareness and its understanding of the material world.

3   Social Constructivism has introduced **process** into the analysis of world politics.
4   The notion of process is central to the theory of Securitization, which has very close links to Social Constructivism.
5   Securitization is dependent upon: (a) an agent to make the securitizing move through a 'speech act'; (b) the referent object that has been threatened and needs to be safeguarded; and (c) an audience that needs to be convinced that the securitization act is necessary.

Recommended reading

Buzan, B. *People, States and Fear: An Agenda for International Security Studies in the Post-Cold War Era*, London: Harvester Wheatsheaf, 1991.

Buzan, B., Waever, O. and De Wilde, J. *Security, A New Framework For Analysis*, London: Lynne Rienner Publishers, 1998.

Dunne, T. 'The social construction of international society', *European Journal of International Relations*, vol. 1, no. 3, 1995, 367–389.

Hopf, T. 'The promise of constructivism in international relations theory', *International Security*, vol. 23, no. 1, Summer 1998, 171–200.

Katzenstein, P. (ed.) *The Culture of National Security: Norms and Identity in World Politics*, New York: Columbia University Press, 1996.

Price, R. and Reus-Smit, C. 'Dangerous liaisons? Critical international theory and constructivism', *European Journal of International Relations*, vol. 4, no. 3, 1998, 259–294.

Ruggie, J. *Constructing the World Polity: Essays on International Institutionalism*, London: Routledge, 1998.

Waever, O. 'Securitization and Desecuritization', in Lipschutz, R. (ed.), *On Security*, New York: Columbia University Press, 1998.

Wendt, A. 'Anarchy is what states make of it: The social construction of power politics', *International Organization*, vol. 46, no. 2, Spring 1992, 391–425.

Wendt, A. 'Constructing international politics', *International Security*, vol. 20, no. 1, Summer 1995, 71–81.

Section 2

Military security

7 Reflecting on war and peace

Bruce Pilbeam

Box 7.1: The nature of war

War is merely the continuation of policy by other means.

Carl von Clausewitz, *On War* [1832/1984: 87)

Introduction

War has been a feature of human societies since their very beginnings. It has been responsible for not only the loss of life on a massive scale, but the impedance of economic development, the spreading of disease and famine, the downfall of governments, and the destruction of whole cultures. Yet at the same time, war has facilitated many positive developments. For example, US government spending in the Second World War may have helped end the Great Depression, and the experiences of soldiers fighting in it led to the desegregation of the nation's military in its aftermath; similarly, in many European societies, rebuilding after the war included the creation of extensive welfare states to provide for citizens in areas like health and education. Furthermore, numerous medical and technological advances owe their development to wartime research and innovation. War is a complicated, contradictory phenomenon.

One of the most famous – indeed, infamous – statements about the nature of war is the one cited above, penned by the nineteenth century Prussian soldier and military theorist Carl von Clausewitz, that war is merely the continuation of policy by other means. To critics, Clausewitz's belief suggests a morally repugnant view of war, treating it as if it were no different to any of the other tools at a statesman's disposal, like diplomacy or sanctions, and thereby failing to appreciate its exceptional and horrifying nature. Yet a different interpretation is that Clausewitz was simply emphasising that war is a *political* instrument – in other words, that it is not a separate, autonomous activity, but is intimately linked to the wider interests, strategies and decision-making processes of those who wage it, usually with some definite end or goal in mind.

At any rate, it is important not to think of war in isolation, but as connected to all the other major issues of international security. Today, this includes not only traditional concerns about power and military force, but others such as many of those discussed in this book, like globalisation and the environment. The purpose of this chapter is to address both the nature and causes of war, especially in the contemporary context, but also – at least as important – to examine the meaning of, and possibilities for, peace.

What is war? What is peace?

The twin questions 'what is war?' and 'what is peace?' may appear deceptively straightforward. However, over the centuries, writers have debated endlessly the meanings of war and peace, and there remains no consensus over either term.

To begin with the definition of war, there have always been disputes as to which forms of conflict to include and which not to include within the category. Another reason that it is not easy to devise an all-encompassing definition is that there are many different types of war – see Box 7.2 for some illustrations of the range of classifications that may be used. Making the task even more difficult today is that the word war has been co-opted by politicians to describe a whole array of policy agendas unrelated to traditional ideas of warfare. For example, there is, or there has been, a War on Drugs, a War on Poverty and a War on Cancer; some have even talked of a War on Litter. Since the 9/11 terrorist attacks of 2001, there has also been the War on Terror, which may not fit comfortably into conventional definitions of war either.

Box 7.2: Typologies of war

There are many different ways of categorising wars, and various typologies have been constructed. Here are some of the major distinctions between types of war that have been suggested:

Inter-state/intra-state/extra-state wars

- **Inter-state** – *between* sovereign states
- **Intra-state** – *within* states. They may be either civil conflicts between states and non-state actors (within nations), or inter-communal conflicts between different non-state groups
- **Extra-state** – between states and non-state actors from *outside* the states themselves (e.g. an international terrorist group).

Declared/undeclared wars

- **Declared** – in which at least one side issues a formal declaration of war
- **Undeclared** – no formal declarations are issued.

Total/limited wars

- **Total** – in which at least one side seeks to mobilise all of its nation's population and resources to secure a complete victory over its enemy
- **Limited** – fought mainly by mobilising only military resources and with clearly defined and restricted objectives (e.g. to expel an enemy from a specific area of land).

Conventional/guerrilla wars

- **Conventional** – fought by professional, organised armies
- **Guerrilla** – in which one side uses small units of combatants, rather than large armies, using tactics such as ambushes and 'hit-and-run' attacks.

Wars of conquest/wars of liberation

- **Conquest** – whereby states seek to invade and perhaps occupy other territories, usually for the purpose of acquiring land or resources
- **Liberation** – waged to free subjugated peoples so that they may gain their independence. They may be fought either solely by dominated peoples themselves or in conjunction with outside assistance.

There are numerous other types of war as well – for example, proxy wars (whereby states, typically major powers, avoid direct confrontation with each other by sponsoring third parties, like smaller states, to fight instead) – but the above serves to illustrate that in reality there is no such thing as 'war in general', but a wide range of different types of armed conflict.

In looking for definitions of terms, the first port of call for many is, unsurprisingly, a dictionary. Considering one of the best known, Merriam-Webster offers this as a definition of war:

> a state of usually open and declared armed hostile conflict between states or nations
> (www.merriam-webster.com/dictionary/war)

However, although this definition accords well enough with ordinary, everyday usage of the word, it also illustrates some of the limitations of relying upon general dictionaries for rigorous, in-depth understandings of concepts. Two issues relating to the above definition will suffice to show this.

First, far from all wars are 'declared', which the use of the qualifier 'usually' does not adequately take into account. For example, under the US Constitution a formal declaration of war can be issued only by Congress, which has happened in only five wars in US history, the last being the Second World War. Consequently, US military actions in Vietnam, Lebanon, Afghanistan and Iraq, to name but a few, have not been accompanied by formal declarations of war, even if many would consider that they are clearly cases of war. Undeclared wars are also multiple – for example, it might be felt that in 2014 Russia was in a state of undeclared war with Ukraine, following the former's military intervention in Crimea and other parts of Ukrainian sovereign territory.

Second, and even more significantly, this definition considers armed conflicts to be wars only when they are 'between states or nations' – in other words, those cases that are *inter-state* wars. However, this excludes wars within states, or *intra-state* wars – principally civil and ethnic wars, such as those that have broken out in Rwanda, Sudan, Libya and Syria. Equally, it does not encompass *extra-state* wars, between states and non-state actors that exist outside the state with which they are in conflict. States engaged in armed conflict with terrorists, warlords or militia groups in other nations, for example, might well be perceived to be at war; proponents of the War on Terror evidently believe this.

It is for such reasons that it is necessary to consider other definitions. To return to Clausewitz, he explicitly addresses the question of 'what is war?' and contends that it is 'an act of force to compel our enemy to do our will' (Clausewitz, 1984: 75). This definition may have some merit to it, but at the very least its language may seem problematic to modern ears, and it may not capture fully all the types of conflict we may consider today to be wars. One of the most useful modern definitions is offered by Hedley Bull, who puts forward the following:

> War is organised violence carried on by political units against each other. Violence is not war unless it is carried out in the name of a political unit; what distinguishes killing in war from murder is its vicarious and official character, the symbolic responsibility of the unit whose agent the killer is. Equally, violence carried out in the name of a political unit is not war unless it is directed against another political unit.
>
> (Bull, 2012: 178)

Bull was a Realist (see Chapter 2), so his analysis focuses very strongly on the role of states. However, although he believes that the involvement of states affects the question of a war's *legitimacy* – for him, in the modern age it is largely only wars between states that have been legitimate – he does not argue that the *definition* of war should be restricted to wars between states.

As such, the first sentence of the above quotation especially, employing the broad category of 'political units', may find favour with both Realists and non-Realists, since it can include a variety of state and non-state actors. Bull's definition is useful as well because it does not limit wars to conflicts fought for particular objectives (for example, conquest or self-defence) or specific methods beyond the use of organised violence. Violence itself is also a wide category that can include not only killing, but other acts such as torture and rape. It is possible to object to the claim that violence must be perpetrated by political units against each other – for example, what about state-sponsored violence against 'non-political' civilians? – but for Bull this is important to distinguish war from, say, the violence used by domestic law enforcement bodies, which they use (for the most part) against people as separate individuals rather than as political units.

However, this still leaves the question of what separates war from less severe instances of armed conflict, such as minor border skirmishes. One of the most widely accepted definitions that attempts to do this is the one used by the Correlates of War (COW) project at the University of Michigan, which maintains a comprehensive statistical database on the incidence and nature of war. To differentiate war, the project sets a threshold of one thousand battle-related deaths as the level of hostilities that distinguishes war from other forms of violence (Sarkees, 2010: 1). Any such figure is, of course, open to dispute, but the COW definition has been adopted by many writers and scholars engaged in the study of war. (It should be noted, though, that – as will be discussed in Chapter 8 – some theorists of contemporary conflicts reject making a minimum number of battle deaths a criterion for defining war.)

Turning to the definition of peace, its meaning may seem obvious: to many, the word simply denotes the opposite condition to a state of war. Yet here, too, there is scope for debate. Perhaps the most important distinction to be drawn between conceptions of peace is between 'negative' and 'positive' peace, which is commonly adopted by those working within the field of peace research. The distinction was originated by Johan Galtung, one of the founding figures of modern peace studies (Galtung, 1964). According to Galtung, negative peace refers simply to the absence of violence. For example, when parties engaged in conflict agree to terminate armed hostilities, this creates negative peace, as fighting is no longer taking place. In many respects, this idea of peace equates to the common understanding of what the word means.

However, according to Galtung and other proponents of positive peace, thinking solely in terms of a negative conception is insufficient because this fails to take into account the deep-rooted causes of conflict, as well as less obvious forms of violence. Here it is worth introducing another distinction that Galtung draws, between direct and indirect violence (Galtung, 1990). Direct violence refers to violence in its most explicit and open manifestations, perpetrated against people directly, such as killing, torture or rape. By contrast, indirect violence is structural (whereby social structures and institutions create embedded inequalities, leading people to die from causes such as poverty and hunger) or cultural (referring to the beliefs and values of a society which underpin either direct or structural violence, such as racial or religious prejudices, which may thereby legitimate the deaths of particular individuals or groups).

Following from this, negative peace should be defined more precisely as the absence of *direct* violence. While positive peace also means the absence of violence, it differs because it entails the elimination of structural and cultural violence as well as direct forms. To create positive peace therefore requires not just bringing about a halt to fighting, but reforming institutions, addressing issues like social and economic inequality, and seeking to change people's attitudes, values and behaviour.

What should be clear from this is that positive peace is a much more full-blooded conception than the negative version. Clearly, too, it is far more demanding, asking us to think about a whole array of political, social and economic questions beyond those simply relating to armed conflict in a narrow sense. Clearly, addressing these questions takes us well outside the boundaries of a traditional view of security, but it would fit with other paradigms discussed in this book, such as Human Security (see Chapter 5).

One criticism of the idea of positive peace is that it may seem 'utopian' and unachievable. After all, we at least know what negative peace looks like, and that it may be a realisable goal – for example, the nations of Western Europe and North America may be said to have achieved a relatively stable state of negative peace among themselves, having not fought armed conflicts with each other for many decades. Yet it is far less certain whether the full achievement of positive peace – ridding societies of structural and cultural as well as direct violence – is a real prospect. Ultimately, the issue comes down to how optimistic one is about humanity's ability and willingness to overcome its prejudices and tackle fundamental inequalities.

The causes of war

When a state goes to war, it normally has a stated casus belli – self-defence, for example, or to protect the human rights of others – but this may not always be the true, or at least, the only reason for its use of armed force. Since we cannot simply rely on the claims made by those who wage wars themselves, we need to address more fully the question of what the causes of war are.

However, as soon as one starts to reflect on this question, further issues immediately arise. For example, do different types of war require different types of explanation – for example, inter-state and intra-state wars? Should we be looking for monocausal or multicausal explanations? And can we devise general theories that apply to all wars, or does every war require its own specific account?

Particular wars can be explained by various motives on the parts of those who wage them – for example: to obtain territory; to acquire natural resources; to build an empire; to fight an empire; to defend against attack; to prevent the possibility of attack; to exact revenge; to protect or aid other peoples; or to spread a political or religious belief system. In most cases, there will be a combination of causes – a mixture of political, economic and social factors – some of which may be short-term while others are long-term in nature. Yet to understand war better within the context of an understanding of international security, it is necessary to consider whether it is possible to provide more general explanations.

The fundamental nature and underlying causes of war have been explored by historians, political philosophers and other thinkers of many types, from ancient writers like Thucydides to modern ones as diverse as Marx, Nietzsche and Freud. However, one of the most influential writers on the contemporary study of war is the Neorealist Kenneth Waltz, and his arguments provide a valuable framework for examining different theories.

In his work, *Man, the State, and War* (first published in 1954) Waltz argues that all of the various explanations that have been offered for the causes of war can be placed under three headings: 'within man, within the structure of the separate states, within the state system' (Waltz, 2001: 12). Waltz describes these as different 'images' of international relations, and the reason why considering the topic in this way is useful is that it suggests a 'levels of analysis' approach that highlights how different theories of war focus on different explanatory levels. Another way to describe Waltz's widely-used notion of three images is to distinguish the following levels of explanation:

- The individual
- The state
- The international system.

i) The individual level

Explanations of war that focus on the individual level examine in particular the qualities and behaviour of political leaders, most notably their warlike, belligerent tendencies. Thus, for example, the outbreak of the Second World War might be explained in terms of the beliefs, attitudes and personality of Adolf Hitler (such as his fervent belief in the need for German territorial expansion) – as well as those of the other major leaders of the time, like Joseph Stalin.

Waltz's account considers specifically the views of classical Realists, like Reinhold Niebuhr and Hans Morgenthau, who placed great weight on the idea of fixed human nature. In particular, it is their belief that human nature is inherently flawed, and that human beings are naturally aggressive, self-interested and competitive, which serves to explain the resort to war. However, Waltz criticises theories centred on human nature on the grounds that if we are to explain human behaviour in terms of human beings' fixed natures, then this must account not only for why societies go to war, but for why they do everything else – including living in peace. As Waltz argues, 'Human nature may in some sense have been the cause of war in 1914, but by the same token it was the cause of peace in 1910' (Waltz, 2001: 28). In other words, if human nature is a fixed constant, how do we explain why human beings may sometimes be antagonistic and bellicose, yet at other times willing to compromise and co-exist with each other peacefully?

Although Waltz was writing in relation to classical Realists, it should be noted that his argument may also apply to other attempts to locate the causes of war in inherent features of human beings' make-up, such as those forwarded by writers within the fields of psychology and evolutionary biology. For example, any theory that claims to explain the drive to war in terms of humans' genetic programming has to account for the fact that humans behave very differently in different times and places.

ii) The state level

Theorists who focus on the state level argue that the causes of war are to be found in the internal organisation of states, including their ideologies, forms of government and economic systems. Wars occur because the characteristics of some types of state make them more likely to use war as an instrument of policy, though different thinkers will identify different features. The main subjects of Waltz's analysis are Liberalism and Marxism, and each of these is worth considering in turn.

The essence of the Liberal view is that non-liberal states are the ones most likely to employ war as a means of achieving their ends. This especially means non-democratic regimes, such as authoritarian and militaristic dictatorships, and ones that do not embrace other Liberal goods like individual rights and free markets. This view was first given clear expression by the Liberal philosopher Immanuel Kant, in his short 1795 essay, 'Perpetual Peace', in which he sets out the conditions he believes are necessary for achieving permanent peace (Kant, 1957). Kant uses the label republican to describe states based on representative government, the consent of the people and the rule of law – which today would more often be called liberal states – and argues that non-republican states are much more likely to wage war. One reason for this is that the leaders of republican (or liberal) states need citizens' consent for their decisions, including the decision to declare war, but because citizens are the ones who suffer most from wars, in having to fight and pay for them, the latter are naturally reluctant to agree to initiating armed conflict. By contrast, rulers in non-republican (or non-liberal) states may declare war when they please, without having to worry about popular opinion or that they themselves will suffer unduly. Similar beliefs have subsequently been avowed by many other liberals, and we shall return to this later in discussing the possibilities for peace.

Marxism, of course, encompasses a number of different strands of thought, which differ as to how war should be explained. For the present purposes, however, it will be sufficient to consider the views of classical Marxists, particularly Lenin's theory of imperialism. Lenin's major study of imperialism, *Imperialism: The Highest Stage of Capitalism*, was written in 1916 while the First World War was raging, as an analysis of this conflict. It is impossible to do full justice to Lenin's argument in the space available here, but its basic tenor can be gleaned from a short passage from one of its prefaces. In Lenin's view:

> the war of 1914–18 was imperialistic (that is, an annexationist, predatory, plunderous war) on the part of both sides; it was a war for the division of the world, for the partition and repartition of colonies, 'spheres of influence' of finance capital, etc.
>
> (Lenin, 1966: 7–8)

In other words, war (in the modern era of advanced capitalism) is the product of the self-interested motives of imperialist states. In particular, it is driven by domestic concerns: having exhausted markets at home, imperialist nations turn their attentions abroad to find new ones. It is this that leads each of them to seek to partition the world for its own benefit, which then brings the major powers into conflict with each other. This is what caused the First World War, as each imperialist state wanted to maximise its access to global markets – to annex, prey upon and plunder other nations.

Clearly, Liberal and Marxist theories differ significantly. Nonetheless, according to Waltz, what they have in common is a shared belief that the main causes of war are defects in the internal structures of states: for Liberals, it is their lack of liberal characteristics, while for Marxists, it is that they are driven to fulfil the rapacious demands of their respective capitalist economies. For Waltz, the crucial failing of such explanations is that, in seeking to explain war in terms of domestic imperatives, they miss the fact that states do not operate in a vacuum, and that their behaviour is heavily determined by the wider international system. As Waltz puts it, 'the international political environment has much to do with the ways in which states behave' (Waltz, 2001: 122–123).

It is not necessary to agree entirely with Waltz's analysis – it may be believed that domestic factors *are* crucial drivers of nations' foreign policies – but it remains useful in highlighting how theories of wars may focus on features internal or external to states.

iii) The international system level

Given the criticisms presented by Waltz already noted, it may come as little surprise to find that his own perspective is one that focuses on the level of the international system. Next, then, it will be valuable to examine the Neorealist view of war. The Neorealist perspective, with its emphasis on the anarchic nature of the international system, has already been explored in Chapter 2, so here we will limit ourselves to the implications Waltz sees in this for war.

To begin, it is necessary to clarify that Waltz does not reject the other two levels of explanation he discusses. Instead, he argues that the causes of war identified by those centred on the individual or state level are what he terms 'efficient' causes, ones that may explain why a *particular* war occurs. So, for example, the acquisitiveness of human nature might be a part of the explanation for why a war of conquest is launched. Yet it is only by looking at the international system as a whole that we can grasp the 'underlying' reason why war is an ineradicable feature of human affairs. A state, being self-interested and operating in a system based on self-help, 'will use force to attain its goals if, after assessing the prospects for success, it values those goals more than it values the pleasures of peace' (Waltz, 2001: 160). Most notably, because the international system is anarchic, meaning that there is no overarching authority to police states' behaviour, the ultimate conclusion is that 'wars occur because there is nothing to prevent them' (Ibid.: 232). The only way to prevent war altogether would be the creation of a world government – which Waltz and other Realists believe to be an extremely unlikely prospect.

How convincing we find these arguments depends on how far we accept the overall Realist depiction of international relations. Specifically in terms of Waltz's account of war, it may be argued that it is by no means certain that anarchy alone is a sufficient condition to explain war's existence. Even if there were nothing to prevent war, it does not follow that war is inevitable. Moreover, as Alexander Wendt argues, 'self-help and power politics are institutions, not essential features of anarchy. *Anarchy is what states make of it*' (Wendt, 1992: 395). Deciding to go to war is a conscious choice, and states may choose to do otherwise. They may decide to co-operate with rather than fight each other; they may even create institutions like the United Nations which – though not a world government – may help them to resolve conflicts peacefully without having to resort to war.

It has not been possible in this brief survey to consider the contributions of every major theoretical perspective on the causes of war, but others also have distinctive views to offer. For example, an interesting Feminist take on Waltz's argument is presented by Jean Elshtain, in an article entitled 'Woman, the State, and War', which examines Waltz's levels of analysis by considering the implications of adding gender as a category (Elshtain, 2009).

War in the twenty-first century

Discussion so far has examined war from a relatively general perspective, but it will be useful next to look at some of the distinctive features of war in the modern era, especially in the twenty-first century. One specific way of understanding the nature of war today is in terms of what is known as the 'new wars' thesis, which posits the idea that contemporary wars are qualitatively different to those of the past. This thesis will be examined in depth in Chapter 8. Furthermore, many specific aspects of twenty-first-century warfare are looked at in other chapters – including terrorism (Chapter 11), the increasing reliance upon private military and security companies (Chapter 14) and the role of natural resources like oil and water in fuelling conflicts (Chapter 15).

Instead, here we will focus on three broad trends and developments.

i) Is war in decline?

One of the most important issues concerning war today is the possibility that it may be in decline. With images of war filling TV screens, and with heated political debates taking place over how the world should respond to armed conflicts around the globe, it may be surprising to learn that the overall picture in terms of war and peace may be far more positive than many suppose.

This view would seem to be borne out by much of the evidence. In particular, statistics suggest that there has been a sharp decline over recent decades in the number of deaths directly resulting from war. This is shown by the line chart in Figure 7.1; battle deaths include all those killed as a direct result of fighting (civilians and soldiers). As one commentator summarises from the available data:

> Worldwide, deaths caused directly by war-related violence in the new century have averaged about 55,000 per year, just over half of what they were in the 1990s (100,000 a year), a third of what they were during the Cold War (180,000 a year from 1950 to 1989), and a hundredth of what they were in World War II ... Far from being an age of killer anarchy, the 20 years since the Cold War ended have been an era of rapid progress toward peace.
>
> (Goldstein, 2011: 1–2)

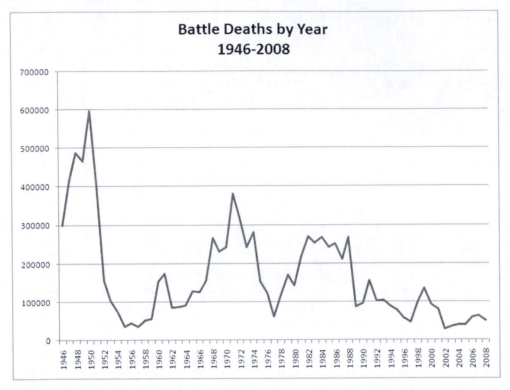

Figure 7.1 The declining trend in battle deaths
Source: Peace Research Institute Oslo (PRIO), www.prio.org/Data/Armed-Conflict/Battle-Deaths/The-Battle-Deaths-Dataset-version-30 (original data from Lacina and Gleditsch 2005).

Others have expressed similarly optimistic views. For example, Stephen Pinker (2011) identifies a long-term historical trend of a decline in violence in human societies (not just war, but all forms including homicide).

In terms of the figures on battle deaths, the principal reason why numbers have fallen is that there has been a major decline in the incidence of inter-state conflicts. Wars between states tend to result in much greater loss of life than those that occur within states, so this has had a crucial impact on casualty figures. Furthermore, the inter-state wars that have been fought in recent decades have not been between major military powers, which are always the most destructive (consider, for example, the two world wars).

Does all this mean that Realists' views about the ineradicability of war are wrong, and that humanity is marching towards a global future of universal peace? In fact, there are many reasons for being cautious about such a belief.

First, measuring deaths from war is always an inexact science, and it is possible to dispute the statistics on which optimists' beliefs rely. Estimates by different organisations of the numbers killed in many modern conflicts, from Bosnia to Rwanda to Iraq, have varied significantly from each other. Furthermore, it can be very difficult to measure accurately the numbers of deaths of non-traditional combatants (like insurgents and guerrilla fighters), especially when fighting takes place in remote areas.

Second, if one takes into account *indirect* deaths – including, for instance, those resulting from the poverty, hunger, homelessness and environmental damage associated with war – then figures would be much higher. They might still show a decline (since indirect deaths would also be added to figures for past wars), but they would nonetheless indicate that war continues to be responsible for far more loss of life than direct battle deaths alone.

Third, the past is not always a reliable guide to the future, and there is no guarantee that the trend of declining battle deaths will inevitably continue. It would seem precipitate to say the least to suggest that the possibility of another major global conflict has been entirely ruled out for all time.

Fourth, even if the number of deaths in war has declined dramatically, this does not mean that there has been a similarly dramatic decline in the incidence of war. As will be examined next, there may still be many wars taking place, but just of different types to traditional inter-state ones.

ii) The changing nature of war

As noted, inter-state wars have declined markedly in number in modern times. Figure 7.2 shows that they have been a small minority of the wars fought in the post-war era – and in the twenty-first century, they have become extremely rare.

However, what the graph also shows is that the post-war era witnessed a rapid growth in the number of intra-state wars (which it divides into civil wars, those fought purely between groups within a state, and civil wars with intervening parties, in which there is some form of foreign involvement in the conflict) over the Cold War period. The numbers peaked during the transitional period of the Cold War's conclusion, as it was drawing to a close at the end of the 1980s through to the immediate post-Cold War years in the early 1990s, but they have since declined. The optimists previously discussed may point out not only the fact of this decline, but also that – as we have already seen – the numbers killed in civil wars are usually much lower than those in inter-state conflicts. Nonetheless, the fact that more than thirty active intra-state wars can be identified in nearly every year of the twenty-first century so far should give pause to anyone who believes that war may be about to disappear completely. Furthermore, the suffering caused by these wars cannot be measured only by numbers of deaths – those who lose their livelihoods, are forced to flee their homes, or are raped or tortured, are still victims of war.

Two further important factors should be noted here. First, the wars that take place today have increasingly become concentrated in particular regions: Africa and the Middle East. War is now extremely rare in the richest, most developed parts of the world. Most notable is the fact that Western Europe, which for centuries was the centre of many of the bloodiest wars in human history, has enjoyed a long period of relative peace.

Yet second, the character of the civil wars fought today is very different to those of the past. For example, civil wars of the twenty-first century are not like the American Civil War of the nineteenth, in which there were clearly defined sides and the state faced a single rebel army (Levy and Thompson, 2010: 13). Nowadays, there will often be a whole host of different groups involved, divided along religious, ethnic and political lines, and states themselves may be far from unified actors. They are, in other words, incredibly 'messy', complex affairs. This is why resolving them can

Conflicts by Type

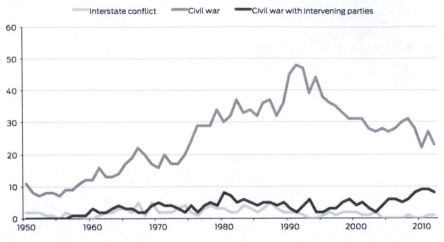

Figure 7.2 Types of war, 1950–2012
Source: B. Stancil (2013) 'Conflict Data on Military Interventions: Will Syria Be Different?', http://bennstancil.com/will-syria-be-different

prove so difficult. The nature of contemporary intra-state conflicts will be discussed further in Chapter 8.

iii) The changing technology of war

War in the twenty-first century is being rapidly transformed by major technological developments. Innovations that even a decade ago would have seemed like the stuff of science fiction are now appearing on the battlefield, including various types of unmanned vehicles (ground-, air- and sea-based) and robots (used for tasks like reconnaissance and bomb disposal). Most of these are remote-controlled by human operators, but the latest designs are fully autonomous. Other advances, like hypersonic weapons and invisibility cloaks, may not be far off.

Box 7.3 examines unmanned drones, one of the most controversial recent developments. States that invest the most in developing advanced forms of technology – with the United States undoubtedly taking the lead – see many advantages in this:

- 'Smart', precision-guided weapons are (supposedly) able to strike specific targets more accurately, rather than killing indiscriminately, thus minimising civilian loss of life.
- Unmanned vehicles can be sent into areas that are too dangerous for or hard to reach by human soldiers.
- Some at least can be cheaper – unmanned drones are certainly less costly than manned aircraft.
- Robots and unmanned vehicles are more expendable than human soldiers. There is undoubtedly a lower political cost to losing the former than the latter, since it does not generate media and public outrage.

Box 7.3: The politics of drones

Unmanned aerial vehicles (UAVs) – or drones as they are commonly called – have become a prominent feature of contemporary warfare thanks largely to their use by the US in fighting the War on Terror. First, under President George W. Bush, and in even larger numbers under President Barack Obama, drones have been deployed in nations including Iraq, Afghanistan and Pakistan. Drones are used in both surveillance and combat capacities, though it is the latter use that is the most controversial. During the first five years of his presidency, the death toll under President Obama was approximately 2,400 people as the result of drone attacks (Sledge, 2014).

The US government defends the use of drones as a vital tool of its counter-terrorism strategy. In particular, it claims that using unmanned drones has allowed it to eliminate a number of leading Taliban and al-Qaeda commanders. Yet critics have raised many objections, including that drone strikes may: violate the national sovereignty of the nations where they are used; constitute targeted assassinations that are illegal under international law; and be responsible, even regardless of how far terrorists and insurgents may constitute legitimate targets, for also killing many innocent civilians.

Drone attacks may also be counter-productive in generating widespread hostility and anger among the populations where they take place. In Pakistan, for example, there have been major protests against drone strikes, and objections raised by many politicians. Nonetheless, their use looks set to continue.

At the same time, though, this technology raises many political and ethical concerns. By giving those states that possess the technology significant military advantages and simultaneously reducing the human costs they have to bear from armed conflict, this may serve to increase the prospects of wars being launched. Automated warfare may also appear to reduce war to a video game, with operators of unmanned vehicles and robots far from the battlefield and never having to confront the reality of death as anything more than something that occurs on a computer screen. Again, by making war 'easy' and 'safe', this sanitises its horrors, and may mean that there are fewer disincentives to initiate hostilities, at least for powerful, developed nations.

Another way in which warfare may be becoming increasingly virtual is in the rise of cyber warfare. This type of warfare involves hacking the computer networks of enemies to disrupt their systems or steal information, and may be perpetrated by both states and non-state groups. A major difference between cyber warfare and the sorts of technological developments discussed above is that whereas the latter are largely the preserve of the richest, most advanced nations, computer hacking can be carried out by very many different sorts of actors, including lesser military powers and terrorist groups. While other forms of technology may be increasing the gap between actors in terms of their capacities to wage war, readily available computer technology may be decreasing it.

Building sustainable peace

All wars end eventually. Yet how they end is another matter, and it is far from always the case that peace proves to be permanent – indeed, there are many cases where it lasts no more than a few years.

Peace, in the form of some type of agreed settlement between warring parties – such as a formal peace agreement – can be achieved in a number of ways. One is simply direct negotiations between the parties involved. However, there are many reasons why this can be difficult, or even impossible. Parties engaged in violent armed conflict are often too hostile or mistrustful towards each other to be willing to sit down together and negotiate a settlement. This is where outside third parties often come in, to act as mediators. Mediators can talk to both sides, suggest new ideas and facilitate meetings, to help parties bridge the trust gap and reach a peace agreement. A famous example of international mediation is when US President Jimmy Carter mediated the Camp David Accords in 1978, which secured peace between Israel and Egypt. Yet it is not only politicians and diplomats that can aid in peacemaking. Non-state actors, like Non-Governmental Organisations (NGOs), can also play significant roles in peace processes, especially because official representatives from other states may not always be trusted by parties in conflict – especially those from the major powers, which may be viewed as having too much self-interest at stake in a conflict for their diplomats to be accepted as neutral and impartial. An example of a mediation success story involving a non-state group is when the Community of Sant'Egidio (a Catholic lay association) helped mediate the 1992 Rome Peace Accords that ended the civil war in Mozambique.

However, the negotiation of a peace settlement is far from a guarantee of lasting peace; many countries have lapsed back into war soon after a peace agreement has been signed. Consider the case of Rwanda. The Arusha Accords were signed by the Rwandan government and rebel fighters in 1993, ending a three-year civil war – yet the following year saw the country descend into a chaotic state of truly horrific violence, with the mass killing of approximately 800,000 people. Indeed, many countries have unfortunately been locked in cycles alternating between periods of relative peace and periods of terrible violence for many decades (such as Somalia). What, then, can be done to build long-term, *sustainable* peace?

This is where it will be useful to return to the distinction between negative and positive peace. Simply ending direct violence between parties in conflict – creating negative peace – is very often not enough to bring about long-term peace. After all, to expect people who have been fighting and killing each other, possibly for many years, to be willing to put the past behind them overnight, and be prepared to live in peace and harmony simply because their leaders have signed a piece of paper, is often highly naïve and unrealistic. This is especially true in the case of civil wars, where peace may mean asking people to live side-by-side with those who have inflicted great pain and suffering on them and their families.

For real peace to have a chance, the root causes of conflicts need to be addressed – and efforts made, perhaps, to create positive peace. In recent times, especially since the end of the Cold War, it has increasingly been the case that one solution in particular has been viewed as the universal answer to the problems of war and conflict: Liberalism. We have already seen the theoretical roots of this idea above, when looking at the Liberal understanding of war; the clear implication of the belief that non-liberal societies are the ones most likely to resort to war is that the more states embrace Liberalism, the more likely they are to be peaceful. This means adopting both the Liberal model of politics (e.g. democratisation) and Liberal economics (free markets), as the way to create permanent peace.

Box 7.4: The liberal peace thesis

Although the theory is sometimes termed the *democratic* peace thesis, the liberal peace thesis is to be preferred as the label for Liberals' contention about the pacific nature of their preferred model of society, as this highlights the fact that regular elections are not the only crucial feature – a free press, individual rights, the rule of law and free trade are others that should be included. One of the most important modern theorists is Michael Doyle, who articulates the viewpoint in a nuanced and sophisticated way (Doyle, 2012).

The basic argument can be stated very simply – liberal states do not go to war with one another; therefore, if all states became liberal, war would disappear. A large part of the justification for the thesis is empirical: although liberal states have often been in *conflict* with each other, it is difficult to identify cases of actual *war* between liberal states. Kant's belief about the problems faced by rulers constrained by the need to secure the consent of citizens to go to war discussed earlier is one reason why this may be, but many others have also been suggested. For example:

- Liberal societies foster values like tolerance and compromise (rather than violence and aggression) through education and socialisation.
- It is easier for free and open societies to trust each other (whereas it is much harder to trust a dictator).
- Leaders in liberal states face many institutionalised checks on their decision-making abilities, such as separations of power between executive and legislative branches of government, meaning that they are unable to wage war without some degree of wider political support.
- The strong economic interdependence created by free trade – accelerated by globalisation – makes liberal states unwilling to go to war with close economic partners (such as member states within the European Union).

However, the thesis has faced numerous criticisms. Three will be noted here.

First, it *may* be possible to identify examples of wars between democracies – in recent times, this may include the war between Israel and Lebanon in 2006, and Russia's 'undeclared' war in Ukraine in 2014. Of course, though, in such cases it is a matter of interpretation as to whether both sides qualify as *liberal* states (regardless of whether we believe that they qualify as democracies).

Second, even if it is hard to identify wars *between* liberal states, there are clearly many examples of wars waged by liberal states against non-liberal ones, some of which have been initiated by the former (consider the US-led invasion of Iraq in 2003). This at least confirms that liberal populations *are* sometimes prepared to bear the costs of war, even wars of choice, and that their leaders *are* willing and able to take their nations to war in certain circumstances – which raises the question of whether wars between liberal states can be entirely ruled out as a possibility for all time.

Third, there is the issue of *how* to achieve a world of universally liberal states, if this is believed desirable – must Liberalism be 'imposed' on those who do not want it? If so, might this require a form of liberal imperialism that contradicts Liberalism's own avowed beliefs in freedom and tolerance?

Box 7.4 examines this belief in the major form in which it has become widely known – the liberal peace thesis. The argument is centrally concerned with Liberalism as a means of ending wars between states, but it is often contended that Liberalism makes societies more peaceful internally as well – less prone to phenomena such as civil wars, revolutions and coups d'état. In any case, the belief in Liberalism as a force for peace has been widely embraced by contemporary actors involved in peacemaking and conflict resolution, including the UN.

Not everyone, of course, accepts the Liberal viewpoint. For example, there are those who are suspicious of what may appear to be the promotion of a specifically Western model of politics and economics around the globe that is insensitive to the values and cultures of other societies.

At any rate, regardless of one's view of Liberal theory, peacebuilding – a term, also owing its origins to Galtung, that describes measures designed to create sustainable peace (Galtung, 1976) – has developed as an approach that makes various practical recommendations for post-conflict societies, many of which may be accepted by liberals and non-liberals alike. Those engaged in peacebuilding seek to implement reforms in key areas such as:

- **Security** – e.g. disarming and reintegrating former combatants; controlling the proliferation of weapons; properly training and making accountable police, military and intelligence forces.
- **Governance** – e.g. rewriting constitutions to protect the rights of both individuals and groups; tackling corruption in public institutions; possibly creating democratic structures.
- **Economy** – e.g. tackling issues like unemployment and poverty; reforming public finances; possibly implementing free-market, liberalising policies.
- **Justice** – e.g. holding those guilty of war crimes to account; incorporating human rights into legal codes; creating better access for all to legal systems.
- **Social** – e.g. measures to promote reconciliation between groups, reforming education systems, and empowering marginalised groups (like women and minorities).

Peacebuilding, too, even leaving aside the extent to which it may also be grounded in Liberal assumptions, has been criticised by some for being based on a top-down approach to change that relies too heavily on outside actors trying to solve other nations' problems. Yet more recent years have seen a growing move towards greater grass-roots involvement in peacebuilding – 'peacebuilding from below' – which may, perhaps, offer the best hope for creating lasting peace within societies.

Conclusion

'War is hell', declared American Civil War general William T. Sherman, and this sentiment has been echoed down the ages by many others. But is war an inevitable part of human existence? Is it sometimes, maybe, even necessary? Self-defence in the face of attack is widely accepted as a legitimate reason to take up arms, even if one regrets having to do so. It is possible, too, to talk of 'just' wars, ones that have a moral justification, such as wars fought to remove an oppressive, murderous dictator. Others, though, have argued that no war is ever justified and believe that the only truly ethical stance is pacifistic opposition to all armed conflict.

War thus raises many difficult issues of principle. Yet as we have also seen, there are many different ways to explain why war occurs. This means, therefore, that we need first to decide which explanation of war we agree with before we can begin to work out how to bring about its end – if we believe this is possible. In recent decades, a widespread consensus has developed that embracing Liberalism is the answer to preventing war, but it remains a matter of dispute whether there are alternative ways to secure peace, and whether, perhaps, other belief systems may contain the resources to do so.

Summary points

1 War may be defined as organised violence between political units.
2 A useful way to distinguish between explanations of war is in terms of different levels of analysis, focusing on the individual, the state or the international system.
3 War in the twenty-first century has changed in many ways – there are now many more intra-state rather than inter-state wars, while technological advances are greatly transforming warfare itself.
4 Creating sustainable peace may entail not just eliminating violence in its most obvious forms, but tackling the structural and cultural underpinnings of conflicts.
5 The promotion of liberal norms and institutions is seen by many as the best way to achieve permanent peace – though critics worry that this may mean trying to impose a Western model on other societies while disregarding their own values and beliefs.

Recommended reading

Clausewitz, C. von [1832] *On War*, rev. ed., ed. and trans. M. Howard and P. Paret, Princeton, NJ: University Press, [1832] 1984.

Darby, J. and MacGinty, R. (eds) *Contemporary Peacemaking: Conflict, Peace Processes and Post-War Reconstruction*, 2nd ed., Basingstoke: Palgrave Macmillan, 2008.

Levy, J.S. and Thompson, W.R. *Causes of War*, Oxford: Blackwell, 2010.

Sobek, D. *The Causes of War*, Cambridge: Polity Press, 2009.

Waltz, K. *Man, the State, and War: A Theoretical Analysis*, rev. ed., New York: Columbia University Press, 2001.

8 New wars, globalisation and failed states

Bruce Pilbeam

Box 8.1: A post-Clausewitzian world?

The previous chapter began with a quotation from renowned military theorist Carl von Clausewitz, which gave an insight into his understanding of war from the perspective of the nineteenth century. Clausewitz's approach remained influential throughout much of the twentieth century, but in recent times it has increasingly come under attack for being outdated, especially since the end of the Cold War. Indeed, many commentators now talk of a 'non-' or 'post-'Clausewitzian world, in which the old rules of war no longer apply.

For example, in a book published in 1991 – as the Cold War era was turning into the post-Cold War one – Israeli military historian Martin van Creveld argues just this, in the revealingly-titled *The Transformation of War: The Most Radical Reinterpretation of Armed Conflict Since Clausewitz*. In this work, van Creveld contends that modern wars are no longer fought primarily between states and their large, professional armies, but involve a whole host of non-state actors, including bandits, guerrillas and terrorists. He also suggests that issues around identity, such as ethnicity, religion and gender, have become much more central to conflicts than the sort of traditional political and economic ones upon which conventional analyses of war (like Clausewitz's) focus. So, is this true? Is it time to consign Clausewitz and other traditional understandings of war to the dustbin of history?

Introduction

In the last chapter, we saw that wars in the twenty-first century may differ from those of the past in various ways. However, if there is one constant in history it is change, so there is nothing in itself remarkable about the fact that war today may not be the same as it was a hundred (or even thirty) years ago; the major wars of the twentieth century were different to those of the nineteenth, which were not the same as those of the eighteenth, and so on. But does this mean that we need a whole new paradigm to understand war, or do we merely need to update older ones to take account of recent developments?

Central to the discussion below will be the examination of a particular argument, the 'new wars' thesis, which suggests that we do need a new framework for understanding the contemporary world. One of the major forces that may be responsible for reshaping the nature of conflict – and much else – is globalisation, so this will also be given a substantial degree of attention. Furthermore, since one of the most challenging problems that may be both a cause and consequence of modern types of conflict is that of failed states, this will similarly be examined in some detail. Finally, we will consider the main criticisms that have been levelled against these concepts and arguments.

The new wars thesis

The label 'new wars' is not the only one that has been forwarded to describe the nature of contemporary wars – others include 'postmodern wars' and 'hybrid wars' – but new wars has achieved the greatest and most lasting prominence. Undoubtedly, the most important theorist of new wars is Mary Kaldor, notably in her book *New and Old Wars: Organized Violence in a Global Era*, first published in 1999. Consequently, it is her work that will be the focus of discussion (others who argue similarly include Münkler, 2005).

Kaldor's argument proceeds by distinguishing new wars from old (with Clausewitz seen as the most significant theorist of the latter). Old wars are typified by the armed conflicts of the nineteenth and twentieth centuries – such as the latter's two world wars – 'involving states in which battle is the decisive factor' (Kaldor, 2012: vi). By contrast, new wars, a type that has flourished especially since the end of the Cold War, 'involve networks of state and non-state actors and most violence is directed against civilians'.

An important point to note is that Kaldor emphasises that new wars should not be conflated with civil wars: 'they are different from both classic inter-state wars and classic civil wars'. New wars are messy and complicated, and blur the line between internal and external. Violence inside a state may be perpetrated by actors originating from within and without, and there will often be transnational connections involving both states and non-state groups. As such, conventional conceptions of either inter-state or intra-state wars are inadequate to explain contemporary conflicts.

Given all this, it should be appreciated that Kaldor examines the nature of war today in a very different manner to traditional approaches (like those examined in the previous chapter, whether Liberal, Realist or Marxist). For example, she rejects the widespread means of defining war in terms of the number of battle deaths (a thousand battle deaths is commonly taken as the minimum threshold for a violent conflict to be considered a war). A crucial reason for this is that we simply do not have sufficiently accurate data on the scale of casualties in new wars because estimates of civilian casualties, their prime victims, are notoriously unreliable. Nor is it possible to say whether or not the number of new wars is increasing or decreasing – since they are different to both conventionally defined inter-state and intra-state wars, graphs of the sort presented in the last chapter simply do not capture the true picture of the many forms of violence that occur within new wars. According to the new wars paradigm, there is for example, no clear distinction between a new war and organised criminal activity.

So, what, specifically, are the defining characteristics of new wars, which distinguish them from old wars? Four in particular are identified by Kaldor (2012: 7–11; 2013: 2–3).

Actors

Whereas old wars were fought largely by the armies of states, new wars involve a mix of state and non-state actors. This includes regular soldiers, but also warlords, jihadists, criminal gangs, paramilitaries, mercenaries and private contractors. A key reason for this change is that states today have lost much of their traditional authority, including in some cases their monopoly on the legitimate use of organised violence.

Goals

The goals of old wars were geo-political (such as the acquisition of strategically important territory) or ideological (such as promoting socialism). By contrast, new wars are fought in the name of identity politics. By this, Kaldor means the claim to power on the basis of a particular group identity – such as ethnic, religious or tribal identity. Although in a sense war has always centred on clashes of identities – for example, between those of different nations or blocs of nations (as in the Cold War) – Kaldor argues that in the past, these identities were tied to some conception of state interest or some 'forward-looking' project. However, identity politics today has a different logic. The aim of today's identity-based politics is to gain access to the state not to implement programmes in the broader social interest, but to promote the agendas of particular groups. The rise of identity politics is intimately connected to the declining purchase of more inclusive (often state-based) ideologies like socialism or post-colonial nationalism. Furthermore, the mobilisation of people around identity politics is not just a cause or instrument of war, but is itself one of new wars' key aims, which again distinguishes them from old wars.

Methods

Kaldor believes that, in old wars, battles were the decisive encounter, and the main mode of warfare was capturing territory through military means. In new wars, battles are much rarer, and the capture of territory occurs through political means – that is, by controlling its population. One technique, for example, is population displacement – forcibly removing those with a different identity. This often leads to the problem of refugees flooding into neighbouring states. To control territory, violence is used principally against civilians, rather than against enemy forces. Women and children are frequently the principal targets of modern wars, and may often be the victims of terrible human rights abuses including sexual violence and torture, as well as being killed.

Finance

Old wars were financed mainly by states (for example, through taxes or borrowing) and war economies were heavily centralised. New war economies are usually highly decentralised, and revenue depends on the use of violence. New wars are often financed by 'predatory' private (rather than public) means like looting and pillaging, hostage-taking, and the smuggling of valuable commodities like oil, diamonds, drugs or even people.

   A notable feature of new wars is their longevity. They tend to persist for many years; even if conflict may abate for a time, it frequently flares up again very quickly. The reason for this persistence is that participants in new wars often gain (politically and economically) from the perpetration of violence itself, rather than from 'winning'. Conceiving of war and peace as entirely separate situations is, therefore, also open to question, as the two often bleed into each other, and the threat of violence is an ever-present one even though its intensity may wax and wane. Another significant feature is that, whereas 'old wars were associated with state building, new wars are the opposite; they tend to contribute to the dismantling of the state' (Kaldor, 2013: 3). As will be discussed later, modern wars are frequently responsible for state failure.

To understand the notion of new wars better, it will be useful to examine a particular contemporary conflict. Kaldor herself examines in depth the wars in Bosnia-Herzegovina, Iraq and Afghanistan as case studies (Kaldor, 2012: 32–70, 151–184). To take a different example, the conflict in Somalia presents another that might seem to fit the new wars model – see Box 8.2.

What, though, explains the shift from old to new wars? Partly, the change may be the result of the end of the Cold War. A common view of the significance of the Cold War's conclusion is that the disappearance of the bipolar world order allowed older identities and enmities to re-emerge that had been suppressed by the superpower

---

Box 8.2: Case study: Somalia

Over the last three decades Somalia has been racked by conflict, but its nature has changed significantly over the years. In terms of new wars theory, it cannot be described simply as a civil war in a traditional sense.

By the mid-1980s, opposition to the authoritarian government of General Siad Barre had begun to organise seriously to overthrow the regime. A coalition of anti-government forces fought the government and military in what might be considered a civil war conflict. Yet even during this phase, matters were more complicated than this label might appear to suggest: the opposition was greatly divided, with little uniting factions beyond a desire to oust Barre, and various outside actors played major roles. For example, Ethiopia supported some of the rebel groups, while US aid had for years propped up Barre's government as Somalia became a client state in the Cold War superpower contest. The withdrawal of US support as the Cold War came to an end was a contributing factor in the regime's fall to the rebels in 1991, as Barre lost the ability to pay for the patronage system that had kept him in power.

Yet it was in the wake of Barre's toppling that the conflict became especially difficult to fit into a traditional framework of war. Somalia descended into a state of chaos in which the opposition that had been (barely) united in fighting Barre rapidly fragmented. In particular, it divided along clan lines, with each clan fiercely defending its status and identity and seeking to promote its own interests – perhaps confirming the notion that identity politics is at the heart of contemporary conflicts. The state itself disintegrated and Somalia plunged into virtual lawlessness – as new wars theory contends about state failure. Furthermore, civilians have been the biggest casualties. It is estimated that during the most intense period of conflict, from 1991 to 1992, 'clan cleansing', drought and famine, and the collapse of basic services caused approximately 250,000 deaths. Human rights abuses were also rampant, including the indiscriminate use of violence and sexual abuse. Moreover, around two million people were forced to flee the country as refugees, while many others were internally displaced.

Other features of the conflict that fit most closely with new wars theory include the importance of religion in defining identities – most notably, with the rise of Islamist groups seeking to establish an Islamic state in Somalia. It also matches the theory's contention about the longevity of conflicts – it has persisted for decades, with many more ordinary Somalis dying and being displaced from their homes; even today, with government re-established, fighting has continued.

conflict. This, then, might explain why so many appear to be driven by ethnic and religious rivalries. Nevertheless, Kaldor, while noting the significance of factors such as the disintegration of the Soviet empire, emphasises rather a different phenomenon to explain the rise of new wars: globalisation (Kaldor, 2012: 71–118). It is this that we will turn to next.

The impact of globalisation

What is globalisation? Globalisation is a highly contested concept, and different writers offer very different understandings. Some focus on its economic aspects, others emphasise its political dimensions, while still others highlight its social and cultural features. There are also globalisation sceptics, who either deny its reality or believe that the various transformations globalisation theorists point to are insufficiently revolutionary to warrant talk of a whole new era. For the moment the sceptical perspective will be put to one side, so that we may understand what it is that some writers on globalisation believe is so significant about it for understanding the nature of war and security.

To return to Kaldor, she presents the following definition of globalisation: 'the intensification of global interconnectedness – political, economic, military and cultural – and the changing character of political authority' (Kaldor, 2012: 4). Like many definitions of globalisation, central to Kaldor's is the idea of increasing interconnectedness, as well as a recognition of the fact that it is multi-dimensional and multi-faceted, affecting all spheres of human activity. In any case, since hers is a relatively general and all-encompassing definition, it will provide a useful starting point for discussion.

Another important preliminary question is, when did globalisation begin? Numerous answers have been given to this question (see O'Rourke and Williamson, 2002). Some date its origins back many centuries, even millennia, others associate its beginnings with the Industrial Revolution that started in the eighteenth century, while others pick various decades during the nineteenth and twentieth centuries. Kaldor chooses to focus on a relatively recent time period, arguing that although it may have earlier roots, it was in the 1980s and 1990s that globalisation emerged as a qualitatively new phenomenon. The significant point about this is that, for her, it nonetheless predates the end of the Cold War. This is why new wars cannot be explained simply as resulting from this conflict's termination: the processes responsible for changing the nature of contemporary wars were set in motion *before* the Cold War had concluded.

In any case, Kaldor is far from alone in seeing globalisation as in various ways responsible for transforming the nature of war; many other commentators do as well, whether or not they embrace the new wars thesis (see, for example, Duyvesteyn and Angstrom, 2004; Jung, 2002; Münkler, 2005; Shankar Jha, 2006). Some of the key debates are discussed elsewhere – for example, the role of globalisation in facilitating terrorism is examined in Chapter 11. Here we will examine four major arguments relating specifically to war put forward by critical writers on globalisation.

It erodes the power and authority of the state

As seen in previous chapters, Realists view the state as the primary actor in international security. Yet writers on globalisation frequently argue that the power and authority of the state has been weakened. At the extreme end of this argument some 'hyperglobalists', like Kenichi Ohmae (2008), argue even that the nation-state is on the verge of extinction thanks to powerful global economic forces undermining it, meaning that we will soon be living in an entirely borderless world. If true, this would render most traditional theories of war and international affairs, not only Realism, entirely redundant.

Few other commentators go this far. Nevertheless, many argue that state sovereignty is under threat, whether due to economic forces such as the power of transnational corporations or political ones like the influence of international organisations. In terms of war, the implications of the state's loss of authority are suggested by Herfried Münkler, another new wars theorist: 'The predominant cause of internal war ... is the erosion of the capability of the state to govern' (Münkler, 2005: 109). Whereas in the past states were able to maintain internal order within their territories, in large part as a result of globalisation this ability has been severely enervated.

This has many consequences. In the face of weakened states, competition and struggle among an array of non-state actors provokes conflicts that states are unable to contain. This is what changes the very character of war – for example, whereas state-waged war is generally governed by some adherence to law and 'the rules of war', wars primarily centred on non-state actors are usually not. Moreover, the weakening of the state helps explain why civilians may be so vulnerable in new wars – we examine in Chapter 20 the argument that states have a responsibility to protect their own citizens, but if the state is too weak to do so, who or what will prevent human rights abuses?

As with all other aspects of globalisation, these developments are very uneven. Thus some states – particularly those in the developed world – retain a high degree of power and authority. Others, particularly in the developing world, may have weakened to such a degree that they cease functioning as states in any meaningful way altogether – as we will see in the discussion of failed states below.

It fosters ethnic, nationalist and religious tensions

One of the most common arguments made in relation to globalisation and war is that it has served to exacerbate ethnic, nationalist and religious tensions, and has therefore helped foster conflicts centred upon them. This includes those that have occurred in places such as the former Yugoslavia, Rwanda, Sudan and Georgia, where different ethnic, nationalist and religious groups have either fought to control power within their respective states, or demanded the right to secede to form new states.

In some respects, it may seem surprising to find globalisation blamed for these types of conflict, since increasing interconnectedness might be thought to produce stronger ties between peoples, both among and within societies, and a weakening of the particular bonds of ethnicity, nationalism and religion. Yet the argument of critics is usually framed in terms of a reaction against the dynamics of globalisation. Thus, those who feel excluded or alienated from, or even threatened by, the modernising and universalising project of globalisation may respond by seeking security in identities rooted in tradition and the past. While some may view these sorts of ethnic, nationalist and religious identities as backward-looking, and grounded in nostalgia and myth, the turn to these identities may nonetheless be understood in very contemporary terms.

In other words, globalisation may be responsible for energising precisely the sort of identity politics that Kaldor writes about as crucial to the shift from old to new wars.

The argument may also be made that globalisation does more than simply force an unwanted interconnectedness upon people, doing something more specific as well. Some argue that globalisation in fact means Westernisation; or, even more specifically, that it means Americanisation. Consequently, globalisation may be understood not just as erasing differences between cultures and societies, but as spreading specific beliefs and institutions – in politics this means liberal democracy, in economics free-market capitalism, and in culture forms of entertainment such as Hollywood films and consumer brands like Coca-Cola or Nike. It is these aspects that people in non-Western societies may react against most strongly. The global promulgation of Western values may be implicated in particular in the rise of 'fundamentalist' religious identities – as found, for example, in radical Islamist movements (see Chapter 12).

Its economic effects inflame conflicts

Another of the most salient arguments is that globalisation reinforces and increases inequality. As Joseph Stiglitz succinctly puts it, the net effect of globalisation is that 'the rich are getting richer while the poor are often not even holding their own' (Stiglitz, 2006: 8). Moreover, inequality is frequently cited as a major cause of conflict, especially within nations – though the relationship between inequality and violent conflict is a complex one (Cramer, 2003). This means that globalisation may again be blamed for fomenting conflict, as competing actors struggle for control of resources and to improve their economic lots.

What is the evidence concerning globalisation and inequality? Many studies suggest that, overall, globalisation has contributed to growing global wealth. Yet this benefit of globalisation has not been distributed evenly. For example, a 2014 United Nations Development Programme (UNDP) report concludes that over what it calls the globalisation era (from the mid-1980s onwards) global inequality has increased (UNDP, 2014: 65). This includes the GDP gap between nations (particularly between those of the developing and the developed world), and incomes within nations. In a sample of 116 countries, household income inequality rose from the early 1990s to the late 2000s by 9% in high-income countries and by 11% in low- and middle-income countries (UNDP, 2014: 64). Various reasons are suggested for why this has occurred, including that technological changes may have increased the demand for skilled, educated workers and reduced that for unskilled, uneducated ones; the impact of economic liberalisation and deregulation upon wages and employment; and the declining bargaining power of collective labour organisations.

Many critics of economic globalisation also highlight the way that nations in the developing world are forced, either by the workings of the financial system or by major international organisations, to liberalise their economies and open themselves up to global capitalism. Yet this may have disastrous consequences, as developing countries' economies are:

> subjected to drastic regimes in order to structurally adjust them to the global market, under the leadership of the IMF and the World Bank ... by embarking wholeheartedly on deregulation, they are periodically shaken by unpredictable and uncontrollable financial upheavals which submerge them anew in the murky waters of underdevelopment.

> (Gélinas, 2003: 22)

This, therefore, creates fragile and unstable environments in which the explosion of violent conflict becomes all too likely.

In terms of the new wars thesis, Kaldor argues that globalisation creates a 'globalised war economy' which, as noted earlier, is highly decentralised, as states lose authority and begin to disintegrate. New wars, she argues, 'take place in a context which could be represented as an extreme form of globalisation' (Kaldor, 2012: 107) and the picture she paints is extremely bleak. In societies where new wars occur, domestic economic production more or less collapses (due to factors such as economic liberalisation, global competition and armed conflict), unemployment is high and inflation rampant. Such economies become greatly dependent on a few valuable commodities (like oil or diamonds) or external resources. In the worst cases, currencies collapse, to be replaced by barter, the use of commodities as currency or foreign currencies (like the dollar) instead. It is hardly surprising in such contexts that conflicts proliferate.

It facilitates the involvement of many different types of actors in conflicts

We have already seen that the new wars thesis suggests that non-state actors, like guerrilla fighters, insurgents and terrorists, play vital roles in conflicts. In what ways does globalisation contribute to this?

A large part of the explanation is connected to the weakening of the state. This creates a power vacuum which others – including warlords and criminal gangs – may attempt to fill. Similarly, globalisation also implies the weakening of state borders, which states may find difficult to police. This is one reason why there may be a blurring of the line between internal and external in new wars, and why both state and non-state actors from outside a nation's territory may find it relatively easy to cross borders into conflict zones.

Yet globalisation produces other significant consequences as well. The processes of economic liberalisation and deregulation associated with globalisation, and the pressures put upon states to lower taxes and cut budgets, may lead to a 'privatisation' of violence and war (Kaldor, 2012: 96; Münkler, 2005: 16). The most important aspect of this is the growing use of 'mercenaries' and private military and security companies in modern conflicts – who may be employed by states (though also by others) but are themselves non-state actors. These are often seen as highly problematic actors – for example, because they are subject to far less oversight and regulation than regular soldiers – and they are discussed in detail in Chapter 14.

Globalisation also shrinks distances between people, creating networks of support for those engaged in conflicts across the globe. Kaldor highlights, for example, the role of diaspora groups in providing financial and political support, even though they may be living far away from conflict areas (Kaldor, 2012: 88–89, 109). Although this is not an entirely new phenomenon, its scale has grown much larger thanks to modern modes of communication and information technology. For example, Tutsis in Zaire and Uganda, Kosovo Albanians in Germany and Switzerland, and Sudanese and Palestinian workers in the Middle East, have all given both material and ideological support to those they see as their own people fighting in conflicts elsewhere.

Finally, it should be noted as well that globalisation also facilitates the entry into war zones of very different sorts of non-state actors than those intent on fighting in conflicts, including journalists, peace activists and humanitarian NGOs.

Many of the features relating to globalisation highlighted above can be found at work in contemporary wars. Box 8.3 offers another case study, of the war in Sierra Leone, to illustrate some of the ways this may be seen.

Box 8.3: Case study: Sierra Leone

The war in Sierra Leone lasted eleven years, from 1991 to 2002. It began when rebel fighters of the Revolutionary United Front (RUF) launched a campaign to overthrow the government of President Joseph Momoh. By its conclusion, more than 75,000 people had been killed and many more had been victims of severe human rights atrocities. Furthermore, many millions were displaced internally and externally as refugees. In what ways can the forces of globalisation be seen as operating in the conflict? Four may be noted.

First, the origins of the war can be traced to the severe economic crisis that hit the country in the 1980s. By the end of the decade, the economy essentially collapsed and the nation fell into extreme poverty – and moreover, the government proved unable to pay many state employees, meaning that vital public services were no longer being provided. Yet when the government turned to the IMF and World Bank, their prescriptions for solving Sierra Leone's crisis may be argued to have made the situation even worse, since they demanded severe austerity measures which led to even greater cuts in social spending. In other words, externally imposed economic liberalisation may have contributed to a deepening social unrest that made Sierra Leone ripe for war.

Second, as a consequence of the dire economic situation and the outbreak of conflict, the state itself collapsed – and as war spread there was little to prevent looting, banditry and the influx of outside actors (for example, from Liberia).

Third, a major source of financing for the conflict was diamond production, one of Sierra Leone's most valuable resources, and both sides fought for control of the nation's diamond mines. Yet the illegal trade in so-called blood diamonds – diamonds mined to fund armed conflict – that fuelled and prolonged the war could only occur because of the existence of a global market for the commodity.

Fourth, the war in Sierra Leone demonstrates the privatisation of war. Private military companies – which some would label mercenaries – Executive Outcomes and Sandline International were both contracted to provide military services. (This was not, though, without controversy – see Chapter 14 for further details.)

The problem of 'failed' states

New wars, Kaldor argues, are concentrated in places where the state is extremely weak or has even entirely collapsed (Kaldor, 2012: 95–96). However, this is an area where terminological difficulties abound. A bewildering array of labels is used to describe circumstances where states face significant challenges to their authority and legitimacy, and may be 'failing' to varying degrees, including 'weak states', 'fragile states', 'quasi states', 'shadow states', 'crisis states', 'failing states', 'failed states' and 'collapsed states'. There is no accepted consensus as to the meaning of many of these terms, the differences between them and if/when they may be used interchangeably. Sometimes the terms are used to suggest a spectrum – for example, weak or fragile states may be ones facing great difficulties, but which are still broadly functioning, while failed or collapsed states are those that have broken down completely. Yet it is also common for a single label to be used to cover all cases, with the label 'failed state' frequently employed in this way.

An illustration of these difficulties can be seen by considering one of the most widely cited sources for the measurement of state failure, an annual report of the Fund for Peace, a non-profit organisation based in Washington DC. Its reports include an index of state failure around the globe, which for the first nine years of reporting (beginning in 2005) was called the Failed States Index. However, in 2014 the name was changed to the Fragile States Index (FSI). This gives some indication of how there is no settled agreement over which term is most appropriate.

Nonetheless, the FSI is a good place to begin for an examination of 'failing' states. The definition the Fund for Peace uses is as follows:

> A state that is failing has several attributes. One of the most common is the loss of physical control of its territory or a monopoly on the legitimate use of force. Other attributes of state failure include the erosion of legitimate authority to make collective decisions, an inability to provide reasonable public services, and the inability to interact with other states as a full member of the international community.
>
> (http://ffp.statesindex.org/faq#5)

In essence, this definition is highlighting circumstances in which states fail to fulfil the core functions they are expected to perform. The best way to understand this is to address the question: what is a state? In a 1918 lecture Max Weber, the German sociologist and philosopher, offered one of the most well-known and influential definitions of a state, that it is a 'community that (successfully) claims the monopoly of the legitimate use of physical force within a given territory' (Weber, 1991: 78). The parallels, and contrasts, with the FSI definition are clear: failing states have *lost* their monopoly on the legitimate use of force – in particular, to hostile non-state actors – and they do *not* have control of the territory within which they exist. New wars theorists may also appear to agree – Münkler, for example, writes in similar terms of 'the weakening of the legitimacy of the state … [and] direct challenges to its monopoly of the use of force' (Münkler, 2005: 109).

Today, of course, there are many more expectations placed on states than when Weber was theorising, so it is not surprising that the FSI definition also includes other elements, such as the responsibility to provide public services and to engage with other states in the international community. In any case, how the FSI is constructed, and the calculations involved, is explained in Box 8.4. The indicators used give a fair idea of the type of factors that many writers on state failure identify as important (see also, for example, Rotberg, 2004). These include the large-scale displacement of people, economic inequality and decline, human rights abuses and the intervention of outside actors.

Box 8.4: Measuring state fragility

The Fragile States Index (FSI) attempts to provide a quantifiable measure of a state's vulnerability to failure. Based on the analysis of a large quantity of data (including from newspapers, speeches, government and non-government reports), for every country assessed each of the 12 indicators below is given a score from 1 to 10, with 1 being the most stable, 10 the least stable. These are added together to give each country a total score out of 120. Countries are then ranked in order – those with the highest score being the most prone to state failure. The indicators are:

Social indicators

1   Mounting Demographic Pressures
2   Massive Movement of Refugees or Internally Displaced Persons
3   Legacy of Vengeance-Seeking Group Grievance or Group Paranoia
4   Chronic and Sustained Human Flight

Economic indicators

5   Uneven Economic Development along Group Lines
6   Sharp and/or Severe Economic Decline

Political and military indicators

7   Criminalisation and/or Delegitimisation of the State
8   Progressive Deterioration of Public Services
9   Suspension or Arbitrary Application of the Rule of Law and Widespread Human Rights Abuse
10 Security Apparatus Operates as a 'State Within a State'
11 Rise of Factionalised Elites
12 Intervention of Other States or External Political Actors

Source: http://ffp.statesindex.org/faq-04-indicators

In 2014, 177 countries were ranked in order by the FSI. The top ten were:

1   South Sudan
2   Somalia
3   Central African Republic
4   Democratic Republic of Congo
5   Sudan
6   Chad
7   Afghanistan
8   Yemen
9   Haiti
10 Pakistan.

(Fund for Peace, 2014)

As is evident, African nations fill a disproportionate number of the index's top slots – the six most 'fragile' states are all African – which has been the case since the FSI was first created. A majority of the ten states have also been torn apart by war in recent years (in some, conflict remains ongoing), indicating the close association between state failure and war – with causality going both ways, as the two phenomena mutually reinforce each other.

What, though, are the underlying causes of state failure? The role of globalisation has already been considered in terms of its role in weakening states, fostering inequality and promoting the rise of identity politics as a counter-reaction to its processes. In particular, as seen, the fact that economic liberalisation and deregulation may be responsible for impacting negatively, especially on countries in the developing world, may help to explain why they are particularly vulnerable to state failure.

However, there are other historical factors to consider, including two worth noting in particular. First, there are the many legacies of colonialism that continue to blight many states in the developing world. This includes the fact that the territorial borders created by colonial powers were frequently artificial in nature – often simply straight lines drawn on maps – which both divided peoples who saw themselves as one, and placed others together in nations who had no pre-colonial history of affinity. Furthermore, it may be argued as well that the whole idea of nation-states is an alien, Western imposition upon parts of the world where other sorts of collective bonds – clan or tribal, for example – were the ones to which people felt, and perhaps still feel, the strongest ties. For these reasons, it may again be less than surprising that states in places like Africa have displayed great weakness and instability.

Second, there are the legacies of the Cold War. During this conflict, the two superpowers created many client states around the world, which were provided with economic, political and military support in return for their allegiance in the Cold War struggle. This encouraged corruption, and meant the propping up of many oppressive and authoritarian regimes. Yet regardless of the disreputable nature of many of these arrangements, their ending once the Cold War concluded also created problems, as the Soviet Union was no longer able and the US no longer needed to support so many states. As seen in the case of Somalia (Box 8.2), this may have been an important contributing factor in the descent of many states into failure and conflict.

State failure has many implications, many of which have already been touched on. Unfortunately it usually means great suffering for people living there. Without a functioning state, people may lack access to all the services modern states provide, including policing, healthcare, education, and benefits for the elderly, disabled and unemployed. In other words, it means a failure not only to provide security in a traditional sense, but also to meet the needs of Human Security. In the absence of the state, people are forced to look elsewhere – which means that the provision of services may be taken on by warlords, criminal gangs, other states or humanitarian NGOs. Yet none of these, regardless of motives or whether or not they use violence, have the same legitimacy or accountability as a properly functioning state.

However, a final implication to mention is that failed states may also impact upon international security. Most notable is the argument that they are a breeding ground for international terrorists. For example, failed states became prominent in policy discussions within the US government after it launched its War on Terror in 2001. As the 2003 *National Strategy for Countering Terrorism* argues, weak and failed states are 'a source of international instability. Often, these states may become a sanctuary for terrorism' (Executive Office of the President United States, 2003: 23). This view has therefore been part of the justification for US interventions in states deemed failed or failing, on the grounds that, as President George W. Bush argued, America 'must take the battle to the enemy' (Executive Office of the President United States, 2003: 11).

Critical perspectives

Despite the influential nature of many of the arguments so far discussed – and the fact that at least some of the concepts have filtered into wider policy debates – they have all also been subject to criticism. Some of these will be examined next.

The new wars thesis

The major thrust of most criticisms of the new wars thesis is that there is little truly new about contemporary wars. For example, Paul Hirst argues that '[m]ost of Kaldor's new wars involve old problems, stemming from the colonial era, or from peace treaties after the First World War, or from the Cold War' (Hirst, 2001: 83). If one considers the conflicts Kaldor examines – including those in Bosnia, Iraq and Afghanistan – all of them indeed have roots that can be traced back to the periods Hirst cites (and even earlier in some cases).

Furthermore, there may be nothing entirely novel about the features supposed to characterise new wars. Part of the problem may lie in the characterisation of old wars – that is, the idea of wars entailing large-scale battles fought by the professional armies of states. While broadly speaking this may be a fair description of *some* nineteenth and twentieth century wars, it can also be criticised for ignoring the fact that many were never like this. For example, there is nothing new about guerrilla and insurgency warfare, as seen in numerous colonial and post-colonial struggles. Similarly, non-state actors like terrorists, warlords and mercenaries have all been involved in these and other types of wars in the past. Mass population displacement during wartime is also nothing new – as occurred, for example, to millions during the Second World War. Finally, identity politics (in the form of assertive ethnic, nationalist and religious movements) is far from unknown historically either. While in some places – such as in the states existing under Soviet domination – these identities may have been suppressed during the Cold War, they nonetheless still existed, and had been central to many conflicts for centuries beforehand.

Another line of criticism is to question some of the empirical assertions made regarding new wars. One of the most significant is the claim that, whereas in old wars the main victims were uniformed soldiers, today the majority are civilians. As Adam Roberts (2010) observes, this is a widespread claim throughout modern academic and policy discussions – with some arguing that as many as 90% of casualties in post-Cold War conflicts are civilians. Yet the evidence base for such claims is decidedly shaky, especially given how difficult it is to obtain accurate data on civilian deaths in war. Moreover, it may again appear to misrepresent wars of the past – many historical conflicts also involved the wholesale killing of civilians (the Second World War being but one).

It should be noted that, in an afterword to the third edition of *New and Old Wars* (Kaldor, 2012: 202–221), Kaldor attempts to answer some of her critics, and it is worth reading this to reflect on both the criticisms and defences of new wars theory that may be formulated.

Globalisation

It has already been observed that some writers are simply sceptical of globalisation – again, therefore, there is a challenge to the supposed newness of the contemporary era. As one set of globalisation sceptics puts it: 'There is no strong tendency toward a globalised economy' (Hirst, Thompson and Bromley, 2009: 186). From this point of view, globalisation does not undermine the state or influence the probability of war because it is not a real phenomenon.

However, a very different perspective can be found among those who not only believe in globalisation, but are much more optimistic about its implications for war and peace. Chapter 7 examined what is known as the liberal peace thesis, the theory that liberal states are much less likely to go to war with one another – the way to ensure world peace, therefore, is to spread Liberalism around the globe. However, while many proponents of this argument focus on the political dimension – principally, the value of democracy in fostering peace – an alternative approach is to emphasise the economic (though the two may be complementary). One writer who sees liberal economics in this way is Erik Gartzke, who forwards a 'capitalist peace' thesis that contends that it is capitalism that is responsible for promoting peace, and that economic globalisation reduces the likelihood of war (Gartzke, 2006, 2007).

Why might this be? There are a number of possibilities. The most widely argued claim is that nations that trade with each other are far less likely to go to war. War disrupts trade and the cost of this disruption is inevitably greater the higher the levels of trade – thus, the more interconnected economies become through globalisation, the less willing states will be to jeopardise their own economic wellbeing by engaging in armed conflicts that will negatively affect their trading relationships.

This argument obviously only has force in relation to inter-state conflicts. However, a second contention, relevant to other types of conflict, centres on the claim that globalisation promotes economic prosperity. The significance of this is that the more prosperous a nation is, it is argued, the higher the probability that it will embrace democracy – and that it will be stable enough for democratic institutions to endure. Since, according to liberal peace theory, democracies are more pacific internally as well as in their international relations, globalisation becomes a force for peace in internal conflicts as well. The answer for nations beset by recurring intra-state conflicts, then, might be to open themselves up even more to the forces of globalisation.

Failed states

One criticism of the notion of failed states is simply that the label itself carries negative connotations – indeed, the reason why the Fund for Peace changed the name of its index from the Failed States Index to the Fragile States Index was because it became sensitive to the fact that the former might appear to suggest that *countries* were being described as failed. Despite its widespread use, therefore, there is an argument for replacing the failed states label with one of the many alternatives.

However, there are also more substantial criticisms. One of these is that the notion of a failed state is often too vaguely and loosely defined, and that too many different characteristics may be attributed to the one concept – social, economic, military and political. This means that states facing greatly varying problems are all placed together in the same category, eliding the significant differences between them. A further argument, which may explain why states in the non-Western world tend to top rankings of failed states, is that the model of 'ideal' statehood against which they are judged is, implicitly or explicitly, a Western one – which thereby unfairly privileges one form of social organisation over all others.

Critics have also focused on the uses to which the label failed states has been put. In particular, they criticise the way it has been used to justify interventions, including military ones, by powerful states into less powerful ones. One of the most notable arguments in this vein is propounded by Noam Chomsky, who attempts to turn the tables by applying the failed state label not to the poorest and weakest nation-states, but to the strongest and richest: the United States (Chomsky, 2006). In ignoring the rule of international law in its military adventures abroad, and endangering the lives of its own and other states' citizens, it is thus the USA which should truly be called a failed state.

Conclusion

Has the character of war changed in recent decades? And if so, what explains this transformation? These are difficult questions to answer, not least because the concepts used in answering them are themselves frequently highly contested. There is certainly no doubt that war continues to plague many parts of the world, but to find solutions, it remains important to seek explanations as to why this is the case. The new wars thesis offers one, with the merit that it links together various notable trends, including increasing globalisation and the proliferation of 'failed' states. Yet more traditional approaches to war – like Liberal, Realist and Marxist ones – may also claim to explain modern forms of conflict, in ways that do not require entirely new frameworks. Wars in places like Bosnia, Somalia, Iraq or Afghanistan might be explained, variously, in terms of the lack of liberal values and institutions, human nature, global and local power politics, class struggle and/or competition for limited resources. In other words, even if different theoretical perspectives may offer different sorts of accounts, these conflicts may still be explicable in ways that are not dissimilar to how older ones may be understood. It remains a case of which perspective one finds the most compelling.

Summary points

1   The new wars thesis posits that contemporary wars are very different to those of the past – in terms of actors, goals, methods and financing.
2   Those involved in new wars include not only regular armies, but non-state actors like warlords, terrorists and guerrillas, who do not fight (at least not only) for traditional geo-political or ideological goals, but to promote particular identities (such as ethnic, nationalist and religious ones).
3   Globalisation may be in large part responsible for the proliferation of new wars – weakening states, fostering tensions between different groups and facilitating the involvement in conflicts of various non-state actors.
4   A failed state is one which has lost its monopoly on the legitimate use of violence and control over its own territory – spawning many problems both for internal and international security.
5   However, all of these concepts – new wars, globalisation and failed states – have been subjected to criticisms, with critics questioning whether trends identified are truly new, and the validity of conclusions drawn.

Recommended reading

Duyvesteyn, I. and Angstrom, J. (eds) *Rethinking the Nature of War*, London: Routledge, 2004.
Kaldor, M. *New and Old Wars: Organized Violence in a Global Era*, 3rd ed., Cambridge: Polity Press, 2012.
Münkler, H. *New Wars*, trans. Patrick Camiller, Cambridge: Polity Press, 2005.
Rotberg, R.I. (ed.) *When States Fail: Causes and Consequences*, Princeton, NJ: Princeton University Press, 2004.
Shankar Jha, P. *The Twilight of the Nation State: Globalisation, Chaos and War*, London: Pluto Press, 2006.

9 Nuclear proliferation

Andrew Moran

Box 9.1: Hiroshima and Nagasaki

At 8.15am on the morning of 6 August 1945, the United States of America detonated the first atomic bomb in a wartime situation. In a matter of seconds, a bomb the size of a small fridge destroyed an entire city and killed over 80,000 people instantly. Three days later a second bomb was dropped on Nagasaki. Estimates suggest that together the total number of deaths attributable to the bombings was over 250,000 people.

The use of the bomb was justified as a means to end the brutal war being fought in the Pacific that was costing thousands of lives. It was also a clear message to the Soviet Union warning it to stay out of the region, and a demonstration of America's new-found military power.

Even today, its use by America to end the Second World War remains controversial.

Introduction

Arguably, no technological change has had a greater impact on security issues than nuclear weapons, both in terms of their influence on the international system and their inability to discriminate between combatants and civilians when used.

In response to the dropping of the atomic bombs on Japan, the United Nations Commission for Conventional Armaments introduced a new category of 'Weapons of Mass Destruction' (WMDs) in 1948. This category includes 'atomic explosive weapons, radioactive material weapons, lethal chemical and biological weapons, and any weapons developed in the future which have characteristics comparable in destructive effect to those of the atomic bomb or other weapons mentioned above'.

Such was the destructive power of these weapons that the superpowers, during the Cold War, chose to fight proxy wars using conventional weapons, fearing that an all-out nuclear war would end human life on Earth as we know it.

Today there are nine states that possess nuclear weapons, but it is feared that more have sought, or are seeking, to develop them. Concerns about their use remain great and the existing nuclear states are resistant to the ownership of weapons spreading, fearing that this will produce instability in the international system.

There are essentially two types of nuclear weapon – the fission and the fusion bomb.

Fission bombs

The first nuclear weapon ever tested was a fission bomb, which was exploded in Alamagordo, New Mexico on 6 July 1945. Most commonly known as the atom bomb, this was the culmination of joint research in the UK/US-led Manhattan Project, which had begun in September 1942.

A fission weapon explodes when one type of atom is split and releases energy. The two elements that can be split to create an explosion are uranium-235 and plutonium. These are known as fissionable materials. Though the physics and engineering needed to produce a fission bomb are well known, and only ten to one hundred pounds of fissionable materials are required to make a bomb, these materials are extremely difficult to obtain. Enriching uranium up to weapons-grade material is expensive, slow and technically complex. Furthermore, the production and storage of these materials is closely monitored by the International Atomic Energy Agency (IAEA).

Plutonium tends to be produced from low-grade uranium in nuclear power reactors. Though nuclear power is used in a number of countries throughout the world, it is harder to build a plutonium bomb than it is one from uranium. One area of controversy is that states such as North Korea and Iran argue they have the right to enrich uranium for peaceful purposes since it is a key component in the production of nuclear energy. It is partly this insistence that has proven to be a sticking point between the West and Iran.

Fusion bombs

Also known as thermo-nuclear weapons or hydrogen bombs, these are much more expensive and are technologically superior to fission bombs. The explosion is caused by fusing two atoms of hydrogen, releasing energy in the process. The explosive power of a fusion bomb can be over a hundred times greater than fission bombs. For example, the first test of a fusion bomb by the US took place at Eniwetok Atoll in the Pacific on 31 October 1952, with a yield of ten megatons, which is equivalent to 10,000 kilotons of TNT. The Russians would detonate the most powerful nuclear weapon ever on 30 October 1961 at the Mityushikha Bay test site. Known as the Tsar Bomba, it had a yield of fifty megatons, and produced a flash of light so bright that it could be seen over a thousand kilometres away. Russian scientists had intended to develop a device twice as powerful.

Arguably, the significance of these bombs has diminished since the end of the Cold War, since they are too difficult for terrorists or a small state to build and they are too powerful for a state to consider using, in part because their destructive yield will reach beyond the boundaries of the military or urban target they are used on.

The effects of a nuclear weapon

Both types of weapons are destructive in four main ways: the electro-magnetic pulse; the thermal light pulse; the blast; and nuclear radiation. The electro-magnetic pulse (EMP) and the thermal light pulse occur at the moment of detonation. The EMP produces a high-voltage electrical charge which can destroy unprotected electronic systems and equipment. If a nuclear weapon was detonated at a great enough height, say 100,000 feet, it would theoretically be possible for it to knock out the electrical systems in a medium-sized state, or, if higher in the atmosphere, it might destroy satellite communications. Given that most economic trade and communications now involve satellite technology, this has become a major concern for security analysts.

The thermal light pulse produces a heat flash that can blind, burn skin, and cause fire. In an extreme example, if the Russians had exploded the Tsar Bomba in an airburst over London, it would have destroyed or set fire to buildings up to twenty miles away, and caused third-degree burns on exposed skin up to forty-eight miles away. The blast, or shock wave, of an explosion follows within seconds of the thermal light pulse. A one megaton airburst, for example, can produce winds of up to 470mph, and would kill or wound up to 50% of the population within a five-mile radius, destroying the majority of buildings in the process.

The fourth effect of an explosion is nuclear radiation, either during the detonation itself, or from fallout in the aftermath. The latter happens when irradiated debris from the explosion is picked up by the fireball and then falls on the population, which can cause lethal radiation sickness. Estimates suggest that as many, if not more, people died because of radiation sickness in the aftermath of the bombs dropped on Hiroshima and Nagasaki than died in the initial explosions.

Box 9.2: Estimated worldwide nuclear warheads, 2014

States are understandably secretive about the number of nuclear weapons they possess. The following figures are based on estimates from a variety of resources.

Country	Deployed Warheads	Non-Deployed Warheads	Total Stockpiled Warheads
United States	1,585	2,661	4,246
Russia	1,512	2,700	4,212
United Kingdom	160	65	225
France	290	10	300
China	–	–	250
India	–	–	90–110
Pakistan	–	–	100–120
Israel	–	–	80–200
North Korea	–	–	6–10

A deployed warhead is attached to a delivery system, such as a missile, and is available for use. For example, the US deploys its warheads on a mixture of delivery systems, including ICBMs and strategic bombers. The UK normally deploys forty-eight warheads on one nuclear submarine.

As well as the above, there are additional warheads, such as those which have been retired and are awaiting dismantlement, which bring the overall estimated total to over 16,000 warheads in the world.

Sources: The Federation of American Scientists,
The Stockholm International Peace Research Institute,
The US Department of Defense,
The US State Department,
and The Arms Control Association.

Delivery systems

One issue often overlooked when discussing the proliferation of nuclear weapons is that although a state may test a bomb, this does not necessarily mean that it can use the weapon effectively. Delivery systems are all-important, and the ability to get the bomb to explode in the right place at the right time is crucial.

When the bomb was first developed in the early days of the Cold War, both superpowers delivered their weapons using long-range bombers, many of which were constantly on standby, with a number always in the air in case of an attack. By the end of the 1950s, however, both countries were experimenting with missile technology. It was for this reason that the Soviet Union's success in launching Sputnik into space so concerned the US – it was not just that the Soviets had successfully placed a satellite in space, it was that they had been able to deliver a payload as planned. Within a decade, the US and the USSR would develop Intercontinental Ballistic Missiles (ICBMs) with a nuclear payload that could hit their targets in under thirty minutes by flying over the North Pole. This would be taken further with the development of Multiple Independently Targeted Re-entry Vehicles (MIRVs), which could deliver a number of warheads from one missile. The assumption was that 'bigger is better', with high numbers, higher yields or multiple payloads driving the development of weapons. Just over two decades after the dropping of the bombs on Japan, both the US and USSR had enough weapons that the principle of Mutually Assured Destruction (MAD) came into play. Put simply, both sides had enough weapons that if one side launched a first strike against the other, enough weapons would survive for the other to retaliate with a second strike. The resulting casualties on both sides would be so great, stretching at least into the tens of millions, that it would deter either state from considering an attack.

This MAD principle was almost undermined at the end of the 1960s and the beginning of the 1970s when the US and USSR began developing anti-ballistic missile systems (ABMs) which were designed to shoot down incoming missiles. Realising the dangers of this technology and how it might encourage one of them to launch a first strike in the hope that any of the enemy's surviving missiles could be destroyed, the US and USSR agreed to an Anti-Ballistic Missile Treaty in 1972 limiting their development. The presidency of Ronald Reagan would see the US attempt to develop an anti-ballistic missile shield in space, called the Strategic Defence Initiative but more popularly known as 'Star Wars'. Though never proven to work, some argue that this concerned the Russians enough that it was a sticking point in nuclear summits between the two sides, most notably in Reykjavik in 1986 when Reagan offered to eliminate all of America's anti-ballistic missiles as long as he could keep Star Wars. Gorbachev suggested abandoning all nuclear weapons within ten years, but would not agree to the continued existence of Star Wars and the summit ended in failure.

Controversially, in the early 1980s the development of Intermediate and Short-Range Ballistic Missiles would see the US place Cruise and Pershing missiles in Western Europe, and the USSR siting SS-20s in Eastern Europe. Less powerful than the long-range ICBMs, their deployment effectively suggested that Europe could become a battleground if the Cold War heated up, leading to a rebirth of the anti-nuclear movement in the region. These weapons were removed from Europe once the Cold War ended.

Though Star Wars was never proven to work, after the terrorist attacks of 9/11 there was a call in America to build a National Missile Defence (NMD) system of surface to air anti-ballistic missiles which could shoot down any incoming missiles fired at the US from rogue states. Not surprisingly, when George W. Bush announced that these missiles, and their early warning systems, would be stationed in the Czech Republic and Poland, this was met with unease from Russia. Bush's proposal for the NMD was widely criticised – it increased tensions with the Russians, was expensive (the Congressional Budget Office put the estimated cost over fifteen to twenty-five years at $238 billion), and it would not have stopped the 9/11 attacks.

The developments in nuclear weapons systems mean that weapons can be divided into two types: *strategic* weapons which can target the enemy's homeland, and *tactical* weapons, which are designed for battlefield use. During the Cold War, both superpowers integrated tactical nuclear weapons into their respective armouries. With the end of the Cold War, however, these weapons were significantly reduced due to fears that if they were used in a conflict situation it would create the risk of escalation to much more powerful weapons.

Part of the psychology of nuclear weapons is that they will not be used – they are the ultimate deterrent. Using them on a small scale would break that taboo and might lead to escalation very quickly. It is for this reason that states are opposed to the development of low-yield nuclear weapons, such as 'bunker busters', which could be used in a battlefield situation. The administration of George W. Bush contemplated the development of these weapons in response to the attacks of 9/11, arguing that they could be used as a tool against terrorists hiding in the mountains of Tora Bora in Afghanistan. They were blocked by the US Congress.

Delivery systems remain important. Though North Korea has, as of 2014, tested three warheads, each relatively small in destructive capacity, it appears to be experiencing difficulties with missile technology with a number of failed launches. In addition, once it has overcome this difficulty, it will then have to succeed in being able to attach a warhead to a missile and then be able to get it to explode at the relevant point for it to be a significant security threat. It is for this reason that the US and Japan express grave concern whenever North Korea tests a missile. The further their missile tests succeed in flying, the greater the potential threat – but at present North Korea has not developed the full range of capabilities required for a fully-armed nuclear missile.

Theories of proliferation and non-proliferation

Today there are nine states that possess nuclear weapons: the US, Russia, the United Kingdom, France, China, India, Pakistan, Israel and North Korea. There have also been a number of states which have developed the capability to construct nuclear devices – for example, Brazil, Argentina and Libya, all of whom moved away from their nuclear programmes, while South Africa dismantled its nuclear capability after it abandoned apartheid and believed it was no longer threatened by external states. Belarus, Kazakhstan and Ukraine returned their nuclear weapons to Russia at the end of the Cold War.

Initial theories seeking to explain the proliferation of nuclear weapons centred on the motivations of states in acquiring this technology, but more recently, particularly since the events of 9/11, there has been an increasing concern about the dangers of sub-state factors, such as nuclear smuggling and nuclear terrorism.

Not surprisingly, it is argued that states believe that possession of the most deadly of weapons will improve their national security. At its most basic level, the deterrence is the driving force – deterring both a conventional attack, particularly when the opponent has a massive superiority in conventional forces, and a nuclear attack. Pakistan, for example, was concerned about India's conventional superiority when choosing to embrace nuclear weapons, not just that India had already tested a nuclear weapon first. As such, it also reflects the classic security dilemma – 'if my opponent has these weapons, so must I'.

For some, international prestige may be a factor, which Bundy argues was most likely the case with Britain and France who wanted to maintain their 'place at the table' (Bundy, 1988). Even if you do not have that place, you most certainly will not be ignored by the international community if you have nuclear capabilities, as North Korea and Pakistan are well aware. At the very least, the possession of nuclear weapons may give you additional leverage when it comes to diplomatic bargaining.

There is also the matter of internal prestige. This appears to have been the case with India, where scientists may have been more persuasive in progressing India's nuclear programme as a matter of national pride and a symbol of the country's development in the post-colonial era. With regards to Iran, for ex-president Mahmoud Ahmadinejad, it was certainly influential in his pronouncements regarding Iran's possible nuclear programme. His speeches suggested the search for nuclear acquisition was not driven solely by the need for regional security, as Iran found itself on America's list of 'Axis of Evil' states in 2002, but also was influenced by internal politics. For him, it was a matter of his own personal standing in the country, as well as Iran's position regionally.

For Israel, it may well be a combination of the above. Though this state does not officially acknowledge the existence of its nuclear programme, it is estimated that it has at least eighty warheads (possibly as many as two hundred). Surrounded by states that are mostly unhappy with its existence, the weapons add an extra layer of security to the powerful conventional forces it already possesses.

For terrorists, the desire to inflict the maximum destruction will remain the most chilling reason for acquisition. Where the terrorists are as extreme as al-Qaeda, the principle of deterrence cannot work because they are non-state actors who are willing to die for their cause. There is no incentive to not use the weapons as they do not fear retaliation.

Waltz vs. Sagan: the debate

Part of the problem with nuclear proliferation is that there is disagreement over what we actually mean by this concept. For example, in 1974 India carried out a peaceful nuclear explosion (PNE), in part to test whether they had developed the technology successfully. South Africa produced a stockpile of six nuclear devices prior to signing the Nuclear Non-Proliferation Treaty of 1968 (NPT), after which it destroyed the weapons. Many states have also developed or are seeking to develop nuclear energy, such as Iran, which, as already noted, may also be a small step away from producing weapons-grade material. Though the IAEA has the authority to monitor such developments, anxiety about a state's motivations can remain.

Central to concerns regarding nuclear weapons is whether nuclear proliferation poses a significant security risk to global stability. Here the debate has been framed by two key theorists, Kenneth Waltz and Scott Sagan.

A Neorealist, Waltz suggested that 'more may be better' (Sagan and Waltz, 2003). For Waltz, the primary goal of any state in the international system is to preserve its security. As such, the acquisition of nuclear weapons is logical because it will enhance a state's security and deter potential aggressors. Waltz believed the spread of nuclear weapons would be slow, a factor borne out by the fact that since 1945 only a handful of states have actually successfully tested a weapon. Furthermore, because of the catastrophic damage these weapons could inflict, he argued that with possession would come constraints and a sense of responsibility not to use them. In short, the possibility of war would decrease as deterrent and defensive capabilities increased, because states would be aware that the use of these weapons in war would probably lead to the end of their own existence as functioning societies. An example he cited to support his argument was the conflict between Pakistan and India, both states with nuclear weapons. Not surprisingly, Waltz is described as a 'proliferation optimist'.

Sagan takes a more pessimistic view, challenging the idea that the spread of nuclear weapons is a good thing. His concern is that the spread of these weapons will see them fall into military-run or weak civilian governments that lack the constraining mechanisms of the original nuclear states and may have military biases which may encourage the use of these weapons.

Sagan notes that there was relative stability between East and West during the Cold War, with a degree of rationality and predictability in political and administrative behaviour, along with orderly communication channels between the two sides to prevent any escalation or misunderstandings. His fear is that this may not be replicated as more states join the nuclear club. Eventually there will be a deterrence failure and a deliberate or accidental war may occur.

Sagan's fears are highlighted by the fact that some analysts suggest that the globalisation of nuclear proliferation has produced a more unstable 'second phase' in which the risks of nuclear conflict are greater. Where proliferation was once vertical, with the US and the USSR simply increasing the strength and numbers of their weapons, it is now horizontal, as more powers seek to acquire the technology. Furthermore, this proliferation may become regionalised, spreading more into Asia and the Middle East. For Sagan, the only way forward is to prevent the spread of nuclear weapons and strengthen the global non-proliferation regime.

Tackling proliferation

During the Cold War the US and the USSR were able to discourage others from developing nuclear weapons, in part because the existence of the security umbrella that both offered to their respective client states was enough. They were also willing to deter states who might consider developing their own nuclear arsenals; for example, the US threatened to withdraw from its security commitments to South Korea and Taiwan if they chose to continue their fledgling nuclear programmes.

Treaty commitments also sought to slow down proliferation, such as the Atmospheric Test Ban Treaty of 1963 and the NPT. The latter, however, suffers from a major weakness in that any signatory state can produce weapons-grade fissile material and explore the non-nuclear components of a weapons programme. It can then leave the treaty under its own withdrawal clause (Article X), which is exactly what North Korea did when it tested its first atom bomb in 2006. Other nuclear states simply never signed it, notably India and Israel.

According to Brown, there are three ways of preventing, inhibiting or delaying the proliferation of nuclear weapons. They are 'preventing the intentional or unintentional spread of weapons and technology, employing sanctions, and offering economic and security incentives' (Brown, 2007–8: 14). In the case of Brazil and Argentina, they stepped back from being nuclear states as they regarded the security risks were greater than being non-nuclear, while the former Soviet satellite states at the end of the Cold War received economic and security assurances in return for giving up the weapons. Sanctions have been applied by the international community against Iran, leading to international talks. To this could be added the use of a pre-emptive military strikes, such as Israeli forces bombing suspected nuclear sites in both Iraq and Syria, or sabotage, as in the use of the Stuxnet virus which targeted the Iranian nuclear programme.

The Clinton Administration had an incentives-based approach to North Korea that led to a freeze of North Korea's plutonium extraction in the late 1990s. When the administration of George W. Bush withdrew America from this, and then announced that North Korea was part of an 'Axis of Evil', it was perhaps unsurprising when the latter then reactivated its nuclear programme.

It is also important to guarantee the security of existing stockpiles to ensure that they do not end up in the hands of unstable states, or, even more concerning, terrorists. It is for this reason that the Clinton administration persuaded the former Soviet satellite states to transfer their weapons to the new Russia in the 1990s.

One solution to a state's desire to produce nuclear energy may be to have uranium enrichment and fuel processing at internationally controlled facilities – something that has been mooted in the current discussions with Iran.

One fundamental sticking point with regard to proliferation is who has the right to determine who can have these weapons and who cannot. Many commentators have noted that though the US punished India after its first nuclear tests in 1974, thirty years later, in 2005, it not only recognised India as a nuclear state but also offered technical advice. Though this was in part because the US wished to deepen its strategic relationship with India, does it suggest that those who wait in isolation may one day be forgiven, and in so doing undermine the NPT? Others asked why it was acceptable for India to be a nuclear state and not Iran.

Indeed, the behaviour of the major nuclear states continues to undermine anti-proliferation efforts. Though Article VI of the NPT commits the nuclear powers to 'pursue negotiations in good faith … to nuclear disarmament' and to 'general and complete disarmament', they are, in fact, continuing to modernise their arsenals. The United States alone is projected to spend $350 billion modernising its nuclear forces, including a new class of missiles for its nuclear submarines and a new land-based intercontinental ballistic missile. It is also continuing with its goal of seeking to install an anti-ballistic missile system in Europe against the possible threat of a launch from a rogue state. Russia has tested a new intercontinental ballistic missile and is building a new class of ballistic-missile submarines. China, as well as modernising its nuclear arsenal, is seeking to equip its submarines with nuclear weapons. India has successfully tested a road-mobile missile which is capable of hitting China, while the UK is seeking a replacement for Trident.

Box 9.3: Iran's nuclear ambitions

According to the NPT, states have the 'inalienable right to develop research, production and use of nuclear energy for peaceful purposes without discrimination'. The Iranian government has used this to justify its attempts to develop nuclear energy, arguing that its oil and gas reserves are finite and alternatives need to be found to guarantee energy security for the future.

However, the US and others are concerned that Iran is seeking to develop more than a peaceful energy programme, and that this is the first stage in Iran's ambition to build a nuclear weapons programme. As a result, the US, with support from some in the international community, has applied sanctions since 2006, something which the Iranians regard as an Anglo-American plot to damage Iran's economic development.

If Iran was seeking to develop a weapon, this would most likely be in response to a number of legitimate security concerns: Israel, a staunch enemy of Iran, already has nuclear weapons; Shiite Iran has an uneasy relationship with a number of Sunni-dominated states in the Middle East; Turkey, to the north, is a member of NATO, an ally of the US, and has political and economic ties with Israel; and to the east is Sunni Pakistan, another nuclear state. Furthermore, Iran has long considered itself a target of the US. In 1953 the Central Intelligence Agency engineered a coup in Iran, installing the West-leaning Shah, who remained in power until the Islamic Revolution of 1979. Many Iranians remember how his brutal regime was supported by the US, and fears remain that the US might seek further regime change again, as it did in Afghanistan in 2001, Iraq in 2003 and Libya in 2011. Developing a nuclear weapon, therefore, would act as a deterrent.

Kenneth Waltz believed that Iran's acquisition of a bomb would bring stability to the Middle East, counterbalancing Israel's regional nuclear monopoly which, he argued, had 'long fuelled instability'. Said Waltz, 'policymakers and citizens in the Arab world, Europe, Israel, and the United States should take comfort from the fact that history has shown that where nuclear capabilities emerge, so, too, does stability. When it comes to nuclear weapons, now as ever, more may be better' (Waltz, 2012).

Many US, European and Israeli politicians and commentators disagree, arguing that a nuclear Iran would actually create serious instability, leading to a probable arms race in the Middle East. Saudi Arabia has already made it clear that it might nuclearise if Iran successfully tests a bomb, while Israel asked approval from President George W. Bush to bomb Iran's nuclear facilities, which the White House refused to support.

Non-state actors

Since the attacks of 9/11, a growing concern is that non-state actors, particularly terrorist groups, may seek to acquire nuclear weapons and would not hesitate to use them to inflict the maximum number of casualties possible. Here, as already noted, deterrence may not work as these groups will have few assets to risk in terms of retaliation.

Despite scare stories in the media, however, it is extremely unlikely that a terrorist would be able to make such a weapon from scratch. Though the information revolution has allowed nuclear information to circulate via the World Wide Web, and there is a black market in materials which has put the technology within the reach of non-state actors, the cost, technological and industrial facilities necessary are most likely beyond the means of terrorist groups. As Talmadge observes, producing plutonium is sophisticated and expensive, while enriching uranium to weapons-grade level requires large buildings and advanced technologies (Talmadge, 2007). Even if terrorists were to succeed in producing, or acquiring, nuclear materials, they would then have to overcome the problem of turning it into a bomb, and be able to design and produce a successful delivery system.

That is not to say that terrorists will not try. Aum Shinrikyo, who carried out the sarin gas attack on the Tokyo underground in 1995, attempted to create its own nuclear material, and when that failed it tried to buy it from Russia (Stern, 1999). It is likely that rather than developing their own weapon, terrorists will choose one of a variety of options: purchasing materials from a group in a collapsing nuclear state; acquiring the weapons from a state which is seeking to promote its own ends; or by theft. It is for the latter reason that the Clinton administration offered support to protect nuclear sites in the former Soviet states after the end of the Cold War. However, theft remains a problem as it is possible that a state may not want to alert the international community that a theft has occurred.

If terrorists ever did acquire a nuclear device, or use one, developments in nuclear forensics now make it possible to identify the signature of a weapon, which would allow states to define the source of a terrorist-deployed weapon. This, in turn, could be used to direct a response at the source, thwarting or disrupting further potential attacks using a nuclear weapon, or it could be used as a possible deterrent to punish a state that may have been the source of materials acquired by a terrorist group. This could be a tool for deterring governments, militaries, and others from assisting or passively assisting terrorist groups. For example, it would not be in North Korea's interests to provide materials to a terrorist group who uses the weapon if the source of the material could be linked back to the state. The same would be true for Iran, if it developed nuclear weapons. Would it really want to provide materials, and tie its fate, to Hezbollah? Arguably such action would be reckless. Having said that, both Iraq and Iran have exposed the problems of information gathering and enforcement in the non-proliferation regime.

Box 9.4: Nuclear accidents

Scott Sagan identified the risks of an accidental use of weapons occurring. One often overlooked security threat posed by nuclear weapons, however, is the risk of an accident occurring where the weapons are sited. There have already been accidents involving the production of nuclear energy, most notably Three Mile Island in 1979, Chernobyl in 1986 and Fukushima Daiichi in 2011. What is less well known is that, according to Eric Schlosser (2013), between 1950 and 1980 there were thirty-two reported 'broken arrows' in the US – the military's term for accidents involving nuclear technology.

Perhaps the most serious occurred at a US Air Force base in Damascus, Arkansas in 1980 when a technician dropped a socket wrench while performing routine maintenance on a Titan II missile – at 103 feet tall, the largest ICBM built by the US. The tool punctured the missile's fuel tank. Though technicians tried to fix the problem, eight hours later the tank exploded, sending the silo's 740-ton blast door more than two hundred yards. The missile's nine megaton W-53 thermo-nuclear warhead – the most powerful warhead ever carried by an American missile, three times the explosive force of all the bombs dropped during the Second World War, including the two atomic bombs – was also found two hundred yards away, relatively intact.

However, this is not the only example. In 1961 a B-52 broke apart in mid-air, dropping two hydrogen bombs near the town of Goldsboro, North Carolina. One of the bombs passed through five of the six steps required to arm the weapon as it plummeted to the ground. If it had been fully armed, the four megaton bomb would have detonated on impact. In 1980, one of the engines on a B-52 bomber caught fire at Grand Forks Air Force base in North Dakota. The plane was carrying four hydrogen bombs and eight short-range missiles with nuclear warheads. Thanks to a combination of strong winds which kept the flames away from the weapons, and a fireman who climbed into the burning plane, disaster was averted.

These events highlight the dangerous mix of human fallibility and complex systems, where apparently trivial events can cause a catastrophic chain reaction.

Schlosser fears that while the US is extremely rich technologically and has the organisational skills and safety culture necessary to manage nuclear weapons, other countries with less experience and fewer resources may not be able to do so. As a result, the threats these weapons pose are as grave to the countries that possess them as they are to everybody else.

Global Zero

Since the end of the Cold War there have been a number of calls for disarmament. Perhaps the most surprising was launched by a number of senior US statesmen in 2007, the group including former National Security Adviser Henry Kissinger and ex-Secretary of State George Schultz. They argued that the doctrine of 'mutual Soviet–American deterrence' was now 'obsolete', that traditional deterrence models would not work against terrorist groups, and that a new era of proliferation was potentially 'more precarious, psychologically disorienting, and economically more costly than was the Cold War'. As a result, they called for a world free of nuclear weapons (Kissinger *et al.*, 2007). This was followed by the Global Zero campaign, and a number of international commissions which called for a nuclear-free world.

The movement was supported by the newly elected president of the US, Barack Obama, when, in a speech in Prague in 2009, he announced 'clearly and with conviction America's commitment to seek the peace and security of a world without nuclear weapons'. Obama's call was driven by what he called a 'strange turn of history': though the end of the Cold War had resulted in the threat of global nuclear war being reduced, he believed that the possibility of a nuclear attack had increased. He warned that the black market in nuclear materials and secrets had allowed nuclear technology to spread, while terrorists were 'determined to buy, build, or steal one'. This in turn placed considerable pressure on the existing global non-proliferation regimes. He feared that 'as more people and nations break the rules, we could reach the point where the centre cannot hold' (Obama, 2009b).

Obama committed the US to reduce the role of nuclear weapons as part of its national security strategy, including reductions in the actual arsenal, and urged others to do the same. He called for ratification of the Comprehensive Test Ban Treaty, a treaty to end the production of fissile materials, strengthening the Nuclear Non-proliferation Treaty, including improved inspections, sanctions, a 'new international effort to secure all vulnerable nuclear material around the world within four years', and a new Strategic Arms Reduction Treaty with Russia, which was signed in 2010. He conceded, however, that the US would not act unilaterally. 'As long as these weapons exist,' said Obama, 'the United States will maintain a safe, secure, and effective arsenal to deter any adversary, and guarantee that defence to our allies.' For the US, the security dilemma would remain.

Opposition to the Zero option

The Global Zero option is not without its critics. Many argue that it would be difficult to verify that all of the world's nuclear warheads had been destroyed, while others note that even if nuclear weapons were abandoned, the knowledge would still exist, ready to be utilised again.

Furthermore, a nuclear-free world would not necessarily result in a more stable world. Conventional forces would still exist, and this would benefit the US disproportionately because of its huge global conventional superiority. In fact, Brown (2007–8) argues that it is the existence of the US's conventional forces, not its nuclear weapons, that was the driving force for states to acquire weapons during the 'war on terror', as they sought to protect their security in the face of the threat of possible regime change. Though nuclear weapons were not used in Iraq or Afghanistan, for example, it may have been North Korea's fear of America's overwhelming conventional forces that pushed it to develop a nuclear weapon because it feared it was next. He also suggests that if Iran did have a nuclear programme, it would not be surprising given the security dilemma posed by America's presence in the Middle East.

For this reason, Brown argues that reducing the number of America's nuclear weapons would have little effect on the behaviour of potential nuclear weapons states. If a state were to abandon nuclear weapons it would have to make that decision in the confidence that its security concerns would not be affected by such a move. This would most likely have to combine a mixture of positive and negative reinforcements, which could include economic benefits, diplomatic acceptance, regional security arrangements and security guarantees.

Box 9.5: The evolution of the global non-proliferation regime

Efforts to prevent nuclear proliferation have involved a wide range of unilateral, bilateral, regional and global measures collectively known as the global nuclear non-proliferation regime. Key moments include:

- The first attempt at controlling nuclear proliferation, which was the Baruch Plan proposed to the United Nations in 1946. This failed due to radical differences between the US and the USSR.
- In 1957 the International Atomic Energy Agency was created by the United Nations to oversee the peaceful use of nuclear materials. By the mid-1960s the IAEA was able to implement a comprehensive monitoring system, known as safeguarding, to ensure peaceful nuclear energy use. The European Community introduced its own successful safeguarding system as early as 1958 with the creation of the European Atomic Energy Community.
- In 1959 the Antarctic Treaty banned all nuclear explosions and the dumping of nuclear waste in the Antarctic.

- In 1963 the Soviet Union, the UK and the US agreed to the Partial Test Ban Treaty which prohibited the testing of nuclear weapons in the atmosphere, underwater and in outer space. Tests would now be carried out underground.
- In 1967 the Treaty for the Prohibition of Nuclear Weapons in Latin America was passed.
- In 1970 the Non-Proliferation Treaty came into force, having been open for states to sign since 1968.
- In 1972 the US and the Soviet Union signed the Strategic Arms Limitation Treaty (SALT 1), which was designed to limit the number of anti-ballistic missiles that could be deployed.
- In 1987 the Intermediate Nuclear Force Agreement limited the range of mid-range nuclear arms.
- In 1993 the Strategic Arms Reduction Treaty II banned the use of MIRVs in ICBMs.
- In 2002 the Moscow Treaty cut Russian and American nuclear forces to 20% of the level they reached during the Cold War.
- In 2010, the New START Accords limited the Russian and US nuclear arsenals to only 1,550 deployed strategic warheads each.

Negotiations continue on a Comprehensive Test Ban Treaty, which was passed by the UN in 1996 but has not yet been fully ratified, and the Fissile Material Cut-Off Treaty to limit the production of fissile material. Other counter-proliferation measures have included the United Nations Security Council Resolution 1540, adopted in 2004, which requires states to prohibit individuals, companies, or other actors from supporting non-state actors seeking to acquire WMDs. There are also increasing regulations to improve international cooperation in efforts to prevent the illegal trafficking of nuclear materials.

Conclusion

It is true to say that since that fateful day in Hiroshima in the closing days of the Second World War, nuclear proliferation has become a global phenomenon, transforming military and political relationships.

At the height of the Cold War in 1985, there were believed to be 65,000 nuclear weapons in the world, as the two superpowers sought to match, and even outpace, each other. Today, there are significantly fewer as the major nuclear powers have reduced their numbers rapidly. Between 2010 and 2013, estimates suggest the number of nuclear warheads fell from 22,600 to roughly just over 14,615, in part as a result of key disarmament treaties between the US and Russia.

However, the Global Zero campaign is unlikely to achieve its aims, as the major nuclear weapons states continue to modernise their arsenals and new states seek to join the nuclear club. The US and Russia in particular will need to set an example by reducing the number of warheads further to help gain support for other measures to limit proliferation. At present, they possess 90% of all the nuclear warheads in the world. Nevertheless, even if states did reduce their stockpiles, or even abandon their nuclear weapons, it would remain extremely difficult to verify that all the world's nuclear weapons had been destroyed.

What motivates states to acquire nuclear weapons may differ from state to state, but ultimately it centres on security. Here, the perceived threat may not always be nuclear, but can be conventional. Nuclear weapons were not used in Iraq or Afghanistan by the United States, for example, but the sheer US superiority in conventional forces may have been enough to push North Korea and Iran towards developing a nuclear programme.

What is clear is that since the end of the Cold War it has proved much harder for the major states to prevent proliferation as the security umbrella they provided has become less important, and though the spread of weapons has been gradual it appears to be regionalising, and so becomes harder for the international community to control.

Summary points

1   Though nuclear weapons have not been used since 1945, they have fundamentally reshaped the nature of relationships between states.
2   During the Cold War the threat posed by nuclear weapons, not least the principle of MAD, allowed for a degree of stability between the two major superpowers.
3   Since the end of the Cold War, concerns have been expressed that proliferation will move from being vertical (within existing states) to horizontal (involving new states or non-state actors, such as terrorists).
4   Some believe that proliferation will provide increased stability whilst others disagree and seek to stop the spread of nuclear weapons.
5   For non-proliferation regimes to be successful, they will need to involve a combination of positive factors (such as security guarantees, diplomatic acceptance, and economic benefits) and negative factors (such as diplomatic isolation, military threats, and economic sanctions).

Recommended reading

Pant, H. (ed.) *Handbook of Nuclear Proliferation*, New York: Routledge, 2012.
Sagan, S. and Waltz, K. *The Spread of Nuclear Weapons: A Debate Renewed* (2nd ed.), New York: Norton, 2003.
Schlosser, E. *Command and Control: Nuclear Weapons, the Damascus Accident, and the Illusion of Safety*, London: Penguin Press, 2013.
Waltz, K. 'Why Iran Should Get the Bomb. Nuclear Balancing Would Mean Stability', *Foreign Affairs*, vol. 91, no. 4, July/August, 2012, 2–5.
Wesley, M. 'It's time to scrap the NPT', *Australian Journal of International Affairs*, vol. 59, no. 3, September, 2005, 283–299.

10 The international arms trade in conventional weapons

Bruce Pilbeam

Box 10.1: 'Merchants of death'

Some of the most significant, and colourful, figures in the international arms trade are the arms traffickers who are willing to provide almost any type of military hardware to virtually any buyer – for a price. Probably the most notorious of all alleged traffickers in modern times is Viktor Bout, a Russian-born arms dealer who ran an operation using over fifty planes to transport weapons and other military equipment. It has been claimed that he supplied arms to everyone from the Taliban in Afghanistan to Charles Taylor in Liberia and Colonel Gaddafi in Libya. These accusations led to him being labelled in 2000 by Peter Hain, then British Foreign Office minister responsible for Africa, as the world's 'chief sanctions-buster' and 'a merchant of death'. In 2012, Bout was sentenced in a US court to twenty-five years in prison for selling arms to a Colombian group designated by the American government a terrorist organisation. Yet in an indication of how blurry the lines of morality (and politics) can be in this world, Bout's fleet of aircraft had previously been used by the US government itself to bring materials into Iraq following the US-led invasion of 2003, and had also transported UN peacekeepers into countries like Somalia. Decried as figures like Bout often are, states and other official actors are frequently willing to work with them when it suits their ends.

Introduction

Given their destructive power, it is perhaps unsurprising that so much attention is paid in Security Studies to nuclear weapons and their proliferation. Yet no nuclear weapon has been used in a conflict since the Second World War, whereas over the subsequent decades conventional weapons have been responsible for tens of millions of deaths around the globe. Not only governments, but a whole array of actors – from rebel groups to warlords to 'terrorists' – rely upon conventional forms of weaponry to pursue their ends, and both state and non-state actors use them not only for 'legal' warfare but to commit the whole gamut of human rights violations, from torture to mass killings. Moreover, the increasing sophistication and lethality of many conventional weapons means that the dividing line between them and so-called Weapons of Mass Destruction (WMDs) like nuclear bombs has become extremely blurred.

For these reasons, understanding the trade in these weapons is vital for an understanding of contemporary international security. However, before turning to the arms trade itself, it is first worth reflecting more deeply on the meaning and significance of conventional weapons.

The world's weapons of choice

What are conventional weapons? It is probably easier to define the meaning of conventional weapons negatively, rather than positively – in other words, to specify what they are *not*. Thus, the simplest way is to argue that all weapons not counted as WMDs – including biological, chemical and nuclear weapons (as discussed in Chapter 9) – should be considered conventional weapons.

However, this way of defining them may seem quite vague. To give a better idea of the types of weapons that may be included under the heading of conventional, it is useful to consider the United Nations Register of Conventional Arms (UNROCA). This register was set up in 1991, with the aim of creating greater transparency in the realm of arms transfers. To this end, UN member states are expected to provide the organisation with details of their imports and exports of seven categories of conventional weapons:

I.   Battle tanks
II. Armoured combat vehicles
III. Large-calibre artillery systems
IV. Combat aircraft
V.   Attack helicopters
VI. Warships
VII. Missiles and missile launchers.

Those included in these seven categories are deemed by the UN to be the most 'offensive' sorts of conventional weapons, so it is not an exhaustive list. Perhaps most noteworthy is that small arms – which may be defined as those that can be used by a single person – are not represented in these categories, although countries may, on a voluntary basis, include these in their reports of arms transfers to be added to the UN register.

In terms of small arms, Box 10.2 presents a list from a 1997 UN report that shows the range of weapons that might be considered to belong to the category often labelled Small Arms and Light Weapons (SALW) – together with associated ammunition and explosives – encompassing weaponry from revolvers and rifles to grenades and landmines. Yet even this list has some crucial absences, as it includes only distinctively modern weapons. This overlooks the fact that there are many other sorts of weapon that may be wielded by individuals which have been used throughout human history, including clubs, knives and machetes, and which continue to be significant even in conflicts today, especially in the developing world.

What is most notable about SALW is that although sophisticated weapons of war, such as tanks, fighter jets and missile systems, may be the most significant economically – sometimes costing billions of dollars – it is these often relatively simple weapons that are responsible for most of the casualties in global conflicts. It is therefore important to consider their nature and impact in some detail.

Box 10.2: Small arms, light weapons, and ammunition and explosives

(a) Small arms

(i)   Revolvers and self-loading pistols
(ii) Rifles and carbines
(iii) Sub-machine-guns
(iv) Assault rifles
(v)   Light machine-guns.

(b) Light weapons

(i)   Heavy machine-guns
(ii) Hand-held under-barrel and mounted grenade launchers
(iii) Portable anti-aircraft guns
(iv) Portable anti-tank guns, recoilless rifles
(v)   Portable launchers of anti-tank missile and rocket systems
(vi) Portable launchers of anti-aircraft missile systems
(vii) Mortars of calibres of less than 100mm.

(c) Ammunition and explosives

(i)   Cartridges (rounds) for small arms
(ii) Shells and missiles for light weapons
(iii) Mobile containers with missiles or shells for single-action anti-aircraft and anti-tank systems
(iv) Anti-personnel and anti-tank hand grenades
(v)   Landmines
(vi) Explosives.

UN Report of the Panel of Governmental Experts on Small Arms (1997)

Source: www.un.org/depts/ddar/Firstcom/SGreport52/a52298.html

The nature and impact of small arms and light weapons (SALW)

According to the Small Arms Survey, an independent research project, there are approximately 875 million SALW in the world today (*Small Arms Survey*, 2014). The UN estimates that these SALW are responsible for 350,000 to 500,000 deaths a year, as well as over a million non-fatal injuries. Not all of these deaths and injuries occur in armed conflicts, since large numbers are the result of criminal activity and suicides. Regardless, globally over 90% of civilian casualties resulting from acts of violence can be attributed to SALW.

One of the important ways in which SALW differ from larger weapons is in terms of ownership: whereas most tanks, warships and combat aircraft are in the hands of states, over three-quarters of SALW are possessed by non-state actors. The majority of these are private individuals, but this category also includes militias, insurgents, criminal gangs and private military and security companies. Related to this are the various characteristics that set SALW apart from larger weapons. These include the facts that they are relatively cheaper, easier to maintain, and much more portable; this last feature means, crucially, that they are much easier to hide. All of these points mean, therefore, that there are often even harder questions raised about the control and regulation of SALW than larger weapons.

SALW also create many particular difficulties in terms of security, conflict and post-conflict situations. The ready availability of SALW often helps protract the duration of conflicts, in poorer countries especially, because even groups like insurgents and rebels, who may not be able to afford or obtain tanks and fighter planes, can commonly acquire smaller weapons with much less difficulty. In wars fought primarily with SALW, there may even be more weapons available than fighters to use them, so they are intimately connected with the problem of child soldiers (children who are coerced into combat), who may be relatively easily equipped with and taught how to use small arms. Another key issue is that external actors involved in conflict situations, from relief workers to peacekeepers, frequently come under fire from SALW, greatly hampering their efforts. Finally, SALW create major problems when it comes to post-conflict reconstruction. Disarming conflict actors, which may be one of the crucial steps in this process, can be enormously difficult in societies awash with SALW. Similarly, the legacy of the use of anti-personnel landmines during conflicts is that, as seen in many African countries in recent decades, they kill and injure long after wars have concluded, again severely hindering the task of rebuilding war-torn societies.

The modern international arms trade

Whether the weapons in question are the latest, most advanced varieties, or relatively simple ones based on centuries-old technology, many states – and non-state actors – are either unable to produce their own, or find it cheaper and easier to purchase them from others. This is where the international trade in arms comes in.

There is nothing new about the selling of weapons in the global marketplace, but this trade has changed and evolved over the years in many ways. For example, in the decades immediately following the Second World War, developed nations' trade in arms with the developing world often consisted of supplying already outdated military equipment left over from the preceding conflict. By the 1980s, states in the developing world were demanding and receiving some of the most sophisticated weapons systems available, as they do today.

Another important development is that the trade's expansion in recent times has been greatly facilitated by the twin trends of globalisation and economic liberalisation. Just as barriers and restrictions in other areas of economic activity have been lowered and eased as part of a global trend towards embracing free markets and deregulation, the same is true in relation to the arms trade. Similarly, advances in information and communications technology have enabled transactions to be conducted faster and more easily, and improvements in transportation – land, sea and air – have greatly aided the physical delivery of weapons.

Also important for understanding the contemporary arms trade are the implications of the ending of the Cold War. During the Cold War, the two superpowers, the USA and the Soviet Union, were very much the dominant players in the international arms trade, since supplying weapons to friendly states was seen by both as crucial for bolstering and furthering their strategic interests. In relation to their respective spheres of influence, therefore, each became the main exporter of military equipment. In doing so, both superpowers were prepared to subsidise these exports very heavily and provide cheap credit, to ensure that they could be afforded by key allies. In many cases, too, the superpowers were willing to turn blind eyes to the natures of the regimes to which they were providing arms – regardless of how corrupt or oppressive a government might be, any concerns about their internal politics were largely subordinated to the over-riding importance attached to their allegiance in the Cold War struggle.

Consequently, the end of the Cold War brought with it significant changes in the global arms trade, with circumstances much less propitious for its flourishing. Partly, this was because military expenditure around the world declined in response to the easing of international tensions (even if some states, especially the USA, kept spending at high levels throughout the 1990s). However, this was also thanks to the fact that the Soviet Union no longer existed to provide a cheap supply of arms to friendly states, and the USA no longer had the same urgent need to do so.

In terms of sales, though, the immediate period in the wake of the Cold War's conclusion may be seen as a temporary blip, because in the twenty-first century arms transfers have once again been on an upward trend. Nonetheless, the reasons for this are very different to those that drove the Cold War arms trade. One factor in explaining rising expenditure on arms is the global insecurities that emerged following the 9/11 terrorist attacks on the United States in 2001, and the subsequent War on Terror that was launched. As well as this, however, in many parts of the world – in Latin America, Asia, Africa and the Middle East – the continuation and proliferation of internal conflicts, together with the growing economic and political power of states outside the West, has led to a growing demand for the acquisition of all types of military weapons.

What, precisely, is the size and nature of the modern arms trade? Accurate information in this area can be difficult to obtain, as different countries define and measure weapons exports differently, and far from all countries disclose full information (China, for example, does not release official figures). As already noted above, the UN keeps a register of major arms transactions, but in practice, far from all member states report all transactions, and small arms are included only on a voluntary basis.

However, various research institutes attempt to keep track of the trade, and provide estimates of its scale that are as accurate as possible. One of the most notable of these is the Stockholm International Peace Research Institute (SIPRI), which publishes research on all aspects of the global arms trade. Its figures indicate that following the dip of the immediate post-Cold War era, since 2002 the trade has grown at a fast rate. Thus, SIPRI estimates that in terms of volume, the trade in major conventional weapons grew by 24% between 2002 and 2006, and the same again between 2007 and 2011 (Stockholm International Peace Research Institute, 2012).

The global economic downturn that began in 2008 has undoubtedly had an impact on the arms trade, with some states reducing military expenditure in response – for example, cuts in this area have formed part of many European nations' austerity programmes. Yet other states, such as in East Asia, North Africa and the Middle East, have continued or increased spending on defence, and arms sales overall have not suffered any precipitous decline.

To give a sense of the trade's absolute size, the total value of global conventional arms exports today is approximately $70 billion. This makes the sale and purchase of conventional weapons one of the largest sectors of international trade. However, at least as revealing as its size are the countries that are the main exporters and the major importers of these weapons.

Table 10.1 reveals the top ten countries in both categories. In terms of exports, the USA is the single largest exporter of weapons, accounting for 30% of the world's total. Indeed, some of its major defence contractors – like Lockheed Martin, Boeing and Northrop Grumman – are among the largest corporations in the world. With Russia the second largest exporter, responsible for 26% of total exports, this shows that at least one aspect of the Cold War has not entirely changed, since the two former Cold War rivals still account for the majority of the conventional weapons trade.

What is also interesting from these figures is that if the sales of France, the UK and China are added to those of the USA and Russia, this accounts for over 70% of the world's total arms exports. Since these five nations are the ones that hold permanent seats on the UN Security Council, it can be seen that those with the greatest power and influence on this body, which is supposed to be centrally concerned with maintaining international peace and security, are also among those who are most heavily responsible for arming the world for war.

To whom do these countries sell their arms? Again, patterns have changed significantly over time. In the 1950s and 1960s, Europe was the single largest market for arms exports. However, by the 1980s nations in the developing world – in Africa, Asia and especially the Middle East – had become the most important markets. Table 10.1 shows that today Asian countries are the largest importers of conventional weapons, with India, China, Pakistan, South Korea and Singapore constituting the top five. In fact, according to SIPRI, if all Asian countries' imports of arms are added together, they account for 44% of the world's total. A whole range of reasons explains the growth in significance of this region for the arms trade, from its nations' efforts to combat piracy and other criminal activity to territorial disputes between them. More broadly, it indicates the growing power (political and economic) of nations in this region, like India, and their desires both to increase and modernise their military capabilities.

Table 10.1 The main importers and exporters of major arms, 2008–2012

Exporter	Global share (%)	Importer	Global share (%)
1. USA	30	1. India	12
2. Russia	26	2. China	6
3. Germany	7	3. Pakistan	5
4. France	6	4. South Korea	5
5. China	5	5. Singapore	4
6. UK	4	6. Algeria	4
7. Spain	3	7. Australia	4
8. Italy	2	8. USA	4
9. Ukraine	2	9. UAE	3
10. Israel	2	10. Saudi Arabia	3

Source: Stockholm International Peace Research Institute (SIPRI), *SIPRI Yearbook 2013: Armaments, Disarmament and International Security,* Summary of chapter on International arms transfers, http://www.sipri.org/yearbook/2013/05.

The two faces of the arms trade: legal and illicit

To understand the global arms trade further, it is important to be aware that the sale and purchase of weapons can take place both legally and illicitly, and that there are significant differences between the legal and illicit markets. As will be seen, these markets are far from wholly separate, yet to begin with, it is necessary to appreciate what distinguishes the legal and illicit trades.

i) The legal arms trade

The primary recipients of legal arms transfers are states. All states have a right to purchase conventional weapons to arm their military and civilian police forces, so in most cases this activity is considered part of the lawful arms trade. The main exception is when states have had embargoes imposed upon them, as will be discussed later. But if no embargo is in place, states are otherwise largely free to purchase whatever conventional weapons (other than those banned by international treaties) they wish.

However, it is not just states that are legally allowed to buy arms. Although few countries permit private citizens to purchase tanks or ballistic missiles, in many places it is perfectly legal to acquire small arms like handguns and rifles. Laws around private gun ownership do, of course, vary enormously. For example, whereas in the United Kingdom the possession of firearms is highly circumscribed by law, in the United States gun rights for private individuals (rooted as these rights are in the American Constitution) are much more extensive, such that it is legal for ordinary Americans to own military assault weapons. In any case, lawful gun ownership by private individuals is widespread around the globe.

For legal sales abroad, arms manufacturers usually require export licences issued by the government of their home nation and allowing them to sell to particular clients, as well as an end user certificate signed by the purchaser. Yet there is no uniformity in this process, as each state has its own rules and regulations governing export licences – while in some countries governments require exporters to obtain a new licence for every sales contract, in others an arms exporter may be allowed to make unlimited sales to a specified customer over a given period of time, without needing a new licence for each sale.

It was noted earlier that economic liberalisation has greatly aided the arms trade. However, this does not mean that the legal trade in arms operates in any sense akin to a pure free market. In particular, the arms industries of most of the major arms-producing countries are heavily supported, promoted and subsidised by their respective governments. For example, the governments of arms-manufacturing countries are frequently involved in organising arms fairs, to facilitate contacts between buyers and sellers. However, they may do much more than this. In Russia, the state-owned corporation Rosoboronexport acts as an intermediary for managing virtually all of the nation's exports and imports of arms. Similarly, in the USA, the Department of Defense operates a Foreign Military Sales (FMS) programme whereby the Department acts as an agent in promoting and selling military arms (and related services and training) to foreign governments. In these cases, therefore, arms manufacturers do not deal directly with the buyers of the weapons that they make, but allow state agencies to secure the deals for them.

Yet governments help their arms industries with more than just sales and marketing. They also underwrite them with large amounts of financial support. Subsidies can take many forms, including direct assistance, funding for research and development, and export credits. One example of this subsidisation is when, in July 2012, the Russian government gave 1.5 billion roubles to its nation's arms industry to help it repay the interest on loans extended to it by banks. In the UK, research commissioned by the Campaign Against Arms Trade (CAAT) calculated that the UK government spends nearly £700 million a year in UK arms export subsidies (Campaign Against Arms Trade, 2011). Support to the arms industry may also take the indirect form of offering loans and credit to foreign buyers. For example, in 2003 the US government loaned the Polish government $3.8 billion, at a very low interest rate, so that it could purchase forty-eight F-16 fighter planes from Lockheed Martin.

ii) The illicit arms trade

The illicit trade in arms consists of two types of market: the black and the grey. The black market is where the trade is simply illegal, violating either national or international law. By contrast, in the grey market, buyers, sellers and brokers do not, strictly speaking, act illegally. Instead, they exploit loopholes and find ways to circumvent regulations; in other words, they may violate the spirit of the law, even if not the letter. Given their natures, it is difficult to assess the sizes of either of these markets accurately, though one estimate puts the size of the illicit small arms market at approximately 10–20% of the legal market (*Small Arms Survey*, 2002). Key actors in the black and grey markets are international arms traffickers, who are to be found behind the scenes in many of the world's conflict zones. Box 10.3 explains how their roles have changed from the Cold War to the post-Cold War eras.

Box 10.3: International arms trafficking: from the Cold War to the post-Cold War

Box 10.1 at the start of this chapter highlighted the role played by international arms traffickers in the global arms trade. The Cold War created many of these figures, as they exploited the need of the two superpowers for third-party brokers to conduct arms deals with their respective client states in secret. This was felt necessary by both sides to avoid political and public scrutiny, since they were often supplying weapons to highly corrupt and authoritarian regimes.

   Yet the Cold War's conclusion did not mean an end to opportunities for international arms traffickers. For example, the deluge of surplus military weapons and equipment, from Kalashnikovs to tanks, that flooded the market from former Communist states after their political systems crumbled proved a major boon for arms dealers, who helped to redistribute them all across the globe. Moreover, the proliferation of intra-state conflicts in the 1990s (particularly in African nations like Angola, Somalia and Sierra Leone) also proved hugely profitable for many arms traffickers, even though they might have to skirt UN embargoes and sanctions to supply the demand for weapons.

Since it involves unlawful transactions, the black market operates without the official consent of governments, although it is quite possible that corrupt government officials may participate. The black market is used by those who do not have access to the legal trade. In the case of states, this is usually because an official embargo has been put in place, which forbids them from purchasing arms (see below). Many other actors may also be prohibited from buying weapons legally, such as those who have been designated terrorists, which is why they also turn to the black market. Small arms are the ones most commonly traded in the black market, and there are few major trouble spots in the world where the illegal smuggling of weapons does not take place.

The grey market is likely much larger than the black, since – though its transactions may raise many ethical questions – it does not actually involve breaking the law. Grey-market transfers proliferated during the Cold War, as both the USA and the Soviet Union clandestinely supplied friendly states. The USA, for example, supported many authoritarian regimes in Latin America in this way, as part of its efforts to contain the spread of Communism. The questionable morality of supporting dictators who committed serious human rights violations against their own people was one reason these arms transfers were carried out in secret, even when they may not have been illegal. States today continue to play roles in the grey market, whenever it suits their foreign policy agendas to provide arms to other states or non-state actors, when the ethical status of those they are supplying may be dubious, and when they wish to avoid public and media scrutiny.

Despite these differences between the legal and illicit markets for arms, it is also the case that they are intimately connected. Most weapons are manufactured legally, by major arms manufacturers, so they begin their existence as part of the legal supply chain. It is only subsequently that they may get diverted into the black and grey markets. This can happen in various ways, including theft (from manufacturers themselves, military and police forces, or private individuals), illegal and fraudulent sales (perhaps using forged documents) and recovering weapons from battlefields. Even when the major states and corporations involved in the arms trade sell their weapons legally, it frequently happens that they are then resold, or otherwise passed on, to third parties who have been proscribed by international law from obtaining them.

Defenders and critics

It will be useful at this point to examine more closely the issue of how the trade in arms should be viewed. It is undoubtedly the case that most media and academic attention focuses on its downsides, but the trade does have defenders as well as critics. As such, it is important to consider some of the arguments that may be made in its defence:

- States may have legitimate concerns in terms of traditional security threats – that is, they may face either internal or external forces, state or non-state actors, which threaten them with violence. Without the international arms trade, many states would be incapable of producing the weapons necessary to protect themselves and their citizens from such threats. Article 51 of the UN Charter upholds the right of states, both individually and collectively, to self-defence, meaning that international law does, in this context, permit the use of coercive force by governments. Without the arms trade, many might be unable to exercise this right.
- Economics may be another factor. Since the arms trade is worth tens of billions of dollars globally, this means that many jobs, even many towns and cities, are dependent upon it. Although it is easy to demonise large corporations and

shadowy arms dealers for making millions of dollars from their activities, many ordinary people also depend on this trade for their livelihoods.

- Another argument might be framed in terms of equality. As seen, the major suppliers of weapons to the world are the world's major powers, but if they were disallowed from selling them to other states, the consequence would be that these few would retain even more monopolies in many areas of military technology, and possess even greater advantages in terms of military superiority, than they already do. Why, it might be asked, should only rich, powerful nations have access to the most sophisticated weapons?

- The use of arms by groups other than states may also, in some cases, be defensible – for example, when used in insurgencies and revolutions to overthrow repressive regimes, or by liberation movements to free a country from external domination. In at least some conflicts, therefore, supplying arms even to non-state actors may be justifiable.

- 'Guns don't kill people, people kill people.' This slogan, popularised by the US gun rights lobbying group the National Rifle Association (NRA), is intended to make the point that a firearm in itself does not kill anyone: the person wielding it is the one responsible for the consequences of its use. Thus, whatever deaths and suffering critics may lay at the door of the arms trade, its defenders might argue that such criticisms are misplaced – it is the people, whether employees of states, or actors like terrorists and insurgents, who use weapons that are truly responsible, not the weapons themselves, or those who make and sell them. (As will be discussed below, it is partly upon this basis that groups like the NRA oppose not only domestic gun control legislation, but also global arms trade regulation.)

On the other side of the debate, critics of the arms trade can marshal many arguments in response to these defences. As noted previously, even considering just the post-Second World War period, conventional weapons have been, and continue to be, implicated in millions of deaths around the world, with small arms being the biggest killers. This human toll is undoubtedly a prime concern of many critics. However, not all of this can be blamed on the global arms trade – not least because many states, especially the major powers, meet the majority of their needs for military equipment from their own domestic industries. So what, specifically, are the criticisms that may be levelled at the international trade in arms?

- The arms trade fuels conflicts. It is very difficult to establish whether the arms trade is itself a cause of conflicts; as discussed in other chapters, conflicts can in any case rarely be explained by single factors. However, there is *some* evidence of a relationship between the global trade in arms and the incidence of conflicts – for example, one study of conflicts in sub-Saharan Africa found that arms transfers were a significant predictor of an increased probability of war (Craft and Smaldone, 2002). Yet whether or not the arms trade actually makes conflicts more likely, it can be argued that it helps increase their duration and intensity. Perhaps most striking are situations where arms-producing nations supply arms to both sides – for example, during the long Iran–Iraq War (1980 to 1988), many countries, including the UK and the USA, provided weapons to both parties. Similarly, in one of the tensest regions of the world today, the same arms dealers have sold weapons to both India and Pakistan.

- Propping up dictators. Arms sales to nations controlled by authoritarian and oppressive regimes help keep their leaderships in power, by giving them the means to suppress internal dissent and carry out human rights abuses. For example, since rebels in Syria launched an uprising in 2011 against the Assad regime – which was responsible for severely restricting civil liberties such as freedom of speech, as well as torture and mass killings – the government has been able to resist being overthrown in part thanks to the arms it has continued to receive from Russia. As well as giving dictators the physical means of repression, selling them arms may also confer a degree of legitimacy upon them, suggesting that they are accepted by the international community as the legitimate rulers of their nations.

- Hampering development. One of the biggest problems faced by poorer countries when it comes to development is the role that armed conflicts play in disrupting efforts in areas such as strengthening the economy, modernising infrastructure, and improving services like education and healthcare. Even regardless of whether the arms trade does indeed cause or fuel conflicts, it may still be accused of leading states to divert resources from these vital areas of development into arms purchases. For example, Zimbabwe, one of the poorest countries in the world – where life expectancy is below forty, and dire problems like food shortages and HIV/AIDs are prevalent – nonetheless spends hundreds of millions of dollars on purchasing fighter aircraft, armoured vehicles and other weapons from abroad, especially from China, which is today its largest supplier.

- Rather than bringing economic benefits, the arms trade may create significant economic problems. The destruction and loss of life resulting from armed conflicts incurs many economic costs for the nations in which they occur. Yet it may be argued that the arms trade also has many negatives for the citizens of arms-manufacturing countries. It has already been seen that governments often heavily subsidise this sector, which must be paid for by the taxpayers of these nations. Beyond this, critics also suggest that the arms industry is often characterised by high levels of waste, and even corruption, with problems such as bribery and price-fixing being rife. A study by Transparency International, a global anti-corruption NGO, found that the majority of governments make minimal efforts to prevent corruption in their defence departments, and they often display little in the way of accountability or transparency, including in terms of their roles in the buying, selling and distributing of arms (Transparency International, 2013). Again, it is ordinary citizens around the world who ultimately pay for this.

- The arms trade may impact negatively on arms-supplying nations in another, even more serious, way. That is, their weapons transfers may eventually rebound against them. For example, in the 1980s the USA provided arms to Mujahideen fighters in Afghanistan in order to aid them in their fight against Soviet occupation, but out of these forces later emerged the Taliban, who would become a major enemy of America in its post-9/11 War on Terror. Similarly, when NATO launched a military intervention into Libya in 2011, it did so against a regime led by Colonel Gaddafi which had previously been armed by NATO members including Italy, France and the UK. Moreover, given that the line between the legal and illicit arms markets is far from fixed, it is often uncertain into whose hands weapons may ultimately fall – including, perhaps, 'terrorists' who may target the very states that produced the weapons that they use – regardless of to whom they are originally sold.

Controlling and regulating the arms trade: past, present and future

Until recently, the arms trade was set apart from most other areas of international commerce in that it was not governed by any globally accepted set of standards or regulations. Indeed, according to research conducted by Oxfam in 2012, there were more international regulations concerning the trade in bananas than in weapons (Oxfam, 2012). Somewhat ironically, perhaps, toy guns were subject to tighter import and export controls than real ones.

However, in 2013 the situation appeared to change, when an international Arms Trade Treaty (ATT) was finally negotiated and signed by over one hundred nations. However, before considering this treaty and its possible impact, it will be useful to consider how matters stood beforehand.

In terms of the regulation that previously existed, what had evolved over time was a patchwork of national, regional and international laws and treaties, which did not constitute a coherent overall framework. Each nation had its own set of laws and practices relating to the import and export of arms, with large variations between them. This enormously complicated the task of arms control, whether in relation to legal or illicit transfers. There were also great differences between states as to their enthusiasm for pursuing and prosecuting illegal arms traffickers.

At the international level, the strongest restrictions on the sale and purchase of weapons have always been arms embargoes. Embargoes are imposed either by international organisations like the UN or by individual nations, prohibiting the sale of weapons to specified nations (or other actors). This occurs in cases such as when states are deemed guilty of severe human rights abuses, or judged to pose a serious threat to international peace and security. Embargoes are intended both to deny states the means to carry out oppressive or threatening acts and – often in combination with other sanctions – to attempt to force them to change their overall behaviour.

Rarely used during the Cold War, arms embargoes have subsequently become much more frequently implemented; as of 2011, the UN had thirteen arms embargoes in force, and the EU had nineteen (Stockholm International Peace Research Institute, 2012). For example, the UN imposed an arms embargo on North Korea in 2006 following its conducting of a nuclear test, to try to make it abandon its nuclear programme; more recently, in 2011, an arms embargo was imposed by the US and the EU upon Syria, in response to the Syrian government's acts of violence against its own people, with the aim of stopping this internal repression.

Prohibitions may similarly be applied to non-state actors like terrorists, rebels and warlords, who often feature on lists of prohibited buyers. For example, the UN Security Council has passed a number of resolutions (the first in 1999) forbidding the sale of arms to the Taliban and al-Qaeda, together with individuals and groups associated with them, and many governments maintain similar lists against these and other such groups.

The major weakness of arms embargoes and prohibitions is that they are widely violated, frequently with impunity. One problem is that they may be weakly or minimally enforced, with the international community often unwilling to devote the resources necessary to implement and monitor them with sufficient robustness. Another key problem is that it is not just clandestine arms traffickers that are responsible for these violations, but states as well. In fact, one study suggests that almost every arms embargo that has been imposed has been systematically broken by arms-exporting nations (Moore, 2010). For example, China has been accused of breaking UN embargoes against North Korea and Sudan, but all the major arms-producing nations have faced similar accusations in relation to embargoes.

As well as these restrictions on who is supposed to be allowed to acquire conventional weapons, there have for some decades been controls on the *types* that may be produced, traded and used. Box 10.4 provides details of two of the major international treaties relating to restrictions on conventional weapons in these respects, which seek to prohibit or limit the use of those like landmines, incendiary weapons and lasers. Yet here, too, there are crucial problems.

First, there is again the issue of verification and enforcement – in many cases, there is little oversight by international actors to ensure compliance with restrictions. As with all treaties, without meaningful commitment to enforcement by its signatories, a treaty is no more than a piece of paper.

Second, treaties apply only to nations that ratify them. This, inevitably, limits their effectiveness, as non-ratifying states are not covered by their provisions. For example, the 1997 Ottawa Treaty banning anti-personnel landmines has not been ratified by a number of major arms-producing (and buying) nations – including Russia, China, the US and India.

Third, these treaties cover only limited categories of weapons. Although many of the weapons included have effects that are shocking and horrific, there is a degree of selectivity and arbitrariness in those covered. To put it in blunt terms, is being blown up by a landmine worse than being shredded by a machine gun, or hacked to death with a machete? Even if there were full and universal compliance with these treaties, this would not eliminate the many horrors of armed conflicts resulting from the use of 'acceptable' conventional weapons.

There have also been various efforts at the regional level to control the spread and misuse of conventional weapons. A good example of this is the Bamako Declaration on an African Common Position on the Illicit Proliferation, Circulation and Trafficking of Small Arms and Light Weapons, which was adopted by members of the Organisation of African Unity (OAU) in 2000. Subsequently, the African Union (AU) – the successor organisation to the OAU – has sought to develop a strategy to implement the Bamako Declaration across Africa. Some of the ideas included in the Bamako Declaration are for all member states to adopt laws (where they do not exist) to: criminalise the illicit manufacture and trafficking of SALW; enhance the capacity of national law enforcement agencies to tackle these problems, as well as increase cooperation and coordination between those of different states; enhance the responsible management of legally owned arms; encourage the voluntary surrender of illicit arms; and destroy surplus or obsolete stocks of weapons to prevent them falling into dangerous hands. Other arms control agreements have been crafted at the subregional level, for example by the Southern African Development Community (SADC).

The rationale behind such regional (and subregional) efforts has been to facilitate progress in tackling conventional weapons proliferation even in the face of failures to do so at the global level. Moreover, it may make particular sense for organisations in Africa to engage with this, since it is here that so many contemporary armed conflicts have erupted. However, the limitations of this approach are twofold. First, a major problem in regions like Africa is that many states simply lack the resources to implement effective arms control programmes. Second, since the arms trade is a global phenomenon, there is only so much a regional approach is able to achieve.

Box 10.4: Major international treaties banning or limiting the use of particular categories of conventional weapons

One of the most significant international treaties concerning conventional weapons is the UN Convention on Prohibitions or Restrictions on the Use of Certain Conventional Weapons which may be deemed to be Excessively Injurious or to have Indiscriminate Effects (usually shortened to the Convention on Certain Conventional Weapons [CCW]).

The CCW was negotiated in 1980, but has subsequently been revised a number of times, with various additions. Originally signed by 51 states, it now has 109 signatories (though not all are signed up to all parts). The treaty aims to protect both military personnel and civilians from certain categories of conventional weapons that, as its full title indicates, are 'excessively injurious' or have 'indiscriminate effects'. Its operative provisions are contained in what are called protocols, of which it presently has five. These are:

- Protocol I – bans weapons that leave non-detectable fragments in the human body (such as tiny pieces of metal or glass).
- Protocol II – restricts (but does not ban) the use of landmines, booby traps and other devices (e.g. landmines must either be placed in clearly marked minefields, or have self-destruct and self-deactivation mechanisms that trigger after a period of time; the government controlling a territory is responsible for clearing landmines after a conflict has ended).
- Protocol III – restricts (but does not ban) the use of incendiary weapons like flamethrowers (e.g. they should not be used against civilians, and forests and other vegetation may be targeted only when being used as cover by military forces).
- Protocol IV (added 1995) – bans the use of lasers specifically designed to blind, and obliges signatories to make every effort to ensure that other laser weapons do not cause permanent blindness.
- Protocol V (added 2003) – relates to the clearance of explosive remnants of war, such as unexploded shells, grenades and bombs. As with landmines in Protocol II, responsibility for dealing with these after conflicts have concluded lies with the government in control of the territory in which they are found.

Another major treaty is the Convention on the Prohibition of the Use, Stockpiling, Production and Transfer of Anti-Personnel Mines and on their Destruction (also known as the Ottawa Treaty or the Anti-Personnel Mine Ban Convention). It was created in 1997, and presently has 161 signatories. Whereas the CCW only places restrictions on the use of landmines, this treaty bans their production and use outright.

Given the deficiencies and limitations of existing treaties and regional approaches, a key ambition of advocates of greater arms control has long been to have a comprehensive ATT adopted at the global level. The major push in this direction began in 2001, developing out of the UN Conference on the Illicit Trade in Small Arms and Light Weapons in All Its Aspects of that year. Since then, the demand for an ATT was promoted in particular by a network of NGOs – including Oxfam, Amnesty International and the International Action Network on Small Arms (IANSA) – that have campaigned together as part of the Control Arms Coalition.

In 2006, the possibility of such a treaty began to be discussed seriously within the UN, and after deliberations by the General Assembly, a Group of Governmental Experts was assembled by the Secretary-General to investigate and consider what its provisions might be. Formal negotiations for an ATT were initiated at a conference in New York in July 2012, with representatives from across the globe. Eventually, after lengthy negotiations – and a further conference in March 2013 – the final terms of a treaty were agreed, which was adopted by the General Assembly on 2 April 2013. As of June 2014, it has been signed by 118 states and ratified by 40. To come into force, it requires ratification by fifty states, so it will do so only if and when this happens. The main provisions are set out in Box 10.5.

To supporters of arms control, the creation of the ATT represents a major step forward. Its merits include that it covers a relatively broad range of conventional weapons, it places some significant obligations on exporting states (including to regulate and monitor arms sales), it should limit the ability of both repressive regimes and dangerous non-state actors like terrorists to acquire weapons, and it creates greater transparency (in the form of annual reporting). Perhaps most important is the simple fact that, for the first time in history, it establishes binding international standards in relation to the trade in conventional weapons.

Box 10.5: The Arms Trade Treaty (2013)

The ATT applies to the trade in the seven categories of conventional weapons covered by the UN Register of Conventional Arms noted earlier, as well as small arms and light weapons. Some of the most important provisions include requiring states:

- To adopt basic legal regulations for the control of weapons transfers across international borders and create oversight mechanisms to ensure compliance.
- Not to authorise transfers that would undermine international peace and security.
- Not to authorise transfers that would violate their international obligations – e.g. to respect UN arms embargoes or treaties like the Geneva Conventions.
- Not to sell weapons to regimes likely to commit severe human rights abuses such as targeted killings of civilians, ethnic cleansing or genocide.
- Not to sell weapons to non-state actors like terrorists or international criminals.
- To take steps to prevent weapons being diverted to parties other than those to whom they are directly selling.
- To submit an annual report detailing their imports and exports of weapons covered by the treaty and how they have been implementing its provisions.

Source:
www.un.org/disarmament/ATT/docs/Draft_ATT_text_27_Mar_2013-E.pdfa

---

At the same time, the treaty has definite weaknesses. First, there are gaps in what the treaty covers – including anything that does not fall within the classifications of the UN Register of Conventional Arms or what may be considered SALW. For example, the UN Register may not cover support systems and vehicles (like those designed for transport and refuelling) or the most modern technological developments, like unmanned combat air vehicles ('drones'). Second, much of the responsibility for control and monitoring is left to states themselves, which may raise questions about how much independent verification is likely to take place. Third, the way the treaty is worded may create loopholes that allow arms-exporting nations to get around its provisions. For example, in assessing whether or not a sale will fall foul of the treaty's prohibitions (such as when weapons are likely to be used to commit severe abuses of human rights), the standard of judgment that states must apply is to determine if there is an 'over-riding risk' of negative consequences resulting. However, since the word over-riding is not defined, it is essentially left to states themselves to evaluate the level of risk – and if they judge that it is limited or minimal, it is uncertain what penalties (if any) a state faces for being wrong in its assessment if it turns out that a buyer of its weapons does use them for prohibited purposes.

However, perhaps the most significant obstacle to the ATT's success is that it may never be ratified by the states that count the most in the global arms trade, the major exporting and importing nations of the world. As of June 2014, although it has been ratified by states including the UK, France and Germany, it has not been ratified by China, Russia, India, Israel or the US.

Many of these non-ratifying states have their own objections to the treaty, as well as domestic opponents to its ratification. To illustrate this point, it is worth considering the position of the world's largest arms exporter, the United States. Although the US Secretary of State John Kerry signed the ATT in 2013, it has not been ratified by the US Senate (which is necessary for its adoption). This is because the treaty is opposed by a number of influential interest groups that defend the right of private individuals to own firearms – including the NRA – on the grounds that they believe that any global arms trade treaty would lead to the domestic curtailment of Americans' rights of gun ownership (Smith, 2013). Although treaty supporters argue that the ATT will not affect domestic gun rights, these groups remain staunchly opposed. Since gun rights groups have significant political influence in the US, this may well make achieving the support necessary for ratification of the ATT among US politicians impossible.

Other non-ratifying states have their own domestic political circumstances that may also make ratification unlikely. The net result may be that, even if the ATT does achieve the required goal of ratification by fifty states to come into force, if this does not include the world's largest exporters and importers of conventional weapons, it will lack the global reach necessary to be truly effective.

Conclusion

As long as there is war and conflict in the world, there will doubtless be an international trade in arms. The nature of this trade is not static, and the nations which are the major sellers and buyers of conventional weapons may change as the twenty-first century continues. Nonetheless, it is almost certain that it will not disappear, at least for the foreseeable future.

In the case of the legal trade in arms, defenders may argue that states – other than those on embargo lists – have every right to procure whatever arms they wish, though critics may point out that this ignores the great harm weapons may cause to the *people* living in states, and that even arms that are bought and sold by 'legitimate' actors in the first instance may often end up in highly questionable hands. Yet efforts at controlling and regulating this trade at the international level have, so far, met with limited success. One of the major difficulties in creating a system of arms trade regulation that can command universal support is that states have dramatically varying interests. While nations that suffer from the trade may have interests in seeing it more strongly regulated, the major arms-manufacturing nations gain not only large profits but significant global influence from their weapons exports, so they have vested interests in very light regulation, at most. It may be only a small handful of nations that dominate the trade in conventional weapons, but without their agreement to any arms control treaty, it is unlikely to be very successful.

Ultimately, though, the arms trade cannot be understood in isolation, but only as part of the broader picture of international affairs. That is, it only exists, at least in the form that it does, because the world is characterised by features such as conflict, poverty, political and social oppression, and power imbalances both between and within states. Those who campaign against the arms trade tend to focus largely on the supply side of the equation, looking for stricter ways to control and regulate the governments and corporations that produce and sell arms. Yet it might be argued that any fundamental solution needs to focus at least as much on the demand side – in other words, to address why states and other actors seek to acquire weapons in the first place. This, of course, requires tackling the deep-rooted causes of conflicts, and issues like global political and economic inequality – even harder tasks than passing new laws and regulations.

Summary points

1   Conventional weapons may be defined as any that do not fall into the category of WMDs, from pistols to battleships – small arms and light weapons (SALW) in particular are responsible for most of the deaths in conflicts around the globe.
2   The international arms trade is big business – globally, arms exports are worth approximately $70 billion a year.
3   There is both a legal and an illicit trade in arms, though the boundaries between the two are not fixed – most illicitly acquired weapons begin life as part of the legal trade, before being diverted.
4   The trade has both defenders (who point out, for example, that all states have a right to arm themselves for self-defence) and critics (who focus on what they believe is the arms trade's role in fuelling conflicts and widespread suffering).
5   Attempts to regulate the arms trade have had only limited success – the 2013 Arms Trade Treaty may be more comprehensive than any previous treaty, but it remains to be seen whether it secures sufficiently wide support to be effective.

Recommended reading

Farah, D. and Braun, S. *Merchant of Death: Money, Guns, Planes, and the Man Who Makes War Possible*, Hoboken, NJ: John Wiley and Sons, 2007.
Feinstein, A. *The Shadow World: Inside the Global Arms Trade*, London: Hamish Hamilton, 2011.
Larsen, J.A. and Wirtz, J.J. (eds) *Arms Control and Cooperative Security*, Boulder, CO: Lynne Rienner Publishers, 2009.
Pierre, A.J. (ed.) *Cascade of Arms: Managing Conventional Weapons Proliferation*, Cambridge, Mass.: World Peace Foundation, 1997.
Stohl, R. and Grillot, S. *The International Arms Trade*, Cambridge: Polity Press, 2009.

11 Terrorism

Andrew Moran

Box 11.1: Terrorism and the aftermath of 9/11

In the aftermath of the al-Qaeda-led attacks on the United States of America on 11 September 2001, concerns about international terrorism rose to the top of the political agenda in many Western countries. America's own response would be to launch a war against terror, which would see it commit itself to two unpopular wars in Afghanistan and Iraq, and carry out increasing surveillance on its own citizens. Cold War concerns about 'Reds under the beds' were replaced by fears of a growing threat from Islamic extremists. Subsequent attacks in London, Madrid, Bali and elsewhere seemed to confirm the anxiety of many. Despite the number of terrorist attacks in the West declining in the years that followed, for much of the public, terrorism remains a tangible security threat.

Introduction

The French Revolution is often cited as witnessing the first use of the word 'terror' as a method of using violence to gain political results. It was then that Robespierre and the Jacobins launched a 'Reign of Terror' (from 1793 to 1794) which involved the mass execution of so-called enemies of the Revolution. Before then, however, there had been many examples of what might be called terrorism. Every year on 5th November the British celebrate a failed terrorist attack by Guy Fawkes and his associates to kill James I and blow up the British parliament in 1605. Earlier examples include the Zealots of Israel against the Roman Empire, or the Thugs of India.

Box 11.2: The four waves of modern terrorism

According to David Rapoport, modern history has witnessed four waves of terrorism.

The first began in the 1880s and was marked by anarchist activity in Russia and Europe, when terrorist groups sought to assassinate monarchs, politicians, and other prominent figures in the hope of turning the masses into revolutionaries. An early example of this was the assassination of Tsar Alexander II on 1 March 1881 by the Narodnaya Volya, or People's Will, a small group of Russian constitutionalists opposed to Tsarist rule.

The second wave began in the 1920s and continued until the 1960s, and was notable for strong anticolonial movements, typified by small states seeking to overthrow their colonial rulers. This would peak with the independence movements in the post-Second World War era in India, Pakistan, Algeria, Indonesia, Nigeria, Kenya, Vietnam, Cyprus, Israel and elsewhere.

The third wave had its roots in the 1960s, when the New Left and communist groups began carrying out terrorist attacks exemplified by so-called 'urban guerrilla' groups which sought to topple corrupt governments and challenge the alleged growing inequalities between the rich and poor. This included the Baader–Meinhof gang in West Germany, anti-Vietnam protest groups such as the Weathermen in the US, and a number of organisations in Latin America.

The final wave began in 1979 with the Iranian revolution and the invasion of Afghanistan by the Soviet Union. This, Rapoport suggests, unleashed a wave of religious terrorism that exists to this day, culminating in the creation of al-Qaeda.

(Rapoport, 2004).

However, definitions of what a terrorist is or what a terrorist does remain controversial.

Defining terrorism

Alex Schmid and Albert Jongman, in their work *Political Terrorism*, argued that there are over a hundred definitions of terrorism that can be identified, including 'violence', 'political goals', 'indiscrimination of targets', and 'victimization of civilians' (Schmid and Jongman, 2005).

Despite numerous attempts, the United Nations has consistently struggled to agree on a definition. In the aftermath of the al-Qaeda-led attacks on the US on 11 September 2001 (known as 9/11) the UN agreed to tackle terrorism, but it could not actually agree on what it was. A common definition used is that adopted by the United States of America, which defines terrorism as 'premeditated, politically motivated violence perpetrated against non-combatant targets by sub-national groups or clandestine agents, usually intended to influence an audience' (Title 22, United States Code, Section 2656f [d]). This definition could be applied to some of the American revolutionaries who fought during the American War of Independence that began in 1776.

Some events attract almost universal agreement that they are terrorist attacks. A good example is 9/11, which saw nineteen men hijack four planes and then crash two of them into the World Trade Center towers and one into the Pentagon, with the fourth plane, most likely intended to hit the White House or Congress, being brought down in a field in Pennsylvania. In total almost 3,000 people were killed. Such was the international condemnation that even the French newspaper *La Monde*, which had been a frequent critic of American foreign policy, declared 'We are all American'. However, as Hammond noted, some Muslims viewed this as an attempt by Islam to 'fight back' against the 'imperial powers' of the US and the West (Hammond, 2003: 83).

Box 11.3: The case of Anders Breivik

On 22 July 2011, Anders Breivik, a white, middle-class Norwegian, detonated a car bomb outside the Prime Minister's office in Oslo, Norway, killing seven government employees and one civilian and wounding thirty other civilians. Two hours later, on Utoya Island, he opened fire on a Norwegian Labour Party associated youth camp. In total, he killed seventy-seven people and injured seventy-five others.

In the lengthy trial that followed his arrest, controversy surrounded the issue of whether Breivik's actions were those of a sane man. The first Court-ordered psychiatric report stated that they could not be, claiming he suffered from 'paranoid schizophrenia', influenced by online gaming culture and right-wing propaganda. This report, however, was met with a barrage of opposition, forcing the Court to take the unusual step of commissioning a second report. This would conclude that Breivik was sane, and, at worst, exhibited a personality disorder.

Breivik himself argued that his actions were a justified response to what he regarded as a threat from an expanding Islamic population in Europe. He also claimed that he was part of a network of similar right-wing activists who opposed multiculturalism and left-wing governments and political groups. In other words, he carried out his attack for political reasons.

Though most people would regard his acts as those of a madman, and a so-called 'lone wolf' who acted alone, can he, in fact, be classified as a terrorist?

The often-quoted cliché that 'one man's terrorist is another man's freedom fighter', though simplistic, does shed some light on the difficulties surrounding the debate. Definitions appear to be subjective rather than objective, and are influenced by a state's domestic politics. For example, to the British government and the Ulster loyalists all violence carried out by the Irish Republican Army (IRA) was terrorism, but to Sinn Fein, the IRA's political wing, it was legitimate violence. To many Israelis, the Hezbollah suicide bombers in Jerusalem or the regular bombings of Israel carried out by Hamas are terrorist acts; to many Arabs, however, Israel is a terrorist state, illegally occupying land and targeting Palestinians in Gaza and the West Bank.

Even Nelson Mandela was classified as a terrorist by the ruling white supremacist party in South Africa, but to many around the world he was a hero in a valid struggle against apartheid. Indeed, the existence of the African National Congress raised a fundamental question about human security. Whose security was more important – the minority whites who governed the country, or the subjugated majority black population who were defined as second-class citizens and treated accordingly? Though the ANC mostly used mass demonstrations and industrial sabotage to further its aims, was it justified in bombing cinemas and churches used by white South Africans?

As Machiavelli famously noted, today's enemy can be tomorrow's friend. Mandela is not the only example. A number of terrorist leaders have become state or political leaders, blurring the boundaries further as terrorists become legitimate leaders. Martin McGuinness, the Deputy First Minister of Northern Ireland, is a good example, having previously been a member of the provisional Irish Republican Army. Menachem Begin and Yitzhak Shamir led the terrorist groups Irgun and Lehi (Fighters for the Freedom of Israel) respectively in the 1940s. Begin would go on to win the Nobel Peace Prize with Yassir Arafat, president of the Palestinian Authority, who had been leader of the revolutionary group Fatah. Shamir would later be elected Prime Minster of Israel.

Bruce Hoffman perhaps offers the best description, arguing that terrorism involves 'the deliberate creation and exploitation of fear through violence or the threat of violence in the pursuit of political change' (Hoffman, 2006: 40).

Box 11.4: Definition of terrorism

Bruce Hoffman suggests the what distinguishes terrorism from other acts is that it is:

- ineluctably political in aims and motives;
- violent – or, equally important, threatens violence;
- designed to have far-reaching psychological repercussions beyond the immediate victim or target;
- conducted by an organisation with an identifiable chain of command or conspiratorial cell structure (whose members wear no uniform or identifying insignia); and
- perpetrated by a subnational group or non-state entity.

Hoffman suggests that 'Terrorism is designed to create power where there is none or to consolidate power where there is very little. Through the publicity generated by their violence, terrorists seek to obtain the leverage, influence and power they otherwise lack to effect political change on either a local or an international scale.'

(Hoffman, 2006: 1–42)

This can take many forms. The *psychological* fear of terrorism can result in people fearing to leave their home, go to a public place, or even use a form of public transport. After the 9/11 attacks in the US there was a notable decline in airline passenger numbers. In the aftermath of the 7 July 2005 (7/7) bombing of the public transport system in London, many took to the streets and cycled.

The target can be *economic* – for example, IRA truck bombs in the City of London in 1992 and 1993 and in Manchester in 1996, the Islamic extremist attacks on the World Trade Center in 1993 and 2001, or the Bali bombing in 2002, which targeted tourism.

It can take the form of *political* assassinations, such as those carried out by the Baader–Meinhof Gang, the Red Brigade, the IRA's assassination of Lord Mountbatten in 1979, the Irish National Liberation Army's murdering of Airey Neave in the same year, and the failed attempt to kill the British Prime Minister Margaret Thatcher in 1994.

Alternatively the focus can be the *military*, such as the use of Improvised Explosive Devices (IEDs) against American and British troops in Iraq and Afghanistan, or the al-Qaeda-led attacks on the *USS Cole* in 1998 and the Pentagon in 2001.

An important distinction also needs to be made between transnational or global terrorism and national or regional terrorism. Here there is a fundamental difference. According to Paul Wilkinson there are a number of different groups that can be distinguished (2006: 4). There are *ethno-nationalist groups*, such as the Basque separatists Euzkadi Ta Askatasuna (ETA), the Tamil Tigers of Sri Lanka, and the nationalists seeking to create a united Republic of Ireland (such as the IRA). There are *ideological groups*, for example the Red Brigade in Italy in the 1970s and 1980s who hoped to create a neo-communist state. *Single issue groups* include militant ecology groups such as the Earth Liberation Front and the Animal Liberation Front, or the anti-abortionist groups in the US. *Religious groups* include the Lord's Resistance Army in Uganda, the Aum Shindrikyo sect that sought to commit mass murder with the use of sarin gas on the Tokyo underground in the 1990s, Hamas in the Middle East, and, of course, al-Qaeda. In all these groups (with the exception of al-Qaeda), the demands of the terrorist groups are national or regional. Al-Qaeda is unusual in that its aims are global.

Box 11.5: Al-Qaeda

Al-Qaeda was originally formed in 1988 by Saudi-born Osama bin Laden to oppose the Soviet Union's invasion of Afghanistan. However, its aims quickly expanded to demand the establishment of a pro-Islamic caliphate across the Muslim world. This would include opposition to America's increasing role in the Middle East in the aftermath of Iraq's failed invasion of Kuwait in 1990–91, which bin Laden argued was propping up corrupt Muslim regimes that he branded as 'apostate' due to alleged Western influence. In February 1998, al-Qaeda issued a statement under the heading 'the World Islamic Front for Jihad Against the Jews and Crusaders', saying that it was the duty of all Muslims to kill Americans and their allies anywhere in the world – whether military or civilians.

Its campaign of violence would be responsible for a number of attacks on the US overseas, including the August 1998 bombings of the American embassies in Kenya and Tanzania, which killed over 200 and injured a further 4,000 people, the October 2000 bombing on the *USS Cole* in a harbour in Yemen, and the 9/11 attacks on American soil.

Since 2002, al-Qaeda has carried out numerous attacks throughout the world, and there are now affiliate groups such as al-Qaeda in the Arabian Peninsula, al-Qaeda in the Lands of the Islamic Maghreb, and al-Qaeda in Iraq.

On 2 May 2011 bin Laden was killed by American Navy Seals at his compound in Abbottabad, Pakistan. He was replaced by his deputy, Ayman Al-Zawahiri, who remains the head of al-Qaeda.

Who are the terrorists?

For security analysts, the issue of who the terrorists are and why they are carrying out their violence is fundamental to addressing the problem. Here, it is important to deconstruct the myths that exist in the popular media and political debate. Public perceptions in the West are that terrorism is a constant threat, and yet the actual number of attacks that have been carried out successfully in the US and Europe have been quite small relative to the rest of the world.

In the ten years that followed 9/11, for example, approximately thirty people were killed in terrorist attacks in the US. Of these, sixteen were killed by Islamic sympathisers, including the thirteen soldiers killed by Major Nidal Hasan at Ford Hood, Texas in 2009, but the remainder had more diverse motivations. Five were killed in 2001 from an anthrax attack most likely perpetrated by an American scientist who later committed suicide; two were suspected to have been killed by members of the Minutemen American Defense group in Arizona in 2009; an abortion provider was killed in Wichita, Kansas in 2009; and two died in Austin, Texas when a man crashed his light plane into a government building over a dispute with the Inland Revenue Service. In August 2012 six people were killed in a Sikh temple in Wisconsin by a known white supremacist.

According to the Global Terrorism Database, the number of attacks in the US has actually fallen significantly since 2001, averaging sixteen a year between 2002 and 2010, in contrast to an average of 41.3 terrorist attacks a year during the period between 1991 and 2000. In the pre-9/11 era the majority of attacks were carried out by domestic terrorists, the most notorious of which was the bombing of the Alfred P. Murrah Federal Building in Oklahoma City in 1995 by Timothy McVeigh, which killed 168 people and injured over 680 more.

High profile events in the West tend to grab the attention of the media, such as the attack on the Boston Marathon in 2013 which left three dead and 264 injured. However, the most damaging terrorist attack that has occurred since 9/11 was actually carried out by Maoist rebels against an army barracks in Nepal in 2004, killing 518 people and injuring 216 others – the majority of whom were the rebels themselves. This event received surprisingly little coverage in the Western media.

In fact, according to the US Department of State, in the last ten years the majority of deaths from terrorism have occurred outside the West. In 2013 there were over 9,700 terrorist attacks in ninety-three countries, resulting in more than 17,800 deaths. The majority were in the Near East and South Asia, with over half of the attacks (57%) in just three countries: Iraq, Pakistan and Afghanistan.

Box 11.6: The ten countries with the most terrorist attacks, 2013

Country	Attacks	Fatalities
Iraq	2,852	7,046
Pakistan	2,212	2,891
Afghanistan	1,443	3,697
India	690	464
Philippines	652	432
Thailand	477	253
Yemen	424	622
Nigeria	341	2,003
Somalia	331	641
Egypt	315	243

Source: Statistics gathered by the National Consortium for the Study of Terrorism and Responses to Terrorism, available at http://www.start.umd.edu/news/majority-2013-terrorist-attacks-occurred-just-few-countries

---

This follows a global pattern since the events of 9/11. It also reflects another development, which is that Sunni extremists increasingly account for the greatest number of terrorist attacks, the largest proportion of which continue to be against Shia Muslims rather than Western forces. In other words, Islamic terrorists statistically kill more Muslims than they do non-Muslims. For example, in 2013 al-Qaeda and its affiliates killed over 2,000 people, whilst the Taliban killed 2,400 in 641 attacks in Afghanistan and Pakistan. Nigeria is now on the list primarily because of the Islamic militant group Boko Haram.

It would be a mistake, however, to assume that all terrorist acts are religiously motivated. Secular, political and anarchist groups were responsible for 2,283 attacks in 2011, resulting in 1,926 deaths. These groups were diverse in nature, including the Revolutionary Armed Forces of Colombia (FARC), the Communist Party of India-Maoist (CPI-Maoist), the New People's Army/Communist Party of the Philippines, and the Kurdistan Worker's Party in Turkey. In 2010 there were over forty terrorist attacks in Northern Ireland carried out by the Real IRA and other dissident groups, leading the British government to conclude that this represented a growing threat to security (*2011 NCTC Annual Report*, 2012; *Contest*, 2011).

Though many expect terrorists to come in the form of a suicide bomber, in actuality these accounted for just 5% of terrorist attacks in 2013, with armed attacks and bombings using IEDs, the preferred method, making up over 75% of all terrorist attacks. However, suicide bombings are extremely effective, being five times as lethal as non-suicide attacks and accounting for 21% of all terrorism-related fatalities. As Bloom notes, they are attractive to certain groups because 'The suicide bomber is the ultimate smart bomb, a thinking and breathing missile that can change directions, cross a street, or delay detonation depending on the circumstances' (Bloom, 2011: 19).

Indeed, Bloom offers an interesting analysis of who the terrorists actually are. The Western image of a terrorist is a suicide bomber who is a young, single Muslim man. Bloom argues that this needs to be challenged, because many terrorists are actually women. Female suicide bombers, for example, are often more effective than men, partly because they do not fit the male stereotype. This was particularly the case in Iraq, where women made up a third of all suicide bombers in 2007, while the Liberation Tigers of Tamil Eelam in Sri Lanka were believed to have the world's largest number of suicide bombers. Of this latter group, their supporters were Hindu, rather than Muslim, and they were nearly 40% female.

Part of the reason why the role of women in terrorist organisations is not fully understood is because they tend not to rise to positions of authority. In many organisations evidence suggests that women actively seek to join terrorist groups rather than being coerced, but even in groups where women number 30–60% of the suicide bombers, they rarely achieve a significant leadership role. Though Astrid Proll and Ulrike Meinhof held important leadership positions in the Baader–Meinhof Group, they were the exception to the rule.

Indeed, from a security perspective the role of women increasingly makes a mockery of so-called profiling. A good example is Muriel Degauque, a Belgian convert to Islam who on 9 November 2005 crashed her car full of explosives into a US convoy in Baquba, Iraq – becoming the first known Western women to be a suicide bomber (Bloom, 2011). She succeeded partly because she did not match what the security forces had been warned to expect.

Can states be terrorists?

Any definition of terrorism must take into account the idea that states can be terrorists too. History is littered with examples. Stalin used terror systematically to consolidate his power, massacring and exiling Communist Party members and ethnic groups during the 1930s. Hitler would do the same in Germany and throughout Europe, including the genocide of over six million Jews, Gypsies, homosexuals and the disabled. The Khmer Rouge would kill over a million people in Cambodia in the mid-1970s as part of their attempt to purge the country of Western influence in its crusade to go back to 'Year Zero'. In the 1970s, so-called 'death squads' in the right-wing military dictatorships of Argentina, Chile and Greece targeted political opponents, human rights and aid workers, student groups, labour organisers, journalists, and others.

Britain does not escape unscathed from this debate. During India's struggle for independence the British massacred 379 civilians in Amritsar in 1919, firing until their bullets ran out in an attempt to squash rebellion in the province of Punjab. Recently released evidence about the activities of the British in Kenya in the 1950s has also highlighted the use of violence and torture on the Mau-Mau tribe.

'What is called terrorism,' Brian Jenkins argues, 'thus seems to depend on one's point of view. Use of the term implies a moral judgement; and if one party can successfully attach the label terrorist to its opponent, then it has indirectly persuaded others to adopt its moral viewpoint' (in Hoffman, 2006: 32). In other words, any definition is inevitably subjective. For example, the National Counterterrorism Centre estimates that in 2011 over 12,500 people were killed in terrorist attacks. During the Second World War, twenty-four hours of air raids by the Allies killed five times as many in one night in Dresden. One is a crime, says international law, the other a legitimate act of war.

Box 11.7: Can states be terrorists? A case study

When seeking to define terrorism, a particular sticking point at the United Nations has been whether state-sponsored terrorism should be included – i.e. should states that illegitimately use violence on their own civilians, or on the civilians of another state, be classified as terrorists?

A number of Islamic states and groups support such an inclusion, citing the Israel–Palestine and Russia–Chechnya struggles which, they argue, have seen the use of state violence within a definition of terrorism. Politicians in the West tend to disagree.

However, some Western commentators have argued for a broadening out. Noam Chomsky regularly argues that the West, and in particular the United States of America, is a practitioner of state-sponsored terrorism, citing the invasions of Afghanistan and Iraq, the continuing support of Israel, and the American-backed replacement of a number of governments in Latin America. This is a view supported by Samuel Huntington, who wrote, 'While the US regularly denounces various countries as "rogue states," in the eyes of many countries it is becoming the rogue superpower ... the single greatest threat to their societies' (Huntington, 1999).

A good example of this is the controversial use of Unmanned Controlled Aerial Vehicles – so-called drones – by the Obama administration. Since coming into office in 2009 President Obama has increased the use of drones sixfold, striking targets in Yemen, Pakistan, Afghanistan, Iraq, Libya, Somalia and the Philippines. In Pakistan alone, the Brookings Institution estimates that between 2004 and 2012 at least 1,932 militants were killed, with a further 1,618 non-militant fatalities. Brookings suggests the actual numbers of deaths are most likely significantly higher (Guerin, 2012; Livingston and O'Hanlon, 2012).

The Obama administration argues that the use of drones is justifiable because they have successfully targeted and eliminated key members of al-Qaeda's leadership, while ensuring that the involvement of American troops on the ground is minimised. However, as the Pew Research Centre argues, the use of drones has fed 'A widespread perception that the US acts unilaterally and does not consider the interests of other countries' (Pew, 2012). It may encourage further terrorism, as each civilian death becomes a recruiting tool for terrorist groups. It also raises serious questions about US compliance with international law, and might possibly constitute a war crime if civilian lives are deliberately put at risk.

Terrorism and globalisation

One interesting outcome of 9/11 is not just that terrorism was catapulted up the international agenda, but also that analysts were forced to examine the links between domestic and international events and to consider the existence of terrorism in the context of globalisation.

There is a startling difference in the technology now available to terrorists in the twenty-first century. The global revolution in transportation, technology and communications has opened up new opportunities for terrorist groups. In particular, the internet has allowed terrorists to transport money and information and build support in an unprecedented fashion. 9/11 itself was planned in Afghanistan, incorporating terrorist cells in both Hamburg, Germany and the US, and it is estimated that 40% of the money used to carry out the attack most likely passed through the financial systems of the World Trade Center in New York. Though the terrorists used box-cutter knifes to hijack the places, they effectively turned the ultimate mode of globalised transport – the plane – into a missile. The attack itself was carried live through global media networks, maximising exposure, striking fear into Westerners, ensuring the event was also a successful recruiting tool, and reinforcing Osama bin Laden's position as the de facto leader of the movement against the West.

Technological change and the resulting revolution in communications and information storage and retrieval has allowed a wide variety of groups to exploit a remarkable range of new approaches to enhance visibility. It is not unusual for terrorist groups to film their activities, distributing propaganda by CD, DVD and the internet. In many ways this is a natural progression from the TV coverage of hijackings in the late 1960s and early 1970s which was instrumental in bringing the cause of the Palestinian liberation groups to the world's attention. In the last decade the extensive coverage of the violence in Afghanistan and Iraq carried out by Western troops, broadcast via satellite television and propaganda websites and videos, has been used by radical Islamic groups to recruit further support. Prisoner abuse in Guantanamo Bay and Abu Ghraib, with estimates suggesting that at least 100,000 people have been detained without trial, further stoked the fire.

The dangers posed by new technology were highlighted further in November 2012, when the entire mobile phone network was switched off in Pakistan during a week of Shia festivals. The fear was that Sunni extremists would target Shia events. It was hoped that switching off the networks would make it harder to use IEDs, which are often detonated remotely by mobile phones. In actuality, the Sunni terrorists switched back to suicide bombing, but the point about technology had been exposed in a remarkable way.

Politicians often speak of their fears that a terrorist may get their hands on a weapon of mass destruction, usually a nuclear device. This fear is made more salient by the illegal trading in nuclear materials and technology that has been exposed, most notably by a Pakistan scientist who sold secrets to other governments, and the development of weapons in rogue states, such as North Korea. This, it has been suggested, may lead to the use of a bomb in a suitcase – a so-called 'dirty bomb'. However, scientists dispute whether this is possible – and, more relevant to the terrorists themselves, there is the matter of cost. Developing such a weapon would take huge sums of money and expertise. A terrorist's preferred choice of weapon is one which is much cheaper – the roadside bomb, or the suicide bomber.

Continuing developments in technology have raised a new concern for security analysts – the 'laptop in a briefcase'. Governments now fear terrorist groups using cyberspace to hack into utility companies, defence networks or financial institutions. This would involve little cost, its source would be most likely untraceable, and it has the potential to cause significantly more damage than a dirty bomb. It is a threat that appears to be exponential in scope, and one which governments are now committing vast sums of money to tackle.

We have also seen the development of 'swarming' by terrorist groups. This involves small numbers of terrorists coming from several directions to hit a target or several targets at the same time, overloading the ability of the security services to respond.

This has been used frequently in Iraq and Afghanistan, but perhaps the most dramatic occurrence was seen in the November 2008 attacks in Mumbai by members of the Lashkar-e-Taiba group. Here ten men broke into five two-man teams and struck simultaneously at a number of different sites. It took more than three days to capture or kill these terrorists, during which period over 160 people were killed. Part of the problem was that the security forces were configured to cope with a single threat rather than multiple, simultaneous ones. Arguably, 9/11 and the 7/7 bombings in London, when four suicide bombers killed 56 and injured 784, were swarm attacks.

The growing use of modern technology touches on another debate within the security community, which is the role of failed states in harbouring terrorist groups. Though the concept of a failed state is difficult to define, we can say that the lack of effective government and policing in states such as Afghanistan, Pakistan, Yemen and Somalia has allowed terrorist networks to flourish. However, terrorists also need infrastructure and modern technology to thrive, and as Smith has noted, al-Qaeda does not 'map onto state structures' but 'works in the spaces between them' (Smith, 2002).

The response of the West to 9/11 failed to fully appreciate this change. By invading Afghanistan, and later Iraq, the West was effectively attempting to impose a Realist, state-centric approach onto a non-state actor, fighting a 'war against terror' through an outdated Cold War mentality in which two forces had mutually exclusive agendas and global interests. It was an approach that could not work. How, asked critics, could a state defeat a stateless organisation?

Furthermore, the West arguably made a strategic mistake in the wake of 9/11 by focusing on global terrorism and the rogue states that support it, while simultaneously de-emphasising national and regional terrorism, misguidedly seeing those as nothing more than a local manifestation of a global campaign of violence. Al-Qaeda would try to take advantage of this by seeking to bring together different national and local conflicts, for example in the Maghreb, against what they saw as the common enemy – oppression by the West, represented by the cultural, economic, political and military power of the United States of America. Al-Qaeda was not entirely successful, as it is clear that it does not represent mainstream Islam, and nor is it typical of the Muslim world. However, many analysts now talk of the 'al-Qaedafication' of terrorism, where individuals carry out acts independently of al-Qaeda but claim to be furthering, or be sympathetic towards, the aims of al-Qaeda, such as the 7/7 bombers in London. Some even suggest that al-Qaeda now operates almost like a multinational, franchising out its operations.

Tackling terrorism

One lesson of the West's response to 9/11 must be to recognise the characteristics and roots of national and regional terrorism rather than seeing all terrorism as being transnational or global in nature. By doing this, it will allow terrorism to be challenged not just militarily, but through other means. Pre-9/11 the most common response to terrorist activity involved traditional methods such as intelligence gathering and policing. The intention would be to thwart an attack before it was launched, or arrest enough members of a group to limit its capabilities, if not force it to decline in influence. Such an approach was used by the FBI in the US when tackling such groups as the Weathermen in the late 1960s.

More recently, British intelligence services were able to thwart an attempt by al-Qaeda to explode up to ten Atlantic planes in mid-flight from Heathrow to the US in 2006. Similarly, plots involving ricin in London's suburbs have been uncovered.

A second approach, which is perhaps more controversial, is for governments to carry out direct military action against terrorist groups. The invasion of Afghanistan and the use of drones to target key members of al-Qaeda's leadership structure have already been noted, but there are many other examples, such as the violent defeat of the Liberation Tigers of Tamil Eelam by the Sri Lankan military in 2009, or the assassination of Hamas leaders by Israeli security forces.

The military solution can prove to be unpopular, effectively becoming a recruitment tool for the terrorists. By embarking on a military strategy against al-Qaeda, for example, the Bush administration effectively elevated bin Laden to an international status vastly out of proportion to his actual power. Instead of labelling him an international criminal, the West's reaction implied that terrorism was a military problem, rather than one that could be won through patient intelligence, domestic security measures, and co-operation between governments, security and law-enforcement agencies. The West may have argued that the intervention in Afghanistan and Iraq would prevent terrorists exporting political violence into neighbouring states and elsewhere, but in actuality it has done little to bring stability or improve security in these countries.

Terrorists have also been known to use unconventional or asymmetrical responses to fight against a more technologically superior opponent. In Iraq and Afghanistan, for example, a guerrilla-style conflict was launched by terrorist groups against the technologically superior coalition forces of the West, with the use of IEDs or brief battles carried out in a variety of sites. Often the objective was not to win a battle but to demoralise the enemy (both the military and the domestic audience at home), in the hope that this would lead to concessions.

A third method is the political solution, addressing the underlying motivations of terrorists and those who support them. This approach has been most commonly used in Europe.

In Northern Ireland all three methods were in use. An extensive policing and intelligence gathering approach was matched by a strong counter-insurgence strategy from the British Army, Northern Ireland forces, and the intelligence services. The IRA bombing of the Remembrance Day parade at Enniskillen in 1987 was a crucial moment in the decline of support for the terrorist group, which the British government sought to build on in the early 1990s by attempting to improve the lives of Catholic nationalists who had a long-standing grievance that they were treated as second-class citizens by the dominant pro-British Protestant unionists. The IRA would eventually agree to a ceasefire in 1994, which became final in 1997 in return for its political wing, Sinn Fein, being granted a voice in the Good Friday Agreement and the government that followed.

It is interesting to note that before ETA announced its permanent ceasefire in 2011 it had allegedly sought the advice of the IRA as how best to do this, and how it might be able to achieve its aims within a democratic framework. In fact, international co-operation between terrorist groups is not unusual: Palestinian militants in the late

1960s and early 1970s were known to have links with terrorist groups in Western Europe and Japan, and the IRA is alleged to have had links with FARC.

Many argue that a solution to the current Israeli–Palestinian conflict would remove one of the key grievances of Islamic extremists around the world. However, this is not the only issue inspiring the ideology of a global jihad. There are significant regional differences. In Algeria, jihadists are provoked by the refusal of the pro-Western military to accept the results of elections won by Islamists in 1991. Pakistani and Kashmiri jihadists direct more of their outrage towards 'Hindu India' than Jewish Israel, while Russia is the major source of grievance for the Chechen jihadists.

The British experience with the IRA is indicative of a general policy found in most European governments in their approach to national terrorism, which has usually been to take into account the political background to terrorist activities. There has always been a shared view that if terrorism is to be undermined, it requires an acceptable alternative in response to their political goals.

As the former head of Israeli military intelligence, Yehoshaphat Harkabi, once said, 'When the swamp disappears, there will be no more mosquitoes' (quoted in Chomsky, 2002). However, this in itself is complicated. A common argument is that if you tackle poverty, unemployment and a lack of education, this will reduce terrorism. However, terrorists are not always poor, and prosperity does not necessarily end terrorism. In fact, in many of the world's fifty poorest countries there is little or no terrorism. There is considerable evidence to suggest that many terrorists tend to be well-educated, and they are unlikely to be poor. In Arab countries, such as Egypt and Saudi Arabia, and in North Africa, terrorists tend to come from some of the wealthiest regions and neighbourhoods. Osama bin Laden came from a very rich family. Furthermore, the failed states model can be questioned given that many terrorist groups have existed, or exist, in democratic states. The IRA, Baader–Meinhof, ETA, and the Red Brigade all existed within democracies. The 7/7 bombers were British citizens. Timothy McVeigh was an American.

Then there is the problem of what the West can offer a member of al-Qaeda. Often the demands of terrorists cannot possibly be met. In Ireland, the offer of political representation was a first step in leading to the Good Friday Agreement being adopted. It was enough to lead to a ceasefire. With al-Qaeda, the cause is driven by an ideology which is extreme and is not truly representative of mainstream Islam (rather like Christian extremists who target abortion clinics in the US, who are not representative of mainstream Christianity). Ultimately the West has no attractive alternative for a suicide bomber who believes that dying will result in him or her going straight to heaven and into Allah's loving embrace.

Conclusion

In the West the threat of a terrorist attack haunts politicians, security analysts and the public. Though the global number of terrorist attacks increased in 2013, in the West the number continues to decline. However, the fear of a successful attack in the West remains ever-present. After all, there have been a number of attacks which have been thwarted. Richard Reid was restrained while trying to light explosives hidden in his shoes on board a flight from Paris, France to Miami on 22 December 2001. Two weeks after the 7 July 2005 bombings in London another group of terrorists attempted to replicate the attack, but were thwarted by explosives that failed to go off. On 25 December 2009 Umar Abdulmutallab unsuccessfully attempted to detonate a bomb hidden in his underwear on board a flight about to land in Detroit.

As a chilling IRA statement made clear after their failed attempt to kill British Prime Minister Margaret Thatcher in Brighton in 1984, 'Today we were unlucky, but remember we only have to be lucky once. You will have to be lucky always' (Clutterbuck, 2012). This is the nightmare security dilemma.

Al-Qaeda has successfully changed perceptions of terrorism within Security Studies. It is no longer the case that only the state can inflict large-scale violence on an international scale. The state's monopoly on violence ended on the morning of 11 September 2001. After that, al-Qaeda sympathisers struck in Bali, Casablanca, Istanbul, Nairobi, London and Madrid, and continue to strike in Iraq, Afghanistan and elsewhere. In a sense, traditional state boundaries have become irrelevant as terrorists now have the technology and resources to strike anywhere.

However, whether al-Qaeda will truly become a global force remains open to question. Undoubtedly its links are widespread, but whether it represents the globalisation of terrorism remains open to dispute.

It is of note that the revolutionary 'Arab Spring', which began at the end of 2010 when Mohamed Bouazizi set fire to himself in Tunisia in protest against police corruption and ill-treatment, was not led, or even inspired, by al-Qaeda. Rather, the demonstrators who brought about change in the Middle East and North Africa demanded jobs and an end to unrepresentative government, leading to the collapse of corrupt regimes in Egypt, Tunisia, Libya and Yemen. Even the civil war that broke out in Syria was about political and economic change and not the establishment of the Sunni caliphate which bin Laden had hoped for.

It is probable, however, that the threat of terrorism from al-Qaeda and its affiliates will remain for at least a generation, driven by the 'blowback' from the West's incursions into Afghanistan and Iraq, the spread of globalisation, and the continuing struggles between Sunni and Shia Muslims. Indeed, the majority of deaths from al-Qaeda and others, such as the Taliban, are most likely to continue to be Muslims killing Muslims. However, it is possible that al-Qaeda may develop new methods of attack against the West, utilising new technologies such as cyberwarfare or even chemical weapons, which have the capabilities to inflict mass casualties on a catastrophic scale. It is for this reason that security services in the West remain ever-vigilant.

Nevertheless, it is important for security strategists to move beyond the stereotype of terrorism being driven by religious extremists. As has been noted, terrorism can be for political, economic or cultural reasons. Furthermore, local and regional terrorism still dominates, rather than international terrorism. For example, British security forces during the Olympic Games in London in 2012 were as concerned about a possible attack from Irish dissidents as they were about al-Qaeda sympathisers.

An effective strategy to tackle terrorism must involve a combination of factors, including effective policing, intelligence gathering, the sharing of information with foreign governments and intelligence services, and the support of the judiciary and the public. An over-reliance on the military can be counter-productive.

What is clear is that the traditional Realist claim that only state actors influence international relations is now seriously challenged by globalisation and the growth of international terrorism. The rapid pace of technological change and global media has given terrorists a worldwide marketplace in which to operate. In the West this has brought to the fore debates over the importance of liberty (i.e. a lack of restrictions on daily life) and privacy (i.e. how far the government should be allowed to scrutinise a citizen's life). For those in Pakistan, Iraq and Afghanistan, however, the issues are more pressing because they, and not the West, bear the brunt of the world's terrorist attacks.

Summary points

1   The events of 9/11 refocused international security concerns.
2   Non-state actors can now inflict large-scale damage.
3   There are fears that terrorists will seek to gain, and use, weapons of mass destruction.
4   The spread of al-Qaeda, aided by the forces of globalisation, has highlighted the dangers of international terrorist networks.
5   Terrorism will not be defeated solely by the use of hard power.

Recommended reading

Booth, K. and Dunne, T. *Terror in Our Time*, Abingdon: Routledge, 2011.

Country Reports on Terrorism, 2013, United States Department of State Publication, 2013. Bureau of Counterterrorism, Released April 2014, U.S. State Department, at http://www.state.gov/documents/organization/225886.pdf (Accessed 18.5.2014).

Farrall, L. 'How Al-Qaeda Works', *Foreign Affairs*, vol. 90, no. 2, March/April 2011, 128–138.

Hoffman, B. (2006), *Inside Terrorism*, Revised and expanded edition, New York: Columbia University Press.

Rapoport, D. 'The Four Waves of Modern Terrorism', in A. Cronin and J. Ludes, (eds) *Attacking Terrorism*. Washington, DC: Georgetown University Press, 2004, 46–73.

Schmid, A. and Jongman, A. *Political Terrorism: A New Guide to Actors, Authors, Concepts, Databases, Theories and Literature*, New Brunswick, NJ: Transaction Press, 2005.

12 Religion and international conflict

Jeffrey Haynes

Box 12.1: The arrival of religion into international politics

The issue of religion and conflict has been of major international concern since the events of 11 September 2001. This was the day when two aircraft commandeered by al-Qaeda followers crashed into the World Trade Center in New York, killing 3,000 people and starting a new phase of world politics. This era is characterised by increasing numbers of conflicts involving 'religion' and key global powers such as the USA. The aftermath of 9/11 included the invasion of Afghanistan in 2001, the takeover of Iraq and the overthrow of Saddam Hussein two years later, and a general growing sense of instability and insecurity in world politics. Religion has become centrally located in the context of conflict both between and within countries in ways that International Relations theorists have struggled to understand. This issue is both timely and controversial and forms the focus of this chapter.

Introduction

Various religious actors are now involved in international relations in significant ways. Some, but by no means all, are linked to international conflict. For many observers, this is new and unexpected in two ways. First, until recently, most International Relations experts believed that religion could be ignored because it appeared to be so insignificant in the mainly secular context of world politics. Second, the end of the Cold War in the late 1980s ushered in a new era of religious involvement in international conflict, with 11 September 2001 (9/11) being a prime example. The consequence of these two developments is that today most observers of international relations would agree that it is impossible to ignore the involvement of religion in international conflict. This chapter examines religion's recent involvement in international conflict, and offers reasons why this has occurred and what it tells us more generally about international relations in the second decade of the twenty-first century.

Religion and international conflict: some general observations

While it is difficult to single out one event that would on its own explain all recent and current examples of religious involvement in international conflict, Samuel Huntington's (1993, 1996) highly influential yet very controversial argument is a good place to start. Although Huntington wrote about what he called 'the clash of civilisations', it was clear that inter-religious clashes were a key focal point of his thesis.

According to Huntington, the (Christian) West's security, and by extension global order, is under attack from international Islamic militancy. For some, Huntington's thesis was given credence by the emergence of overtly anti-Western Islamist regimes in Afghanistan and Sudan in the 1990s, a contemporaneous and concerted attempt to introduce a similar regime in Algeria, the tragic events of 9/11, when around 3,000 people were killed in the USA in al-Qaeda attacks, subsequent bomb attacks in Madrid and London, and the US-led invasions of Afghanistan (2001) and Iraq (2003), as well as Islamist militants' responses in Somalia, Nigeria, Mali and elsewhere. Around the world, many people responded to both 9/11 and subsequent US retaliation against the al-Qaeda attacks in broadly religious and cultural terms. On the one hand, Western governments, including those of Britain, Italy and Spain, strongly supported the American people against al-Qaeda, and more generally against Islamist terrorism. On the other hand, many 'ordinary' Muslims – although not necessarily their governments – appeared to view the events rather differently: while they acknowledged the undesirability of the loss of thousands of innocent people as a consequence of a terrorist outrage, for some Muslims 9/11 also represented an attempt to 'fight back' against what some saw as a globally destructive state – the USA (and by extension the 'West' more generally) (Dolan, 2005). In addition, many Muslims also regarded punitive US-led actions against both Afghanistan and Iraq as unjust, designed to unfairly 'punish' fellow believers for 9/11 – a tragic event over which they had no control (Shlapentokh, Woods and Shiraev, 2005).

No doubt, al-Qaeda envisaged Muslim reactions to the 9/11 outrage (Haynes, 2005a). Clearly Al-Qaeda's purpose was to wreak terrible destruction on the USA – but that was not all. In addition, al-Qaeda wished to create a global media spectacle, to show the mass of 'downtrodden ordinary Muslims' that bin Laden personally – already a hero for some Muslims following his anti-Soviet exploits in Afghanistan in the late 1980s – and al-Qaeda collectively acted on *their* behalf. Thus, around the world, 'ordinary' Muslims were an important target audience for the highly visual spectacle of the destruction of the Twin Towers and the contemporaneous attack on the Pentagon. For bin Laden and al-Qaeda a key goal of 9/11 was to grab the attention of ordinary (Sunni) Muslims, and to encourage them to make connections between the attacks and widespread Muslim resentment against the USA. Prior to 9/11 this was already simmering as a result, *inter alia*, of the earlier US-led invasion of Iraq in 1990–1 and, over time, successive American governments' apparently unwavering support both for Israel's resolutely harsh treatment of the Palestinians and for many unelected and – according to al-Qaeda – 'un-Islamic' rulers in the Muslim world, such as the King of Saudi Arabia.

However, even if such areas of specific concern to many Muslims were speedily resolved, it may be that associated resentment and antipathy towards the USA, and by extension the (Christian) West, would not necessarily dispel speedily. This is because rather than a finite list of specific issues, potentially resolvable via negotiation and compromise, there are also sources of antipathy and disquiet that go much deeper and have been in place for much longer, and as a result these issues are likely to be much more problematic to resolve. Thus, even if solutions for specific sources of complaint are quickly found, this would not necessarily deal fully with all sources of Muslim disquiet at the status quo, including an international environment apparently dominated by the (Christian) West. In addition, as Hurrell (2002: 197) notes, it 'seems plausible that much [Muslim] resentment has to do with the far-reaching and corrosive encroachments of modernization, westernization and globalization'. So, there are both specific and more general reasons for the development of international conflict based on religious divisions, which collectively are difficult to deal with.

This chapter looks at the issue of religion's involvement in international conflict. It begins by surveying the context and background of today's international relations, dominated until recently by the idea that world politics is inherently secular – that is, non-religious. The next part of the chapter looks at the 'return' of religion to international relations and what this has meant for international conflict. The third part of the chapter returns to Huntington's argument and assesses the extent to which he was right in assuming that post-Cold War international conflict would be focused upon battles between the (Christian) West and the Muslim world.

Religion, secularisation and international conflict

Looking for a starting point for the re-engagement of religion in international conflict, the Iranian revolution of 1979 is difficult to ignore. Not only starting decades of conflict between the USA and Iran, the revolution was also highly significant in focusing attention on religious actors in international relations, and even more important for highlighting how religion can be a focal point of conflict. Prior to this epochal event, religion was widely seen as insignificant in international relations. This lack of concern was at least in part derived from the prominence of secular international security issues during the Cold War (Almond, Appleby and Sivan, 2003). Underpinning such a view were two widely accepted assumptions in Western social science: (1) rationality and secularity go hand in hand; and (2) 'modern', political, economic and social systems are found in societies that have modernised via a process of secularisation that publicly marginalises or 'privatises' religion (Casanova, 1994). In short, the secular cannot be viewed as a successor to religion, or be seen as on the side of the rational. It is a category with a multi-layered history, related to major premises of modernity, democracy, and the concept of human rights.

Box 12.2: The notion of secularisation

Secularisation implies a significant diminishing of religious concerns in everyday life, a unidirectional process whereby societies move from a sacred condition to an increasingly irreligious state until a point where the sacred becomes both socially and politically marginal. According to 'secularisation theory', both religion and piety are destined *universally* to become 'only' private matters; consequently, religion would no longer be an important public actor. As Shupe (1990: 19) notes, 'the demystification of religion inherent in the classic secularization paradigm posits a gradual, persistent, unbroken erosion of religious influence in urban industrial societies'. Such was secularisation theory's claim to universalism that, according to the sociologist José Casanova (1994: 17), it 'may be the only theory which was able to attain a truly paradigmatic status within the modern social sciences'. This was partly because leading figures in late nineteenth and twentieth century social science – including Emile Durkheim, Max Weber, Karl Marx, Auguste Comte, Sigmund Freud, Talcott Parsons and Herbert Spencer – all maintained that secularisation is an integral facet of modernisation, a global trend of relevance everywhere as societies moved from the 'traditional' to the 'modern'. They shared a view 'that religion would gradually fade in importance and cease to be significant with the advent of industrial society. The belief that religion was dying became the conventional wisdom in the social sciences during most of the twentieth century' (Norris and Inglehart, 2004: 3). As modernisation extended its hold, so the argument went, religion would everywhere be 'privatised', losing its grip on culture and becoming a purely personal matter. Thus religion would no longer be a *collective* force with significant mobilising potential for social change. In short, Donald Eugene Smith (1970: 6) proclaimed nearly half a century ago that secularisation was 'the most fundamental structural and ideological change in the process of political development'. Secularisation was a one-way street: societies gradually – but inexorably – move away from being focused around the sacred and a concern with the divine to a situation characterised by significant diminution of religious power and authority.

The secularisation thesis was a core assumption of Western social sciences for decades, including in the decades immediately following the Second World War. It animated two highly significant sets of ideas: modernisation theory in the 1950s and early 1960s, and dependency theory in the late 1960s and early 1970s. Both schools of thought maintained – or rather, implicitly accepted the conventional wisdom of the day, then at its most unchallenged – that the course of both international relations and integrated nation-states necessarily lay squarely in secular participatory politics. In an example of theory guiding 'real world' politics, many political leaders – especially in the developing world, vast areas of which were emerging from colonial rule at that time – worked from the key premise that, sometimes irrespective of their own religious beliefs and cultural affiliations, they must for ideological reasons *necessarily* remain neutral in respect of entanglements stemming from particularist religious and cultural claims *if* they wanted to build successful nation-states and conduct flourishing international relations. Not to do so would serve to encourage dogmatism, reduce tolerance and invite conflict ('isn't this what "history" tells us?', they queried), and as a result be antipathetic to the development of viable nation-states, democracy and the smooth running of the (secular) international system. As Juergensmeyer (1993: 27) notes, 'secular nationalism was thought to be not only natural but also universally applicable and morally right'. In sum, as a consequence of the global advance of secular, centralised states from the seventeenth century via colonialism and an international system from which religion was expunged from the eighteenth century onwards – because of its demonstrable 'bad influence', reflected in numerous religious wars between Christians on the one hand, and between Muslims and Christians on the other – religion was relegated to the category of a potentially dangerous but actually rather minor issue that must not be allowed to intrude on the search for domestic national unity and international political stability and progress. In terms of international conflict, this implied that battles would be between secular actors and associated ideologies, and during the Cold War (from the late 1940s to the late 1980s) this appeared to be empirically true as the USA and the Soviet Union fought for global domination.

'Resurgence' of religion and international conflict

Two key events – the end of the Cold War in the late 1980s, and the dissolution of the Soviet Union a few years later – were accompanied by a third: a resurgence of religion, with ramifications for our understanding of international relations, including international conflict. As the 1990s drew to a close it was clear that something quite extraordinary was happening: the century was ending 'with a resurgence of religion, with great new cathedrals, mosques, and temples rising up, with the symbols and songs of faith everywhere apparent' (Woollacott, 1995). Astonishingly, religious resurgence was not restricted to one country or even a handful of states; instead, it was a near-global religious resurgence with important ramifications for international relations (Petito and Hatzopoulos, 2003; Thomas, 2005; Haynes, 2013). To explain how surprising this was, it is necessary to make a brief historical detour in order to put recent events in context.

Following the Peace of Westphalia in 1648 and the subsequent development of the current international system, religion lost its earlier international political significance. Previously – that is, before the mid-seventeenth century – both Islam and Christianity had been key political actors. Islam had expanded from its Arabian heartland in westerly, easterly, southerly and northern directions for nearly a millennium. As a consequence, vast territories in Africa and Asia and smaller areas of Europe (parts of the Balkans and much of the Iberian Peninsula) came under Muslim control. However, unable to deal with the consequences of increasingly centralised Christian polities in Western Europe – with their superior firepower and organisational skills – Islam found itself on the back foot. The consequence was a significant reduction in the faith's influence in Europe from the late fifteenth century. Overall, however, despite this setback, elsewhere Islam developed into a holistic religious, social and cultural system, over time becoming a global religion via the spread of transnational religious communities.

Box 12.3: Theoretical perspectives and religious resurgence

The recent resurgence of religion noted on all levels of social activity – including international relations/International Relations[1] – calls into question the stubbornness of Western social sciences, which are apparently unwilling (and unable) to treat religions as important social factors on their own terms, on a par with secular discourses. Four generic approaches to international relations – Realism, Liberal internationalism, neo-Marxism, and Constructivism – are briefly reviewed next, in order to assess how each understands the issue of religion in international relations. The conclusion of the short survey is that none of the four perceives religion to be a consistently important component of contemporary international relations, including international conflict. Put another way, this indicates that the 'return' of religion to international conflict, highlighted by Huntington, is indeed *sui generis* and explains why International Relations theories, with the partial exception of Constructivism, struggle to explain this phenomenon.

First, the Realist perspective contends that the state is *always* the most important factor in international relations because there is no higher authority; international organisations are regarded as always subservient to the state. The global system is a global *states* system grounded in competition, conflict and cooperation. States must rely upon their own resources to achieve the power they need to thrive, even if they are prepared, as most are, to collaborate with others to achieve general goals. Serious conflict is not the usual status of the international system because peace is maintained through local and global balances of power. Realism emphasises how hegemonic powers, such as the United States, have an important role in establishing and maintaining order in the international system, and stresses that the structure of power in the international system shapes the character of the political order. In short, Realist analysis places great stress on the significance of military power, because states must ultimately rely on their own efforts to achieve their goals. It ignores or seriously downplays the role of religion, not least because very few – if any – states proclaim that their foreign policies are driven by religious factors (Haynes, 2013: 58–60).

Second, the Liberal paradigm begins from the premise that the state is no longer automatically the primary actor in world politics. The growth of transnational relations points to the significance of non-state actors, especially transnational corporations and international organisations of various kinds – including cross-border religious groups, such as al-Qaeda – which can be independent of the control of any individual state or group of states (Haynes, 2005a). Indeed, the state itself is not regarded as a unitary actor. Rather, it consists of a body of bureaucratic organisations and institutions. The global system is perceived as an aggregate of different issue areas, such as trade, finance, energy, human rights, democracy and ecology, in which domestic and international policy processes merge. The management of global interdependencies is carried out through processes of bargaining, negotiation and consensus-seeking. Order is maintained not by a balance of power, as Realists contend, but by the consensual acceptance of common values, norms and international law. In other words, global order is maintained because states have a vested interest in so doing, while the global political process does not involve states alone but also includes a variety of non-state actors. Despite the fact that the Liberal internationalist perspective recognises that religious actors can be important transnationally, their importance is seen in terms of particular issues – for example, human rights – rather than more generally.

Third, the neo-Marxist views political processes at the global level primarily as expressions of underlying class conflicts on a global scale; and religion is not seen as an important facet of class issues. Neo-Marxists differ from Realists in not conceiving of global order as based upon the structure of military power, nor as sustained by networks of interdependence as Liberal internationalists do. One of the dominant characteristics of the global order for neo-Marxists is the structural differentiation of the world into core, peripheral and semi-peripheral centres of economic power. While this was traditionally regarded as the division between the 'North', the 'South' and the communist Eastern bloc, the emergence of the East Asian Newly Industrialising Countries and the demise of the Eastern communist bloc have comprehensively undermined the simple (and increasingly simplistic) three-way international economic division. In short, for neo-Marxists, global order is preserved through the power of the leading capitalist states, by international agencies such as the United Nations, by transnational corporations, and by international regimes which together serve to legitimate a global diffusion of a dominant ideology of Liberalism and Western-type modernisation (Haynes, 2013: 64–65).

Finally, Constructivism is an approach to international relations that is not restricted to one form, view or paradigm. Instead, what Constructivist approaches have in common is the aim of understanding the behaviour of agents, states and non-state actors alike, in social and cultural contexts. For Constructivists, political decision-making is understood in both ideational and material terms. Theoretically, then, Constructivists might be expected to consider, to a greater degree than Realists,

Liberal internationalists and neo-Marxists, factors such as culture, history and religion. This is because they have a say in helping craft significant players in international relations, including, but not restricted to, states. In short, Constructivism, with its central role for identity, norms, and culture, provides a potentially more favourable theoretical environment in which to bring religion into International Relations theory (Haynes, 2013: 65–67).

International conflict involving religion after 9/11: does Huntington's argument stack up?

In order to put some empirical flesh on what might otherwise be rather abstract bones, I want to focus on 9/11 as a key example of the return of religion to international conflict and suggest some reasons why this is the case. 9/11 emphasised two questions of sudden crucial importance: first, how can we prevent such conflicts developing in the first place? And second, when they do erupt, how can they be brought to a speedy peaceful conclusion? Regarding the first question, some inter-faith religious organisations – for example, Religions for Peace (RfP; http://www.religionsforpeace.org/about/), established in 1970 – have for decades devoted a great deal of time, energy and commitment to trying to build inter-faith harmony in order to prevent associated conflicts from breaking out. However, it is impossible to know how successful RfP is because *if* a conflict related to religion does *not* break out, how do we *know* that conflict has *not* occurred? On the other hand, RfP efforts are important in helping more general efforts to stress what religious traditions have in common and what can be done to minimise conflict and increase cooperation between religious faiths in international relations.

What *is* clear is that inter-religious dialogue and cooperation can be made extremely difficult – although not necessarily impossible – by sudden, unexpected and damaging developments. I want to illustrate this contention in relation to the 9/11 attacks, subsequent US-led invasions of Muslim-majority Afghanistan (2001) and Iraq (2003), and successive bomb attacks in Europe, including Madrid (2004) and London (2005), both of which were connected to ideas about international conflict advanced by al-Qaeda. Together, these specific events, as well as continuing resentment at what many Muslims see as US/Western attempts to dominate the world, have almost certainly made inter-religious dialogue between Christians and Muslims more problematic than it might otherwise have been.

To return to our specific issue: twenty years after Huntington's thoughts on the topic of Western–Muslim world conflict linked to religious difference, to what extent do his ideas stand up to scrutiny? To what extent does Huntington's thesis explain where we are today in terms of inter-faith conflict in international relations?

In 2013 in Mali and in 2014 in northern Nigeria, Islamist militants claimed allegiance to the ideas of al-Qaeda in seeking to pursue their goal of an Islamic state and the forcible expulsion or conversion of Christians and other non-Muslims (Minteh and Perry, 2013). We have already noted that the revolution in Iran in 1979 was an early sign of the return of religious difference to international conflict, specifically in relation to the continuing hostility between Muslim Iran and the USA. The conflict between the two highlights the near-impossibility of finding common ground between two countries and their governments, differentiated by very different sets of values, norms and beliefs, and the problematic issue of how they live in harmony in an increasingly globalised world where they frequently come into contact.

My argument in this section of the chapter is not that Huntington's article and book were collectively important because they were 'correct' or 'right'. My claim instead is twofold. First, Huntington's article was and is important because it captured perfectly the end-of-the-Cold War *zeitgeist*, a way of seeing the world which endured in these uncertain times we call 'globalisation'. Second, it has proved to be an abiding statement about globalisation and the hopes and fears that it conveys.

It is almost irrelevant that his focal point – the impossibility of the West (read 'the USA') and Islam (read 'Islamic fundamentalism') living together in harmony – was laughably over-simplified, redolent of the paranoia of someone experiencing the shattering of a stable, safe and unchanging world, suddenly and demonstrably confronted with the scenario of the post-Second World War paradigm smashed to smithereens. What was a card-carrying Realist such as Huntington to do? One approach, the one he adopted, was to find a new enemy ('Islamic fundamentalism') and dress it up in the same 'baddie' clothes that had exemplified the treatment of the USSR by US Realists since the start of the Cold War, transferring the characteristics of the old enemy to a new international 'religious' 'actor', 'Islamic fundamentalism'.

It is worth recalling that in the early 1990s, when Huntington first presented his 'clash of civilisations' thesis, the world had just emerged from a fifty-year period of secular ideological polarisation and conflict. Despite the claims of some today in the USA, the US did not 'win' the Cold War; rather, the Soviet Union 'lost' it. Unable to compete with America in a competition for global dominance, its shaky, dysfunctional and misanthropic political/social/economic system spectacularly imploded within a seemingly impossibly short period of time: apparently as strong as ever in the mid-1980s, by 1991 the Soviet Union and its system, as well as its parasitic coterie of attendant nations, was no more. This left a gulf, a hole, a vacuum. How, and with what, to fill it?

If globalisation was the force which defeated the USSR, it was also the trend that enabled religion to resume its long-abandoned place in global politics. Exiled to marginalisation after 1648, the sudden demise of the Cold War and the USSR and its attendant secular ideology opened the way for a new focus on 'religion'. Now, as everyone knows who has ever played a word association game, 'religion' is almost a synonym for 'culture', because often the thing that most obviously differentiates one culture from another is religious difference.

The 9/11 attacks on the United States were a key event in the debate about the role of cultural and religious difference – especially 'Islamic fundamentalism' – in international conflict, especially in the way that they focused attention on al-Qaeda's brand of globalised cultural terrorism. For some scholars, analysts and policy-makers – especially but not exclusively in the United States – 9/11 marked the practical onset of Samuel Huntington's 'clash of civilisations' between two cultural entities: the 'Christian West' and the 'Islamic world', with special concern directed at those entities which might attract the nomenclature 'Islamic fundamentalists'. Of course, this is not to claim that Huntington had it all his own way; many have addressed his claims of global cultural conflict between the 'Christian West' and the 'Islamic fundamentalists' with the counter-argument that 9/11 was not the *start* of a clash of civilisations, but rather the *last gasp* of transnational Islamist radicalism. (It remains to be seen if recent events in Mali and those involving Boko Haram ['Western education is forbidden'] in Nigeria are the start of a new phase.) It is hard to disagree with the claim that the events of 11 September thrust culture (and religion) to the forefront of the international conflict agenda, providing Huntington's 'clash of civilisations' thesis with a new lease of life as a result. Over the next decade, many commentators – especially those inhabiting the conservative political spectrum in the USA – were not inhibited in attributing essentialist characteristics both to the 'Christian West' and to the 'Muslim world'. That is, after 9/11, there was a pronounced penchant in some quarters to see the world in terms of a Huntingtonian – albeit very simplistic – division. This polarisation was characterised by straight lines on maps – 'Islam has bloody borders' (Huntington, 1993: 35) – which was apparently key to a pictorial representation of a world where borders still meant something even in this era of globalisation, as long as those divisions were underpinned by cultural and religious difference.

Box 12.4: 9/11 and Huntington's thesis

Some characteristics of the post-9/11 world are beyond dispute. 11 September 2001, as well as many subsequent terrorist outrages, were perpetrated by al-Qaeda or its followers, and all involved Islamist extremists who shared the goal of wanting to cause destruction and loss of life against 'Western' targets that nevertheless often led to considerable loss of life among Muslims, for example in Istanbul and Casablanca. The US response – the Bush administration's 'war on terror' – targeted Muslims, many believe indiscriminately, in Afghanistan, Iraq and elsewhere. Some have claimed that these events 'prove' the correctness of Huntington's thesis of the 'clash of civilisations'. In such views, the 9/11 attacks and the US response suggested that Huntington's prophecy about clashing civilisations was now less abstract and more plausible than when first articulated in the early 1990s. Others contend, however, that 9/11 was not the start of the clash of civilisations, but, as already noted, the last gasp of radical Islamists' attempts to foment revolutionary change in, *inter alia*, Algeria and Egypt in the 1980s and early 1990s. Nevertheless, we can also note that 9/11 not only had major effects on both the USA and international relations, but also contributed to a surge in Islamic radicalism in Saudi Arabia. This was a result not only of the presence of US troops in the kingdom, as highlighted by bin Laden, but also due to a growing realisation that the function of Saudi Arabia's *ulema* was and is overwhelmingly to underpin and explain away the unearned and unrepresentative dominance of the ruling king, his extended family and parasitic entourage.

More than a dozen years after 9/11 and two decades since the publication of Huntington's article (1993) and book (1996), what do we now know about the 'clash of civilisations'? Huntington did note in his article that he was aware of differences of opinion and outlook *within* 'civilisations', but he appeared to think this was much less important than an apparently clear 'clash' of values, norms and beliefs, which for him characterised the division 'between' the 'West' and 'Islam'. It is clear – to me, at least – that the very idea of a world divided into 'seven, or eight major civilizations', as Huntington (1993: 25) posited, is absurd. (In parentheses, as it were, the very idea that there is 'possibly [an] African civilization' (ibid.) is belied by events in Nigeria in 2014, involving murderous conflict between Islamist extremists and run-of-the-mill Christians. Just *one* African civilisation? What, pray tell, would this comprise?) Once again time has shown, at least to me, that anyone who can possibly take seriously the idea of a world divided into 'seven, or eight major civilizations' lacks the capacity to have any possible understanding of our fascinating mosaic of a world filled with myriad ideas, norms, beliefs and conceptions of how the world is.

Since Huntington's contributions in the mid-1990s to the debate about civilisations and their propensity for violence and conflict with each other, a growing literature has emerged on the topic of religious involvement in both international conflict and its opposite: international cooperation.

Box 12.5: Criticising Huntington

There are numerous critics of Huntington's arguments. Some have noted that it is one thing to argue that various brands of political Islam have qualitatively different perspectives on liberal democracy compared to many forms of Christianity, but quite another to claim that Muslims *en masse* are poised to enter into a period of conflict with the West. Critics also pointed out that there are actually many 'Islams', and only the malevolent or misinformed would associate the terrorist attacks with the apparently representative quality of a single – necessarily, extremist – idea of Islam. Second, the 11 September atrocities – as well as subsequent bomb outrages in London, Madrid and elsewhere – were not carried out by a state or group of states or at their behest, but by al-Qaeda, an international terrorist organisation, as vilified by Muslim governments, including those in Pakistan, Saudi Arabia and Libya, as it is by Western states.

Third, the idea of inter-civilisational conflict is also implausible for another reason: it is very difficult or impossible to clearly delineate territorial boundaries between 'civilisations', and even more tricky to perceive them as acting as coherent units. This underlines that, problematically, Huntington's scenario of 'clashing civilisations' focuses attention on a one-dimensional, undifferentiated category – 'civilisation' – and as a result places insufficient emphasis on various trends, conflicts and disagreements occurring *within* all religious and cultural traditions, including Islam, Christianity and Judaism. The wider point is that cultures are not usefully seen as closed systems of essentialist values, and it is not helpful to try to understand the world as comprising a strictly limited, discrete number of civilisations or cultures, each with its own unique core beliefs.

Finally, the image of 'clashing civilisations' ignores the very important sense in which radical Islamist revolt generally and al-Qaeda terrorism in particular is primarily aimed at governments *within* the Islamic world, especially those consistently accused of both corruption and 'un-Islamic' practices. Yet the rise of Islamist groups across a swathe of Arab countries and elsewhere in the Muslim world is not *only* consequential to failings of *individual* regimes – it is also the result of the failure of modernisation promises to deliver generally beneficial outcomes. That is, the contemporary Islamist resurgence – of which al-Qaeda is an aspect but not the whole story – carries within it popular disillusionment at developmental and societal failures, as well as widespread disgust at the spectre of corrupt and unrepresentative governments – which, to add insult to injury, consistently refuse to meaningfully democratise political systems. As a result, confronted by state power that seeks to destroy or control communitarian structures and replace them with an idea of a national citizenry based on the link between state and individual, to many Muslims Islamist groups are important vehicles of popular political aspirations (Strindberg and Wärn, 2011).

It is useful to think of 'political Islam' as a variable and varied political ideology, since it is not necessarily associated with radicalism or extremism. Various expressions of political Islam are undoubtedly radical – for example, post-revolutionary Iran or Afghanistan, when governed by the Taliban between 1996 and 2001 – or extremist, such as al-Qaeda and assorted Islamist terrorists from Morocco to Indonesia. But what the latter examples have in common – a willingness to use extremist tactics in order to achieve their political goals – does not imply that they see the world in the same way, from a shared religious perspective. For example, the government of Shia Iran has evolved a unique system of administration which has almost nothing in common – beyond the rather opaque idea of a pursuit of 'Islamic principles' – with the form of government expressed in neighbouring Afghanistan by the Sunni Taliban from 1996 to 2001. Much more common are the myriad groups in the Muslim world which can be described as 'moderate', implying that they eschew extremist tactics. Over the last two decades, Islamically-orientated candidates and political parties in Algeria, Tunisia, Morocco, Egypt, Lebanon, Turkey, Jordan, Kuwait, Bahrain, Pakistan, Malaysia and Indonesia have all sought to utilise pluralistic pathways to electoral success. They have contested and won seats at both local and national levels, been invited to serve in cabinets, and in some cases achieved power, as in Turkey, Egypt and Tunisia. Over the last decade, elections in, *inter alia*, Bahrain, Egypt, Iraq, Kuwait, Morocco, Palestine, Pakistan, Saudi Arabia, Tunisia and Turkey have served to highlight the political salience of 'Islam' in numerous countries. Some such groups, it should be noted, are highly controversial, espousing militancy which has not necessarily endeared them to democrats everywhere; examples include Hezbollah in Lebanon and Hamas in Palestine. In both cases, however, the organisations combine the attributes of successful guerrilla groups with those of viable, grassroots-orientated political parties, which have achieved massive electoral successes.

Seeking to come up with workable policies in order to respond adequately to both 'moderate' and 'extremist' political Islam, Western foreign policy-makers must learn to acquire better understandings of how global Muslim majorities see the world, including the West. A 2011 opinion survey, involving nearly 14,000 people in fourteen countries in both telephone and face-to-face interviews, was conducted by the US-based Pew Research Center, and found that majorities in several mainly Muslim countries – the Palestinian Territories, Turkey, Lebanon, Egypt and Jordan – believed that 'relations are poor' between Muslims and Westerners, as did majorities in France, Germany, Spain and Britain. The same poll revealed that large majorities in Russia, Germany, USA, Britain, France and Spain were concerned about 'Islamic extremism', as were over half of the respondents in various Muslim majority countries: the Palestinian Territories, Egypt, Lebanon, Pakistan, and Turkey (Pew Research Global Attitudes Project, 2011).

Petito (2007, 2009) notes that partly in response to Huntington's claims, attempts have developed to pursue a *dialogue* of civilisations, which has become institutionalised as the 'Alliance of Civilisations' under United Nations auspices. The more general context for this development was the post-1989 debate on the future of world order – that is, how to develop what is increasingly seen as a political necessity: a more peaceful, multicultural and just world order. Since 9/11, the idea of a dialogue of civilisations – and its related components of inter-cultural and inter-religious dialogue – has been the subject of a proliferation of public initiatives and international meetings.

A former UN Secretary-General, Kofi Annan, formed an eighteen-person expert group – known as the 'High-level Group' – to look into the issue of civilisational (read 'inter-religious') conflict.[2] The High-level Group sought to achieve two main tasks: first, to explore what currently causes 'polarisation' between different societies and cultures; and second, to determine a practical programme of action to address this issue. At the end of their deliberations in the mid-2000s, the High-level Group compiled and circulated a report providing analysis and practical recommendations forming the basis for the implementation plan of the United Nations Alliance of Civilizations (UNAOC). Following the report of the High-level Group, in April 2007 the former president of Portugal, Jorge Sampaio, was appointed as the High Representative for the UNAOC by the current UN Secretary-General Ban Ki-moon. Sampaio's main task was to lead the implementation phase of what is now known as the 'Alliance of Civilizations' (www.unaoc.org). From 2007, the UNAOC Secretariat, based in New York, sought to work with a network of partners, including: governments, international and regional organisations, civil society groups, foundations, and the private sector. The overall objective was to improve cross-cultural relations between sometimes diverse nations and communities. At the grassroots level, UNAOC promotes various projects focused in four areas: youth, media, education, and migration, which collectively seek to build trust, reconciliation and mutual respect.

In addition to the Alliance of Civilizations there are also other high-level international attempts aiming to help build inter-civilisational trust. They include: actions by the United Nations Educational, Scientific and Cultural Organization in support of the dialogue of civilisations (www.unesco.org/dialogue2001); the Islamic Educational, Scientific and Cultural Organisation (ISESCO) programmes on dialogue of civilisations, under the auspices of the fifty-seven-member Organisation of Islamic Cooperation (www.isesco.org.ma); a Russian-led initiative, the World Public Forum 'Dialogue of Civilizations' (http://www.wpfdc.org/index.php?lang=en); and an initiative organised by a lay Catholic organisation, the Sant'Egidio community, entitled 'International Meetings: Peoples and Religions' (www.santegidio.org/).

The UNAOC in particular has been critiqued by those who are not convinced of its ability to make a beneficial difference. Riem Spielhaus, a research fellow at the Centre for European Islamic Thought, Copenhagen, contends that the UNAOC starts from a disadvantage 'when it comes to making concrete progress as it is shackled by its own terminology. The two sides are often portrayed in simplistic terms'. In a 2010 interview in the German newspaper, *Deutsche Welle*, Spielhaus argued that the main problem with the UNAOC approach is that it stems from a 'binary' approach – that is, an approach comprising two autonomous parts – emphasised in the terminology of 'the West' and 'Islam'. While 'dialogue and direct communications between individuals are to be preferred to violent conflicts', she added, 'it remains questionable whether they will lead to solutions or further partitions if the terminology remains binary'. Another negative appraisal of the UNAOC comes from David Bosold, head of the German Council for Foreign Relations' Forum on International Strategic Thinking, who argues that the UNAOC lacks fundamental ability to achieve its desired results (Amies, 2010). For Bosold, the main problem is that the UNAOC is top-down and lacks consistent connection with civil society organisations.

UN initiatives such as the AoC are only useful in terms of symbolic politics by creating a more open atmosphere for political discussions among political leaders … In order to achieve concrete results, AoC lacks at least three aspects: it is not able to connect with civil society in both the Islamic world and the West in order to bring significant parts from both sides into a permanent dialogue; it is elite-driven and not a grass roots-level endeavour, notwithstanding its pretension to achieve that very end.

Bosold, quoted by Amies (2010)

The problem is made worse, according to Bosold, because the UNAOC does not have a framework outside that of the UN. Many now argue that the UN is simply not central to international relations in the ways it was planned to be when it was founded in 1945 after the Second World War. This is a problem because the UN is recently seen to have lost relevance in international affairs. As Bosold argues, 'Since the Secretary-Generals of the UN have increasingly lost the ability to set the international agenda, I don't see how this problem might be remedied when it comes to the AoC' (Amies, 2010).

Conclusion

The chapter noted that, following the Peace of Westphalia in 1648 and the subsequent development of the modern international system, religion lost its earlier international political significance in much of the world, including the West. Given this historic context, it came as a major surprise when many observers and analysts claimed to see a recent resurgence of religion, noted on all levels of social activity – including international relations/International Relations – in many parts of the world, again including the West. This obviously calls into question the stubbornness of Western social sciences, including International Relations theory, to treat religions as important social factors on their own terms, on a par with secular discourses. Four approaches to International Relations – Realism, Liberal internationalism, neo-Marxism and Constructivism – were briefly reviewed, in order to assess how each understands the issue of religion in international relations. The conclusion of the short survey was that none of the four approaches perceives religion to be a consistently important component of contemporary international relations. Finally, the chapter paid attention to Samuel Huntington's still-controversial 'clash of civilisations' thesis, twenty years after his influential claims were first made. Problematic two decades ago because of the lack of empirical data to back up his arguments, Huntington's ideas stack up even less well today than they did then. What he saw as inter-civilisational clashes based on incompatible Western–Muslim values turned out to be egregiously simplistic, and, 9/11 excepted, they were not an important continuing source of international conflict. For that, we need to refocus not on the Muslim world but on the anti-liberal values of Russia and China, whose international values are not the same as those of the West and may well pose a much greater threat to international peace and stability than those of a mere handful of Islamist extremists who are able to make a stir but cannot win the battle for hearts and minds.

Summary points

1   Various religious actors are now involved in various significant ways in international relations. Some, but by no means all, are linked to international conflict.

2   Following the Peace of Westphalia in 1648 and the subsequent development of the modern international system, religion lost its earlier international political significance in much of the world, including the West.

3   The end of the Cold War in the late 1980s ushered in a new era of religious involvement in international conflict, with 11 September 2001 (9/11) a prime example.

4   None of the 'traditional' approaches to theorising about International Relations perceives religion to be a consistently important component of contemporary international relations.

5   There is little evidence for the claim that we are witnessing inter-civilisational conflict based on religious differences.

Notes

1 The academic discipline of 'International Relations' (initial capitals) is the study of 'international relations' (lower case).

2 Membership of the group can be found at: http://www.un.org/News/Press/docs/2005/sgsm10073.doc.htm

Recommended reading

Haynes, J. 'Al-Qaeda: Ideology and action', *Critical Review of International Social and Political Philosophy*, vol. 8, no. 2, 2005a, 177–191.

Haynes, J. 'Review article: Religion and International Relations after "9/11"', *Democratization*, vol. 12, no. 3, 2005b, 398–413.

Haynes, J. *An Introduction to International Relations and Religion*, 2nd ed., London: Pearson, 2013.

Huntington, S. *The Clash of Civilizations*, New York: Simon & Schuster, 1996.

Strindberg, A. and Wärn, M. *Islamism. Religion, Radicalism and Rresistance*, Cambridge, UK: Polity, 2011.

13 Intelligence and security

Andrew Moran

Box 13.1: Stuxnet

In 2009 the Iranian nuclear facility at Natanz was targeted by a highly sophisticated computer virus called Stuxnet. Thought to have been introduced by a USB flash drive, the virus attacked computers and centrifuges, slowing down Iran's uranium enrichment programme.

Evidence suggests that Mossad, Israel's intelligence agency, was responsible for the attack, most likely with the support of the US.

For Israel, Stuxnet was an alternative to bombing Iran's nuclear programme, which Mossad feared would lead to an escalation of violence, possibly drawing in Hezbollah, Hamas and even Syria.

It was, arguably, the first cyber-weapon of global significance, delaying the Iranian nuclear programme by at least two years, and was a major success for Mossad.

Introduction

Definitions pose a problem when studying intelligence. To most laymen, the work of the intelligence community tends to be shaped by the extremes reflected in popular culture, such as the exciting world of Ian Fleming's James Bond, or the almost drab, shadowy underworld of the spies depicted in John LeCarré's *Tinker, Tailor, Soldier, Spy*. The more historically-minded might look back to the spies of Ancient Rome or the court of Queen Elizabeth I.

More than ever before the general public are aware of the results of the work carried out by various intelligence services around the world. The use of drones to target terrorists in Afghanistan or Yemen, a police raid on a suspected terrorist hideout in London, or the introduction of restrictions on the liquids passengers can take on an aeroplane are all examples of intelligence which has been acted on.

However, the role of intelligence agencies is controversial, particularly in democratic countries where openness and accountability are important, and most especially when agencies are collecting data about their own citizens, whether through eavesdropping or covert action, or are engaged in torture to gain information about terrorists' networks or plots.

Box 13.2: Intelligence organisations

There are a number of organisations involved in intelligence around the world. The following are, arguably, the most influential.

The US has a number of intelligence agencies, of which the most famous is the Central Intelligence Agency (CIA), which collects foreign intelligence and carries out covert actions outside the borders of the US. The National Security Agency (NSA) collects signals intelligence from a variety of sites around the world. Since 11 September 2001 the Federal Bureau of Investigation (FBI) has played an increasing role in counterintelligence and counterterrorism within the US, while the Department for Homeland Security ensures that intelligence information relating to terrorist activities is shared throughout the intelligence community and between state and local law enforcement officials.

In the United Kingdom the most well-known intelligence agencies are MI5, which is entrusted with domestic counterintelligence and security, the Secret Intelligence Service (also known as MI6), which concentrates on foreign intelligence, and the Government Communications Headquarters (GCHQ), which gathers intelligence from communications, and also provides assistance to the Government and the public sector on the security of communications and electronic data.

In Russia, the Federal Security Service of the Russian Federation (FSB) is the successor to the Committee of State Security (or KGB, as it was better known during the Cold War), with responsibility for counterintelligence, counterterrorism and surveillance. The Foreign Intelligence Service (SVR) has responsibility for intelligence and espionage outside the Russian Federation.

In China there are believed to be at least five Ministry of State security bureaus which have two main goals. One is to target and crack down on dissidents to maintain internal security, while the other is concerned with foreign intelligence operations.

Israel has two main intelligence services, Mossad, which deals with foreign intelligence and special operations, and Shin Bet, which concentrates on domestic security. Their main concern is the survival of the Israeli state, with the threat of terrorism and the development of Weapons of Mass Destruction by aggressor states being a priority.

Defining intelligence?

Though the work of the intelligence community can undoubtedly be violent, and even involve death, it also involves painstaking research and the collection of information through a wide variety of means.

Indeed, information is a key concept when considering intelligence, because, as Michael Warner notes, every bit of information that exists is not intelligence (2002). It is what is done with the information that makes it intelligence. Even here, however, there are differing views of what is meant by intelligence.

Mark Lowenthal, once a National Intelligence Council officer in the US, defines intelligence as 'the process by which specific types of information important to national security are requested, collected, analysed, and provided to policymakers; the products of that process; the safeguarding of these processes and this information by counterintelligence activities; and the carrying out of operations as requested by lawful authorities' (2012: 8). Abram Shulsky added to this definition the concept of secrecy. Warner agrees, suggesting that 'without secrecy, it is not intelligence', it is simply information (2002: 20). This secrecy is essential, Shulsky wrote, because of the ongoing 'struggle' between nations 'with an enemy who is fighting back' (2002: 1–3, 171–176).

To put it more succinctly, as Lowenthal (2012) argues, governments seek to hide some information from other governments. This, in turn, leads to the latter seeking to find out what this information is by using methods that they themselves wish to keep secret.

The role of intelligence

Secrecy is important because, as Warner argues, intelligence is a form of information that enables policymakers, or operational commanders, to make effective decisions (2002). Good intelligence should aid policymakers and military planners by providing warnings of potentially threatening events and the required information to make the correct decisions to meet those threats.

Box 13.3: The purpose of intelligence

Mark Lowenthal (2012) suggests that intelligence agencies exist for four main reasons:

1   To avoid strategic surprise. The main goal of an intelligence agency is to be aware of the threats to the security of a state (this may not always work, as was highlighted by the 9/11 attacks, Pearl Harbor in 1941, and the attack by Egypt and Syria on Israel in 1973).
2   To provide long-term expertise. Unlike politicians, who are transient, whether elected or not, intelligence officers are bureaucrats who have built up a wealth of experience and knowledge on specific issues. Politicians will need to rely on their advice. In theory they offer stability and impartial advice, although this has been progressively undermined in some countries where the intelligence agencies are increasingly politicised.
3   To support the policy process. Policymakers need timely and detailed intelligence on risk assessments, background information and context, benefits, and likely outcomes to enable them to make decisions. In theory, the intelligence agencies provide intelligence while the government makes decisions.
4   To maintain the secrecy of information, needs and methods. It is the secrecy that makes the intelligence agencies unique.

For Lowenthal, intelligence refers to issues related to national security, i.e. defence, foreign policy, and certain elements of homeland and internal security.

As a result, intelligence becomes both an activity and a product, conducted in confidential circumstances. Traditionally, in organisations such as the CIA and MI6, intelligence was gathered and analysed to enable policymakers to understand foreign developments and the impact they might have. During the Cold War it tended to concentrate on military information, such as weapons capabilities, troop numbers and movements. Clandestine operations were carried out with the aim of causing certain effects in a foreign land, and intelligence was designed to influence foreign governments in ways that were unattributable to the acting government. As Warner notes, if they were open, it would be diplomacy.

Michael Herman (1996) defined intelligence as a form of power, similar to military and economic power, that allows states to project military force on a global scale. However, intelligence is also gathered on a whole variety of areas, including political, economic, cultural, social, and environmental. With the rapid pace and complexity of globalisation, intelligence is not just targeting states, but is increasingly tracking the actions of non-state actors such as terrorist groups, drug and human traffickers, and smugglers of nuclear materials. Indeed, the risks posed by these new threats have seen intelligence agencies increasingly cross the divide between the domestic and the international.

Furthermore, as Shulsky notes, intelligence does not just relate to foreign activities. Its emphasis can be solely domestic. For example, non-democratic states may regard any form of internal political dissent as a threat, with intelligence agencies being tasked to detect and challenge or even prevent that dissent, as is the common accusation made against the intelligence and security services in China. In the former Soviet Union, the KGB served an important role as an internal law enforcer as well as coordinating foreign intelligence.

Controversially, in democratic states intelligence can also be gathered on individuals or organisations that may be deemed to be a threat, or potential threat, within a state. In Britain, for example, it is well documented that MI5 targeted members of the Irish Republican Army, right-wing groups, and has now become increasingly concerned about home-grown Islamic jihadists, such as those who targeted the transport network in London with a series of bombings on 7 July 2005 (7/7).

One confusing element of intelligence for the general public is the fact that states spy on their allies. The US, for example, has often been accused of this. Yet it is not surprising that a state would engage in such activities. The US may have many allies in the European Union, but it is also competing with the same states for resources and markets. Alternatively, an ally may be pursuing a relationship with a third state which might put it in conflict with the first. A good example of this would be the disagreements between the US and the European Union regarding sanctions in the aftermath of the annexation of Crimea in 2014, or the US spying on friendly countries in the run-up to the invasion of Iraq in 2003.

States also appear to use intelligence in different ways. As noted, British intelligence is primarily concerned with home-grown terrorism. Since the 7/7 bombings there have been a number of attacks which have been thwarted, such as an attempt to blow up at least four transatlantic aeroplanes. However, terrorism is not the only issue. In December 2007, for example, the then Director General of MI5, Jonathan Evans, warned the heads of Britain's banking interests of possible attempts at espionage by Chinese hackers. The UK government has continued to express its concern at the death of the former KGB officer Alexander Litvinenko, who was most likely murdered by Andrei Lugovoi, a KGB agent, who poisoned him with a radioactive element called polonium which was traced back to Russia.

A common accusation made about Chinese intelligence is that it is engaged in espionage and cyberspace activities which seem to be centred on scientific and technological targets, whether civil or military. Indeed, both China and Russia have attempted to steal intellectual property, saving the expense and resources needed to develop their own, whether for civilian or military use.

During the Cold War, West Germany experienced terrorism carried out by the Baader–Meinhof Gang, including kidnappings, bombings, murders, and hijackings, while the Munich Olympics in 1972 saw Arab extremists take Israeli athletes hostage. Today, like many other Western states, German intelligence is concerned about the threat of right-wing and left-wing extremists, Islamic terrorists, and espionage.

The links between intelligence and law enforcement are also interesting. In the USSR the KGB served as an internal law enforcer, as does the current Chinese intelligence service. MI5 does this in the UK in cooperation with the police, but it is not something that the CIA or MI6 would engage in.

The intelligence cycle

The process by which intelligence is requested by policymakers or operational commanders and is then collected, analysed, and passed on to the consumers of that intelligence, i.e. the decision makers, is known as the 'intelligence cycle'.

David Omand (2010: 118) suggests that a classic linear intelligence cycle was demonstrated by NATO during the Cold War. This began with *direction setting requirements*, which identified the priorities and requirements to be given to intelligence agencies by those who needed the intelligence. It was followed by the *collection* of intelligence, which was sent back to the relevant agency's headquarters; *processing* and *analysis* followed, leading to an *all-source assessment* that brought different strands together and enabled judgements about the meaning of the intelligence, before the *dissemination of the finished product to the end-users,* allowing feedback on its value.

A similar cycle is common in most intelligence agencies. The CIA, for example, has five intelligence cycle stages: planning and direction; collection; processing; analysis and production; and dissemination. The FBI model adds evaluation and feedback at the final level.

During the Cold War the bipolar struggle gave intelligence agencies in the West and the Soviet Union an easily understood point of reference. What the intelligence communities were doing was rarely questioned and resources were committed to a struggle that had a clear enemy and purpose.

Since the end of the Cold War, however, and particularly since the events of 9/11, it has become apparent that the enemy has become more difficult to define as security threats have changed. For example, terrorists do not operate from easily identifiable infrastructures, as both the US and Soviet Union did. Indeed, in an age in which more is known about intelligence agencies and how they operate, terrorists have found ways of avoiding detection. It is known that Osama bin Laden stopped using mobile phones and fax machines for fear of being located – his eventual detection took years of painstaking intelligence work.

Omand suggests that what is now needed is not a cycle but rather an interactive network, because intelligence work has become internationalised as there are now common threats that pose problems for the international community (2010: 119). As a result, intelligence agencies are increasingly being forced to share information where they may not previously have done, creating a culture of intelligence globalisation which has moved from a 'need to know' to a 'need to share'. As a result, the FBI now has several overseas liaison officers serving with the CIA, while MI5 has officers working overseas with MI6. In the wake of 9/11 intelligence agencies in the West cooperated with partners in Jordan, Egypt, Syria, Libya and a number of African countries in an attempt to track down al-Qaeda's leadership and combat the spread of terrorist cells in the Middle East and Africa.

Necessity being the mother of invention has led to states being willing to compromise their values in what has become known as 'low politics', where cooperation in pursuit of a common intelligence goal is seen as being more important than disagreements in the broader political sense. Hence, Britain was prepared to share secrets with the Gadaffi government in Libya after he announced he was abandoning his nuclear programme, even allegedly agreeing to render a Libyan family from Hong Kong back to Libya where they were subsequently tortured. Indeed, the Arab Spring which eventually deposed Gadaffi posed particular dilemmas for a number of Western intelligence agencies who had previously cooperated with the security services in the region, not least the much feared 'Mukhabarat' in Jordan and Egypt.

Interestingly, Herman (2001) argues that even when intelligence agencies are competing with each other, together they can create a collective, or 'international good', such as a combined effort to tackle terrorism which can result from different agencies piecing together and sharing information, creating a bigger, more coherent picture. This, of course, assumes that competing intelligence agencies are willing to share – something that did not tend to happen before 9/11. A good example would be the use of seismology and air sampling which was used to verify North Korea's three nuclear weapons tests, which drew on information collected by a number of agencies.

Box 13.4: Sources of intelligence

Six common sources of intelligence are:

HUMINT – Human Source Intelligence. This involves the collection of information from individuals who know, or have access to, sensitive information.

SIGINT – Signals Intelligence. This derives from signal intercepts, however they are transmitted, whether between humans or electronic devices.

IMINT – Imagery Intelligence includes representations of objects produced electronically or by optical means on film, electronic display devices, or other media. This tends to be derived from visual photography, infrared sensors, radar sensors, lasers, and electro-optics.

MASINT – Measurement and Signature Intelligence. This can include radar intelligence, nuclear intelligence, or chemical and biological intelligence.

OSINT – Open-Source Intelligence is publically available information which can appear in a variety of forms, such as print or electronic form, radio, television, the internet, and commercial databases. Search engines have revolutionised the collection of open source intelligence.

GEOINT – Geospatial Intelligence is gathered from satellite, aerial photography, mapping and terrain data.

The problem of failure

One of the major concerns for all intelligence agencies is failure – missing the terrorist plot that kills hundreds, failing to prevent an assassination, or allowing a major criminal to slip through the net. US intelligence agencies were criticised for failing to predict the Japanese attack on Pearl Harbor in 1941. Though the CIA predicted the outbreak and outcome of the 1967 Six Day War between Israel and neighbouring Arab states, it could not prevent it. It did not foresee the attack by Egypt and Syria on Israel in 1973, and it failed to predict the Iranian revolution of 1979.

Most dramatically, the attacks of 9/11 are viewed by many as representing a massive intelligence failure. It is worth noting, however, that the threat had been predicted. During the late 1990s the US intelligence agencies had monitored al-Qaeda and bin

Laden's activities, and had warned the Clinton and Bush administrations of the dangers. The problem was that information was not collated and shared, leading to a failure in joining up the relevant dots. This was demonstrated again in 2009 when Umar Farouk Abdulmutallab attempted to bring down a Northwest Airlines flight as it landed in Detroit, using plastic explosives hidden in his underpants that failed to detonate correctly. Abdulmutallab had been placed on a CIA list of suspected terrorists, but had not yet been placed on the US' 'No Fly List' at the time of his journey.

Part of the problem is that there will always be events which are completely unpredictable (so-called 'black swans'), such as the Boston Marathon bombings carried out by two 'lone wolves' who were not on the intelligence radar. Events may also be too complex to model or predict. For example, US intelligence agencies did not anticipate the speed with which the Arab Spring would gather pace after Mohamed Bouazizi immolated himself in Tunisia on 17 December 2010.

There will always be unpleasant surprises and new challenges. As Donald Rumsfeld famously said, there will always be 'unknown unknowns'. Furthermore, it may not be that the answers are not known – it might be that intelligence may discover that the wrong questions are being asked. Importantly, what intelligence can do is provide a strategic understanding and help manage the uncertainty, but it cannot eliminate it.

Failures of intelligence may stem from other causes. As Jervis (1976) noted, states often interpret information to fit the image they have of other nations, with one state assuming that the other will always follow a predictable pattern. As such, perceptions are rigidly set.

Richard Betts (1978) took this further and examined why surprise attacks might be successful. The answer, he said, was not because of the weak collection of data, but rather because of three things: bureaucratic dysfunction, psychological perception issues or 'cognitive dissonance', and too much political interference by policymakers. As Pillar notes (2012), with regards to the foreign policy of the US, intelligence may not be a decisive factor in a President's actions. Any given President will have their own world view, personal experience and a perception of history and domestic politics which will shape the decisions they make. So despite Lyndon Johnson being warned in the mid-1960s about the weaknesses of South Vietnam's military forces and the enormous commitment that the US would be required to make, he chose to allow his fear of South East Asia falling under the spread of Communism, like a series of dominoes, to shape his decisions. He was also influenced by domestic considerations and the need to appear strong against Communist aggressors while pursing a liberal agenda at home.

With regard to the invasion of Iraq in 2003, it is arguable that the intelligence community warned against the dangers of going to war in Iraq, something that Bush chose to ignore. The intelligence community reports did not see Saddam as a threat and warned of the dangers of invasion leading to collapse in the country. Thus, it was not a failure of intelligence, but rather the manipulation of information by politicians who wished to tell a particular story to the public and media. The intelligence was manufactured to justify a decision already taken. However, this was not the only reason for mistakes being made. 'Group think' appears to have been operating, with dissenters unwilling to question unsound information and judgements, and there was poor source validation particularly concerning some of the information provided by the UK government, not least the outdated claims that Saddam was seeking bomb-making materials from Africa. It appears to have been the needs of policymakers that drove the process by which intelligence was selected, analysed, and interpreted.

The events of 9/11 and the failure to find WMDs in Iraq have led a number of states, notably the US, the UK, Israel and Australia, to conclude that the solution was to throw more money at a failed system. Indeed, evidence has repeatedly shown that failure to predict a major disaster tends to result in an increase in intelligence budgets. After 9/11 the US intelligence budget doubled within ten years. Today, it is estimated to spend at least $80 billion a year on intelligence, but, by nature of its activities being mostly secret, the figure may be much higher.

The 'grey' areas of intelligence

Intelligence agencies not only gather information, but they seek to covertly shape events – what Henry Kissinger once called the 'grey areas' of foreign policy. This might involve a political assassination, influencing the outcomes of elections, helping remove a foreign government from power, or sabotage.

An early example of this was the assassination of Stalin's former rival, Leon Trotsky, in Mexico City in 1940, by Russian intelligence services. In 1973 the CIA was involved in a coup in Chile, while the Israeli intelligence services are credited with tracking down and killing the perpetrators of the terrorist attack at the 1972 Olympic Games in Munich, and are also blamed for the deaths of a number of Iranian nuclear scientists and members of Hezbollah. In addition, France targeted the Greenpeace ship *Rainbow Warrior* in a harbour in New Zealand in July 1985, blowing the ship up and killing one person on board. Greenpeace activists had been campaigning against French nuclear tests in the region.

Though these actions are often carried out in a way that attempts to ensure plausible deniability, i.e. the perpetrator may cover their tracks enough to deny involvement, it is the case that those who are affected will have a good idea of who the perpetrators are, or, at least, which country's intelligence agencies were involved. For the US this has created a problem identified by Chalmers Johnson (2000) known as 'blowback', meaning the unintended consequences of covert actions that were deliberately hidden from the American public.

Evidence suggests, for example, that over forty governments were replaced in South America with involvement from the US during the twentieth century, leaving a legacy that has made it problematic for the US to have normalised relations with the region in recent times. Noam Chomsky, a frequent critic of American foreign policy, argues that the US has played a major role in subverting democracies in the underdeveloped and developing world, secretly funnelling money into the coffers of their favoured candidates (Chomsky and Otero, 2003).

The same accusation could also be made about Iran, where the American-backed removal of the democratic regime in 1953, followed by the coming to power of the corrupt, dictatorial rule of the pro-Western Shah of Iran, helps explain the continuing distrust of the US in that region – something not helped by the invasion of Iraq in 2003.

Perhaps the most dramatic example of blowback was US funding of the Mujahideen in the 1980s in Afghanistan against the Soviet Union. Out of this would come al-Qaeda.

Indeed, the emergence of al-Qaeda, partly in response to America's perceived influence in the Middle East, demonstrates how blowback can create confusion for the public because often it occurs without any context. The intelligence agency's actions which will have encouraged the blowback will, by nature, have been secretive. Thus, after the events of 9/11 many Americans were left wondering why the US had been attacked in such a violent manner.

There are some who argue that covert action can promote democracy without the use of direct military intervention, such as the CIA's support of the trade union movement 'Solidarity' in Poland in the 1980s, or the financial support the US currently offers to democratic movements in Iran. As Newton (2011) also notes, intelligence agencies have played an important role in facilitating dialogue between states and non-state actors such as terrorist groups, or even between states that do not have diplomatic relations. Politicians in the West regularly claim they would never talk to terrorists (as President Ronald Reagan and Mrs Thatcher both famously stated), but their intelligence agencies will, giving them a possibility of deniability and access that might not otherwise have existed.

Accountability

According to Cogan, the aftermath of 9/11 and the hunt for bin Laden saw the US intelligence community move beyond just gathering intelligence, becoming 'hunters not gatherers' (Cogan, 2004). Wrote Shafer: 'With little or no public input, the US government has kidnapped suspected terrorists, established secret prisons, performed "enhanced" interrogations, tortured prisoners, and carried out targeted killings' (2014). Chomsky, and others, argue this reflects a shift away from 'watch and wait' intelligence to 'capture and kill'. Where once pre-emptive action, including assassinations, was regarded as a fringe activity for intelligence services, it moved centre stage during the Bush administration. Even the Obama administration has admitted it has a 'hit list' of names of Taliban and al-Qaeda members who have been regularly targeted and assassinated by drones. As noted earlier, the UK government was also implicated in rendition and now has a 'secret court' in London where cases involving national security can be held out of the gaze of public scrutiny.

The morality of such actions is highly controversial, with some regarding it as illegal. For the West, these grey areas obviously raise issues surrounding accountability in a democratic society. In particular, can the ends ever justify the means? Furthermore, how can politicians, and the public, ever know the truth given that the intelligence agencies have the power to declare information secret?

Senator Patrick Moynihan argued in 1998 that excessive secrecy could possibly harm national security by preventing policymakers from learning valuable information required to make informed decisions, citing a case during the Truman presidency when the FBI had withheld information on intercepted communications from Soviet spies intent on espionage within the US because it was concerned that the intelligence might be leaked.

The revelations of the CIA contractor Edward Snowden in 2013 drew attention to how intelligence agencies in the US and UK had gone beyond keeping the enemy at bay to becoming almost a state within a state. His leaking of thousands of documents from the National Security Agency's computers exposed how the NSA and GCHQ were involved in a mass-surveillance programme which involved carrying out warrantless wiretaps, weakening public encryption software, collecting and storing huge amounts of metadata from phones and e-mails by mass-intercepting data from fibre-optic cables, and undermining the security standards upon which the internet, commerce, and the banking sector rely. This massive collection of data was highlighted when the NSA constructed a new facility in 2003 designed to house all the internet data it could collect in three years. It filled the site in eleven months.

Snowden's leaks are not without precedent. In 1971 a military analyst, Daniel Ellsberg, leaked the so-called 'Pentagon Papers' to the *New York Times*, which exposed America's covert escalation of the war in Vietnam. In 2010 the leak of diplomatic cables stolen by Bradley Manning and made available by Wikileaks certainly embarrassed America. The problem with the latter is that they were followed by Snowden.

One of the most damaging revelations was that the NSA had intercepted phone calls made by at least thirty-five allied leaders around the world, including the German Chancellor, Angela Merkel, who would retaliate by expelling the CIA's station chief in Germany in 2014. The President of Brazil, Dilma Rousseff, cancelled a state visit to the US in protest. The leaks also brought together the major internet companies, including Google, Facebook, Microsoft, Twitter and Yahoo, in December 2013 to protest against the spying revealed by Snowden.

Sir John Sawers, the chief of MI6, argued that the Snowden revelations had left al-Qaeda 'rubbing their hands with glee'. It is possible that Snowden's leaks, by detailing how the NSA intercepts al-Qaeda's communications, might enable the latter to avoid surveillance, but this most likely will not be for long.

Many argue that Snowden's activities amount to treason, but others regard him as a valuable whistleblower who has exposed abuses being carried out by the state. A common argument is that an official who leaks may not be able to fully determine if their disclosures will serve the public interests or not. In the case of Bradley Manning, for example, there appears to have been no quality control in what Wikileaks placed online (that was introduced by the media who chose to follow the story). Snowden, however, appears to have been more careful, deliberately exposing the lengths to which intelligence agencies in the US and UK are capable of going. In doing so, he drew attention to the fact that the intelligence agencies do not feel that they have done anything illegal. What they may have done is interpreted laws passed by Congress and the UK government in a very broad manner. The collection of personal data was approved by both the President and Congress, and by the UK Parliament.

The Snowden leaks have also drawn attention to another development within the intelligence community, which is the increasing link between private and public services. Evidence suggests that up to a third of CIA employees are private contractors, which means that it is no longer possible to claim that intelligence is solely a state-based activity. The intelligence gathered by the NSA is allegedly seen by up to 850,000 private employees from 2,000 companies, with 483,000 contractors holding top-secret clearance. Secrecy at the highest levels is no longer the domain of state employees only.

Furthermore, the laws that have been passed by governments in the US and the UK have seen private companies, such as telecommunications and internet service providers, airline companies and banks, increasingly required to become intelligence gatherers on behalf of the state by storing information on their customers. This is not without controversy. In 2014 the European Court of Justice declared invalid an EU law requiring telecoms firms to store citizens' communications data for up to two years. The Court ruled that the EU Data Retention Directive violated two basic rights – respect for private life and the protection of personal data. The UK government responded by passing emergency phone and internet data laws to ensure that the police and security services could continue to access this information, citing the need to protect the public from criminals and terrorists.

We are all intelligence officers now

As well as the gathering of information by intelligence agencies, many companies now gather information about the individuals who use their services. Supermarket loyalty cards keep records of how, what and when their consumers buy, often supported by personal information submitted by the customers about themselves and their family for free. 'Oyster' cards in London keep a record of where and how a person has travelled.

Social media sites, such as Facebook and My Space, have introduced a new level of self-surveillance. Facebook, for example, allows an individual to gather a whole wealth of information about their friends, what they like and do not like, which is provided willingly and for free as a type of 'offermation'. Mobile phones can be used by an ordinary citizen to track the whereabouts of their friends. Per person, the UK has the highest number of CCTV cameras in the world, with 4.2 million, roughly 20% of the world's cameras. There are thirty-two of them within two hundred yards of the flat that George Orwell, the writer of *1984*, lived in.

According to David Lyon (2007) this has allowed surveillance to become normalised, and, by implication, it makes surveillance at a higher level more acceptable. This leads to the clichéd defence: 'If you have nothing to hide, why should the state not practise more surveillance?' Though campaign groups, such as Liberty in the UK, argue that the government is unnecessarily intruding into the privacy of individual's lives, some in the intelligence community have noted, with more than a hint of irony, that the public seem more than willing to give highly personal information to private companies over which they have no control.

Though this may be true, the danger here is that where once democratic states had the view that they did not spy on their own citizens, now it appears to be the case that they increasingly do – all in the name of security. Though in the past it was known that the security services tracked the activities of particular individuals or groups if they were perceived as a threat – such as members of the IRA during the 'Troubles', Nixon's list of individuals he regarded as a threat to American society, or even J. Edgar Hoover's obsession with Martin Luther King and members of the Civil Rights movement – the scale of this surveillance was minuscule in comparison to the levels Snowden revealed. Simply buying a plane ticket to the US requires the British government to share fourteen pieces of information about the purchaser with the American security services.

Intelligence agencies and cyber warfare

New technologies have helped change the way in which covert activities may be carried out. John Ferris (2004) argues that the 'Revolution in Military Affairs' led by the then Secretary of Defence Donald Rumsfeld at the beginning of the 'war on terror', helped reshape the way in which war was conducted as it relied heavily on streamlining troop numbers based on an ability to utilise significantly larger amounts of complex data and new technology, such as the CIA's escalated use of Unmanned Combat Air Vehicles (UCAVs), or drones, to assassinate members of al-Qaeda and the Taliban. Though the drones have raised serious questions about US compliance with international law, some even arguing that the collateral deaths of innocent civilians constitute a war crime, the majority of Americans support their use.

Perhaps the most dramatic example of the use of new technology, however, is the development of digital weapons. Analysts dispute when the first use of these weapons occurred. Some believe the earliest known example was a so-called 'logic bomb' allegedly used by the CIA to blow up a pipeline in Siberia in 1982, while others cite a chip used to shut down Syria's defence system in 2007 which allowed Israel to bomb its secret nuclear facility. In the same year Russia was alleged to have launched a massive cyber attack on Estonia. The success of Stuxnet has already been noted. In each example, the relative country's intelligence agencies were thought to be involved.

The benefits of digital weapons are many. Like drones, they do not put military personnel in harm's way, they produce less collateral damage, they can be deployed stealthily, and they are relatively cheap. The US now defines a cyber attack as a conventional act of war, and arguably this has changed the nature of global military strategy in the twenty-first century.

It is not just state intelligence services that are using these new weapons. There are a growing number of non-state actors operating in the so-called 'dark net', launching attacks on networks around the world (so-called intrusion or penetration), utilising Distributed Denial of Service programmes (capable of disabling websites and networks and a favourite tool of internet anarchists such as 'Anonymous', as well as being the method used to attack Estonia), or complex malware.

In 2010 large businesses and government institutions were reporting four major targeted attacks a day to the UK's Office of Cyber Security. By 2012, that figure had risen to over 500 an hour and was still rising. The flood of attacks on Britain prompted the head of MI5, Jonathan Evans, to warn of the damage inflicted by this increasingly systematic assault on networked systems in Britain. Describing the increase in attacks as 'astonishing', he pointed out that in 2011 one UK company lost £800m because of a single breach of its computers (Glenny, 2011).

Governments and intelligence agencies in the West now regard protection against computer hackers and viruses as a priority security issue, with global agreements being signed and organisations being formed to tackle this potentially catastrophic development as fears mount that banks, defence systems, and utilities will increasingly be targeted.

Conclusion

During the Cold War, the struggle between East and West ensured that the role of the intelligence services was very clear, namely to stop either side gaining an advantage. However, the collapse of the Soviet Union and the changing nature of security concerns saw the role of the intelligence agencies redirected towards a growing number of issues, not least international crime, weapons proliferation, and the spread of terrorism. This movement away from state-centric surveillance led to an explosion in intelligence gathering.

The spread of globalisation has also undermined the traditional Westphalian state-centric model, which has led to an increasing integration of foreign intelligence operations and domestic surveillance. For example, the Independent Commission that looked into the events of 9/11 in the US concluded that one of the reasons why the intelligence community was unable to predict the attack by al-Qaeda was because the domestic and international intelligence agencies did not share information with each other. That divide no longer exists. Even in the UK, though MI5 and MI6 may be on different sides of the Thames, there are now clear points of contact between the two organisations. Home-grown terrorism, for example, cannot be understood within the context of domestic or international politics alone.

The growing role of private companies within intelligence organisations has increased, as has the informal role of major companies who, thanks to improvements in technology, are now able to gather mass intelligence about their customers. Unlike the secret gathering of data by intelligence agencies, customers will often offer this information both willingly and for free. In the wrong hands, this information has the potential to be misused in very damaging ways.

In the West, revelations such as those by Edward Snowden have ignited a debate about privacy and transparency, while the leaking of documents implicating the US (and to some extent the UK) in extraordinary rendition, torture and secret detention sites has raised fundamental questions surrounding the legality of some activities carried out by the intelligence agencies in the name of protecting the freedom of citizens.

Ultimately, the fact that secrecy is central to intelligence creates the most controversy. What methods are acceptable in seeking to guarantee the security of the state and its citizens? Is it necessary to compromise principles of human rights and individual privacy? For many non-democratic states these are not important questions. For the West, they remain central to the debate surrounding the role intelligence plays in promoting security, and they will continue to do so long into the future.

Summary points

1   Intelligence involves a range of activities, including analysis, collection, and covert activity.
2   The analysis informs policymakers' day-to-day decision making, and can identify threats that they might otherwise ignore.
3   Covert action, such as political assassination and torture, are very controversial.
4   Since the end of the Cold War, intelligence agencies have increasingly moved from a state-centric view of intelligence to concentrating more on the role of non-state actors, such as terrorists or international criminal gangs.
5   The failure to find weapons in Iraq raised questions about the intelligence agencies.
6   Globalisation and the rapid pace of technological change have challenged what is meant by intelligence and how intelligence should be gathered and used.

Recommended reading

Aldrich, R., Andrew, C. & Wark, W. (eds.) *Secret Intelligence: A Reader*, London: Routledge, 2008.
Johnson, L. (ed.) *Handbook of Intelligence Studies*, London: Routledge, 2009.
Lowenthal, M. *Intelligence: From Secrets to Policy*, 5th edition, Washington DC: CQ Press, 2012.
Omand, D. *Securing the State*, London: Hurst and Company, 2010.
Warner, M. 'Wanted: A Definition of Intelligence', *Studies in Intelligence*, vol. 46, no. 3, 2002, 15–23.

14 The rise of private military and security companies

Bruce Pilbeam

Box 14.1: Concerning mercenaries

I say, therefore, that the arms with which a prince defends his state are either his own, or they are mercenaries, auxiliaries, or mixed. Mercenaries and auxiliaries are useless and dangerous; and if one holds his state based on these arms, he will stand neither firm nor safe; for they are disunited, ambitious, and without discipline, unfaithful, valiant before friends, cowardly before enemies; they have neither the fear of God nor fidelity to men, and destruction is deferred only so long as the attack is; for in peace one is robbed by them, and in war by the enemy. The fact is, they have no other attraction or reason for keeping the field than a trifle of stipend, which is not sufficient to make them willing to die for you.

Niccolò Machiavelli, *The Prince* (1532/2010: 90)

Introduction

The idea of employing military and security personnel whose primary motivation is financial remuneration, rather than any deep-rooted allegiance to the state (or individual) to whom they provide their services, is not new: since classical times, mercenaries have fought alongside regular troops in conflicts around the globe. However, as indicated by the quotation above from *The Prince* by the sixteenth-century Italian diplomat and writer Niccolò Machiavelli, still one of the world's most famous 'how-to' manuals for political leaders on acquiring and maintaining power, many have viewed such swords-for-hire with suspicion or even disdain. It is for this reason that modern private military and security companies usually vehemently reject the mercenary label, even if they may have much in common with their historical antecedents. As this chapter will show, there are many reasons why these private companies are increasingly relied upon to perform a wide variety of military and security activities. Whether we approve of them or not, they are likely to remain key actors in the field of international security.

What are private military and security companies?

Until recently, the presumption in international affairs, dating back to the Treaty of Westphalia in 1648, had been that the main entities that fight wars were states, meaning that wars were usually conceived as clashes between two or more regular armies. However, as discussed in other chapters, a notable trend in contemporary conflicts has been the increased involvement of non-state actors such as guerrillas, insurgents, warlords and 'terrorists'. This group of actors also includes private military and security companies, so it is within the context of the growing prevalence of non-state actors in the waging of conflicts that these organisations are best understood.

The private military and security industry has become a highly significant one, not least in economic terms, and companies within it are used by both governments and non-government organisations. In terms of the industry's composition, it is a mixture of very large companies – usually headquartered in the US or Europe – with high numbers of employees, and many hundreds of smaller companies distributed around the globe. However, given the sensitive and sometimes secretive nature of the work carried out by firms in this sector, obtaining precise figures on the size and value of the industry is difficult. There is no single set of reliable statistics covering the entire industry. However, estimates suggest that as a whole it is worth between $100 and $400 billion a year (Pingeot, 2012: 11); even the lower end of this range is a sizable figure.

Perhaps the best way to give a sense of just how important the sector has become, and how rapidly it has grown, is to consider the extent to which some states have come to rely on private firms for military and security services. For example, in the military intervention in the former Yugoslavia in the early 1990s there was approximately one private contractor employed for every fifty US soldiers, but in Iraq from 2003, the US Department of Defense employed roughly the same number of private contractors as regular troops (Krahmann, 2010: 2).

But how do we define and categorise private military and security companies? One of the difficulties in this area is that there is very little consistency in the use of terminology. For example, some writers draw a distinction between private security companies (PSCs) and private military companies (PMCs), while others use the terms interchangeably. If the two are distinguished, probably the most common way of understanding the difference is that it is similar to the distinction between police and military forces employed by states. That is, whereas a PSC refers to an organisation that provides services similar to those of the police, such as the protection of individuals and property, a PMC is more akin to an army, either working alongside or replacing regular soldiers in the planning and conducting of military operations.

Yet many other classification systems have been offered. For example, one of the leading writers in the field, Peter Singer, suggests that there are three types of what he terms private military firms: military provider firms, military consultant firms and military support firms (Singer, 2003). However, the problem with all such categorisations is that in practice distinctions tend to break down, because the major firms that now dominate the sector typically provide all types of military and security services, and to both commercial and government clients. As such, the single umbrella term of private military and security companies (PMSCs) is generally to be preferred, and will be used throughout this chapter.

One definition of PMSCs that will be valuable to consider is that offered in the Montreux Document on Private Military and Security Companies, a code of conduct for these organisations drawn up in 2008 by the Swiss government and the International Committee of the Red Cross (ICRC). According to this code, PMSCs are:

> private business entities that provide military and/or security services, irrespective of how they describe themselves. Military and security services include, in particular, armed guarding and protection of persons and objects, such as convoys,

buildings and other places; maintenance and operation of weapons systems; prisoner detention; and advice to or training of local forces and security personnel. (www.icrc.org/eng/resources/documents/misc/ montreux-document-170908.htm)

A number of features of this definition are worth highlighting. First, PMSCs are businesses – thus, they share the characteristics of all such enterprises, such as being owned by and answerable to shareholders, having to compete in the marketplace for contracts, and, most important, being run for profit. Second, the definition hints at the fact that many companies may not describe themselves in terms that immediately make clear that they *are* PMSCs – using labels such as 'contractor' or 'advisor' instead, perhaps thanks to the negative public image this sector often has. Third, they engage in the full range of military and security activities that might conventionally have been conducted by states, rather than just – or even mainly – combat-related activities in a narrow sense.

For some examples of PMSCs, four of the leading organisations operating today are listed in Box 14.2. Most PMSCs maintain websites with substantial amounts of information about the services they offer. It is notable, however, that no company uses the word 'mercenaries' in its 'About Us' section. It will be useful next to turn to the question of whether or not they should.

Box 14.2: Four major PMSCs

(1) Academi – academi.com

This is the company formerly known as Blackwater, one of the most notorious PMSCs in the world thanks to its highly controversial activities in Iraq (see Box 14.3). Blackwater was founded by ex-US Navy Seal Erik Prince in 1997, and after various rebrandings became Academi in 2011. Its website explains that it 'serves both government and corporate clients that require elite training and security services for static site protection, executive protection, cyber and physical protection strategies, logistics planning and more'. Based in the United States, it is the US State Department's largest private security contractor and boasts a 7,000-acre training facility in North Carolina.

(2) Triple Canopy – www.triplecanopy.com

Established in 2003 by former US Special Forces personnel, Triple Canopy is also well known for providing security services in Iraq, most notably protecting the thirteen headquarters of the Coalition Provisional Authority. The company's website explains that it provides 'mission support', 'integrated security' and 'training' to both government and non-government actors, including NGOs, it has clients in countries including Afghanistan, Uganda and Indonesia, and it employs around 5,500 personnel. Sometimes, though, PMSCs can fall out with their clients, as occurred in 2012 when the US government sued Triple Canopy for alleged fraud over some of its Iraq security contracts (although the case was subsequently dismissed by a judge).

(3) Aegis Defence Services – www.aegisworld.com

This is a British company, founded in 2002 by Tim Spicer, previously a director of the controversial PMSC Sandline International (see later discussion below). Aegis Defence

Services operates across the globe, for government and non-government clients, with services including 'Kidnap for Ransom, technology integration, advisory and intelligence, training, consultancy, strategic communications and protective services'. It employs over 3,500 people at any one time and has a fleet of over 300 vehicles. One controversy it was embroiled in occurred in 2005, when so-called 'trophy videos' emerged seemingly showing several of its contractors in Iraq firing rounds indiscriminately into civilian vehicles.

(4) Defion Internacional

Based in Peru, Defion Internacional trains military and security personnel, mainly from Latin America, for deployment around the globe in roles such as drivers, bodyguards and logistical support. It has offices in Sri Lanka, the Philippines, Dubai and Iraq. The firm became most prominent when it contracted with Triple Canopy to supply personnel for security duties in Iraq, protecting the Green Zone in Baghdad. One controversy attached to Defion Internacional has been its comparatively low rates of pay, paying its operatives as little as $1000 a month for work in often highly hazardous situations.

The new mercenaries?

There are three related questions that need to be asked. What is a mercenary? What – if anything – separates PMSCs from mercenaries? And what is the status of mercenaries and PMSCs within international law? Answering these questions will be the task of this next section.

As noted at the beginning, the term mercenary usually carries with it negative connotations. Whereas soldiers who serve in the armies of states may be perceived as doing so for 'noble' reasons – for example, to protect their nation and fellow citizens, or to fight for some other worthy cause – mercenaries appear to fight purely for self-interest; specifically, they fight for money. However, in truth, the distinction between regular soldiers and mercenaries has never been entirely clear-cut. Indeed, the etymological derivation of the word soldier is from the Latin word *solidus*, a Roman gold coin. In other words, its original meaning indicates that soldiers are men and women who fight for pay, whatever other motives they may have. Moreover, it remains true today that self-interest is likely to be at least a factor in any individual's decision to join his or her nation's military (other than in cases where individuals are compelled to, through compulsory national service or because of a draft). This may be because of the salary on offer, benefits like educational scholarships, or the training and career opportunities military service can provide.

Therefore the motivation of self-interest is not by itself a distinguishing feature of mercenaries. Consequently, we need to consider more formal definitions to get a better idea of what precisely is distinctive about them. This is where we must turn to international conventions and international law.

Despite the fact that mercenaries have been around since ancient times and are common throughout human history thereafter, by the beginning of the twentieth century they had largely disappeared as major actors in armed conflicts. However, during the 1960s and 1970s they reappeared in significant numbers, in response to the turmoil and upheavals created by decolonisation. Thus, mercenaries became active in many of the post-colonial conflicts in Africa (and elsewhere), often acting with little respect for human rights or international law. The modern problem of mercenaries in conflicts was first brought to the attention of the United Nations (UN) in 1961, when the province of Katanga employed mercenaries in its secessionist war against Congo; subsequent mercenary activities across Africa were also thrown into the international spotlight. These led to vigorous condemnations by international bodies, including the UN General Assembly and the Security Council, together with a search for clearer definitions and more stringent prohibitions.

It was against this background that probably the most important starting point for understanding the international legal status of mercenaries today was created, namely the 1977 Protocol I amendments to the 1949 Geneva Conventions (the Protocol is a set of amendments relating to the protection of victims of international armed conflicts). A key value of the Protocol is that it has now been ratified by 174 states, meaning that it possesses – in theory, at least – widespread acceptance and legitimacy (although the group of states that have not ratified it include some very significant ones, like India, Iran and, perhaps most important, the United States). In any case, it states the following:

1   A mercenary shall not have the right to be a combatant or a prisoner of war.
2   A mercenary is any person who:
    (a) is specially recruited locally or abroad in order to fight in an armed conflict;
    (b) does, in fact, take a direct part in the hostilities;
    (c) is motivated to take part in the hostilities essentially by the desire for private gain and, in fact, is promised, by or on behalf of a Party to the conflict, material compensation substantially in excess of that promised or paid to combatants of similar ranks and functions in the armed forces of that Party;
    (d) is neither a national of a Party to the conflict nor a resident of territory controlled by a Party to the conflict;
    (e) is not a member of the armed forces of a Party to the conflict; and
    (f) has not been sent by a State which is not a Party to the conflict on official duty as a member of its armed forces.

(www.icrc.org/ihl/WebART/470-750057)

The first point suggests some very definite consequences for those who are given the designation of mercenaries. Since they have no right to be considered combatants, if mercenaries do engage in combat they may be liable for criminal prosecution for their actions – including, potentially, facing the death penalty (consider that, unlike with regular soldiers, any killing by a mercenary may be deemed murder). Moreover, if they are captured on the battlefield they do not have the right to be treated as prisoners of war, with all the safeguards the Geneva Conventions offer such captives, including the right to be repatriated once a conflict has concluded – a mercenary may remain imprisoned for years or even decades after the conflict. (Note, though, that the Protocol says only that mercenaries do not have the *right* to be accorded the statuses of combatants or prisoners of war, which does not preclude the possibility that they *may* be given them. Furthermore, even without these statuses, mistreatment – in the form of torture or the denial of necessary medical treatment, for example – would still be prohibited by the Geneva Conventions, as it is in the case of anyone considered a non-combatant.)

Turning to the definition of mercenary itself, attention may be drawn to some of the specifics of the Protocol's subsections. Section (a) includes the phrase *specially recruited*, so as to distinguish mercenaries from those who choose to serve in foreign armies on a permanent or long-term basis (for example, non-French recruits to the French Foreign Legion). Section (b) limits the category to those who take a *direct* part in combat – thus excluding those who provide services such as training, advice, intelligence or technical assistance.

Section (c) is perhaps the heart of the definition. By employing the word *essentially* to describe the mercenary's motive of personal gain, this takes account of the fact that all soldiers may have self-interest as *a* motive, but the mercenary differs in having this as the *main* or *over-riding* motivation. Furthermore, the paramount importance of this motive, explaining why an individual might choose the path of the mercenary over that of enlisting in a regular army, is that he or she will receive far greater remuneration by following the former rather than the latter.

Sections (d) and (e) are both intended to limit the idea of a mercenary to someone who is an 'outsider', not a member of any of the parties directly involved in the conflict. Condition (e) is deemed a necessary addition to (d) for the reason that not every member of a nation's armed forces is necessarily a national – many states employ foreign soldiers in their militaries.

Section (f) suggests that even when someone is an outsider to the conflict, to qualify as a mercenary he or she must be participating under their own motivation, not acting on behalf of another state. This is why the military personnel of other states – when acting on *official* duty – are also disqualified from being considered mercenaries.

What may be immediately obvious about the Protocol's definition is that it is very restrictive, and it does not entirely capture the everyday understanding that many people have of what a mercenary is. It is especially limiting in that to be considered a mercenary, an individual must meet *all* of the six criteria. Examples of its restrictiveness include the fact that anyone who carries out activities that fall short of direct engagement in combat cannot be considered a mercenary, even though this leaves a very large scope for providing *indirect* support to those who are direct combatants. Some of the conditions in particular, especially (e), can be criticised for providing very easy loopholes for states that wish to employ outside military and security operatives. Thanks to condition (e), even in the case of individuals who do take part in combat, who are not members of the parties in conflict and who are motivated primarily by personal gain, they might simply be designated by a state that employs them a member of their armed forces, and thus fall outside the definition.

Other important attempts to define, and prohibit, mercenaries include regional ones, like the Organization of African Unity [the precursor to the African Union]'s Convention on the Elimination of Mercenarism in Africa, which was signed in 1977 and came into force in 1985. Globally, the most significant is the UN's 1989 International Convention against the Recruitment, Use, Financing and Training of Mercenaries, which entered into effect in 2001. This Convention explicitly bans mercenaries, so it is important for this reason alone. Article 1.1 contains a definition of a mercenary based on that found in Protocol I of the Geneva Conventions, and is virtually identical, but Article 1.2 adds an additional set of conditions. A mercenary is also any person who, in any other situation:

(a) Is specially recruited locally or abroad for the purpose of participating in a concerted act of violence aimed at:
   (i) Overthrowing a Government or otherwise undermining the constitutional order of a State; or
   (ii) Undermining the territorial integrity of a State;

(b) Is motivated to take part therein essentially by the desire for significant private gain and is prompted by the promise or payment of material compensation;

(c) Is neither a national nor a resident of the State against which such an act is directed;

(d) Has not been sent by a State on official duty; and

(e) Is not a member of the armed forces of the State on whose territory the act is undertaken.

(www.un.org/documents/ga/res/44/a44r034.htm)

Of note here is that in subsection (a) there is not a requirement of direct involvement in combat – so in the case of a coup, for example, any outside individual simply 'participating' could potentially be considered a mercenary. However, he or she would still have to meet the other conditions as well; as with the Protocol, all of them have to be met simultaneously. It should also be noted that this Convention has been ratified by only thirty-three states – those that have not include Russia, China, France, the UK and the US (all five of the permanent members of the UN Security Council).

In terms of these definitions, where does this leave PMSCs? It is quite likely that many PMSCs meet *some* of the criteria set out in the Geneva Protocol or the UN Convention, but it is much less clear how many might meet *all* of them, as they are supposed to with either the Protocol or the Convention, if they are to be officially considered mercenaries under international law. Specifically, while it frequently is the case that PMSCs would tick the boxes as outsiders in relation to the conflicts in which they become involved (in terms of the Protocol, subsections d to f), the others are more difficult to determine.

For example, the question of motivation can be a very subjective issue, and while 'private gain' is by definition the goal of any profit-seeking organisation, as will be seen below, PMSCs themselves also emphasise their roles in such areas as protecting civilians and promoting humanitarian goals, which many might accept as being of wider public benefit. Nevertheless, perhaps the biggest difficulty with these definitions is their emphasis upon direct participation in combat. The problem here is that it is in fact quite rare today for PMSCs' employees to take direct part in combat operations, especially in an offensive capacity. As will be discussed below, their main roles tend to be in the broader fields of security and supporting military action, rather than frontline combat.

Overall, the problem with trying to fit PMSCs into established definitions of mercenaries is that the relevant laws and regulations were designed for an earlier age, to deal with the sorts of situations that existed in the immediate post-colonial era. Today, PMSCs operate in a different world and in different ways; apart from anything else, many today present themselves in a much more professional and 'business-like' fashion than traditional mercenaries. Only if a much broader definition of mercenaries is adopted, taking account of their changed nature, can PMSCs readily be placed within the category.

The issue is about more than just semantics, entailing the very legitimacy and legality of PMSCs. If they are considered to be no different from mercenaries, then the 1989 UN Convention might imply that they should be prohibited outright. If they are not, they may be considered simply akin to any other private businesses – in need of regulation, perhaps, but nonetheless legal organisations.

As matters stand, PMSCs are widely accepted as legitimate entities by most states, even if some have misgivings about them. Furthermore, even if they were considered to be mercenaries, so few states are signatories to the 1989 Convention that they might only be prohibited in a very limited number of places. Most telling, perhaps, is that the majority are headquartered in states that have not ratified the Convention.

Moreover, even international bodies like the UN have at best ambiguous views of PMSCs, not least because they, too, often work with them.

What this all means is that if the operatives working for PMSCs are not mercenaries (under internationally accepted definitions), but neither are they officially members of the armed forces participating in conflicts, then under international law – as contained, for example, in the Geneva Conventions – they are considered to be civilians. As such, while they may be permitted to perform supportive and defensive roles, they should not be direct participants in conflicts.

We will return to this issue of the legal status of PMSCs later on when we examine efforts at their regulation. For now, though, it will be useful to reflect on why it is that PMSCs have grown to be such an important part of the international security landscape.

The rise and rise of PMSCs

One way of understanding the rise of PMSCs is in terms of the changing nature of war itself. This has already been touched on in the discussion of 'new wars' theory in Chapter 8, which places the role of private military actors in the broader context of an argument about the transformation of war in the contemporary era. Here we shall draw upon elements of such theories, but we will also consider other factors.

As we have seen, the modern debate around mercenaries began in the 1960s, due to their roles in post-colonial conflicts. However, PMSCs specifically have grown in significance most notably in the post-Cold War era, for a variety of reasons. A large number of these are connected to the end of the Cold War itself:

- Various states responded to the conclusion of Cold War hostilities by downsizing their militaries, including the United States and many in Western Europe. In the absence of the Soviet threat, leaders in these states imagined at the beginning of the 1990s that it was simply no longer necessary to maintain such large standing armies. Therefore, when new threats did emerge, either real or imagined, these states did not have sufficient personnel to meet the perceived need.
- This downsizing also meant that there was a great influx of ex-military personnel into the labour market, whose skills could be harnessed by private companies. Indeed, many new PMSCs were created by former military figures (as illustrated by some of the examples in Box 14.2).
- Whereas during the Cold War many states in regions like Africa, the Middle East, Asia and Latin America were able to rely on one or other of the two superpowers for military and security assistance – as proxies in the US–Soviet struggle for supremacy – once this conflict ended, so too did much of the support. As such, these states have had to turn elsewhere for their military and security requirements.
- The post-Cold War era has seen an explosion of different types of security threat, including civil wars, ethnic conflicts and the rise of violent non-state actors like terrorists and militias. These threats have also appeared to create increased requirements for military and security responses.

As a result of these developments, PMSCs have flourished by filling the vacuum left by the collapse of the old bipolar order, and by responding to the rise of new security threats. Yet the ending of the Cold War is only part of the story. In relation to the first bullet point above, states have reduced the sizes of their armies before in history during periods of peace and stability, only to expand them again when new crises emerged. Why have private companies increasingly been seen as part of the solution in the present period?

Another crucial element of the explanation for the proliferation of PMSCs is the broader economic and political context, specifically the spread of globalisation and the rise of neoliberal agendas. Since the 1980s, policies of deregulation, privatisation and outsourcing have been adopted by governments across the world as part of a resurgence of free-market thinking, together with the belief that powerful global forces have undermined the capacity of states to provide the extensive range of services they may once have done. As a consequence, in areas from health to education to criminal justice, many governments have sought more and more to employ market mechanisms in providing services. The increasing reliance upon PMSCs can be understood as part of the same trend: while no state is ever likely to go as far as entirely privatising its armed forces, many nonetheless believe in complementing them with market-based provision.

In any case, the trend is one which appears to have accelerated in the twenty-first century, especially since the launching of the War on Terror in 2001. The largest deployments of PMSCs in modern times – and the sources of some of the most lucrative contracts – have been in Iraq and Afghanistan following the American-led interventions. In Iraq, at their peak numbers in 2008 there were approximately 163,000 private contractors operating under the aegis of the US Department of Defense, while in Afghanistan the peak came in 2012, with approximately 117,000 (Schwartz and Church, 2013: 23–24). At least in terms of numbers, therefore, it seems reasonable in these cases to talk of 'armies' of private contractors; moreover, in both countries there were periods when the number of the latter equalled, or even outstripped, the number of regular troops.

Who employs PMSCs – and why

Although it is private contractors working for governments that tend to gain the most attention, another distinctive feature of PMSCs is the variety of clients for whom they work. This will be explored next.

However, first it is important to be aware of the range of services that PMSCs provide, as this helps to explain why they attract an array of different clients. The conventional image of PMSC operatives is of thick-set men in quasi-military garb and dark glasses, brandishing heavy-duty weapons – in other words, individuals suited largely or exclusively to combat. Yet in reality, direct combat roles are not the most common ones that PMSCs today fulfil (indeed, the majority of private contractors do not even carry firearms).

Partly, this is because PMSCs do not wish to be classed as mercenaries, and partly because of the negative press that has attended PMSCs that have focused on combat in the past (as will be seen below). However, the main reason is simply that the greatest demand for PMSC services is in other areas.

Box 14.3 details some of the key services PMSCs supply. To return to the cases of Iraq and Afghanistan, PMSC contractors have been responsible in these two countries for such tasks as feeding and housing troops, guarding buildings, acting as bodyguards, maintaining weapons systems, providing transport, rebuilding roads and other infrastructure, and training the police and military.

Box 14.3: The main services PMSCs provide

There are various ways of categorising the services PMSCs offer, but one useful way is to divide them into the following six areas (Ortiz, 2010: 45):

(1) **Combat** – May encompass a spectrum of activities, from direct engagement to providing assistance to regular troops.
(2) **Training** – Including not only weapons and combat training, but training in areas such as tactics, off-road driving, survival skills and field medicine.
(3) **Support** – Covering areas such as logistics (managing the supply of goods and services, often to inhospitable areas), construction, maintenance and IT services.
(4) **Security** – Most obviously, the protection of individuals, buildings and other infrastructure, as well as transport (from private cars to convoys). Yet today, this may also include data and computer security.
(5) **Intelligence** – Information collection and analysis, through methods such as research and surveillance.
(6) **Reconstruction** – In post-conflict situations, activities such as mine clearing, rebuilding infrastructure and the restoration of critical services (like water and electricity).

Turning to the range of clients to whom PMSCs provide services, this includes:

- Governments
- Private individuals
- Private businesses
- Intergovernmental organisations (IGOs)
- Nongovernmental organisations (NGOs).

As this list shows, it is far from only governments that employ PMSCs. For all types of client, it is most often in contexts where existing state security is felt to be inadequate that PMSCs are contracted – particularly in the most volatile regions of the globe, and especially in failed states.

Private individuals employ PMSCs to protect themselves, their families and their property, while businesses do so to protect their operations, their infrastructure and their workers. In terms of private businesses, those in areas like mining, oil and gas (i.e. extractive industries) often operate in highly dangerous parts of the world, so they often have a need for PMSCs' security services.

The most significant IGO to examine in relation to PMSCs is the UN. As already seen, the UN has been one of the key international bodies involved in efforts to outlaw mercenarism, but in what may be seen as a contradiction, it has also worked with many PMSCs. One of the difficulties the UN faces is that it does not possess a military or security force of its own, so it is dependent upon member states to supply personnel when it wishes to carry out operations. In many cases, however, members have proven reluctant to do so. One of the most well-known cases of the international community's failure to act was in relation to the mass killings that occurred in Rwanda in the mid-1990s. Subsequently the UN Secretary-General at the time, Kofi Annan, revealed that he had in fact considered hiring private troops to intervene in the crisis. In the event, he did not, having concluded that 'the world may not be ready to privatize peace' (Annan, 1998). However, even though the UN has not yet gone so far as to use PMSCs as peacekeepers, both before and after the crisis in Rwanda it has contracted private companies to assist in many of its other activities (Østensen, 2011). For example:

- Defence Systems Limited (DSL) has provided protection for United Nations Children's Fund (UNICEF) staff in Sudan and Somalia, and to the World Food Programme (WFP) in Angola.
- ArmorGroup was contracted by the UN High Commissioner for Refugees (UNHCR) for security services in Kenya.
- DynCorp supplied helicopters and satellite network communications to the UN-sanctioned peacekeeping force in East Timor.
- Pacific Architects and Engineers (PAE) contributed civilian police personnel to the UN missions in Haiti and Liberia.

As these examples illustrate, PMSCs have been used by a number of different UN bodies to support various humanitarian and peacekeeping activities, in similar capacities to those in which PMSCs have been employed by NGOs. The Red Cross, CARE International and World Vision are just some of those that have done so. NGO workers, whether delivering immediate humanitarian relief or engaging in long-term development projects, have often found themselves under attack from armed forces. These workers are themselves unarmed, which is why some NGOs have felt the need to employ the services of PMSCs to safeguard their staff. Furthermore, even organisations like the Worldwide Fund for Nature (WWF) have hired PMSCs, to help protect endangered species including rhinos and elephants.

To defenders of PMSCs this again shows how they differ from traditional mercenaries, in that they appear to be serving not just self-interested ends, but humanitarian, peacebuilding and environmental ones. Yet regardless of who hires them, what are the (perceived) benefits of employing PMSCs?

A range of arguments is put forward by supporters of employing PMSCs, many of which mirror the ones put forward by proponents of free markets in favour of the private provision of services more generally. They include:

- **Cost** – perhaps the most important argument, especially relevant in a climate where many governments around the world are seeking to cut budgets, is that utilising the private sector brings efficiency and cost-savings. Whereas armies are normally monopolies within their respective states, and so they may have little incentive to be efficient or avoid wasteful expenditure, PMSCs exist in a competitive marketplace which therefore forces them to be cost-efficient. One way that PMSCs can operate more cheaply is that whereas state militaries must pay for their standing armies – not only their soldiers' salaries, but their food, accommodation and so on – whether they are being deployed on active service or not, many PMSCs employ personnel on specific contracts for particular operations. Consequently, they do not need to pay them once an operation has concluded.
- **Choice** – another of the claimed advantages of the free market is that it brings greater choice. Again, in contrast to the monopolistic nature of state militaries, the private market offers a range of options to potential contractors of PMSCs. This means that specific organisations can be chosen for their expertise in particular

areas, while in a different context another PMSC might be chosen. It also means that if a firm does not perform as expected it may be possible to terminate its contract, or at least not award it new ones, and find another firm that performs better. By contrast, a poorly performing army cannot be so easily replaced.

- **Innovation** – a third contended feature of free markets is that they promote the generation of new ideas and technologies much better than do state bodies. Whereas state militaries can be highly bureaucratic and slow to embrace change, PMSCs may be more streamlined in their hierarchies and able to adapt more quickly.
- **Flexibility** – a further benefit of PMSCs is that they can allow states to deploy additional forces very quickly, providing so-called 'surge' capacity to complement their existing units in the field. While it takes a long time to recruit and train new soldiers, PMSCs can be contracted much faster. This was one of the reasons that so many were hired by the US government in Iraq and Afghanistan.
- **Skills/Experience** – for less militarily capable nations, PMSCs give them access to the skills and knowledge of personnel who have been trained by the most advanced militaries in the world (since many of their personnel are former soldiers of armies from the US, the UK and Russia) that might well be greatly superior to their own. Yet even for the major powers, there are possible benefits in this area. Many PMSCs recruit internationally, meaning that they have at their disposal military expertise from every corner of the globe, which the militaries of even leading nations may not possess.
- **Politics** – as will be seen, relying upon PMSCs can be very controversial. However, there are political advantages to doing so as well. Images of dead soldiers coming home in body bags is often very damaging to the politicians responsible for having sent them to the wars in which they died. Yet while these are often broadcast by the media, along with army casualty figures, the deaths of private contractors are much less widely reported – and less likely to cause public outrage. From politicians' points of view, this may well be a key consideration in their employment.

The darker side of PMSCs

In the 1990s, various examples grabbed the headlines where PMSCs appeared to act little differently to conventional mercenaries, taking direct part in combat. Two of the most notorious were Executive Outcomes (EO), established by former members of the South African Defense Force, and the British company Sandline International; these companies also had links with each other.

EO was hired by governments in a number of African states, but the two most significant cases were when it was contracted in 1992 by the Angolan government to aid in its conflict against UNITA rebels, and in 1995 by the Sierra Leone government in its struggle with Revolutionary United Front (RUF) insurgents. Similarly, Sandline International helped the governments of Papua New Guinea in 1997 and Sierra Leone in 1998 in fighting rebel groups. (See Chapter 8 for further discussion of the Sierra Leone conflict and the involvement of EO and Sandline.)

Defenders of EO and Sandline International may point out that the governments they were hired by had a legitimate right to seek to quash internal rebellions that threatened to plunge their nations into chaos, and that it is unfair for Western critics – living in stable societies with sophisticated police forces and militaries to protect them – to denounce regimes that may not have had the capacity to contain insurgencies alone. Moreover, many of the rebel groups they combated, like UNITA and the RUF, were accused of committing atrocities and human rights abuses (although so, too, were the governments for which the PMSCs fought). Yet EO's and Sandline's participation in these conflicts was controversial for a number of reasons.

First, to return to the definitions of mercenaries contained in the 1977 Geneva Conventions Protocol and the 1989 UN Convention, it is more than possible that EO and Sandline International *would* meet all of the criteria, since they did take direct parts in hostilities. As such, they might well have been categorisable as mercenary organisations, and under the terms of the UN Convention, this would mean that they should have been banned (though most of the countries in which they operated in the 1990s had not signed the Convention).

Second, there was the secretive – and possibly illegal – nature of their activities. For example, Sandline International was involved in a number of scandals. This included what became known as the 'Sandline Affair', in which the government of Papua New Guinea contracted the company in secret to help put down rebels in the Bougainville region – when the scandal emerged, its repercussions included the fall of the government itself. Furthermore, Sandline International was accused of supplying weapons in Sierra Leone in breach of a UN arms embargo.

Third, their operatives may have paid scant regard to human rights concerns or international humanitarian law – they participated in combat without being part of any formal armies, and there was often little oversight of their activities.

Fourth, they may have leveraged their services for major economic concessions from the governments for which they worked. For example, EO was accused of receiving mineral rights to valuable resources such as oil and diamonds in return for their military and security work. Even if they did help the nations in which they operated in some respects, this may nonetheless have been at a significant cost.

Both EO and Sandline International have since been disbanded, and in the twenty-first century there have been fewer instances of PMSCs operating in such clearly mercenary ways. Yet this does not mean that contemporary PMSCs have been without controversy.

There have been scandals involving PMSCs everywhere from Bosnia to Colombia to the Democratic Republic of Congo and they have been accused of everything from financial irregularities to rapes and killings. Yet the most famous cases have been in Iraq and Afghanistan – unsurprising, perhaps, given the sheer numbers of private contractors employed in these two countries. Box 14.4 gives examples of some of those in Iraq.

Box 14.4: Alleged PMSC abuses in Iraq

There have been multiple scandals involving PMSCs in Iraq (including the 'trophy videos' noted in Box 14.1). For example:

- 2003/4 – the abuse of prisoners at Abu Ghraib prison involved both US soldiers and employees of CACI International and Titan Corporation.
- 2005 – contractors working for Zapata Engineering were detained by US Marines for allegedly firing weapons at both civilians and Marines.

Yet a whole category of scandals belongs to a single company, Blackwater. These include:

- 2005 – Blackwater guards shot seventy rounds into an approaching car, which a subsequent investigation deemed unjustified.
- 2006 – an employee allegedly shot and killed a member of the Iraqi Vice President's security detail.
- 2007 – in Nisour Square in Baghdad, Blackwater operatives killed seventeen civilians, including women and children, and wounded another twenty-four. Both the Iraqi government and US military officials condemned the shootings as unjustified.

The Nisour Square killings, the most serious scandal involving PMSCs in Iraq, eventually led in 2009 to the Iraqi government refusing to renew Blackwater's licence to operate in the country.

As well as the many abuses of which PMSCs have been accused, there are other potential downsides to their employment. For example:

- **Costs** – the cost-cutting that may allow PMSCs to operate more cheaply than regular armies can come at a price, including putting themselves and others at greater risk. For example, another Blackwater controversy occurred in 2004 when insurgents ambushed two Blackwater SUVs, killed four operatives and displayed their mutilated bodies on a bridge in Fallujah. Yet this may have occurred because the company cut costs by having two rather than three operatives in each vehicle, and did not provide higher levels of armour protection. Furthermore, there are hidden costs in employing PMSCs. In particular, since many personnel are ex-military, they will possess years of training and experience already paid for by governments, not the PMSCs themselves. Finally, studies have disputed whether employing PMSCs does indeed bring the savings claimed (Chassy and Amey, 2011: 21–26).
- **Motivation** – it may be argued that the reason PMSCs are so often involved in abuse scandals is because their primary motive is profit maximisation, rather than any real concern for either the cause their employers are fighting for or the people among whom they work. Whereas regular militaries may, for example, be concerned about trying to win the 'hearts and minds' of local populations, this may not be a primary consideration for a PMSC.
- **Oversight** – the other side to PMSCs' flexibility and ability to innovate is that since they are not part of regular army bureaucracies they are typically not subject to the same degree of oversight or regulation. They are, of course, bound by the terms of their contracts, but these are frequently vaguely worded, and stipulate few requirements in relation to matters such as respecting human rights. Overall, therefore, there may be a distinct lack of accountability and transparency.
- **Politics** – scandals such as the Blackwater killings in Nisour Square do not damage only the reputations of the companies involved, but also those of their employers – in the Nisour Square case, the US government. Indeed, the use of PMSCs has likely served to greatly undermine America's image in Iraq and Afghanistan (and beyond), and has been a contributory factor in the decline in support for these interventions. Regardless of any economic savings, using PMSCs may come with significant political costs.

Regulating the market

Given the problems associated with PMSCs and their employment, how might oversight and accountability be strengthened? Individual nations where PMSCs are based and operate have their own regulatory mechanisms, but for the purposes of this chapter, the focus will be on efforts to regulate at the international level.

One answer to the issues might be to persuade more states to become signatories to the 1989 UN Convention. However, given the fact that modern PMSCs generally do not fall within the definition of mercenaries that it sets out, even if every state in the world ratified it, this might not make much difference.

More recent efforts at regulation have sought to take into account the fact that today's PMSCs are not the same as the mercenaries of the past. In 2009, the UN Working Group on the Use of Mercenaries (established in 2005) produced a Draft International Convention on the Regulation, Oversight and Monitoring of Private Military and Security Companies. The title alone reveals that, despite the Working Group's remit being mercenaries, it recognised the need to deal with the PMSC industry as a distinct concern.

The draft convention's approach was to make *states* primarily responsible for regulating the PMSCs headquartered or contracted in their territories. Some of its key suggestions include demands that states:

- accept responsibility for the military and security activities of private entities registered or operating in their jurisdiction;
- should not delegate or outsource 'fundamental state functions' (such as the direct use of force) to non-state actors;
- undertake to pass legislation to regulate the contracting and licensing of the export and import of military and security services;
- ensure that the non-state actors they contract are trained in and respect international humanitarian law and human rights norms.

(mgimo.ru/files/121626/draft.pdf)

Of note is the use of the terms 'non-state actors' and 'private entities' in the draft's stipulations, which clearly apply to PMSCs; this thereby sidesteps all the thorny definitional problems involved in deciding whether or not they should be classed as mercenaries.

However, the draft gained only limited support from UN member states and very little from the major powers, meaning that a ratified convention did not materialise. This reveals the difficulties of getting states to agree to the use of 'hard' international law in the regulation of PMSCs – that is, law which creates binding obligations.

By contrast, the 2008 Montreux Document on Private Military and Security Companies, noted earlier in this chapter, is more akin to 'soft' law (although it is not a law or treaty in itself), since it does not impose binding obligations. Instead, it highlights the existing laws that do apply to PMSCs, as well as suggesting examples of good practice. These include improving procedures for their licensing, making certain that personnel are properly vetted, and ensuring that proper training is given not only in areas such as the use of weapons, but others such as human rights. As of 2013, the Montreux Document had been signed by forty-nine states (including the US, the UK, France and China) and three international organisations (including the European Union).

While the Montreux Document was intended for states, in 2010 the Swiss government also produced an International Code of Conduct for Security Providers specifically for PMSCs. It highlights similar areas of good practice as the Montreux Document, in areas like vetting and training staff, and shows an awareness of accepted international norms on human rights. By 2013, over six hundred companies had signed up to the code.

For those concerned about the lack of regulation of PMSCs, these developments may seem like positive ones. However, the problem with both the Montreux Document and the International Code is that, since they are not binding and – crucially – there are no enforcement mechanisms to ensure compliance, it is essentially left to states and PMSCs whether or not they fulfil their obligations. Only time will tell if this proves to be an effective approach.

Conclusion

For the foreseeable future, PMSCs are here to stay. Indeed, for their supporters, there is room for expanding their use – perhaps, for example, allowing them to take on roles such as peacekeepers. Yet critics worry about not only the abuses perpetrated by some PMSCs but also the broader issues relating to the outsourcing of activities conventionally undertaken by states to private firms: does this imply the transformation of public security into a private good? At any rate, attempts at further regulation of the industry have proven as difficult as securing greater international regulation in other areas, such as the arms trade or the environment. The underlying reason is the familiar one that the world's major powers simply do not see it as in their interests to enact restrictions that will affect them. Moreover, if not only powerful states but also international organisations like the UN regularly employ PMSCs for their military and security needs, it may be impossible to institute anything more than voluntary codes of practice. A more robust regime, with real teeth, is unlikely to be implemented any time soon.

Summary points

1   One of the main questions regarding PMSCs concerns whether their personnel should be considered mercenaries. Although many critics believe they are, because most these days do not take direct part in combat operations they are generally not classed as mercenaries according to international legal definitions.
2   PMSCs have increasingly been relied upon to provide military and security services in the post-Cold War era – not only by states, but also by others such as businesses, IGOs and NGOs.
3   PMSCs are used for a variety of reasons, including because their personnel may be cheaper than regular soldiers, and because they can be deployed relatively quickly and easily.
4   Some of the problems in relying upon PMSCs are that there is often insufficient oversight of their activities, and they have been involved in various unethical, even illegal, activities – including torture and killings.
5   Attempts to regulate PMSCs at the international level have met with only limited success – by and large, it has been left to states and PMSCs themselves to agree to voluntary codes of conduct, which do not have binding force.

Recommended reading

Abrahamsen, R. and Williams, M.C. *Security Beyond the State: Private Security in International Politics*, Cambridge: Cambridge University Press, 2010.

Krahmann, E. *States, Citizens and the Privatisation of Security*, Cambridge: Cambridge University Press, 2010.

Ortiz, C. *Private Armed Forces and Global Security: A Guide to the Issues*, Santa Barbara, CA: Praeger, 2010.

Scahill, J. *Blackwater: The Rise of the World's Most Powerful Mercenary Army*, New York: Nation Books, 2007.

Singer, P. *Corporate Warriors: The Rise of the Privatized Military Industry*, Ithaca, NY: Cornell University Press, 2003.

Section 3

Non-military security

15 Environmental security

Peter Hough

Box 15.1: The environment at the UN Security Council

In 2007 the Foreign Minister Margaret Beckett used the UK's presidency of the UN Security Council to push through, with some resistance from other members, the first discussion on an overtly environmental topic in reasoning that climate change carried implications that 'reach to the very heart of the security agenda' (Beckett, 2007). A major influence on this stance was *The Stern Review* of the previous year, compiled by a British economist on behalf of the UK government, which provided an economic security rationale for prioritising action on climate change. Stern calculated the cost of inaction on climate change as amounting to, at the very least, 5% of global GDP forever. Set against this, the costs of effective action to curb climate change would cost around 1% of global GDP per year (Stern, 2006).

Securitising the environment, though, remains unusual in international relations and contentious in International Relations for reasons that will be discussed in this chapter.

Introduction

The notion and practise of treating questions of environmental change as matters of security have evolved over the last half century, but they remain contentious both in terms of a traditional Realist view that non-military issues do not warrant such treatment, and an ecological concern that these concerns should not be militarised. Of course, securitisation need not mean militarisation, but the Human Security (freedom from want variation) rationale, that the millions of annual deaths from pollution and potential global armageddon from climate change or ozone depletion are enough to merit emergency treatment, has suffered by being in the shadow of these two camps.

The two major geopolitical shifts that affected the world in the 1970s and then at the end of the 1980s served to bring the environment into a widened security purview, firstly due to heightened fears over resource depletion, and then when the opportunities to deal with such concerns were able to emerge from under the shadow of superpower rivalry. For many, a link between resource depletion and military power political calculations began to become apparent in the economic downturn of the 1970s, and then became firmly established after the conclusion of the Cold War.

The economic downturn that accompanied the oil crises of the 1970s shook international relations practically and academically. The US and Western economies thrived under the Bretton Woods monetary system centred on Washington through the 1950s and 1960s, but it all came unstuck in the 1970s. This era of US hegemony came to an abrupt halt amid the global economic recession of 1971 to 1974. The sudden rise in oil prices, instigated when the Organisation of Petroleum Exporting Countries (OPEC) took advantage of having secured political control of this crucial commodity from multinational corporations (MNCs), allied with the spiralling costs of the Vietnam War, led to the US budget deficit (the amount of debt acquired through borrowing) getting so large that bondholders and other governments began to lose faith in the dollar holding its value in relation to gold. Additionally, the revival of European economies and the emergence of Japan as a major player in the international economy meant that the US' hegemony was not what it had been and other currencies were emerging to rival the US dollar, leaving it ill-equipped to serve as a world currency in the way that it had from the Bretton Woods Conference in 1944.

Having passed their peak in oil production and recognising that a post-hegemonic future lay ahead in the global economy, the 'Carter doctrine', announced by the US President in 1980, made it plain that questions relating to the economic resources of distant states would enter into the calculations of the American national interest by stating that military action to secure oil imports and other economic interests was a possibility:

> An attempt by any outside force to gain control of the Persian Gulf region will be regarded as an assault on the vital interests of the United States of America, and such an assault will be repelled by any means necessary, including military force.
>
> (Carter, 1980)

A preparedness to fight to secure international economic interests had, of course, been evident long before 1980. Securing access to resources was a key rationale behind the autarky of economic nationalism that marked the first half of the twentieth century and the imperialism that had marked much of the millennium. Just twenty-four years before the announcement of the Carter doctrine the UK and France had launched an invasion of Egypt in order to secure supply routes which they felt were threatened by President Nasser's nationalisation of the Suez Canal. The rise to high politics of oil pricing in the 1970s prompted greater scrutiny of the importance of threats to the supply of key economic resources to states. This became allied to the rise in neo-Malthusian concerns that global overpopulation could drain the world's resources, which had gathered momentum in the late 1960s with the rise of ecological social movements and greater recognition that resources could be threatened by environmental degradation as well as through political action. Paul Ehrlich's influential *Population Bomb*, for example, used dramatic language and metaphors in the cause of securitising overpopulation: '[W]e can no longer afford merely to treat the symptoms of the cancer of population growth: the cancer itself must be cut out'. 'The battle to feed all of humanity is over' (Ehrlich, 1968: xi).

However, it was not until the 1990s when the agenda of international politics was allowed to broaden, that environmental degradation as a potential state security threat began to take prominence in academia and mould the thinking of some foreign policy makers. Economic statecraft had been revived as an instrument of foreign policy by the oil crises (a second occurred in 1979, triggered by the Iranian revolution), but it was not until the strategic constraints of the Cold War had been lifted that a full manifestation of the Carter doctrine was put into practice with the US-led action against Iraq in the Gulf War. A just war and a long-awaited display of collective security the liberation of Kuwait may well have been, but few would dispute that securing oil supplies was a key additional motivation for the action of the allied forces.

Environmental securitisation in theory

While it was the post-Cold War optimism of the early 1990s that encouraged the 'securitisation' of environmental problems, such an approach was already being articulated as far back as the early 1970s on the basis of resource depletion. The Liberal arch-critic of Realism, Richard Falk, in *This Endangered Planet* (1971), articulated that: 'We need to revamp our entire concept of "national security" and "economic growth" if we are to solve the problems of environmental decay' (Falk, 1971: 185). In a similar vein the Sprouts' *Toward a Politics of the Planet Earth* trumpeted the need for IR to focus on global as opposed to national security because of the scale of threat posed by resource scarcity and overpopulation (Sprout and Sprout, 1971). Going back further still, in 1948 Osborn opined that resource scarcity could be a cause of war nearly half a century before this notion came to be popularised: '…one of the principal causes of the aggressive attitudes of individual nations and of much of the present discord among groups of nations is traceable to diminishing productive land and to increasing population pressures' (Osborn, 1948: 200–201). Written before the Cold War had fully set in place, this highlights just how that conflict came to dominate the security agenda in the second half of the twentieth century.

State securitisation

Towards the end of the Cold War such thinking began to permeate the political mainstream and even find the ear of a superpower. An influential article by US diplomat Jessica Mathews for the conservative and influential journal *Foreign Affairs* highlighted the need for states to give proper concern to the newly-apparent threats posed by environmental problems. Mathews, a former member of the US government's National Security Council, followed the line of reasoning of Osborn, Falk and the Sprouts but in a more state-centred, Realist analysis. In addition to calling for greater consideration in foreign policy of the effects of resource depletion on the political stability of poorer states, Mathews argued that environmental problems with global ramifications, such as ozone depletion, climate change and deforestation, should become issues of state security concern because they were the underlying cause of regional instability (Mathews, 1989). Though less heralded, four years earlier legendary US diplomat George Kennan, in the same journal, had argued that the world faced 'two unprecedented and supreme dangers', which were nuclear war and 'the devastating effect of modern industrialization and overpopulation on the world's natural resources' (Kennan 1985: 216).

From these seeds sewn by Kennan and Mathews in the 1980s a new strand of IR enquiry emerged in the post-Cold War New World Order era, positing that heightened competition for resources would increasingly be a cause of war, particularly in LDCs. Canadian academic Homer-Dixon and US journalist Kaplan were at the forefront of this area of study (Homer-Dixon, 1994; Kaplan, 1994). 'Environmental scarcities are already contributing to violent conflicts in many parts of the world. These conflicts are probably the early signs of an upsurge of violence in the coming decades that will be induced or aggravated by scarcity' (Homer-Dixon, 1994: 6). Around the same time that the Homer-Dixon/Kaplan thesis was emerging, increased competition for that most precious of all resources triggered a similar and significant 'water wars' literature, highlighting how arid regions, such as the Middle East, could increasingly see access to water used as a weapon (Starr, 1991; Bullock and Adel, 1993).

Many others have come to link scarcity with war, and a subsequent strand of the resource war literature has emerged specifically in relation to climate change. Dupont and Pearman, for example, posit that a warming world has increased the likelihood of conflict in five key ways: resource scarcity, land being rendered uninhabitable due to either water scarcity or inundation, the effects of disasters and disease, greater refugee movements, and an increased scramble for remaining resource sources (Dupont and Pearman, 2006). In an empirical study by Columbia University, similar in style to Homer-Dixon's research, it was found that countries affected by the El Niño/Southern Oscillation extreme weather phenomenon between 1950 and 2005 were twice as likely to experience major civil or international conflict (i.e. causing at least twenty-five fatalities) as those countries which were not affected. Cases in point highlighted in the study included the fact that El Niño struck Peru in 1982 in the same year as the Shining Path insurgency took off, and that civil wars in Sudan had flared up in parallel with the emergence of extreme weather conditions. The study concluded that 'when crops fail people may take up a gun simply to make a living' (Hsiang *et al.*, 2011).

Human securitisation

Going beyond the 'widened security' Realism of securitising environmental issues where national interests are seen to be invoked are Critical and Human Security approaches, which focus on the threats that environmental changes pose to people. The clearest case of how environmental change can become an issue of Human Security is in the threat posed by climate change. Earth's average temperature has risen consistently over the last century and it is now almost universally accepted that this is more than a natural development and is likely to accelerate if not responded to. The central cause of global warming is an exacerbation of the natural phenomenon of the 'greenhouse effect', caused by increased industrial emissions. Increased releases of carbon dioxide and methane over the years, principally through the burning of fossil fuels, have served to exaggerate the natural tendency of the atmosphere to trap a certain amount of infrared sunlight after it is reflected from Earth's surface. The implications of this are various but include increased desertification, a rise in sea levels due to the polar ice caps melting, more extreme weather events, and the spread of the range of tropical diseases, all carrying significant threats to human life in various forms. The World Health Organization suggests that around 150,000 deaths a year since the early 1970s can be attributed to the gradual rise in temperatures across the world (McMichael *et al.*, 2004). The human cost of ozone depletion caused by the accumulation of chlorofluorocarbons in the upper atmosphere, exacerbating the threat posed by cataracts and skin cancer, also became apparent towards the close of the Cold War and was key to propelling environmental change much higher up the international political agenda than had been seen before – and, probably, since. Aside from these globally-threatening forms of pollution, more general contamination by smog and smoke and long-range contamination of the air and water by pollutants claims over seven million lives a year (see Table 15.1).

Table 15.1 Global deaths due to pollution in 2010

1	Household air pollution (smoke)	3,546,399
2	Outdoor air pollution (ambient particulate matter)	3,223,540
3	Lead poisoning	674,038
4	Water/sanitation pollution	337,476
5	Ozone	152,434
6	Residential radon exposure	98,992

(Lim *et al.*, 2012)

Other issues of environmental change have come to be framed in Human Security terms. In 2008 the Economics of Ecosystems and Biodiversity (TEEB), a thinktank funded by the EU and the German government, put a new face on a classically ecocentric issue somewhat put in the shade by the politics of climate change. The TEEB review posited that global GDP would be likely to decline by 7% by 2050 if greater commitment to preserving fish stocks, forests and other species needed by humanity was not given (Sukhdev, 2008). Released against a backdrop of unprecedented rises in global food and energy prices, this was a particularly pertinent warning.

Environmental security in practise

As discussed elsewhere in this book designating an issue as a matter of security is not just a theoretical question but one that carries 'real world' significance. The traditional, Realist way of framing security presupposes that military issues (and certain economic issues for Neo-realists) are security issues and as such they must be prioritised by governments above other 'low politics' issues, important though these might be. The logic informing this stance is that human needs and ecocentric concerns cannot be addressed unless the country is secure in the first place. While Realism is undoubtedly apparent in real world international relations, some securitisation of environmental issues has been evident in the corridors of power, mirroring the academic dialectic previously discussed.

National environmental securitisation

Many states have taken a widened approach to security since the 1990s. The US Clinton administration made extensive use of academic advisers and the burgeoning literature on the 'national security' imperative of taking on board non-military concerns once the Soviet threat had receded. The impact of this was made explicit in the 1994 'National Security Strategy', the US' annual foreign policy manifesto:

> Not all security risks are military in nature. Transnational phenomena such as terrorism, narcotics trafficking, environmental degradation, rapid population growth and refugee flows also have security implications for both present and long term American policy.
> ...an emerging class of transnational environmental issues are increasingly affecting international stability and consequently present new challenges to US strategy.

> (USA, 1994: 1)

Clinton's widening approach to security owed much to his special adviser Strobe Talbot, who, in turn, was inspired by Joseph Nye's concept of 'soft power' (Nye, 1990). Soft power for Nye denotes the non-military dimension of state power, particularly rooted in the world of information. For US governments, being 'on top' of information on global issues was useful not only for better comprehending problems like ozone depletion but also for advancing the US' standing in the world. The resource wars literature was particularly influential on the Clinton administration in the early 1990s, convincing them that environmental degradation represented a potential source of military insecurity. Homer-Dixon is known to have been invited to brief Vice President Al Gore and the State Department on several occasions (Floyd, 2010: 75–76). In 1993 a new government position in the Defense Department was created with the Deputy Under Secretary for Environmental Security, and the Environmental Task Force was set up as part of Washington's intelligence network.

While it was the lifting of the Cold War shadow that permitted some securitisation of the environment, these concerns were periodically aired in international diplomacy in the 1970s and 1980s. Although the 1972 UN Conference on the Human Environment at Stockholm did not securitise environmental change and put it at the top of an international political agenda, nevertheless, in spite of détente, dominated by the Cold War and impending global recession, some 'high politics' did take place at the Conference. Most notably, the Swedish Prime Minister Olof Palme used the event to denounce the use of herbicides in war as 'ecocide'. Palme made no explicit reference to the recent American use of the infamous jungle defoliant Agent Orange in Vietnam, but the implied criticism caused grave offence to the Nixon administration, who responded by withdrawing the US ambassador from Stockholm. Full diplomatic relations between the two countries were suspended for over a year.

A less predictable environmental champion than Sweden was the Soviet Union, which chose to play the 'green card' on occasion during the Cold War. In the mid-1970s the Soviets were able to exploit the backlash against the US over Agent Orange and become the unlikely pioneer of international legislation proscribing deliberate environmental destruction in warfare (the 1976 Environmental Modification Treaty (ENMOD) and Geneva Conventions Protocol I of 1977). A decade later a changing Soviet Union under Gorbachev used environmental cooperation in the Arctic as an olive branch as part of his strategy of accommodation with the West, most notably in his Murmansk address of 1987 (Gorbachev, 1987).

In the new Western-oriented Russia that emerged after the end of the Cold War and the exit of Gorbachev, Moscow, rhetorically at least, appeared to become a full convert to the cause of securitising the environment. In 1994 the government Commission on Environmental Security adopted a declaration stating that:

> Environmental security is the protection of the natural environment and vital interests of citizens, society, the state from internal and external impacts, adverse processes and trends in development that threaten human health, biodiversity and sustainable functioning of ecosystems, and survival of humankind. Environmental security is an integral part of Russia's national security.
>
> (Russia, 1994: 55)

Similarly, post-Communist Hungary made environmental security an explicitly-expressed foreign policy concern in the 1990s:

Problems appearing in the context of environmental protection and threats to civilisation spreading across borders constitute some of the largest-scale challenges to mankind. The protection of our natural resources, our natural habitat and values, as well as the preservation of the environmental balance is putting an ever-increasing burden on our societies. Such global problems as the destruction of rain forests, damages to the ozone layer, the greenhouse effect and the increase of air, water and soil pollution constitute a threat to our entire Earth.

(Hungary, 1998)

More predictable converts to making the environment the stuff of high politics have since emerged in North America and northern Europe. Finland's Security and Defence Policy of 2004 recognises the interlinkages between the environment and security in terms of the extent to which resource scarcity and degradation, allied to unequal access, 'have increased the likelihood of conflict' (Finland, 2004). Canada's foreign policy declares one of six core goals to be understanding 'the interaction among the social, economic, and environment pillars of sustainable development, and of how human security and human rights relate to sustainable development' (Canada, 2002). In 2008 the UK followed a similar path to the US over a decade earlier; following up on the Security Council initiative, climate change was referred to in the UK's inaugural National Security Strategy and, a year later, a new role of Climate and Energy Security Envoy was created. The Netherlands' 2006 Foreign Policy Agenda also specifically acknowledges the role that environmental degradation plays in threatening global security. However, the Dutch also go beyond national security widening in declaring one of the eight goals of this policy to be 'to protect and improve the environment' (Netherlands, 2006).

This ecocentric trend towards making the environment the referent object of security has also been advanced in a different political form in recent years outside the Western world, appearing as part of the 'new left' wave in Latin America from the late 2000s. The critical stance on Western capitalism and focus on indigenous people that marks this political movement has found expression in the empowerment of nature. In 2008 Ecuador's new constitution declared that nature had the 'right to exist, persist, maintain and regenerate its vital cycles, structure, functions and its processes in evolution', and mandates the government to take 'precaution and restriction measures in all the activities that can lead to the extinction of species, the destruction of the ecosystems or the permanent alteration of the natural cycles' (Ecuador, 2008).

While many countries have cited environmental protection in their constitutions, none have done so in such unambiguously ecocentric terms. This 'rights of nature' approach has also been followed by the Morales government in Bolivia where the 'Law of Mother Earth' defends the right of nature 'to not be affected by mega-infrastructure and development projects that affect the balance of ecosystems and the local inhabitant communities' (Bolivia, 2011). For both countries this idea of environmental rights has come from the twin impact of the empowerment of indigenous people and a legacy of environmental pollution. The rights of long-marginalised indigenous Americans (of which Morales is one) have become an important domestic political concern aided by greater international discourse on this realm of politics, which is promoted within the UN system by the Trustee Council, the Working Group on Indigenous Populations, the Human Rights Council and the International Labour Organization (particularly

Convention 169). In addition, the long-standing problem of pollution from oil in Ecuador and tin in Bolivia has heightened environmental concerns beyond those witnessed in most developing countries.

Some states have even securitised the environment in the most explicit and traditional way by sending in troops to tackle ecological disasters. In 2009 Bangladesh deployed armed forces to lead the national response to the cyclone Aila. More significantly, Brazil established the National Environmental Security Force to combat deforestation in 2012, employing a combination of armed forces and police to tackle the huge problem of illegal logging in the Amazonian rainforest.

While it could be argued that none of the aforementioned political announcements or initiatives really make environmental change the number one diplomatic priority, this is clearly the case for some states affected by climate change. For low-lying island states the prospect of a rise in the level of the oceans is a human and state security threat of the utmost gravity:

> We want the islands of Tuvalu, our nation, to exist permanently forever and not to be submerged underwater merely due to the selfishness and greed of the industrialised world.
>
> Saufatu Sopoanga, Prime Minister of Tuvalu,
> at the 2002 World Summit on Sustainable Development (Sopoanga, 2002)

These governments have sought to emphasise the urgency of international action in diplomatic forums and in media-friendly stunts such as the holding of a cabinet meeting of the Maldives government underwater in 2009. However, in a realistic assessment of the likelihood of their pleas being acted upon, the governments of the Maldives and Kiribati have already made plans to shift their entire populations to other locations.

Intergovernmental environmental securitisation

In the politics of intergovernmental organisations we can see the notion of securitising the environment begin to emerge in the early 1970s before properly flourishing in the aftermath of the Cold War. Once again, Swedish Prime Minister Olof Palme was pivotal in securitising the environment at the United Nations. At the UN Commission on Disarmament and Security in 1982 Palme called on member states to move beyond considering collective security and embrace 'common security', bringing into focus threats emanating from overpopulation, environmental degradation and resource scarcity (Palme, 1982). Two years earlier Palme had been part of the Independent Commission on International Development Issues which gave rhetorical support to securitising the environment, stating that 'few threats to peace and survival of the human community are greater than those posed by the prospects of cumulative and irreversible degradation of the biosphere on which human life depends' (ICIDI, 1980).

In the 1980s the onset of the second Cold War limited the advance of this environmental security agenda, but the mantle was picked up again in the revival of multilateralism during the 1990s, and has found expression in several elements of the UN system. In 2004 the United Nations Secretary-General's High-Level Panel on Threats, Challenges, and Change produced a report endorsed by many governments at the Millennium Review Summit the following year, setting out a new vision of comprehensive security, reminiscent of Palme's Common Security, that addresses six clusters of threats with which the world must be concerned now and in the coming decades. These include poverty, infectious disease and environmental degradation (UN, 2004). Following the Security Council discussion of climate change two years earlier, in 2009 the UN General Assembly also took up this theme with a resolution entitled Climate Change and its Possible Security Implications calling on all UN agencies to prioritise climate change, drafted by the government of low-lying Nauru and unanimously adopted (A64/350).

Perhaps, though, the clearest illustration of the environment becoming the stuff of widened security comes from its embrace by the Cold Warriors of NATO:

> Based on a broad definition of security that recognizes the importance of political, economic, social and environmental factors, NATO is addressing security challenges emanating from the environment. This includes extreme weather conditions, depletion of natural resources, pollution and so on – factors that can ultimately lead to disasters, regional tensions and violence.
>
> (NATO, 2013)

Human Security approaches highlighting the necessity of tackling vulnerability to environmental problems have also been strongly advocated within the UN system by the two most recent Secretary-Generals, the Human Security Unit of the Office for the Coordination of Humanitarian Affairs within the Secretariat, and, most notably, the UN Development Programme (UNDP):

> The concept of security must change – from an exclusive stress on national security to a much greater stress on people's security, from security through armaments to security through human development, from territorial to food, employment and environmental security.
>
> (UNDP, 1993)

Merits and demerits of environmental securitisation

Is the securitisation of the environment to be welcomed? The question of whether environmental problems merit the politically significant label of 'security' is a complex and highly contested one. On the one hand, the complexity and uneven human impact of environmental issues leads to disputes about the scale of the threat they pose, or else an attitude of denial in the face of 'inconvenient truths' often geographically or chronologically distant. On the other hand, there is a lack of consensus as to what 'security' actually means. For some who are unable to break free of a militarised and state-centric view of IR forged in the three global wars of the twentieth century, environmental challenges can only be considered the stuff of security if they can be seen to cause wars or threaten the sovereign apparatus of states. For others who may be receptive to ontological and epistemological challenges to the conventions of IR that emerged following the end of the Cold War, environmental threats can and should be securitised by abandoning the preoccupation with the state and the military and facing up to a different nature of threat. A third perspective agrees with the second in terms of the scale of threat posed by environmental problems, but resists securitisation because of concerns that this risks invoking inappropriate, militaristic 'national security' responses.

Deudney cites three key arguments for not extending the reach of Security Studies to incorporate environmental issues:

1. It is analytically misleading to think of environmental degradation as a national security threat, because the traditional focus of national security – interstate violence – has little in common with either environmental problems or solutions.
2. The effort to harness the emotive power of nationalism to help mobilize environmental awareness and action may prove counterproductive by undermining globalist political stability.
3. Environmental degradation is not very likely to cause interstate wars.

(Deudney, 1990: 461)

Point three is a direct rebuttal of the Homer-Dixon approach of coupling certain environmental issues with military security, which is certainly open to challenge. Despite its influence on the thinking of the US government and others, the approach of framing environmental scarcity as a military security matter has not been without its critics. The empirical evidence linking environmental degradation and political conflict is, by Homer-Dixon's own admission, not straightforward, prompting scepticism as to whether other variables are the real causes of conflicts in situations where environmental scarcity can be demonstrated. The assumption that changes in the balance between resources and people create political problems is viewed as flawed logic by the resource war sceptics. Critics have reasoned that it is easy to link droughts in Sudan to the Darfur Crisis and other civil conflicts in the country, but such events are unfortunate facts of life in the Sahel and the responsibility for the bloodshed lies squarely with the Janjaweed insurgents and the Sudanese government for giving a green light to their murderous campaigns (Brown and McLeman, 2009: 297). History also can provide plenty of evidence of environmental disasters and extreme weather conditions *not* prompting conflict. The devastating dustbowls that struck the US Great Plains in the 1930s did not trigger conflict (Brown and McLeman, 2009: 296). Neither was conflict a consequence of the 2010 earthquake in the far more politically volatile state of Haiti, in spite of the widespread assumptions that it would be. Australia has been as much affected by El Niño as Sudan or Peru, but has not been struck by civil war for obvious economic and political reasons. The cited cases could suggest a correlation between conflict and underdevelopment and a lack of democracy, more than with environmental scarcity.

Deudney's second point rightly implies that global problems require global responses rather than relying on individual state calculations of rationality, a standard challenge presented by environmental problems to the traditional statist national interest-based model of how foreign policies should be constructed. For Human Security advocates, however, the weakness in Deudney's argument comes from a statist bias in another way. Nationalism is indeed an inappropriate political ideology to tackle most environmental problems, but who has ever proposed this as a solution to climate change or pollution? Deudney, in common with most traditionalists, conflates 'security' with 'something that requires a military response by the state', rather than seeing it as a condition which relates to people's lives and which can be acted upon at various political levels. 'Both violence and environmental degradation may kill people and may reduce human well-being, but not all threats to life and property are threats to security' (Deudney, 1990: 463). This represents an explicit admission that 'security' can have no meaning other than being a synonym for 'military defence against other states'.

For Human Security advocates, the scale of threats to people posed by environmental change are so far removed from the way in which issues are conventionally ordered on the political agenda by states that International Relations theory and international political practise needs to find ways of accommodating them, or else they will cease to be connected in any meaningful way with human behaviour and needs. Eight million people a year already die from pollution, and this is set to get much worse. War and terrorism, in contrast, represent much lesser threats (around 170,000 deaths per year). Most of these deaths from pollution or natural disasters could be avoided by political action, and therefore if steps are not taken to avoid them, a political failing has occurred. Are people who are indirectly killed by a known problem not insecure?

However, another concern with securitising the environment is the lack of consensus and subsequent confusion over what this actually means. De Wilde points out that there is a fundamental problem in very different ideas coming to be conflated in the environmental security literature: i) the environment as the referent object to be secured by urgent human action; and ii) human civilisation as the referent object to be secured against environmental change (De Wilde, 2008: 598–599).

This argument has validity since securitisation does mean different things to different thinkers, governments and international organisations. Civilisational security can and has been invoked on occasion, but it risks accusations of exaggeration, particularly in light of the hysteria prompted by overpopulation concerns in the late 1960s. Securing the environment against human harm can be understood as the fundament of political ecology, and as such it could be accused of merely representing a new and unnecessary label for ecocentric policy. However, while it has been criticised for its vagueness and comes in different strengths, Human Security does have a clear referent object – the human. Given the transboundary and global nature of environmental problems, the human is also a more clear-cut reference point for security than the state in this area. 'Territorial security, for delimited groups may once have been fundamental to achieving "the good life", but it now seems more likely that the security of the global environment (incorporating localities) is the basic condition for human security' (Dyer, 2001: 449).

Human Security is still somewhat problematic from an environmentalist perspective since this is, by definition, an anthropocentric rather than ecocentric way of framing problems. However, so long as Human Security is understood in the context of us being part of a global biosphere, the safeguarding of which enhances both human and non-human interests, this need not be a problem. Dalby argues that the key to safeguarding Human Security in issues such as climate change and resource depletion is to cease framing such problems in the context of 'environmental threats'. Dalby defines security in terms of a referent object which is the global totality: 'the assurance of relatively undisturbed ecological systems in all parts of the biosphere' (Dalby, 2002: 106). Thinking in such ecological terms means that social and economic transformations are not treated as distinct from atmospheric or biological developments in terms of their consequences. Human Security can then be incorporated into this logic of ecological security. 'When people do not have enough options to avoid or adapt to environmental change such that their needs, rights and values are likely to be undermined, then they can be said to be environmentally insecure' (Matthew, Barnett, McDonald and O'Brien, 2010: 18). Appreciating that human phenomena like urbanisation or increasing consumption have effects in the natural world with implications for Human Security can improve the management of threats. Security threats can be more subtle than the rapid emergence of a hole in the ozone layer, and the solutions more complex than switching from the use of CFCs to replacement chemicals. A better appreciation of this complexity could help alleviate these difficulties before they become imminent crises. The traditional practises of international relations, though, are much better suited to responding to crises rather than tackling the long-term, underlying causes of these sources of insecurity.

A further consequence of this residual Realism still permeating real-world international politics is that securitising the environment for many still invokes a perception of militarisation which, apart from some utility for deploying armed forces in the aftermath of a natural disaster, offers few solutions while presenting further problems. National securitisation may be welcomed in terms of getting governments on board and giving environmental issues the spotlight they often deserve, but old habits die hard, and this does tend to frame the issues in Realist terms. The discourse of environmental change in venues of intergovernmental 'high politics' invariably becomes reduced to the resource wars thesis or the apparent threat posed by a rise in environmental migration. Environmental degradation is deemed important because it might be a cause of war and instability rather than because it **is** a threat to life in itself. The UK UN delegation in 2007 cited the following security implications of climate change: border disputes due to the melting of ice sheets and rising sea levels; increased migration with 'the potential for instability and conflict'; conflict over energy supplies; conflict due to scarcity; conflict due to poverty; and conflicts related to extreme weather events (UNSC, 2007).

Hence the UK advocacy of action on climate change at the UN Security Council in 2007 was as Realist as the Chinese and South African objections to debating the issue. The British had been won over by the resource war thesis of Homer-Dixon and others, believing that mitigating global warming was a route to peace and also calculating that it made economic sense given the conclusions of *The Stern Review* they had convened, which concluded that the costs of inaction on climate change greatly exceeded the price of action. Compassion for the fate of peoples most affected – those living in arid, low lying or polar regions – doubtless played a part in the thinking of Beckett, Blair and the Labour government, but a clear self-interest was apparent and British permanent membership of the Security Council provided a good opportunity to attempt a 'tactical securitisation' of the issue. The Chinese and South Africans, in disputing this securitisation move, were not rejecting the notion that climate change was an important concern, but calculating that it was not in their national interests to debate this in the Security Council.

The playing of the national security card over climate change by some countries is instinctively treated with suspicion by others because of what national security is understood to stand for in the discourse of international relations that all have been engaged in over the past century. It invokes a militarisation of politics with an aggressive interference in the affairs of others or a defensive retreat behind strengthened armed borders, neither of which are relevant for the multi-dimensional threats posed by climate change. The rhetoric of climate change securitisation has done little to dispel this notion. The debates in the Security Council in 2007 and 2011, the foreign policy statements of the US, the UK and others, plus the academic arguments of the likes of Homer-Dixon, have highlighted national security threats to do with failed states, resource conflict and mass migration. Tightening up borders to deter environmental migrants is directly contradictory to the human interest, and the armed humanitarian intervention solution to lawlessness deployed in other contexts is unlikely to be either welcome or useful.

The misgivings of the Chinese and South Africans over debating climate change in the Security Council doubtless had something to do with their determination not to compromise their economic development, but there is some merit in the argument that it is an issue better tackled elsewhere. In theory it is appropriate that climate change should be debated at the high table of global politics, but the problem with this in practise is that the UN Security Council has always been an arena of great power realpolitik. It is the arena where Soviet and US Cold War adventurism was ignored, and, in the present age, where violations of International Law by countries like Israel and Syria are still ignored because of their continued sponsorship by Washington and Moscow.

Furthermore, militarisation may not only be unwarranted but also, possibly, inaccurate. Environmental change may even be a source of peace rather than conflict. Contrary to many assumptions, there is no real evidence of transboundary environmental problems or greater resource scarcity prompting war, and indeed the environment can be 'used' in the context of peace building. Gorbachev's initial westward-reaching olive branches were to propose environmental cooperation in the Arctic and to tackle pollution. In a more concrete example of peace building, in 1998 the Peru–Ecuador Cordillera de Condor 'Peace Park' was consciously established by both governments to dampen the long-running border dispute between the Andean neighbours by consigning a contested mountainous region as a zone of conservation (Conca and Dabelko, 2002).

An additional problem with securitisation is that it fuels accusations of scaremongering and exaggeration from vested interests seeking to downplay environmental problems. The overpopulation hyperbole of the late 1960s and subsequent expansion of the food supply though technological innovation in the Green Revolution fed the dangerous climate change scepticism which stifles requisite urgent international action today. Concentrating on highly speculative and unproven links between environmental change and war rather than on rigorously researched and already evident negative consequences of climate change, pollution or deforestation does not help in overcoming such accusations.

Conclusion

The consideration of environmental issues as matters of security has gathered momentum academically and politically but remains highly contested. This is not only a consequence of environmental issues being given different levels of priority by different ideological perspectives, but also a question of appropriateness. Those resisting securitisation are not only the environmental sceptics, but also environmentalists alarmed at the apparent coupling of the issue with the politics of national interest and militarism.

Where the military assumption can be overcome, the national securitisation of the environment can still lead to inappropriate solutions. Technological quick fixes, reactive responses after a crisis and headline-grabbing stunts are often more politically attractive than the slow, unspectacular politics of tackling underlying causes of vulnerability. However, low-key, gradual, technical solutions are usually what are needed to address insecurities arising from environmental change. It was the careful, prolonged work of transnational scientists and civil society actors rather than grand government gestures that achieved the international political successes seen in combating ozone depletion, based on the Montreal Protocol of the 1985 Vienna Convention, which UNEP claim has averted 1.5 million cases of skin cancer and 130 million cataracts (UNEP, 2012). Put in these terms, this is environmental policy clearly in the cause of Human Security, but putting limits on industrial emissions is not what most people think of as the politics of security. The problem of securitising the environment remains; as Prins and Stamp memorably put it, 'you can't shoot an ozone hole' (Prins and Stamp, 1991: 12).

Summary points

1   Issues of environmental change have often been framed as (widened) national security concerns – both academically and governmentally – through fears of resource depletion triggering conflicts, but this thesis is disputed.
2   Issues of environmental change are also often framed as Human Security concerns because of the considerable death toll attributable to pollution, but this is contentious, both to traditional security theorists and to some ecologists fearful that the 'label of security' will prompt inappropriate political responses.

Recommended reading

Dalby, S. *Security and Environmental Change*, Cambridge: Polity, 2009.
Floyd, R. and Mathew, R. *Environmental Security. Approaches and Issues*, London and New York: Routledge, 2013.
Hough, P. *Environmental Security. An Introduction*, London and New York: Routledge, 2014.
Mathew, R.A., Barnett, J., McDonald, B. and O'Brien, K.L. (eds), *Global Environmental Change and Human Security*, Boston: MIT Press, 2010.

16 Crime and security

Peter Hough

Box 16.1: Cocaine and security

Colombia's cocaine industry illustrates the multi-dimensional links between crime and security. The national security of Colombia and the Human Security of its citizens have long been inextricably linked to the production and trade of the notorious narcotic, owing to the power of criminal syndicates who have fought, corrupted and killed in order to control this commerce and the fact that both sides in a long and brutal civil war have also utilised it in order to fund their insurgencies.

The security ramifications of Colombian cocaine extend well beyond its borders, though. The lucrative cocaine trade has implications for the national security of Mexico and other parts of Central America and the Human Security of the people who live there as the corruption of state officials and internecine wars between gangs seeking to escort the cargoes periodically spiral out of control. The security dimension of cocaine then also extends to the destinations of this trade in North America, Europe and beyond, where the illegal sale and consumption of the drug claims and undermines thousands of lives to addiction and the criminality that sustains the industry.

The 'securitisation' of cocaine in international political affairs is classically illustrated by the deployment of US and UK troops sent to assist the Colombian government in their war against drug barons and 'narco-terrorists'. What is also clear, though, is that such traditional national security measures have not succeeded in stifling the cocaine industry, such are its international tentacles. In a telling illustration of the complexities of securing people and countries against crime, the Colombian government, at the same time as hosting British and American troops, has despatched government ministers and diplomats to London and Washington to call upon those governments to do more to stop their citizens taking cocaine, recognising that this is the root cause of their and the world's problem with the addictive white powder.

Introduction: the globalisation of crime

The complexities and paradoxes that globalisation brings are very apparent when examining the case of international crime. The political and economic coming together of the world over the past quarter of a century may have enhanced personal and national security in many ways, but it has also served to heighten some forms of insecurity, and international crime is notable among these.

Crime has always been a Human Security concern and the maintenance of law and order has always been a key aim of sovereign government and domestic politics. Indeed, it can be argued that this is the main rationale for sovereign statehood becoming the cornerstone of political order from the seventeenth century, marking the end to an era of the arbitrary justice of warlords, barons and invaders. In some cases there is also a long history of crime becoming a concern to governments to the point of it being a matter of national security. The level of influence held by organised crime gangs in southern Italy since their emergence in the mid-nineteenth century, when sovereign authority from Rome was yet to be established, is a case in point, as is the influence of drug barons in Colombia. International crime is also far from new if we consider the export of Italian mafia operations to the US in the early twentieth century and the long history of trading in cocaine and other illegal commodities. However, the national and human security implications of international crime have significantly heightened over recent decades, making law and order the stuff of international, rather than just sovereign, domestic politics.

Since the late 1980s crime has become much more internationalised as a side-effect of post-Cold War political change and the onset of globalisation in its various forms. Statistical support for this is inevitably uncertain, but nevertheless pretty compelling. The IMF estimates that the amount of criminally acquired money in the world grew from $85 to $5000 billion between 1988 and 1998 (Kendall, 1998: 264). One of the most comprehensive and reliable studies of international crime, by the Council of Europe, showed that the number of convictions for completed homicide rose from 1.5 per 100,000 people in 1990 to 2.9 in 1996 (CoE, 1999: Table 3.B.1.2). This economic trend has continued and the global black market now accounts for over $2 trillion per year or 6% of global GDP (UNODC, 2011a). Indeed, this may be a conservative estimate since UN data does not give a full account of financial crimes, and Glenny, for one, has suggested that 15% of the global economy is black (Glenny, 2008).

The end of the Cold War

The end of the Cold War can be understood to have facilitated the rise in the significance of and priority given to crime in several ways. The rise of 'failed states' is a striking symptom of post-Cold War insecurity with repercussions for a number of international political issues. Since the 1990s this term has come to be attributed to those countries where a single government could not be said to be in effective political control within its own borders beyond what could be understood as any sort of period of transition or temporary civil strife. In effect, such territories can be seen to be in a permanent state of insurgency or general lawlessness. The preponderance of failed states increased after the ending of the Cold War partly because many such countries lost the patronage of a superpower in a New World Order where they ceased to hold such a strong military security attraction.

The classic case of the failed state is Afghanistan. Invaded by the USSR in 1979, Afghanistan became the focal point of the Second Cold War, with the US providing substantial financial and military backing to the mujahideen resistance fighters. The thawing of relations between the US and the USSR saw Soviet Premier Gorbachev announce the withdrawal of troops from the bloody and intractable conflict in 1988. This ended the proxy war between the two superpowers but did not end the conflict in Afghanistan, where rival factions continued to fight out a civil war in the power vacuum created by the sudden disinterest of the world's two most powerful states. The political legacy of this for the US in terms of the rise of anti-American terrorist groups from the mujahideen is well documented, but Afghanistan also rose again as a crucial haven for the global heroin industry. Ironically it was the toppling of the Taliban by the US-led invasion of 2001 that served to increase lawlessness in the country and led to a resurgence in the export of opiates to the West, since that government had begun to clamp down on narcotics production.

Somalia represents another quintessential failed state, with much of the country existing in turmoil since the collapse of the Soviet-backed Barre government in 1991. Against this backdrop we can easily see how gangs of pirates have been able to thrive off the coast and become a scourge of international cargo and tourist liners travelling through the region. The pirates themselves have even cited the lack of sovereign authority as a justification for their actions in seizing control of their country's waters from international criminals:

> We don't consider ourselves pirates. We consider pirates those who illegally fish in our seas and dump in our seas and carry weapons in our seas. Think of us like a Coast Guard.
>
> (Ali, 2008)

Failed states are significant in International Relations because they stand in contradiction to conventional notions of the sovereign state system. Sovereignty is traditionally viewed as the cement that holds together the state system and maintains international order. The crucial component of the multi-faceted concept of sovereignty, enshrined in International Law in the 1933 Montevideo Convention on the Rights and Duties of States, is that a sovereign state has a government in 'effective control'. The rise in cases where countries cannot be said to have a sovereign government in effective control – such as in Afghanistan, Somalia or Colombia – is, of course, a recipe for increased lawlessness in the world.

Short of the complete sovereign meltdown that characterises failed states are the 'mafiocracies' that have emerged as a consequence of weakened state structures resulting from post-Communist change (Godson and Williams, 2000: 113). One of the most prominent features of the post-Cold War political landscape has been the process of transition of many former Communist countries towards the Western model state with a partially free market economy and a democratic political system. Welcomed by most Western governments and analysts as reducing the likelihood of military conflict in the world and even signalling 'the end of history' (Fukuyama, 1992), this wave of democratisation can also, however, be construed as having brought with it new security threats to the world.

Transition from a one-party state to a multi-party democracy, and from a centrally-planned economy to a more diverse mixed economy with private industries and shareholders, is a very difficult process. Poverty and social upheaval are always favourable conditions in which crime can thrive, and even the successful transition states have witnessed increased social problems with black marketeers and illegal traders of various kinds. EU states have helped alleviate this by providing policing advice and training to their eastern neighbours through aid and EU accession preparations, and it is the former Communist countries further east, which have found most difficulty in making the transition to capitalism and democracy, where crime has become most prevalent and of greatest concern to the rest of the world. Rapid, wholesale privatisation programmes in countries without experienced businessmen, shareholders and private bankers inevitably run the risk of leaving key industries in the hands of black marketeers and unscrupulous individuals.

Between a quarter and a third of Russia's economy is widely held to be black, and the murder rate has rocketed since the fall of Communism. Criminal gangs or *mafiya* are a prominent feature of Russian life, with extortion rackets rife in most cities. These syndicates are generally far from new and can be traced back to gangs that were successfully suppressed in the Communist era. However, additional recruits came from newly-redundant military and security personnel as some of the post-Cold War peace dividend turned to filthy lucre. The influence of the *mafiya* has also extended into operations in many parts of Europe and elsewhere in the world.

Perhaps the clearest illustration of a new security threat emerging in international politics with the ending of the Cold War, and souring the toasts being made to global peace, is the rise in black market trading in weapons-grade nuclear material. Nearly seven hundred incidences of such operations were documented in the 1990s, principally focused in the successor states of the Soviet Union (Williams and Woesner, 2000). Here, President Yeltsin had assumed control from Gorbachev of a country shorn not only of fourteen of its fifteen republics and six colonies, but also of a large chunk of its huge nuclear arsenal.

A further example of how post-Communist transition can serve as a catalyst for international crime at the same time as enhancing wider state security is provided by Kosovo. The Yugoslav successor state, fought for and sustained by Western compassion and interest, has become a haven for criminality while its sovereignty slowly evolves. The 2005 UN Drug Report identified Kosovan organised crime groups as the key controllers of heroin trafficking into Western Europe, and the 2007 Report additionally noted that they were becoming important players in the transport of cocaine from South America to Western Europe (UNODC, 2005, 2007).

The rise of criminal gangs in the former Communist world and their diffusion into the Western world hence encapsulates the dark side of three generally positive developments in international relations in the 1990s: the fall of the Iron Curtain, democratisation, and globalisation. However, it is, of course, naïve to suppose that transnational crime, and narcotics trading in particular, did not occur during the Cold War years. As well as increasing in incidence in the 1990s, narcotics trading was able to receive greater priority from governments with the shadow of the Cold War no longer obscuring other political issues. It is incontrovertible that the superpowers were prepared to tolerate corrupt governments being involved with or even directing criminal operations if they were in charge of important military allies or client states. Returning to the theme of cocaine and security, we can see several clear instances of Cold War *realpolitik* trumping serious international crime in superpower foreign policy. The US invasion of Panama in 1989, in the dying days of the Cold War, is a prime example. One of the principal reasons for the breakdown in relations between the two countries, which led to the overthrow of the Panamanian government, was the refusal of President Noriega to yield to US demands to act to curb the flow of cocaine passing through his country to their cities. Noriega's connections to the drugs underworld were well known to the Americans throughout the 1980s, as a military general until 1987 and as the President thereafter. At that time this was not viewed in such a negative light since he had aided the US in anti-leftist operations in Central America (Tatham and McCleary, 1992). The US' security for the majority of the 1980s was construed almost entirely in terms of the Communist threat, which Noriega had stood as a bulwark against, rather than in the threat posed by cocaine addiction and related crime in US cities. By 1989 this was beginning to change.

Similarly, the Soviet Union, whilst no supporter of narcotics, backed the fiercely conservative Communist regime of Eric Honecker in East Germany despite surely being aware of the leader's personal involvement in importing and selling cocaine. The Soviets also helped supply the Colombian revolutionaries FARC, despite their well-known links to local cocaine cartels.

Economic globalisation

Globalisation, denoting the increased level of cross-border economic activity and increasingly global political framing of such change, can be seen to have influenced the rise in prominence of global crime in a number of ways.

One of these is simply the increased volume of traded goods. The opportunities for trading in legal commodities are much greater than ever before in terms of costs, speed and the existence of global regulations favouring free trade over state protectionism. However, such opportunities are also present for the trade in illegal commodities. It is easier and cheaper for criminals to operate internationally, and the sheer volume of traded goods makes it ever more difficult for state authorities to detect the movement of drugs, arms shipments and other illicit cargoes.

Drug traffickers, for example, have come to make effective use of that very symbol of globalisation, the internet, to boost their operations. Gangs are known to have used encrypted websites to communicate and share information on their activities while employing information technology experts as hackers to alter information held on customs databases and create phantom websites to put state officials off the scent of the real sites. A simple illustration of how modern technological aids to commerce can serve murkier purposes also comes with evidence that Australian drug traffickers have brazenly used the web service offered by legitimate couriers, allowing customers to track the location of the goods they are having delivered (INCB, 2002: 2).

In addition, the growth of cross-border financial transactions has also presented opportunities to international criminals as much as to international businessmen. Large-scale criminal activity is usually accompanied by money laundering as crime groups seek to protect their ill-gotten gains from state authorities by moving the money around or investing it in legitimate businesses. This process is becoming increasingly globalised as criminal organisations learn to exploit the inadequacies of the sovereign state system by moving money from country to country. Investing the proceeds of crime into legitimate businesses in a state other than where the crime took place illustrates the nature of criminal globalisation's challenge to the state system. A crucial aspect of a crime may not be construed as criminal in the country where it occurs, and may even be considered to be a beneficial overseas investment.

The globalisation of 'white collar crime' is another price that governments and individuals have paid for reaping some of the benefits of financial liberalisation. Many governments, such as the US and the UK, consciously began taking a more 'hands off' approach to banking and financial services from the 1990s in order to accrue inward flows of investment. While this bore many fruits for a while, such a voluntary relaxation of sovereign controls came to appear more questionable from 2008 when a global recession unfolded as a consequence of widespread shoddy banking practices. Some bankers exploited the laxer regulatory environment, while others went further and blatantly broke laws, feeling sure that they would never be caught. US financier Bernie Madoff was able to carry out frauds to the tune of $65 billion for several years on Wall Street before finally being caught and sentenced to 150 years in prison in 2009.

Political globalisation

Globalisation not only provides criminals with the opportunities to widen their operations; it can also sometimes be seen to create new opportunities for crime. Political integration is a by-product of an increasingly interdependent world where states recognise the limitations on independent action in the global economy and work towards 'pooling' their sovereignty by creating new, wider economic and political communities with nearby states. By far the most extensive case of such political integration is in Europe with the European Union. The EU is very much a leap of faith since no comparable project has been attempted before, and, as a result, merging together the economic activities of twenty-eight states has had some unintended side-effects. For example, organised crime groups are known to have exploited the complexity of the EU's costly and highly bureaucratic Common Agricultural Policy (CAP). The payment of subsidies to olive producers has inadvertently helped finance the mafia who have long had an 'influence' on that industry in Sicily. The opening up of borders between the member states of the EU since the late 1980s has provided a further boost to the mafia by creating a market for safe passage for illegal immigrants across the Adriatic from East Europe to southern Italy, since from there migrants can more easily head north to wealthier parts of the Union. Drugs and counterfeit cargoes have followed in the same direction. Hence we see the boon to business provided by the EU's Single Market accompanied by a 'single market for crime'.

The EU has responded to such developments with the establishment of a Justice and Home Affairs 'pillar' to accompany measures furthering economic integration and measures to improve coordination between national police forces.

Cultural globalisation

The global trend towards urban living is a factor behind the rise of crime since city dwellers are statistically far more violent and lawless than their rural counterparts. The homicide rate in the urban municipalities of Brazil is over three times that of the rural municipalities (*Small Arms Survey*, 2007: 230–231). Deprived urban living is closely associated with the development of criminal gangs, and this is a growing phenomenon in many megacities in both the global North and South. Around one sixth of the world's population lives in urban slums, the majority of which are in the global South (UN-Habitat, 2003). Urban gang culture is nothing new, but it appears to be globalising not only via migration routes but through the global media. Hence the notorious Los Angeles *MS-13* gang have, in recent years, become the biggest gang, and significant societal and governmental menace, in Honduras and El Salvador, two countries with among the world's highest homicide rates (Hagerdorn, 2005).

A further form of global cultural change fuelling international crime is the increasingly internationalised consumption of the products of criminal enterprise. A key reason for global crime is the existence of a global market for such products and services. Rudimentary criminology recognises that controlling crime is about tackling the demand as well as the supply side of the activities, but such logic is often lost in the traditional conduct of international security so focused on externalising threats.

Sending troops to Colombia to fight drug barons seems like a 'tough' response to the problem, but the tougher challenge for Washington and London is to make cocaine less attractive to their citizens. As with many security issues, there is a tendency to see global crime as emanating solely from the 'badlands' when much of the problem actually lies closer to home. The consumers of drugs, cheap pirated goods and sex worker services perpetuate these areas of global crime, and these people generally reside in wealthy and apparently respectable countries.

Criminal globalisation

A key factor in the globalisation of crime is the increased tendency for organised criminal groups to follow the lead of transnational corporations and work with the phenomenon, consciously setting up operations in a number of other countries. Cheaper international travel costs favour criminals as much as they do other profit-seeking individuals. Godson and Williams describe how transnational criminal organisations can come to utilise a *home state* from where they direct operations, a *host state* where they carry out crimes or sell their produce, a *transportation state* where criminal activities will seek to ensure an unhindered passage of goods to the host state, and a *service state* in countries where favourably secretive banking laws allow for profits to be secured (Godson and Williams, 2000: 115). Hence, a genuinely transnational operation can be established where, for example, a Colombian-based narcotics gang could secure access to markets in the US by bribing Mexican officials to permit the transit of the drugs, and then invest the proceeds in a Cayman Islands offshore bank account. The greatest security threats may not be at the point of source or distribution of the criminal enterprise. Over 40,000 Mexicans were killed between 2007 and 2012 in the context of internecine criminal wars based on the transit of South American narcotics into North America (BBC, 2011).

At the 1994 United Nations Conference on Internationally Organised Crime, UN Secretary-General Boutros-Ghali referred to an 'empire of criminals' to highlight the problem of globally operating criminal gangs, but also to illustrate the fact that many of these organised gangs were cooperating with other, likeminded groups to extend the reach of their operations. There is a long history of criminal gangs extending their influence into other countries, but this has traditionally been in line with patterns of migration. Hence the mafia's influence in the US from the 1930s followed large-scale Italian migration, and, to a far lesser extent, Jamaican *yardies* and Hong Kong *triads* extended operations to the UK from the 1980s. The 1990s, however, witnessed the increased formation of strategic alliances between transnational criminal organisations exploiting changing political rather than demographic circumstances. Russian *mafiya* are known to have linked with South American criminal cartels in 'guns for drugs' marriages made in hell (Williams, 2001: 75–76). International criminal cooperation can sometimes even thrive where societal and governmental cooperation is absent. Serb and Albanian gangsters, for example, are known to have worked together extensively in human trafficking operations in the Balkans (Williams, 2006: 198).

Crime and national security

In some countries state security has long been as much a domestic political issue as an international one. In Italy during the Cold War, for example, the domestic threat posed by political violence (most notably the Red Brigade) and criminal violence (most notably the mafia) dominated state security policy to much the same extent as the Soviet threat preoccupying the rest of Western Europe. This fact manifests itself in the existence and prominence in Italy of the paramilitary police force the *Carabinieri*, in contrast to its relatively modest military capabilities. This situation, though, has become more common as more countries have turned to paramilitary policing in recent years as a blurring of the distinction between internal and external security has prompted a commensurate blurring of the traditional roles of the military and police. For example, the US has seen the number of Special Weapons and Tactics (SWAT) police operations rise from 3,000 per year in the 1980s to around 40,000 per year in the 2000s (Kraska, 2005).

Colombia epitomises the security threats posed by crime. The technologically advanced and international military operation mounted to assassinate Colombian drugs magnate Pablo Escobar in 1993 illustrates how crime had entered into the realms of 'national security' in the post-Cold War years. Escobar was finally killed after US special troops the Delta Force and various crime-fighters from the US were brought in to help by an exasperated and pressurised Colombian government. As well as representing a major Human Security threat to ordinary Colombian and foreign citizens, criminal organisations (in tandem with violent political organisations) have seriously undermined the capacity of the government to rule the country. Foreign troops have been called in to fight drugs barons while a large tract of Colombian territory was, for a number of years, conceded to 'narco-terrorists'. Colombia is an extreme case, but in many countries throughout the world governments are increasingly threatened or undermined by armed groups terrifying their citizens, damaging their economy and corrupting their institutions.

However, the limits of a traditional national security response to organised crime become apparent when the criminals infiltrate, corrupt or even become the state. As previously discussed, *mafiocracies*, where criminal syndicates buy into crucial aspects of the state apparatus and win political influence, and failed states, where law and order breaks down completely, have become more commonplace in recent decades. Longer established are *kleptocracies* where the governing institutions are themselves the source of criminality, with elites wilfully exploiting their citizens through embezzlement and corruption. The term was coined in particular reference to the notorious rule of Mabuto in the Congo from the mid-1960s to the 1990s, when huge amounts of taxes and foreign aid were siphoned off for ornate palace furnishings and secret bank accounts, but it has continued currency in reference to several contemporary tyrants in Africa and Central Asia.

Crime and Human Security

Perhaps most pertinent to the consideration of security is the fact that nearly half a million people per year are murdered (UNODC, 2011b) and one in five of all people fall victim to serious contact crime (robbery, sexual crimes or assaults) (Newman, 2002: Chapter 1). The pattern is variable, though, and it is in the Americas and Africa where life-threatening crime is most prevalent. The availability of firearms appears to be a major factor in explaining international variation in homicide rates. Nearly three-quarters of all homicides in the Americas are committed using firearms, a rate over three times that of Europe (UNODC, 2011b). The human and economic costs of some of the most prominent forms of transnational crime are summarised in Table 16.1.

Table 16.1 The cost of transnational crime

		Annual Economic cost (US$)	Annual Human Cost
1	Corruption	1.6 trillion (vii)	
2	Cyber crime	1 trillion (vi)	
3	Drug trafficking	400 billion (i)	200,000 deaths (i)
4	Counterfeits	250 billion (ii)	
5	Environmental crime (oil, wildlife, timber, fish)	33.6 billion (ii)	
6	Human trafficking	31.6 billion (ii)	27 million victims (v)
7	Stolen goods	20 billion (iii)	
8	Maritime piracy	9.5 billion (iv)	11 deaths, 1,000 hostages (iv)
9	Human organ trafficking	0.9 billion (ii)	7,000 victims
10	Arms trafficking	0.6 billion (ii)	99,000 deaths (viii)
	Total	2.1 trillion (excluding tax evasion) of which 1.6 trillion is laundered. (i)	450,000 homicides

Sources:
(i) UNODC (2011b)
(ii) Global Financial Integrity (2011)
(iii) Baker (2005)
(iv) IMO (2011)
(v) US State Department (2011)
(vi) UK FCO (2011)
(vii) BBC (2009) http://news.bbc.co.uk/1/hi/business/8350239.stm
(viii) Author's estimate extrapolated from estimates that a quarter of small arms trade is illegal and small arms account for three-quarters of the world's 526,000 violent killings (*Small Arms Survey*, 2007)

International political responses to transnational crime

The value of international cooperation in policing is well established, but international politico-legal measures to combat crime are relatively recent and generally held to be, as yet, insufficient in the face of the growing problem.

Interpol

Established in 1923, Interpol is undoubtedly the best known global institutional response to the problem of transnational crime. Its membership is impressively universal with 190 member-states. Each member-state is represented by delegates at the organisation's headquarters at Lyon, France and each hosts a National Crime Bureau (NCB) which serve as the nodes in an information network to aid state police forces and promote cooperation among them. The 190 NCBs are linked by a computerised database which contains pooled information resources on known criminals and stolen goods, such as cars, to aid in the detection of transnational criminals and speed up the process of their extradition (although the process of extradition is still a bilateral matter between the governments concerned). In addition to this chief function of facilitating the exchange of information, Interpol also seeks to promote greater regional cooperation between police forces (as for example with the Mercosur countries; Brazil, Argentina, Paraguay and Uruguay) and act as a 'value-added service provider', giving advice to governments on how to develop extradition agreements and to state police forces on updating their information technology resources. Interpol as an intergovernmental organisation has a conventional decision-making structure. Each member-state is represented by a government-appointed delegate at an annual General Assembly, which votes by simple majority on the adoption of new procedures. The General Assembly also elects an Executive Committee of thirteen member-state delegates, which meets three times a year and prepares the agenda for the General Assemblies, as well as managing the implementation of decisions. Day-to-day administration is carried out by a permanent secretariat at Lyon headed by the Secretary General, elected for a five-year term of office by two-thirds majority of the General Assembly (Interpol, 2012).

Despite proclaiming among its objectives that it aims to act 'in the spirit of the Universal Declaration of Human Rights' (Interpol Constitution, Article 2), Interpol has always sought to play a non-political role. Article 3 of its constitution makes this clear: 'It is strictly forbidden for the organisation to undertake any intervention or activities of a political, military, religious or racial character'. This somewhat contradicts the previous Article since racial and religious persecution are among the crimes renounced in the Universal Declaration of Human Rights, but it would, of course, be impossible for an organisation of this nature to maintain its broad membership without such a precondition.

Another limitation to the work of Interpol is its modest budget, derived from member-state contributions calculated on the basis of population and GDP. This point has been clearly expressed by Secretary General Ronald Noble: 'we have a multi-billion dollar problem being tackled by an organisation running on just 30 million euros' (Interpol, 2002). Sheptycki, with provocative irony, has argued that where Interpol has grown it has evolved like a series of protection rackets. As a largely informal arrangement, without an explicit treaty or fixed budget, Interpol inevitably 'chases the money' and focuses on illicit trade cases referred to it by state police in wealthy countries, rather than tackling global crime in the global interest. Hence issues uncomfortable for any particular state, such as the corruption of government officials or the dumping of toxic waste, rarely occupy the time of Interpol officers on temporary secondment from national jobs (Sheptycki, 2003). Interpol is clearly a valuable resource to police forces around the world in arresting transnational criminals, but in its present guise it can only be a limited player in the development of global policies to arrest the rise of transnational crime. '…[W]hat is needed is an agreed calculus by which to allocate policing resources in order for them to be efficiently and effectively targeted on criminal activities that cause social harm' (Sheptycki, 2003: 53).

The World Customs Organisation

A similar body to Interpol, the WCO aims to facilitate cooperation between customs officials and coordinate national customs procedures in order to combat illicit trades. Based in Brussels, the organisation is impressively universal with 177 member-states and has been in operation for over fifty years, but like Interpol, it is limited in what it can do in the face of increasingly sophisticated global criminals. By the WCO's own admission, 'efficient and effective performance is not spread evenly among all Customs administrations, or in all regions of the world' (WCO, 2006).

The United Nations

The role of the UN with regards to transnational crime originated in efforts to coordinate action against the trade in narcotics before evolving into activities dealing with other realms of global criminal activity. The UN took over the management of the League of Nations' work on tackling the narcotics trade, as it did with many functional agencies established by its forerunner. The League's well documented failures with regards to military security should not obscure its pioneering work in developing global responses to other great threats to humanity. The League's Committee on the Traffic in Opium and Other Dangerous Drugs was transformed into the Commission on Narcotic Drugs (CND), but the UN soon expanded its role and the 1961 Single Convention on Narcotic Drugs created a sister organisation to the CND, the International Narcotics Control Board (INCB). This signalled an attempt by the UN to deepen the global response to an increasingly contentious issue, but the further creation of various groups and programmes over the next three decades served to confuse the picture and prompt a rationalisation, in line with other structural changes to the UN at the close of the Cold War.

A special session of the UN General Assembly in 1990 recognised the growing threat posed by narcotics and instigated the creation of a single programme to replace the 'alphabet soup' of small UN groups that had developed in this policy area. The UN International Drug Control Programme (UNDCP) started operations in 1991 to coordinate UN policy, with the CND and INCB taken under its wing as committees. A further rationalisation of UN operations occurred in 1997 when the UNDCP married its operations to a new body, the UN Centre for International Crime Prevention (CICP) as subsections of the UN Office for Drugs and Crime (UNODC). This step marked a recognition by the UN of the growing significance of a range of transnational criminal operations first evident in the sponsorship of a major conference in Naples in 1994 attended by government ministers from 136 states.

The CICP did not appear from nowhere, representing a greatly souped-up version of its predecessor, the UN Crime Prevention and Criminal Justice Division (CPCJD). The CICP is very much the junior partner within the UNODC, with a permanent staff of fifteen compared to over three hundred in the UNDCP. It is, however, assisted by a separate forty-strong body, the Commission on Crime Prevention and Criminal Justice (CCPCJ), which is a subsidiary of the Economic and Social Council, the UN's chief steering mechanism for developing global policy on non-military issues. The CCPCJ cooperates with pressure groups, academics and politicians in organising congresses which produce draft resolutions to direct the CICP in its work of defining 'internationally recognised principles for criminal justice'.

The culmination of the work of these congresses, and a Global Action Plan initiated by the 1994 Naples Conference, was the UN International Convention Against Transnational Organized Crime which was adopted by the General Assembly in November 2000 and entered into force in 2003. Article 1 of the Convention succinctly describes its purpose as being 'to promote cooperation to prevent and combat transnational organised crime more effectively' (UN, 2000: 1). Subsequent articles of the convention deal with a wide range of issues relating to transnational organised crime. These are summarised in the following table.

Table 16.2 The UN Convention on Transnational Organized Crime

Articles 2 to 4	definitions and scope of the convention
Article 5	criminalising the participation in an organised crime group
Articles 8 to 10	corruption
Articles 11 & 12	punishment
Articles 13 & 14	international cooperation on confiscation
Article 15	jurisdiction
Articles 16 & 17	extradition
Articles 18 to 22	mutual legal assistance and investigative cooperation
Article 23	criminalising the obstruction of justice
Article 24	witness protection
Article 25	victim protection
Article 26	encouraging public notification of crime
Article 27	law enforcement cooperation
Article 28	sharing information
Article 29	law enforcement training programmes (initiation or improvement)
Article 30	assistance to LDCs in implementing the convention
Article 31	prevention of organised crime at the domestic level
Articles 32 to 41	implementation

Protocols:

1   Trafficking in persons.
2   Smuggling of migrants.
3   Illegal trading in firearms.

A 'Conference of the Parties' has met regularly since 2003 to oversee the implementation and development of the Convention. The Convention is a step forward in terms of providing the basis for greater international harmonisation in tackling money laundering and corruption, but as with most intergovernmental arrangements of this kind, there are no enforcement measures beyond peer pressure. The compulsory sharing of information among parties, for example, is cited as a necessary next step by the UNODC (UNODC, 2010).

Europol

The rise in cross-border crime in the European Union due to the relaxation of border controls, referred to earlier in this chapter, prompted the organisation in the early 1990s to instigate an Interpol-style institution of its own to coordinate the work of its member-state police forces. Europol was agreed upon at the 1992 Treaty on European Union (the Maastricht Treaty), in line with the creation of a 'Justice and Home Affairs' dimension to the EU's political integration process, and came into being in January 1994. Like Interpol, Europol has a central database, The Europol Computer Systems (TECS), serving a system of offices in the member-states. Still in the early stages of its evolution, Europol has already outgrown its global 'parent'. Its budget for 2011 was 84 million euro, more than double the amount it ran on ten years previously. In addition to a permanent secretariat in The Hague, Europol employs 137 'Europol Liaison Officers' (ELOs) in the twenty-seven member-states, principally made up of experienced policemen and customs officers (Europol, 2012).

A further way in which Europol has moved beyond the role of facilitating the exchange of information between police forces is in the promotion of judicial cooperation. The European Judicial Network was set up in 1998 as an information exchange service for lawyers in the member-states. In 2001 this development was augmented by the creation of Eurojust, a sister organisation to Europol made up of representatives of the legal professions, such as magistrates and prosecution services. Again, this is spillover in practice, with the drive to improve the detection of transboundary crime being accompanied by a desire to achieve a commensurate improvement in the capacity to arrest tranboundary criminals. The 2008 Lisbon Treaty brought Europol fully into the EU political system with the possibility of unilateral national vetoes ending, with its decisions now made on the basis of qualified majority voting. Given its budgetary and political growth we can thus expect the informational, legal and political roles of the EU in fighting crime to continue to evolve.

Conclusion

That crime is a matter of security is beyond dispute, whichever political or theoretical standpoint is employed. While the appropriateness of giving security status to many non-military issues is questioned by many, the maintenance of law and order is almost universally acknowledged as a political priority and in the interests of the state and its people. The legitimisation of sovereign force to uphold the law and maintain internal security may be interpreted very differently from country to country, but it is evident in every functioning state.

However, the increasing evidence that sovereign force may no longer be enough to best uphold law and order, due to the rise of transnational crime, has yet to find international political expression. The Head of Interpol, Ron Noble, has expressed this eloquently in an appeal to the international community:

> No one country can effectively fight transnational organized crime within or outside its borders. Therefore, I submit, countries must relinquish some of their procedural or substantive sovereignty in order for the purpose for which sovereignty exists in the first place to remain intact.
>
> (Noble, 2003)

At the heart of this issue is a paradox. Historically, the maintenance of law and order is the best argument for sovereignty. In the pre-Westphalian age, without sovereign borders and police forces, justice and protection was arbitrarily applied. Hence, surrendering full and exclusive control over law and order in order to better secure its people and institutions is anathema to most of the world's sovereigns. To many Realists this would represent a reckless lurch back to the lawless 'New Medievalism' of the pre-Westphalian age, but to others, renegotiating sovereignty would be a pragmatic and necessary step towards that most central of political tasks – upholding law and order.

Criminals used to exploit the lack of holism in domestic law enforcement by operating across (US) state boundaries or even (UK) county borders until such inappropriate de-centralisation was addressed politically by creating federal/national police forces. Many Liberals contend that this situation has now arisen globally, and that steps towards a global police force are required.

Summary points

1   Organised crime on an international basis is not a new phenomenon, but it has become a heightened national and human security threat over recent decades by groups exploiting the opportunities provided by post-Cold War socio-political change and globalisation.
2   International political measures seeking to tackle this rising problem of global crime have advanced, but remain stifled by the continuing tendency to treat law and order as a sovereign and domestic concern.

Recommended reading

Edwards, A. and Gill, P. (eds) *Transnational Organized Crime: Perspectives on Global Security,* London and New York: Routledge, 2006.

Glenny, M. *McMafia: Crime Without Frontiers,* London: The Bodley Head, 2008.

Madsen, F. *Transnational Organized Crime (Global Institutions)*, Abingdon: Routledge, 2009.

UNODC, *Global Study on Homicide,* Vienna: UN Office for Drugs and Crime, 2011. http://www.unodc.org/documents/gsh/pdfs/2014_GLOBAL_HOMICIDE_BOOK_web.pdf, 2013 (Accessed 12.4.14).

Williams, P. 'Strategy for a New World: Combating Terrorism and Transboundary Crime' in J. Baylis, J. Wirtz, E. Cohen and C.S. Gray (eds) *Strategy in the Contemporary World* (2nd ed.), Oxford: Oxford University Press, 2006, 192–208.

17 Food security

Peter Hough

Box 17.1: 2007–8 African food riots

Major riots against rapidly rising food prices and consequent heightened hunger problems occurred in fourteen countries across Africa (and at least sixteen elsewhere in the world) over around twelve months from the Spring of 2007: Guinea, Mauritania, Morocco, Senegal, Cameroon, Mozambique, Burkina Faso, Ivory Coast, Ethiopia, Egypt, Madagascar, Somalia, Tunisia and Zimbabwe. Protestors were killed by security forces in the uprisings in Mozambique, Ivory Coast, Egypt, Somalia and Tunisia. There is a long history of food riots on a national scale but no real precedent for this kind of internationalisation of such protests. Prices stabilised after a 2007–8 spike, but underlying factors promoting food insecurity remain. In 2011 food riots reignited in Algeria and Tunisia, the latter sparking the revolution that toppled the Ben Ali government and the subsequent wave of protests and revolutions across much of the Arab world.

Introduction

The deployment of national security forces and force against the African protestors of 2007–8 testifies that food anxieties can be deemed the stuff of national security by governments, and history tells us that this is with good cause. The French and Russian revolutions and many other notable insurgencies had at heart questions about 'who gets what', with powerful political systems delegitimised and toppled through their failure to ensure that their whole population was fed. More starkly, though, access to food is a critical dimension of Human Security. 'Who gets what' at the global level is a particularly pertinent question to ask since there is demonstrably enough food in the world for all, but not everyone is getting their required share. Most challengingly for the conduct of international relations, the pursuit of national food security – by stockpiling and protecting what you have – serves to heighten this problem.

This chapter examines this political dilemma and 'collective goods problem' by examining in turn the causes and political responses to the periodic onset of famines and the more persistent problem of underlying hunger.

Famine

The most acute and immediate economic threat to Human Security comes in the form of famine. However, precisely estimating deaths from famine is extremely difficult for several reasons. First, famines are functionally related to other threats such as disease, drought and flooding. Floods and droughts wipe out crops and can cause famine, but they can also kill directly, while diseases are generally more virulent when infecting a malnourished population. Hence, determining the precise cause of death for people beset by such natural catastrophes is problematic, and as such, figures on famine fatalities are inexact. Second, even allowing for the blurring of the causal factors of death, disaster mortality statistics are notoriously unreliable. Governments tend to underestimate figures while anti-government voices often exaggerate them for opposing political purposes. Notwithstanding these reservations, estimates suggest that the 1958–62 Great Famine in China can lay claim to being the worst in history with around thirty million fatalities (Becker, 2000). China was also the scene of the second worst famine in history between 1876–8 when at least twelve million died (Davis, 2001). Of other famines widely considered to have claimed over a million lives, at least seven occurred in India (1770, 1845–7, 1865–6, 1869, 1876–8, 1897, 1943–4) along with the disasters in Ukraine in the Soviet Union in 1932–3, Ireland in 1845–7, and North Korea from 1995 (Hough, 2013).

The causes of famine

Invariably there are a combination of factors that can explain famines. As with their mortality figures, the causes of famines are frequently disputed by analysts and politicians. Most famines are the result of a combination of both natural and political factors, and disputes on causation centre on determining the relative weighting of the two contributory factors. For example, the aforementioned famines in India and Ireland had natural causes (potato blight in the latter and principally droughts in the former), but these disasters are generally considered to have been exacerbated by an ignorance of the local situation born of colonial rule. The North Korean famine had natural origins (a combination of droughts and floods) but was undoubtedly greatly worsened by the government's drive for economic self-sufficiency, which saw food imports reduced at the same time as the domestic food supply dwindled. The clearest cases of man-made political famine are the horrific twentieth-century disasters in Communist China and the USSR. The Chinese famine was influenced by the effects of excessive rainfall on harvests, but there is little doubt that its principal cause was Mao Tse Tung's determination to pursue his 'Great Leap Forward' economic reform plan, regardless of the human consequences. The Ukrainian famine did not have any obvious natural causes and appears to have been entirely political, deliberately engineered by Stalin to punish the farmers in the region for their lack of enthusiasm for Soviet collectivisation.

There are three fundamental explanations for any particular famine related to the balance between the supply of and the demand for food.

1   A fall in the food supply.
2   An increase in the demand for food.
3   Disruptions to the normal distribution of food.

The third of these is most particularly influenced by politics and economics. All three explanations can variously be applied to the situation in states where famines are occurring. The food supply in countries can fall below the level sufficient to meet demand because of poor harvests, or the population can grow at a rate that the food supply is unable to match.

Overpopulation is a condition that has certainly affected most of the principal arenas of famine over the last century, such as in China and India, where it has sometimes prompted drastic domestic political action to curb population growth. A provocative argument from prominent American economists the Paddock brothers in the late 1960s went so far as to argue that India and other countries prone to famine had only themselves to blame, and they should be left to suffer for their own and everyone else's good. Overpopulation, added to endemic poor government meant that, for some states, food aid was a waste of time and that they should be considered as part of a 'can't be saved' group and ignored by the USA and other benefactors. 'Waste not the food on the "can't be saved" and the "walking wounded". Send it to those nations which, having it, can buttress their own resources, their own efforts, and fight through to survival' (W. and P. Paddock, 1967: 229).

The ecologist Garret Hardin advanced a similar idea in formulating the analogy of lifeboats in a post-shipping disaster sea to characterise states in a world where food supplies will eventually be used up in the face of population growth. Hardin's thesis argued for the application of 'lifeboat ethics' to combat this, which essentially argued that international action to tackle famine was folly as wealthy countries would risk sinking their own 'lifeboats' in doing so. Better to let the overcrowded lifeboats of the Third World sink than ensure that we all drown (Hardin, 1995). Such apocalyptic views of the global security implications of overpopulation were common in the 1960s and 1970s and can be dated back as far as the eighteenth century and the works of Thomas Malthus (Malthus, 1798). However, they are rarer today since the central plank of the Malthusian and neo-Malthusian prediction, that world population will come to exceed world food supply, has not happened and does not look likely to do so in the near future. The demand for food continues to increase in the less developed world and natural disasters continue to blight many of the same countries, creating food shortages, but most contemporary analysts of famine emphasise distributive factors in their explanations of particular cases. Modern governments can insure against future crop shortages by stockpiling reserves of food and protecting the price of agricultural products.

The leading writer in this approach to explaining famine is economist Amartya Sen. Sen expounds the 'entitlements approach', in which he argues that all individuals should by rights be able to expect to be protected from famine by their government, regardless of changes in food supply or population. In a convincing application of the democratic peace argument to economic rather than military security, Sen draws on extensive evidence to propose that:

> no substantial famine has ever occurred in any independent and democratic country with a relatively free press...
>
> ...Even the poorest democratic countries that have faced terrible droughts or floods or other natural disasters (such as India in 1973, or Zimbabwe and Botswana in the early 1980s) have been able to feed their people without experiencing a famine.
>
> (Sen, 1999: 6–7)

Democratic governments are compelled to be responsive to the needs of ordinary people whose security is imperiled, whether directly or indirectly through the pressure of the media or other concerned citizens, in a way that tyrannical dictators or neglectful colonialists are not. Democracy can thus save people as well as empower them, and the spread of democratisation in the world offers hope in the fight against famine. Food shortages will still occur from time to time but these can normally be planned for by governments, and when they cannot be dealt with the international community can step in. Countless lives in North Korea would have been saved were it not for the fact that the state had virtually cut itself off from the rest of the world as part of their isolationist *Juche* philosophy, so that external assistance was not possible. Being part of the global economy could have saved the lives of many North Koreans. Being a state in which human entitlements were valued and responded to could have saved more still.

Global policy on famine relief

The principal instrument for coordinating famine relief at the global level has traditionally been the UN's World Food Programme (WFP), a hybrid of the Food and Agricultural Organization (FAO) and the World Health Organization (WHO). Created in 1963, initially as an ad hoc three-year project, the WFP has evolved into the 'food arm of the UN' (WFP, 2002a: 1) with all of the characteristics of an IGO. Based like the FAO in Rome, the WFP is governed by an Executive Board and served by a permanent secretariat. The Executive Board votes on where to allocate food aid from an annual budget of around $5.5 billion (WFP, 2011). Through the course of its working life this food aid has increasingly been targeted at countries suffering food shortages due to the effects of natural disasters or conflict rather than for general development purposes.

The stated aim of the WFP's work is '...eradicating hunger and poverty. The ultimate objective of food aid should be the elimination of the need for food aid' (WFP, 2002b: 1). In reality, though, the WFP is a global emergency service and the broad aim of achieving 'food security' – 'access of all peoples at all times to the food needed for an active and healthy life' (FAO/WHO, 1992) – is a more profound goal beyond the reach of its budget and operations.

Hunger

Global political action, coordinated inter-governmentally by the WFP and also non-governmentally by pressure groups such as OXFAM, CAFOD and War on Want, has in recent decades helped curtail the onset of famines, but such groups are quick to point out that these periodic disasters are merely the tip of the global hunger 'iceberg'. Far more people in today's world die due to malnutrition through plain poverty rather than as a result of short-term regional imbalances between the supply of and demand for food. The WFP claims that some 25,000 people die every day as a result of hunger and related ailments, and that over one billion people in the world suffer from malnutrition (WFP, 2009).[1] This may well be a conservative estimate, but this death toll undoubtedly outstrips any other threats to human existence.

Institutionally the FAO is at the centre of global policy with regards to global food production, given that its principal tasks have been to increase food production in the world and create a framework of standards for the distribution of this food. While acknowledging the scale of global hunger, the FAO makes a case for their contribution to tackling the problem: 'Food production has increased at an unprecedented rate since the FAO was founded in 1945, outpacing the doubling of the world's population over the same period' (FAO, 2002). Most notably they spearheaded the 'Green Revolution' of the 1970s and 1980s in which neo-Malthusian fears that global population growth would surpass the planet's food supply were averted by technological transfers from North to South. Modern agricultural techniques, including the use of synthetic fertilisers and pesticides, were successfully incorporated into developmental programmes leading to big improvements in food production. With the neo-Malthusian apocalypse overcome, why, then, does this relentless death toll persist in a world in which the food supply is sufficient to permit every person in the world at least 2,720 calories per day (FAO, 2002)?

Many factors contribute to this striking inequity and the failure of international politics and economics.

Global population growth

The sheer existence of more people increases the demand for food and the land to cultivate it, thereby contributing to further strains on resources through pollution, desertification, deforestation and climate change. However, there is a danger of over-simplification in seeing people and resources as the two sides of a global see-saw. Blaming overpopulation overlooks the fact that most of the growth in demand for food and resources comes from rising consumption in the global North rather than rising populations in Africa, Asia and Latin America. It has been estimated that North American inhabitants consume an average 90kg of resources per year, compared with 10kg for their African counterparts (FoE, 2009: 21). Notwithstanding this, there must be some correlation between the number of people in the world and the amount of resources they utilise.

Poverty

Poverty kills directly in huge numbers when people are unable to secure sufficient food to live because they lack the economic means to purchase or produce it. Economic inequality in the world has always existed, but it is more pronounced today than it has ever been and there is little evidence that this trend is likely to be reversed in the foreseeable future. The 80/20 ratio is a well-known and effective means of expressing this global inequality: 80% of the world's people live in the 'global South' but only 20% of the world's wealth is possessed by those same countries. Hence, the reverse of this is that the 'global North' has 20% of the world's people but 80% of its resources. The terms North and South are increasingly losing currency as labels given the economic growth of southern countries like China, India and Brazil, but nevertheless, the statistic gives us a useful snapshot of the 'haves' and 'have nots' in today's world. Over a billion people live on an income equivalent to no more than $1.25 per day, but perhaps most striking is the fact that the disparity between the haves and the have nots has significantly widened over recent decades. The world's richest 20% of people (not countries) had a cumulative wealth thirty times greater than the poorest 20% in 1960, but by 1999 this ratio had widened to 74:1 (UNDP, 1999: 36–38).

Feeding humanity is not solely an economic task, but without doubt it is principally achieved by the possession of money, personally and at a societal level. Money is not the root of all of humanity's ills, and neither is it the sole cause of starvation and hunger. On the one hand, droughts and other natural phenomena can disrupt the food supply, and on the other, it is possible to feed yourself without buying food. However, money can secure people against natural hazards or insure them against fluctuations in the food supply caused either by natural or economic disruptions. In addition, self-sufficiency in food production, either for individuals or states, is an increasingly difficult means of achieving security. There is no precise correlation between wealth and life expectancy, but the match up, particularly at the bottom of the scale, is striking. Most of the same states of sub-Saharan Africa that populate the bottom of the league tables that rank the world's countries according to GDP per capita also feature at the bottom of UN Millennium Development Goal on progress in reducing hunger. In 2013 the country considered to have fallen the furthest short of the MDG target of reducing hunger was Burundi (where the situation had actually worsened since 1990), which also ranks second to lowest (ahead of the Congo DR) in GDP per capita. The world's poorest people are also, by and large, the world's most insecure (UNECA, 2013; World Bank, 2013).

Supply disruptions due to conflict or disaster

There is also some correlation between peace and food security. The aforementioned state of Burundi is not only poor but particularly war torn, with ethnic civil conflict between the Hutu and Tutsi a near-permanent feature since the mid-1990s. In a civil war situation food distribution inevitably becomes less equitable as it is distorted by military demand and increased societal rivalry. Hunger and famine may even occur deliberately as well as collaterally in conflict situations. In Sierra Leone in the 1990s the Revolutionary United Fund notably used food as a weapon, destroying crops in opposition villages and diverting food to the diamond industry (Sanchez *et al.*, 2005: 27). Natural disasters, most notably floods or droughts, can also shrink the food supply and have Human Security consequences beyond the immediate aftermath of the catastrophe.

Increased price volatility

Agricultural prices are traditionally more volatile than for most goods because of the simple economics of supply and demand. While the demand for food will always be there – and will probably rise – the supply of crops or meat is subject to the vagaries of climate. Fears of a bad harvest are deeply ingrained in the human psyche and partly explain the cautious and protective attitudes of governments and the public towards national agriculture, even in wealthy countries where food shortages are unlikely. In developing countries, where sudden price rises are more critical, inter-governmental coalitions such as the Group of 77 (G77) have, from the 1960s, called for the establishment of 'common funds' to stabilise the international price of food exports. The European Community, for example, introduced the STABEX mechanism, providing compensation for loss of earnings due to price drops in certain crops as part of the 1975 Lomé Convention regulating its trading relations with African, Caribbean and Pacific former colonies.

STABEX was discontinued in 2000 in line with the expiry of Lomé (to be replaced by a less extensive FLEX system), and, in general, demands for common funds declined as food prices stabilised in the 1990s and early 2000s after a period of volatility in the 1970s and early 1980s. However, the major spike in prices that occurred between March 2007 and March 2008 saw the world average price of food soar by 56%, with rises of 130% in wheat and 74% in rice (FAO, 2008). Numerous factors were behind this, including supply-side problems such as particularly poor wheat harvests in Australia and Europe. On the demand side, the economic growth of emerging markets, particularly in India and China, has increased the market for milk, cereals and meat. A significant rise in the price of oil also had an impact on food prices because of its consequences for the cost of transportation. In addition, the speculative, short-term buying and selling of grain, in line with the unregulated bubble building up in the financial world at the time, also affected world prices. Several issues behind the global economic collapse of 2008 negatively affected food prices, but longer term underlying factors explain the more general rise either side of the 2007–8 spike.

Environmental degradation of productive land

The well documented environmental changes of desertification and deforestation have obvious and dire consequences for food supply, and the twin phenomena are both symptoms and causes of the wider threat to the world's productive capacity posed by climate change.

Contrary to popular assumption, the phenomenon of desertification is about persistent, irreversible land degradation rather than simply the advance of deserts. It is a phenomenon that is more long-term than droughts, which are symptoms of this wider problem of progressive land degradation. Hence a large proportion of the world, including much of North America, thirteen EU states (principally in the Mediterranean region) and 110 countries overall are affected by desertification (WER, 2009:4). Degraded land can rarely be reclaimed for agriculture, so the food security implications are obvious. In Haiti, for example, grain production is estimated to have halved between the 1960s and the 1980s as a result of the progressive loss of fertile land (Brauch, 2003). Degraded land also destroys natural habitats which can have knock-on human food security effects. For example, 12% of mammals and 8% of birds in the arid zones of Australia became extinct in the twentieth century, much higher rates than in the non-arid zones. This has undermined the hunting and food security of several aboriginal tribes (Pickup, 1998: 56–57).

The once vast freshwater Lake Chad, spanning the borders of Chad, Cameroon, Niger and Nigeria, stands as a stark illustration of desertification, having shrunk by 90% from over 25,000 square kilometres in the 1960s to just 2,500 square kilometres today. The flow rates of the lake's two principal feeding rivers, the Chari and Logone, have fallen progressively over recent decades due to drought, a gradual overall decrease in rainfall and increased water demand. The region has suffered the consequences of declining fish stocks in the lake and the erosion of surrounding farmlands. The four countries, together with neighbouring Libya and the Central African Republic, have coordinated politically to combat this decline through the Lake Chad Basin Commission and have succeeded in improving the management of surrounding lands, but overall their efforts have been undermined by climate change.

Like desertification – and indeed linked to it – deforestation refers to the progressive decline in the world's trees. Also like desertification, it is a centuries-old phenomenon that is to some extent natural, but which has accelerated due to human exploitation, particularly in line with industrialisation and industrial-scale agriculture. In the 2000s there was a net loss of 5.2 million hectares per year (equivalent to the size of Costa Rica), which, while shocking, does represent a reduction from an annual average net loss of 8.3 million hectares in the 1990s (FAO, 2011a). Unsustainable agricultural practices, such as the growth in soy plantations, accounts for 80% of this global total with logging for timber, paper and fuel responsible for much of the rest (Kissinger, Herold and De Sy, 2012: 5). Other contributory factors include the expansion of mining plants and urbanisation.

Forests supply fruit and other key human foodstuffs and provide habitats for many animals useful for the human diet, as well as other creatures important to agriculture such as pollinating bees. In addition, deforestation exacerbates desertification since the removal of sun-blocking cover dries up the land and tree roots serve to bind the soil. In addition, the water cycle is disrupted by deforestation, prompting changes in patterns of precipitation and river flow which heighten water scarcity.

Switching of production to non-food crops

Switching from producing cereals and sugar to the newly profitable biofuel market has also served to shrink the world food supply. Among the most prominent biofuels are ethanol from sugar cane and biodiesel from grains. A World Bank paper has estimated that between 70% and 75% of the rise in food prices between 2002 and 2008 was a consequence of the subsidisation and tariff protection of the biofuel industries in the US and EU, which decreased food production and bucked the market by squeezing out cheaper sources in Brazil and Africa (Mitchell, 2008).

International sale of productive land

Also affecting the food supply in certain countries is the increasing phenomenon of 'land grab' whereby croplands in the global South are being sold off to Western or Chinese investors for a quick profit. This also serves to shrink the global food supply, since such investors often switch production to biofuels as well as creating more localised shortages and being sources of political discontent. One estimate suggests that in the 2000s over 200 million hectares (an area of land eight times the size of the UK) was sold or leased externally (Anseeuw, Wily, Cotula and Taylor, 2011).

Agricultural trade distortion

While global food production has increased since the rise of neo-Malthusian concerns that supply would be outstripped by demand in the late 1960s, the global trade in food is far from a free market and the Economic Liberal ideal of unlocking comparative advantage by allowing efficient producers to export as much as the rest of the world demands is notably absent. The agricultural industry in the global North has managed to remain largely exempted from the international trade liberalisation of the last sixty years, and in many countries it enjoys heavy government subsidisation and protection. This undermines the capacity of the global South countries – who tend to have a much higher proportion of their economy based on agriculture – to export their food produce to Northern markets. Over $250 billion per year is spent in OECD countries to artificially prop up domestic farmers (*The Economist*, 2010), and the losses for developing countries resulting from this distortion of the free market are generally held to far exceed the sums given to them in foreign aid transfers. Developing countries have campaigned relentlessly for a liberalisation of agricultural trade through the World Trade Organization since its inception in 1995, but thus far vested agribusiness interests in the global North have resisted this in an illustration of 'beggar thy neighbour' economics that is as clear as any you might find.

Overfishing

Like agricultural production, fishing and the consumption of the produce of this practice has accelerated with population growth and beyond, in line with consumption patterns over the past seventy years. The global market in 1950 was 19.3 million tonnes of fish, but by 2009 this had risen to 163 million tonnes (FAO, 2011b: 4). However, unlike the Green Revolution in agriculture, human ingenuity has succeeded only in terms of learning how to catch more fish and not in increasing or maintaining the supply, in a clear collective goods problem. The FAO estimates that 57.4% of fish stocks are now 'fully exploited' and 29.9% 'over-exploited', meaning that less than 13% are being sustainably harvested (FAO, 2011b).

Such a growth in fishing and fishing depletion is due to the industrialisation of the practice with the deployment of much bigger 'factory vessels', more indiscriminate harvesting of 'bycatch', and the rise of aquaculture (fish farming). The underlying problem is that fishing tends to be treated politically as an economic and social issue rather than as a matter of conservation. Governments in domestic policy tend to focus on subsidising the industry and in foreign policy they tend to play 'beggar thy neighbour' in the face of a collective goods problem, while in development policy they encourage the modernisation of LDC fishing in aid programmes. Globally it is estimated that $26 billion per year is paid to the fishing industry, mostly encouraging modernisation, including $6.4 billion on fuel subsidies (World Bank, 2009). In this way the classic development policy maxim of 'giving a man a fishing rod rather than the fish' is undermined, since 'the man with the rod' is, in reality, often put out of business by the focus on industrialisation in aid programmes. In addition, the 'sea grab' phenomenon whereby developing countries sell the rights to fish in their waters to industrialised countries has grown. Since the 1980s West African states like Mauritania and Senegal have signed deals with the EU and then China granting them the right to fish within their Exclusive Economic Zones. Initially this seemed to satisfy both sides, but over time local fishing industries have been undermined by competition that is able to utilise more sophisticated equipment, driving down prices because of their subsidisation. Overall, the global fishing industry actually runs at a loss of around $5 billion per year, but if it was run in an optimal, sustainable manner it could deliver a $45 billion profit (World Bank, 2009).

Theories of International Political Economy and food security

Reasoning why some should go hungry in a world of sufficient food is probably the most fundamental question of International Political Economy and defines the four broad schools of thought that inhabit that discipline, each with a different take on the equity of the globalising capitalist system.

Mercantilism

Mercantilism is the economic philosophy of 'looking after number one', the IPE version of IR Realism. For Mercantilists food security lies in self-sufficiency and they are wary of globalisation, advocating the importation of food and other goods only where absolutely necessary. Self-sufficiency through imperialism or conquest is an aggressive version of Mercantilism that has marked much of history. A more subtle contemporary version is the economic nationalism of protectionism witnessed in much of the world today. Mercantilism can be witnessed when apparent proponents of free trade – such as the US, EU and Japan – maintain high tariffs on agricultural imports and subsidise their farmers and fishermen and their food exporters (in what is commonly known in the countries affected by such market manipulation as 'dumping').

Marxism

Marxist analysis argues that structural economic factors account for famines and hunger as much as the inadequate political responses of particular governments to crop failures. It is indeed striking that so many of the worst famines in history occurred in the late nineteenth century, an era of then-unparalleled global economic liberalisation when the trade in foodstuffs greatly increased. Marx himself considered the famines of his era to be the product of capitalism, and his latter day protégés, such as Davis, cite persuasive evidence that colonised or semi-colonised countries, like India and China, finding themselves thrust into a global market economy, exported food to the developed world while their own nationals starved (Davis, 2001: 27). Those deaths should serve as a powerful warning from history of the need to temper contemporary economic globalisation with political measures in order to be ready to deal with the rise of unexpected threats to economic security.

Marxist explanations for the persistence of poverty-induced hunger hold that like famine, it is actually caused by the global economy and is more a case of wilful ignorance by the world's wealthy. In the 1960s Norwegian peace studies scholar Johan Galtung, using language deliberately designed to securitise poverty and hunger, coined the phrase 'structural violence' to encapsulate the nature of the phenomenon:

> ...if people are starving when this is objectively avoidable, then violence is committed, regardless of whether there is a clear subject–action–object relation, as during a siege yesterday or no such clear relation, as in the way economic relations are organized today.
>
> (Galtung, 1969: 170)

Hence, Marxists are unconvinced that reforming global institutions is a route to feeding the world. Uvin, in an angry polemical work in the mid-1990s, described the combined work of the FAO and its offspring the WFP as amounting to an 'international hunger regime' (Uvin, 1994: 73–74). Uvin contends that the FAO, in line with other UN agencies and IGOs, is interested in facilitating greater international trade through mechanising agricultural production in LDCs rather than confronting the nutritional needs of people in poverty. The FAO stands accused of having undergone a value shift from its original aspirations and becoming an agent of Northern economic gain rather than relieving human suffering. For Marxists, the world's hungry will never be fed by waiting on the compassion of its well-nourished. *Developing* states are nothing of the sort; they are dependent states, systematically and deliberately exploited by their wealthy counterparts. The global economic system requires underdeveloped states in order to feed the voracious capitalist appetite for more wealth in the developed states.

Economic Liberalism

Economic Liberalism stands in direct opposition to the Marxist perspective by advocating that LDCs can best mimic Northern development by integrating themselves into the global economy to permit export-oriented industries to flourish and gain from the inward investment provided by multinational corporations (MNCs). For these globalists – proponents of globalisation – hunger can be eradicated by those countries affected pursuing economic development of the kind experienced by Northern states. The conditions for modernisation can then be created – wealth, democracy, education, state-welfarism and smaller families – all of which can serve to alleviate poverty. The clearest articulation of this view came from the influential US economic historian Rostow with his 'Stages of Growth' thesis in the 1960s. Rostow analysed the process of development in the North and concluded that all states pass through five similar stages of progression towards 'take off' and an end stage of a wealthy consumer-driven society (Rostow, 1960). The successful economic development of the Newly Industrialised Countries (NICs), such as the 'Asian Tigers' of Taiwan, South Korea, Hong Kong and Singapore, after opening themselves up to foreign investment and developing export-oriented manufacturing industries, served to reinforce the notion that a global route out of poverty is available for those states stuck in pre-modernity.

Economic Liberals contend that more rather than less liberalisation of the global economic order is needed for Human Security to be enhanced. The Liberal International Economic Order (LIEO) we have inhabited since the end of the Second World War has allowed the people of the world to get richer by limiting the capacity of their governments to buck the market in claiming the money for themselves in tariffs. Free from meddling governments, international trade can increase in volume and serve the interest of humanity through the logic of 'comparative advantage'. Rather than having states pursue self-sufficiency, freer global trade allows countries or regions to produce what they are best suited to rather than 'a bit of everything'. Hence, in the logic of Liberalism, more is produced and more is traded. The pioneer of this perspective was the eighteenth century Scottish economist Adam Smith, who greatly influenced British international policy in the following century.

Some of Smith's contemporary protégés put the world's economic failings down to the LIEO not being sufficiently Liberal, and are concerned at recent shifts towards more socially-minded 'compensatory liberalism' in global bodies like the World Bank. Peter Bauer, an exponent of true global free market economics, once said of foreign aid that it is 'an excellent method for transferring money from poor people in rich countries to rich people in poor countries' (*The Economist*, 2002a). This view that charity from the north tends to be squandered by elites in the south and produce dependency provides an interesting instance of the political right and left reaching the same conclusions about the world. Where they differ, though, is in terms of trade. Economic Liberals advocate liberalising the global agricultural market in the same way that has happened to industrial trade under the LIEO, thereby allowing LDCs to export their way out of poverty. Marxists (and Mercantilists) favour a more endogenous economic approach focusing on the 'food sovereignty' of national self-reliance.

Economic Liberalism was revived in global economic discourse and practice in the 1980s and 1990s in the guise of the 'Washington Consensus' (so named to highlight the importance of the US government and the IMF, based also in Washington) after a period in the 1970s when the New International Economic Order (NIEO) agenda, calling for protectionist measures to be specially permitted for developing countries, made some inroads. The debt crisis of the 1980s provided an opportunity for New Right 'monetarist' economic policies to be put into practice on the international political stage. Faced with the prospect of countries defaulting on their loan repayments, the emphasis of the World Bank and the IMF in bailing out Third World countries in economic crisis shifted from lending more money towards 'Structural Adjustment Policies', tying assistance to the enactment of measures to control inflation and seek economic growth through private rather than state-led enterprises. Just as it was felt that poor citizens of the US and the UK could best be helped by allowing them to help themselves by becoming less dependent on state benefits, saving their money and becoming more entrepreneurial, the neo-Liberals felt that poor states needed to keep their own finances in order and allow the invisible hand of market forces, rather than handouts, to fuel their development.

Alter-globalist

Dissatisfaction with the 'free trade good'/'free trade bad' debates in IPE theory and practice has prompted the emergence of a less rigid and more consensual position on the causes of hunger, led by Critical Theorists who accept that global structural forces have been damaging but who are dissatisfied with the inflexibility of classic Marxists and 'Compensatory Liberals', and who still believe in free trade but not as dogmatically as the Economic Liberals. This reformist *alter-globalist* (as opposed to being pro- or anti-globalisation/capitalism) does not accept that hunger is inevitable in a capitalist world economy, but argues that global political failings are still culpable for the persistence of poverty. Something of a global consensus in the discourse of IPE emerged from the 1990s in the guise of the post-Washington Consensus which, while still advocating economic development through globalisation, acknowledges structural failings in the contemporary global economic system. Former World Bank Chief Economist Joseph Stiglitz, for example, has argued that globalisation has been both harmful and helpful in terms of poverty, and what is needed is global social justice as well as global economics (Stiglitz, 2002).

For alter-globalists, alleviating hunger is possible without abandoning global capitalism by reforming international institutions and encouraging governments to act less selfishly in international trade. The 'Make Poverty History' campaign of the 2000s, for example, sought to increase public awareness of the daily death toll due to hunger, as well as pressure governments into structural political actions to alleviate this tragedy. Hence 'trade not aid' became a mantra of the Make Poverty History campaign, in contrast to the charity-focused Band Aid/Live Aid movement of the 1980s which had inspired it. Hence alter-globalists argue for a 'mixed economy' for the world in which more political intervention is required in some cases, but in other instances the invisible hand of the free market should be allowed to do its work.

In line with this post-Washington Consensus, and in order to move international development policy beyond rhetoric and build a genuine consensus, a new global reformist agenda, the Millennium Development Goals (MDGs), were adopted by the UN General Assembly in 2000. Importantly, unlike the NIEO, the MDGs were also adopted by the IMF, the World Bank, the Organisation for Economic Cooperation and Development and G7, institutions dominated by the global North and with more political muscle than the UN's talking shop. The eight broad goals of the MDGs included three with food security implications:

- Reduce extreme poverty and hunger by half
- Ensure environmental sustainability
- Develop a Global Partnership for Development (fair trade and more aid).

Hence the MDGs were far from a utopian wish-list, representing an attempt to set pragmatic and verifiable targets by which the international community could be judged. The baseline for the calculations of the various indicators was as of 1990, and judgements about whether the goals have been met will be made in 2015. However, progress towards meeting the goals could best be described as 'mixed'. The proportion of the world living on less than $1.25 has fallen significantly, but hunger levels have not improved. The World Food Programme estimates that the number of malnourished people in the world topped the one billion mark for the first time in 2009, significantly up on the 1990 level (WFP, 2009). On unpicking these figures a general trend for all the goals emerges. Asia, Latin America and North Africa have seen significant progress, and are likely to meet many of the targets on a regional basis, but sub-Saharan Africa is out of step with this improvement.

Concerns at the MDGs not being met and heightened anxieties over food security prompted by the post-2008 global economic downturn have seen renewed efforts to construct more reformist global political and economic institutions and policies. The UN Secretary General Ban Ki-moon established a High-Level Task Force on the Global Food Security Crisis in 2008, which adopted a Comprehensive Framework for Action the following year, a two-track strategy pledging food assistance to the most vulnerable in times of crisis as well as seeking to reduce vulnerability in the longer term. In 2009 Ban then suggested building on this pledge at a Madrid Food Security Meeting: 'We should be ready to add a third track, the right to food, as a basis for analysis and accountability' (Ban, 2009). The 2009 Madrid meeting launched the Global Partnership for Agriculture and Food Security, a global network of NGOs and IGOs, and established a fund of $900 million.

In a similar vein a Human Rights Council resolution in 2008 called upon states to 'consider reviewing any policy or measure which could have a negative impact on the realization of the right to food' (A/HRC/S-7/L. 1/Rev. 1). A desire to tackle global hunger at the high table of economic interests was also evident when the G8 (the 'Group of Eight' – the world's seven biggest economies plus Russia) adopted the L'Aqilla Food Security Initiative at its 2009 Summit which (along with several other states and private donors) pledged $20 billion for projects supporting food production in the global South over the next three years. In 2012, on the initiative's expiry, this was then followed up by a similar commitment under the 'New Alliance to Improve Food and Nutrition Security'. In 2013 the targets identified for taking governance beyond the 2015 deadline for the Millennium Development Goals – the UN High-Level Panel post-2015 development targets – set several new challenges for the international community in recognition that intergovernmental policy and law had not served the global interest: highlighting deforestation, desertification, climate change and the over-subsidisation of farming and fishing (see Box 17.2).

Box 17.2: Post–2015 development targets concerning food security

5   *Ensure Food Security and Good Nutrition*
   a) 'end hunger and protect the right of everyone to sufficient, safe, affordable and nutritious food'
   b) reduce infant deaths from malnutrition
   c) focus on sustainably increasing smallholder yields
   d) adopt sustainable agricultural and fishing practices
   e) reduce post-harvest loss and food waste.

9   *Manage Natural Resources Sustainably*
   c) safeguard ecosystems and biodiversity
   d) reduce deforestation and increase reforestation
   e) improve soil quality and combat desertification.

Hence, in spite of the persistence of hunger for one seventh of the world's people, there has been normative progress on the notion that the international community has a 'responsibility to feed' as well as protect. The rise of a global discourse about the right to food – like the right to health – is evident in civil society, looser grassroots activists, the United Nations and even the world's wealthiest countries, and it may be early evidence of a globalisation of the entitlements thesis. It may be some way from being put into practice, but the idea of a global right to food has made great strides.

Conclusion

Food security clearly exposes the 'referent object' dilemma in the politics of security. On a global scale food security is not synonymous with national security and is frequently directly contradictory to it, since national interests have tended to be seen as being served by hoarding rather than sharing produce. Agricultural protectionism in the global North keeps northern farmers and food producers wealthy, but abandoning it would not imperil their lives. Lives in the global South, however, are threatened by the distorting effects of this protectionism. For Human Security advocates and opponents of Realism and Mercantilism, this illustrates clearly the failings of state-centrism in the pursuit of Human Security. The post-Washington Consensus has put development more to the forefront of international politics than ever, but the persistence of absolute poverty in a world of sufficient food and resources for all is indicative of a similarly persistent global political failing. From a Marxist perspective this failure is not one that can be dealt with by better governance of these resources, since it is deeply rooted in the exploitative nature of capitalism. However, while it can scarcely be doubted that short-term economic interests are a barrier to effective sustainable governance, it is possible to argue from the opposite end of the political spectrum that the problem is the lack of free enterprise distorting the market through the over-subsidisation of food and fuel. A global consensus on how to secure access to food has progressed, but the debate goes on and the problem remains. In the course of you reading this chapter, hundreds of people – needlessly and avoidably – died of hunger.

Summary points

1   Famines can be triggered by natural factors such as droughts, but invariably they are also explained by political factors influencing the distribution of food.
2   Food insecurity today is more associated with the general underlying problem of hunger arising from distributive failures than periodic famine, and this affects over one billion people.
3   A variety of particular factors can explain the global political failing that is hunger in a world of sufficient food for all, but on a global scale, anti-globalists see it as an inevitable and deliberate consequence of capitalism, while globalists argue the opposite and see it as due to a lack of market forces in agricultural trade and fisheries.

Note

1   Malnutrition is defined by the WFP as a daily intake of below 1,800 calories.

Recommended reading

Paarlberg, R. *Food Politics: What Everyone Needs to Know,* Oxford: Oxford University Press, 2013.
Sanchez, S. and Dobie, Y. *Halving Hunger: It Can Be Done,* UN Millennium Project Task Force on Hunger, London: Earthscan, 2005.
Sen, A. 'Democracy as a Universal Value', *Journal of Democracy*, vol. 10, no. 3, 1999, 3–17.

18 Health and security

Peter Hough

Box 18.1: Bush and the 'war on AIDS'

In his 2003 State of the Union address, George W. Bush announced the launch of a new scheme, the President's Emergency Plan for AIDS Relief (PEPFAR), which would allocate $15 billion to combating the international spread of HIV/AIDS over the next five years. In appraisals of its record, the Bush administration is generally remembered for presiding over a period in which the US experienced the worst terrorist attack in history, initiated one of the most controversial wars in modern history and triggered the second worst global economic depression in history. PEPFAR rarely warrants a mention in such accounts, but it was an initiative unprecedented in its scale and later claimed by some to have saved over a million African lives (Bendavid and Bhattacharya, 2009). This illustrates two general truisms about global health issues: they tend to be underrepresented in international political analysis, but nonetheless they are increasingly considered to be important, even to more Realist-minded statesmen.

Introduction: the globalisation of ill-health

Disease has long been the biggest threat of all to humankind, and despite the continuing advances of medical science, it looks set to continue to be so for the foreseeable future. The Black Death of the fourteenth century claimed more lives than any military conflict before or since, while the great influenza epidemic of 1918–20 killed far more than the Great War that it closely followed. The 'Plague of Justinian', which started in sixth-century Constantinople and spread throughout the Mediterranean, was a classic 'national security' issue since it precipitated the fall of the Byzantine Roman Empire (McNeill, 1989: 101–106). In addition, the threats posed by diseases, like some environmental problems, tend to be transnational and as such represent a security challenge not easily countered by a human race artificially subdivided into independent, though not impervious, units. Today, AIDS (Acquired Immune Deficiency Syndrome) is the second biggest killer in history and represents a far greater threat to life than armed conflict for most sub-Saharan Africans and for many millions more in all of the inhabited continents of the world.

As with famines and hunger, however, major epidemics and pandemics (international epidemics) of diseases represent only dramatic periodic escalations of an underlying and persistent threat. By the end of the 1970s there was optimism that humanity's war against disease was being won. Disease is an enemy of humanity which can probably never be entirely defeated, but in the decades which followed the

Second World War a growing belief emerged that scientific and medical advances could eliminate many diseases and at least contain the others. The attack was led by the use of synthetic (organic) insecticides, following the 1939 discovery of dichlorodiphenyltrichloroethane (DDT), against disease-carrying insects such as mosquitoes and Tsetse flies. The defence against disease was strengthened by significant medical advances which discovered and refined antibiotics, such as long-acting penicillin, which could directly attack the microbes themselves or immunise whole vulnerable populations against threatening diseases. Coordinating this joint strategy was a new global body set up as part of the United Nations – the World Health Organization (WHO).

Fuelled by the breakthrough inventions of penicillin and DDT in the 1940s, global health security appeared to be a realisable dream for the WHO, but many of the battles in this major war have not been won. In 1955 a global eradication programme for malaria was launched, the largest of its kind in public health history. The use of DDT around human dwellings in the late 1950s and 1960s rapidly killed all mosquitoes that came into contact with it, and virtually eliminated the disease in all areas in which it was used. An illustration of DDT's success in eliminating malaria comes from comparing the numbers of infections before and after its extensive use in Sardinia, Italy. There were 78,000 cases of malaria on the island in 1942 prior to the use of DDT, compared with only nine in 1951, after several years of treatment with the insecticide (McEwen and Stephenson, 1979: 23). Replacement insecticides have not matched the success of DDT in its early years, and malaria has resurged in Africa, South-East Asia and South America. In Ceylon (now Sri Lanka), where DDT had reduced the annual number of malaria outbreaks to seventeen by 1963, its withdrawal prompted a resurgence of the disease to greater levels than ever, reaching an estimated two million cases in 1970 (Hicks, 1992).

A WHO-led immunisation campaign entirely eradicated smallpox in 1978, saving around two million lives a year, while the use of DDT in WHO-led operations quickly curbed the annual death toll attributable to malaria to a similar degree without actually eradicating the disease. In line with these and many other successes, the WHO optimistically declared in 1977 that victory against disease was in sight, setting the target of 'Health for All by the Year 2000'. By the end of the century, however, the WHO's hope that it could shift its main focus to Primary Health Care (ensuring all people have access to health care, clean water and sanitation) had been overtaken by events with the revival of apparently dormant illnesses and the arrival of new, even more virulent diseases.

Although human history is replete with peaks and troughs of disease pandemics, a number of factors particular to the contemporary world can be offered as explanations for the marked proliferation and internationalisation of this over the last quarter of a century.

Demographic globalisation

History shows that epidemics and pandemics of diseases have tended to occur when previously isolated human populations mix. The Roman Empire was beset by periodic plagues of previously-unknown magnitude, new diseases entered Europe from Asia in the wake of Marco Polo's establishment of links in the thirteenth century, and diseases left Europe for the Americas with Columbus and his successors from the late fifteenth century (Pirages and Runci, 2000: 176–180). Over time human groups can evolve immunities to certain strains of disease which can be deadly when encountered by humans who have evolved (genetically) from other geographical areas. The prevalence of holiday ailments, often erroneously blamed on foreign food, bears testimony to the fact that this phenomenon persists. Ever-greater levels of contact between people ultimately should diminish the deadliest impacts of this by making human immunities more similar, but in the meantime, contemporary global social change is a root of the problem rather than the cure.

The much more frequent movement of people around the globe also serves to transport diseases dangerous to all to new parts of the world in ever-greater quantities. Aeroplanes and international shipping are well established hosts for the spread of dangerous pathogens, carried either directly by the human tourists or on insect or rodent vectors. Between 70% and 86% of the measles outbreaks in Europe are believed to have been imported from travellers returning from Asia and Africa (Chen and Wilson, 2008: 1421). Of course, immigrants will tend to be 'vetted' for alien diseases by state authorities before admission into the country, but this is neither feasible nor politically acceptable for tourists and other visitors entering, or particularly for citizens returning from abroad.

Just as more frequent voluntary movements of people have increased outbreaks of diseases, so have more frequent enforced movements, as a consequence of natural or human disaster. People fleeing countries beset by war or famine will obviously be far more likely to be carrying diseases, and also more vulnerable to contracting them. Recipient countries can help refugees and prevent the further spread of disease, at least if they are fortunate enough to seek asylum in a developed and welcoming country. At much greater risk are peoples coerced into moves to other parts of their own state rather than abroad, who are not technically refugees but 'internally displaced persons (IDPs)'. Such people are less likely to receive assistance, either domestic or international, and tend to be forced to settle in overcrowded and unhygienic locations. For example, in 2011 cholera claimed hundreds of lives in Mogadishu, Somalia among IDPs crowded into unsanitary accommodation to escape civil conflict. As with the growth of other causes of human insecurity, the increased number of 'failed states', associated with the contemporary age, has exacerbated the dangers posed by disease. Political upheaval in sub-Saharan African states such as Sudan, Somalia and the Democratic Republic of Congo has contributed to poverty and the limited development of public health and sanitation provision. Even in states less anarchic and less naturally prone to disease epidemics than some of those in sub-Saharan Africa, health threats to security have emerged in line with political upheaval. One of the side-effects of Russia's difficult process of political, social and economic transition since the fall of Communist rule in 1991 has been the rise of vaccine-preventable diseases like tuberculosis and diptheria, largely attributed to poverty and cuts in health expenditure. Of course, failed states also encourage migration and the global spread of disease in addition to localised resurgences.

Economic globalisation

As with travel, the link between trade and the spread of disease is well established. The Black Death arrived in Europe directly via goods imported from the Orient, and although trading standards have evolved somewhat since that time, the rapid proliferation of trade links in recent years has opened up more potential routes for disease to spread. In particular, the globalisation of food production and movement has been accompanied by the globalisation of food-borne illnesses. In 2011, for example, over forty people were killed by a sudden outbreak of *Escherichia coli* (E. coli) in Germany. Despite the high levels of bureaucracy that characterise the European Union's Common Agricultural Policy, scientists could not be sure where the vegetables infected by the bacterium originated, while politicians in Germany, Spain and elsewhere pointed the finger of blame at each other. Once localised outbreaks of disease, due to hygienic failings in food production, are now more likely to become globalised since consumers come from increasingly far afield.

Economic globalisation has some negative implications for human health beyond the side-effects of creating a single market for food. The profits from trade and tourism have become such a major element of the state exchequer that governments have been known to downplay or deny disease outbreaks for fear of the economic costs of doing so. Pirages and Runci note that a pneumonia outbreak in India in 1996 was not reported to the WHO as is customary, because of these sorts of fears (Pirages and Runci, 2000: 190). This decision was, doubtless influenced by the estimated loss of $1.7 billion to the country as a result of a well-publicised plague epidemic two years earlier (Heymann, 2001: 12). States have lost huge slices of income as a result of international panic in the response to an epidemic. Tourism to the UK was affected by the 2001 outbreak of 'foot and mouth', even though it was a cattle disease and represented no threat to human life. The likelihood is that many human lives have been sacrificed on the altars of profit and national pride.

Global environmental change

Even if a small number continue to question whether global warming is natural or man-made, it is beyond dispute that average temperatures on Earth have risen over recent decades and this has had, and will continue to have, a considerable bearing on the spread of certain diseases. Tropical diseases, associated with insect vectors native to equatorial areas, are becoming increasingly common in areas with traditionally more temperate climes. The warmer the weather the more readily mosquitoes breed and bite, and malaria and other diseases have recently become a health threat in countries outside of the insects' usual habitat. The USA, for example, has been hit by West Nile virus as far north as New York every summer since 1999. A record number of cases of the bacterial lung infection Legionnaire's disease in the UK in 2006 led the Health Protection Agency to claim that the country had suffered its first casualties from infectious disease due to global warming (Laurance, 2006). The WHO estimates that air pollution accounts for 5% of the annual global deaths from heart disease, and climate change is responsible for 3% of malaria and diarrhoea fatalities (Hughes *et al.*, 2010: 93).

The erosion of the ozone layer is believed to be a significant factor in the rise of cases of skin cancer (malignant melanoma) over recent years. Increased levels of ultraviolet radiation resulting from ozone depletion appear to be a major explanation for why the disease should have risen in prevalence in the US, increasing by 1800% from 1930 to the end of the century (the increased popularity of sunbathing is another factor) (UNEP, 2002: Chapters 3 and 4).

The general onset of urbanisation, associated with globalisation, is also a contributory factor to heightened disease epidemics and pandemics. The trend for population growth in urban areas at the expense of rural areas has been witnessed since industrialisation began in Europe in the eighteenth century, but it has become particularly prominent in the global South over recent decades. This has had profound implications for the spread of disease in two dimensions:

a) Overcrowding in megacities has led to many people living in squalor, providing the conditions for diseases associated with poor sanitation to emerge and for other diseases to be more readily transmitted among a large population. Examples of this include dysentery and cholera, chiefly spread by unsanitary food and water.

b) Urban encroachment on traditionally distinct rural areas can cause diseases associated with the rural environment to contaminate the urban population. Deforestation, for example, has contributed to the spread of tropical diseases such as malaria and Leishmaniasis since the tropical insects have come into contact with more people. In addition, entirely new human ailments are believed to have emerged as a result of greater contact with other animal species, allowing for cross-species transmission of *zoonotic* diseases. Of the three hundred new diseases to have emerged since 1940, 60% have crossed to humans from other animals (Laurance, 2010), It is widely held that AIDS was transmitted to humans by monkeys.

Human-driven changes to the environment other than urbanisation can also upset the equilibrium in a given ecosystem and cause a resurgence of certain diseases. For example, large dam projects in Africa have been found to have contributed to the proliferation of water-breeding disease vectors such as mosquitoes and water snails, causing the spread of Rift Valley Fever and schistomiasis (NIC, 2000).

Technological globalisation

The globalisation of modern medicine and pest control has brought huge benefits to human health, but it is important to note that these gains have been accompanied by some (admittedly much lower) costs. A major factor behind the counter-attacks of disease against man in the war against disease since the 1970s has been the increased redundancy of human weaponry. The globalisation of the human strategy has had the side-effect of globalising resistance. Both pathogens and the pests by which they are transmitted have increasingly developed immunities to the pesticides and antibiotic drugs used against them. Many insects and rodents have become resistant to insecticides and rodenticides used against them over the last fifty years, with diseases like malaria resurging from near-elimination as a result. Similarly, many antibiotics have become increasingly ineffective in treating illnesses they once could be relied upon to combat. That most renowned panacea penicillin, for example, can no longer be guaranteed to treat gonorrhea or pneumonia. Additionally, resistance requires increased innovation in antibiotic development, increasing the costs of treatment and exacerbating the vulnerability of people in the world's poorest states. For both pesticides and antibiotics, overuse has been a partial cause of target resistance, and more cautious application is now understood to be the best strategy against an enemy more ingenious than was imagined in the 1950s and 1960s. Nobody today seriously imagines that malaria can be eradicated and resources are increasingly targeted on preventative strategies, like the supply of sleeping nets, than on efforts to eliminate the anopheles mosquito. The 'eradicationist' period of the conflict between man and disease looks ever more like a temporarily victorious phase in a protracted war.

A further but inverted link between economic development and disease can be seen in the spread of certain diseases associated specifically with technologically advanced societies. There can be no doubt that modern medicine saves more lives than it claims, but the death toll is still considerable. Around 37,000 people a year across the European Union die of nosocomial (hospital-acquired) infections such as Staphylococcus aureas (the bacterium causing Toxic Shock Syndrome), which are associated with modern invasive medical procedures and which have become more prevalent in recent years (WHO, 2010).

Cultural globalisation

The diffusion of disease around the world is not entirely a one-way process of transmission from south to north. Globalisation has also seen certain non-communicable 'lifestyle illnesses', associated with mass-consumption societies of the global North, head southwards as people in Less Developed Countries (LDCs) adopt some of the unhealthy practices associated with modernisation. For example, the consumption of high-fat and high-sugar foods has led to previously minor health problems such as obesity, heart disease and diabetes becoming more prominent in many LDCs. Diabetes claims as many lives in Asia as AIDS and is estimated to become the sixth leading case of all deaths by 2030 (Mathers and Loncur, 2006). Tobacco smoking has become more common in a number of LDCs (encouraged by northern MNCs faced with a declining market at home), leading to a rise in lung cancer. Alcohol and narcotic drugs in LDCs may not be being supplied by the North but their increased usage, and associated problems of addiction and infection via needles, is believed to be a cultural import (McMurray and Smith, 2001).

Rising health insecurity among indigenous peoples of the Arctic can also be linked to the globalisation of culture. A rise in rates of obesity and diabetes has resulted from the nutrition transition to Western consumption patterns. The mechanisation of travel and the decline in hunting in some communities has also added to the obesity problem as the Arctic lifestyle has become less active (Sharma, 2010). Native Alaskans are nearly nine times more likely to die of alcohol-related health problems than the average US citizen (Seale, Shellenberger and Spence, 2006). Cancers were near non-existent in the Arctic until the last hundred years, but lung, colon and breast cancers have soared due to social change (Friborg and Melbye, 2008). Overall, non-communicable diseases account for 63% of all deaths in the world (WHO 2008).

The state securitisation of health

The WHO Constitution states that 'the health of all peoples is fundamental to the attainment of peace and security' (preamble). Hence it was recognised at the birth of the United Nations that military stability and the security of states, the chief aims of the overall UN system, rested on more than the blend of collective security and great powers concert politics that makes up the Security Council. This reflected both the spirit of Idealism and an appreciation of security in a fuller form that marked international relations at the time, although this was soon transformed by the Cold

War. Though the WHO proceeded to carry out some remarkable public health work during the Cold War years, greatly enhancing Human Security, the state security dimension to health was largely forgotten until the Idealist renaissance that came with the passing of that conflict.

The WHO Secretary General Nakajima took steps to reestablish the state security–world health link and revive state interest in the organisation's work in a 1997 article and series of speeches (Nakajima, 1997). A further development came in 2000 when the UN Security Council adopted a resolution in response to the threat to the international community posed by AIDS. Speaking ahead of that meeting, US Vice President Al Gore articulated the case for securitisation:

> The heart of the security agenda is protecting lives – and we now know that the number of people who will die of AIDS in the first decade of the twenty-first century will rival the number that died in all the decades of the twentieth century.
>
> (Gore, 2000)

Despite this fanfare the resolution was modest, calling upon the UN agencies to increase collaboration and reasoning that the 'HIV/AIDS pandemic, if unchecked, **may** pose a threat to stability and security' (UN Security Council, 2000: 2) (emphasis added). Such understatement in the face of a scourge killing millions of people and economically undermining many states is, on the one hand, breathtaking, but on the other hand, still significant in that it marked the first occasion when a health issue was debated at the high table of *realpolitik*.

The recent 'securitisation' of infectious disease has, like the securitisation of the environment in mainstream politics, often been more a case of considering the implications of this threat for military security than the general security of individual people. The term *microbialpolitik* was coined by Fidler to describe this phenomenon (Fidler, 1999). The Security Council resolution refers to the dangers posed by UN peacekeepers being infected with HIV, while the US State Department interest has focused on the potential for disease to 'exacerbate social and political instability in key countries in which the United States has significant interests' (National Intelligence Council, 2000: 2). Southern Africa is most frequently cited in this context. In Zambia several government ministers have died of AIDS and it has been estimated that half of the police and armed forces are HIV-positive (Price-Smith, 2001: 14). In particular, the threat of diseases being deliberately unleashed in acts of warfare has, since the 2001 anthrax attacks in the US, elevated to matters of high politics questions on the availability of antidotes and the preparedness of emergency forces for combating epidemics. A 2003 article by Prescott in the avowedly 'traditional' security journal *Survival* argued for greater northern aid for southern health problems and applauded the greater international cooperation of medics in the wake of the SARS outbreak as it augured well for preparing for a bio-terrorism attack (Prescott, 2003). The state securitisation of health has had some positive benefits for enhancing Human Security. The US was better able to deal with recurrence of West Nile virus from 2002 because of a strengthening of information links between hospitals motivated by fear of biological terrorism (*The Economist*, 2002b). Horrific though the spectre of biological warfare is, it is pertinent to remember that only a handful of people have ever died in this manner, whereas millions every year perish as a result of diseases which, although naturally occurring, are nonetheless preventable by human endeavour.

The human securitisation of health

While the impact infectious epidemics and pandemics can have on one's own or another state's power capabilities is increasingly something governments factor in to their foreign policy decision making, the security most threatened by disease is that of ordinary people rather than states. The inappropriateness of the high politics/low politics distinction in international relations is most clearly apparent when considering health issues, since they transcend boundaries and threaten far greater numbers of people than any other issues (see Table 18.1). As with other non-military issues, though, health solutions provided by traditional agents of security can be inappropriate. In 2011, for example, a cholera epidemic occurred among Haitians being re-housed by UN troops after a major earthquake due to the installation of inadequate sanitary systems in the new dwellings.

Table 18.1 The world's deadliest diseases

	Disease	Cause	Main areas affected	Annual deaths
1	Cardiovascular – ischaemic and cerebrovascular heart disease	Poor diet, obesity	Global, particularly significant in East Asia and Europe	17.3 million
2	Cancers	Tobacco smoking, poor diet	Global, particularly prevalent in East Europe and N. America	7.6 million (lung cancer = 1.4, stomach 0.7, liver 0.7)
3	Upper respiratory disorders, e.g. bronchitis	Tobacco smoking	Global, particularly significant in East Asia	4.2 million
4	Lower respiratory diseases	Influenza and pneumonia viruses, passed by coughing and sneezing	Global but most deadly in LDCs	3.5 million
5	Perinatal	Infections contracted by babies via their mothers, such as streptococcus	LDCs, particularly sub-Saharan Africa	2.6 million
6	Diarrhoeal	Various diseases carried by waterborne viruses, bacteria and parasites (e.g. cholera, dysentery, E. coli)	LDCs, particularly sub-Saharan Africa	2.5 million
7	Digestive, e.g. cirrhosis, peptic ulcers	Poor diet, alcohol consumption	Global, particularly significant in Asia	2.2 million
8	AIDS	Virus transmitted by bodily fluids	Global but principally sub-Saharan Africa	1.8 million
9	Tuberculosis	Bacterial infection transmitted by coughs and sneezes	LDCs, principally Africa and SE Asia	1.3 million
10	Diabetes mellitus	Poor diet, excessive sugar	Global, particularly prevalent in N. America, East Europe and Middle East	1.3 million

(*Source:* WHO, 2009)

Although the WHO is an intergovernmental organisation it has developed an independent and global perspective informed by a right to health ethos and in line with Human Security, due to the epistemic communities of experts and serving medics who carry out its work. Its track record in the provision of the global good of public health is unprecedented in human history. It is inconceivable that the charitable cooperation of governments could have achieved the eradication of smallpox and thereby saved the lives of two million people a year. The logistics of mounting a genuinely global vaccination campaign, which had to overcome political and cultural obstacles to the intervention of foreign doctors, could only be dealt with by a body representing the whole world, rather than a powerful subset of it. In spite of setbacks, which occurred when resistance and disease resurgences increased in the 1980s and 1990s, overall the WHO has presided over a period of unprecedented improvements in human health.

Life expectancies in the global South have improved markedly despite the fact that these countries continue to bear the brunt of health problems. World life expectancy (at birth) in the first fifty years of the WHO increased from 46.5 years to 64.3 years, an increase of 38%. While some of this can be attributed to economic growth, great improvements have occurred in parts of the world where economic development and modernisation have not advanced significantly. African life expectancy has increased by 36% (from 37.8 years to 51.4 years) while US–Canadian life expectancy has increased by 11% (from 69 years to 76.9 years). The highest growths have been in Asia where economic and health developments have both been significant (41.3 to 66.3 years, 61%) (WHO, 1999). However, public health interventions are the major explanation for longer life. In a major study evaluating the reasons for reduced mortality in the twentieth century, Preston estimated that contrary to popular assumption, economic development accounted for only 15–20% of the global improvement in life expectancy between the 1930s and the 1960s. Overwhelmingly, this improvement was attributable to better public and professional knowledge with regard to disease prevention and cure (Preston, 1975). Subsequent studies by the World Bank (1993) and the World Health Organization (1999) have corroborated this finding.

In common with the other areas of security, globalisation is for health a double-edged sword. It brings with it new threats and challenges, but also new opportunities for improved coping with threats both old and new. Although the opportunities for diseases to diffuse throughout humankind are greater than ever before, the means of mobilising resistance to this are also greater than ever before, and can only get stronger. The widening and deepening of politics characteristic of the modern global condition offers a number of possibilities which could enhance the health security of all people, particularly those in the global South who are the most insecure.

Harnessing technological globalisation

Over recent years there have been major advances in the use of computer and communications technology to advance the knowledge of, and means to contain and control, the spread of disease. The WHO launched the HINARI Programme for Access to Health Research in 2002 in an effort to offset the perennial criticism that the fruits of globalisation are rarely enjoyed globally. To improve medical knowledge in LDCs, in line with its horizontal strategy, the WHO has promoted free or low-cost internet access to over eight thousand online medical journals and helped make available cheap software for improving medical delivery systems. Private information systems such as ProMED and TravelMED perform similar services, but the WHO's global reach and public orientation give their network greater significance and scope for future development.

IT advances have also served to strengthen the capacity to detect and respond to disease outbreaks at the global level. The WHO, with its near universal membership and undoubted epistemic leadership, has been able to put itself at the forefront of this development and has given greater authority to existing global rules on disease notification and opened the way for the development of further ones. An Outbreak Verification System was initiated in 1997 to improve upon the previous system of relying on official state notifications of significant disease outbreaks to the WHO. As mentioned earlier, some governments can be coy about releasing such information, while some might lack the capacity to do so effectively. Part of this system is the Global Public Health Intelligence Network (GPHIN), which routinely scans media sources for epidemiological information and passes it on to the WHO to verify and inform relevant authorities in an early warning system. The significance of this development is shown by the fact that of all initial reports gathered under the system in the first two years of its operation, 71% came from unofficial (generally media) sources rather than official ones (Grein *et al.*, 2000: 100).

The Global Outbreak and Alert Response Network (GOARN) in 2000 further developed this capability by globalising and coordinating various regional and disease-specific surveillance networks into a single 'network of networks'. GOARN has also worked on pooling the resources of participating states and organisations so that international teams of experts can be quickly assembled and dispatched to outbreak scenes. For example, the 2000 Ebola outbreak in Uganda prompted a rapid international response led by GOARN, while in 2003 the notoriously secretive Chinese government was quickly forced into coming clean after initially attempting to downplay the outbreak of Severe Acute Respiratory Syndrome (SARS). China is estimated to have lost $1000 billion due to the SARS outbreak of 2003, but when the second wave of the disease struck the following year the government reported it immediately and fired the officials deemed responsible for covering up the facts in the original outbreak (Upton, 2004: 76). David Heymann, head of the WHO's communicable diseases operations, has even gone so far as to suggest that '[h]ad this system been in place in the early 1980s, AIDS might never have become a global epidemic on the scale we see today' (Heymann, 2001: 12).

Harnessing political globalisation

Health is the longest established and one of the most prominent dimensions of global civil society. Many pressure groups, such as OXFAM and Save the Children, have a long history of highlighting the plight of disease victims, but recent years have seen a significant deepening of NGO activity in this field. A new breed of pressure groups is increasingly using advanced communications technology to assist medics in LDCs. For example, the US-based group SatelLife makes use of satellites to link medics in LDCs to the developed world. TEPHINET (Training Programs in Epidemiology and Public Health Interventions Network) was set up in 1997 and disperses help on a not-for-profit basis. The medical profession itself increasingly lobbies at the global level. MedAct is a group comprising health professionals which campaigns for governments to give greater consideration to the health impact of their policies in areas such as military security and economic development. This is a more overtly political stance than the traditional neutrality of groups such as the Red Cross, seeking to provide relief to human suffering in crisis situations. The radicalisation of pressure groups, in public health and in international relations in general, is best characterised by the work of the group Médecins Sans Frontièrs (MSF, Doctors Without Borders). MSF consciously chooses to ignore the constraints of sovereignty in its operations, sending in medical teams to countries without being specifically requested to enter by the government and making overtly political statements on the rights of individual people to receive medical attention: a global 'right to life'. The UN–NGO symbiosis, best known in the global politics of the environment and human rights, is also evident in health. Public health pressure groups enjoy a healthy relationship with the WHO and have been extensively consulted and utilised in initiatives such as GOARN.

As with the 'greening' of petrochemical firms witnessed in the politics of the environment, the growth of global civil society and greater consumer awareness has prompted MNCs operating in the developing world to improve their public image. The cynic can point to tax breaks often open to MNCs who make charitable contributions and to the advertising pay-offs of apparent philanthropism, but the fact remains that businesses are donating significant sums to global public health and can be said to be contributing to a global good. At the same time, blatantly cynical activities by MNCs which undermine public health are increasingly likely to be highlighted by pressure groups and used to damage their image in the eyes of ever more enlightened consumers. The backtracking of pharmaceutical firms and the US government over the patenting of HIV drugs in Brazil and South Africa in 2001 provides a clear instance of this. Several US pharmaceutical firms and the US government were persuaded to drop legal challenges preventing South African and Brazilian firms from marketing cheaper versions of generic HIV drugs. In both instances the legal cases had sought to uphold WTO Trade Related Intellectual Property Rights (TRIPS). A global public outcry over the cases prompted the backdown and marked a significant victory in this particular recurring clash between competing international laws satisfying the sometimes-competing values of wealth maximisation and Human Security.

The spread of democracy and the notion of a citizen's right to health protection from their government have also been significant factors in global health improvements. The logic of the Sen thesis, that famines are less likely under democratic conditions, holds also for public health in general. Citizens empowered with the vote are unlikely to tolerate governments that are negligent in securing their health. The Indian state of Kerala has been highlighted by Sen and others as a case study of human development in the face of economic adversity. The state government of Kerala in the 1970s introduced a major reform package of social security provision and land redistribution in the face of significant political protest. Despite insignificant economic growth in the state, Keralan citizens' lives improved markedly over the next two decades, including a major advance in life expectancy. Sen's advocacy of a 'support-led' approach to development does not simply equate democratic political systems with better health, since he emphasises how countries like China and Cuba have achieved better health for their people than wealthier, more democratic states by having well-funded public health and education systems (Dreze and Sen, 1991: 221–226). Marxist/Maoist governments generally have an instinctive, ideological commitment to public health which does not need to be prompted by society (the Keralan government was also lefitist). It is the globalisation of socially-responsive government, then, rather than simply democratisation, that has contributed to improved standards of public health.

Conclusion

The state securitisation of global health and the injection of private money into WHO programmes that has occurred since the 1990s has brought with it fears that policy could be transformed from the 'Health for All' social security approach to a more uneven charitable approach. Garrett, for example, contends that the international community's emphasis on HIV/AIDS has actually worsened the overall health of many countries blighted by the infection because HIV medics are often segregated from other health workers and money has drained out of public health budgets. This separation occurs because of the stigma associated with the disease and the preference of international donors for working through NGOs, and is exacerbated by the brain drain of global South medics to the North:

> Guinea-Bissau has plenty of donated ARV [HIV anti retroviral drug] supplies for its people, but the drugs are cooking in a hot dockside warehouse because the country lacks doctors to distribute them.
>
> (Garrett, 2007)

Some voices are more cynical about the whole concept of directly involving industry in global public health ventures. Oxfam's response to the development of partnerships between the UN and the manufacturers of HIV-retroviral drugs has been particularly sceptical: '...[C]orporations in the pharmaceutical sector are offering islands of philanthropy, while promoting a global patents system which would enhance their profitability, but which could also consign millions to unnecessary suffering' (Oxfam, 2002: 8).

Similar fears were expressed when developed democracies began undergoing a 'welfare backlash' from the mid-1970s. Then the cost of state support began to spiral due to aging populations and higher levels of unemployment, causing more people than ever envisaged to fall into the welfare safety net. Countries in Western Europe and North America responded to varying degrees by incorporating private solutions to public health in what has been described as a 'welfare mix' (Rose and Shiratori, 1986). However, the wholesale dismantling of welfare state provision has not happened in any country, despite economic and political arguments favouring this, partly because public opinion considers state health provision a right and partly because public health practitioners have powerfully resisted this. Similarly, medics and scientists operating at the global level provide a powerful lobby in favour of maintaining the WHOs human-focused 'Health for All' strategy. The epistemic community for global public health is an influential one since its opinions are generally seen as informed and clearly inspired by the provision of a public good rather than any sectional interest. The standing of the WHO was evident in 2003 during the SARS outbreak when governments and the general public interpreted their recommendations not to travel to the affected cities of Beijing and Toronto as authoritative 'bans', and they again became the source of global authority when the swine flu pandemic caused panic in 2009. Appreciation of the WHO from the global general public is increasing on both a pragmatic level, spurred by personal security fears, and on an empathetic level, due to greater awareness of the suffering of others. The growth of new NGOs, internationally-oriented doctors and the persistence of the WHO have together helped formulate a culture in the politics of global health where the dominant discourse is based on a right to health for all, even though this is proving harder to achieve than was imagined in the 1970s.

Despite some contradictions, recognition is growing that national and human security can be advanced mutually through global health governance. Aside from the Human Security logic of acting on global public health issues, a simple widened security state-utilitarian logic also supports action. Benatar, Daar and Singer argue that:

> it is both desirable and necessary to develop a global mindset in health ethics, we also suggest that this change need not be based merely on altruism, but could be founded on long-term self interest. For example, it has been shown by mathematical modelling for hepatitis B that resources needed to prevent one carrier in the United Kingdom could prevent 4,000 carriers in Bangladesh, of whom, statistically, four might be expected to migrate to the UK. Thus it would be four times more cost-effective for the UK to sponsor a vaccination programme against hepatitis B in Bangladesh than to introduce its own universal vaccination programme.
>
> (Benatar, Daar and Singer, 2003: 133)[1]

Such logic is slowly coming to inform intergovernmental politics. Hence President Bush (Jr.), as clear an exponent of the 'national' interest as you could find, felt able to initiate the US' global campaign against AIDS in 2003. Political stability in Africa may have been the chief aim of the initiative, but Human Security was additionally enhanced as a result. There is scope for optimism that, so long as national interests are harnessed to global governance, essentially self-motivated policy can contribute to the global common good and thereby enhance both human and state security.

Summary points

1   Disease has long had profound implications for both national and human security.
2   Social, economic and environmental changes associated with contemporary globalisation have heightened transnational health threats.
3   However, globalisation also offers great opportunities for tackling transnational health problems by harnessing IT for disseminating medical knowledge and bolstering the work and recognition of the World Health Organization.

Note

1 This estimate is based upon Gay, N. and Edmunds, W. 'Developed Countries Should Pay for Hepatitis B Vaccine in Developing Countries', *British Medical Journal*, vol. 316, 1998, 1457.

Recommended reading

Elbe, S. *Security and Global Health: Toward the Medicalization of Insecurity*. Cambridge: Polity Press, 2010.
Garrett, L. 'The Challenge of Global Health', *Foreign Affairs*, vol. 86, no. 1, 2007, 14–38.
Pirages, D. and Runci, P. 'Ecological Interdependence and the Spread of Infectious Disease', in M. Cusimano, (ed.), *Beyond Sovereignty: Issues for a Global Agenda*, 4th ed., Boston, MA: Wadsworth, Cengage, 2011, 264–281.

19 Disasters and security

Peter Hough

Box 19.1: The 2011 Japanese tsunami

On 11 March 2011 the most powerful earthquake ever to strike Japan (9.0 on the Richter Scale) triggered a tsunami that swept vast waves over towns along the north-east coast of the country and then prompted a leak at the Fukushima Daiichi nuclear power station. 28,050 people were left dead as a result of the waves (CRED, 2011) including three workers at the nuclear plant. In addition, many thousands of people in the surrounding area had to be re-housed as a result of both wave damage and the nuclear crisis. Although levels of public radiation exposure were officially reported as not being dangerous, many fear that longer-term health defects will emerge.

Aside from the horrific death toll and lingering fears associated with the nuclear fallout, the Japanese disaster particularly highlighted the following points:

- The interconnectedness of different forms of natural hazards.
- The interconnectedness of natural and industrial disasters.
- That, even in a wealthy democracy with a long history of dealing with earthquakes and a strong industrial safety record, people can be insecure in the face of disasters.

Introduction

Of all of the issues considered in this book, disasters in their various forms are least frequently thought of, and hence acted upon, as matters of security. However, 'natural' or man-made disasters or accidents represent a very major risk to human life throughout the world, which has grown over recent decades and looks likely to continue to do so. Consequently, this chapter will examine and evaluate a number of interlinked factors, including: first, the various forms of disaster, both 'natural' and 'man-made'; second, the factors that make people vulnerable to such disasters; and finally, international policy on disasters and the case for treating them as matters of security.

Table 19.1 Global causes of death in 2008

- Disease/ill-health – 52.25 million
- Disasters/accidents – 3.63 million
- Suicide – 0.78 million
- Criminal violence – 0.54 million
- War/political violence – 0.18 million

Source: WHO, 2011. Previously published in Hough (2013).

As Table 19.1 indicates, you are 381 times more likely to be killed in a disaster or accident than by a political enemy. In the United States, road crash fatalities alone equalled the death toll of the 11 September attack every 26 days in 2001 (Wilson and Thomson, 2005). The death toll by natural disaster is somewhat variable, as can be seen in Figure 19.1, but in terms of sudden deadly impact, events like the 2010 earthquake in Haiti and the 2004 Indian Ocean tsunami – which both claimed well over 200,000 lives – far outstrip any recent wars or insurgencies.

The Centre for Research on the Epidemiology of Disasters (CRED), the UN's chief source of data in this area, groups natural disasters into four types; geophysical, hydrological, meteorological, and climatological. In practice, though, many are interlinked and classifying a particular disaster as one or the other type can be difficult.

Geophysical

Seismic forces – natural movements originating from within the earth – can prompt disasters in several ways:

Volcanic eruptions

The threats to human life from volcanic activity come in many diverse forms. The most familiar threatening image of volcanicity is the sight of molten lava flowing

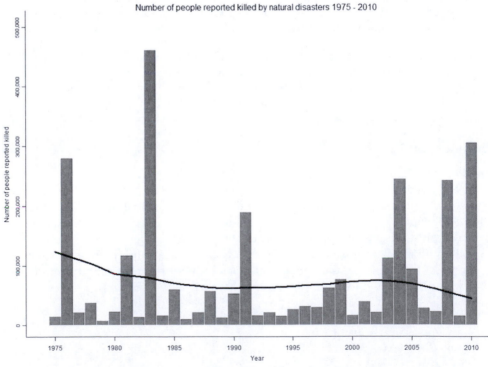

Figure 19.1 Global deaths by natural disaster: 1975–2010
Source: CRED, 2011. Previously published in Hough (2013).

down a hillside. Today, however, lava flows represent a minor threat to life since they are generally slow enough and well enough observed to permit the evacuation of nearby settlements. Generally more deadly than lava flows are 'pyroclastic flows' – the movement of mixtures of volcanic gases and debris that can be formed on the side of a volcano. The Roman city of Pompeii was famously destroyed in this way and the highest death toll from volcanicity in the twentieth century was also caused in this way, when 29,000 people were killed near Mount Pelee, Martinique in 1902. Volcanic debris mixed with water – 'lahars' – can also be deadly, principally since this moves further and more quickly than lava or pyroclastic flows. The 1985 Nevada del Ruiz eruption in Colombia killed 23,000 people in this way when a relatively small eruption produced pyroclastic flows which mixed with snow at the summit and flowed many kilometres down a valley, engulfing the town of Armero.

Also potentially dangerous is 'tephra', the various solid objects that can be spat out at high speed during a volcanic explosion. Chunks of molten lava chill in the air to form 'volcanic bombs', while volcanic glass and ash may be showered onto residential areas. Eruptions of Mount Pinatubo in the Philippines in 1991 killed over two hundred people, principally as a result of tephra collapsing the roofs of houses in nearby settlements. Tephra may also create knock-on disasters by downing aeroplanes, instigating lightning and damaging infrastructure and crops. A famine occurred following the 1815 Tambora eruption in Indonesia, the largest and most deadly volcanic eruption in history, which killed 82,000 people in addition to the 10,000 direct deaths from tephra and pyroclastic flows (University of North Dakota, 2002). In addition, many toxic chemicals can be emitted by volcanic eruptions, including carbon dioxide, carbon monoxide, sulphur dioxide, hydrogen sulphide and gaseous forms of hydrochloric and sulphuric acid. It is even possible for poisonous gases to be released from a volcano without any eruption. In Cameroon in 1986, 1,700 people were killed by a cloud of carbon dioxide released from Lake Nyos, a crater on a dormant volcano (a *caldera*). The gas had seeped out of underground magma into the lake and was then released into the atmosphere owing to some sort of disturbance in the water (Coch, 1995: 97).

Earthquakes

Earthquakes, more clearly than any natural hazard, demonstrate the centrality of the social component in the onset of a disaster. Though the scale of seismic shocks in Earth's crust cannot be entirely predicted, the places where such shocks occur are well established. Seismic activity is most pronounced on the margins of Earth's tectonic plates, such as along the San Andreas Fault Line which marks the point at which the Pacific plate meets the North American plate. The threat to humanity posed by earthquakes is almost entirely due to the secondary effects of seismic waves destroying the man-made infrastructure built in such susceptible areas, rather than the event in itself.

Direct death by earthquake is rare, but possible if someone is killed by a fall into a fault line which has been widened or moved by seismic waves. More commonly, though still a relatively minor form of earthquake-related fatality, people can be killed by buildings being dislodged in this way. Of far greater significance than surface faulting is the shaking effects of seismic waves on Earth's surface. A combination of the waves' amplitude, frequency and duration will determine how much ground motion they create. This is generally most pronounced near the earthquake's epicentre (the point on the surface directly above the source of the seismic wave, the focus). Ground motion in itself is not especially hazardous to man but the effects it has on the human environment can be devastating.

- *Falling buildings*: The most common cause of death during an earthquake is as a result of the collapse of dwellings or other constructions. Recent history's most calamitous earthquakes, in Tang-shan in China in 1976 and Haiti in 2010, killed nearly a quarter of a million people in this way. Most of the cities' buildings were destroyed during the principal earthquakes, and those that survived were then toppled by the aftershocks that followed. Hence, the design and location of buildings in earthquake-prone areas is a critical factor in the scale of the security threat they represent. In some cities in locations vulnerable to earthquakes, such as Tokyo and San Francisco, the security threat to citizens is significantly diminished by the implementation of regulations requiring particular safety-conscious engineering techniques in the construction of buildings.
- *Fire*: The structural damage caused by earthquakes can prove lethal in ways other than crushing victims with masonry or causing them to fall to their deaths. A common knock-on effect is the spread of fire through a town hit by an earth tremor. Most of the casualties of the famous earthquakes that hit San Francisco in 1906 and Tokyo in 1923 were killed in fires caused by damage to cookers and heating equipment. In Tokyo fire swept through wooden dwellings specifically designed to avoid the sorts of casualties associated with the collapse of stone buildings.
- *Liquefaction*: Deaths may also result from earthquakes when geological conditions permit ground water to seep to the surface due to seismic disturbance, in a process known as *liquefaction*. This can result in major land subsidence or flooding. It was in this way that many of the victims of the 1985 Mexico City earthquake perished.
- *Landslides*: Earthquakes can also pose a hazard by prompting the fall of stones or soil from a hillside overlooking a town.

Tsunamis

The Japanese term 'tsunami' (meaning literally 'harbour wave') is the more correct term for what are still sometimes referred to as 'tidal waves'. These giant sea waves are not produced by tides but by volcanic eruptions or, most usually, earthquakes. Tsunamis have a wave length of between 100 to 150 kilometres (around 100 times the size of an ordinary sea wave) and can travel hundreds of kilometres at speeds ranging between 640 and 960km/h. On the high seas, however, they can be very difficult to detect since their height may be no more than a metre (Whittow, 1984: 554). By far the most devastating tsunami in history occurred in December 2004 in the Indian Ocean, triggered by earthquakes along the margins of the Indian and Eurasian tectonic plates near Aceh, Indonesia and the Andaman Islands of India. Around 230,000 people were killed as a result of rapid coastal flooding in Indonesia, Sri Lanka, India, Thailand, Malaysia, the Maldives and Somalia (CRED, 2011).

Hydrological

Extreme rainfall can prompt disasters in a range of forms.

Floods

Historically floods are far and away the biggest security threat to humanity from the non-living world. Floods in China in 1931 and 1959 claimed 3.7 and 2 million lives respectively, figures surpassed by few wars and in a much shorter space of time (CRED, 2011). Although overtaken in terms of deadliness by windstorms and tsunamis in recent years, most of these fatalities were also the result of flooding triggered by the effect of cyclones. Floods often occur as secondary effects of other natural phenomena, but they can present a direct hazard to human life in a number of ways.

'Flash floods' occur when heavy rainfall exceeds the capacity of the ground to absorb the water and causes a rapid, widespread deluge. Nearly 2,000 people were killed in Northwest Pakistan in this way in 2010. 'Riverine floods' occur when precipitation causes a river to burst its banks. This is the most dangerous type of flooding since it is relatively common and rivers frequently run through densely populated areas. The Huang Ho river system in China can lay claim to being the most hazardous natural feature on Earth, having claimed millions of lives over the centuries. Additional flooding hazards can occur when an excessive inflow from rivers or as a result of snow melt causes lakes or seas to flood.

Drowning is obviously the major means by which floods can kill, but this can happen in a number of ways. People may simply be engulfed by rising waters, become trapped in buildings or cars or caught in river sediment deposited by the waters. Collapsing buildings and trees form an additional significant hazard, and structural damage may also lead to deaths by electrocution and even, with grim irony, fires. Hypothermia and water-borne diseases are also often associated with flooding. However, flooding only represents a hazard when it is not predictable. The regular, seasonal flooding of rivers can not only be managed but utilised for its benefits to humankind, since silt deposits from rivers bursting their banks provide fertile soils. It is instructive that the Bengali language has two distinctive words for 'flood'. *Barsha* refers to the usual and beneficial floods, whilst the word *bona* is reserved for more infrequent and destructive large floods.

Avalanches/landslides

Sudden mass movements of snow and ice down a mountainside, known as avalanches, can kill by directly smothering people in a valley or, more commonly, by destroying buildings. 'Wet' snow avalanches, which tend to occur in spring when mountain snows begin to melt, tend to be the most destructive. The biggest ever avalanche disaster occurred in Peru in 1970 when nearly all of the 20,000 inhabitants of Yungay were killed when an earthquake triggered a wet 'slab avalanche' of ice and glacial rock to fall down the side of the country's highest mountain, Nevado Huascaran. Airborne powder snow avalanches are less hazardous, but they can also kill as they are frequently preceded by avalanche winds which can cause houses to explode as a result of rapid changes in air pressure (Whittow, 1984: 45).

Landslides are a common knock-on effect of other geothermal and meteorological phenomena and are sometimes man-made, but they can occur independently by the natural process of gravity acting on soil and rock accumulated on a hillside. Typically, rainwater is the catalyst for this process. For example, a period of torrential rainfall in northern China in 2010 prompted mudslides in Gansu which led to 1,765 fatalities (CRED, 2011).

Meteorological

Potentially damaging windstorms, resulting from particular atmospheric conditions, come in two main forms:

Cyclones

Known variously as hurricanes (in North America) or typhoons (in East Asia), cyclones are storm systems based around an area of low atmospheric pressure in tropical climes. Storm force winds circulate around the calm 'eye' of the storm (anti-clockwise in the northern hemisphere, clockwise in the southern) usually accompanied by torrential rains. The most devastating consequence of a cyclone is coastal flooding caused by a storm surge, when winds create huge sea waves. It was in this way that upwards of 300,000 people were killed around the Ganges delta in Bangladesh in 1970. Wind damage and riverine flooding can also result from cyclones and claim lives.

Tornadoes

Similarly to cyclones, tornadoes are storms which rotate around an eye of low atmospheric pressure. However, in contrast, they tend to be narrower and faster and generally originate inland rather than at sea. The world's most deadly tornado also occurred in Bangladesh in 1989, when 1,300 people were killed around the town of Saturia (Castello-Cortes and Feldman, 1996: 27). Owing to their narrow, funnel-like shape the destruction caused by tornadoes tends to be quite localised, although they move across the surface of the earth in an unpredictable manner. Damage from tornadoes tends to be of three forms: i) high winds associated with tornadoes can cause significant damage to buildings, either directly or through the propelling of debris; ii) the circulatory winds and low-pressure vortex – the updraught – can cause large objects and even people to be 'sucked up' the tornado funnel and deposited up to several kilometres away; and iii) the extremely low air pressure in the eye of the tornado is the most hazardous element of the phenomenon, and buildings caught in the eye are prone to explode because of the difference in pressure inside and outside of the walls.

Climatological

Extreme weather in terms of temperature can also be a cause of disaster.

Extreme temperatures

Both 'hot waves' and 'cold waves' can kill. The deadliest recorded heat waves hit western Europe in 2003 and Russia in 2010, both claiming over 50,000 lives (CRED,

2011). Excessive cold represents the first and excessive heat the second biggest annual causes of death by natural hazards in the US (Goklany, 2007). Short-term dramatic rises in temperature can kill through heatstroke, and cold spells can kill directly by hypothermia or frostbite. Most cold-related deaths, however, are caused indirectly as a result of power lines freezing or heavy snow crushing dwellings. Unpredictability is the key danger in these events. The 38°C temperatures that Moscow and other Russian cities experienced in August 2010 would not have killed in other parts of the world, but they were unprecedented and the resultant heat and smog led to a sudden rise in heatstroke and served to exacerbate illnesses in the old and infirm.

Wildfires

Wildfires are common in woodland regions with an arid climate and strong winds. Droughts and hot winds can dry vegetation which may then be ignited by lightning or other forces, causing fires which spread to other trees or shrubs carried by the wind. The US and Australia are particularly prone to wildfire in the summer. The worst ever disaster occurred in 1871 in the US states of Wisconsin and Michigan, when around 1,500 people perished (Smith, 2001: 248). The Australian bushfires of 1974/5 burned around 15% of the whole country (ibid.) and those in 2009 claimed 180 lives (CRED, 2011).

However, it is debatable whether wildfires should be considered natural disasters at all since an estimated 80% of them ultimately are man-made, resulting from negligence or ignorance in forestry, farming or some other form of land use (Goldammer, 1999: 69). Indeed, it has become increasingly apparent in recent years that many wildfires not only are not natural, but are not accidents either. It has been suggested that around a quarter of wildfires in California occur as a result of arson (Smith, 2001: 256). There was a public outcry in Australia in 2002 when it appeared that the 2001/2 'Black Christmas' fires that devastated large areas of New South Wales were deliberately started by a number of youths and young adults with no clear motive. The human aspect, whether deliberate or accidental, has become more significant with the increased encroachment of settlements into wooded areas, and wildfires are becoming more common and even a regular phenomena in certain places.

Floods and earthquakes have historically been the most deadly of natural disasters, but improvements in flood defences have lessened their impact over time. Windstorms, tsunamis and extreme temperatures, though, have become notably more prevalent and deadly in recent years (see Table 19.2).

Table 19.2 Average annual death toll from types of natural disaster 2000–2010

1	Earthquakes	40,888
2	Tsunamis	22,798
3	Windstorms	15,636
4	Extreme temperatures	13,884
5	Floods	5,673
6	Avalanches/landslides	1,038
7	Wildfires	71
8	Volcanic eruptions	54

Source: CRED, 2011. Excludes droughts.

Man-made disasters/accidents

Transport

Major transport disasters have politicised safety issues over the last one hundred years with domestic security measures frequently enacted by governments after the event. Many states re-wrote maritime safety legislation after the infamous 1912 *Titanic* disaster exposed weaknesses in the provision of lifeboats and other procedures in the classic tradition of 'closing the stable door after the horse has bolted', which have also informed other domestic and international political initiatives. It is a similar story with air and rail travel.

However, just as the iceberg that sank the *Titanic* revealed but a tiny fraction of its full dangerous form to the doomed ship, the chief risk to life posed by travelling is largely unappreciated. Road traffic accidents claim well over a million lives per year worldwide, far in excess of all political and criminal casualties combined. Such deaths occur so regularly and so universally that they tend not to attract the sort of attention given to sporadic ferry, rail or air crashes and so are less controversial. This has begun to change somewhat, at least in the developed world, as statistics showing national variations in road deaths have become better known. Hence the French government in 2003 initiated a campaign to reduce deaths on the road through better enforcement of safety rules, which resulted in a 20% cut in annual deaths (WHO, 2004: preface). In general, though, domestic political action on accidents has tended to be more stringent for public rather than private transport since the greater clusters of deaths provoke more publicity and public anxiety. Nonetheless, most of the deaths on the roads, rail, sea and air today are in the developing world. Western Europe and North America have 60% of the world's vehicles but experience only 14% of the deaths (Jacobs and Aeron-Thomas, 2000).

Structural

Like transport accidents, disasters due to structural failure have occurred for as long as such human activity has occurred, but they have become far more common and dangerous in the industrialised age. Public buildings collapsing or burning down became much more commonplace in Europe and North America in the nineteenth century. In contrast to transport accidents, however, the threat posed by structural accidents in the industrialised world has lessened over recent decades rather than coming to be accepted, as health and safety legislation has evolved to make such buildings more secure.

Industrial

The phenomenon most clearly associated with modern living is industrialisation, which is itself associated with far more hazardous forms of employment and production than pre-industrial economic activity. Like structural disasters, major industrial accidents can be prevented. Most of the worst disasters in history have occurred in countries in the early stages of industrialisation and economic development. Again, the nineteenth century was when such disasters were most prominent in the West, but the death toll reduced in the twentieth century with the advance of industrial safety legislation, and the developing world has been the main arena for accidents in recent decades.

The world's worst ever industrial accident occurred at Bhopal, India on 3 December 1984. During the production of the pesticide Carbaryl the Union Carbide plant accidentally released forty tonnes of the highly toxic chemical methyl-isocyanate (MIC) used in the production process. At least 2,500 people living near the plant were killed and around 180,000 others have since suffered from a range of long-term health effects and birth defects.

Personal

In addition to those encountered while travelling, working and congregating in public buildings, people increasingly face risks to their lives at home and at leisure. Electrical appliances and cooking facilities characteristic of modern living present a component of 'everyday danger' confronting an ever-increasing proportion of the world's population. The WHO estimates that over 300,000 people – mainly children playing – drown every year (WHO, 2011). Many accidental deaths result from personal, domestic activities such as fires caused by deep fat fryers and people falling off ladders while carrying out household repairs. Again, domestic safety legislation has served to improve safety in the home in most countries, but there is an observable tendency to accept the possibility of such 'mundane' ways to die.

Vulnerability to disasters

A number of factors contribute to the increased frequency and deadliness of disasters in recent decades:

Poverty

Between 1991 and 2005 the death toll from natural disasters in developing countries was ten times that in OECD countries (Ferris and Petz, 2011). Clearly money can buy some degree of security from natural disasters. More particularly, it is the sort of well-evolved legal environment associated with economic development that brings security to people. 'It is not an "Act of God" that no more than 10 per cent of the multi-storey structures in Indian cities are built according to earthquake resistant norms' (Wisner, 2000).

However, Bankoff cautions that shifting the focus for dealing with natural disasters from technical responses to tackling underlying vulnerability carries a danger of conflating securing those at risk with modernisation and traditional notions of economic development. Designating large proportions of the population of the global South as 'vulnerable' reinforces the notion that such people can only be 'saved' by technical assistance from the North (Bankoff, 2001). Prioritising economic growth over safety has sometimes served to make LDC populations more vulnerable at the same time as furthering their 'development' by encouraging them to live in overcrowded cities or commute to work on unsafe forms of transport. In addition, the 2005 New Orleans flooding in the wake of Hurricane Katrina demonstrated that inadequate governance and social exclusion can render sections of the population of wealthy, developed countries insecure. In thinking about natural disasters, then, 'vulnerable' should not simply be conflated with 'undeveloped' or 'poor', even though there is clearly some correlation. This was graphically evident in Japan in

2011, as it had been earlier that same year when an earthquake struck Christchurch in New Zealand. Various factors, natural and social and local and global, combine to render certain individuals vulnerable to natural hazards.

Better information

There is a case to be made that one key factor behind the rise in natural disasters is simply that more disasters are being reported in the world's media. The ever extending lenses of the global media and the concerted efforts of a developing global epistemic community continue to bring more events into focus than ever before. The annual number of recorded natural disasters in the world was consistently in double figures in the 1970s and 1980s, but it has been in triple figures since 1990. Similarly, annual man-made 'catastrophes' (large-scale accidents) were recorded in double figures between 1970 and 1986, but have consistently been in triple figures since then (Swiss Re, 2012).

Population growth

Since 'if people are not involved there is no disaster' (Loretti, 2000), the more people there are in the world the increased likelihood there is of a natural hazard having Human Security implications and becoming a natural disaster, or an accident having lethal consequences. As significant population growth in the world is now largely confined to the global South, where disaster mitigation policy tends to be as underdeveloped as the economy, ever greater numbers of people are being exposed to natural hazards and accidents.

Urbanisation

The burgeoning population of the global South in the main manifests itself in the growth of major cities. Around half of these new *megacities* which have emerged are located in areas prone to seismic or storm activity. Most of the quarter of a million people who perished as a result of the Haiti earthquake in 2010 were residents of shanty towns clinging to the hillsides that surround the capital, Port au Prince. At Bhopal in 1984 the death rate was so severe because of the poorly constructed dwellings that had sprung up around the plant to house the workers and their families.

Accidents are much more likely in urban settings, but improved safety standards for public buildings in most countries have seen deaths reduced from a highpoint in the latter half of the nineteenth and the early twentieth century. However, accidents of this form cannot be eliminated altogether in a modern world characterised by crowded urban living and working. It is instructive to note that the Great Fire of London in 1666, which destroyed most of the city, only claimed an estimated five or six lives.

Refugees

Increased flows of refugees and internally displaced people over recent years has also contributed to the increase in number and deadliness of natural disasters. Desperate and frequently unwelcome people are likely to settle in insecure places. The exodus of around two million Afghans to neighbouring Pakistan over the last three decades has presented many of these people with a choice of relocating either to urban slums or rural margins, such as mountain sides (Matthew and Zalidi, 2002: 74–75). Either option brings heightened vulnerability to hazards, the former from earthquakes or structural failures, and the latter from landslides.

Environmental change

Natural disasters often occur for rational, natural reasons. Tropical cyclones can be understood as 'safety valves' which dissipate the excessive build-up of heat in the ocean or atmosphere (Ingleton, 1999). This has prompted many climatologists to suggest that the increased prominence of the El Niño effect from the 1990s, associated with more frequent cyclones and other extreme weather phenomena, could be linked to global warming (Mazza, 1998; Trenberth, 1998). The 2003 and 2010 European heatwaves provided even clearer evidence of a correlation between global warming and natural disasters.

In another side-effect of environmental change, many cases of natural disasters are triggered or exacerbated by the loss of natural defences. Hence, changes in land use can have disastrous side-effects. For example, the loss of traditional vegetation on river banks can increase the likelihood of flooding, and on hillsides it can make land slips more likely (UNEP, 2002: Chapter 3, p. 10).

Pushing for development

Preparedness for coping with natural disasters can be diminished by prioritising development over Human Security. It has been suggested that the capacities of the Nicaraguan and Honduran social services to deal with the effects of Hurricane Mitch in 1998 were diminished by Structural Adjustment policies put in place in both countries to meet the conditions of IMF loans (Comfort *et al.*, 1999).

Smith posits that 1984 was a watershed year for technological disasters. As well the Bhopal disaster, that year also saw a petroleum fire in Cubatao, Brazil which killed 508 people and a petroleum gas explosion in Mexico City which claimed 540 lives (Smith 2001: 322). In total, more people were killed in major incidents that year than in all the technological disasters during the previous forty years. In particular, the three prominent disasters were in LDCs avidly pursuing industrial development. This served to demonstrate that, as with natural disasters, there was a socio-economic dimension to industrial accidents. The vast majority of such deaths prior to 1984 had been attributable to small-scale accidents in the developed world, giving credence to the notion that these were an unfortunate but inevitable form of collateral damage offset by the overall social gains to be had from sustained economic growth and mass consumerism. However, it is in the 'emerging markets' where industrial accidents are now most prominent. Between 1998 and 2001, in contrast to stable or falling figures in the developed world, work fatalities in China rose from 73,500 to 90,500 and in Latin America from 29,500 to 39,500 (ILO/WHO, 2005).

The 1984 disasters also illustrated that technological accidents had become an international political economy issue in another dimension. Union Carbide were a US-based multinational corporation (MNC) and it became clear on investigation that safety standards at their Bhopal plant were far more lax than at their home plant in

West Virginia. The disaster gave ammunition to pressure groups and commentators concerned that globalisation was a 'race to the bottom' in which MNCs would escape domestic safety constraints and seek out low-wage, low-safety sites for their operations.

Modernisation

In the same way that new health and environmental threats can be linked to social change prompted by global economic forces promoting modernisation, so too can natural hazards. Changes to the human–environmental equilibrium can prompt natural hazards or make people more susceptible to 'regular' hazards. Lopez noted how subsistence farming tribes in the Philippines had become more at risk from tropical storms and landslides in the 1980s as a result of being pushed onto higher ground by the establishment of modern farmsteads (Lopez, 1987). In addition, the traditional relationship between people and natural phenomena may be weakened by globalisation. Societal coping mechanisms can develop over time in areas prone to extreme meteorological or geothermal events, and these can be undermined by profound socio-economic changes related to modernisation and development. Well-meaning outside interventions can sometimes even prove unhelpful. Traditional tactics for dealing with flooding in Bangladesh, which include building portable houses, burying precious possessions and responding to certain behaviour patterns in animals associated with an imminent cyclone, have tended to be overlooked by outside agencies. A report on NGO activity in Bangladesh found that well-equipped relief agencies were sometimes less prepared for a flood than the local population, with serious consequences since they had assumed control of response operations (Matin and Taher, 2000).

Deaths by accident are very much a feature of the modern world. Of course, there have always been accidental deaths, but this form of threat to human life is closely associated with technological development and has risen in conjunction with industrialisation and the onset of modernity. In fact, it is possible to argue that accidents, in terms of their perception as such, did not exist for most of human history. The pre-industrial advance of science was significant in providing a means for comprehending unfortunate acts as something that could be explained and hence avoided. Green argues that 'Before 1650, an accident was merely a happening or an event, and there appears to have been no space in European discourse for the concept of an event that was neither motivated nor predictable' (Green, 1997: 196). Modern technology and legislation can enhance our safety, but at the same time modern living in urban areas located on floodplains, coasts or fault lines is inherently less safe.

International policy on disasters

Political measures to protect people against disasters can be dated back to the rise of 'social security' measures in the late nineteenth century, when accidents at work rose dramatically in countries undergoing industrialisation. Health and safety measures to secure people against accidents and the effects of natural hazards are now well-established in industrialised countries, particularly in democracies where such measures can be insisted upon. However, international policy on disasters to date is more sporadic and less influential.

Traditional security responses

Natural disasters present a straightforward basis for governments to 'widen' state security since armed forces can easily be utilised for relief operations. The post-Cold War 'peace dividend' in Europe has seen armies increasingly engaged in this non-military function as illustrated by the increased prominence of NATO in this sphere of activity. In 1998, part of the post-Cold War restructuring of NATO saw the establishment of a unit at its Brussels headquarters to utilise military resources to protect citizens from natural rather than military threats. The Euro-Atlantic Disaster Response Coordination Centre (EADRCC) is a tiny cog in the NATO machine, but its creation epitomised not only a widening of its notion of security but also the widening of its sphere of operations beyond the defence of NATO member-states. A Euro-Atlantic Disaster Response Unit (EADRU), comprising both military and civilian experts from the EAPC countries, has been despatched by EADRCC to many prominent recent disasters within the EAPC area, such as to the US for Hurricane Katrina, and outside, most notably to Pakistan in 2005 when the government requested help with earthquake relief operations. The success of the EADRCC has prompted the Association of South East Asian Nations (ASEAN) to develop a Regional Programme on Disaster Management which has conducted military and civilian cooperation exercises since 2004.

Disasters can sometimes inspire acts of security cooperation and conciliation which are at odds with diplomatic hostility. A special edition of the Cambridge Review of International Affairs in 2000 dedicated to 'disaster diplomacy' demonstrated how 'security communities' can emerge between neighbouring states facing a common threat, in which information is shared to minimise a common risk. The warming of relations between Greece and Turkey after earthquakes ravaged both countries in 1999 is a classic case of two governments and societies overcoming cultural and political differences when faced with a common difficulty. At the one level this was a case of basic human empathy at the societal level triumphing over realpolitik and then being reciprocated, but Ker-Lindsay demonstrates that the case is more revealing than that. The level of cooperation between the two governments, which surprised the rest of the world, was a result of an agreement reached at a meeting of foreign ministers a few months before the earthquake (Ker-Lindsay, 2000). Similarly, in 2001 the destruction wreaked by earthquakes in India prompted offers of relief from Pakistan and the first contact between the two countries' leaders for two years. Such occurrences may assist in improving relations, but security communities require more systematic levels of cooperation and information-sharing to be able to develop. NATO's role in natural disaster relief looks set to develop and become a routine feature of risk sharing and mitigation between its member states and associates.

There is much less precedent for 'national' security agencies getting involved in intergovernmental policy with regard to man-made accidents as the scale of such disasters tends to make them less prominent and military solutions are rarely relevant.

As with other areas of security, however, widening rather than deepening can lead to inappropriately militaristic solutions and a misallocation of resources. The concern that the 'war on terror' may be hampering governments in dealing with other threats to their citizens became apparent in 2005 with the US administration's response to the New Orleans flood disaster. The first batch of relief supplies sent to the area by the Federal Emergency Management Agency (FEMA) was made up of materials intended for dealing with the aftermath of a chemical terrorism strike.

International and institutional responses to natural disasters

UN action on disasters steadily grew from the 1990s, which were designated as the International Decade for Natural Disaster Relief by General Assembly Resolution 46/182 in 1989. The decade inspired unprecedented levels of international cooperation in this policy area and the formation or deepening of numerous epistemic communities for particular disaster forms. However, the decade also witnessed an upsurge in the number of fatalities from natural disasters, which served to illustrate that transnational scientific cooperation, though welcome, was not enough.

The IDNDR approach was largely about applying technical solutions rather than addressing underlying vulnerabilities. A number of sectoral initiatives were launched, such as the Global Fire Monitoring Centre, the Tsunami Inundation Modelling Exchange Programme and the Tropical Cyclone Programme, which improved transnational early warning capacities. Britton comments: 'There is little doubt that IDNDR was effective in encouraging nations to focus attention on the threat posed by natural hazards and in creating an environment wherein greater international collaboration was fostered. Nevertheless, the fundamental task of reducing societal consequences of disaster reduction remained' (Britton, 2001: 45). The Secretariat of the IDNDR itself admitted: 'The application of science and technology was recognised as being essential for reducing the risk of natural disasters, but in the early years of the decade, it became evident that this was not sufficient by itself' (Jeggle, 1999: 24).

At the global level, in a similar manner as seen in the politics of health, the social dimension to securing people against natural hazards has come to prominence from epistemic communities and operates alongside more prominent technical strategies. The International Strategy for Disaster Reduction (ISDR), established after the IDNDR, maintains research on technical solutions to particular forms of hazard but has a far more holistic approach than that seen during the IDNDR. UN agencies have also shifted the emphasis towards a more socially-oriented strategy. From 2001 the UNDP began work on a World Vulnerability Report, an annual index to aid disaster mitigation based on identifying where the world's most vulnerable populations, from a socio-economic perspective, are located. While it might be expected that the UNDP would approach the problem of natural hazards from a socio-economic perspective, a more surprising convert is the World Bank, which has moved well beyond lending money only for post-disaster reconstruction. The Disaster Management Facility (DMF) established in 1998 aims to improve state preparedness through insurance and better public education (Arnold and Merrick, 2001). In the sphere of global civil society the Global Disaster Information Network was also launched in 1998 linking experts from academia, industry, IGOs, pressure groups and governments with the express purpose of providing information to potential victims rather than money to victims after the event. A further development came in 2005 when the Central Emergency Response Fund (CERF) was established after a resolution of the UN General Assembly to manage the dispersal of emergency aid (for war and disease as well as disasters).

Box 19.2: Humanitarian emergency response review 2011

The UK politician Paddy Ashdown was commissioned by the British government to lead a review of international disaster relief operations in 2011. The report considered that 'the UN is the only legitimate authority that can lead but is often too weak and slow to do so', and proposed that the following key factors should be given greater emphasis in its work on disasters:

- **Resilience**: invest in infrastructure to avoid disasters occurring.
- **Leadership**: the UN should invest in 'leadership cadre'.
- **Innovation**: more thought is needed on how best to respond to disasters. For example, money may be more effective than blankets or food.
- **Accountability**: recipients of relief aid must be consulted so that social issues, such as vulnerability and gender, can be accounted for.
- **Partnership**: relief should be multi-lateral and involve NGOs.
- **'Humanitarian Space'**: there is a need to think about the political context of a disaster – e.g. work with 'neutral' NGOs where states are not welcome, and be prepared to get UN support for military support where this is necessary.

(Ashdown, 2011)

Despite all of this, there is still a notable unevenness in international disaster aid donations. In 2010 eight times as much was spent on each earthquake-affected Haitian as on each flood-affected Pakistani (Ferris and Petz, 2011: 23). Currently, though, international responses to disasters still tend to be after the event rather than pre-emptive. This is not only ineffective but also often wasteful. In 2006 the government of Mozambique requested £2 million of emergency aid which would have been sufficient for them to prepare them against imminent floods, but without tragic images to project to the world, no supply of funds was forthcoming. When the subsequent floods duly arrived the international community dug deep to find £60 million, but too late (Ashdown, 2011). Hence there remains dissatisfaction with the capacity of the 'international community' to respond to disasters, as illustrated in Box 19.2.

International Legal and institutional responses to man-made disaster

Efforts to enhance Human Security in the face of man-made accidents through international law can actually be traced back to the early twentieth century, but the impact has been minimal. Worker safety has always been a cornerstone of the work of the International Labour Organization (ILO) which was founded in 1919 as part of the League of Nations system, absorbing the work of the International Association for Labour Legislation which had been set up in 1901. The ILO's 1929 Prevention of Industrial Accidents Recommendation (R31) incorporated a resolution of the previous year's International Labour Conference (ILC) that information on accidents and their causes should be collated systematically. Numerous ILO Conventions dealing with worker safety have been drafted and signed in subsequent decades, culminating in the 1993 Prevention of Major Industrial Accidents Convention (C174) which obliges ratifying states to disseminate accident safety information and site hazardous installations away from residential areas. These provisions are in accord with received wisdom on industrial safety and the domestic legislation of most industrialised countries, but a major limitation comes from the fact that it is also written into the agreement that the provisions do not apply to the nuclear industry, to military installations, or to off-site transportation (except pipelines). Despite this, ratification of the Convention has been poor and it is evident that governments do not have much interest in international safety policy. 'If all ILO member states used the best accident prevention strategies and practices that are already in place and easily available, some 300,000 deaths (out of the total of 360,000) ... could be prevented' (Takala, 2002: 6).

Prompted by the 1986 Chernobyl disaster and the end of Cold War secrecy, the UN's International Atomic Energy Agency (IAEA) codified their most extensive legal instrument to date in the 1990s with the Convention on Nuclear Safety, which came into force in 1996. The Convention covers a range of issues including the siting and construction of power plants and emergency preparation. However, despite the implied strengthening of IAEA standards with the use of the term 'convention' in place of 'principles' and 'codes of practice', this is not a robust piece of legislation. In the IAEA's own words: 'The Convention is an incentive instrument. It is not designed to ensure fulfilment of obligations by Parties through control and sanction' (IAEA, 2012).

Global standards on the safety aspects of business and employment are limp when set against comparable standards for facilitating the trade in the produce of this process. The ILO and the IAEA do not have the same sort of authority in compelling states to protect workers and citizens living near areas of industrial production that the World Trade Organization has in compelling them to allow goods into their countries. Hence we see one reason why many political activists have come to view economic globalisation as a dangerous exercise in unfettered Liberalism, guided only by the profit motives of the global North. However, 'unfettered Liberalism' is not the political system which has emerged from the political evolution of states which have industrialised and modernised, and there is no reason to believe that it will be for the global polity. The industrialisation of Western European and North American states prompted the emergence of policies to protect those put at risk by these social changes, based both on compassion and the political pragmatism of winning support. An ideological consensus emerged in industrialised countries in the late nineteenth century in support of the notion of state welfare, and such a proposition is slowly gathering advocates at the global level.

Conclusion

Disasters are atypical security matters and yet they represent a much bigger threat to most people's lives than those most typical of security concerns; war and terrorism. If the 'referent object' is the individual, as in the Human Security approach, then there can be little doubt that natural and man-made disasters are matters of security. If the referent object is the state, as in the traditional, 'national' security approach, then 'securitisation' is less clear cut since there is no precedent for a disaster destroying or threatening the *whole* of a country. Japan in 2011 was not threatened to the same degree that it was when faced with nuclear attack from the US in 1945. Nevertheless the 2011 Fukushima Daiichi disaster was the most devastating event to hit the country since 1945, and many would argue that such non-military threats will be likely to be the biggest emergencies Japan and most other countries are likely to face in the future.

A further barrier to the 'securitisation' of disasters for some is the absence of explicitly threatening causal factors with 'malice aforethought'. Even MacFarlane and Foong Khong, while purporting to advocate Human Security, opine that natural disasters and accidents 'fail the "organized harm" test – tsunami waves, traffic accidents, the spread of viruses and crop failure are usually not organized by individuals to do their victims in' (MacFarlane and Foong Khong, 2006: 275). For most Human Security advocates, though, there is a fatal fatalism in assuming that only direct and deliberate threats to life can be deemed worthy of security status. There is a human component to all disasters. Natural disasters are not purely 'natural', they occur only when potentially hazardous events – like earthquakes – interact with social factors that render people insecure. Hence people can be made more secure through political actions, such as regulations governing the construction of earthquake-proof buildings. Unlike at Fukushima, though, most man-made accidents are wholly unnatural and rooted entirely in contemporary human societal practices which are becoming more widespread throughout the world. Securing people against such accidents is, again, a political task accepted by industrialised governments from as far back as the late nineteenth century, when 'social security' policies began to evolve in response to changing economic and social conditions. Therefore, disasters are actually no more unavoidable than other social systemic problems like war and crime and people can be secured against them, at least to some degree.

There can also be no doubt that disasters are now – at least to some degree – global problems requiring global solutions. Natural disasters are global problems in both a geological and human sense. State borders are irrelevant in both regards. The natural dimensions can better be countered by a pooling of human efforts and ingenuity, and the socio-economic dimensions of vulnerability can better be addressed by global action. Incidents of workers or residents near industrial plants in LDCs being killed are no longer unfortunate problems unconnected with the relatively safe lives of people in the global North. Developed world consumers are functionally connected to these systemic failures as never before, and they are increasingly aware of this fact. Inter-state competition and sovereignty have little to offer when it comes to dealing with disasters, other than on the occasions when troops can be despatched to help in their aftermath. Intergovernmental responses to disaster can be impressive, such as those which followed the 2004 Indian Ocean tsunami and the 2010 Haiti earthquake, but such events – as well as those that do not attract the world's media – also serve to show how unnecessarily insecure large swathes of humanity are in the contemporary world. Global governance, driven by Human Security rather than sporadic bouts of human compassion, could have saved most of the victims of these tragedies, as well as the less well-reported ones which occur every day. They could have been saved specifically through the implementation of early warning systems and building regulations, and more generally through an appreciation of the ways in which vulnerability turns natural and man-made hazards into disasters.

Summary points

1   Disasters claim nearly four hundred times as many lives as wars, terrorism and other political killings combined, but they are not usually treated as matters of security.
2   Human-caused disasters and accidents are mostly avoidable and are, as such, political matters rather than mere strokes of fate.
3   Natural disasters are also socio-political phenomena since human vulnerability, rather than the events themselves, chiefly accounts for the threat they pose.

4   Global policy on disasters has tended to be reactive, despatching relief operations after the event, rather than proactive, addressing underlying causes of human vulnerability.

Recommended reading

Centre for Research on the Epidemiology of Disasters (CRED), http://www.cred.be/, 2011.

Coppola, D. *Introduction to International Disaster Management* (2nd ed.), Oxford: Butterworth-Heinemann, 2011.

Smith, K. and Petley, D. *Environmental Hazards. Assessing Risk and Reducing Disaster*, 5th edn, London and New York: Routledge, 2009.

Section 4

Institutions and security

20 The United Nations and the responsibility to protect

Bruce Pilbeam

Box 20.1: Mass killings in Rwanda

Between April and July 1994, during the civil war in Rwanda, approximately 800,000 people were massacred, most of whom were Tutsi civilians murdered by Hutu militias. Victims, including children, were slaughtered not only with guns but also with knives and machetes, while women were systematically raped. Yet as this took place, the United Nations Security Council refused to expand the small peacekeeping mission the United Nations (UN) had in the country, or give it a mandate that would allow it to intervene in the carnage – thus, the organisation did virtually nothing to stop the killings.

This and other cases of apparent UN 'failure' in the 1990s helped spark major debates about the role the UN should play in global conflicts, which continue in the twenty-first century.

Introduction

Recent decades have witnessed an explosion of humanitarian crises, especially as a result of the proliferation of civil and ethnic conflicts that has occurred following the end of the Cold War – including in Bosnia, Rwanda, Somalia and Syria.

It is these crises that often prove the hardest cases with which the United Nations has to deal. The global outrage provoked by stories and images of terrible atrocities and human suffering have fuelled calls for a much more vigorous and proactive approach by the organisation. In particular, the common demand is for it to authorise and oversee so-called 'humanitarian interventions' to protect civilian populations.

Yet despite the widespread sentiment that the UN ought to be doing more to respond to cases of severe human rights abuses, it is important to recognise that there are many difficult questions to be answered when external actors intervene in the internal affairs of nations. These include:

- When, if ever, is it legitimate to violate the principle of national sovereignty?
- At what stage in a conflict should an intervention occur?
- Who precisely should be empowered to make an intervention?
- What form should an intervention take?
- Is it necessary to pick sides in conflicts, to determine who is 'right' and who is 'wrong'?

These, and other such questions, will be a major part of the focus of this chapter.

Collective security: the solution to war and conflict?

The common assumption today when considering who should take the lead in resolving international conflicts, and addressing violations of human rights, is that it should be the United Nations. However, to understand the hopes and expectations that have been vested in the UN as an instrument of world peace, it is worth beginning by considering that the quest for a solution to the problems of war and conflict has preoccupied politicians and thinkers for centuries. For many of those who have sought to eliminate armed conflict from world affairs, the answer has been the creation of a system of collective security, and since this idea is at the heart of how the founders of the United Nations believed the organisation could secure global peace, it is worth examining in some detail.

Traditional Realist approaches to security (see Chapter 2) are based on a 'self-help' model, in which every nation is responsible for preserving its own security, since self-interest is seen as the primary motivation of all states. This may entail nations forming alliances, but these are likely to involve relatively limited numbers of states and will last only as long as they remain in participants' self-interests to maintain them. By contrast, proponents of collective security see it as a more long-term, perhaps permanent, approach, in which very many nations will participate.

The basic idea of a collective security arrangement is that a threat to the security of one member is treated as a threat that *all* members must confront; thus, they will present a united front in responding to the security threats faced by any of their number. Advocates of collective security argue that it is a much more effective way for nations to preserve their security than if they had to rely solely on their own resources. It can also help prevent destructive arms races from occurring, which frequently happens, it is argued, with the balance-of-power approach that Realists typically favour. The latter operates by nations continually striving to match the power of their rivals, to prevent any one nation gaining a predominant advantage. This approach is thus centred on competition and conflict, whereas collective security is to be preferred, supporters argue, because it fosters cooperation instead.

Another crucial way in which this conceptualisation of security differs from Realist approaches is that the idea of collective security is frequently understood in moral terms – it is not just self-interest that motivates individual nations to come to the aid of others (though this may be a factor), but because it is believed that they have a moral obligation to do so.

However, for a collective security arrangement to work clearly depends upon a variety of conditions being met. For example, all participants must:

- share broadly similar views of what constitutes a security threat;
- agree in identifying who is responsible for a threat;
- be equally committed to responding to threats, from whatever source they may come (even if from a nation that is on good terms with some members of the arrangement);
- be willing to subordinate their own interests in the defence of other nations';
- be willing to pay the price (in money and lives) necessary to deal with threats to other nations.

The demands of such conditions explain why Realists tend to be sceptical about the long-term viability of collective security systems: after all, why should we expect country A to get involved in a conflict between countries B and C, if no interests of its own are at stake but it may still have to bear significant costs? Or worse, what if involvement actually damages country A's own interests?

Despite its critics, collective security has been seen by many as the best hope for achieving world peace. How, though, to put the idea into practice? One way is to create some form of international authority, charged with the responsibility of ensuring that nations behave pacifically towards one another. The first serious attempt at doing this occurred after the First World War, with the founding of the League of Nations in 1919. The League was established with the aim of promoting international peace and cooperation through a system of collective security. At its height, fifty-eight nations were members.

However, the League of Nations ultimately proved an unsuccessful experiment. One of the most important reasons for this was that the US – despite the fact that it was US President Woodrow Wilson who had originated the idea of the League – did not join. Furthermore, those major powers that did, like Britain and France, did not give the League serious support. Overall, the League lacked the power, resources and willpower of its members to respond meaningfully to major acts of aggression when they occurred in the 1930s, including those committed by Italy, Japan, Germany and the Soviet Union. In the eyes of many, its dismal record in this decade showed that it was little more than a toothless talking shop.

The effective demise of the League occurred in 1939 with the outbreak of the Second World War (though its formal dissolution would have to wait until after the war had concluded in 1946). Its inability to avert another worldwide conflict is what finally sealed its fate. Yet the lessons of the League's failures would prove important for the creation of its successor, the United Nations.

The United Nations: aims and history

Like the League of Nations, the United Nations was created in the aftermath of a global war, this time the Second World War. It was formally inaugurated on 24 October 1945 after a majority of its founding members had ratified its Charter, the document which sets out its aims, organisational structure and rules of operation. In the words of the Charter's Preamble, its lofty ambition was to 'save succeeding generations from the scourge of war'. In a similar spirit, the very first of its purposes mentioned in Article 1 is 'To maintain international peace and security'. Article 1 also contains aims such as the promotion of human rights, but originally these were very much seen as secondary to the UN's primary purpose – based on a traditional notion of security – of preventing military conflicts between states.

When it was first established, the UN had fifty-one members. Unlike the League of Nations, one advantage it had in terms of its prospects for success was that its membership included the USA. Since 1945, the UN's membership has grown to the point where it now has 193 members, including virtually every sovereign state in the world. This is seen by supporters as conferring upon the UN a clear legitimacy, since it can claim to be speaking for virtually the whole of the international community – although as will be seen, members are far from equal in terms of the power and influence they wield.

Upon joining the United Nations, members agree to adhere to its rules and abide by its decisions. Yet at the same time, national sovereignty remains a key principle to be respected. As stated in Article 2, 'Nothing contained in the present Charter shall authorise the United Nations to intervene in matters which are essentially within the domestic jurisdiction of any state'. The UN was not intended to be a world government, but a forum for resolving disputes between independent sovereign states.

The term collective security does not appear anywhere in the Charter explicitly, yet the idea is present implicitly. For example, Article 1's declaration that the UN seeks 'to take effective collective measures for the prevention and removal of threats to the peace' is clear evidence of this. Throughout the Cold War, the major focus of the UN's collective security efforts remained inter-state military conflicts. However, the understanding of collective security it employs has not remained fixed, and more recent debates about expanded notions of security (discussed in previous chapters of this book) have been taken on board. Thus, in a 2004 report commissioned by the UN Secretary-General, entitled *A More Secure World: Our Shared Responsibility*, the case is made for adopting what it calls a 'comprehensive' concept of collective security, which goes beyond a traditional military-centred understanding (United Nations High-Level Panel on Threats, Challenges and Change, 2004). The report identifies six clusters of threats, arguing that since they all pose problems for the entire world, they need to be tackled collectively:

- Economic and social threats, including poverty, infectious diseases and environmental degradation
- Inter-state conflict
- Internal conflict, including civil war, genocide and other large-scale atrocities
- Nuclear, radiological, chemical and biological weapons
- Terrorism
- Transnational organised crime.

While the focus of this chapter is numbers two and three on this list, it will be useful to bear in mind the extent to which the UN has latterly sought to expand its remit in tackling a much wider range of security threats than in the past.

Organisation and powers

The organisational structure of the United Nations is presented in Figure 20.1. As this shows, it has six principal organs. Of these, the Security Council is the most important in dealing with security issues; as Article 24 specifies, the UN's members 'confer on the Security Council primary responsibility for the maintenance of international peace and security'.

However, before looking at the role of the Security Council in more detail, it is worth briefly examining the roles of two of the other major organs, the General Assembly and the Secretariat.

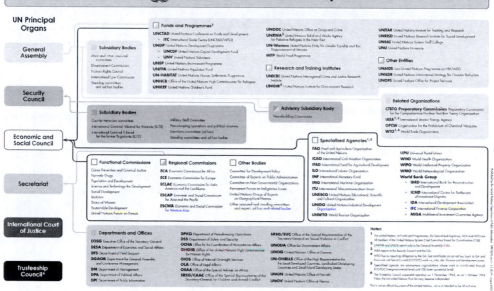

Figure 20.1 The United Nations System
Source: www.un.org/en/aboutun/structure/org_chart.shtml

The General Assembly

The General Assembly is the main deliberative, policymaking and representative body of the UN. It includes all 193 UN members, who are formally regarded as equal, meaning that each gets a single vote regardless of size or population. Decisions on major questions, such as those on peace and security, require a two-thirds majority to be approved.

The General Assembly's commitment to formal equality might seem to give small countries a large advantage, since although the major powers (like the US, Russia and China) may be economically and militarily powerful, they are nonetheless far fewer in number. Yet a crucial limitation of the General Assembly's powers is that the resolutions it passes count only as recommendations: thus, they are non-binding. In relation to security matters, one of the most notable areas where this has proved significant, throughout UN history, is the Israeli–Palestinian conflict. Since the Israeli state was founded in 1948, not long after the UN itself, the General Assembly has repeatedly passed resolutions relating to this conflict, the vast majority supporting the Palestinian cause. Yet since they are non-binding, these resolutions have had minimal impact on the conflict's resolution.

The Secretariat

The Secretariat carries out the day-to-day work of the UN, with staff stationed around the world. It is headed by the UN Secretary-General and has a staff of some 44,000. Its duties include administering peacekeeping operations and mediating international disputes, through departments and offices such as the Department of Peacekeeping

Operations (DPKO) and the Office for the Coordination of Humanitarian Affairs (OCHO). The Secretariat's crucial importance in security affairs is therefore that, although the Security Council may make the key decisions, it is the body that has to implement them. Moreover, the Secretary-General often makes recommendations to the Security Council about which issues to address.

The Security Council

As already noted, the Security Council has the main role in security matters. It is composed of fifteen members. When the UN was established after the Second World War, the five main victors – China, France, the USSR (now Russia), the UK and the US – ensured that they each had permanent seats on the Security Council. Alongside these five, known as the P5, there are also non-permanent members. Originally there were six of these, but in 1965 the number was expanded to ten. These ten are elected for two-year terms and are not eligible for immediate re-election. They are selected by the UN's five regional groups of nations, ensuring that there is at least some geographical distribution of power on the Security Council, and confirmed by the General Assembly.

Permanency clearly gives the P5 a major advantage over all other nations. A second important advantage they possess is the power of veto. The Security Council's fifteen members each have one vote when it comes to making decisions, which require the affirmative vote of nine members. On procedural matters – such as what issues and topics to discuss – this may be any of the nine. However, on substantive matters such as the approval of sanctions or military force, all of the P5 must give their agreement. In effect, therefore, each of the P5 is able to veto major decisions with which it disagrees, by withholding its affirmative vote. Between 1945 and 2012 China used its veto on 9 occasions, France 18, the United Kingdom 32, the United States 83, and the USSR/Russia 128 (Global Policy Forum, 2012).

Both of these advantages are sources of great controversy. Why should the P5 members enjoy the privileged position that they do? One argument in favour is that it is necessary to keep the major powers on board; without this, some (such as the US) may not even have joined in the first place. Not having such nations as members would threaten the long-term viability of the organisation, being one of the factors that had undermined the League of Nations.

Another argument is based on recognising that since power and resources are not equally distributed between nations, those with the most ought to have a greater influence over decision-making since their agreement is the most important for resolutions' successful implementation. What should also be noted is that all of the P5 are nuclear powers, and even though other nations have also now acquired nuclear weapons, it remains the case that the states with the capacity to initiate global nuclear warfare are among the P5. Thus, it might be felt unwise not to have such powers always represented on the Security Council, and allowed the power of veto, to reduce the likelihood of this latter possibility.

Nonetheless, many critics have argued that the original set-up of the Security Council, even if justifiable in 1945, is anachronistic in the twenty-first century. In particular, it may be deemed both undemocratic and inegalitarian.

In terms of the issue of permanent membership, suggestions for reform have included abolishing this altogether, so that all seats are non-permanent elected ones;

or alternatively, expanding the number of permanent seats. Candidates for becoming permanent members include Japan and Germany, since both are major economic powers as well as large funding contributors to the UN. Yet shifts in the distribution of economic and political power in the world since the UN was founded mean that there are also strong arguments for considering increasingly significant nations such as India and Brazil.

The veto power of permanent members has also been the subject of proposals for reform, the most obvious idea being simply to do away with it. Supporters of this argue that it would allow the UN to be much more effective than it has been in the past, as one of the major obstacles to decisive action has always been the ability of even a single veto-holder to override the wishes of the majority.

However, reforming the Security Council depends on the backing of the P5 – and it is not at all clear when, or if, this support will be forthcoming.

Powers for dealing with international conflicts

What, though, are the UN's – and especially the Security Council's – powers when it comes to dealing with disputes and conflicts? Unlike the League of Nations, the UN was given real teeth by its Charter. For example, although it was not given an army of its own, it is able to draw upon the military resources of members to enforce its decisions. In relation to the resolution of disputes, two of the Charter's chapters in particular are most significant.

Chapter VI is entitled the 'Pacific Settlement of Disputes'. It is mainly concerned with *prevention*: stopping disputes from escalating into armed conflicts by trying to persuade those involved to find other means of resolving them. To this end, Article 33 calls for parties in dispute to seek, in the first instance, 'a solution by negotiation, enquiry, mediation, conciliation, arbitration, judicial settlement, resort to regional agencies or arrangements, or other peaceful means of their own choice'. Coercive interventions into conflicts are, therefore, supposed to be a last rather than first resort.

Chapter VII, by contrast, contains provisions concerning 'Action With Respect to Threats to the Peace, Breaches of the Peace, and Acts of Aggression' – in other words, its focus is on instances where disputes *have* escalated into open hostilities, and coercion is believed to have become necessary. Some of Chapter VII's main Articles are presented in Box 20.2. As can be seen, Article 41 gives the Security Council the power to use action short of military force, including, for example, economic sanctions. Should such measures prove inadequate, Article 42 authorises the use of military action to maintain or restore peace. Article 43's insistence that all members make available the resources necessary to do so again shows the importance of the principle of collective security. Interesting, too, is the fact that not all non-Security Council mandated uses of force are prohibited, with Article 51 permitting nations the independent right of self-defence.

Box 20.2: The UN's powers in dealing with threats to peace

UN Charter

Chapter VII:

Action With Respect to Threats to the Peace, Breaches of the Peace, and Acts of Aggression

Article 39

The Security Council shall determine the existence of any threat to the peace, breach of the peace, or act of aggression and shall make recommendations, or decide what measures shall be taken in accordance with Articles 41 and 42, to maintain or restore international peace and security.

Article 41

The Security Council may decide what measures not involving the use of armed force are to be employed to give effect to its decisions, and it may call upon the Members of the United Nations to apply such measures. These may include complete or partial interruption of economic relations and of rail, sea, air, postal, telegraphic, radio, and other means of communication, and the severance of diplomatic relations.

Article 42

Should the Security Council consider that measures provided for in Article 41 would be inadequate or have proved to be inadequate, it may take such action by air, sea, or land forces as may be necessary to maintain or restore international peace and security. Such action may include demonstrations, blockade, and other operations by air, sea, or land forces of Members of the United Nations.

Article 43

All Members of the United Nations, in order to contribute to the maintenance of international peace and security, undertake to make available to the Security Council, on its call and in accordance with a special agreement or agreements, armed forces, assistance, and facilities, including rights of passage, necessary for the purpose of maintaining international peace and security.

Article 51

Nothing in the present Charter shall impair the inherent right of individual or collective self-defence if an armed attack occurs against a Member of the United Nations, until the Security Council has taken measures necessary to maintain international peace and security.

Source: www.un.org/en/documents/charter/chapter7.shtml

To understand how the UN has attempted to maintain international peace and security in practice, and how its efforts have evolved over the years, it will be useful next to examine how the organisation has operated from its beginnings to the present day.

The Cold War: from collective security to peacekeeping

Soon after the UN was founded, the Cold War commenced. This had major repercussions for the organisation. Most significant, the rivalry between the US and the Soviet Union, characterised as it was by animosity and distrust, meant that the cooperation upon which collective security depends became unachievable. Any hope that the UN might realise its goal of eradicating the scourge of war remained a forlorn one throughout this period.

The US and the Soviet Union regularly took different sides on major international issues. They also proved willing to use their Security Council vetoes to block resolutions in order to stymie the wishes and interests of their opponents; indeed, during the first ten years of the UN's existence, the Soviet Union used its veto power seventy-nine times. This therefore prevented the Security Council from presenting the united front needed to use the full powers granted by the Charter to maintain peace and security.

In 1950 the Security Council did authorise the use of force in Korea – a country divided between the Communist North and non-Communist South – in response to the former's invasion of the latter. A task force composed of soldiers from sixteen countries (though predominantly American) thus intervened in the ensuing war under the auspices of the UN. Its success in confronting aggression led defenders to hail this as an example of collective security's effectiveness. Yet leaving aside the rights and wrongs of the Korean War, what is important to note is that this UN action was possible only because at the time the Security Council made its decision, the Soviet Union was boycotting the organisation (over its failure to recognise Mao Tse-Tung's Communist regime as the official government of China). It was therefore unable to use its veto, which it almost certainly would otherwise have done. Once the Soviet Union returned to the UN in 1951, stalemate between the powers resumed and it again became impossible to orchestrate concerted action. When the US intervened militarily in the Vietnam War – another conflict within a country divided between a Communist North and non-Communist South – in the 1960s, it was without UN Security Council support.

It is within the context of Cold War tensions, and consequent Security Council paralysis, that a different strategy to full-fledged military action emerged for responding to conflicts. That strategy was peacekeeping. The origins and growth of UN peacekeeping operations may thus be understood as a response to the organisation's failure to create an effective system of collective security. In effect, horizons and expectations were lowered. The UN was not going to be able to *end* the problems of war and conflict; instead, it would attempt to contain and ameliorate them.

Defining peacekeeping is enormously difficult, complicated by the fact that, like the concept of collective security, it is not explicitly mentioned in the UN Charter. In terms of this, peacekeeping has often been understood as existing somewhere in between the non-military mechanisms for conflict resolution set out in Chapter VI and the military ones authorised by Chapter VII; for this reason, it has been characterised – by Dag Hammarskjöld, the second UN Secretary-General – as belonging to 'Chapter VI and a Half' of the Charter.

A useful starting point for understanding what peacekeeping means is to recognise that it is but one type of peace activity, alongside many others relating to the pre-, during and post- phases of conflicts. Box 20.3 shows the spectrum of activities that the UN engages in relating to peace and security. Here it can be seen that the UN's own definition of peacekeeping is as follows: 'a technique designed to preserve the peace, however fragile, where fighting has been halted'. In other words, peacekeeping is supposed to be an activity that takes place *after* armed hostilities have ceased, aimed at safeguarding whatever peace has been achieved. Of course, this definition leaves many questions unanswered. However, since the nature of peacekeeping has changed greatly over the years, it is perhaps impossible to give a single, static definition that will encompass every activity that has been undertaken under this label.

Box 20.3: The spectrum of peace and security activities

Conflict prevention – involves the application of structural or diplomatic measures to keep intra-state or inter-state tensions and disputes from escalating into violent conflict.

Peacemaking – generally includes measures to address conflicts in progress and usually involves diplomatic action to bring hostile parties to a negotiated agreement.

Peacekeeping – a technique designed to preserve the peace, however fragile, where fighting has been halted.

Peace enforcement – involves the application, with the authorisation of the Security Council, of a range of coercive measures, including the use of military force.

Peacebuilding – involves a range of measures targeted to reduce the risk of lapsing or relapsing into conflict by strengthening national capacities at all levels for conflict management.

United Nations Peacekeeping Operations: Principles and Guidelines (2008)
Source: pbpu.unlb.org/pbps/library/capstone_doctrine_eng.pdf

Instead, to understand better the type of peacekeeping operation that occurred during the Cold War, it is worth attending briefly to their history (UN, 2014).

From 1948 to 1988 the UN undertook thirteen peacekeeping missions, largely in places sufficiently removed from the centres of Cold War rivalry that they would be acceptable to both superpowers. Significantly as well, the countries that supplied troops for operations were generally neutral or non-aligned ones – such as Sweden, Norway, Ireland, Canada and India – and not the P5.

The vitality and impact of UN peacekeeping operations waxed and waned throughout this period. The first mission to be deployed was the United Nations Truce Supervision Organization (UNTSO), which in 1948 was sent to observe the ceasefire between Israel and the Palestinians; in 1949 the UN Military Observer Group in India and Pakistan (UNMOGIP) undertook a similar operation to observe the ceasefire in Kashmir. In both cases, the strength and remit of the missions were modest: they were limited to observing and monitoring; personnel numbered in the low hundreds; and they were unarmed. (What they also have in common is that they are both still in situ today.)

Yet from the mid-1950s onwards, the scale and scope of peacekeeping operations began to expand. The first armed operation was the UN Emergency Force (UNEF I) deployed in 1956 to monitor the withdrawal of British, French and Israeli troops from the Suez Canal. This was also the first to which the label peacekeeping was applied. The first large-scale operation was the UN Operation in the Congo (ONUC), established in 1960. At its peak, it had nearly 20,000 military personnel, making it the largest peacekeeping operation of the Cold War period. Over the following years, further missions in places such as Cyprus and the Middle East saw the role of UN peacekeeping operations continue to grow.

However, the mid-1970s marked the beginning of a retreat. After 1975, only a single major operation was initiated – the UN Interim Force in Lebanon (UNIFIL) in 1978 – until the Cold War began to thaw at the end of the 1980s. This decline was caused by continued Cold War tensions, coupled with financial constraints. Only as the Cold War was coming to its conclusion was another significant operation launched, when a peacekeeping mission was sent to monitor Soviet withdrawal from Afghanistan in 1988.

The Cold War period of peacekeeping has come to be known as the era of traditional peacekeeping. It represented a shift away from the idea of large armies setting out to quash the world's aggressors, towards that of relatively small units monitoring adherence to peace agreements, troop withdrawals, ceasefires and buffer zones; the major exception to this was the Congo operation, which did involve a large force with more ambitious goals. Despite there being significant differences between operations, the peacekeeping efforts of this period were largely informed by three guiding principles:

- Consent of the parties involved in a conflict
- Impartiality (i.e. peacekeepers should not take sides)
- Non-use of force, except in self-defence and defence of the mandate.

To return to the questions asked at the start of this chapter, operating under these principles clearly heavily circumscribes when and in what circumstances peacekeeping may take place, and how peacekeepers may act when they do. If peacekeepers can operate only with the permission of those involved in disputes, must maintain a stance of neutrality, and are greatly restricted in when they may use force, there are obviously major limits on the roles they can play in resolving conflicts. Certainly, they do not provide the basis for eliminating war altogether, or perhaps even mass atrocities. In part, these restrictions were developed so that operations would be as uncontroversial as possible, not least to make them acceptable to both sides in the Cold War. However, they were also important so that the principle of national sovereignty would continue to be respected, as enshrined in the UN's own Charter. As we turn to examine how matters have developed in the post-Cold War era, it will be useful to reflect upon whether it has become necessary to adopt different principles because of the changed context.

The post-Cold War era: a changed UN for changed times?

On 2 August 1990, Iraqi forces launched a surprise attack against the small nation of Kuwait. After mere days of fighting, the army of Saddam Hussein proved victorious and Kuwait fell into his hands. What, though, would be the international response?

Very soon after, the UN Security Council met and passed a resolution condemning the invasion and demanding Iraqi withdrawal. Over the following months, more resolutions were approved, until finally, Resolution 678 – passed on 29 November – set a deadline of 15 January 1991 for Iraq to withdraw. If it did not, then 'all necessary means' would be used to enforce the resolution. When compliance by the appointed date was not forthcoming, a coalition of forces from thirty-four countries, led by the US, was dispatched under UN authorisation. After a relatively brief campaign, the occupying army was dislodged from Kuwait. On 28 February 1991 the US President George H.W. Bush declared that Kuwait had been liberated and that fighting would end.

The Gulf War, as it became known, had many critics, some labelling it an imperialist adventure undertaken at America's behest to gain control of Middle Eastern oil, extend its influence in the region and/or reassert its global hegemony. Yet to many of the UN's supporters, the war's significance was the central role that the organisation played, and what this augured for the future. What was critically different about the context in which it now operated was that the Cold War rivalries of the past had ended – crucially, the Soviet Union (which did not finally dissolve until December 1991) did not veto the resolution allowing force to be used against Iraq. This appeared to suggest that it might at last be possible for the major powers to cooperate instead of compete, and work together to create an effective system of collective security. President Bush described the post-Cold War era as representing a 'New World Order', and great hopes arose that a strengthened UN would be central in shaping it.

However, events did not develop as optimists anticipated. Confidence in the belief that the post-Cold War era might produce a new order of peace and harmony was shaken by the proliferation of conflicts around the world, most of which were intra-state rather than inter-state in nature. These raised particular dilemmas for organisations like the UN. Whereas the international action taken during the Gulf War seemed to defenders (though not to many critics) to have unambiguous legal, political and perhaps moral justifications – as a legitimate response to one sovereign state committing an act of aggression against another – the civil wars of the 1990s presented much more complex scenarios. Crucially for the UN, and despite claims about a New World Order, nor was there any clear consensus over how the international community should respond to them.

Humanitarian interventions and new forms of peacekeeping

What raised particular concerns about the conflicts of the 1990s was the impact they had upon civilian populations. Consequently, the notion that came to the fore in the 1990s, and which was regularly used to justify the international community's involvement in these intra-state conflicts, was that of humanitarian interventions.

A humanitarian intervention may be defined as the threat or use of force to prevent or halt widespread suffering and violations of human rights, without the consent of the host state in which they are undertaken. A major question raised by this is, of course, the implications it has for state sovereignty, the right of nations to manage their own domestic affairs as specified in Article 2 of the UN Charter. Yet the use of humanitarianism as the basis for sanctioning the overriding of state sovereignty points to another crucial characteristic of post-Cold War interventions: that rather than being justified in traditional security terms, they have frequently been grounded in broader notions of Human Security (as discussed in previous chapters) that look beyond the simple security of the state.

Peacekeeping operations, too, began to change. One way in which this was so is simply in terms of the number of operations initiated once the Cold War started drawing to a close and stalemate on the Security Council began to ease. Thus, from 1988 to 1993, twenty new operations were begun, more than in the previous forty years combined (as of 2014, there are sixteen UN peace operations deployed on four continents). Moreover, a much wider range of countries began to contribute troops, including members of the P5, once the reduction of Cold War tensions made this more acceptable (though it is worth noting that most peacekeeping forces today are drawn from developing nations, like India, Pakistan and Bangladesh).

Yet most significant was that with the changing nature of conflicts came important changes in the natures of peacekeeping operations. The intra-state conflicts of the post-Cold War era were triggered by multiple, interlinking factors, including political, economic, religious, ethnic and nationalist tensions. They also frequently involved the breakdown of nations' social, political and economic structures. In response, there was a shift from traditional peacekeeping operations – which, as seen, were generally limited to activities such as observation and monitoring – to much more ambitious ones, aiming both to alleviate widespread humanitarian suffering and also to lay the foundations for long-term, sustainable peace.

To distinguish types of peacekeeping operation, traditional ones are often labelled 'first generation' peacekeeping, whereas those with more large-scale and elaborate goals are given different labels. Thus, 'second generation' peacekeeping refers to efforts that are more complex and multidimensional, aiming at peacebuilding (see Box 20.3) for the long term; while 'third generation' operations involve peace enforcement – that is, the use of force – to secure humanitarian ends. (What may be confusing is that these generational designations are not strictly chronological – thus, although the majority of Cold War operations were first generation, the operation in the Congo mentioned earlier was an example of third generation peacekeeping, in that it involved the proactive use of force.)

In concrete terms, the styles of operations that have developed since the 1990s have differed from traditional peacekeeping efforts in a number of ways. For example, the range of activities undertaken has much expanded, to include those such as:

- Delivering humanitarian aid
- Monitoring human rights
- Protecting civilians – e.g. establishing 'safe havens'
- Disarming and demobilising combatants
- Building sustainable institutions of governance and economic development
- Monitoring elections.

One consequence of this is that a much wider range of personnel are involved in contemporary peacekeeping operations, including not just the military, but human rights monitors, humanitarian workers, legal experts and economists.

Most important, modern operations have raised many questions about the principles that have traditionally governed peacekeeping. For example, in the 'messy' conditions of intra-state conflicts, where there are often not just two clearly defined sides but a whole range of participants – which may include, say, various tribes, factions or militia groups – it is not always possible to operate with the consent of every single actor. Perhaps most significantly, operations that engage in peace enforcement clearly challenge the principle that the use of force should be limited to self-defence. For example, the United Nations Operation in Somalia II (UNOSOM II), in place from 1993 to 1995, was authorised to use force to fulfil its goals of disarming those engaged in fighting and distributing humanitarian aid. Yet moving away from traditional peacekeeping principles has many significant implications, not least of which is that it may compromise the UN in terms of how far it is perceived as a neutral and impartial body.

The UN under scrutiny

Throughout the 1990s, humanitarian interventions proved extremely controversial. To advocates, they were seen as a long overdue acceptance by the international community of the need to uphold universal values and standards concerning human rights and justice, whereas to critics they represented unjustifiable infringements of the sovereign rights of states. What helped fuel these debates was that the UN's record in practice was often not strong, either in preventing and resolving conflicts or in protecting civilians from harm. Thus, in numerous cases, the UN was widely judged to have 'failed', regardless of any rhetoric about humanitarianism. For example:

Bosnia and Herzegovina – From 1992 to 1995, despite the presence of the United Nations Protection Force (UNPROFOR), approximately 200,000 people were killed, including atrocities such as the mass killings in Srebrenica of five to eight thousand unarmed Muslim men and boys. Many others suffered major upheavals and dislocations, together with religious and ethnic persecution.

Somalia – From 1991 to 1992, in the first two years alone of the Somali civil war, approximately 350,000 people died, not only from fighting but also from famine and disease. The United Nations Operation in Somalia I (UNOSOM I) did little to prevent this, and even with the peace enforcement efforts of the United Nations Operation in Somalia II (UNOSOM II), violence was not stopped. The death toll rose to approximately 500,000 by the decade's end, and many hundreds of thousands more lost their homes and became refugees. The conflict remains unresolved to this day.

Rwanda – From 1990 to 1994, as well as the 800,000 killed in the massacres noted at the start of this chapter (together with those killed during earlier fighting), millions of refugees were created, many of whom fled to the neighbouring countries of Zaire (now the Democratic Republic of the Congo), Burundi and Tanzania. The United Nations Assistance Mission for Rwanda (UNAMIR) was given by the Security Council neither the personnel nor authority to halt the terrible human suffering.

What is notable about the UN's operations of the 1990s is that the organisation was accused of failing both when it did intervene, as in Bosnia and Somalia, and when it did not, as in Rwanda. In all these cases, common complaints from commanders on the ground were that the mandates they were given to operate under were too weak or unclear (such as in specifying when force was permitted and the exact nature of objectives), and that resources (troops and equipment) were inadequate – see, for example, the memoir of Lieutenant General Roméo Dallaire, the commander of the Rwandan mission (Dallaire, 2003). Behind these issues was a lack of both international will and agreement about the need for and nature of interventions.

Bringing the debates about humanitarian interventions to a head at the end of the decade was the case of Kosovo in 1999. Once more conducted in the name of humanitarianism, NATO conducted a bombing campaign to force Yugoslav forces out of Kosovo. Yet this exposed serious divisions among the major powers and raised even more questions about humanitarian interventions. The UN Security Council was divided over the issue, with both Russia and China vetoing a resolution for action; moreover, a majority of the General Assembly also opposed it. Consequently, the NATO campaign took place without UN authorisation. This therefore led to many uncertainties about the moral and legal status of the intervention, as well as whether or not this was a challenge to the UN's authority in security matters. Moreover, critics argued that the bombing campaign caused more harm than good, raising concerns about what measures could and should be used in the name of humanitarianism.

All of these instances meant that by the end of the 1990s there were still no clear answers to the major questions concerning the when, how and who of humanitarian interventions.

The twenty-first century: a responsibility to protect?

It was in 2000, against this background of division and uncertainty about the legal, political and ethical status of humanitarian interventions, that Secretary-General Kofi Annan posed the following question to the General Assembly:

> ...if humanitarian intervention is, indeed, an unacceptable assault on sovereignty, how *should* we respond to a Rwanda, to a Srebrenica – to gross and systematic violations of human rights that affect every precept of our common humanity?
>
> (Annan, 2000: 34).

In response to this challenge, in September 2000 the Canadian government, together with a group of major foundations, established the International Commission on Intervention and State Sovereignty (ICISS). The Commission was tasked with examining the whole range of issues relating to humanitarian interventions, and to produce a report that might provide clearer principles and guidelines for their initiation and conduct, which would be able to establish common ground between critics and supporters of previous actions.

The Commission's report, entitled *The Responsibility to Protect*, was published in 2001 (ICISS, 2001). It formulated a new doctrine – sharing its name with the report's title, the Responsibility to Protect (R2P) – that the Commission hoped would fulfil the goals of providing greater clarity and generating greater consensus. In 2005, at the UN World Summit, heads of state and government from 150 countries unanimously agreed to adopt R2P. In 2006 the Security Council also passed a resolution affirming its support for R2P. Subsequently, in 2009, Secretary-General Ban Ki-moon published a report, *Implementing the Responsibility to Protect*, which sought to establish how the aims of R2P might be realised.

What, then, does the doctrine say? There is much in the 2001 report worth reflecting on (though it is important to be aware that not all of its ideas and recommendations have been adopted by the UN). For example, it suggests that the Responsibility to Protect encompasses three major responsibilities – to prevent, to react and to rebuild. In other words, it extends to all phases of a conflict situation, meaning the pre-, during and post- stages. Furthermore, the report offers a set of principles for determining when military interventions are justified (and, therefore, when they are not). These are set out in Box 20.4.

Box 20.4: The Responsibility to Protect – principles for military intervention

(1) The just cause threshold

Military intervention for human protection purposes is an exceptional and extraordinary measure. To be warranted, there must be serious and irreparable harm occurring to human beings, or imminently likely to occur, of the following kinds:

A. **large scale loss of life,** actual or apprehended, with genocidal intent or not, which is the product either of deliberate state action, or state neglect or inability to act, or a failed state situation; or
B. **large scale 'ethnic cleansing',** actual or apprehended, whether carried out by killing, forced expulsion, acts of terror or rape.

(2) The precautionary principles

A. **Right intention:** The primary purpose of the intervention, whatever other motives intervening states may have, must be to halt or avert human suffering.
B. **Last resort:** Military intervention can only be justified when every non-military option for the prevention or peaceful resolution of the crisis has been explored.
C. **Proportional means:** The scale, duration and intensity of the planned military intervention should be the minimum necessary to secure the defined human protection objective.
D. **Reasonable prospects:** There must be a reasonable chance of success in halting or averting the suffering which has justified the intervention, with the consequences of action not likely to be worse than the consequences of inaction.

(3) Right authority

A. There is no better or more appropriate body than the United Nations Security Council to authorise military intervention for human protection purposes. The task is not to find alternatives to the Security Council as a source of authority, but to make the Security Council work better than it has.

(ICISS, 2001: 12)

However, to understand R2P in terms of its translation into practice, it is worth turning to the Outcome Document that was produced from the 2005 summit, as this gave the final shape to the doctrine as it was accepted by the international community (UN General Assembly, 2005). Two paragraphs from this provide an understanding of what R2P means:

> **Para 138** – 'Each individual State has the responsibility to protect its populations from genocide, war crimes, ethnic cleansing and crimes against humanity.'

> **Para 139** – 'The international community, through the United Nations, also has the responsibility to use appropriate diplomatic, humanitarian and other peaceful means, in accordance with Chapters VI and VIII of the Charter, to help protect

populations from genocide, war crimes, ethnic cleansing and crimes against humanity. In this context, we are prepared to take collective action, in a timely and decisive manner, through the Security Council, in accordance with the Charter, including Chapter VII, on a case-by-case basis and in cooperation with relevant regional organizations as appropriate, should peaceful means be inadequate and national authorities manifestly fail to protect their populations ...'

There is a number of points of interest here. First, these paragraphs explain the doctrine's scope – that is, that R2P relates to four specific areas (genocide, war crimes, ethnic cleansing and crimes against humanity). Thus, it does not apply to every possible case of human rights abuse, only to the most egregious transgressions. Second, they make clear that, in the first instance, the responsibility belongs to states themselves, authorising the UN (alongside regional organisations) to intervene only when states have failed in their responsibility. Third, that force should be only a last resort, once peaceful methods of conflict resolution have been exhausted.

In these ways, the aim of R2P is to attempt to balance competing claims – the particular claims of state sovereignty and the universal claims of human rights and humanitarianism. Even so, opinions concerning the doctrine's validity have been sharply divided, and some of the main arguments forwarded by both supporters and critics are shown in Box 20.5.

Box 20.5: Arguments for and against R2P

Arguments of Supporters	Arguments of Critics
• It shifts the focus from the emphasis placed by traditional humanitarian interventions on the right of interveners to intervene, to the rights of those suffering abuses	• Some argue that its scope is too limited – why should the responsibility be restricted to just the four circumstances specified?
• It offers guidelines for understanding when interventions are justified – to prevent atrocities – while balancing this with respect for state sovereignty	• Others argue that it goes too far – even R2P's criteria may not place sufficient limits on the trespass it represents on state sovereignty; criteria are always open to interpretation, and thus potentially abuse
• It emphasises not just military/coercive measures, but non-coercive ones (e.g. diplomacy)	• Is it a tool of Western imperialism – i.e. to justify powerful countries intervening in weaker ones? Many critical voices have come from the global South, suspicious for this reason
• It considers all stages of a conflict (pre-, during and post-)	
• It aims to prevent interventions being used (and abused) for purposes other than humanitarian ones	• Will it only ever be applied selectively? In particular, the P5 will likely never allow it to conflict with their own interests – e.g. Russia would not allow it to be applied to Chechnya, or China to Tibet

What bearing, though, has any of this had upon the actual practice of interventions? Even after its seeming embrace by the international community in 2005, in many people's eyes there was little evidence that it had much impact on the world's ongoing conflicts. In places such as Darfur, Sri Lanka, Gaza and Chechnya, human rights abuses and humanitarian emergencies occurred, with few signs that any supposed Responsibility to Protect had been accepted, either by states or the international community.

There are many explanations for why interventions into specific conflicts may not have taken place, but there is one major factor that has undoubtedly dominated all discussions about military interventions in the twenty-first century. R2P came into being to try to reshape the debates about interventions that had occurred in the 1990s, but it is important to realise that the original report came out at a time when these debates were already being radically reshaped.

The report was published in December 2001, but only a few months previously, in September 2001, US President George W. Bush had launched the War on Terror. The significance of this, and the subsequent US-led invasions of Afghanistan (2002) and Iraq (2003), was that these events came to overshadow thinking about the ethics of military interventions. In particular, even though R2P may not have justified the sort of interventions America initiated in the name of fighting terrorism – which appeared to make regime change the priority more than human rights – the controversies which surrounded these latter cases meant that all theories of international intervention became heavily tainted by association.

In any case, support and enthusiasm for intervening in the world's conflicts on humanitarian grounds has remained uncertain as the twenty-first century has progressed. During the first decade since the 2001 report, it seemed as if R2P would remain an idea existing purely in the realms of argument and rhetoric. Yet what appeared to give real life to the doctrine was the wave of protests and uprisings in 2011 that became collectively known as the 'Arab Spring'. During this, R2P not only moved back to the centre of debate, but was used to justify international action in relation to Libya as this country descended into violence and civil war. Thus, one of the key Security Council resolutions passed relating to the Libyan crisis, Resolution 1973, was suffused with the language of R2P, reiterating the 'responsibility of the Libyan authorities to protect the Libyan population' and justifying the authorisation of 'all necessary measures', short of invasion and occupation, 'to protect civilians and civilian populated areas' from attack (UN Security Council, 2011). A no-fly zone was imposed, and NATO air strikes also took place – this time, with full UN sanction.

Nonetheless, while some supporters of R2P took this as evidence of a new commitment to the doctrine by the global community, others were more critical. For example, India's UN ambassador, Hardeep Singh Puri, argued that 'Libya has given R2P a bad name' (quoted in Bolopian, 2011), in that a resolution ostensibly aimed at protecting civilians was ultimately used by NATO for the cause of regime change by supporting the rebels who eventually ousted Libya's leader Colonel Gaddafi.

In any case, subsequently R2P appears to have lost favour once more. Most notable has been the case of Syria. After the eruption of civil war in 2011, there has not been the necessary consensus on the Security Council to secure similar resolutions as enacted in relation to Libya. Thus, as of June 2014, Russia and China have vetoed four proposed resolutions that threatened action against the regime of Syrian President Assad (largely because Assad has long been a close Russian ally). As a consequence, various commentators have questioned whether R2P might not in fact be dead (see, for example, Gottlieb, 2013).

However, regardless of whether or not R2P can be revived, and whatever its strengths and weaknesses as a doctrine, it seems clear that it has not managed to create the consensus its originators hoped that it would or, perhaps, given the whole idea of humanitarian interventions, firmer foundations.

Conclusion

After the United Nations was established in 1945, it very soon became apparent that the hope that it might rid the world of the scourge of war through a system of collective security was not going to succeed. This was largely thanks to the dynamics of the Cold War and the paralysing effect this had upon the Security Council. Similarly, expectations that the Cold War's end might produce a New World Order of peace and cooperation were also quickly dashed, and the UN found itself confronted with the array of difficulties that arise from responding to complex and involved intra-state conflicts. In the twenty-first century, the question that remains is whether it will ever be possible – via the Responsibility to Protect or any other doctrine – to discover sufficient common ground and agreement for the organisation to fulfil its original goals.

Summary points

1   The UN was created to maintain international peace and security – optimists even hoped that it might help to eradicate war altogether.
2   Its Charter would appear to give the UN extensive powers to resolve conflicts between states, including the authorisation of coercive force – yet to use these effectively requires consensus on the Security Council which is often not forthcoming.
3   Peacekeeping has developed as one of the UN's main tools for aiding states in the resolution of their conflicts, though missions have far from always been successful.
4   Recent times have seen increasing demands placed upon the UN to intervene in humanitarian crises, especially since the development of the Responsibility to Protect doctrine, but there remain significant disagreements over if, when and how it should do so.
5   Many reforms have been suggested to make the UN more representative, responsive and effective – such as reforming the composition of the Security Council or the operation of peacekeeping missions – though there are many obstacles (such as member-states' self-interest) to change within the organisation.

Recommended reading

Bellamy, A.J. *Global Politics and the Responsibility to Protect: From Words to Deeds*, London: Routledge, 2011.

Bellamy, A.J., Williams, P. and Griffin, S. *Understanding Peacekeeping*, 2nd ed., Cambridge: Polity Press, 2010.

Chandler, D. *From Kosovo to Kabul and Beyond: Human Rights and International Intervention*, London: Pluto Press, 2006.

Weiss, T.G., Forsythe, D.P., Coate, R.A. and Pwase, K.-K. *The United Nations and Changing World Politics*, 6th ed., Boulder, CO: Westview Press, 2010.

Weiss, T.G. and Daws, S. (eds) *The Oxford Handbook on the United Nations*, Oxford: Oxford University Press, 2007.

21 The North Atlantic Treaty Organization
Continuity and change

Andrew Moran

Box 21.1: NATO

The North Atlantic Treaty Organization (NATO) was founded in 1949 to deter the Soviet Union from spreading its influence into Western Europe. Since then, it has become the most successful political-military alliance in modern history and has outlasted the collapse of its Cold War enemy. However, the certainty of Cold War conflict has now been replaced by the uncertainty of a complex collection of security risks and challenges that range from terrorism, nuclear proliferation and cyber warfare to energy security and failed states.

   The question many now ask is whether NATO is fit for purpose when dealing with the rapidly changing international environment.

Introduction

NATO is not the first recorded alliance, nor will it be the last. Alliances have played a fundamental role in the relationships between states for centuries, regularly formed and often broken. Walt (1987: 1), in probably the most influential study of alliances yet published, describes them as 'a formal or informal relationship of security cooperation between two or more sovereign states' which is formed to balance against a threatening state. Weitsman (2004: 27) takes a similar approach, defining them as 'bilateral or multilateral agreements to provide some element of security to the signatories'. For Walt, the importance of alliances is significant as 'the factors that determine how states choose partners will shape the evolution of the international system as a whole' (Walt, 1987: 1).

   The reasons why individual states join an alliance may differ from state to state. According to Waltz (1979), states do so to maintain their security if they believe their sovereignty is at risk because they do not possess adequate resources. As a result, they will join with other states which share their goals, or perceive similar threats to their security, whether those threats are external or internal. For smaller states with limited resources, an alliance may be the only option to guarantee survival, and becomes a key component in ensuring a balance of power by preventing a stronger power dominating.

   When joining an alliance, Waltz (1979) argues, states may seek to strengthen and enlarge their own alliance or to weaken an opposing one. Walt (1987) suggests the shape that alliances take will be influenced by how large a threat each of the states faces and how much help they can expect when joining the alliance. These factors will also affect how long an alliance will last. Mearsheimer (1990) contends that the stronger the perceived threat is, the greater cohesion an alliance will have. Indeed, Realists emphasise the fluidity of alliances – that they are not marriages of love, but of convenience, in which national interests maintain a balance of power.

Weber (1997) suggests that alliances can be hierarchical or egalitarian, the latter where power is distributed relatively evenly amongst most members, and the former where there are imbalances of power and capabilities. Others argue states may 'bandwagon', allying with a winning hegemon (Thompson, 1977). Here, one state will be more dominant than others within an alliance, effectively spreading a protective umbrella over weaker states. Though Keohane (1984) has argued that this may be driven by enlightened self-interest on the part of the hegemon, tension may exist where, for example, the hegemon may use the alliance to project its own self-interest, or, alternatively, the weaker alliance members are accused of 'free riding' by not being able to contribute fully in terms of resources to the alliance. Indeed, Masala (2003) notes that when a threat decreases, there is a risk that smaller or weaker alliance members will not necessarily continue to subordinate their interests to those of a hegemon.

Intuitively, it would follow that alliances tend to be formed of members who share a common set of values and ideas. Risse-Kappen (1996), for example, argues that NATO was formed partly as the result of the common values and world-views that emerged from the Second World War among the triumphant Allied powers. As such, it developed as an alliance founded on identity rather than being threat-based. Gaubutz (1996) goes further, suggesting that alliances are likely to prevail between liberal democratic states as there is greater continuity in leadership and public preferences, as opposed to less stable states where political coups or revolutions can lead to alliances weakening as partners may suddenly withdraw. Indeed, it would follow that cohesion is increased when national interests and cooperation converge and become institutionalised and habitual. Russett (1971) and Walt (1987), however, question whether such 'affinity theories' of common cultures and identities are instrumental in shaping the creation of alliances.

Though diplomacy and economic interaction, and even economic support, may be notable within an alliance, many theorists argue that alliances are strictly centred on military power, and are formed for the purpose of waging war, ceasing when the war has ended. Osgood (1968), for example, defined an alliance as 'a formal agreement that pledges states to co-operate in using their military resources against a specific state or states and usually obligates one or more of the signatories to use force, or to consider (unilaterally or in consultation with allies) the use of force in specified circumstances' (p. 17). Synder (1997) suggests that 'Alliances are formal associations of states for the use (or non-use) of military force, in specialised circumstances, against states outside their membership', adding that their 'primary function is to pool military strength against a common enemy, not to protect alliance members from each other' (p. 4).

Interestingly, some argue that alliances may not necessarily contribute to a state's military security, but rather can be destabilising factors for the international system as they generate opposing alliances. For example, once NATO was created, the Soviet Union responded with the creation of the Warsaw Pact. What is unusual about NATO, though, is not just that it has lasted so long, but that it was formed during peacetime, and has continued long after its reasons for being have ceased. Also, supporters of NATO note that it was created almost out of a sense of self-deterrence. None of the original members wanted war, and self-deterrence limited that possibility.

NATO's origins

NATO's roots can be traced back to the end of the Second World War and British and French concerns that Germany might remilitarise, combined with a fear that the US would become less interested in Europe and retreat back into isolationism. Though the Marshall Plan went some way to reassure Europe of America's financial commitment to the rebuilding of the continent, the United Kingdom and France signed the Treaty of Dunkirk in March 1947, creating an alliance based on mutual security and assistance. One year later, in March 1948, this was expanded to include Luxembourg, Belgium and the Netherlands in the Treaty of Brussels, which called for greater military cooperation and collective security, laying the ground for what became the Western European Union (WEU) in 1954. It could be argued there was some degree of 'affinity' in this, but there were also two common enemies. One was Germany, the other the Soviet Union, which in 1948 covertly supported the Communist Party of Czechoslovakia in overthrowing the democratically elected government, and had also blockaded Allied-controlled West Berlin, leading to the Berlin airlift. It was as a result of these developments, and a belief that the security of Europe and the deterring of Soviet aggression could be best achieved through a stronger transatlantic agreement, that the Washington Treaty was signed in April 1949, creating NATO and ensuring that America remained committed to Europe.

The twelve original members stated in the preamble to the NATO Charter that they were 'resolved to unite their efforts for collective defence and for the preservation of peace and security'. Though the original treaty did not refer to a specific enemy, it was clear that it was created in response to the perceived growing threat of the Soviet Union. In 1947 President Truman of the US had already announced that his country was committed to the containment of Communism, something that was reinforced by the Marshall Plan and later by his National Security Council team who, in a document entitled NSC-68, advocated that the policy of containment be both militarised and globalised. During the Cold War, the United States would station 300,000 troops throughout Europe.

NATO's creation, however, was not just about keeping the Soviets at bay. There were also political reasons for its creation, not least securing the bridge between the US and Europe and providing a morale boost to the people of Western Europe who were being encouraged by the US to resist left-wing movements. Significantly, following on from the Treaty of Dunkirk, a number of member states signed up in fear of the future possibility of a resurgent Germany.

These concerns were reflected by the first Secretary General of NATO, Lord Hastings Ismay, who when asked to define its purpose famously remarked it was to keep the Russians out, the Americans in, and the Germans down.

What was clear was that collective security was central to the purpose of NATO, as enshrined in Article V, which stated: 'The Parties agree that an armed attack against one or more of them in Europe or North America shall be considered an attack against them all', and that following an attack, each ally would take 'such action as it deems necessary, including the use of armed force', in response.

The Soviet Union would react to the creation of NATO with its own military alliance, the Warsaw Pact, which was formed in 1955, partly in response to the prospect of a 'remilitarised' West Germany being admitted to the alliance, but also because of the Soviet's need to maintain control over Central and Eastern European military forces.

Box 21.2: NATO's member states

At present, NATO has twenty-eight members.

In 1949, there were twelve founding members: Belgium, Canada, Denmark, France, Iceland, Italy, Luxembourg, the Netherlands, Norway, Portugal, the United Kingdom and the United States.

Greece and Turkey joined in 1952, Germany in 1955 and Spain in 1982.

In 1999, membership was widened to include the Czech Republic, Hungary and Poland.

In 2004 Bulgaria, Estonia, Latvia, Lithuania, Romania, Slovakia and Slovenia joined.

In 2009 Albania and Croatia became the most recent members.

Article 10 of the North Atlantic Treaty defines the terms for enlargement, stating that membership is open to any 'European State in a position to further the principles of this Treaty and to contribute to the security of the North Atlantic area'.

The North Atlantic Council, NATO's principle decision-making body, has the authority to invite a country to join, based on a consensus among all of the allies. Bosnia and Herzegovina, Georgia, Montenegro, and the former Yugoslav Republic of Macedonia are all aspiring members.

Institutionally, the alliance had a modest structure to begin with. In fact, when the treaty was signed, it did not have a clear military structure that could coordinate its actions to any great effect. That would change after the Soviet Union tested its first atomic bomb in 1949 and the Korean War broke out in 1950. A Council of Members in permanent session was established in Paris, to be followed by a more elaborate decision-making structure, including a Secretary General and a Military Committee. This was combined with a more integrated military planning and command structure, the most prominent part of which would be the Supreme Allied Commander Europe (SACEUR), the first of whom was the US General, and soon to be US President, Dwight D. Eisenhower.

From the outset disagreements existed over issues of state sovereignty, competing national interests, and how best to meet the threats NATO faced. One notable example came in 1966 when, at General Charles de Gaulle's urging, the French withdrew from NATO's integrated military structure, primarily because they wished to maintain their own independent defence policy which now included a developing nuclear weapons programme. Though France continued to participate in NATO's political structures, and even made contributions to its ongoing missions, NATO moved its headquarters to Brussels, Belgium. Interestingly, although the headquarters have remained in Europe, traditionally the 'Allied Supreme Commander' has always been a US general.

Though disagreements did exist, most commentators agree that during the Cold War the fear of the political and military threat posed by the Soviet Union was enough to hold NATO together, creating a consensus between the military and politicians. Furthermore, a much understated achievement of NATO during this period was that it allowed the resurgent West Germany to emerge as a key ally without destabilising the region.

Why did NATO survive the end of the Cold War?

After the collapse of the Berlin Wall and the ending of the Cold War a number of commentators suggested that NATO had outlived its purpose and should be wound up. Early advocates of this included John Mearsheimer (1990) and Kenneth Waltz (1993), who argued that there would be no need for NATO to remain as an alliance in the absence of a clear and present danger, i.e. the Soviet Union. This seemed particularly to be the case as the Warsaw Pact began to crumble in 1989 and was officially disbanded in 1991.

Surprisingly, they were wrong. NATO did not go into decline. In fact, since 1990 it has added twelve new members, almost doubling its size. Its first actual use of force would come in Bosnia in 1994, followed by significant roles in combat operations as far afield as Libya, Bosnia, Kosovo, Afghanistan, in counter-piracy operations in the Gulf of Aden, giving logistical support to the African Union's mission in Darfur, assisting the tsunami relief effort in Indonesia, and helping in the clean-up operation after Hurricane Katrina.

In addition, Article V of the NATO treaty, which obligates members to provide assistance should one or more of them be subjected to an armed attack, would be invoked for the first time in response to the terrorist attacks of 11 September 2001.

In doing so, NATO has effectively moved from being a military alliance designed to deter a specific enemy to becoming one committed to the maintenance of peace and security across Europe and beyond, moving beyond its traditional sphere of influence. As a result, it has adapted its purpose to meet the changing geopolitical landscape of the post-Cold War world, moving 'out of area' in its responses to conflicts, no longer concentrating solely on Europe in geographical terms, but forcefully arguing that global security issues, such as terrorism or energy and food security, will impact on the security concerns of its member states. Rather than being a regional collective security arrangement, it has become what Wallander and Keohane (1999) describe as a 'security management institution'.

Since the end of the Cold War there are a number of issues that NATO has addressed and which offer some explanation of its continued existence.

NATO enlargement and the 'partnership for peace'

The most significant step taken by NATO to adapt to the post-Cold War era was to begin to absorb the very states it had been opposed to by expanding its membership eastwards, beyond the east–west dividing line of the Cold War. This was not without its problems, as NATO had to ensure that the alliance was not destabilised, balancing the concerns of its existing members, some of whom were wary of working with Warsaw Pact states, with the interests of the newly joining states, who, having broken free of the control of the former Soviet Union, feared a resurgent Russia.

In 1999 Poland, the Czech Republic and Hungary joined the alliance, followed in 2004 by Estonia, Latvia, Lithuania, Slovakia, Slovenia, Romania and Bulgaria. In 2009, Albania and Croatia also joined. All were former Soviet-bloc countries. NATO justified this expansion on the grounds of securing and strengthening new democracies, but to many it seemed like an attempt at securing protection against future Russian aggression. Indeed, in the 1990s NATO walked a difficult line between seeking to avoid alienating Russia while not disappointing the newly independent Eastern European states.

NATO tried to lessen fears by creating a symbolic membership – the 'Partnership of Peace' – which was joined by most Eastern European and former Soviet states, including Russia. This was drawn up in January 1994 at a NATO Brussels summit. The move was controversial. Where Germany advocated admitting former communist states into the alliance, Britain and France were less favourable to the idea. Germany believed it would help to stabilise the new democracies, and argued that Russia should not see NATO as a threat. Conversely, those who opposed enlargement argued that if Russia was not a threat, NATO enlargement was not necessary – particularly as these new states could be weak in military terms as well as financially dependent.

In May 1997 the NATO–Russia 'Founding Act' created a permanent joint command to discuss security problems, which would include nuclear safety, peacekeeping operations and anti-terrorist activities. Though NATO and Russia no longer considered themselves adversaries, with Russia even announcing that its nuclear missiles would no longer target NATO countries, the 'Founding Act' was part of a process that saw a weakened Russia reluctantly accepting that enlargement would occur.

Russia and NATO

In contrast to the Cold War years it could be argued that the relationship between the West and Russia improved in the 1990s, with regular summits, a willingness to accept the initial expansion of NATO, and a degree of cooperation over the war on terror, including joint action in Afghanistan to target poppy fields. However, there were disagreements, including over the Kosovo war of 1999, the invasion of Iraq in 2003, how best to deal with Iran's nuclear ambitions, whether to intervene in Syria as it descended into civil war, and growing Russian opposition to the US desire to place its anti-ballistic missile system (the so-called National Missile Defense system) in Eastern and Central Europe.

According to Charles Kupchan, however, the US and its NATO allies made a strategic mistake from the outset by seeking to construct a post-Cold War order that excluded Russia. Though Central and Eastern European states were embraced, he suggests that Russia was treated as an outsider, made worse by the West ignoring the potential consequences of Russian discontent. Daniel Deudenny and G. John Ikenberry put this more bluntly, observing that 'Washington policy makers increasingly acted as though Russia no longer mattered and the United States could do whatever it wanted' (Kupchan, 2010). In so doing, NATO also missed an opportunity to support the consolidation of democracy in Russia in the 1990s, which would see an eventual shift towards more authoritarian, anti-Western rule under Vladimir Putin.

It is now unclear how this relationship will develop. The Baltic states that border Russia pose a particular problem as Russia seeks to increase its regional influence and prevent further encroachment in Eastern Europe by the West, while NATO has sought to increase stability and security throughout Eastern Europe. Russia has perceived the expansion of NATO, and to some extent the EU in the post-Cold War era, as a humiliating attempt by the West to expand its influence during a time of Russian weakness. Though Georgia and Ukraine have expressed an interest in joining NATO, Russia regards this as redrawing the dividing lines of power in Europe closer to Russia's borders, putting its security at risk.

Furthermore, some argue America, and by implication NATO, now faces a Russia that conceives itself as reborn in strength as both a regional power and as an active contradictory player to America. In Munich in 2007, for example, Vladimir Putin openly criticised George W. Bush's foreign policy and America's belief that it was the sole global superpower. The Ukrainian crisis has also shown that Russia is still willing to assert itself, sometimes by coercive means. The problems for NATO are whether it can allow Russia to have a wider sphere of influence and what the long-term implications of this might be.

Though some NATO members, particularly the US and even the UK, see the role of the alliance reaching beyond Europe to address more global problems, for most of NATO's members, particularly in the eastern half of Europe, territorial defence is still the primary concern. Part of the difficulty here, which Russia perhaps capitalised on when annexing Crimea in 2014, is that NATO seemed unable to articulate a message of reassurance to its new allies with regard to a commitment to collective defence under Article V. Some of NATO's members, and certainly parts of the EU, appeared willing to compromise the position of their eastern neighbours because they are dependent on Russian gas and oil imports. It was noticeable to many that the EU states sought to enforce weaker sanctions on Russia than the Americans probably for this very reason, and because they did not want to be flooded with potentially large numbers of refugees (a problem the US would not have encountered because of being so far away). This undermined any sense of solidarity of commitment among the European states. This is ironic given that it appears to be the case that some of NATO's easternmost allies fought in Afghanistan because they felt their security was linked to NATO and the US, not because the security of Afghanistan directly impacted on their own national security. Whatever the cause, division in Europe suits Russia best.

Globalisation and the emergence of new threats

Since the end of the Cold War the world has witnessed a growing number of complex security issues, ranging from terrorism, nuclear proliferation, cyber warfare, energy security, to the problems posed by failed states. NATO has sought to keep pace with these developments.

An early example of its response to the emergence of new threats came during the break-up of the former Yugoslavia. The first actual use of force by NATO was in Bosnia in 1994, culminating in the use of airstrikes in 1999 during the Kosovo crisis. The increased use of force by NATO was motivated by two key factors. The first was public and political pressure for humanitarian intervention to prevent a repetition of 'ethnic cleansing', most graphically illustrated by the massacre of over 8,000 men by Bosnian Serb forces in a Muslim enclave in Srebrenica, previously designated a 'safe area' by the UN. The second was a concern that the conflict would spread into neighbouring countries, possibly drawing European nations into a wider war.

In this instance NATO was seeking to protect people who were not within the organisation's membership, in essence metamorphosing into a peacekeeping organisation and allowing the US to intervene under the umbrella of NATO as both the UN and Europe struggled to achieve a consensus on action.

The 'war on terror' has also led to a greater role for NATO, not least in Iraq, where NATO forces trained Iraqi military forces after the overthrow of Saddam Hussein, but also in Afghanistan, where NATO took command of the International Security Assistance Force (ISAF) in Afghanistan in 2003.

Against the backdrop of globalisation and the increasing complexity of security concerns, NATO has played an ever-greater role in enforcing UN Security Council resolutions, not just in Bosnia but, as noted earlier, elsewhere in the world as well, including supporting regime change in Libya.

Box 21.3: Libya

As Libya descended into a brutal conflict in the wake of the Arab Spring and attempts to remove Colonel Gaddafi from power, the UN Security Council passed Resolution 1973 authorising action to protect civilians by 'all necessary means'. As a result, a small coalition of forces, initially led by the US but including France, Britain, Italy and Canada, began military action to enforce a 'no-fly' zone over Libya to protect civilians. Furthermore, the US and Britain used cruise missiles to destroy Gaddafi's air defences, while France bombed Libyan units close to Benghazi. America, however, sought to 'lead from behind' rather than becoming more deeply involved in a conflict in the Islamic world, allowing other NATO members to take charge. Divisions existed, however, within NATO's European allies, with some, such as Germany and Turkey, wanting solely to protect civilians with a no-fly zone, while others, such as Britain and France, wanted to play a more active role in attacking Gaddafi's forces. NATO airstrikes would wear down Gaddafi's forces, with the Colonel eventually being killed by his own people on 20 October 2011 as he tried to flee the country.

According to Anders Fogh Rasmussen, the Secretary General of NATO in 2011, the action in Libya was a reminder of how important it was for NATO to be 'ready, capable, and willing to act', and how 'Any shortfalls have been primarily due to political, rather than military, constraints' (Rasmussen, 2011). In other words, the military might be ready and willing, but the politicians might not be willing to act, or at the very least they have to seek greater consensus if their actions are to be successful.

Libya also highlighted a divide in the Obama administration between those who felt it was important to support the Arab Spring for humanitarian reasons and others, such as Bob Gates, the then US Secretary of Defense, who argued that there was no American national or strategic interest at stake and so America should only offer enough support to ensure the Europeans did not fail.

Europe vs. NATO?

NATO plays an important role in maintaining positive relationships between its member states. This has been particularly the case when absorbing the newly unified Germany into the fold in the 1990s, allaying potential fears in the process. By ensuring such things as transparency, balances of power and the denationalisation of security policies, it plays a role in reducing suspicions (Duffield, 1994/95). Germany has found this to be of notable benefit in reassuring its neighbours since the 1990s (Duffield, 1998).

Initial concerns about the future of NATO in Europe were addressed in 1990/1 when the European Community (EC) discussed the creation of a Common Foreign and Security Policy (CFSP), which was included in the February 1992 Maastricht Treaty. For America this posed an interesting dilemma – as the Cold War receded and many Americans argued that the US should prioritise domestic concerns, there was a justification for asking Europeans to take on more responsibility for their own security needs, but not at the risk of endangering NATO.

However, this does not mean that Europe has not attempted to strike out in its own direction. It actually first sought to do this in the mid-1950s when the Western European Union was created, which the French President François Mitterrand attempted to revive in 1984 as a possible defence arm of the EC. During the Clinton presidency the Americans tolerated WEU activities to the extent that Europeans contemplated military operations independent of the US. In 1994, for example, France and Germany created the 'Eurocorps', and in 1996 there was an agreement on 'Combined Joint Task Forces' where the WEU could carry out operations on its own while using the NATO infrastructure. One outcome of this agreement was that it allowed France back into the alliance's military structure after thirty years of self-exile. Furthermore, the European Union created its own rapid deployment force, sending its first military forces to the Democratic Congo in 2003 – the first multinational European military operation to occur outside NATO – and in 2004, after NATO forces withdrew from Bosnia, peacekeeping operations were passed on to the European Union, with NATO forces remaining in Kosovo.

It is clear, however, that for the moment European states are aware of the limitations of their power and are not prepared to compromise the US security guarantee that NATO offers.

Political cohesion and political reform

Though it is agreed that a key component of NATO's continued existence is the bridge that has been built between the US and Europe since the end of the Second World War, so too is the integration of military planning and organisational and command structures since the Cold War that has helped NATO engage in a relatively smooth transition from Cold War priorities to the emerging threats of the twenty-first century.

The need to keep unity within this structure is evident in NATO playing a role in promoting democratic reform and upholding human rights in the post-Cold War era. Though during the Cold War NATO was happy to accept Greece, Turkey and Portugal while they were under military rule, today liberal democratic practices and institutions are seen as prerequisites for membership. In part this reflects democratic peace theory, but it is also designed to ensure cohesion within the alliance, an essential element as the alliance has grown. As a result, as the former Soviet satellite states joined, they were encouraged to adopt a number of democratic reforms, including increased civilian control of the military.

However, like the debate surrounding the expansion of the European Union, many critics have wondered if NATO has reached capacity. Though some argue that its democratisation mission will continue to bring greater stability, others suggest that NATO needs to consider curtailing its expansion.

Interestingly, after the events of 9/11 and the resulting collaboration in Afghanistan with states such as Australia, Sweden and North Korea, the then NATO Secretary General Jaap de Hoop Scheffer attempted to broaden the alliance to include closer relationships with those states, plus Finland, Japan and New Zealand. His plan failed, partly because the states themselves did not want to join, but also because there were concerns expressed by some European members that the transatlantic focus of NATO would be lost, and that NATO would become nothing more than a tool for American military and hegemonic interests around the world – particularly as this expansion was supported by George W. Bush. If NATO were to expand 'out of area', it would require a revision of Article X of the NATO treaty, which allows for enlargement of the alliance only to European countries. The debate over expansion highlighted once again a fundamental concern relating to NATO – if its role is to be an increasingly global one, external relations are important; if it is to concentrate solely on Europe, arguably they are not, or else at best they are peripheral.

There is also a broader argument concerning NATO expansion which centres on its accountability. Hill and Smith argue that, like the UN and the African Union, it has a democratic deficit because there is no clear provision for significant public interaction with power holders and senior partners (Hill and Smith, 2005). Indeed, in an era of revelations by Edward Snowden relating to the questionable, and sometimes unaccountable, behaviour of intelligence agencies, there is a notable lack of transparency in NATO. Perhaps this is a result of it being primarily a military alliance that engages in military activities, but it remains a problem.

One way that this issue has been overcome is that the differing national priorities and interests of its member states have been tolerated since its formation. Indeed, this is arguably an important binding agent for NATO. The Iraq War of 2003, for example, saw the UK support American interests while France and Germany opposed the invasion, and Turkey refused to allow US ground forces to cross its territory into Iraq. In 2011, only eight out of twenty-eight allies conducted air strikes over Libya. Germany actually abstained on the UN resolution authorising the mission, and then withdrew its crews from NATO's warning and control aircraft and from its warships on other NATO missions in the Mediterranean. In fact, Germany remains resistant to the use of force in most situations.

Money has often been a cause of friction between Europe and the US. The economic power of NATO is significant, its membership making up almost one half of the world's GDP. However, this does not always translate into financial support for NATO. When the Cold War ended, for example, European countries accounted for 34% of NATO's military spending. By 2012, partly as a result of the economic collapse of 2008 that saw many European states tightening their budgets, this had fallen to 21%, with only four European countries meeting the alliance's defence-spending target of 2% of GDP – Britain, France, Greece and Albania.

This fall in European contributions has resulted in increasing unease amongst policy-makers in the US. Bob Gates (2011), in his last speech to NATO as US Secretary of Defense, criticised Europe for not contributing enough, accusing it of effectively getting a 'free ride' on American defence spending (which as a share of GDP is approximately three times the European average). He suggested that there needed to be a more equitable sharing of financial burdens for NATO to function effectively, with Europe being more willing to take greater responsibility for security in its own backyard – no longer a 'consumer' of security, but becoming a 'producer' of security.

One of Gates' concerns was that a two-tiered NATO might develop, between those who were willing to fight and those who were not. In Afghanistan, for example, not all NATO members were willing to send forces, with the UK contributing far more than France and Germany.

Gates' speech came at a time when many in Europe complained that the Obama administration seemed to be losing interest in Europe as the US continued to 'pivot' towards the Asia-Pacific region, where it saw an increasing number of security concerns. The fear was that Europe's economic austerity and America's apparent semi-detachment would lead to NATO doing less, or doing nothing and possibly fading away. In comparison, that same year, Asian defence spending was predicted to outstrip that of Europe.

The issue of austerity has been addressed by Fogh Rasmussen, who argues that if NATO is to do more with less it must adopt what he calls 'smart defence', with states pooling and sharing equipment and capabilities, encouraging them to specialise in what they are best at and avoiding duplication. Rasmussen has warned that concentrating on homeland security is not enough. External threats, such as the resurgence of Russia, terrorism, the volatility of regions such as North Africa (close to Europe), the proliferation of nuclear weapons and cyber warfare, will all require investment and cooperation if NATO is to continue and succeed in its mission (Rasmussen, 2011).

Box 21.4: Connected forces initiative

After the end of the ISAF mission in Afghanistan in 2014, NATO was 'expected to shift its emphasis from operational engagement to operational preparedness'. This would mean that NATO would have to remain capable of performing its core tasks while maintaining its forces at a high level of readiness. The Connected Forces Initiative, which formed part of a review called 'NATO Forces 2020', sought to ensure this through expanded education and training, increased exercises, and better use of technology. It was hoped that this would increase opportunities for NATO's allies to validate and certify their ability to 'communicate, train, and operate together', combining with the NATO Response Force as a 'test bed' for the transformation of the alliance.

www.nato.int/cps/en/natolive/topics_98527.htm, accessed on 30 June 2014.

The future of NATO

There is universal agreement that NATO succeeded in its original mission of providing collective security for Western Europe and the United States, and that it has played an instrumental role in securing peace and stability in Europe since the collapse of the Berlin Wall in 1989. But does this mean that NATO will continue into the twenty-first century, particularly as many commentators argue that its aims are unclear?

The veracity of this argument is difficult to gauge. Waltz (2000) believed that the reason NATO existed ten years after the Berlin Wall fell was because the US was keen to maintain its 'grip' on developments in Europe, whilst Walt (1997) agreed that the US hegemony was key to understanding why NATO had survived. Wallander (2000), however, notes that NATO has been adept at adapting its assets to a new security environment, allowing it to move from being a military alliance designed to deter a specific enemy to becoming one committed to the maintenance of peace and security across Europe and beyond. In so doing it effectively redesigned itself to meet the changing geopolitical landscape of the post-Cold War world, evolving beyond its original purpose of collective security to embrace peacekeeping and humanitarian missions, and developing partnerships with over forty countries.

What is interesting about this is that some of its older members value this expansion and consider it worthwhile, whilse more recent members are more interested in NATO providing a means of security against a resurgent Russia in the future. This may create tensions when it comes to deciding alliance priorities. A good example of this is the response of NATO to the rise of international terrorism, where member states have adopted different approaches to this new security threat, resulting in a lack of cohesion in NATO's approach.

Indeed, critics have argued that a significant problem for NATO is that the US and Europe need to have a much more precise agreement on common threat perceptions than the one that currently exists. Without this, there will be a continual problem for

NATO in articulating a coherent vision in the future. It is a sense of shared threats that will, arguably, bind NATO's member states together. Perhaps for this reason, the actions of Russia in 2014 in Ukraine will provide an impetus to NATO.

Putin made it quite clear in March 2014, in his announcement of the annexation of Crimea, that he is willing to use military force in support of his coercive diplomacy when he feels Russian interests are being challenged, in essence claiming he has the right to intervene whenever he wishes. Not surprisingly, this is a matter of great concern to Central and Eastern European states.

Putin's actions have, as a result, potentially revalidated NATO and breathed new life into the Atlantic partnership. However, this has also made it more difficult for states such as Ukraine, Georgia and Moldova to join NATO. Though they have all expressed an interest in becoming members, Putin will not tolerate this, as his actions in Ukraine have demonstrated. This in turn has severely damaged NATO's attempts to engage with Russia. Significantly, the belief that hard power no longer has a place in Europe has also been undermined, with many fearing that Putin is seeking to create a Eurasian Union of post-Soviet states.

The problem NATO faces now is how it can unite its members against this new challenge. In principle all the NATO states are opposed to Russia's actions, but how far are they willing to uphold collective security and what elements of compromise exist? Though Eastern and Central European countries feel a sense of insecurity that began with the war between Russia and Georgia over South Ossetia in 2008 and worsened with the Crimean incursion of 2014, do citizens in Germany, France or the UK really believe that they will be next – the very fear that motivated the foundation of NATO?

Interestingly, though Crimea provided a new focus, during the preceding decade European countries had begun to express a political identity that was at odds with the goals of the US, and particularly the Bush administration, as Europeans increasingly articulated their own interests and values. Bush himself was a keen advocate of NATO becoming global in its reach, in part to fight the 'war on terror', but also because he felt Europe should spend more on its military forces to relieve America from further increasing its rapidly escalating budget deficits.

However, increasing unease in Europe regarding Bush's foreign policy agenda, and the accusation that America was seeking to remain a hegemonic power, increasingly caused some European states to question the actions of their transatlantic partner, such that some argued that one possible challenge to NATO, in the long term, could come from the European Union developing its own coordinated policy-making structures in foreign, security and defence policy. Though only in its infancy, this may undermine the purpose of NATO in the future.

Conclusion

What is clear is that in an era of globalisation, security is no longer linked solely to territorial defence. In short, the security of the US and Europe is no longer solely a regional issue, but a global one. This raises questions about whether NATO's role in the future is solely a military one, or whether it should engage in peacekeeping, state-building and disaster relief, as it has done since the end of the Cold War.

It is possible that once NATO withdraws from Afghanistan it will return to its regional European roots, and the notion of a 'global NATO' which gathered pace in the 1990s may be diminished. It is certainly unlikely that NATO will engage in another mission like the one in Afghanistan in the immediate future (particularly as America provided most of the troops and resources).

However, the politics of such a large organisation are complex. The question is what the alliance wants to do in the twenty-first century, and how it can achieve its goals on mutually acceptable terms between the US and Europe, particularly as allies may differ on what they want to do. NATO allows Europe to project hard power, while also serving to provide legitimacy for United States actions overseas. If NATO does not play a global role, however, will the US lose interest? As Walt (1997) noted, in an increasingly multipolar world alliances will most likely be less robust because major powers would have more options. As a result, existing alliance commitments may no longer be taken for granted.

Indeed, Walt (1998/99) compared the Atlantic alliance to Oscar Wilde's Dorian Gray, 'appearing youthful and robust as it grows older – but becoming ever more infirm'. Walt warned that 'the danger is that NATO will be dead before anyone notices, and we will only discover the corpse the moment we want it to rise and respond'. Recent actions by Russia may have revived the NATO alliance, but for how long?

Summary points

1   NATO is the most successful military-political alliance of the modern era.
2   Though it has remained together since the end of the Cold War, its aims remain unclear.
3   In particular, should NATO concentrate on Europe and its original role as a defensive alliance, or should it proactively tackle global security issues?
4   As long as it remains a cost-effective way of dealing with agreed threats it will continue.
5   Europe must create solidarity with the US over perceived threat perceptions for US policy-makers to remain loyal to NATO.
6   What is unusual about NATO as an alliance is that it has existed for so long, and that it is a peacetime alliance.

Recommended reading

Gates, R, (2011), 'The Security and Defense Agenda (Future of NATO)', 10 June, available at http://www.defense.gov/speeches/speech.aspx?speechid=1581, accessed on 10 July 2014.
Kaplan, L.S. *NATO Divided, NATO United: The Evolution of an Alliance*, Westport, CT: Praeger, 2004.
Modelski, G. 'The Study of Alliances: A Review', *Journal of Conflict Resolution*, vol. 7, no. 4, 1963, 769–776.
Synder, G. *Alliance Politics*, New York: Cornell University Press, 1997.
Theis, W.J. *Why NATO Endures*, New York: Cambridge University Press, 2009.
Walt, S. *The Origins of Alliances*, New York: Cornell University Press, 1987.
Waltz, K. *Theory of International Politics*, Reading, MA: Addison-Wesley, 1979.

22 Regional security organisations

Peter Hough

Box 22.1: IGOs and the Libyan intervention of 2011

When a major massacre in the rebel stronghold city of Benghazi led by Libyan dictator Gadaffi seemed imminent, several Intergovernmental Organisations (IGOs) established emergency meetings to discuss how this could be averted. UN Security Council Resolution 1973 called on the international community to take 'all necessary measures' to stop the bloodshed, but this was interpreted differently by an array of regional IGOs concerned at the situation and keen to assert their leadership. The African Union (AU) called for a ceasefire and put forward a transition plan for the country. The Libyan rebels – mindful that Gadaffi had long been an important AU sponsor and that the organisation had a poor track record in averting government massacres – rejected this and called instead on other IGOs to act. Consequently, a London meeting brought rebel group representatives together with NATO, the EU, the Arab League and the Organisation of the Islamic Conferences (OIC), but with no AU delegation. This meeting agreed to the idea of putting together a 'no-fly zone' plan in which government forces could be attacked if they defied the decree and Gadaffi would be removed from power. This policy was duly implemented by NATO and the rebels then completed a successful revolution in which Gadaffi was killed.

Was this intervention a successful illustration of intergovernmental security cooperation? From a positive point of view it was, since an imminent major massacre appeared to have been averted and the civil war was ended with the chief villain in the affair deposed. However, the intervention was also controversial. Many analysts and onlooking governments asserted that NATO had exceeded their UN-granted authority in an old-fashioned example of Western neo-imperialist meddling in the affairs of an oil-rich Middle Eastern state. Muscling in on the scene in this way may, additionally, have served to undermine the UN and make countries like China and Russia suspicious of future UN 'Responsibility to Protect' missions. The intervention could also be said to have undermined regional bodies more obviously relevant to deal with Libya, as well as confusing the mandate of NATO to defend Europe.

Introduction

This chapter reviews the growth of regional IGOs with a security dimension and examines rival opinions as to whether this phenomenon is good or bad in the pursuit of order and security in the world.

Military security is the most traditional basis for intergovernmental cooperation, but is among the least likely of bases for establishing an intergovernmental organisation

(IGO). Sovereignty explains this paradox. Fear of losing sovereignty through invasion has long prompted governments to create alliances to coordinate with friendly states or their enemy's enemies. Sovereignty, though, has also tended to dictate that defence is off-limits when friendly states join together more formally to reap mutual economic or diplomatic gains via IGOs. However, the complexity of contemporary sovereignty, in both non-military and military forms, has seen many IGOs that were originally set up for economic or diplomatic purposes come to adapt security measures in the face of less imminent and less clear-cut threats than an armed invasion.

An intergovernmental organisation (IGO) is a formalised kind of cross-border cooperation characterised as involving explicit rules and a clearly-defined decision-making process. Hence an IGO is more than a treaty, although they are often established as the result of one. An IGO has a 'life of its own' in that it is intended to be permanent and to evolve according to changing circumstances. It will have a fixed headquarters staffed by its own secretariat, and some form of policy-making process by which new binding rules can be developed as and when required by its member-states. Most security-oriented IGOs are relatively recent developments, reviewed later in this chapter, but less-formalised intergovernmental cooperation on security matters is more common and has a much longer history, and this is considered first.

Non-institutionalised regional security cooperation

Alliances

There is a long history of states working together in 'coalitions of the willing' to reap mutual security rewards, but such alliances usually fall short of an IGO. Alliances are usually temporary marriages of convenience which 'use cooperation as a means to an end rather than a good in itself' (Bailes and Cottey, 2006: 199). Since the crystallisation of sovereignty in international relations (at least in Europe) at the Treaty of Westphalia in 1648, military alliances have been forged in times of crisis when the balance of power has been perceived to be threatened by another state's or alliance's adventurism. French expansionism in the eighteenth and nineteenth centuries was thwarted by the construction of Grand Alliances of other European powers. In the twentieth century two European alliances then came into collision in the First World War. This calamity blotted the copybook of alliances and promoted an experiment with collective security in the form of the League of Nations. When this experiment proved unsuccessful the great powers reverted to form in order to defeat Germany and Japan in the Second World War. Allied cooperation in the Second World War was extensive – and in some senses institutionalised – but did not amount to an IGO because it was purely for the purposes of prosecuting a particular war. Churchill's response to criticism of him brokering an alliance with the Soviet Union that he would 'do a deal with the devil' in order to defeat Germany makes this plain, as does the quick dissolution of these ties after 1945.

Since the end of the Second World War some longer-term, less functional alliances have become established, blurring the distinction with formal IGOs. US bilateral ties with Japan, Israel, Australia and the UK (beyond their NATO relationship) since the 1940s have involved a high degree of military and intelligence cooperation without explicit organisational frameworks, although there is a treaty underpinning the Washington–Tokyo axis. 'Coalitions of the willing' have also been a prominent feature of recent international relations with alliances forged to prosecute wars against tyrants of a lesser order of threat than the likes of Bonaparte, Kaiser Wilhelm II or Hitler. These have generally been put together in the context of UN or NATO operations, but the 2003 Iraq War, circumventing both of these organisations, showed the strength of the US–UK–Australian 'Alliance of English-Speaking Nations'.

International regimes

Forms of intergovernmental cooperation less formal than IGOs but also less overt than alliances, covered by the term international regimes, can increasingly be seen in security politics. International regimes encompass a broader definition of international cooperation than IGOs, coming to prominence in the 1980s as representing: 'implicit or explicit principles, norms, rules and decision-making procedures around which actors' expectations converge in a given area of international relations' (Krasner, 1983: 1). One prominent form of international security regime that has grown over recent decades is cooperation based on regional arms control agreements. For example, the 1990 Conference on Conventional Armed Forces in Europe (CFE) was concluded between the NATO and Warsaw Pact countries as part of the curtain call of the Cold War, limiting troop and combat aircraft numbers. The treaty came into force in 1992 and survives today, although Russia suspended its involvement in 2007 in protest at the plans for the US missile shield system to be extended to Europe.

Nuclear Free Zones, outlawing the production or internal or external use of such weapons (by the official nuclear weapons states of the US, Russia, UK, China and France) in given regions, have developed since the 1960s and are encouraged by the 1968 Nuclear Non-Proliferation Treaty (NPT). The Treaty of Tlatelolco – or Treaty for the Prohibition of Nuclear Weapons in Latin America and the Caribbean – applies to all states of that broad region and has apparently succeeded in its aims, most notably in serving as a basis for diplomatic leverage on Brazil to abandon a weapons programme in the 1970s. The Treaty of Rarotonga binds most of the states in Oceania, including Australia and New Zealand, and has greater relevance than might be imagined since the South Pacific was the scene of French weapons testing in the early 1980s. In a similar vein 'The Stans' of the former Soviet Union (Kazakhstan, Uzbekistan, Tajikistan, Kyrgyzstan and Turkmenistan) became bound by a Central Asian Nuclear Free Zone under the Treaty of Semipalatinsk in 2009. On a more geopolitically benign basis, the 1959 Antarctica Treaty was given a nuclear weapons free dimension in the 1960s.

Globalisation increasingly presents both the opportunities and necessity for defence or justice ministers to meet their counterparts in other countries and for this to become informally regularised. It was in this way that crime and security gradually became part of the EU's remit, having previously been consciously kept out of the Treaty of Rome. The Arctic Council (AC), for example, was set up in 1996 with the explicit statement that issues of defence were off-limits (at the insistence of the US government). This remains the case, but, nevertheless, military chiefs of staff of the eight Arctic states met for the first time in Newfoundland in 2012 where it was announced that these meetings would become annual events, cooperating in the provision of military support for civil emergencies and building on the AC's first binding policy (a maritime search and rescue agreement). In a similar vein, defence ministers of the Americas have met biannually since the mid-1990s to discuss common concerns outside the Organization of American States (OAS) framework. In an example of civil society getting involved in high politics, the Shangri-La Dialogue between Asian-Pacific defence ministers and military leaders was initiated by the International Institute of Security Studies in 2002 (Bailes and Cottey, 2006: 205).

The rise of transnational organised crime is a common threat that has also prompted increased intergovernmental cooperation and the emergence of international regimes. The Kimberley Process is a certification scheme introduced in 2003 to try and stem the trade in 'blood diamonds' on the basis of a UN General Assembly Resolution (A/RES55/56). Over eighty-nine states have participated in the scheme which seeks to 'ensure that diamond purchases were not financing violence by rebel movements and their allies seeking to undermine legitimate governments' (Kimberley, 2013). Another prominent international regime prompted by criminal security threats has emerged to tackle the persistent problem of piracy off the East African coast, particularly in the 'sovereign' waters of the failed state that is Somalia. A far-reaching and successful set of cooperative measures has emerged, leading to extensive intelligence sharing and joint naval actions between several governments in conjunction with the UN, Interpol and the EU.

Security communities

The notion that informal transnational (private, societal) cross-border links, more than formal intergovernmental ones, can serve to enhance regional security dates back to the seminal work of Karl Deutsch in the 1950s (Deutsch *et al.*, 1957). Deutsch's Security Communities are more psychological than institutional and his research measured societal cross-border links to show that everyday communications were the route to peace. The research appeared to confirm that awareness of 'the other' allows for differences to be resolved peacefully since there is greater appreciation of other perspectives. Prominent examples of Security Communities included the Nordic states and Canada–US, before these relationships went on to become institutionally formalised. Security Communities are still a widely applied concept, better understood today as developing in accordance with regional IGOs as regulations and political cooperation 'spill over' into other domains.

Security spillover from regional IGOs in Europe

NATO, discussed in the previous chapter, represents an unusual example of a military alliance transforming itself into an intergovernmental organisation. It is more typical for the reverse to be the case, i.e. for an IGO to evolve to a point where the member-states decide to embark on some degree of security cooperation as a knock-on effect of the successful co-management of other policy areas – the phenomenon recognised in the study of political integration between states as 'spillover'.

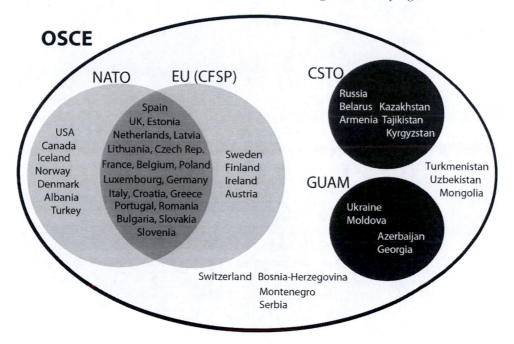

Figure 22.1 Overlapping membership of security IGOs in Europe

OSCE

Alongside the CFE, the transition to a post-Cold War order in Europe was negotiated under the auspices of the Conference on Security and Cooperation in Europe (CSCE), set up in 1973 in the context of the new spirit of détente that was seemingly bringing the Cold War to an end. The Conference procedure spawned the 1975 Helsinki Treaty, under which the Soviets agreed to improve civil and political rights on their side of the Iron Curtain in exchange for a Western guarantee not to interfere in their sphere of influence. The CSCE process was kept alive in the early 1980s, in spite of the flaring up of East–West tensions after the détente era, and was then able to become the focus for the formal ending of the Cold War at the end of the decade. The Charter of Paris for a New Europe in 1990, ratified by the NATO and Warsaw Pact countries, effectively consigned the Cold War to history and seemed to forge the basis of a new institutional framework for European security that succeeded the two Cold War warrior groupings.

While the CSCE formalised into the OSCE in 1975, with a permanent headquarters in Vienna and a membership growing to fifty-seven (including all of Europe as well as the US, Canada and Mongolia), it never became the main focus of European security cooperation that was envisaged in 1990. Of course, this was because NATO never left the scene. Nevertheless the OSCE remains an arena for pan-European dialogue on issues of peace and security. The OSCE hosts an information exchange facility that underpins the CFE regime, played an important role in the 'nation building' process in Bosnia-Herzegovina from its independence in the mid-1990s, and, in the field of transnational crime, has a counter-human-trafficking office which forms a key plank of international political cooperation on this problem extending well beyond the confines of Europe.

EU

Defence or security cooperation were consciously not part of the 1957 Treaty of Rome which set up the European Communities, but they were added to the competencies of the IGO when it deepened into the European Union under the Maastricht Treaty of 1992. The Common Foreign and Security Policy (CFSP) has grown since then but remains contentious among the member-states, and integration lags far behind most other of the growing roster of policy areas decided in Brussels. While peace and security were key motivations for the Treaty of Rome and the cooperation between France, West Germany, Netherlands, Belgium, Luxembourg and Italy which preceded this from the formation of the European Coal and Steel Community (ECSC) six years earlier, defence and formal foreign policy coordination were considered off-limits for two key reasons: the failure of the European Defence Community (EDC), and the popularity of NATO. The EDC was a French initiative of 1950 to initiate a process of developing a common army among the six countries that would go on to form the ECSC and EC, with the aim of tying down the Germans militarily. However, the EDC never came into force after the French government scuppered their own project in 1954 by refusing to ratify the 1952 Paris Treaty through a combination of fears that a Western European army without the UK on board (since that nation's Euroscepticism had ruled them out of the EDC and ECSC) was weak, and internal political opposition to such a compromise to their sovereignty. NATO had been supportive of the EDC, but with this failure the question of German rearmament was taken into their remit and West Germany was invited into the Western alliance/IGO in 1955. This move was opposed by the USSR who responded by bringing East Germany into a military alliance along with the other five of their Eastern bloc allied states. When French efforts to revive defence cooperation in the EC then failed to get off the ground in the mid-1960s, they withdrew from the military structure of NATO (while maintaining membership) in 1966. Hence, foreign policy and security remained off the formal agenda of the EC until the 1990s, with that role essentially assumed to be taken care of from Washington via Brussels.

In the early 1990s the CFSP was born of both the revival of European integration (after a period of stagnation in the 1980s mainly due to the recalcitrance of the UK and Denmark following their admission in 1973) and the practical necessity for a community now fully unified in international trade to speak with a more unified voice on diplomatic issues. The CFSP managed to get off the ground in spite of the opposition of the Danes (who were allowed to opt out despite this technically being contrary to community law), since the British changed course and gave their support to the initiative. This time a revival of the 'German question' served to bring Paris and London together. While German reunification in 1990 was hardly comparable to fears of a fourth Reich rising in the early 1950s, balance of power considerations did come into play through concerns that the enlargement of the already most powerful economy in the EC could diminish the influence of the two premier military powers. At the time, it was also far from inevitable that NATO would live on, meaning that the British needed to look at alternatives to their 'special relationship' with the US.

NATO's persistence did not kill off the CFSP, however, as Washington, while still committed to the defence of Europe, favoured a more equal relationship than during the Cold War, in which the Europeans would do more in defending themselves. Hence it was hoped that the EU could play a security role within the confines of

NATO. Towards this end a long-forgotten European security institution was brought out of cold storage – the Western European Union (WEU). The WEU was the predecessor of NATO formed by the Brussels Treaty of 1948 as a defence pact between France, the UK and the Benelux countries, attempting to provide a guarantee against any future German military revival. Once it became apparent that the Soviet Union was a far greater potential threat to Western Europe than the Germans, the US were brought on board and the WEU was absorbed into NATO. However, this WEU revival plan never materialised, because whilst in the late 1950s all EC countries were also NATO members, this was not the case in the 1990s (see Figure 22.1).

The WEU was therefore wound up in 2011 and the issue of how to avoid an overlap of functions with NATO remains, but EU cooperation on security matters has nonetheless evolved. The 1998 St Malo Declaration heralded closer defence cooperation between the French and British, paving the way for the European Security and Defence Policy (ESDP) the following year which finally provided the basis for European cross-border military brigades, albeit on a much smaller scale than envisaged in the early 1950s. Hence in 2005 an EU-FOR peacekeeping force led by the UK was deployed in Bosnia-Herzegovina after a NATO mission. Two years later an EU foreign policy chief position was established, filled initially by the former NATO Secretary General Solano. In general, though, EU security cooperation remains more at the diplomatic than at the military level, with important differences in foreign policy orientation remaining among its membership. Irish, Swedish, Finnish and Austrian neutrality remains an obstacle to a more substantive military role for the EU, as does the Atlanticist indifference of Denmark. As discussed in the previous chapter, however, NATO's future is still somewhat uncertain owing to the divergent levels of commitment to its recent role in Afghanistan among its membership, and the issue of Europeans being ready to defend themselves remains. Most crucially, the British and French have – with the notable exception of the 2003 Iraq War – come closer together than at any time since the 1940s, and have maintained a twin-track approach to European security cooperation utilising both NATO (who France became fully integrated into again in 2009) and the ESDP.

In the domain of crime EU cooperation is a similarly recent development, but it is already well advanced and set to deepen in a more clear-cut instance of spillover. The rise in cross-border crime in the European Union that accompanied the relaxation of member-state border controls in the Single Market programme in the early 1990s prompted the organisation to instigate a devolved but souped-up version of Interpol to coordinate the work of its member-state police forces. Europol was agreed upon in the 1992 Maastricht Treaty, in line with the creation of a 'Justice and Home Affairs' dimension to the EU's political integration process, and came into being in January 1994. Its budget doubled through the 2000s and in 2008 the Lisbon Treaty brought Europol fully into the EU political system – unlike CFSP – with the possibility of unilateral national vetoes ending and decisions now made on the basis of qualified majority voting (i.e. without national vetoes). Thus, further deepening of EU-level crime fighting is likely.

Pre-dating the EC/EU and significantly wider, with a membership of forty-nine (spanning all of Europe, east and west, except for the dictatorship of Belarus), the Strasbourg-based Council of Europe has largely been left in the shade by Brussels-centred integration, but it has made a notable contribution to Human Security on the continent through its Convention and Court of Human Rights. The ECHR is the most far-reaching international human rights regime in the world, exceeding UN instruments in giving protection to individuals, such as sexual minorities, by regularly prosecuting governments who violate these rights.

Post-Soviet IGOs

Unlike NATO, the Warsaw Pact was dissolved at the end of the Cold War, leaving the former Soviet states and allies somewhat in the shade of their erstwhile foe. Moscow's six Eastern bloc partners ultimately joined NATO, as did the three Baltic states from within the Soviet Union (Latvia, Lithuania and Estonia), leaving the remaining twelve Soviet Socialist Republics (SSRs) to maintain links through the Commonwealth of Independent States (CIS). Given the rapid and unforeseen break-up of the USSR difficult issues remained unresolved in spite of fifteen declarations of independence. Large ethnic Russian populations remained in most of the new states (previously encouraged by Russification policies) and economic reliance on Moscow was still apparent in spite of policies of decentralisation and privatisation being quickly ushered in by the new Yeltsin government. Security was also an issue since many of the Russians now stranded outside Russia were troops that Moscow wished to remain there, and who many non-Russians also felt might be needed to maintain order.

In 1994 the CIS agreed on a Collective Security Treaty (CST) in parallel with the launch of a free trade area. By the time the CST came up for renewal in 1999, though, many CIS members had grown bolder and more westward in their outlook and were more interested in joining other ex-Eastern bloc states in tying themselves to Washington and Brussels than in preserving links with Moscow. Georgia, Ukraine, Uzbekistan, Azerbaijan and Moldova refused to re-ratify and put their faith instead into the loose GUUAM alliance they had formed in 1996. These five former SSRs had become concerned at excessive Russian military interference, particularly in Georgia and Moldova where Moscow remained committed to defending large Russian enclaves outside the sovereign control of Tblisi or Chisnau. The rise to power of the Taliban in Afghanistan in 1996 had also caused increased Russian interest in Central Asia and a rise in general Islamophobia. Russian support for Christian Armenia in their territorial squabble with Azerbaijan was an added factor in the latter's desire to cut the old apron strings. The fact that GUUAM's founding treaty was signed in Washington provided an obvious clue to the geopolitical orientation of these states, some of whom aspired to NATO membership. Uzbekistan, though, turned GUUAM to GUAM in 2006 and moved closer to the CIS/CST when their authoritarian secular government, previously indulged by the West in classic Cold War *realpolitik* style for cracking down on Islamic fundamentalism, went too far in the 2005 Andrjan massacre and prompted criticism from the US and other Western countries. The six remnants of the USSR remaining loyal to Moscow now comprise what was renamed the Collective Security Treaty Organisation (CSTO) in 2002. In spite of the loss of numbers it is probably a case of leaner and meaner for the CSTO, with rapid reaction forces now established with Russian troops operating in joint brigades in Armenia and Belarus and peacekeepers deployed in the face of civil unrest in Tajikistan. This, taken in conjunction with the 2008 Russo-Georgian war, made it evident to the world that Moscow had drawn new lines in the sands of Central Asia.

Security spillover from regional IGOs in Africa

African union

Under its charter, African Union (AU) members can request an intervention from the organisation and there is an obligation on them to act in the face of genocide or war crimes. The track record of the AU (previously the Organisation of African Unity [OAU]) in peacekeeping and peacemaking is, though, limited. In the 1990s and 2000s they played diplomatic roles in efforts to quell civil unrest in Angola, Ivory Coast, Madagascar, Somalia, Sudan and the Comoros, but most notably failed (as did the UN) to prevent genocide in Rwanda in 1994. The OAU helped broker the Arusha peace process in 1992, but the Rwandan catastrophe led to the development of the Mechanism for Conflict Prevention Management and Resolution in 1993. In the 2000s a further determination to play a meaningful peacekeeping and conflict resolution role saw the launch of the Common African Defence and Security Policy, featuring a Peace and Security Council, a Commissioner for Peace and Security, and African Standby Forces organised into five brigades in different parts of the continent.[1] Subsequently peacekeeping roles were played by the AU in Burundi (2003/4), Darfur (2004) and Somalia (2007). In Burundi the AU despatched 3,000 troops who were able to disarm some militia and facilitate the flow of humanitarian aid, paving the way for a UN force to intervene the following year (who had previously prevaricated because of the chaotic nature of the ethnic civil conflict). In Somalia the AU intervention also served as a prelude and preparatory mission for a more extensive UN operation. The Darfur mission, though, relied much on external support and emphasised the limitations of the AU's powers, going some way to explaining the marginalisation of the organisation over the Libyan crisis seven years later. This pattern of a limited role for the AU supporting an external great power was repeated in Mali and the Central African Republic in 2013/4, when key peacekeeping responsibilities came to be assumed by their former colonial masters, the French.

In another dimension to AU efforts to maintain a peaceful continent, the African Nuclear Free Zone, based on the Treaty of Pelindaba, came into force in 2009. An AU role in peacekeeping has thus evolved, but it has so far been highly reliant on wider international support.

ECOWAS

The Economic Organisation of West African States, in a similar fashion to the AU, has evolved a peacekeeping dimension but has still to assume primary responsibility to protect the Western part of the continent. Formed in 1978 as a trade bloc of sixteen states with an Abuja headquarters, within three years ECOWAS had agreed to a protocol on non-aggression and then followed this up with the 1981 Mutual Defence Pact. However, its first major role, based on mediation and the deployment of a peacekeeper force in the Liberian Civil War in 1990 (ECOMOG), was not successful. A ceasefire that was established failed to hold, and in 1993 a UN peacekeeping force was despatched, with ECOMOG playing a supporting role. Initially the ECOWAS action had been taken without UN authorisation and there was concern within the membership about the dominant role played by Nigeria. Hence in 1997, when civil war erupted in Sierra Leone, the government called not on the AU or ECOWAS but on their former imperial rulers in London to provide the troops which succeeded in quelling the insurgency. In 1999 ECOWAS sought to assume greater responsibility with the establishment of the Mechanism for Conflict Resolution, but European peacekeepers have still tended to be favoured by governments in crisis. Hence in 2011 the overthrow of Ghagbo and measures to damp down the Ivorian Civil War saw ECOWAS play only a supporting role in a French-led mission.

More promisingly, ECOWAS has unexpectedly come to have a Human Security dimension through its court, which – while it is not ostensibly a human rights judiciary – passed a landmark verdict in 2008 against the government of Niger for failing to protect a girl from being sold into slavery.[2]

SADC

The Southern African Development Community, set up as a trade bloc in 1992, also quickly established a security dimension, and can cite some evidence of success and self-reliance. The successful intervention by South Africa, Botswana and Zimbabwe into Lesotho in 1994 (at that government's request) ended civil unrest and prompted the launch of the Politics, Defence and Security organ in 1996. The region has been relatively stable – on an intergovernmental level – since that time, and cooperation has spilled over into intelligence sharing and joint crime fighting.

Security spillover from regional IGOs in the Middle East

The Arab League and the OIC

The Arab League was launched in 1945 and has twenty-two members spanning the Middle East and North Africa. The wider Organisation of the Islamic Conference, formed from a 1969 summit in Rabat, comprises some fifty-seven states from four continents. While united on the Palestine question, both fora have struggled for unity since the 1979 Iranian revolution heightened sectarian Shia–Sunni divisions, followed by the in-fighting of the Iran–Iraq and Iraq–Kuwait wars. Both organisations played diplomatic roles in Bosnia and Somalia in the early 1990s, but sectarian-based divisions have persisted and any more substantive roles have not been possible.

Gulf Cooperation Council

Greater Arab unity has been possible through the more tightly knit GCC, established in 1981 as an economic and diplomatic bloc of Saudi Arabia, Kuwait, Bahrain, Qatar, Oman and the UAE with a headquarters in Riyadh. The GCC's founding treaty makes no mention of military cooperation, but in the organisation's first year of operation its Supreme Council agreed upon a defence pact. The GCC presented a peace plan to Iran and Iraq in response to their bloody war in 1983, but it had not had to deal with an issue directly concerning its membership until it was jolted into life by the Iraqi invasion of Kuwait in 1990. The GCC demanded an immediate Iraqi withdrawal, formed the joint 'Peninsular Shield' to defend north-east Saudi Arabia from any expansion of Saddam's adventurism, and then joined the UN force which succeeded in driving him out. The Peninsular Shield remained after the war and has subsequently more than doubled in size to a force of over 100,000. A combination of internal and external security concerns explains this. A fear of internal insurgency bonds together these monarchical regimes, and this has heightened in recent years with the revolutionary wave that has washed through the Arab world. Consequently, a predominantly Saudi force was despatched to Bahrain in 2011 to suppress a popular uprising against monarchical rule. Externally Iran provides the chief common foe, since that nation is considered by many to be behind the fomenting of Shia opposition in the Gulf states and it has also asserted some historical sovereign claims to Bahrain. A 2008 Wikileaks exposé illustrated these fears, but also the determination of the Saudis to bring in the US to 'cut off the head of the snake' (*Guardian*, 2010).

Security spillover from regional IGOs in Asia and the Pacific

ASEAN

Dating back to 1967, the Association of South East Asian Nations always had a security community motivation which has persisted and been better realised than the aim of economic integration, hampered by the diversity of a membership which includes the wealthy democracy of Singapore and the developing dictatorship of Myanmar. The 1976 Treaty of Amity and Cooperation in South East Asia and the 1994 ASEAN Regional Forum have provided the basis for some joint military exercises, which have brought in the US and involved China in an observer capacity. The ASEAN also played a diplomatic role in Cambodia in the late 1990s, using the fact that that country was in the process of negotiating entry to insist, as a condition of this, that political reforms be enacted to stabilise civil turmoil. Fear of Japanese or Chinese domination was always a key spur to regional cooperation and the maintenance of mainly cordial relations with their northern neighbours suggests that it has succeeded in this regard. In 2003 China signed up to the Treaty of Amity in spite of some sovereign quarrels in the South China Sea, mindful that good relations and an orderly South East Asia is in their economic interest.

In other security dimensions ASEAN has also agreed to a nuclear free zone under the treaty of Bangkok, and has followed the NATO lead in developing a capacity to collaborate in natural disaster relief with the Agreement on Disaster Management and Emergency Response (AADMER), which entered into force in 2009. South East Asian political cooperation is widely held as successfully bringing its diverse membership together, in spite of limited formal integration, through the emergence of 'The ASEAN way', characterised by informal, consensual mutual consultation promoting sovereign order and non-interference.

Pacific Islands Forum

Founded in 1971 as a diplomatic forum for the islands of the South Pacific and Australasia, the PIF took on an explicit security dimension with the Biketawa Declaration in 2000, which pledged the supply of military or police cooperation – principally from Australia or New Zealand – in the event of crisis. Concerns that the rise of civil disorder in some of the small but independent South Pacific islands in the 1990s could render them failed states provided a mutual interest in such cooperation for the 'Big 2' and the remaining small members. This agreement provided the basis for Australian-led 'Regional Assistance Missions' in the Solomon Islands in 2003, Nauru in 2004 and Tonga in 2006. In a different dimension the PIF agreed to the suspension of Fiji from the organisation in 2009 for persistent anti-democratic actions and human rights abuses by its government. In an illustration of the organisation's success, ten years on the Solomon Islands mission began to scale down, having disarmed the insurgents, restored order and shifted operations to a 'nation building' approach of re-training the local police force and carrying out development projects.

Security spillover from regional IGOs in the Americas

On a pan-American basis the Organization of American States (OAS) has the potential for regional peacekeeping through its Office for the Prevention and Resolution of Conflicts. In 2005 the OAS got involved in mediation in the Nicaraguan civil war, but in general its role has been limited in the post-Cold War era because of greater South American confidence not to acquiesce to US hegemony.

The Common Market of the South (Mercosur), comprising Brazil, Argentina, Uruguay, Paraguay and Venezuela, has always had an explicit political as well as an economic rationale, but security cooperation has been limited to date. There have been some coordinated military exercises, such as joint naval drills on the Uruguay River in 2013, but no peacekeeping instruments have been developed. However, the lack of major international disputes in South America over recent decades is both a cause and an effect of this, and Mercosur stands as a good case study of a security community. The maintenance of cordial relations between the two chief powers, Brazil and Argentina, represents a less spectacular version of the Franco-German relationship that underpins European integration.

Organised crime represents more of a common threat to most South American governments than war or insurgency, and special police cooperation between the Mercosur countries has been facilitated by an Interpol Regional Bureau. In addition, a Conference of the Home Secretaries has provided a forum for crime fighting cooperation since 1996. Similarly, in Central America, the Central American Integration System (SICA) trade bloc, established in 1993, developed a Security Initiative in 2007 to facilitate greater intelligence sharing in the face of the region's persistent drug crime problem.

Linking Mercosur with the neighbouring Andean Community of Nations is the Union of South American States (UNASUR), signed in 2008, which features the South American Defence Council (CDS). Possibly heralding a new dawn for South American security cooperation, UNASUR was involved in Bolivia in the first year of its operation, supporting President Morales against an insurgency and instigating an investigation into a rebel massacre.

Is regionalism a route to global security?

The proliferation of IGOs tackling matters of security is a part the 'new regionalism' phenomenon, better recognised in the field of International Political Economy (IPE) in the rapid growth of trade blocs of various forms since the 1990s (having previously been largely confined to Western Europe from the 1950s). The debate on the implications of this phenomenon can be understood as broadly the same as in IPE. Are regional security organisations stepping stones to wider global peace or a complicating impediment to this? Proponents of regional trade blocs argue that they represent small, practical steps in the pursuit of global free trade, and the same line of argument can be advanced in favour of regional security cooperation. In the early 1990s UN Secretary-General Boutros-Ghali's Agenda For Peace subscribed to this line of thought, describing regional organisations as 'resurgent spheres of influence but as a complement to healthy institutionalism' (Boutros-Ghali, 1992). The dismal track record of global organisations in activating collective security provides a strong case for devolving this most fundamental of all international political tasks. In Europe this has been apparent since the mid-1990s when NATO stepped in where the UN had failed as Yugoslavia imploded. In other parts of the world regional frameworks provide the opportunity for localised security solutions that can avoid the need to wait on the largesse of the Big Five on the UN Security Council.

However, just as many see regional trade groupings as stumbling blocks rather than stepping stones to freeing up global trade, the 'alphabet soup' of organisations and intergovernmental initiatives that has emerged in international security politics can, equally, be viewed as a complicating distraction from the maintenance of global peace and order. The 'practical devolution' argument could only really apply if regional organisations worked in tandem with the UN, but while this has often happened, for most governments these arrangements are seen more as an alternative to the utopia of global collective security. The circumvention of the UN by NATO over Kosovo in 1999 and the circumvention of both the UN and NATO by the US, the UK and Australia in 2003 over Iraq served to undermine the authority of the global body, the stock of which had been at an all-time high in the early 1990s.

A strong case can be made that NATO was making up for UN deficiency rather than causing it over Kosovo, but the Western alliance is a highly atypical regional body in containing three-fifths of the UN's Big Five, including a global military 'hyperpower'. This is far from the case with other regional organisations, most of which have not proved themselves to be up to the job of regional policeman. With the probable exception of the CSTO, where the projection of Russian power into her faithful former Soviet allies is mutually beneficial and realistic, it is hard to make a case for regional security arrangements being up to the job. The GCC have well-developed security arrangements and common interests and have proved themselves capable of maintaining sovereign internal order among themselves, but beyond that they recognise their limitations and look to Washington as an ultimate guarantor of protection. GUAM is really nothing more than an appeal to Washington. ECOWAS, like the GCC, strives for a role in West African peace enforcement but also understands its limitations in this regard and has a track record of deferring to former colonial masters in Paris and London. SADC has stronger credentials in keeping its house in order, but this is only an imperfect sovereign order if we consider that its membership of five includes two barely sovereign dependent entities (Swaziland and Lesotho) and the humanitarian nightmare that is Zimbabwe. The PIF has proved its worth but is similarly diverse and amounts to little more than an offer of protection by Australia for several small and barely sovereign island states. NATO's assumption of responsibility in Libya in 2011 tells the story that the AU, the OIC and the AL were, ultimately, not up to the job. ASEAN, Mercosur and EU cooperation have helped forge security communities among once rival neighbouring powers, but they have yet to demonstrate that they could police their part of the globe if it came to the crunch.

Regional security organisations can be viewed as problematic from either a Realist or a Liberal perspective. For Liberals they can undermine and distract from the proper functioning of International Law, the UN and collective security; 'regionally based arrangements for peace and security could become iron spheres of local dominance, not golden circles of a more enlightened world order' (Henrikson, 1996: 70). Similarly, in response to the 2011 NATO action in Libya Köchler summarised a view of many international lawyers:

> It is obvious that the delegation of virtually unlimited authority to interested parties and regional groups – as has become customary since the Gulf War resolutions of 1990/1991 – is not only incompatible with the United Nations Charter, but with the international rule of law as such.
>
> As long as it encourages member states to act as they please, allowing them to further their own national interests in the disguise of enforcement action on behalf of the United Nations, the Security Council's practice will itself constitute a threat to international peace and security.
>
> (Köchler, 2011)

For many Realists, organisations global or regional offer a 'false promise' (Mearsheimer, 1995) and serve to distract from the key route to order that comes from the balancing of state power, best served by looser and more flexible alliances. Alliances reinforce sovereign order rather than undermining it and so avoid the 'New Medievalism' concern prophesied by Bull in the 1970s and revived by anti-globalists in the 1990s. New Medievalism refers to the dangers of sleepwalking into a post-sovereign chaos by allowing states to wither on the vine of global governance, comparable to the pre-sovereign chaos of Europe before order was established at the Treaty of Westphalia in 1648. In a complex world of overlapping organisations political responsibility and accountability become muddied, and, in terms of security, there would be a danger of the buck continually being passed and no Great Powers being around or prepared to step up to the mark in a crisis (Bull, 1977: 254).

Equally, though, it is possible to paint a positive picture of regional security organisations on either a Liberal or Realist canvas. The security communities of Western Europe, North America, South America, South East Asia and the Gulf States are testimony to the pacifying force of intergovernmental cooperation if viewed in Liberal, integrationist or English School Realist 'society of states' terms. The English School-inspired Copenhagen School's notion of a Regional Security Complex, for instance, views as a source of order 'a group of states whose primary security concerns link together sufficiently closely that their national securities cannot realistically be considered apart from one another' (Buzan, 1991: 190). For Structural Realists regional security organisations may even represent a way of avoiding New Medievalism by providing arenas for the projection of power by hegemons. Mearsheimer qualifies his scepticism of IGOs by observing that 'the most powerful states in the world create and shape institutions so that they can maintain their share of world power, or even increase it' (Mearsheimer, 1995: 13). US power underpins the undoubtedly successful NATO and indirectly supports the GCC and other less formal regional groupings. Russia performs the same function with the CSTO. On a less grand scale, regional security organisations provide regional powers like Brazil, South Africa, Saudi Arabia, Australia and Nigeria with an arena to help preserve sovereign order in their 'backyards' and project their power in the wider interest.

For Social Constructivists and Critical Theorists the debate on organisations needs to mature beyond the classic dialectic of intergovernmentalism versus supranationality, recognising that sovereignty is an evolving and subjective concept. New regionalism is about more than the given region; it is 'extroverted rather than introverted' (Soderbaum, 2003: 5), given that threats to security are globalising. These organisations are far from alliances constructed to deter imminent threats; they are responses to the more complex world of variable, longer-term threats we now inhabit, and they represent attempts at the management of the future by being reflexive rather than reactive (Rasmussen, 2001).

Regional security organisations and the UN

While the idea of the UN devolving some peacekeeping responsibilities to regional security organisations has only really been put into practise over the past twenty years, the notion of such an arrangement was around at the start of its history. However, like much of the global body's potential, this was stymied by the Cold War. Chapter VIII of the UN Charter deals explicitly with 'Regional Arrangements', noting 'the existence of regional arrangements or agencies for dealing with such matters relating to the maintenance of international peace and security as are appropriate for regional action'. Article 53(1) of the chapter determines that '[t]he Security Council shall, where appropriate, utilize such regional arrangements or agencies for enforcement action under its authority. But no enforcement action shall be taken under regional arrangements or by regional agencies without the authorisation of the Security Council'. However, regional organisations were barely in existence when these words were written in the 1940s, and when they did emerge, they were never going to be able to work in tandem with all of the Big Five at the UN.

The New World Order of the early 1990s permitted the late flowering of these seeds in UN politics, half a century after their sowing. In 1993 the Security Council invited regional organisations to improve coordination with them and play a stronger peacekeeping role (Res. 25184), and the following year the General Assembly pledged its support for this in its 'Comprehensive Review of Peacekeeping' (A/RES/48/42). Also in 1994 Secretary-General Boutros-Ghali held a meeting with his counterparts in several regional organisations including NATO, the EU, the AU, the CIS, the AL, the OAU and the OAS. This was the first of its kind, but these summits are now established events and have widened while remaining in keeping with the overall informal trend.

Box 22.2: The UN–regional security partnership

In 2006 on the basis of UNSC Resolution 1631 the previous year, the UN Secretary-General Kofi Annan produced the report *A Regional–Global Security Partnership: Challenges and Opportunities*, which stated that;

'The United Nations claims no monopoly on the settlement of disputes. There may be times when it would be better for other mediators such as those from regional partners to handle a given situation' (UNGA and UNSC, 2006: 7).

'At times, a regional response may be the best means to prevent or end conflict; at other times, direct involvement of the United Nations, either alone or with regional partners, may be the only way to act effectively' (UNGA and UNSC, 2006: 9).

The report went on to recommend that a clarification of responsibilities was needed to improve cross-organisational cooperation, and that it was necessary to address the uneven capacity of regional organisations – particularly in Africa. As a particular measure to improve coordination further, it was mooted that a dedicated unit towards this end should be set up within the UN's Department of Political Affairs.

UN–regional interactions have also become more routinised. 'Desk to desk' dialogue between the UN and the EU was established in 2003, and between the UN and the CoE in 2005 when the first UN-OSCE staff level meeting was also held. NATO and CSTO have also signed joint declarations on secretariat-level cooperation with New York (in 2005 and 2010). Broad global support for this trend was made apparent in 2005 when the General Assembly, in the 2005 World Summit Outcome, declared: 'We support a stronger relationship between the United Nations and regional and sub-regional organizations, pursuant to Chapter VIII'.

Conclusion

A subsidiarity of sorts is emerging in which global and regional responsibilities for peace and security are being mutually agreed between these two layers of governance through common interest. The results of this are a little messy and lack the neatness – in theory at least – of intergovernmental power balances or global collective security systems, but a symbiotic relationship has emerged on the basis that the UN cannot police the globe without them, and the fact that most of the regional organisations cannot police their regions without the UN. The picture is uneven with some regions better policed than others and several grey areas where overlapping interests exist. National security concerns are generally tackled better than non-military Human Security threats, but the latter category is improving and is better covered than at any time in the past. This is obviously not the subsidiarity of a federal system, but that is inevitable in such a diverse and unevenly globalised world. After all, even the EU is moving in a 'Europe à la carte' direction. The UN–regional organisation relationship needs fine tuning, but this is going on. The differences on Libya in 2011 were due to ambiguous wording in the Security Council resolution, and such ambiguity can be expected to recede through learning to adjust to these relationships.

Amid the debate as to whether the emergence of regional security organisations over recent decades helps or hinders the quest for global peace, the decline in wars presents a good case for a new order based neither on a classic balance of power nor on global collective security. Interstate wars have become rare events, and civil wars were half as frequent in the 2000s as they were during the early 1990s. Overall conflict deaths have fallen from 164,000 per year in the 1980s to 92,000 in the 1990s, to 42,000 in the 2000s (World Bank, 2011: 52; Uppsala/PRIO, 2010). This pacific trend is not conclusive evidence of a productive role for regional IGOs, since an array of other explanatory factors could be offered, but a more peaceful world certainly cannot be explained by the existence of a global balance of power or a fully-functioning global system of collective security.

Summary points

1   Regional IGOs with a security dimension have grown significantly across the world over recent decades with a mixed record of success in maintaining order.
2   Non-institutionalised forms of regional security cooperation have also grown.
3   For some this development is unwelcome: either – for some Realists – for undermining power-balancing alliances, or – for some Liberals – for undermining the United Nations.

4   For others, this new regionalism is a positive development, allowing for regional groups to step in where the UN fears to tread.

Notes

1 North, East, Central, South and ECOWAS.
2 Hadijatou Mani Koraou v. Niger, 2008.

Recommended reading

Bailes, A. and Cottey, A. 'Regional Security Cooperation in the Early 21st Century' in SIPRI, *SIPRI Yearbook 2006: Armaments, Disarmament and International Security,* Stockholm International Peace Research Institute, 2006.
UNGA and UNSC, *A Regional-Global Security Partnership: Challenges and Opportunities,* Report of the Secretary General, A/61/204–S/2006/590, 28 July 2006.

Section 5

Case studies

23 The United States

Finding a role in the post-Cold War and post-9/11 eras

Andrew Moran

Box 23.1 The end of unipolarity?

In the immediate aftermath of the Cold War many writers argued that the world had entered a unipolar moment. Charles Krauthammer (1990) went so far as to predict a prolonged era of American dominance which would last thirty to forty years. America, he proclaimed, was the world's sole superpower, preponderant both economically and militarily.

However, where the Cold War had provided direction for American foreign policy, namely the containment of Communism, the sudden end of that war made America's security concerns less clear, particularly as it was now part of a rapidly globalising and increasingly complex world. President Bill Clinton would seek to reprioritise America's interests, arguing that it must be at the forefront of this new global process, supporting the spread of democratisation and liberal capitalism around the world, and placing economic policy at the centre of America's long-term security. For example, America provided aid to the former Soviet bloc countries to promote these aims and increase the likelihood of regional stability. By the end of the decade, America appeared to be a more prosperous nation, at peace with the world. Then came the al-Qaeda-led attacks of 11 September 2001.

Security and the Bush presidency

It is difficult to overestimate the devastating affect of 9/11 on the American psyche. In a single day, nearly three thousand people were killed by nineteen men armed with box-cutter knives who hijacked four planes and smashed them into the symbols of American power – the World Trade Center (economic) and the Pentagon (military), while the fourth, brought down in a field in Pennsylvania, would most likely have hit the White House or Capitol Hill (political). More Americans died that day than on any since the bloodiest days of the American Civil War of 1861 to 1865, and it was the first attack on Washington DC since the British burned the White House in 1812.

President George W. Bush responded by launching a 'war on terror' against al-Qaeda and its leader, Osama bin Laden, that would see America take the fight outside its borders to Afghanistan and Iraq, and covertly to countries such as Pakistan and Yemen. Reflecting a more Realist agenda, his National Security Strategy in 2002 would proclaim 'our best defence is a good offense' (NSS, 2002). Terrorism was now America's top security concern. Initially lacking in foreign policy experience, Bush surrounded himself with skilled, experienced foreign policy specialists who shared

Krauthammer's view that America was now the dominant power in the world. They quickly sought to change Clinton's more multilateralist approach to one centred on unilateralism, combined with a more aggressive diplomatic style. This was demonstrated early on by the Bush administration's rejection of the Kyoto Protocol on climate change, a refusal to sign up to the International Criminal Court, and opposition to the international ban on landmines.

This new approach was influenced by the so-called 'neo-conservatives', many of whom where members of the influential Project for a New American Century, a think-tank which advocated 'unchallenged American global leadership and the expansion of the American empire of liberty, democracy, and free markets backed up by a mighty military machine' (Williams, 2005; Nuruzzaman, 2006: 248).

The Bush Doctrine

To fight the war on terror, Bush proposed a new grand strategy for America. Central to this was the strategy of pre-emptive war – the right to strike an enemy who posed an imminent threat before they attacked first. Though America has long reserved the right to do so as a means of self-defence, it had never been so explicitly stated. Significantly, Bush announced that this would involve the abandonment of the Cold War doctrines of deterrence and containment, which he argued were ineffective against a violent, non-state actor such as al-Qaeda whose members were prepared to die for their cause and kill others in the process.

The Administration also advocated regime change and the aggressive promotion of democracy. Bush argued that Iraq, Iran and North Korea were 'rogue states' that were part of an 'axis of evil', which sought to aid terrorists and threaten world peace. As a result, they must be challenged and their leadership replaced, by force if necessary.

This approach implied that the 'war on terror' required a military solution, rather than being a war that could be won through intelligence and cooperation between governments, security and law-enforcement agencies. Bush framed the war in Realist terms, warning: 'We will pursue nations that provide aid or safe haven to terrorism. Every nation, in every region, now has a decision to make. Either you are with us or you are with the terrorists' (Bush, 2001).

In addition, Bush called for the development of a controversial National Missile Defence system composed of Anti-Ballistic Missiles (ABMs) designed to shoot down any incoming missiles fired at the US from rogue states. This was viewed with suspicion by Russia, who noted that these missiles, and their early warning systems, would be stationed close to their borders in the Czech Republic and Poland. This was made worse by Bush unilaterally withdrawing the US from the anti-ballistic missile treaties with Russia from the early 1970s, which had originally been designed to limit the development of ABMs for fear that they might tempt one side to launch a first-strike attack against the other, knowing they could knock out there opponent's retaliatory weapons. As many noted, this new system also would not have stopped the 9/11 attacks. To fulfil these aims the defence budget doubled within five years reaching $604 billion in 2006 – equal to 45% of all the world's defence spending. Bush reinforced the unilateral nature of his policy by proclaiming that 'America will never seek a permission slip to defend the security of our country' (Bush, 2004).

Though it was framed in moral terms, with the President frequently using terms such as 'good', 'democracy', 'liberty' and 'freedom', and calling bin Laden and other terrorists 'evil-doers', this new foreign policy was not without its critics. The Harvard political scientist Stanley Hoffman suggested that 'In context, it amounts to a doctrine of global domination' (Hoffman, 2003), while others feared that the US was becoming a unilateral, imperialist state.

Afghanistan

The invasion of Afghanistan in 2001 was the first application of the Bush doctrine, with the US taking the fight directly to the enemy and removing the Taliban government that had harboured bin Laden and his al-Qaeda network. Few states around the world opposed this action, particularly as only two countries in the world had granted the Taliban government diplomatic recognition, it had been denied its seat at the UN, and it had one of the worst records on human rights in the world.

American-led forces quickly removed the Taliban from power, but many of its leaders and members of al-Qaeda, including bin Laden, escaped capture. America soon found itself bogged down in a long war where it became increasingly unclear who the enemy was. By the end of the Bush presidency a rudimentary democracy had been created and the first elections held, but there was little security outside the capital, Kabul, and the Taliban returned, regularly carrying out attacks against military and civilian targets. The American public began to question their country's involvement and demanded the troops come home. The administration would also make the tactical mistake of fighting a second war in Iraq, drawing troops away from one war zone to another.

Iraq

According to the journalist Bob Woodward, very soon after 9/11 the Secretary of Defense, Donald Rumsfeld was asked by Bush about the status of military planning for a possible invasion of Iraq (Woodward, 2002). Neo-conservatives had consistently argued that Saddam Hussein's replacement by a democratic regime would inspire democratic revolutions throughout the Middle East (Rothkopf, 2005).

Though there had been widespread support for the war in Afghanistan, the invasion of Iraq in March 2003 divided the United Nations, the NATO allies, and the American public. Bush justified action against Iraq on security grounds, arguing that Saddam Hussein was a brutal dictator who abused his own people and threatened stability in the Middle East and beyond. This would be linked to Saddam's alleged development of weapons of mass destruction and his encouragement of terrorism, with the Bush administration making frequent links between Iraq and the 9/11 attacks. Both would prove to be unfounded. Given its large oil reserves, many argued the war was driven by a need to acquire this valuable commodity in an age of growing resource scarcity (America being the world's leader in oil usage).

America's 'shock and awe' tactics guaranteed a swift victory. Initially this enhanced the credibility of American power within the region, and was instrumental in persuading Colonel Gaddafi in Libya to announce that he was abandoning his nuclear proliferation programme, most likely in fear that he would be next. In May 2003 Bush announced that combat missions had ended, but the euphoria proved short-lived. The removal of Saddam would be followed by widespread violence and bloodshed.

Unlike the war in 1990/1 which saw half a million troops remove Saddam Hussein from Kuwait, America only deployed 200,000 to Iraq in 2003, reflecting its confidence in more potent battalions using state-of-the-art technology. However, these troops quickly found themselves trapped in a 'hit and run' war where opposition forces engaged in asymmetrical warfare, much to the frustration of the American commanders. Furthermore, the disbanding of the Iraqi security forces put almost 700,000 unemployed Iraqis on the streets, which helped fuel an insurgency made worse by jihadists from across the Middle East crossing into Iraq. The country descended into a near all-out civil war between Iraq's rival Muslim sects – Shiites and Sunnis. By the end of 2012, 4,000 Americans had been killed and 30,000 wounded. Iraqi casualties included over 100,000 dead, countless thousands injured, and several million made refugees.

For America, the costs of the war were enormous in financial terms. However, the wider costs were much greater. Many suggested that the limits of US power had been exposed. Though arguably it had won the wars in both Afghanistan and Iraq, it had certainly not secured the peace. America found itself increasingly isolated, with an international community opposing the invasion and refusing to finance the subsequent state-building programme. A strategy which had hoped to facilitate US-friendly democracies in the Middle East had, instead, produced a more emboldened Iran. It also marked a new low in relations between the US and the UN, and the Bush doctrine raised fears of open-ended American military operations around the world.

In the US, Bush's pursuit of the "war on terror" led to accusations that his administration had been distracted from other security problems, being unable to stop North Korea's detonation of its first nuclear device in 2006, and failing to act soon enough to tackle growing concerns regarding Iran's ongoing enrichment of nuclear fuel, possibly to develop their own nuclear weapon, raising fears of an arms race in the Middle East. Moreover, America's non-proliferation agenda was accused of hypocrisy as it continued to support Israel, which already had weapons of mass destruction, and had signed an agreement to trade in nuclear technology with India.

The Bush years also saw a resurgence of Russian nationalism under Vladimir Putin, who, in a stark warning, challenged America's claim to unipolarity in a speech in Munich in 2007. Indeed, Putin forcefully pursued an agenda that placed Russia as an active contradictory player to America. Russia opposed the invasion of Iraq, and increasingly threatened the developing democracies of Ukraine and Georgia which had expressed an interest in joining NATO. Russia also weakened American resolutions in the UN Security Council regarding Iran and North Korea, and opposed the installation of the National Missile Defence System. Meanwhile in Latin America, a region that America regarded as its backyard, anti-Americanism grew, led by the formidable and well-resourced Hugo Chávez of Venezuela.

To make matters worse, America's credibility plummeted as Bush enforced a set of practices that Stephen Walt described as being 'normally associated with brutal military dictatorships' (Walt, 2010). This included 'the systematic use of torture, the suspension of habeas corpus, secret renditions of suspected terrorists, targeted assassinations, and indefinite detention without trial at Guantanamo and other overseas facilities'. To this could be added the PATRIOT act, the controversial extension of the National Security Agency responsibilities exposed by Edward Snowden, and establishing military tribunals to try suspected terrorists without due process. All were justified by the administration as key to securing the safety of America's borders, something many questioned.

The Bush legacy

The presidency of George W. Bush remains one of the most controversial in recent American history. However, Melvyn Leffler (2004) argued that the Bush administration actually represented continuity, rather than discontinuity, with regard to America's foreign policy traditions. He suggested that pre-emptive war was not unusual, and that the administration's commitment to promote democracy overseas reflected America's belief in its own exceptionalism.

Bush himself believed that his policies had been successful, noting that there were no further successful terrorist attacks on the US on his watch after 9/11. He had also sought to develop relationships with India, accepting its regional importance as a counterweight to China and as a global economic power, and increased the aid budget to Africa well beyond any limits reached by the Clinton administration. More difficult to back up is the assertion made by some Bush supporters that there is a direct link between the fall of Saddam Hussein and the pro-democracy movements of the Arab Spring that began in 2011.

Perhaps the most influential assessment of Bush's foreign policy came from the American academic Joseph Nye, who argued that during the Bush years the aggressive use of hard power in Iraq was matched by a decline in America's soft power as the situation deteriorated and many feared that America was seeking to export its values by force. In effect, Bush squandered the boost in America's soft power generated in the wake of 9/11, damaging America's international standing (Nye, 2011).

The foreign policy of Barack Obama

Like Bush, Obama lacked foreign policy experience, but where Bush received from Clinton a country at peace with the world and with a budget in surplus for the first time since 1969, Obama became president at an extraordinarily difficult moment, inheriting two unpopular wars (in Iraq and Afghanistan), a broader war against terror, and an economy in decline.

From the outset, Obama sought to pursue a more discriminating foreign policy, suggesting that America had overextended itself in Iraq and Afghanistan, and fighting a more general war against terrorism, which had resulted in it neglecting other significant security issues including economic security, nuclear proliferation, climate change and cyber warfare. America, he argued, needed to reduce its overseas commitments while avoiding the open-ended interventions of the Bush era (NSS, 2010).

This suggested a more multilateralist position than Bush, stressing the importance of global institutions and emphasising America's role in promoting democratic values in a multipolar world, rather than relying on pre-emptive war. Diplomacy would be a crucial component of this new agenda, and would involve reaching beyond traditional allies in Europe to embrace the new security and economic challenges posed by globalisation.

Obama sought to prioritise relations with rising powers, such as China, India, Russia and Brazil, adopting a strategy of setting aside smaller issues as a bargaining chip to cooperate on bigger ones. A controversial example of this was his decision to downplay human rights during his initial dealings with China. He also made it clear that a major goal would be to develop stronger links, economically and politically, with countries in the Asia-Pacific region. This became known as the 'Asian Pivot', and reflected a growing view among many analysts, such as Niall Ferguson (2011) and Joseph Nye (2011), that economic and political power was shifting from the West to the Asia-Pacific region. The Pivot was also a badly-disguised attempt to develop relations with countries in the region as a counterbalance to the emerging power of China.

Obama also attempted to rebuild relations with Islamic countries, rejecting Samuel Huntington's claim that a clash of civilisations would happen between the Christian and Islamic worlds. In his first year in office he gave a landmark speech in Cairo, making it clear that America's relationship with the Muslim world would be based on mutual interest and respect. Though dialogue is clearly important, Obama has not shied away from the use of force. This is most graphically seen in the continued targeting of al-Qaeda members by drones in Pakistan, Yemen and elsewhere, and the dramatic death of Osama bin Laden at the hands of US Navy Seals in May 2011.

However, Obama has also stressed that 'our power alone cannot protect us, nor does it entitle us to do as we please' (Obama, 2009). There is what Hilary Clinton called the application of 'smart power' – a greater reliance on soft power (unlike Bush), but with the contingent use of hard power when necessary (Clinton, 2009). First put forward by Joseph Nye (2004) and Suzanne Nossel (2004), smart power is evident in many areas of Obama's foreign policy. A good example was his approach to Iran's nuclear ambitions, where Obama built an international coalition willing to engage in a mix of constructive dialogue and tough sanctions to persuade Iran to limit its nuclear programme as part of a wider agenda designed to secure peace in the Middle East.

Simultaneously, he has not ignored America's traditional relationships. After the souring of the Bush years, Obama sought to reset relations with Russia. A new Strategic Arms Reduction Treaty was signed in 2010, significantly cutting the nuclear arsenals of both countries, and Obama announced that he would be abandoning the National Missile Defence System as envisaged by Bush – although a scaled-down version will be developed, it will be open to inspection by Russia. However, these positive developments were put at risk when Russia reasserted its regional power by annexing Crimea in 2014, in the wake of a newly emboldened President Putin having gained the upper hand in Syria after Obama and the American Congress stumbled over taking action when chemical weapons had been used. Though the relationship has not returned to a Cold War scenario, it has clearly chilled.

The relationship with China is equally unclear. Obama has sought to establish a new 'US–China Strategic and Economic Dialogue' reflecting the administration's awareness of the challenges China represents, both politically and economically. In the long term, however, many regard China as America's biggest threat as it continues to develop an international portfolio of client states in Africa, Latin America and the Middle East, while simultaneously expanding its military and economic powers. It is also unclear as to whether India will allow itself to be used as a counter-balance to Chinese influence in the region.

With regard to Iraq, Obama was a critic of the invasion from the very beginning. He achieved his pledge to end combat missions by 31 August 2010, and by the end of 2011 all American troops had left the country. In June 2014 the legacy of the invasion became apparent when the Sunni jihadist group the Islamic State in Iraq and the Levant (ISIS) attempted to take control of much of Iraq. The violence that ensued forced the Obama administration to send special advisors to the country to protect American interests there. Such were the concerns about the crisis spreading into surrounding states in the region that the Americans took the dramatic step of entering into talks with the Iranian government about how best to contain ISIS forces.

In Afghanistan, Obama has reshaped policy from the goals of spreading democracy and promoting human rights to a military mission which is now solely committed to providing security in the region with a view to American troops eventually leaving. This approach is complicated by Pakistan, a nuclear-weapons state whose security services have links to the Taliban and which many suggest supports members of al-Qaeda. It is difficult to see how America can withdraw without some form of compromise allowing a degree of Taliban control, particularly as American attempts to train up Afghanistan's own military and security forces have not been as successful as they would have liked. Many fear that the security failures experienced in Iraq once American troops had left will be repeated in Afghanistan.

The war on terror has also left a difficult problem in that on becoming president, Obama distanced himself from the abuses of the Bush administration by ordering the closure of the prison at Guantanamo Bay, a review of detention and interrogation policy, and prohibiting the use of torture. Frustratingly for Obama, Guantanamo Bay remains open, in part due to the reluctance of other countries to take any of the prisoners, or a fear that if they are repatriated they might be released. Furthermore, though Obama could claim a victory against terrorism when Osama bin Laden was killed in May 2012, the celebrations proved short-lived when Islamic militants attacked the US consulate in Benghazi, Libya four months later, killing the US Ambassador and three other Americans.

What is clear is that, long term, Obama wants to scale down America's commitments overseas to focus on domestic reforms at home. His instinct is to reduce and move away from 'out-dated Cold War systems', preferring disarmament agreements to military build-ups (Obama, 2012). This approach is evident in his handling of the Arab Spring. One adviser described the President's actions in Libya as 'leading from behind', but it reflects Obama's reluctance to commit America to another war, and his desire to avoid any further damage to America's standing in the Muslim and Arab world (Lizza, 2011).

It is also driven by economic necessity. The financial economic collapse of 2008 exacerbated the enormous deficits Obama inherited from Bush, such that the Chairman of the Joint Chiefs of Staff, Michael Mullen, identified the national debt as the single largest threat to US security. This was starkly highlighted at the beginning of 2012 when it was announced that the following decade would see the Pentagon's military budget cut by $487 billion. Ultimately Obama is seeking a world in which security burdens are shared, rather than America having unilateral commitments. Within this the United States would still remain the dominant power, but with fewer demands on its resources and a reduction in the dangers of being drawn into a new military conflict.

Perhaps the clearest statement of this was when Obama gave his address at West Point Military Academy in 2014, when he made it clear that it was not a question of whether America would lead, but how it would lead. For Obama, military solutions should not be the only tool in the box; he declared, 'Just because we have the best hammer does not mean that every problem is a nail' (Obama, 2014). Instead, he proposed a new foreign policy doctrine focused on soft power diplomacy and launching financial grants to fight terrorism through international partnerships. For many Americans, however, this felt like retrenchment – an America seeking to scale back its global responsibilities after a decade of war, with little sense of where the country goes next.

The future of American power

In February 1941 Henry Luce, the publisher of *Time* magazine, famously wrote that the twentieth century would be 'America's century'. As the twenty-first century began the magazine suggested the current century would be the same, reflecting America's victory in the Cold War and the rapid spread of liberal capitalism throughout the world. America, it argued, was at peace with the world, and its economy was prospering.

The events of 11 September, 2001, the failure in Afghanistan and Iraq, and the economic collapse of 2008 appeared to shatter America's unipolar moment before it really got going. By 2004, America's National Intelligence Council was describing a future in which America would not be the dominant power, but simply a strong power among many, as the empowerment of individuals and the diffusion of power among states and from states to informal networks would result in a shift away from dominance by the United States and the West (National Intelligence Council, 2004, 2008 and 2012).

Many analysts suggest that China poses the most significant security challenge to the US. Its rapidly expanding economy and international ambitions have seen it develop strong links with a growing number of emerging economies around the world. What is notable about this is that China and the emerging powers often have foreign policy preferences at odds with the US; in particular, China does not consider liberal capitalism or democracy promotion to be an important part of its foreign policy, in contrast with America's post-Cold War mission. More worryingly for America, perhaps, is China's intention to develop its military forces, not least its navy, as it seeks to assert itself as a regional power.

As Fareed Zakaria notes, however, fears of America's, and the West's, decline may be misjudged – it might be that everyone else is rising (Zakaria, 2009). Indeed, Richard Haass believes the world has entered an era of 'non-polarity' or 'apolarity', with globalisation forcing an era of interdependence, particularly as America experiences chronic fiscal deficits and military overstretch (Haass, 2008). It is unlikely that any other power will be able to challenge the power of the United States, even China, in the short term. America still has most of the world's largest companies, many of the leading universities, and militarily it remains the strongest force in the world – by some considerable distance. As a result, suggests John Ikenberry, 'In this new age of international order, the United States will not be able to rule. But it can still lead' (Ikenberry, 2011b). It will remain what Josef Joffe defines as the world's 'default power' (Joffe, 2009).

Conclusion

America's security concerns have changed since the end of the Cold War. The simple containment and deterrence of Communism was initially replaced by a desire to ensure America remained at the forefront of globalisation in the 1990s through an approach that combined economic security with the search for peace through democratic expansion. The attacks of 9/11 reshaped the agenda, placing terrorism at the top and enabling the Bush administration to pursue an aggressive doctrine of pre-emption and military expansion that saw it take the fight to the enemy in Afghanistan and Iraq, while fighting a broader war on terror. Many argue that in doing so Bush failed to engage fully with an increasing number of complex security concerns that included the rise of China, the re-emergence of Russia as a regional power, and the broader shift of power from the West to the Asia-Pacific region, resource scarcity, nuclear proliferation, climate change, and cyber warfare. President Obama has sought to readjust America's foreign policy to address this growing list of problems, but, as Joseph Nye concludes, 'The problem of American power in the twenty-first century … is not one of decline but what to do in light of the realization that even the largest country cannot achieve the outcomes it wants without the help of others' (Nye, 2010: 12). In the end America's security may depend on working with others rather than against them.

Recommended reading

Foreign Affairs at www.foreignaffairs.org.

Foreign Policy at www.foreignpolicy.com

The Washington Quarterly at www.twq.com.

Ikenberry, G.J. *American Foreign Policy: Theoretical Essays*, 6th Edition, Boston: Wadsworth, 2011.

Jentleson, B. *American Foreign Policy: The Dynamics of Choice in the 21st Century*, 5th Edition, New York: W.W. Norton, 2014.

Kupchan, C. *No One's World: The West, the Rising Rest, and the Coming Global Turn*, New York: Oxford University Press, 2012.

Nye, J. *The Future of Power*, New York: Public Affairs, 2011.

24 Russia, the Black Sea region and security

Tunç Aybak

Box 24.1: New Cold War?

The Georgian war of 2008 and the subsequent crisis in 2014 between Ukraine and Russia provoked security concerns about whether Russia and the West are heading towards a new Cold War. In 2014 the Russian Prime Minister Dimitriy Medvedev, bristling at Western criticism and sanctions levelled at his country for the annexation of Crimea from Ukraine, echoed sentiments widely expressed in the West in stating: 'we are slowly but surely moving toward a Second Cold War' (Bloomberg TV, 19 May 2014).

Introduction

To fully grasp these developments in Russia's foreign and security policy in the Black Sea region and towards the West, it is necessary to understand these conflicts not as minor skirmishes but as a geopolitical shift in the post-Cold War order in Europe. The 2008 conflict in the Southern Caucasus was the first war that Russia had waged outside its legitimate borders since the disintegration of the Soviet Union. In fact, the invasion of Georgia undermined the post-Cold War order in Europe with serious implications for territoriality and sovereignty in the wider Black Sea region and beyond. The Russian advance confirmed that its sphere of influence now directly bordered the expanded 'Western neighbourhood' which is located in the wider Black Sea region.

In this context the 2014 crisis between Ukraine and Russia over Crimea was the culmination of a series of events and changes in the security perceptions of Russian foreign policy with regard to the West. The conflict in Georgia and the annexation of Crimea must be assessed against the background of competing perceptions and discursive strategies that have been shaping and informing the thinking of Russian state elites regarding the geopolitics of greater Europe and Russia's geopolitical place under the Putin regime.

From marginality to the centre

The Russian presence in Europe has always been a dominant one, but this dominance has not always been stable and secure. Russia has had a self-contained Eurasian empire for nearly five hundred years, and the sudden break-up of the Soviet Union in 1991 had a deep impact on their state and society. Since the disintegration of the Soviet Union, Russian state elites have been adjusting themselves to post-Cold War realities. In the 1990s the Clinton administration made successful inroads into the post-Soviet space while his Russian presidential counterpart, Boris Yeltsin, was far too preoccupied with domestic troubles and a bitter, costly, ongoing war in Chechnya to match his moves. While the state elites in Russia struggled to manage the marginalisation of Russia in the international politics of Europe, the Yeltsin era failed to produce consistent and coherent foreign policy objectives to consolidate her international standing. Combined with the deepening and widening process of the EU, the economic and military influence of the West has continued to increase in the immediate neighbourhood of Russia. It was also clear that senior Russian officials were becoming concerned about the growing presence of NATO and the extension of the European integration project into the Black Sea area on their western frontier. On the other hand, the Russians were incapable of reversing the projection of Euro-Atlantic presence in their backyard. The financial crisis of 1998 was a final blow to Russia's international standing. The construction of new western pipeline projects connecting the Caspian energy resources to the west via the BTC pipeline and the eastwards extension of NATO's military facilities seriously undermined Russia's geopolitical sphere of influence. For the state elites and societies in Russia, the 1990s were the years of economic decline and political marginalisation.

The key turning point in Russia's relationship with the West was Moscow's assertive reaction to NATO's war in Kosovo in 1999, which raised concerns that she might start restoring her influence in the 'near abroad'. At a critical moment, on 31 December 1999, Vladimir Putin was appointed President by Yeltsin, and in 2000 he was elected to a full four-year term in office. Boris Yeltsin's chaotic nine-year rule ended with the emergence of an as-then virtually unknown technocrat and ex-KGB officer. Putin's gradual ascendance in power reached its zenith in 2005, during his second term as President, when he openly expressed his nostalgia for the Soviet Union during the celebration of the sixtieth anniversary of the Great Patriotic War. In his speech, he referred to the disintegration of the Soviet Union as the 'greatest geopolitical catastrophe of the twentieth century'. While avoiding open and direct confrontation with the West, Putin's popularity at home grew as he appealed to the people of Russia, who felt that Russia and Russians had been treated badly and humiliated by the West during the Yeltsin period. The key goal of Putin has been to restore Russia's position on an equal footing with the West as a 'normal power' and reverse the humiliations of the 1990s. It is misleading to apply epithets like 'empire' and 'empire building', as Putin's critics do. This suggests taking direct responsibility and assuming formal control of other nations' territories. Overall, Russia has refrained from directly interfering in the territorial sovereignty of the newly independent states of Eurasia. The military intervention in Georgia was an exception to this rule, which may be seen as an extraordinary reaction to extraordinary circumstances. In general, the Russians have relied on diplomatic means, energy diplomacy and soft power.

Indeed, Putin's speech in February 2007 at a security conference in Munich was a clear signal of Russia's determination to return to, in Trenin's words, 'the traditional status of an independent player on the international stage, unencumbered by any relationship "of complex subordination" to the west' (Trenin, 2006). Post Cold War hopes of integrating Russia into the West have been abandoned as Russia increasingly re-emerges as a key factor in Eurasian politics. In his speech at the Munich International Conference on Security in February 2007 Putin openly criticised the expansion of the Euro-Atlantic institutions into its western neighbourhood, stating:

'NATO has put its frontline forces on our borders. It does not have any relation with the modernisation of the Alliance itself or with ensuring security in Europe. On the contrary, it represents a serious provocation that reduces the level of mutual trust. And we have a right to ask: against whom is this expansion intended? And what happened to the assurances our western partners made after the dissolution of the Warsaw Pact?' (Putin, 2007). In the eyes of the Russian strategic elites these were seen as violations of the guarantees made by NATO states and in the NATO–Russia founding act of 1997. Fifteen months after Putin's speech and two months before the Russian invasion of Georgia, the newly-elected President Medvedev in a speech in Berlin openly criticised NATO and the Organisation for Security and Cooperation in Europe (OSCE), arguing that 'The end of the Cold War made it possible to build up genuinely equal cooperation between Russia, the European Union, and North America as three branches of European civilization. It is my conviction that Atlanticism as a sole historical principle has already had its day. We need to talk today about unity between the whole Euro-Atlantic area from Vancouver to Vladivostok. Life itself dictates the need for this kind of cooperation'. He also warned against 'marginalising and isolating countries, creating zones with differentiated levels of security' (Medvedev, 2008).

The Kremlin has repeatedly argued that the current post-Cold War security architecture is not working. Apart from proving unable to prevent the August 2008 war in South Ossetia, the post-Cold War European security architecture's failures as seen by the Russian leadership also include: NATO's eastward expansion; the bombing of then-Yugoslavia by NATO in 1999; US plans to deploy ballistic missile systems in Eastern Europe; the demise of the adapted Conventional Forces in Europe treaty; and the declaration and recognition of Kosovo's independence in 2008. The 'Medvedev doctrine' actually reflected the underpinnings of an evolving cluster ideology and geopolitical perceptions of what can be possibly called 'Putinism'. For these reasons, Medvedev's declared foreign policy principles cannot be seen as a knee-jerk reaction to a single event, but as carefully designed Russian geopolitical statecraft consisting of a set of principles and discursive practices that has developed over the last twenty years. The basic principles of Russian foreign policy have been consistent: Russia as the guarantor of the rights of the Russian-speaking people; the use of force to protect Russian-speaking communities and Russian unity; and recognition of the sovereignty and territorial independence of the post-Soviet states only on the basis of good neighbourly relations with Russia. In March 2012, Vladimir Putin was elected as President for the third time. Since then he has been refining his doctrine of Russia as a civilisation at the centre of the Russian world. Unlike the previous documents, the new Russian Foreign Policy Document, released in 2013, pronounced the ideological principles of Putin's doctrine more strongly. While the 2008 concept noted the steady overcoming of the Cold War legacy and the 'end of the ideological era', the emphasis in the 2013 concept is on the 'civilisational diversity' and ideological differences between Russia and the West (Russia, 2013).

Frozen conflicts in the Black Sea region

The Black Sea has long played a central and strategic role in Russia's history and identity. During the Cold War the Black Sea region was simply a frontline region between NATO and the Warsaw Pact military alliances and the competing ideological blocs of the Atlantic countries and the Soviet Union. This was a region where relations between East and West were frozen and the territorial borders and membership of regional organisations were defined on ideological lines between two competing models of free market capitalism and socialist command economies.

With the disintegration of the Soviet Union, the Russian Federation's presence in the Black Sea diminished substantially. Russia had to share the common Soviet borders with the other independent Black Sea states. The Black Sea coastline inherited by the Russian Federation was reduced to 30% of its former length. Russia has also lost crucial port cities and major coastal centres. The era when the Russian Empire and the Soviet Union controlled the entire northern and north-eastern part of the Black Sea coast had come to an end. Several geopolitical developments in the Black Sea area have substantially changed the context of Russian foreign policy. In particular, the extension of NATO's military framework to Bulgaria and Romania and beyond in varying degrees of institutional and bilateral links and the following enlargement of the EU brought the Euro-Atlantic institutions to the shores of the western Black Sea.

In the context of the Black Sea region, Russia's geopolitical 'privileged interests' can be identified with particular reference to its historical, cultural, political and militaristic ties. The South Caucasus as a sub-region has traditionally been Russia's 'troubled' southern frontier, which is closely connected to developments in the North Caucasus. Historically speaking, the Greater Caucasus region located between the Black and Caspian Seas has played an important role in the historical formation of the Russian identity. The Russian Empire and the Soviet Union acted in this sub-region as the agents of modernisation and progress. It is in the Caucasus where the clash of civilisations thesis was put to the test in terms of the Russian Empire and Islam. The Caucasus has been the permanent frontier of Russian identity. In his annual 2005 annual address Putin declared that 'Russia should continue its civilising mission on the Eurasian continent'.

Following the disintegration of the Soviet Union, strong ethnic identities and nationalist forces emerged from the control of the titular Soviet nationalities system. The combination of weak statehood and strong ethnic and national identities generated a conducive environment for conflict and manipulation by regional and extra-regional powers. The systemic transition has been a highly uneven and incomplete process. The situation remains largely the same today since the states in the Caucasus are still trapped between zones and different trajectories and models of modernity.

Russia has been trying to maintain its military, political and economic presence in the independent states of the South Caucasus (Armenia and Azerbaijan) while trying to contain the Chechen uprising of the North Caucasus within its borders. As the independent states in the South Caucasus increasingly looked to the EU and NATO for their national development and modernisation, the main Russian concern remained how to restrain the extending military and political influence of the Euro-Atlantic institutions, while officially recognising the territorial integrity of the Commonwealth of Independent States (CIS). However, Russia has increasingly become more assertive and supportive of the self-declared de facto separatist states: the Pridnestrovyan Moldovan Republic (Transnistria) inside Moldovan borders, the Republic of South Ossetia and the Republic of Abkhazia within Georgian borders, and the Nagorno-Karabakh Republic of Azerbaijan. Russian counter-measures have included political, economic and diplomatic support, state-building assistance, maintaining the status quo, making use of the 'Kosovo precedent' and taking over some of the institutions of the secessionist entities. In fact, Putin's second term has marked the end of Russia's declining influence and the beginning of the re-assertion of its great power status by exerting its economic, political dominance in its near-abroad.

Beyond the Caucasus sub-region, Russia is still able to exert her influence across the Black Sea. Prior to the peninsular's annexation in 2014 the Russian naval presence in Crimea, through its contractual ties with Ukraine, was of great symbolic significance to the Russians, demonstrating that despite a diminishing coastal border she was still a Black Sea power. So the domestic developments in Ukraine, and in Georgia for that matter, are directly related to Russia's regional power status and its Black Sea identity.

More importantly, since the end of the Cold War the Black Sea's importance as an energy transport corridor has increased significantly. As Russia's oil and gas exports and its wealth grew exponentially, the construction of new pipelines across and around the Black Sea turned the region into a new corridor of energy transportation. For the Russian Federation energy has gradually become a new foreign policy instrument, alongside its military muscle. However, it would be too simplistic to reduce the geopolitics of the Black Sea to energy issues and pipeline politics because there are other issues underlying the nature of discord in this region.

Sovereign democracy

The crisis in Georgia shook the foundations of the bilateral strategic partnership between the EU and the Russian Federation. As one Brussels-based senior analyst put it, 'the small war between Georgia and Russia from 8 to 22 August 2008 has shattered any remaining illusions over the frontiers of the normative map of Europe. This was Europe's first war of the twenty-first century, which has seen Russia acting in line with the European realpolitik models of the nineteenth and early twentieth centuries' (Emerson, 2008). However, the sources of the bilateral crisis of confidence between Russia and the EU can be traced back to Russia's reaction to earlier events around the Black Sea. The so-called coloured revolutions in Ukraine and Georgia in the mid-2000s posed serious challenges to the post-Cold War order in the Black Sea region and beyond. Its transformative impact was felt not only in international politics but at the very heart of the Kremlin's political establishment. One of the key consequences of the coloured revolutions was the re-conceptualisation and re-evaluation of Russia's specific place and status in Europe. On the other hand, it would be too simplistic to reduce Russian conduct to the basics of 'realpolitik' as demonstrated in Georgia. Indeed, under Putin's leadership Russia's foreign policy increasingly became more normative. Russian foreign policy is conducted not only according to Realist pragmatism, but also by a set of values and practices in what Makarychev calls Russia's 'normative offensive' as a soft power. The normative elements of Russian foreign policy, Makarychev argues, stem from two sources: a set of ideas as opposed to material interests; and multilateralism as opposed to unilateralism. The normative discursive strategies and concepts developed under Putin's leadership aim to arrest Russia's marginalisation and carve an authentic inclusive identity in the new European order, rather than challenging the foundations and the basic principles of the post-Cold War order (Makarychev, 2008).

The coloured revolutions in Ukraine and Georgia had a deep transformative impact on Russia's self-perception as a great power. Russia's main concerns were to prevent the rise of anti-Russian neighbouring regimes in its Black Sea neighbourhood, and block the projection of another coloured revolution into Russia. As Krastev observed in the aftermath of the Orange Revolution in Ukraine, 'the major objective of the Russian policy was to introduce an efficient infrastructure of ideas, institutions, networks and media outlets that can use the predictable crisis of the current orange-type regimes to regain influence not simply at the level of government but at the level of society as well. Russia will not fight democracy in these countries. Russia will fight for democracy – its kind of democracy' (Krastev, 2005). Underpinning this is the key concept that was invented in the Kremlin as a response to the coloured 'revolutions' backed by the West: 'sovereign democracy'. In a seminal article, Krastev argues that the 'sovereign democracy' project does not mean separation from Europe, but an attempt to become 'the other Europe'. The concept of sovereign democracy which was constructed by Surkov, Putin's senior adviser, has been inspired by the anti-populism of the nineteenth-century French political thinker Francois Guizot and the anti-pluralism of the German political philosopher Carl Schmitt. In Surkov's words: 'I often hear that democracy is more important than sovereignty. We do not admit it, we think we need both. An independent state is worth fighting for, it would be good to flee Europe but they will not receive us there. Russia is a European civilization. It is a badly illuminated remote area of Europe but not Europe yet. In this regard we are inseparably tied with Europe and must be friends with it; they are not "enemies". They are simply competitors. So it is more insulting that we are not "enemies". To lose in a competitive struggle means to be a loser. And this is doubly insulting. It is better to be "enemies" and not competitive friends as is the case now' (Svetlichnaja and Heartfield, 2010).

In the eyes of the Russian political establishment the state is the ultimate expression of the society and the institutions of Russia (Makarychev, 2008). In Putin's Russia, the state extends deep into society. In his speeches Putin often stated that strong civil society will not flourish unless the state initiates it. Civil society is seen as the basis of unity among all sections of society, as opposed to divergent values and pluralistic interests. During the parliamentary elections in 2007 Putin openly attacked the critics of the Russian regime. Given the active role of civil society organisations during the Orange Revolution in Ukraine, Putin's administration and the political establishment around him grew increasingly more suspicious of the activities of the civil society associations sponsored by Western governments. As Shlapentokh argues, 'the emergence of the foreign threat to the regime as a major political and ideological issue in Moscow was deeply influenced by political developments in Ukraine in 2004'. The perception that the same methods used in Ukraine might be employed to weaken the regime in Russia was a real concern for Putin (Shlapentokh, 2007). While civil society associations, NGOs and social movements sponsored and endorsed by the West were seen as the extension of the influence of foreign agents and governments, the formation of civil society in Russia is intrinsically different from the trajectory of Western civil societies. In Russia civil society is inherently statist in its direction, where society completes the state rather than diminishing it.

This Russian sovereignty stands in opposition to the post-modern understandings of European governmentality. Russia's path to modern sovereignty differs fundamentally from European modernity. According to Neumann the new rationality of governing that developed in Europe, which began in the sixteenth century and which Foucault refers to as governmentality in terms of the emergence of new Eurocentric standards of liberal and civilised society, has been particularly problematic in the history of

Russia's alternative modernisation. In Neumann's words, the tradition of a strong state as the basis of the system of governance hampered Russia's quest for equity with Europe (Neumann, 2008). The Russian state exercises sovereignty in the name of and through Russian society. Neumann also concludes that 'as long as Russia's rationality of government derives from present-day hegemonic neo-liberal models by favouring direct state rule rather than indirect governance, the West will not recognize Russia as a fully fledged great power' (Neumann, 2008: 151). However, it is this Russian quest for equity and authenticity that lies precisely at the core of the concept of 'sovereign democracy'. Sovereign democracy implies that Russia is unwilling to accept either Western criticism or hegemony and wants to be treated as part of the international society on an equal footing. Even though both Putin and Medvedev avoid using the concept of sovereign democracy explicitly in public, its discursive significance in underlying the mindset of the Russian elites cannot be overestimated.

Eurasianism versus Atlanticisim

If the sovereign democracy discourse is Russia's alternative to the enlargement of the post-modern and post-Westphalian European political order, the rise of Eurasianism is another discursive strategy to challenge the Euro-Atlantic ordering of the post-Soviet Eurasian space. Following the demise of the Soviet Union, old geopolitical visions have returned. Eurasianism as a geopolitical discourse has been gaining influence since the mid-1990s in its various forms and directions. Eurasianism in a sense is a civilisational vision as a solution to Russia's identity crisis following the disintegration of the Soviet Union (Tsygankov, 2007). Eurasianism takes different meanings in different contexts and derives its inspiration from diverse sources in Russian history. In her book on Eurasianism, Laurelle gives a comprehensive and authoritative definition of Eurasianism: 'Eurasianist terminology suggests that Russia and its "margins" occupy a dual and median position between Europe and Asia, that their specific traits have to do with their culture being a mix born of the fusion of Slavic and Turko-Muslim peoples, and that Russia should highlight its Asian features. Eurasianism thus conflates the centre and the middle. It rejects the view that Russia is on the periphery of Europe, and on the contrary it interprets the country's geographic position as grounds for choosing a messianic "third way"' (Laurelle, 2008). This is Russian 'exceptionalism' par excellence, offering a model between market and state and between Asia and Europe. In this sense, the frontiers of Eurasia both include and exclude the fuzzy borders of the wider Europe. Eurasianism in this sense departs from the Eurocentric modernisation project with its emphasis on social justice and egalitarianism between the nations and restoring lost national dignity. In this broader sense, Eurasianism is the product of Russian modernity heavily borrowing from and mixing the ingredients of other ideological trends in Russian history.

Since the beginning of the 2000s, according to Laurelle, Eurasianism has become a highly diversified and influential concept in political imagination in Russian intellectual circles and statecraft. For example, in 2003 Tsygankov argued that rather than perceiving Eurasianism as a singular homogenised discourse in the geopolitical imagination of Russian state and society, it would be more meaningful to see it as a highly diverse discourse of discursive strategies consisting of several intellectual strands and schools varying from West-friendly, geo-economical versions to those that are highly isolationist and expansionist (Tsygankov, 2003).

Post-Soviet regionalism confronts European integration

Another key driver behind Russia's Eurasianist strategy was to re-integrate the post-Soviet states and economies within the framework of Eurasian regional organisations. In 1991, Russia established the Commonwealth of Independent States to sustain its legacy in the post-Soviet Eurasia. Among other things, as an alternative to the Western election monitors, the CIS introduced its own election monitoring process to counterbalance intervention in the democratic processes in CIS countries following the coloured revolutions in Ukraine and Georgia. However, the CIS has failed to serve Russia's long-term interests as several members have formed their own regional organisations seeking to join the EU and NATO, while others have left the organisation altogether. Following the Russian intervention, Georgia left the CIS and Ukraine never signed the charter from the very beginning. For Russia, the CIS summits were disappointing as attendance by high representatives has been poor.

In order to re-assert its weakening influence, Russia adopted a strategy to include the willing post-Soviet states of Belarus, Armenia, Uzbekistan, Kyrgyzstan and Tajikistan within the Collective Security Treaty Organisation, the institutionalised version of the CIS Collective Security Treaty. From the very beginning, Russia used the CSTO as a security alliance of the post-Soviet countries to counterbalance NATO's expansion and influence and as a response to Georgia's and Ukraine's interest in joining NATO. In addition to the CSTO, Russia played an active role in the Shanghai Cooperation Organisation (SCO), which also included four Central Asian states plus the influential Eurasian player, China. The SCO legitimises the involvement of China in the post-Soviet space, even though some Russian and Central Asian states are wary of China's regional motivations. While the CSTO and the SCO are essentially regional organisations whose mandates focus on security and defence related issues, Russia's recent initiative to introduce the Eurasian Customs Union (consisting of Russia, Belarus, Kazakhstan and the newest member, Armenia) to the post-Soviet space is in direct response to the European Union's influence in its own neighbourhood.

In general, Russia's state-driven Eurasian regional economic integration project must be seen as an alternative to the market-based policies of Western neo-liberal globalisation and a response to the detrimental impact of globalisation on the societies of the CIS. The proposed Eurasian Union is not an alternative to the capitalist world economy, but rather an integral part of Russia's strategic vision to offer an alternative soft landing in the world economy. Its timing is meaningful in the sense that the proposal for the Union followed Russia's full membership of the WTO. In this context, Armenia's declaration of intent to join the Eurasian Customs Union over the Association Agreement within the framework of the EU's Eastern Partnership initiative was a boost to the Eurasian Union. However, following the November 2013 Eastern Partnership summit in Vilnius, the protests in Ukraine prompted an escalation of Putin's strategic vision for Eurasian economic integration. Thus the case of Ukraine is worth assessing in its own context.

The Ukrainian crisis

In November 2013, the Ukrainian government declared that it had suspended its preparations for signing an Association Agreement and Comprehensive Trade Agreement with the EU. In its statement, the Ukrainian government justified its decision in terms of 'reasons of national security', as well as to improve its trade relations with Russia and the CIS countries. In December 2013 President Yanukovych instead signed a deal with Putin to reduce gas import prices. For Ukraine, the Russian deal seemed to offer a much more attractive financial incentive than what the EU could offer, particularly since no conditionality was attached to it. In fact, the dilemma of whether to join the Eurasian Economic Union or sign an association agreement with the EU revealed deep societal divisions between the pro-EU western and the pro-Russian eastern regions of Ukraine. In fact, the deal with Russia sparked mass protests in the western cities of Ukraine, and then similar reactions against the pro-Western agreement from the Russian-speaking minorities in eastern Ukraine. The stark choice between oligarchic structures faced by the Ukrainian people is not promising for the future of democracy in the Black Sea region.

Even though the annexation of Crimea, where the majority of the population are Russian, was a key strategic victory for Russia, in the long run the possible Balkanisation of Ukraine will have ramifications for stability in the Black Sea region and beyond. Ukraine has always had a special place in Russian history and geopolitics. First of all, the presence of the Russian Navy in the Crimean port of Sevastopol, with its extended lease until 2025, was strategically indispensable for Russian access to the Eastern Mediterranean and its naval base in the Syrian port of Tartus. Secondly, Russia has always been concerned with the presence of Russian-speaking populations in Crimea as well as in its eastern regions. As long as Ukraine remained a buffer zone between Russia and Western influence, Moscow tolerated Ukraine's overtures towards membership of NATO and the EU. However, another attempt at regime change against the largely pro-Russian elected government in Ukraine, with the encouragement of outside powers, reminded the Russian decision makers of populist uprisings that were plotting against Russia's privileged interests in its own backyard.

For these reasons, the annexation of Crimea must be seen as a reaction to the changes taking place beyond Russia's political influence. While Russia effectively secured Crimea from Ukraine, it then showed a reluctance to intervene directly in mainland Ukraine and has seemed to be content with the proxy Russian insurgencies in the eastern regions of Ukraine proper. Indeed, the Crimean crisis could not prevent the subsequent Poroshenko government from signing an association agreement with the EU, demonstrating the limits of Russian intervention.

The existence of a Russian-speaking population in the eastern regions of the country provides Russia with additional political leverage to influence Ukraine's domestic politics. Until the Ukrainian crisis the EU and Russia had not been open and direct geopolitical competitors, but in a way the developments revealed the limits of NATO and the EU expansionist ambitions in the Black Sea region. Putin also openly warned that 'if NATO extends its influence to Ukraine, Russia will be pushed out of the Black Sea' (Putin, 2014). The Crimean crisis has confirmed the underlying differences between the West and Russia and drawn red lines in the Black Sea region in the competition between Euro-Atlanticist and Eurasianist visions. The strategically important Crimean peninsula has now been reintegrated into the Russian Federation for the first time since 1954. It did not make a big strategic difference then, as Ukraine was part of the Soviet Union, but the annexation of Crimea has irreversibly altered the context of regional security by making Russia again the most significant Black Sea power.

Conclusion

Is there a new Cold War between Russia and the West? Answering this question is not as clear as it was between 1945 and 1990. The original Cold War was about a clear ideological competition between capitalist and socialist blocs which took place under a bipolar nuclear balance of power. These sharp and clear-cut ideological and strategic differences are now gone. There are no major differences in terms of economic models. Russia wants to join the global capitalist political economy, but on its own terms, and it offers a more state-centred regionalist strategy as opposed to the market-based models presented by the West. Russia also effectively uses its energy card to influence the outcomes of regional and global processes, but at the same time it is dependent on the demand side of the energy markets and is at the mercy of global markets, unlike in the Soviet era.

Under Putin, Russia has been striving to revive its 'great power status' and to escape from marginalisation. Under Putin's rule, Russia's foreign policy has increasingly emphasised her civilisational identity, which may be characterised as 'Russian exceptionalism', as a way of adapting to the post-Cold War order. Russian foreign and security policy has departed from the bipolarity of the Cold War and resisted US unipolarity. The conditions under which Russian foreign policy operate are very different and much more complex than during the Cold War period. The key challenges Russia now faces are about how to manage complex economic interdependence in the multipolar global political economy while exercising its influence and protecting its existential interests in its immediate neighbourhood.

Recommended Reading

Allison, R., Light, M. and White, S. *Putin's Russia and the Enlarged Europe*, Blackwell: London, 2006.

Laurelle, M. *Russian Eurasianism: An Ideology of Empire*, Baltimore, MD: John Hopkins University Press, 2008.

25 China

Security and threat perceptions

Peter Hough and Shahin Malik

Box 25.1: China's national security strategy

In 2014 the Chinese President Xi Jinping launched a new government agency, the
Central National Security Commission, and in its inaugural speech he listed – in order
of rank – his view of the country's eleven greatest priorities:

- Political security
- Homeland security
- Military security
- Economic security
- Cultural security
- Social security
- Science and technology security
- Information security
- Ecological security
- Resources security
- Nuclear security.

Introduction

The list in the text box above is striking in that it seems to represent a more nuanced
approach to security than customarily seen in the West. Military security is not
considered the ultimate priority, and internal threats are deemed more acute than
external ones. While this new, high-profile trumpeting of China's interests in itself
revealed a more external orientation to her security thinking than in the past, this
was really only a public airing of a long-established comprehensive strategy. China's
sense of security has long differed markedly from the orthodox Western model in
terms of its multi-dimensionality and emphasis on internal rather than external
order. This chapter explores the contemporary significance of this conceptualisation
of security for the Chinese state, its inhabitants and the wider world.

National security

Though never articulated as explicitly in the past, the national security priorities listed
in 2014 are very much part of a long-established tradition of Chinese political thinking,
albeit revamped in line with technological changes. National security for Chinese

governments has always been more multi-faceted and more internally-orientated than for the other great powers. Of course, Realism is not an alien notion to Chinese policy makers, and during the Cold War its national security strategy would have mirrored that of the other great powers – and understandably so, since it would have felt threatened by both the United States and the Soviet Union. However, the changing circumstances at the end of the Cold War and the evolving debates regarding the concept of security have meant that the Realist orientation of the discipline of Security Studies has come under intense scrutiny. The impact on China of the removal of the Soviet threat, its dramatic economic growth as well as increasing connections with the global economy have meant that since the end of the Cold War China has enjoyed a relatively benign international environment. Furthermore, despite the ongoing tensions in Sino-American relations, one can conclude that China does not perceive the United States to be an immediate threat to its security. This is especially the case since the US has remained preoccupied elsewhere, first with the War on Terror, and second with the continuing diplomatic fallout over Russia's annexation of Crimea in March 2014 which has left Ukraine on the verge of civil war. Elsewhere, in the South China Sea, China faces other states (Philippines, Vietnam, Malaysia, Brunei and Taiwan) that are laying claim to the potentially oil-rich seas around the islands of Paracel and Spratly. However, as of June 2014 there has been no military face-off between any of these states, and even in the case of Vietnam, where the greatest level of aggression has been shown, both states have referred their grievances to the United Nations in the hope of avoiding military action.

In addition to these issues, China's relations with Japan have deteriorated in recent years, especially after Japan's nationalisation of the Senkakus – uninhabited islands surrounded by abundant natural gas fields and fishing grounds which were claimed by both states. Particularly worrisome is the possibility that any military clash between the two states is likely to draw the US into the dispute, given its long-standing commitment to Japanese security. This would undoubtedly place the US in an unviable position since China is fast becoming a major economic and military player in the international system. Ultimately, however, China remains an undemocratic state with a regime that does not easily tolerate dissent. Consequently, the focus for the state's security structures are as much on preventing internal unrest as they are on protecting China's borders and interests internationally.

Political security

Preserving the institutions and ideology of the state against internal opposition are acknowledged as the ultimate political priority for Chinese governments, trumping defence against external aggression. This fear of social disorder is not purely a reflection of a Maoist prioritisation of the state and the ruling party over the individual; it has deeper roots in Chinese politics and culture. An ideologically hard-line stance on law and order can be traced as far back as the third century BC, when the thinker and elite adviser Han Fei outlined the influential philosophy of Legalism in response to the perceived weakness of Confucian and Taoist ethics in the 'warring states' era of civil unrest: 'benevolence, righteousness, love and generosity are useless, but severe punishments and dire penalties can keep the state in order' (Armesto, 2003: 146–147). Pre-dating European totalitarianism by two millennia, this state-centric view of security helps to explain the fierceness of the 1989 massacre of

Tiananmen Square protestors and the general intolerance of views within the Party that deviate from the line at the top.

Recent events demonstrate that little has changed since the events of 1989. For instance, a pro-democracy movement (inspired by the Jasmine Revolution in Tunisia) began on 20 February 2011. The objectives of the organisers were primarily political in nature, and called for greater state accountability and transparency. However, a heavy police presence in Beijing and other cities soon put an end to these fledgling protests. We must also question whether China was ever likely to experience the mass movements that took hold in states such as Tunisia or Egypt. The differences between the states are significant in the sense that China was delivering on economic growth, some of which has been filtering down to the masses. Egypt and Tunisia were failing to deliver economic benefits to their citizens. Furthermore, neither Egypt nor Tunisia had a leadership succession system; in the case of Egypt, for instance, Hosni Mubarak ruled for almost thirty years. Although there is only one party in China, leadership succession does take place, whereby a new Paramount Leader is appointed after two five-year terms.

Despite appearances to the contrary, political demonstrations in China are rare, but during recent years there has been an increase in the protests about specific issues whereby citizens have begun to air their grievances by taking to the streets. The types of issues that have led to protests have primarily included police brutality, corruption among officials, land grabs and other local grievances. Indeed, between the years of 2006 and 2010 the number of protests almost doubled to 180,000 'mass incidents' – more than the entire Arab world. However, what is perhaps most surprising is that, despite these protests, China remains far more stable than most Arab states. There are a number of reasons for this, including the fact that most protests appear to be the result of local issues, and often the central authorities yield to complaints. This gives the impression that rather than seeking to overturn the political system, most dissenters appear to want to work within the system and continue to see the Communist Party as the legitimate authority. The protests act as a release, and as long as the Party gives way over what are often minor issues, this has the effect of maintaining stability in the absence of actual democracy. However, one factor has enabled this dissent to remain small in scale and 'within the system', namely real economic growth, but the possibility of such dissent turning revolutionary in the event of a major economic downturn cannot be discounted. Indeed, this is perhaps one reason why China is now spending more of its defence budget on domestic security than on what it perceives to be external threats. In 2013, for instance, the figures stood at 740.6 billion Yuan ($119 billion) on the People's Liberation Army, while the domestic security budget was 769.1 billion Yuan.

Homeland security

China has faced pacifist resistance in Tibet and some violent insurgency in Xinjiang, but on the face of it this seems a limited threat when compared to many other large, ethnically-diverse states such as India or Russia. Nevertheless, the National Security Commission's first meeting aired the view that even domestic insurgents armed with sticks represent a serious threat to the state. Again, an ultra-cautious pursuit of domestic order is apparent. The present insurgency in Xinjiang has its roots in centuries-old political, cultural and religious persecution of the Uighurs (descendents of Turkic-Mongolian tribes from eastern Turkey who migrated eastward in AD 740) at the hands of the majority Chinese. The unrelenting aggression by successive Chinese leaderships provided the Uighurs with a modicum of Western and international support. However, there is also little doubt that current Chinese policy towards the region has allowed al-Qaeda-inspired terrorists to infiltrate the political, social and cultural processes within Xinjiang, and this is resulting in an increasingly violent Uighur insurgency which has greater links to external global organisations such as al-Qaeda. The US-led global War on Terror has further complicated the legitimate desires of the Uighur population to live without persecution. Indeed, it has allowed Chinese authorities to label Uighur groups fighting for equality and greater rights as terrorists, and as a consequence they have been able to intensify their persecution of this population without any repercussions or criticism from the international system.

Another region which has featured prominently in the context of China's human rights record and persecution of minorities is the autonomous region of Tibet. Tibetans claim that they have been colonised by the Chinese, whereas China argues that its sovereignty over the region stretches back centuries. This belief led to the 1950 invasion of Tibet by thousands of Chinese troops, and since then not only has the region been a serious security concern for China, but also many Tibetans have suffered persecution and serious human rights violations. A failed uprising against the Chinese in 1959 led to the exile of the fourteenth Dalai Lama (the spiritual leader of all Tibetans) and the establishment of a 'government in exile' in India, from where he continues to draw the world's attention to the plight of his people. Tibet is clearly a strategic issue for China, and Tibetans are unlikely to achieve independence in the foreseeable future. Tibet lies on China's western frontier, has a long border with the restless Xinjiang province, and also borders India, China's long-time rival in Asia.

Both of these examples highlight serious shortcomings on the part of China's political centres in dealing with its minorities. Despite almost three decades of military and economic advances, many minority groups (numbering around fifty-five) continue to be persecuted and denied the benefits which China's rapid growth have brought to the state. Although such groups total less than 8% of the national population, their location in critical regions along China's periphery means that their stability is crucial in ensuring future economic and energy co-operation with Russia and Central Asian states. Uprisings in Tibet in 2008, in Xinjiang in 2009 and many more elsewhere reflect a general dissatisfaction among these minorities, and at the very least this translates into demands for greater autonomy from the centre, or even outright independence from China. One must also consider this concern with the periphery in the context of Taiwan, where there is convincing evidence to support the premise that China is likely to risk conflict with the United States should Taipei actively seek independence. Indeed, if Taiwan were to gain independence from China, it would be likely to lead to more active attempts by Xinjiang and Tibet to follow suit, thus signalling the end of the Chinese empire – something which the political centre cannot tolerate.

Military security

China is undoubtedly a great military power, but the third-place ranking of this domain of security by the government, while surprising to many in the West, is borne out by some evidence of restraint despite possessing the largest armed forces, as regards numbers, in the world. The Chinese nuclear arsenal remains far behind the US and Russia and must be understood as a minimum deterrent, as in the cases of

France and the UK, rather than a push for global dominance. Similarly, the Korean War of the early 1950s represents China's only external military engagement in modern history, a far less adventurist track record than the other four in the UN's 'Big Five'. However, China has been prepared to bare its teeth in defending its borders and hinterlands, as was seen in the border disputes with the USSR and India that flared up in 1960 and the continuing claims to Taiwan, as well as several island groups in the East China and South China Seas. This defensive Chinese strategy of securing borders is not wholly external. Geopolitical thinking has long stressed the notion of a Han 'island' surrounded by the natural barriers of the Himalayas to the south-west, the wastes of the Gobi desert and Siberia to the north and seas to the east and south-east, thereby keeping foes from Japan, India and Russia at bay. In this context, control of the potential weak spots, namely the buffer zones inhabited by the Buddhists of Tibet in the south and Muslims of Xinjang in the west, is a vital task.

Foreign policy analyses of China have consistently emphasised the twin core goals of regional hegemony and global great power status. Competitive rivalries with India, and particularly Japan, are perennial features of Chinese external affairs, as is the aim of being taken seriously by the great powers of the West. The Western notion of China that has prevailed since the end of the Second World War, as a rising power looking to join their elite, is not how Beijing views the recent growth. From Beijing, Chinese great power status is considered a return to the normal order after an unfortunate interregnum between the middle of the nineteenth and twentieth centuries, a period of weakness when being caught off-guard allowed rivals from near and far to take advantage. From the time that the British Opium Wars ushered in a period of semi-colonialism for several European powers to the Japanese invasion of the 1930s, China experienced an uncharacteristic and humiliating period of subservience, out of step with its long former history as Asia's premier power and a major global trader.

In line with this historical paradigm of power politics one (slightly less alarmist) line of Western analysis sees the rise of China as another facet of a defensive mindset, seeking to ensure that they are never again subservient through deterrence and power parity rather than seeking global hegemony. One strand of this thinking foresees the future emergence of a loose 'G2' marriage of convenience between China and the US, unlikely bedfellows since they are divided by ideology and superpower suspicion, but sharing a common interest in the maintenance of the status quo and too intertwined by trade and monetary links to become dangerously estranged (Brzezinski, 2009a). A more pessimistic and traditionally-Realist prophecy (from a Western perspective) envisages a time 'When China Rules the World', where it inevitably comes to topple the US and ushers in a new era of history and International Relations (Jacques, 2012).

Economic/resource security

China's century of decline is understood in the context of falling behind the Europeans, Americans and Japanese economically in the nineteenth century when those nations became industrialised. Mao's Great Leap Forward of the late 1950s and early 1960s was a radical drive to catch up in this regard, and subsequent 'Great Leaps Outward', which have seen China embrace capitalism and globalisation, can also be understood in this context.

In an outward manifestation of the pursuit of economic and resource security, trade ties with Russia and South-East Asia have been strengthened, and, further afield, Chinese interests in Africa and the Arctic have grown rapidly during recent years. In Africa a huge push to advance economic ties has seen trade grow from $10 billion to $200 billion between 2000 and 2014. China has had a steadily-growing presence in Arctic affairs over the last thirty years, driven by the fact that climate change has opened up the possibility of northern trade routes and readier access to undersea resources. Regular Chinese polar expeditions have been organised since the 1980s and they have an established presence on Spitsbergen. China also possesses the world's biggest non-nuclear icebreaker, the Xue Long (Snow Dragon), and has growing interests in commercial shipping and securing new energy supplies. Hence Beijing has intensified diplomatic activity in the northern latitudes in recent years. China has the biggest embassy in Reykjavik, and the seemingly mundane matter of the Icelandic Premier's 2007 visit to Beijing was made into a lavish affair by the hosts. In 2008 China supported Iceland's campaign to gain a seat on the UN Security Council, and it has made some significant economic investments in the country, including the controversial purchase of a 300 sq. km tract of wilderness in the north-east by the tycoon Huang Nubo. In 2012 Wen Jiaboa made the first visit by a Chinese Premier to Iceland in forty years as part of a North European tour which also took in Sweden. Beijing has also courted the support of Sweden and Norway for gaining permanent observer status on the Arctic Council, at which they have previously observed in an *ad hoc* capacity.

Economic and resource security questions have become increasingly externalised as a result of the growth in demand that has accompanied Chinese economic enlargement. This represents a break with the recent past, but is also something of a return to the past prior to the nineteenth century, when China was a major economic player globally.

Cultural security

Cultural security is more clearly a new Chinese concern, and Hu's Presidency from 2002 to 2012 featured many speeches citing its importance. In essence this is the external dimension of political security; the fear that greater coexistence with the West risks the import of destabilising ideas and norms. Strategies to enhance Chinese cultural security have taken both defensive and proactive forms. Censorship of 'dangerous Western media', most notoriously of internet search engines through the so-called 'Great Firewall of China', is one dimension. So too, though, is an attempt to embrace the concept of soft power and project positive images of China. Examples of this include the lavishly organised Beijing Olympic Games of 2008 and the charm offensive that has accompanied African investment – such as the building of a new headquarters for the AU in Addis Ababa.

Overwhelmingly Western influences upon China are not new and the state has had to contend with the import of ideas since the nineteenth century. Periodically these have heightened concerns regarding cultural identity; however, it is only now, within the context of its rapid rise, that China can finally begin to use its soft power to redress what it sees as a powerful Western military, political and media effort to impose Neoliberal ideas throughout the world. It is likely that the Chinese see Western Neoliberalism as a form of imperialism where the key objective is not physical, in an attempt to control resources, but rather ideological dominance. Countering this influence by exporting its own ideology may not be official policy, but the examples highlighted can certainly be viewed as attempts to meet Western challenges at the international level. Internally, minimising dissent through a regular crackdown on dissenting individuals and the media alongside propaganda campaigns is a way of ensuring compliance with official views of cultural identity and ideology.

Information security

In recent years, Beijing has been preoccupied with its concern at being behind the US in terms of information technology. The Chinese state is alleged to have been at the forefront of numerous cyberwar activities in recent years, hacking and corrupting Western business websites for the purposes of industrial espionage and competitive advantage. In 2014 US courts issued the first arrest warrants for Chinese military personnel alleged to have been involved in such activities. Indeed, evidence has been mounting that China is at the forefront of spying on Western companies, politicians and other strategic assets. In April 2014, a US government report suggested tighter controls on space technology due to the fear that China was seeking to steal it. Similarly, in 2013 European diplomats learned of attempts by China to spy on them, but as always the Chinese responded with a denial, followed as usual by counter accusations levelled against the US and Europe. According to Jeffrey Carr, the author of *Inside Cyber Warfare: Mapping the Cyber Underworld*, numerous states, such as India and Russia, are behind attempts to steal Western (especially US) intellectual property. However, China has been singled out by many security agencies as well as companies as being responsible for up to 80% of all such thefts from US companies.

Ecological security

China's embrace of ecological security appears surprising from afar, but again it reflects its high regard for internal order. China has witnessed a growing environmental social movement over recent years, out of line with what might be predicted in such an undemocratic and socially conservative setting. In 2007 there were protests in Xiamen against the location of a chemical plant producing paraxylene which ultimately forced its relocation. A similar scenario unfolded in 2012 over plans to construct a waste pipe for a paper factory in Qidong, and again the following year in a series of protests in Kunming in Yunnan province against the development of a petrochemical plant aiming to produce paraxylene. In 2013 the Chinese government, clearly responding to rising protests, announced a package of significant anti-pollution policies aimed at reducing key emissions by 30% over the next four years: 'smog is visible and affects the life of everyone, rich and poor. It has been proven that environmental crises can stir controversy and greatly undermine social stability' (Coonan, 2013).

Human Security

Human Security, predictably, has little currency in a country politically defined by Communism, hierarchy and a long-standing culture that is more communal than individual. In this context individuals have often paid a heavy price in the pursuit of national economic advancement. As discussed in Chapter 20, China has the worst record in the world in terms of fatalities from both natural and industrial disasters, with safety standards well behind those in the West or Japan. Two notorious 'deliberate disasters', dating from before and during the Communist era, starkly illustrate the elevation of the national interest over Human Security. The deliberate flooding of the Yellow River was carried out by the Chiang Kai-Shek government when resisting the Japanese invasion of Manchuria in 1938. In destroying dykes the Chinese slowed down the invaders by creating a bigger barrier and destroying farmland, but they also sacrificed hundreds of thousands of their own citizens and left millions more homeless in an act both desperate and appalling. Under the Maoist regime that succeeded Chiang Kai-Shek, the 1958–62 Chinese famine was the worst in history. While it was influenced by the effects of excessive rainfall on harvests, there is little doubt that its principal cause was Mao's determination to pursue his 'Great Leap Forward' economic reform plan and forcibly relocate farmers into industrial work, regardless of the human consequences.

At the same time, though, it has to be noted that China's state-centric security has enhanced the security of many of its citizens. The Chinese health system has many admirers and delivers better levels of wellbeing than most other countries of a comparable GDP per capita. Alongside this, the impressive economic growth of recent decades has lifted millions out of poverty.

Conclusion

This case study has shown that as China rises as a regional and global power, it is beset by a number of threats emanating from outside as well as from within its borders. The collapse of the Soviet Union, Russia's war against the Chechens, the Kashmiri Muslims in India, the Kurds in Turkey, and the Hutus in Burundi are just some examples which show that under-represented people often rise up to demand greater rights. China also faces such problems. Given the increasingly violent insurgency in Xinjiang, calls for independence in Tibet and demands for autonomy elsewhere, the potential for ethnic-nationalist wars certainly exists – especially if China's political centre is unable or unwilling to meet those demands. There is little doubt that as China rises it is seeking more of a say in the world, especially in Asia. It is therefore taking steps to safeguard its territory, political ideology, and culture while at the same time using its increasingly abundant soft power to safeguard economic and resource interests in far-off places such as Africa. For the moment the United States remains the pre-eminent global power, including in the Asia-Pacific region, but as China seeks to assert itself, it will be interesting to see how the US accommodates those increasing demands, since it is already obvious that they are beginning to encroach on US interests.

Recommended reading

Carr, J. *Inside Cyber Warfare: Mapping the Cyber Underworld*, 2nd Edition, Sebastopol, CA: O'Reilly Media, 2011.

Craig, S.L. *Chinese Perceptions of Traditional and Non-traditional Security Threats*, http://www. StrategicStudiesInstitute.army.mil/, March 2007 (Accessed 14.7.2014).

Jacques, M. *When China Rules the World: the End of the Western World and the Birth of a New Global Order*, 2nd Edition, London: Penguin, 2012.

Ong, R. *China's Security Interests in the 21st Century*, London and New York: Routledge, 2007.

US–China Security Perceptions Survey: Findings and Implications, http://carnegieendowment.org/ files/us_china_security_perceptions_report.pdf (Accessed 12.7.2014).

26 Security in Europe

The triumph of institution-building?

Dermot McCann

Box 26.1: Violence in Europe

Europe has witnessed some of the most violent and destructive conflicts in human history. Throughout the twentieth century it lay at the epicentre of global inter-state rivalry. Following the end of the Cold War it appeared that the development of innovative forms of institutional cooperation had finally enabled it to establish a sustainable peace. However, recent events in Georgia and the Ukraine raise justifiable concerns that a return to the violent instabilities of the past is a real possibility.

Introduction

Following a prolonged period of violent conflict and profound insecurity, in recent decades Europe has enjoyed a substantial degree of peace and stability. With few exceptions, European states no longer regard each other as a threat to their security. Military expenditure has fallen substantially. The response to newly emerging security threats, ranging from terrorism to climate change, has been characterised by a high degree of collective, cooperative action among states. Indeed, in many respects, Europe has become a reference model for other regions in the world that seek to contain and overcome inter-state conflict and to develop a capacity to respond to new security challenges collectively. This case study will examine the institutional mechanisms and policies that have enabled the continent to transcend its traumatic past, stabilise its inter-state system and address the myriad new challenges to its security that have developed in recent decades. Finally, it will assess the durability of Europe's relatively happy condition in the face of the intense economic and political stresses that are increasingly evident across the continent.

Stabilising the inter-state system: building a 'security community'

International politics in Europe has long been characterised by inter-state rivalries that have manifested themselves in balance of power politics, the creation of competing alliances and, ultimately, outright conflict. Within the last century alone, two world wars and a Cold War have consumed the continent, threatening the security of its states and its peoples in the most profound way. Viewed in this light, the current relatively stable and peaceful condition of Europe is remarkable. While inter-state rivalries and conflicts of interest persist, the outbreak of war among the continent's major states is widely regarded as unthinkable. When war does break out, as it did in the Balkans in the 1990s, neighbouring states have sought to contain the conflict rather than generalise it, as they so often did in the past. In explanation of this surprising turn, many analysts have focused on the rich process of institution-building that has taken place in the last half century or so. Inter-state relations are mediated and managed by a complex tapestry of international organisations, the most important of which are the North Atlantic Treaty Organization (NATO) and the European Union (EU). It is argued that together these institutions have served to establish a 'security community'. Within this community, conflicts between states 'are resolved by peaceful means, so there is a high expectation that this norm will be maintained and that war would therefore be extremely unlikely, if not inconceivable' (Cottey, 2013: 13). Indeed, much of European security policy is now informed by a belief that the primary threats to the continent's security arise from outside this community (ibid.: 14).

The North Atlantic Treaty Organization (NATO)

NATO plays a fundamentally important role at the heart of Europe's security community. Founded in 1949, for the four decades of the Cold War NATO was the bedrock of security in Western Europe. It was a mutual defence pact composed of most of the states of Western Europe and subject to the de facto leadership of the United States. Its core purpose was to contain the military threat to its members presented by the Soviet Union and its allies. To that end, it developed a large, integrated military capability focused on repulsing any attack from the east. Inevitably, with the end of the Cold War and the break-up of the Soviet Union, doubts were raised about its future role. Given the disappearance of its enemy, what was its function? Given its origins, organisation and objectives, its suitability as an agent for the management of the radically transformed condition of post-Cold War Europe seemed highly questionable. Moreover, the alliance was the institutional embodiment of US power in Europe. With the disappearance of its principal foe, would the US wish to maintain its (expensive) presence in Europe?

By the mid- to late 1990s, after a period of considerable uncertainty, the broad outline of a new strategic role for NATO began to emerge. Four features of this strategy are of particular importance. First, after a period of equivocation and limited disengagement, the US determined to maintain its leadership role and military presence both in NATO and in Europe more generally. The US is a central player in Europe's defence community. Second, NATO began to diversify both its operational objectives and its geographical sphere of engagement. Founded as a defensive alliance, it began to formulate a broader and more flexible set of criteria for action. As early as 1992 it intervened in the Yugoslavian war to enforce a no-fly zone over Bosnia-Herzegovina. As the conflict evolved, its participation deepened. In 1999 it launched a seventy-eight-day bombing campaign against Serbia to enforce a change in the latter's policy in Kosovo. Subsequently, the alliance deployed ground troops in Kosovo as part of the KFOR peacekeeping force. Marking an even more dramatic break with its Cold War origins and European focus, in 2001 it deployed forces in Afghanistan in support of the US invasion of that country following the 9/11 attacks. Having never engaged in military action during the Cold War, NATO established itself as a willing and capable security enforcer in Europe and beyond. Third, NATO responded to the end of Europe's division into two mutually antagonistic armed camps by incorporating into its membership many central and eastern European states which had previously belonged to its rival military bloc, the Warsaw Pact. Indeed, in the case of Estonia, Latvia and Lithuania, it took into membership former republics of the Soviet Union itself. A membership of sixteen states at the end of the Cold War had grown to twenty-eight by 2009 as NATO sought to manage Europe's inter-state security relations by internalising key aspects of them. Fourth, where membership incorporation was deemed to be unfeasible or undesirable, NATO sought to build stable and cooperative relations by establishing a complex web of bilateral relations and cooperative practices. Twenty-two states, including Russia, have signed up to the alliance's Partnership for Peace framework which is designed to build cooperative relations between individual non-member states and the alliance. Its activities encompass a wide range of fields, including defence reform, defence planning, civil–military relations, military-to-military cooperation and exercises, disaster response, etc.[1] By 2010 NATO had successfully transformed itself from a Western Cold War defence alliance into an encompassing pan-European military alliance. Its policy remit was much broader and more flexible and its relationships with surrounding regions and states were much more complex, institutionalised and cooperative. NATO has come to play a pivotal role in the management of the post-Cold War European inter-state system.

The European Union

The European Union forms the second principal pillar of Europe's security community. Though its membership, structure and focus of activity are very different to that of NATO, from its inception the building of security in Europe has also been one of its core objectives. Founded in the aftermath of the Second World War, it was designed to stabilise and manage relations among participating Western European states, many of which had recently been at war with each other. In particular, it was designed to reconcile France and Germany, two countries that had engaged in three increasingly violent confrontations since the latter's creation in 1870. However, rather than focusing on defence or foreign policy issues, it sought to achieve these objectives by fostering the integration of its member states' economies. Cross-border trade was facilitated, markets were opened up and common 'supranational' institutions established in order to formulate, legislate and enforce common policies and market regulations that were deemed advantageous by its members. The economic growth and prosperity that these innovations facilitated served to buttress and sustain the habits of inter-state cooperation that the system embodied. By greatly deepening the interdependence of its member states and creating mechanisms of shared governance the security of Europe was enhanced.

As in the case of NATO, the end of the Cold War profoundly altered the context within which the EU operated and presented a fundamental challenge to its role. One element of its response was the establishment a *Common Foreign and Security Policy* (CFSP), following the negotiation of the Maastricht Treaty (1991). CFSP's broad objectives are to 'preserve peace and strengthen international security; to promote international cooperation; and to develop and consolidate democracy, the rule of law and respect for human rights and fundamental freedoms'.[2] Running alongside national member states' foreign policies, it seeks to formulate common positions that can be pursued collectively through diplomatic means. Following the coming into force of the Lisbon Treaty (2009), a European External Action Service has been created to support its international diplomatic mission. In addition, following the embarrassing failure of its efforts to resolve the Yugoslavian crisis during the 1990s, the EU has sought to create a military capability to intervene in conflict zones, whether on the continent or further afield (*Common Security and Defence Policy*). Thus, for example, in 2003 troops under EU command were deployed in the former Yugoslavian republic of Macedonia and the Democratic Republic of the Congo as part of UN-sanctioned peacekeeping missions. The EU has developed a modest but significant capacity to act alone in the foreign policy and defence field.

Yet, while it has been important, the EU's greatest contribution to the stabilisation of the post-Cold War European inter-state system lay not in its acquisition of a foreign policy instrument, but rather in its decision to extend the prize of membership to the emerging capitalist Liberal democracies of Central and Eastern Europe. In return for a commitment to adapt their domestic political and economic institutions to EU standards and norms, these vulnerable states were offered the prospect of economic opportunity and political influence. Eleven former Communist states of Central and Eastern European became members (including three former Soviet Union republics). In addition, six more former Soviet republics have participated in the EU's European Neighbourhood Policy. This seeks to foster good relations between the EU and its neighbours by providing grant aid for development projects, agreeing favourable terms for access to European markets, and easing visa entry arrangements for work and study. Moreover, the strategy of stabilisation through incorporation continues to be deployed in Europe. While its efforts to contain and end the Yugoslavian war in the 1990s largely failed, the EU's strategy of offering membership to the successor states that emerged from the country's break-up as a *quid pro quo* for their adherence to the rules of market economics and liberal democracy has proven to be far more successful. Croatia and Slovenia are already in membership, with Serbia at an advanced stage of negotiations.

Security: beyond inter-state relations

The security of Europe is not only threatened by potential inter-state conflict. In recent years growing challenges have been evident from a broad range of issues stretching from the growth of international terrorism, through the destabilising impact of climate change to problems of poverty, economic development and state failure in neighbouring regions. Terrorists have demonstrated a significant capacity to strike hard in Europe over the last two decades. Climate change is acting as a 'threat multiplier which exacerbates existing trends, tensions and instability' and threatens to overburden states and regions on Europe's borders 'which are already fragile and conflict prone'.[3] Economic underdevelopment generates large-scale population movements into Europe, contributes to political instability and, in some instances, fuels terrorism. The threat to Europe's security in such cases comes not from state aggression but, rather, from state weakness or even failure. As in respect of inter-state rivalry, however, Europe's response to these challenges is distinctive for its reliance on collective institutions, most notably the EU, to develop and implement a coherent policy response. Partly, this reliance is a reflection of the nature of the problems themselves. European states do craft individual national policies to address them, but given their character and scale the effectiveness of unilateral national action will certainly be inadequate. It is the essence of international terrorism that it operates across national borders. States must act cooperatively to combat it successfully. Addressing the causes and managing the consequences of climate change can only be achieved through regional and global collective action. Similarly, the scale of the poverty and underdevelopment that exists in Europe's neighbouring states and regions is beyond the capacity of any single state to resolve. However, it is also the case that the heavy reliance on the EU as an instrument to address these security challenges partly reflects the familiarity of European states with collective, highly institutionalised forms of problem solving and their confidence in its efficacy.

The nature of the role played by the EU in shaping policy in these areas varies considerably from case to case. In some, its contribution is designed to enable and enhance cooperation and coordination within Europe between national agencies. Thus, for example, in respect of anti-terrorism strategies, the European Arrest Warrant introduced in 2002 facilitates the arrest anywhere in the EU of persons indicted in another member state for terrorism or other serious crimes. National legal systems now mutually recognise judicial orders to freeze and confiscate assets as a consequence of an EU agreement. A common EU definition of terrorism offences has also been agreed, and a list of terrorist individuals, entities and offences drawn up. An EU agency, Frontex, was created in 2005 to oversee and enforce a high and uniform level of monitoring and control of the Union's external frontiers. European laws have been introduced to combat terrorist money-laundering activities. The effectiveness of national anti-terrorist policies is predicated on a high level of legal integration and operational cooperation that would be unfeasible without EU involvement.

In other policy areas, the focus of EU action is on mitigating the threat to European security by reshaping the continent's external environment. Thus, for example, in respect of climate change the EU has adopted the '20–20–20' formula to control the growth of greenhouse gas (GHG) emissions. This commits member states to reduce EU GHG emissions by 20%, to ensure that 20% of all energy comes from renewable sources and to reduce primary energy use by 20%, all to be achieved by the year 2020. Simultaneously, however, it has sought to extend the logic of this policy globally by developing a system of legally binding emission reduction targets that encompasses all developed states. This strategy met with some initial success with the negotiation of the Kyoto Protocol on climate change, signed in 1997. Subsequent EU efforts to build on Kyoto at Copenhagen (2009) and Durban (2011) have largely failed to bear fruit. Nevertheless, the logic of its strategy remains unaltered and the centrality of its role in the global politics of climate change is striking. In the case of development, the EU's strategy of reducing the security threat to Europe by reshaping its external environment has taken the form of attempts to induce underdeveloped states to reform their internal structures and policies in ways that it believes will render them more stable and, by extension, less of a threat to the security of others. Thus, for example, under the terms of the Cotonou Agreement, signed in 2000 between the EU and seventy-eight underdeveloped African, Caribbean and Pacific states, it has formulated a complex policy which offers the prospect of economic aid and trade concessions in return for the introduction of democratic and market enhancing domestic reforms. Such reforms range from the strengthening of protections for human rights through the entrenching of the rule of law to requirements for transparent and accountable management of all of a country's development resources (Holland and Doidge, 2012: 76). The EU's strategy reflects a belief that politically stable states that are integrated into the liberal international economic order present fewer threats to European security.

Challenges to stability

While the success of Europe in achieving a high degree of peace and security since the end of the Cold War is undeniable, the durability and the continuing effectiveness of the institutions that underpinned it cannot be presumed. Political, economic, social and military tensions have intensified across Europe in recent years. The ability of institutions such as NATO and the EU to manage and contain these tensions, and the willingness of national states to concede such a pivotal role to them, is open to question. Though the nature and sources of these problems are very diverse, they can roughly be divided into those stemming from internal weaknesses within European institutions and those stemming from external challenges to their operation.

Weaknesses within the 'security community'

The euro crisis represents a major challenge to the integrity and effectiveness of the EU as a security actor. The severity of the crisis and the complex interactions it has generated between creditor and debtor states has provoked enormous political and popular controversy. Greek resentment of German 'diktats' has led to abusive mutual recriminations in each country's popular press. More substantially, the crisis has exposed deep conflicts of interest between member states and raised fears that the Union may become an instrument through which stronger states exert their power, enabling them to impose their preferred policies on the resentful populations of weaker, more vulnerable states. Such developments corrode the mutual trust necessary for the EU to perform effectively and undermine one of the key institutional components of Europe's security community. It is as yet unclear whether this crisis can be surmounted without transforming the relationship between states within the Union. However, already it has served as a reminder of the inherent fragility of collective institutions. The potential for destabilising shifts in relations between member states is always present.

Doubt also exists about the effectiveness and durability of the NATO pillar of Europe's security community. Partly this stems from uncertainty about the commitment of the US to maintaining its leadership role in Europe following President Obama's announcement of a 'pivot' towards Asia in its strategic orientation. The implications of this shift in policy focus are far from clear, but it is evident that the geo-political importance of Europe for the US is diminishing, and that this is likely to affect the nature and extent of its involvement in the continent in the future. At the same time, however, there is growing doubt about the capacity of European states to assume full responsibility for their own security. It is notable that in the recent Anglo-French-led intervention in Libya, the campaign would have been impossible without the logistical and technical support of the USA. Thus, while European countries conducted 75% of the strike sorties, 90% of the strikes and contributed 85% of the ships and naval aircraft to the mission, some '75% of Intelligence, Surveillance and Reconnaissance (ISR) capabilities, 75% of aerial refuelling and 90% of targeting' were provided by the USA (Chatham House, 2012: 2–3). Without such support European states would have struggled to mount an effective military operation. Yet this incapacity is unlikely to be overcome in the near or medium-term future as across Europe countries continue to cut defence spending. Whereas in 1990 six of the sixteen NATO member countries spent at least 2% of their GDP on defence, in 2012 only three to five did (depending on the measuring method used) out of twenty-eight. Norway and Estonia are currently the only NATO countries that are not cutting back on spending (Chatham House, 2012: 4). The combination of uncertainty about the extent of US commitment to maintaining its leadership role and the unwillingness of European states to substitute for any reduction in its military presence casts into doubt the longer-term durability of key elements of Europe's security community.

Threats from without: Russia and the resurgence of inter-state rivalry

Many international relations analysts question the capacity of complex institutional arrangements to contain inter-state rivalries indefinitely. Partly this reflects broader theoretical debates about the nature of the international system. Realists have long been sceptical about the transformative power of institutions and 'security communities'. Thus, for example, in respect of Europe a leading 'Offensive Realist' observer argued at the turn of the millennium that powerful countries such as Germany or Russia would inevitably come to seek hegemonic status which 'is likely to result in dangerous security competition among the great powers' (Mearsheimer, 2001: 396). The logic of inter-state rivalry will reassert itself. Since the mid-2000s Russian policy under President Vladimir Putin has manifested some of the behavioural features that Mearsheimer anticipated. Putin's primary concern has been to re-establish Russia as a great power, endowed with the economic and military capacity to pursue its interests effectively on the world stage. In the early stages of his rule he adopted a broadly pro-Western policy focused on the joint combating of Islamic terrorism. Thus, he acquiesced in the deployment of US troops in Uzbekistan and Kyrgyzstan, former republics of the Soviet Union. In the last decade, however, relations with the West have deteriorated. Attempts to renew an EU–Russia Partnership and Cooperation Agreement signed in 1997 have stalled, and further cooperative economic initiatives, such as the EU–Russia Partnership for Modernisation, have petered out. Russia has increasingly come to perceive the eastern advance of NATO and the EU as a threat, reviving long-standing fears of encirclement by aggressive Western powers. In the case of Georgia, a former republic of the Soviet Union, the attempt by its strongly pro-Western leader George Saakashvili to break free of Russian influence and gain entry to NATO prompted a Russian invasion. Russia justified its actions by attributing genocidal intent to the Georgian government in its dealings with the pro-Russian South Ossetian minority in the country. The war ended after only five days with Russia gaining the controls and guarantees that it had demanded. It had successfully demonstrated its capacity to intervene in foreign states in defence of ethnic Russian minorities and its own wider interests. More broadly, the conflict revealed the growing gulf in perception between Russia, NATO and the EU. Where NATO and the EU presented their policies as exercises in cooperation and peacemaking, Russia perceived them to be quasi-imperial in nature, designed to extend Western power at its expense. The Georgian war effectively halted NATO's eastern expansion. For its part, the EU continued to pursue the same strategy of engagement and institution-building that it had employed since the end of the Cold War. However, the Ukrainian crisis of 2013–14 casts the continuing effectiveness of this approach into grave doubt. In late 2013 an EU–Ukrainian trade deal was struck.

At the last minute the Ukrainian government declined to sign the agreement, partly in response to Russia's opposition to its terms. This prompted 'pro-deal' groups in Ukraine to protest, and ultimately they succeeded in deposing the government. This, in turn, prompted Russian intervention in eastern Ukraine and its effective annexation of Crimea. These events constituted the most serious crisis of the post-Cold War period. The integrity of the state of Ukraine came into question. More fundamentally, these developments raised serious questions about the capacity of Europe's highly institutionalised 'security community' to sustain the continent's security in the longer term in the face of re-emerging inter-state rivalries.

Conclusion

Given its history of violent conflict, the attempt by states to stabilise the European continent through the creation of powerful regional institutions has proven to be remarkably successful. The tensions of the Cold War, the difficult political and economic re-integration of the continent following the end of the Cold War, and the challenges to security stemming from the process of globalisation, have all been managed with considerable effectiveness. Indeed, with some degree of plausibility Europe has been able to present itself to other regions plagued by political rivalries and economic weakness as a model to be emulated. However, the sustainability of this success cannot be assumed. The commitment of the US to maintaining its European role is in some doubt. The strength of the European Union is threatened both by economic and monetary crisis and the potential defection from membership by Britain, an important player in European security politics. Moreover, the belief that institutional innovation has enabled Europe to transcend the dynamics of great power politics has been shaken by recent events in Georgia and Ukraine. It remains to be seen whether the pacifying influence of Europe's 'security community' over the last few decades represents a definitive change in the nature of European politics or merely a short, happy interlude in its long turbulent history.

Notes

1 http://www.nato.int/cps/en/natolive/topics_50349.htm, accessed 14 April 2014.
2 European Union, Foreign and Security Policy http://europa.eu/pol/cfsp/index_en.htm, accessed 21 March 2014.
3 Climate Change and International Security, Paper from the High Representative and the European Commission to the European Council, 2008, p.3 http://www.consilium.europa.eu/uedocs/cms_data/librairie/PDF/EN_clim_change_low.pdf, accessed 1 May 2014.

Recommended reading

Chatham House, European Defence and Security 2012: Commitments, Capabilities and Cash, Conference Summary, Rapporteur: Benoît Gomis, 2012. http://www.chathamhouse.org/sites/default/files/public/Research/International%20Security/0112confsummary.pdf (Accessed 10 January 2014).

Cottey, A. *Security in 21st Century Europe*, New York: Palgrave Macmillan, 2013.

Holland, M. and Doidge, M. *Development Policy in the European Union*, New York: Palgrave Macmillan, 2012.

Mearsheimer, J.J. *The Tragedy of Great Power Politics*, New York: Norton, 2001.

27 Security in Africa

Peter Hough

Table 27.1 Single biggest fear for Africans[1]

1	Economic insecurity[2]	37%
2	Disease[3]	21%
3	Corruption	7%
4	Illiteracy	6%
5	War	6%
6	Political conflict	5%
7	Environmental destruction	3%

Source: BBC (2004)

Introduction

While it is a large and diverse continent too often generalised about, Africa, nevertheless, presents a revealing case study on the meaning of security. Whilst politics on the 'Dark continent' has been blighted by many wars and armed insurgences since it began to overthrow colonial rule in the 1950s and 1960s, the traditional prioritisation of national military security over 'low politics' has never been a satisfactory way of understanding or addressing the plight of most Africans. Indeed, the first articulation of Human Security in international politics came at a Pan-African conference co-sponsored by the UN and the Organisation for African Unity in 1991, two years before the concept's now well-known adoption by the UN Development Programme in their Human Development Report:

> The concept of security goes beyond military considerations. [It] must be construed in terms of the security of the individual citizen to live in peace with access to basic necessities of life while fully participating in the affairs of his/her society in freedom and enjoying all fundamental human rights.
>
> (African Leadership Forum, 1991)

Even in the 'heyday' of national security during the Cold War, prior to the conceptualisation of Human Security, the most pressing problems in Africa were not the same as the fears of nuclear annihilation preoccupying North America and Eurasia. Famine, hunger and disease have always represented much greater threats than war and terrorism for the vast majority of Africa's inhabitants, and this continues to be the case in the present age. Table 27.1, showing the results of a poll asking respondents to name the single greatest threat to their life, illustrates clearly how traditional security priorities are out of step with the concerns of African people. This case study chapter, examining some of the key dimensions of national and human security across Africa, illustrates the disparity between the two approaches more clearly than could be achieved by looking at any other of the world's continents.

National security

Africa epitomises the limitations of traditional approaches to security in two key ways: i) the 'nation-state' as a referent object of security is rarely evident; and ii) military threats from other state governments are rarely major sources of insecurity. Hence the Realist definition of security as relating to the 'threat, use and control of military force' (Walt, 1991: 212) has little currency in the case of Africa. Contrary to much popular assumption, in intergovernmental terms Africa is a comparatively peaceful continent with only a limited history of classic state-to-state wars. In this regard the continent compares well with the more developed and democratic Europe, and has even prompted some to refer to an 'African peace' (Henderson, 2008). The only major inter-state wars since the 1960s, when the continent began to rule itself, have been the 1978–9 invasion of Uganda by Tanzania (which is often viewed as a humanitarian intervention) and the wars between Ethiopia and Eritrea (1998–2000) and Sudan and South Sudan (2013–), both of which followed the secession of the succession of the latter part. Africa has not witnessed the regular spiral into great power conflict that marked European history from the Middle Ages to the twentieth century or, more sporadically, Asian history.

However, Hendricks considers the African Peace notion to be a misnomer based on an outmoded interpretation of inter-state wars. While there are few classic inter-state wars in recent African history, this is also the case the world over with fully fledged or partial civil wars now the norm. Hendricks suggests that 30% of the world's conflicts since 1945 have been African, and that most supposedly civil wars have in fact been internationalised disputes (Hendricks, 2012: 52). In the mid-1990s the challenge presented to the notion of a pacific post-Cold War New World Order by the rise in African conflicts was instrumental in prompting the emergence of the Resource Wars and New Wars theses, which predicted that this was a prelude to a new era of conflict triggered by environmental scarcity and failed states, discussed elsewhere in this volume (Homer-Dixon, 1994; Kaldor, 1999). The prominent US journalist Robert Kaplan particularly popularised this line of thinking with *The Coming Anarchy*, which painted a pessimistic picture of post-Cold War Africa as a dangerous place characterised by 'disease, overpopulation, unprovoked crime, scarcity of resources, refugee migrations, the increasing erosion of nation-states and international borders and the empowerment of private armies, security firms and international drug cartels' (Kaplan, 1994: 144). The chaotic civil conflicts in Congo, Somalia and Sierra Leone in the 1990s did seem to support this notion of widespread anarchy, with warlords using criminality and grabbing resources to fund insurgencies against weak governments.

This 'anarchy' was actually a predicted acceleration and globalisation of problems that had been apparent in Africa for some time. A number of general explanations can be advanced to account for the prominence of internal insurgency on the continent over the past fifty years.

The 'strongman' phenomenon

The optimism generated by the wind of change that swept Africa in the 1950s and 1960s in many cases did not last. Of the ten self-ruling democracies that emerged from the ashes of empire, six had turned authoritarian within a decade (Lesotho, Nigeria, Sierra Leone, Somalia, Sudan and Uganda) (Marshall, 2006: 13). As we now better appreciate, democracy needs time to bed in, and if it is ushered in quickly it is often vulnerable to collapse. Sudanese democracy was snuffed out by Abbud in 1958 and has never properly been restored. It is now surprising to think that Sierra Leone was a democracy before Stevens ripped up its constitution in 1971. In these countries and many more, post-colonial strongman leaders emerged and were able to pull the drawbridge up behind them with little to stop them doing so. The charismatic Kenyatta of Kenya, who had fashioned his own brand of African socialism admired across much of the world, in 1969 banned opposition parties and closed the National Assembly. Much of the continent subsequently became dominated by military rule, cronyism and a chronic level of corruption as elites plundered sovereign wealth in a phenomenon that came to be known as *kleptocracy*. In the Congo, for example, Mobutu overthrew the democratically elected Lumumba in 1965 (with the support of the US and the country's former colonial masters Belgium) and proceeded to run the huge country for over thirty years for his own gratification, snaffling billions for personal luxuries and to swell secret bank accounts. Internal checks and balances were not in place to support these new African democracies, and Western powers were more interested in deterring Soviet interests on the continent than nurturing democracy. Strongman leaders remain a significant feature across Africa, as the Arab Spring uprisings against this form of tyranny in 2011–12 served to testify.

The artificiality of state borders

A cursory glance at a map of Africa tells the story that the notion of national self-determination as a route to inter-state order has never been close to being put into practice, in spite of the successful overthrow of European colonial rule in the second half of the twentieth century. Huge and diverse countries, usually with ethnically arbitrary borders – revealingly often straight-lined – characterise Africa. Many of these are literally lines in the sand, drawn by the British and French in their imperial disregard for local culture. Nigeria contains at least 250 different ethnicities and Uganda at least forty, including people of Arab and Asian origin alongside myriad tribes from three distinct African language groups. In addition, many of the continent's ethnic groups transcend its borders, such as the Akan who inhabit parts of Ghana and Ivory Coast, or the Hutu and the Tutsi who divide both Rwanda and Burundi as well as living in the Congo DR and elsewhere in East Africa.

One consequence of this nation/state mismatch is that civil conflicts have frequently internationalised due to the opportunistic intervention of neighbouring 'vulture states' (Hendricks, 2012) seeking to exploit and exacerbate state collapse in order to buttress their own state power. Cases in point include incursions by Uganda into Rwanda, Ethiopia into Somalia, Sudan into Chad, and, at various times, Angola, Rwanda and Zimbabwe into Congo.

Resource curse theory

If the ingredient of sudden lucrative mineral discoveries is added to the volatile mix of huge, ethnically divided and corrupt states, an exacerbation of those problems is likely. Export earnings from oil in Nigeria, Angola and Equatorial Guinea have been closer to breaking than making these countries, by fuelling insurgencies over 'who gets what'. More recently, the income to be made from minerals such as diamonds and cobalt has worsened criminality and ethnic divisions in the Congo DR and elsewhere in central Africa.

Religious fundamentalism

Africa is also particularly characterised by religious cleavage with the southward advance of Islam producing something of a fault line with Christianity across the Sahara, which has fuelled conflict in countries such as Nigeria, Sudan, Ivory Coast and Mali. Islamic fundamentalism has also clashed with secularity in predominantly Islamic states in the north such as Algeria and Egypt. One report claims that 70% of African countries with populations that are at least 40% Muslim are unstable, as opposed to 33% of the others (Marshall, 2006: 31). However, Christian fundamentalism is also a source of African instability with the most notorious example being the persistent, brutal insurgency of the Lords Resistance Army in northern Uganda, operating chiefly out of South Sudan.

Signs of stability

However, there is scope for optimism in looking at the data on wars with regard to Africa. While there are cases in support of Kaplan's thesis, the violent anarchy of sub-Saharan Africa has lessened rather than intensified since the mid-1990s. The Peace Research Institute of Oslo (PRIO, 2014) posit that thirty (or 66%) of sub-Saharan African states have experienced conflict since independence, and that much of this was accounted for by an accelerating trend in civil wars from the 1960s to the 1990s (PRIO, 2014; Strauss, 2012) . However, this trend has not continued since then, and civil wars in the 2000s were around half as prevalent as in the 1990s. A 50% decrease in major armed conflicts in Africa has occurred since a peak rate in 1991 (Marshall, 2006: 2; Strauss, 2012). Indeed, over the broad period of 1960 to 2008 sub-Saharan Africa was less warlike than Asia, with an average 1.65 conflicts per country set against 1.88 (the Middle East, spanning both continents, is more pacific than either with only 1.14 conflicts per country) (Strauss, 2012: 183–185). In addition, the tendency has been for African wars to become shorter and less bloody, with most recent conflicts taking the form of brief, factionalised insurgencies. There was an initial flare-up of African conflict after the end of the Cold War with the defrosting of conflicts frozen in time, such as in Liberia, Sierra Leone, Rwanda and the Congo DR. Subsequent to this, though, Liberia and Sierra Leone appear to have stabilised, and the long-standing conflicts in Mozambique, Ethiopia–Eritrea and Angola seem to have come to an end. With the notable exceptions of Sudan and the Congo DR, Africa's festering sores are healing.

Factors contributing to this retreat from rather than descent into anarchy include the role played by the African Union (AU), which has encouraged respect for borders, arbitrary though they may be, and sovereign order, and has shown pragmatism in compensating for its military weakness by a preparedness to use external help towards this (see Chapter 22). Recent Chinese investment in the continent has also helped fill the void that has been in place since the main Cold War protagonists largely lost interest, and, despite Western alarm, this has not been accompanied by significant political strings or seen Beijing playing divide and rule by supporting insurgent groups. Despite institutional weaknesses and a lack of homogeneity, the state system of Africa appears, on the face of it, to be reasonably stable and resilient. African insecurities, in the main, do not emanate from the kinds of intergovernmental power rivalries from which the concept of national security was forged.

Human Security

In contrast to the clear limitations of thinking in terms of national security, the rationale for a Human Security approach is starkly apparent in Africa, which contains many of the world's most impoverished and poorly governed states. For example, half of the world's lives lost to HIV/AIDs have been in sub-Saharan Africa over recent years (UNAIDS, 2011: 7), and at least 90% of those accounted for by malaria (WHO, 2013).

Poverty

Money, so the saying goes, 'can't buy you love', but it can buy you a certain measure of that other of life's most precious commodities – security. Table 27.2 illustrates the point that the wealthy of the world live longer while the poor die young. There is not a precise correlation between wealth and life expectancy, but the match up, particularly at the bottom of the scale, is still striking. The world's poorest people are also, by and large, the world's most insecure, and many of these live in Africa. As is illustrated in Table 27.2, sub-Saharan African states rank poorly in relation to Europe and Asia (and also, though this is not represented in the table, to North America).

Table 27.2 The price of poverty – wealth and life expectancy

2009 Ranking by GNP per capita, P.P.P.[4]	2009 Ranking by life expectancy (out of 194)	2009 Ranking by HDI (out of 187)
TOP (over $40,000)		
1 Qatar	39 (79.4)	37
2 Luxembourg	26 (80)	25
3 United Arab Emirates	49 (76.5)	30
4 Norway	13 (81.1)	1
5 Singapore	3 (81.1)	26
BOTTOM (under $700)		
183 Niger	171 (54.7)	186
184 Eritrea	154 (61.6)	177
185 Liberia	166 (56.8)	182
186 Burundi	184 (50.4)	185
187 Dem. Rep. of Congo	194 (48.4)	187

Source: UNDP (2011)

There are, however, some anomalies which emerge from comparing income and life expectancy and which demonstrate that there is more to security than money. Equatorial Guinea is Africa's richest country, ranked forty-five in the world by GDP per capita, but its citizens have a life expectancy of only fifty-one, the thirteenth worst in the world. The country has acquired great export earnings from oil production, but at the same time it is beset with corruption, poor governance and civil turmoil. The United Nations Development Programme (UNDP), to get over the limitations of judging development purely in economic terms, calculates a 'Human Development Index' to rank a country's progress. This figure combines income, life expectancy and educational attainment to give a more thorough picture of whether a state's wealth is being utilised to the benefit of its people. Hence states which, for various reasons, do not utilise their resources for the benefit of all of their people, like Equatorial Guinea, are judged to be less developed than their GDP would suggest. Equally, some countries, such as Madagascar, can be understood under HDI as more developed than their income would suggest, due to relatively good health and educational systems securing their citizens. At the same time, the most developed countries by HDI are rich but not necessarily the richest. There is more than money when it comes to achieving Human Security, since good governance can compensate for it, but there is no doubt that it helps.

As is made evident in several of the chapters in this volume, poverty is a key cause of most insecurity, heightening vulnerability to disease, disasters, criminality and conflict. The end of the Cold War, although providing an opportunity for non-military issues to gain global attention, represented a setback for the Third World since there was no longer a First and Second World to play off against each other. In the 1970s and 1980s many African countries were able to compete for the attention of the two superpowers, who saw it as in their strategic interests to help them. Additionally, the ending of the Cold War shifted the focus of Western Europe and North America to the transition of the former Communist countries and further marginalised the global South, and particularly Africa. The very notion of a Third World was further undermined throughout the 1980s and beyond by the fact that, while it was always a diverse grouping of states, its 'membership' gradually became so disparate that they ceased pulling in the same direction. The OPEC countries had helped to inspire Third World countries not fortunate enough to possess bountiful oil deposits, but the economic growth of countries like Libya and Algeria saw them move closer to the developed world. Similarly, the 'Asian Tigers' or 'Newly Industrialised Countries', like Thailand, South Korea and Taiwan, had joined the developed world by taking them on at their own game and producing modern manufactured goods more efficiently.

While kleptocracy and poor governance can be cited in some of the African states locked in underdevelopment (like the Congo DR), many of them have also been held back by the inequity of the Bretton Woods' Liberal International Economic Order (LIEO). The LIEO has only really succeeded in liberalising the trade in manufactured goods, allowing countries like the Asian Tigers and Brazil to take on the West at their 'own game', but agricultural exports – the main focus of most African economies – remain stifled by protectionism in the global North. The Asian Tigers had followed a broadly Western script, but many African countries found the Structural Adjustment development model's prescription of opening up their economies to foreign competition a bitter medicine with no remedial effects. In

Mozambique, for example, the once major cashew nut industry collapsed in the early 2000s when they were compelled to stop subsidising the sector as a condition of World Bank loans.

Recognition that sub-Saharan Africa has not been given the opportunity to lift itself out of poverty and thereby enhance the Human Security of its citizens by export earnings or opening itself up to foreign competition prompted the emergence of a new, more reformist global development agenda in the 2000s: the Post-Washington Consensus. A greater emphasis on human needs than the previous Washington Consensus paradigm's focus on privatisation, monetary conservatism and debt-settling saw the Millennium Development Goals (MDGs) adopted by the UN General Assembly in 2000. The MDGs were also adopted by the IMF, the World Bank, the Organisation for Economic Cooperation and Development and the G7 –institutions dominated by the global North and with more political muscle than the UN's talking shop. The eight broad goals of the MDGs, which have a distinct flavour of Human Security, are as follows:

- Reduce extreme poverty and hunger by half
- Achieve universal primary education
- Promote gender equality and empower women
- Reduce child mortality by two-thirds
- Reduce maternal mortality by three-quarters
- Reverse the spread of HIV/AIDS, malaria and other diseases
- Ensure environmental sustainability
- Develop a Global Partnership for Development (fair trade and more aid).

As can be seen, the MDGs are far from a utopian wish-list and represent an attempt to set pragmatic and verifiable targets by which the international community can be judged. The baselines for the calculations are the various indicators as of 1990, and the judgement deadline for meeting the goals was set as 2015. Progress towards meeting the Millennium Development Goals in 2015 could at best be described as 'mixed', indicating that a similar division in the ranks of the global South persists, despite a more socially-oriented model of global development policy. The proportion of the world living on less than $1.25 per day has fallen significantly, but hunger levels have not improved. The World Food Programme estimates that the number of malnourished people in the world topped the one billion mark for the first time in 2009, significantly up on the 1990 level (WFP, 2009). On unpicking these figures, a general trend for all the goals emerges. Asia, Latin America and North Africa have seen significant progress, and are likely to meet many of the targets on a regional basis, but sub-Saharan Africa is out of step with this improvement. Judged globally, the poverty reduction target has already been met, but only nineteen of the forty-five sub-Saharan African states had achieved this by 2013 (IMF, 2013). Goal 8 includes the sub-aim of completing the Doha Round of WTO trade negotiations and so liberalising global agricultural commerce comparable to what has been achieved in the trade in manufactured goods. This has yet to happen, and this failure has not been compensated by increases in foreign aid (a further sub-aim of Goal 8) largely due to the post-2008 global economic recession. Much of Africa thus has been unable to fulfil its potential, develop and lift its people out of poverty and vulnerability due to the persistence of vested global economic interests.

Governance

As has already been discussed, Africa has been particularly blighted by domestic political instability, the most chronic forms of which have come to be seen as producing 'failed states', defined by Rotberg as those which are 'consumed by internal violence and cease delivering positive political goods to their inhabitants' (Rotberg, 2004: 1). Prominent among such political goods is, of course, security. According to the 2013 rankings, compiled by the widely cited pressure group Fund for Peace, fifteen of the top twenty most failed states were African, headed by a top five of Somalia, Congo DR, Sudan, South Sudan and Chad (FFP, 2013). The top two epitomise the key explanatory factors behind the failed state phenomenon: instability born of post-colonial adjustment, and the post-Cold War political change. The Congo became independent in 1960, following the rapid departure of the Belgian King Leopold II who had run the vast territory as a personal fiefdom and in a particularly brutal manner. The inevitable resultant power vacuum led to a complex civil war sucking in neighbouring countries, which even an international intervention born of an as-then unique display of UN Security Council solidarity was not able to stifle. The net result was the despotic rule of Mobutu and the ethnic and criminal turmoil that continues to this day. In Somalia the fall of the Barre regime in 1991, previously propped up by the USSR, prompted a civil war and another unsuccessful UN intervention comparable to the Congo mission. Organised crime has flourished in Somalia, as in the Congo, and both are also ravaged by disease and malnutrition resulting from a lack of public health structures.

Leaving aside Africa's 'basket cases' among the more celebrated success stories, the problem of traditional national security trumping human security (a worldwide problem) is often still seen in domestic political prioritisation. For example, the government of South Africa trebled its allocation of the state exchequer for fighting AIDS for 2002–3 to $1 billion over the previous financial year, responding to criticism that they had not done enough to tackle this massive threat to life. However, the increased expenditure needs to be set in context. For the same financial year the slice of the budget set aside for military defence was $21 billion, even though there seems little doubt that few South African citizens would consider the prospect of armed invasion from Mozambique, Zimbabwe or any other state more of a threat to their lives than AIDS.[5] At the time around five million people in South Africa (11% of the population) were infected with HIV, and AIDS has long been the country's biggest killer, responsible for an estimated 40% of all deaths in 2002 (Dorrington, Bradshaw and Budlender, 2002). In comparison, South Africa has no obvious external military threat. Straight comparisons between government expenditure on different areas are problematic since different policy goals cost different amounts of money. Similarly, one could posit that South Africa's lack of military adversaries is a measure of the success of its defence policy. Even if this were to be accepted, however, the threat of AIDS remains acute in South Africa and there is little doubt that more could be done to alleviate the problem. The government of poorer and war-torn Uganda, for instance, cut HIV prevalence by half in the late 1990s through a concerted public information campaign (Ammann and Nogueira, 2002).

Again, though, there is scope for some optimism in looking at the politics of Africa. Democratisation has advanced in recent years with the number of autocracies falling from a peak of thirty-six (out of forty-one) in 1989 to just five (out of forty-three) in 2004 (Marshall, 2006: 3). The Arab Spring revolts and their aftermath from 2011 have furthered this trend. Human rights have also advanced, with state discrimination against minorities falling by an estimated 70% between the mid-1980s and the mid-2000s (Marshall, 2006: 3). Like the picture with conflict, with notable exceptions such as Sudan, Congo DR and much of Somalia, governance is generally improving in Africa.

Conclusion

The traditional concerns of national security politics – war and insurgency – remain major problems in Africa, but they are far from the most pressing concerns and the traditional high-low politics distinction is close to irrelevant. Security in Africa is not all about war and not all about the state (other than the consequences of its weakness or absence). As the World Bank has observed: 'the remaining forms of conflict and violence do not fit neatly into "war" or "peace", or into "communal violence" or "political violence"' (World Bank, 2011). Faced with this, conventional notions of 'defence' or 'deterrence' hold little currency. Vulnerability is complex and consequently the job of securing people is not straightforward, with a variety of 'securitising agents' invoked. Domestically there have been governmental improvements across much of the continent and regional governance via the AU has also contributed to greater stability. It is global governance and the persistence of inequitable trading rules, where there is the most room for improvement, holding African economies back.

Notes

1 BBC World Service poll of 7,671 people from Kenya, Tanzania, Mozambique, Ghana, Nigeria, Cameroon, Malawi, Zambia, Rwanda and Ivory Coast.
2 'Economic Insecurity' conflated from the poll's categories of 'poverty' (24%), 'unemployment' (10%) and 'poor economic development' (3%).
3 This category collates 'HIV/AIDS' (14%) and 'poor health' (7%).
4 GNP is 'Gross National Product', the total earnings of all citizens of a country. This divided by the population of the country gives the GNP per capita. This figure is factored by PPP, 'purchasing power parity', the relative worth of that country's money.
5 4% of South Africans identified war as their biggest security threat in a 2005 opinion poll (Human Security Centre, 2005).

Recommended reading

Henderson, E. 'Disturbing the Peace: African Warfare, Political Inversion and the Universality of the Democratic Peace Thesis', *British Journal of Political Science* 39(1), 2008, 25–58.
Hendricks, K. 'African Vultures: The New Prevalence of Interstate War in Africa', *Amsterdam Social Science* 4(1), 2012, 49–66.
Marshall, M. *Conflict Trends in Africa 1946–2004*, Report for UK Government, London: Department for International Development, 2006.
Strauss, S. 'Wars Do End! Changing Patterns of Political Violence in sub-Saharan Africa', *African Affairs* 111/443, 2012, 179–201.

28 The Arctic

Peter Hough

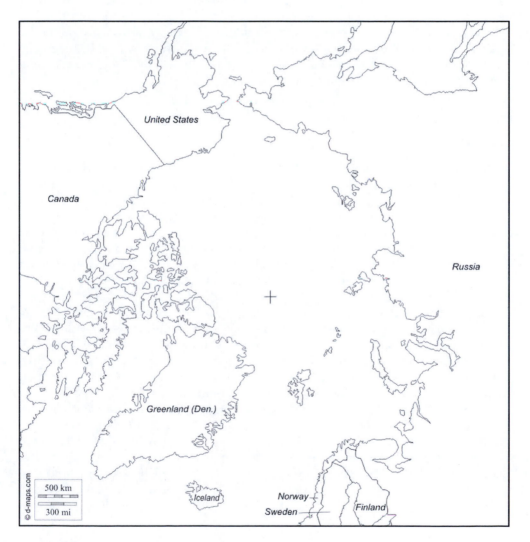

Figure 28.1 The Arctic
Source: http://d-maps.com/carte.php?num_car=3197&lang=en

Introduction

Climate change is literally and metaphorically bringing the Arctic in from the cold in international affairs, with new economic opportunities appearing to emerge with the retreat of the ice sheets. Prominent among these is the prospect of previously inaccessible oil and gas sources in the High North becoming available for extraction. A spate of extended maritime claims by the states of the region and some high-profile diplomatic posturing has prompted much anticipation of a new scramble for resources and even a new, more literal Cold War. However, the reality appears to be more mundane, with the Arctic oil rush so far proving to be more of a slow and cooperative saunter as the Arctic powers, and others, survey the new riches with a degree of caution, employing – and even sharing – lawyers and geologists rather than deploying troops. In as clear an illustration as you could have of the misprioritisation of political concerns that can occur with a traditional security perspective, while the national security dimensions of Arctic environmental change have been greatly exaggerated, the profound Human Security plight of the region's indigenous people is only just coming to the attention of the world.

The Arctic and state security

New Cold War?

In 2007 the Arctic was uncharacteristically thrust to the forefront of the world's media when a robot from a Russian submarine placed the national flag on the exact location of the North Pole for the first time in history, in a symbolic act of conquest both retro and futurist. The Russophobic response of the Western media and politicians to this stunt was also reminiscent of fears from yesteryear provoked by 'the Bear', and seemed to many to be a likely precursor for a new, modern and high-tech geopolitical struggle between East and West. The Canadian Foreign Minister Peter MacKay epitomised Western irritation at the Russian initiative by stating to television reporters: 'You can't go around the world and just plant flags and say "we're claiming this territory"' (MacKay, 2007). However, the governments of Canada, along with fellow Arctic littoral states Denmark and Norway, have also been busy claiming extra (underwater) territory in recent years, albeit in a less extravagant fashion. The melting of the Arctic ice sheets has opened up new possibilities for navigation, fishing and, most particularly, the exploitation of underground resources once thought too costly to extract, awakening the interests of governments and multinational corporations (MNCs).

At around the same time that the Russian robot was at the North Pole the US Geological Society was carrying out a 'Survey of Undiscovered Oil and Gas in the Arctic', the results of which further thrust the region into the media spotlight and the realms of realpolitik. The much quoted survey, carried out in conjunction with fellow geologists from Canada, Denmark, Greenland, Norway and Russia, estimated that the region contained 22% of the world's undiscovered fossil fuels: 13% of oil and 30% of gas (see Table 28.1). These findings are, of course, in addition to proven reserves already being extracted near the northern coasts of Alaska, Canada and Russia, amounting to 10% of the world's known remainder. 84% of all the undiscovered deposits are offshore, and much of it lies under parts of the Arctic Ocean beyond the two-hundred-mile Exclusive Economic Zone (EEZ) of the states, and is hence, as yet, not under any sovereign control (USGS, 2008).

Table 28.1 Estimated oil and gas deposits in the Arctic

	Oil – billion barrels	Liquified Gas – billion barrels	Natural Gas – trillion cubic feet	TOTAL – billion barrels equivalent
Undiscovered	90	44	1,669	412
Known	40	8.5	1,100	240

Source: USGS (2008)

The combined effects of the Russian robot and the geological survey prompted some shrill and bellicose reactions in the Western media and academia. A 2008 article in *Jane's Intelligence Review*, widely cited in the UK popular press, reasoned that Russia's recent war against Georgia and the general high stakes could see them, and possibly other Arctic states, 'make pre-emptive military strikes' to secure resources (Galeotti, 2008). Similarly, another widely cited article, by a former US Coast Guard Officer in the conservative journal *Foreign Affairs*, warned of 'armed brinkmanship' due to the anarchic nature of the emerging Arctic political landscape. 'Decisions about how to manage this rapidly changing region will likely be made within a diplomatic vacuum unless the United States steps forward to lead the international community toward a multilateral solution' (Borgerson, 2008: 73). Cold War stereotyping also came out of cold storage in a special edition of the *Eurasian Review of Geopolitics* on 'The Polar Game', which declared: 'Russia's decision to take an aggressive stand in the polar area has left the US, Canada and the Nordic countries little choice but to forge a cooperative High North strategy and invite other friendly countries, such as Great Britain, to help build a Western presence in the Arctic' (Cohen, 2008: 36).

Seemingly supporting such reactions was a notable reassertion of energy security interests in foreign policy statements by the Arctic powers. The *Fundamentals of Russian State Policy in the Arctic up to 2020 and Beyond* vowed to establish military and coastguard groups to protect new economic interests in line with their extended continental shelf claim, and stated that the Arctic would become 'the country's top strategic resource base by 2020' (Russian Government, 2009). One of the last acts of the Bush (Jr.) government was to release a Homeland Security Directive on the Arctic, the first official US foreign policy statement on the region since 1994, which announced that Washington would 'assert a more active and influential national presence to protect its Arctic interests' (US Government, 2009). The release of the Canadian government's *Comprehensive Northern Strategy* in the same year was in the context of their already well-established 'use it or lose it' strategy, which had prompted regular naval manoeuvres around the Arctic islands and promised the construction of a major military base at Resolute Bay on Cornwallis Island. The Canadian government under Prime Minister Stephen Harper and Foreign Minister Peter MacKay have set a notably militaristic tone on Arctic issues. In an incident that came to be described in some sections of the North American media as MacKay's 'Dr Strangelove moment', during a visit of President Obama to Ottawa in 2009 he despatched fighter planes to 'meet' Russian jets over the Beaufort Sea, only to be corrected by US military officials that the Russians had not entered Canadian airspace (Byers, 2010: 2–3). Also in 2009, in a seemingly symbolic move, the Norwegian government moved their national military headquarters from Jalta near Stavanger to Reitan, near Bodø, north of the Arctic Circle.

Norway, Canada and Denmark are, like the Russians, claiming extended continental shelf territory a further 150km from the edge of their EEZs. This has been done by submitting geological evidence to the International Tribunal for the Law of the Sea, established by the United Nations Conference on the Law of the Sea (UNCLOS). The United States have not been part of this process since they are not party to UNCLOS. Isolationist opposition in the Congress to the notion of being beholden to an international political body has hence prevented the Americans from being able to participate in the new 'carve up'. This provides a classic example of 'bureaucratic politics' in foreign policy, as favoured by Liberal analysts, over the 'rational actor' model of the Realists. The US government has not been able to implement a self-identified national interest policy due to internal politicking. Presidents Bush and Obama, Secretary of State Clinton and the US navy have all promoted ratification, but it has not happened and the Americans are, so far, left behind in the 'race'. The Russian, Norwegian, Danish and Canadian continental shelf claims overlap in several places, including on the Lomonosov Ridge which runs to the North Pole and which is claimed by Copenhagen, Moscow and Ottawa. Longer running territorial and particularly maritime disputes in a number of the shared seas of the Arctic Ocean have also been given prominence in the media.

Hot air over the Arctic?

However, it increasingly seems apparent that, while the Arctic natural environment is undoubtedly changing, the economic and political climate is not heating up at anything like the rate that was widely predicted. Despite the way it was reported and commented upon, the USGS survey was not revelatory. Its findings were not out of step with previous estimates of untapped Arctic energy supplies, and were broadly similar to its previous 2000 report. It does appear to have been the spectacle of the robotic Russian flag bearer which elevated the significance of the survey. However, the Russian North Pole flag planting exercise was, as Dodds notes, an act of 'stagecraft rather than statecraft' (Dodds, 2010: 63). As Russian Foreign Minister Lavrov was quick to point out at the time, this was a piece of exploratory showmanship comparable to the 'Stars and Stripes' being planted on the Moon in 1969. Indeed, it is usually overlooked that some of the money for the expedition came from Western sponsors (Baev, 2010).

The rise of interest from the 'supermajor' oil companies in the region is not necessarily indicative of a new black gold rush. Increasingly they have been compelled to look further afield as a result of the rise in 'resource nationalism', with the increased state control of hydrocarbon reserves. The Russian government in particular has acquired more direct influence over domestic energy companies and foreign investment ventures as part of the centralisation that has occurred since Putin succeeded Yeltsin as President in 1999. The expertise of the supermajors, though, is still needed by the Russian government, leading to a series of cooperative international ventures at odds with the nationalistic scramble popularly portrayed and predicted.

The USGS survey itself warns that 'no economic considerations are included in these initial estimates; results are presented without reference to costs of exploration and development which will be important in many of the assessed areas' (USGS, 2008). Of course, evaluating energy opportunities is not simply a matter of estimating the likely amounts of oil and gas under the ice and rock of the Arctic and comparing them to estimates in the rest of the world. The costs of exploration, extraction and transport are much different in the High North. The economic downturn the world has experienced since 2008 has made such costs all the more significant, and many of the companies that have acquired drilling licences for new Arctic fields have not yet set to work. For example, the Shtokman LNG field project, a much heralded joint venture between Gazprom, TOTAL and Statoil launched in 2007 in the Russian Barents Sea, has yet to begin operations due to the increasing doubts of shareholders which have prompted a series of postponements.

Even with warming temperatures the Arctic drilling season will only be three months long for the foreseeable future. Despite its retreat, thick ice cover will still be a reality in most of the Arctic for most of the year, and twenty-four-hour darkness will always be a fact of life in the winter months. Offshore prospecting, extraction and transport are much more expensive than onshore anywhere in the world, and the costs are multiplied when operations are sited in such remote locations. Shipping in the Arctic will gradually become more straightforward with global warming, but it still will not be easy. Many of the new routes, such as the fabled North West Passage, will only be open for short seasons, and an increasing number of icebergs from melting glaciers will present new hazards.

In April 2010, while President Medvedev was visiting Oslo, the Russians and Norwegians concluded an agreement ending a low level forty-year diplomatic dispute over how to partition the Barents Sea by amicably splitting it in two. In a joint communiqué that followed, the two Foreign Ministers announced: 'We firmly believe that the Arctic can be used to demonstrate just how much peace and collective interests can be served by the implementation of the international rule of law' (Store and Lavrov, 2010). This initiative took much of the world by surprise, but it should not have done, given that it was a win–win result. Doggedly sticking to their divergent claims had created a 'grey zone' amounting to some 12% of the Sea in which neither side could prospect for oil. Russian policy in the Arctic has, in fact, been far less belligerent and more cooperative than portrayed in the West. This can be dated back to Gorbachev's 1987 Murmansk speech when he declared: 'What everybody can be absolutely certain of is the Soviet Union's profound and certain interest in preventing the North of the planet, its Polar and sub-Polar regions and all Northern countries, from ever again becoming an arena of war, and in forming there a genuine zone of peace and fruitful cooperation' (Gorbachev, 1987). Russian overtures to the West on the Arctic have been consistently conciliatory since then, while maintaining their claims to the Seas to their north. Gorbachev's words were re-echoed in 2010 by Prime Minister Putin at a meeting of an International Arctic Forum in Moscow, when he stated: 'We think it is imperative to keep the Arctic as a zone of peace and cooperation', since, 'We all know that it is hard to live alone in the Arctic' (Putin, 2010).

There is only one territorial question to be resolved in the Arctic – a somewhat surreal, ridiculous but generally good-natured dispute between Canada and Denmark over the tiny and uninhabited Hans Island in Baffin Bay – and this looks increasingly likely to be resolved by either dividing or co-ruling the icy slab. Maritime disputes still exist, but this is far from unusual in international relations and there is little precedent for fighting over fish and water. Areas of contention remain in the Bering Sea between the US and Russia and between the US and Canada over the North West Passage and Beaufort Sea, but these are lower level disputes than the Barents Sea which was amicably resolved. In practice the US and Canada have cooperated in the disputed areas, with arrangements for coordinating coast guard work and special permission for navigation having been in operation since the 1980s. Again it appears to be dawning on both sides that a compromise would be a win–win situation, since the Canadian claim in the Beaufort (based on extending the territorial border northwards), while giving them a larger slice of the Sea up to the two-hundred-mile EEZ limit, would also actually give them less of the Sea beyond this than under the terms of the US claim (based on equidistance). This is because, at this distance, Canada's Banks Island comes into the equation. Hence, in a bizarre twist, the Canadian's claim could favour the Americans and the US claim favour the Canadians (Byers, 2011). There has been a deal on the table over the Bering Strait since 1990, but it has never entered into law due to a reluctance by the Duma to sanction what some Russian nationalists see as a sell-out to the Americans by the, in their eyes, discredited Gorbachev government. In practice, though, both sides have since stuck to the delineation agreed by Foreign Ministers Baker and Sheverdnadze and what we, in reality, see is realpolitik for domestic consumption masking the reality of peaceful coexistence at the intergovernmental level.

Foreign policy statements assert national interests and zero-sum characterisations of energy security because that is what foreign policy statements are supposed to do and what most of us expect to read. Formal Realism, though, often masks a truer discourse of cordial cooperative relations, and that is the case with the 'Arctic Five'. The toughest posturing has come not from the Russians or the Americans but from Canada, but nonetheless this is still more rhetoric than reality. Grant suggests that 'claims of protecting Arctic sovereignty seem little more than paper sovereignty' (Grant, 2010: 418) given that no new icebreakers have been constructed and the Resolute Bay military base has not advanced in spite of the tough talk. In addition, Canadian public opinion is much more sensitive about their Arctic hinterlands than the rest of the world generally appreciates (MSGA, 2011) and the Harper–MacKay government has been playing to this audience more than an international one.

Arctic intergovernmental cooperation can be viewed as vindicating a Liberal model of IR, but it is also possible to view this through the lenses of Neo-Realist and English School thinkers if one considers that the world's two premier military powers have come to accept a balance of power, consolidating their influence in the region by playing constructive roles in vehicles like the Arctic Council, which might limit their manoeuvres a little but also help to reinforce the status quo and keep other rising powers – like the EU or China – at a distance. Like the Concert of Europe in the nineteenth century or the EU or World Trade Organization in the present age, perhaps Arctic institutions and regimes represent mutually convenient vehicles for states, rather than evidence of creeping devolved global governance.

The continental shelf claims are being pursued in a distinctly legalistic manner with the Russians, Canadians, Danes and Norwegians patiently presenting claims to UNCLOS and showing every indication that they will abide by their arbitration. This was made public with the 'Ilulissat Declaration', which followed a meeting of the Arctic Five in Greenland in 2008, stating: 'We remain committed to this legal framework [UNCLOS] and to the orderly settlement of any overlapping claims' (Ilulissat, 2008). While this declaration irked the governments of the three other Arctic states and the members of the Arctic Council who were not consulted (Sweden, Iceland and Finland, who are not Arctic **Ocean** states), it was very much indicative of the fact that a peaceful carve-up of the Arctic between the sovereign powers is in their mutual interests. Hence the declaration also stated the opposition of the Arctic Five to the alternative model of governance frequently suggested by other countries and environmentalists, of an Antarctic-style 'world park' conservation area outside of sovereign jurisdiction. Danish Foreign Minister Møller hence saw fit to announce after the Ilulissat release that 'we have hopefully quelled all of the myths about a race for the North Pole once and for all' (Møller, 2008).

Human Security in the Arctic

Globalisation has come belatedly but rapidly to the Arctic, with profound environmental and social changes transforming the lives of its peoples. As with globalisation elsewhere in the world, industrialisation, modernisation and MNC investment are bringing great opportunities for some, but, at the same time they are also bringing new Human Security concerns.

Environmental change

Climate change: The increased spotlight that has been cast on the Arctic due to climate change has also served to begin revealing the Human Security implications of this phenomenon. The world's most profound form of environmental change is being felt most profoundly of all in the Arctic. The United Nation's Intergovernmental Panel on Climate Change reported that average Arctic temperatures had increased at nearly twice the global average rate over the past century, and that Arctic sea ice had shrunk by 3.3% over the previous decade (IPCC, 2007).

As described in Chapter 16, one key implication of climate change is the raising of sea levels due to the polar ice caps melting. This carries significant threats to human life in the more frequent and lengthy heatwaves and droughts, coastal flooding, ocean acidification due to carbon dioxide affecting fish stocks, and more frequent and stronger riverine flooding. While most of these Human Security impacts are coming to be felt worldwide, they are manifesting themselves most dramatically in the Polar North due to its differentially rapid rate of warming. Pollution is being exacerbated as northerly winds become more intense, precipitation increases and the flow rate in rivers accelerates. The flow rate in the great Siberian rivers has already increased by between 15–20% in the twenty years since the mid-1980s (Usher *et al.*, 2010). Further effects on pollution and food supply will then be experienced, since melted ice entering the sea affects salinity and ocean circulation patterns. Together with its antipodean counterpart, changes in the Arctic also contribute to the exacerbation of global warming by altering the albedo effect of Earth, since sea ice reflects sunlight.

Pollution: In a graphic illustration of the globalisation of environmental problems, the Arctic region has become particularly prone to several forms of long-range pollution, mainly associated with industrial activities in Europe, North America and Asia. Arctic Haze, a smog resulting from the accumulation of sulphur, nitrogen and carbon emissions in the atmosphere in winter and spring over the High North, is likely to accelerate with the further onset of warming and social change in the Arctic, since it is linked to local shipping traffic emissions (Law and Stohl, 2007).

Persistent Organic Pollutants (POPs), described in Chapter 16, have come to affect the environment and human health in the Arctic despite the fact that such pesticides and industrial chemicals are barely used in the region. Since they are so slow to break down and tend to be stored in fat, POPs can end up deposited in animals thousands of kilometres from where they were used. Through the process of bioaccumulation fish and aquatic mammals build up deposits of these toxins, which can then pass through predators higher up the food chain. Hence polar bears and wolves, at the top of Arctic food chains, have been found to be contaminated by POPs (Tenenbaum, 2004).

The Arctic is also prone to extreme manifestations of long-range transboundary pollution in the context of the accumulation of mercury and lead residues in food. While mercury emissions from North America and Europe have progressively fallen since the 1980s, due to political actions, the growth of Chinese coal-fed power plants has served to counter this and led to a continuation of contamination by long-range atmospheric transport which has particularly affected Arctic fish stocks, again through bioaccumulation. Mercury can be transported in the air and then fall as snow in springtime and come to be ingested by sea birds and marine mammals.

Health

Human security among the peoples of the High North has been affected by the social changes brought about by globalisation as well as environmental change.

Disease exposure: Increased exposure to harmful strains of disease is a well-established side-effect of globalisation. It is well documented that political colonisation has often been accompanied by biological colonisation. There were sudden outbreaks of spiral meningitis, tuberculosis, influenza and pneumonia among Canadian Inuit in the early 1940s owing to the increased wartime presence of military and administrative staff from the South. This represented an escalation of a phenomenon previously witnessed after the arrival of supply ships from Quebec. Most strikingly, it came to be appreciated that the common cold could be fatal to natives of the Polar North since these people had not developed the genetic resistance that renders this a trivial ailment in most of the world (Duffy, 1988: 87–89).

Recent years have seen a resurgence of diseases in the Arctic that were thought to have been consigned to history in the developed world. In 2010 there were ninety-nine recorded cases of tuberculosis in Canada's Nunavut Territory, a rate sixty-two times the national average. Living standards out of step with one of the world's wealthiest countries are a contributory factor to this phenomenon, but so is the biological and psychological persistence of the epidemics of the 1940s and 1950s. Many elderly Canadian Inuit carry a dormant version of the disease retained from that time, while memories of the clumsy and insensitive handling of the epidemics by Federal authorities leave many reluctant to undertake the lengthy antibiotic treatment courses (White, 2010). Given that around 10% of Canada's Inuit were relocated in the mid-twentieth century (sometimes forcibly) to southern sanitaria, from where many never returned, this is not surprising (Grygier, 1994).

Lifestyle illnesses: Arctic peoples have been particularly affected by the rise of 'lifestyle illnesses'. In a side-effect to the rise of pollution in the region referred to as the 'Arctic dilemma', health problems have arisen as a result of people consuming less of their traditional foodstuffs through fears of poisoning by lead, mercury or POPs. The relative poverty of native Arctic peoples allied to the relatively high costs of processed foods, due to their long-range transport, makes the 'nutrition transition' away from their traditional diet particularly damaging. The types of 'Western' foods best suited to long-range transport are, of course, not fresh fruit and vegetables but processed snacks like crisps, biscuits and fizzy drinks.

The globalisation of culture also explains the appeal of Western food, and this has served to heighten health insecurity in the Arctic. A rise in rates of obesity and diabetes has resulted from the nutrition transition to Western consumption patterns. The mechanisation of travel and a decline in hunting in some communities has also added to the obesity problem as the Arctic lifestyle has become less active (Sharma, 2010).

Native Alaskans are nearly nine times more likely to die of alcohol-related health problems than the average US citizen (Seale, Shellenberger and Spence, 2006). Cancers were near non-existent in the Arctic until the last hundred years, but lung, colon and breast cancers have soared due to social change (Friborg and Melbye, 2008). Lung cancer rates in the Canadian Inuit are the highest in the world (Krummel, 2009: 515).

Suicides: Suicide rates among Northern natives in Russia are over three times those of the overall population of a country with one of the world's highest incidences. East Greenland has one of the highest regional rates in the world (1,500 per 100,000) (Krummel, 2009: 511). A Canadian report found that suicide rates among male Nunavut Inuit between the ages of 19 and 24 were around fifty times the rate found in the equivalent demographic group in the rest of the country. Although stereotypically explained by cold, dark and lonely lifestyles, this phenomenon is very much a product of globalisation. Suicide was a phenomenon barely known in the Arctic in the pre-modern age. There was only one suicide in Nunavut in the whole of the 1960s, but since then the 'historical trauma' of rapid social change has seen young men exposed to the forms of alienation linked to depression in the developed world – educational failure, sexual frustrations, alcohol, drugs and petty crime – but to a much greater degree. Mental illnesses are not fifty times more prominent in young Nunavut men, so explanations have to be social rather than biological, and patterns of social change appear to support this. Suicides began to rise in the Alaskan Inuit in the 1960s, among the Greenland Inuit in the late 1970s and then in the Nunavut Inuit in the 1980s, at the same time as modernisation, in the form of colonial education, settled communities and a decline in traditional hunting employment, occurred (Nunavut, 2008: 16–17).

Globalisation has brought new opportunities for Arctic peoples, but it has also rendered them more vulnerable to a range of new insecurities. The uneven nature of globalisation witnessed worldwide is illustrated in microcosm here, since Inuit life expectancy is considerably lower than the average for citizens in the Arctic states. In Canada and Greenland the difference is more than ten years. Life expectancy for Canadian men, for example, is 77.2, but for Inuit in Nunavut it is just 66.6 (Krummel, 2009: 509).

Conclusion

Rhetoric and reality are often not the same thing in international relations, but particularly, it seems, in the politics of the Arctic, where foreign policy posturing and pronouncements are often the howls of sheep in wolves' clothing. Arctic exploration, be it for adventure or profit, has always seemed to be accompanied by much symbolism, jingoism and bombast as man seeks to conquer nature at its most brutal in something of a 'masculinist fantasy' (Ditmer *et al.*, 2011). However, this flies in the face of the reality that making money in remote, difficult conditions necessitates cooperation rather than nationalist rivalry. Instead of the old maxim that a successful foreign policy requires one to 'speak softly but carry a big stick', what we are witnessing in the Arctic is more a case of 'talk tough but carry a big bag of carrots'. The cordial cartel that is the 'Arctic Five' and the energy-seeking ventures bringing together Western MNCs and the Kremlin represent transnational symbiosis rather than new Cold War nationalism. Far from the lucrative scrambles produced by the discoveries of Yukon gold in the 1920s or Alaskan oil in the 1960s, future energy exploration in the High Arctic is set to be much more long term and speculative – or, as Emmerson terms it, a 'slow rush for Northern resources' (Emmerson, 2010: 197). While global warming is rightly bringing much-needed attention to the needs of its indigenous populations, whose lives are being transformed by a transforming physical and economic climate, an awful lot of hot air has been spoken about an Arctic oil rush and new Cold War. To most Arctic observers the hope is that the national security false alarms that have been ringing in response to environmental change in the Arctic can serve as a wake-up call for the Human Security plight of the region's indigenous peoples.

Recommended reading

Arctic Governance Project – collation of papers from researchers from all eight Arctic states. http://www.arcticgovernance.org/.

Byers, M. *Who Owns the Arctic? Understanding Sovereignty Disputes in the North,* Vancouver: Douglas & McIntyre, 2010.

Hough, P. *International Politics of the Arctic: Coming in From the Cold,* London and New York: Routledge, 2013.

Young, O. 'The Future of the Arctic: Cauldron of Conflict or Zone of Peace?' (Review Article), *International Affairs,* vol. 87, no. 1, 2011, 185–193.

29 The Arab Spring and democracy

Problems and prospects

Jeffrey Haynes

Box 29.1: The Arab Spring

For six months, we have witnessed an extraordinary change taking place in the Middle East and North Africa. Square by square, town by town, country by country, the people have risen up to demand their basic human rights. Two leaders have stepped aside. More may follow. And though these countries may be a great distance from our shores, we know that our own future is bound to this region by the forces of economics and security, by history and by faith.

(Remarks by the US President on the Middle East and North Africa, 19 May 2011, The White House, Office of the Press Secretary[1])

Introduction

The Arab Spring began in October 2010 in Tunisia. It was an important focal point of political concerns, affecting many Arab-majority countries in the Middle East and North Africa (MENA). Four years later, nothing is clear in terms of whether the Arab Spring events will (eventually) lead to more democracy in the countries of the MENA. That is, no uniformity is to be seen in what has occurred politically, although in some cases old dictators remain in power (Syria) while in others (Egypt) a new dubiously democratic leader appeared via the ballot box. Despite uncertainty about political outcomes, the concerns of the Arab Spring are still alive and relevant – that is, popular concerns with political reform and economic growth – although we are not really any the wiser about what will be the eventual outcome. Throughout the Arab Spring events, the issue of the role of religion in political reforms – especially political Islam – has been of central importance, and as a result, in this case study we examine both the political context of the Arab Spring and the relationship between political Islam and politics.

Politics, religion and the Arab Spring

Contemporary political debates in the context of the Arab Spring, involving both democratising countries (for example, Tunisia), truncated democracies (for example, Egypt) and not-yet-democratising polities (for example, Libya and Syria), all focus on demands for political reform. In addition, throughout the region there is a widespread political involvement of religion, and its overall role in public life is now a pertinent and controversial political question. Put another way, as the countries of the MENA struggle for meaningful political changes, the role of religion in this context inevitably takes centre stage.

The general question of how religious actors might affect political outcomes has long been a controversial issue, not only in the MENA but in many countries and regions in recent decades. Immediately after the Second World War, scholars of comparative politics stressed the importance of what was called 'political culture' in explaining the success or failure of democratisation in various countries influenced by US policy, including West Germany, Italy and Japan (Linz and Stepan, 1996; Stepan, 2000; Huntington, 1991). Also at this time, religious traditions – for example, Roman Catholicism in Italy and Christian Democracy in West Germany – were said to be important in the (re)making of those countries' political cultures following the traumatising effects of totalitarian regimes before and during the Second World War (Casanova, 1994). Later, during the 'third wave of democracy' (mid-1970s to late 1990s), attention was also paid to the political role of religion in democratisation (Huntington, 1991). For example, it was widely noted that in Poland, the Polish Roman Catholic Church, in tandem with a Polish pope, John Paul II, played a key role in undermining the existing Communist government, a significant factor in helping to establish a post-Communist, democratically accountable regime in the country (Weigel, 2005, 2007).

In addition, the democratic impact of the Roman Catholic Church had a wider political effect beyond Poland, extending to Latin America, Africa and parts of Asia during the1980s and 1990s. Contemporaneously there was the rise of the Christian/ Religious Right in the US, and since then its considerable and continuing impact on the electoral fortunes of both the Republican and Democratic parties. Add to this the emergence, growth and spread of various kinds of political Islam – including Islamist movements such as the Muslim Brotherhood – across the Muslim world, from Morocco to Indonesia, which has had significant ramifications for electoral outcomes in various countries, including Algeria, Egypt, Morocco, recent electoral success for the *Bharatiya Janata* Party in India, and substantial political influence over time for various political parties rooted in Judaist interpretations of the world in Israel, and we see irrefutable evidence for religion's clear and sustained political involvement around the world. Most recently, as a new wave of challenges to authoritarianism continues to significantly affect a region previously apparently isolated from democratic trends and currents, it is clear that in the Arab countries of the MENA religion substantially affects political and, more specifically, democratisation outcomes.

But how might it do this? Earlier research established that various kinds of religious actors – including Christian and Islamist entities – are not necessarily pivotal to democratisation processes, either successful or unsuccessful. For example, focusing on the formerly communist Central and East European region and its democratising experience in the 1980s and 1990s, Juan Linz and Alfred Stepan argue that religion (Christianity) was *not* generally the – or even a – key explanatory factor in associated democratic outcomes (Linz and Stepan, 1996). Turning to Muslim-majority countries in the MENA and writing in the mid-1990s, Fred Halliday (2005) argued that the general failure to democratise during the third wave of democracy was not primarily due to the characteristics of Islam. Instead, Halliday argued that the failure to democratise when democratisation was otherwise a global trend was essentially the outcome of entrenched non-religious social and political impediments. These included decades-long experiences of rule by 'strong' individualistic leaders, associated patterns and structures of authoritarian rule, weak and often powerless institutions, and frail, fragmented civil societies, which were demonstrably incapable of pushing sustainably or collectively for democratisation. Halliday also contended that while some such features might be legitimised by the state in terms of extant 'Islamic doctrine' (*viz.* Wahhabism in Saudi Arabia), there was in fact nothing specifically 'Islamic' about them; in other words, being Muslim did not mean you were necessarily anti-democracy or culturally and religiously content with an unelected, unrepresentative, often capricious rule by self-proclaimed 'strongmen'.

Samuel Huntington (1996) articulated a third view on the role of religion in democratisation. In contrast to Linz and Stepan and unlike Halliday, he averred that religions had a crucial impact, whether for 'good' or 'bad', on democratisation outcomes during the third wave of democracy. Huntington controversially claimed that Christianity, in both Protestant and Catholic forms, was strongly connected to the remarkable spread of democracy during the third wave, a crucial component of the majority of successful democratisations during the period of the third wave (the mid-1970s to the late 1990s). Several other religious faiths, Huntington asserted, including Orthodox Christianity, Islam, Buddhism and Confucianism, were either not as supportive of democracy or even resolutely opposed to it. In sum, there is no consensus regarding the role of religion in recent democratisation; various prominent scholars have drawn differing conclusions in this respect. The following observations can be inferred from the views of Linz and Stepan, Halliday and Huntington:

- Religious traditions have core elements which may be *more* or *less* conducive to democratisation and democracy;
- Religious traditions are always multi-vocal. However, at any given moment there are voices in the ascendancy which are *more* or *less* receptive to and encouraging of democratisation;
- Religious actors *rarely if ever determine* democratisation outcomes. On the other hand, they may be of significance in various ways for democratisation, with a range of outcomes.

These observations will inform our examination of the Arab Spring which follows.

Religion, democratisation and civil liberties in Arab countries

Rebellions occurred in early 2011 in both Egypt and Tunisia, while the Gaddafi government in Libya was overthrown later in the same year following decisive international intervention. From 2011 there were also major, and in some cases continuing, political upheavals in Syria, Bahrain and Yemen, and smaller although still notable expressions of political dissent in Algeria and Morocco. Events took an unexpected turn in May 2011 with the killing by US agents in Pakistan of the al-Qaeda leader, Osama bin Laden. Perhaps surprisingly, however, bin Laden's death did not appear to lead to political ramifications in the context of the 'Arab uprising' despite his supposed iconic status for thousands of regional Islamists.

On the other hand, not since the end of Communism in Central and Eastern Europe a generation ago has the role of religion in democratisation and post-authoritarian political arrangements been so centrally and consistently to the fore as it is today in discussions and analysis of the Arab Spring. However, a simple question – 'What is to be the general political outcome of the Arab Spring for the Arab/ Muslim countries of the MENA, a region largely untouched by the third wave of democracy?' – is not likely to elicit a clear or simple response. Another question – 'What is the role of religion in the Arab Spring events?' – is also not conducive to a simple or short satisfactory reply.

Nevertheless, since the demands for fundamental political changes in the MENA region unexpectedly but widely surfaced in the autumn of 2010, international attention has consistently focused on the Arab countries of the MENA, albeit without clear or consistent patterns of religious involvement in the continuing events and developments. This is partly because, at the time of writing, the Arab Spring has not reached a clear conclusion. In particular, the question of whether there will eventually be widespread, epochal political changes in the region is not resolved, and the issue remains of profound international importance, not least because of the continuing – and increasingly successful – attempt by the Assad government in Syria to hang on to power in the face of sustained (albeit fragmented) domestic challenges to its rule, and an almost total lack of support by anti-regime external actors compared to the strong support supplied to Assad by foreign governments, notably that of Iran. In sum, after four years the Arab Spring shows no sign of winding down or abating, while the unresolved civil war in Syria has served both to internationalise the conflict, with unforeseeable results for the region, and highlight the serious dangers of sectarian division which could lead to state failure or even collapse.

Turning to the specific role of religion in the Arab Spring since late 2010, while across the affected countries various identifiable religious actors have been, and continue to be, conspicuous by their involvement in anti-authoritarian and pro-democratisation, it is not possible to discern a clear pattern in terms of outcomes related to democratisation. What we do know is that rebellions in Egypt and Tunisia unseated incumbent governments and ushered in recognisably democratic elections which, in both cases, various Islamists won. Yet in both Egypt and Tunisia, while Islamists won power via the ballot box, we did not see a clear or inexorable transition either to a recognisably democratic regime or to an Islamic state. In fact, in both Egypt and Tunisia, Islamists are very significantly divided between what we might call 'moderates' and 'extremists'.

These outcomes provide further evidence that 'Islam' does not provide a demonstrable, one-size-fits-all blueprint for how to rule once an *ancien régime* has been ousted, and whether authentically democratic regimes become ensconced in Egypt and Tunisia or not would appear to have little to do with the fact that both are overwhelmingly Muslim countries. What is of much more importance for stability, security and regime longevity, and hence the prospects of democratisation, are material considerations: can new governments deal with pressing challenges from fast-growing populations who want more jobs and improved welfare? However, to the many, many people in both countries who want instant change for the better – and these include a majority of the young, especially those who were most prominent in the globally observed anti-government demonstrations which led to the overthrow of incumbent regimes – the religious complexion of a government is almost certainly much less important than its ability to bring about swift, desirable improvements in living standards. Evidence for this assertion comes from Turkey where the *Adalet ve Kalkınma Partisi* (AKP; Justice and Development Party) government has presided over a sustained period of economic growth since coming to power in 2002, with beneficial ramifications in terms of jobs, welfare and security. The governing party has also seen its share of the vote increase to over 50% of the ballots cast in the most recent election in 2011. This was not due to the government becoming 'more religious' – in fact, the ruling party and its leaders are at pains to stress that the AKP is not a religious party *per se*, but is actually a 'conservative democratic' party along the lines of Germany's Christian Democrats (Haynes, 2012).

Given the significant – perhaps increasingly fundamental – political changes that have recently occurred in Egypt, Tunisia and Libya, and which may also be slowly unfolding in Syria, all of which are staunchly Islamic countries with majority Muslim populations of over 90% in each case, then it seems uncontroversial to argue there is nothing inherent in Islam which means that Muslim countries – whether in the MENA or elsewhere – necessarily lack the capacity to fundamentally change their political arrangements, including in a pro-democracy direction. Not that we need evidence from the 'Arab uprising' to make this assertion. Significant recent democratic advances in a number of Muslim countries – including the above-mentioned Turkey, as well as Indonesia, the world's most populous Muslim country with a population of over 200 million, and Bangladesh, with more than 150 million people, mainly Muslims – make it certain that Islam *per se* is not an insurmountable barrier to democratisation.

On the other hand, the domestic environment, including the political role of Islam, is but one side of the story. The overthrow of the Gaddafi government in Libya and the lack of consistent purposive action by the 'international community' in Syria to encourage President Assad to stand down highlight the problematic issue of foreign intervention in democracy promotion during the Arab Spring. Western governments have been torn between generally wishing to see more democracy in the MENA and the potential dangers to Western security of having hostile Islamist governments in power, as occurred in Afghanistan during the period from 1996 to 2001 during Taliban rule. The West's contention is that extremist Islamists thrive in a context of instability, insecurity and a lack of hope, such as engendered in some regional countries as a result of the 'Arab uprising'. In response, the UK Prime Minister David Cameron announced in May 2011 that the UK would make a major financial donation in support of democratisation and improved social welfare in several Arab Spring countries. The UK government announced that £110 million ($165 million) would be siphoned off from the existing Department for International Development budget, to be focused upon encouraging democratisation in the MENA. In addition, the UK's Foreign and Commonwealth Office announced that up to £40 million ($60 million) would be spent over the 2011–15 period to try to improve three democratic cornerstones in the Arab countries: increased political participation; improved rule of law; and greater freedom of the press. Finally, the UK government pledged to donate a further £70 million ($105 million), focused generally on economic reforms and specifically on aiming to boost youth employment, strengthen anti-corruption measures and promote private sector investment. In sum, in response to the events of the 'Arab uprising', the UK government committed both short- and medium-term funding increases both to help build democracy in the MENA and to make it less likely that extremism, especially Islamist extremism, would be able to take power in political vacuums and threaten UK and other Western security interests.

However, a word of caution is necessary. For three main reasons, it is unlikely that the MENA region is about to jump from authoritarianism to democratisation and then on to democratic consolidation, as many post-Communist Central and Eastern European countries did following the implosion of Soviet power and authority in the early 1990s. First, the MENA region has widespread sectarian divisions – leading to sustained and often deadly conflict between different religious sects, including intra-Muslim (Iraq, Syria, Bahrain) and Muslim–Christian (Tunisia, Egypt) tensions. Despite the coming together of people from all faiths in the protests that brought down their governments, both Egypt and Tunisia have experienced sectarian tensions and conflict, while Syria is immersed in a deeply polarising sectarian conflict fuelled by deadly rivalries between Iran and Saudi Arabia, on the one hand, and Russia and the US on the other. Egypt was the scene of a bloody attack against a Coptic church in Alexandria in December 2010, followed by a clash in the Imbaba district of Cairo which killed at least fifteen, both Copts and Muslims. Tunisia saw the murder of a Polish-born Catholic priest, Father Marek Rybinski, killed on the premises of an inter-denominational school in Tunis, while Islamist protesters gathered together outside the Great Synagogue of Tunis and a chapel was burned near Gabes. In Bahrain, the political violence pitted Shias against Sunnis. In Syria, the Assad-led Alawite minority government has exploited the country's hitherto latent sectarian divisions in its increasingly desperate bid to stay in power.

Second, religious competition and conflict is but one dimension of a more generalised threat to democratisation in the Arab countries of the MENA. In addition, there are also endemic, widespread economic problems engulfing most of the region's countries, which is one of the key reasons why incumbent authoritarian governments were challenged by popular protest in the first place. Overall, the MENA region is undergoing a serious and sustained economic slide, notwithstanding the relatively high extant global oil prices. Across the region, gross domestic product (GDP) is well down and social welfare is declining, and all this is occurring in the context of some of the fastest growing populations in the world. Egypt is a good example of what is happening. Arguably, much of the cause of the uprising which led to the overthrow of the Mubarak government in early 2011 was the result of economic frustration, especially among the young who were in the forefront of the rebellion. Tourism revenue, the mainstay of the economy and the biggest single element in GDP, fell by 80% in the same year, the stock market plummeted and continues to underperform, and the International Monetary Fund noted a mere 1% growth in 2011, down from 5.1% in 2010.

Third, Saudi Arabia and Iran are deadly rivals in the MENA. Saudi Arabia has had to deal with the loss of its closest ally, the Mubarak government. Iran contemplates the fall of its ally, the Assad regime. The government of Bahrain is bolstered – but for how long? – by the injection of Saudi troops, while Iran seeks to exploit the growing anarchy in Yemen in order to destabilise its Saudi arch enemy.

Overall, evidence suggests that the prospect of the Arab countries of the MENA region taking a clear path to democratisation is currently poor, and the chances of widespread democratic consolidation are worse. The unwelcome but most likely outcome is a gradual slide into entrenched and long-term political instability culminating in some cases in state failure with serious ramifications for regional and international instability.

The role of religion in these developments is unclear. On the one hand, various Islamists have shown themselves to be willing to play by the democratic rules of the game where elections have been held (Egypt and Tunisia), although this has not necessarily helped to dispel fears, especially among secularists, that the ruse of the

Islamists is to get into power and then use circumstances to make sure they stay there. The same kind of argument was used in relation to Algeria in the early 1990s to justify a military coup that ushered in a two-decade-long civil war, which did nothing for the country's long-term political or economic development.

Conclusion

This case study seeks to engage with the issue of the relationship between religion – especially political Islam – and democratisation in the context of the Arab Spring in the MENA, which began in late 2010. We have seen that on occasion religious actors can be pivotal in relation to democratisation outcomes, as in Egypt and Tunisia. Most of the time, however, religious actors in general, including Islamists, have a rather ambivalent relationship with democratisation. This is partly because they are not necessarily recognised as legitimate actors in this context, a terrain where secular political actors are normally much more influential than religious actors. The only way to be sure is to enable the Islamists to take power, if it is achieved legitimately through the ballot box, and then see what they do with it. If they try to truncate or diminish democracy, or undermine its veracity, then there is always the option to take to the streets again in order to pressurise incumbent rulers to change policies in a pro-democracy direction.

It is impossible to overlook the external dimension when assessing the prospects for democratisation in the Arab countries of the MENA. Western governments were often key supporters of the third wave of democracy, including in many Central and Eastern European countries, in the 1980s and 1990s. Embarking on often ambitious programmes of democracy promotion in the 1980s and 1990s, backed up by large sums of money in order to improve the prospects of democratisation, over time this fulsome support gave way to growing Western ambivalence about encouraging democracy, especially in regions such as the MENA where a shift to democracy was likely to mean an increase in the capacity of Islamists to play a role in government, as events in post-revolution Egypt and Tunisia underline.

However, overall neither the course nor the outcome of the 'Arab uprising' is clear or unidirectional. In some cases Islamists have achieved power (Egypt, Tunisia, only to lose it again soon after in Egypt), while in others secular actors appear to be (perhaps temporarily) in charge following the overthrow of an existing regime (Libya). In sum, the longer-term role of religious actors in political events in the MENA is by no means clear, and it appears that the relationship with democracy that Islamists and others have varies from place to place and context to context.

Note

1 http://www.whitehouse.gov/the-press-office/2011/05/19/remarks-president-middle-east-and-north-africa.

Recommended reading

Halliday, F. *The Middle East in International Relations: Power, Politics and Ideology*. Cambridge: Cambridge University Press, 2005.

Haynes, J. 'Religion and democracy: The Case of the AKP in Turkey', in J. Fox (ed.), *Religion, Politics, Society, & the State*, Oxford: Oxford University Press, 2012, 73–88.

Huntington, S. *The Third Wave: Democratization in the Late Twentieth Century*, Norman: University of Oklahoma Press, 1991.

Huntington, S. *The Clash of Civilizations and the Remaking of World Order*. New York: Free Press, 1996.

Linz, J. and Stepan, A. *Problems of Democratic Transition and Consolidation. Southern Europe, South America, and Post-Communist Europe*. Baltimore and London: John Hopkins University Press, 1996.

Stepan, A. 'Religion, Democracy, and the "Twin Tolerations"', *Journal of Democracy*, vol. 11, no. 4, 2000, 37–57.

Weigel, G. *Faith, Reason, and the War against Jihadism: A Call to Action*, New York: Doubleday, 2007.

30 The Israeli–Palestinian conflict

Ronald Ranta

Box 30.1: National anthems

As long as in the heart within,
The Jewish soul yearns,
And towards the eastern edges, onwards,
An eye gazes towards Zion.
Our hope is not yet lost,
The hope that is two thousand years old,
To be a free nation in our land,
The land of Zion, Jerusalem.
(Israel's national anthem)

With the resolve of the winds and the fire of the weapons
And the determination of my nation in the land of struggle
Palestine is my home, Palestine is my fire,
Palestine is my vendetta and the land of withstanding
By the oath under the shade of the flag
By my land and nation, and the fire of pain
I will live as a Fida'i, I will remain a redeemer,
I will die as a Fida'i – until my country returns
Fida'i.
(Part of the Palestinian national anthem)

Introduction

The Israeli–Palestinian conflict is an ongoing situation that began at the end of the nineteenth century. It plays an important role in Middle Eastern and international politics and is part of the wider Arab–Israeli conflict. Some of the main conflict issues, such as refugees, water and security, affect not only the two sides, but also neighbouring states and international actors further afield. Despite claims that it is religious or ethnic, the Israeli–Palestinian conflict is, at its core, a dispute between two nations over land and sovereignty. This chapter aims to broaden the reader's understanding of the conflict and relate it to some of the key concepts and terms discussed in the core chapters of the book.

There are different ways of analysing the Israeli–Palestinian conflict. It can be viewed as a conflict between two sides that have clear and identifiable concerns and objectives relating to issues such as land, sovereignty and resources. However, the longevity and intractability of the conflict give rise to other forms of analysis. Issues such as psychology, fear and hatred of the other, sense of victimhood, and religious and ideological considerations sometimes create the impression that there is more to the conflict than land and sovereignty. Therefore, it is vital that students are aware of the different narratives woven by each side, their history and psychology.

Additionally, it is important to note that the sides are not as coherent and unitary as sometimes presented. Although Israel is a state, a multitude of different factions and interest groups operate within it – for example, the Israeli peace movement, Jewish settlers, and different political parties, each pursuing different aims as regards the conflict. The Palestinians do not have a state and are geographically divided. They are also politically divided, with the Gaza Strip ruled by Hamas and the West Bank ruled by the Palestinian Authority (PA).

Historical introduction

The name Palestine was given to the region by the Romans after the suppression of a Jewish revolt in 135 CE, and it has remained in use ever since. The modern borders of Israel/Palestine were drawn by the British and the League of Nations in 1923.

At the end of the nineteenth century the overwhelming majority of the population in Palestine was non-Jewish (mostly Muslim, but with a significant Christian minority). The process of Jewish immigration to Palestine as a consequence of the rise of Zionism (Jewish nationalism) and anti-Semitism stood in stark contrast to rising national awareness among the local Arab-Palestinian population. The main aim of Zionism was the return of Jews to Palestine (in Hebrew *Eretz Israel* – the historic-Biblical land of Israel and the birthplace of Judaism) and the establishment of a Jewish state there. Both national groups claim the same land – Israel/Palestine – as their homeland. The often violent struggle between these two nations took place amid the collapse of the Ottoman Empire, the establishment of a British Mandate (1919–48) and the Second World War and the Holocaust (1939–45).

During the period of the British Mandate several solutions were put forward, including a partition plan, but none gained the acceptance of both sides. Taking into account the horrors of the Holocaust (when six million Jews were killed and several hundred thousand more became refugees), and Britain's inability to resolve the conflict, the United Nations General Assembly voted on partitioning Palestine into a Jewish and an Arab-Palestinian state (29 November 1947 – Resolution 181).

A war ensued in 1948, first at a civil level between Jews and Palestinians, and later between Israel (the Jewish state) and neighbouring Arab states. The war ended in an overwhelming victory for Israel, which took over most of the land. The Arab-held parts of Palestine were reduced to the West Bank and the Gaza Strip (22% of historical Palestine), controlled by Jordan and Egypt respectively. The war also resulted in a massive refugee problem. Approximately seven hundred and fifty thousand Palestinians became refugees as a direct consequence of the war. Despite a UN resolution, Israel did not allow the refugees to return. For Palestinians the war is known as the *Nakba* (the Catastrophe) and is characterised by dispossession and expulsion: for Israelis this was their war of independence. As a consequence of Jewish suffering in the Holocaust and the Palestinian refugee tragedy, both nations share a strong sense of victimhood. Therefore the conflict is sometimes seen as one between two groups of victims.

Palestinian refugees: According to the UN there are around 4.7 million Palestinian refugees (2012), the majority of whom are descendents of refugees from the 1948 war. There are around two million refugees in the Occupied Territories, two million in Jordan, and half a million in both Lebanon and Syria respectively. Many refugees are supported by the UNRWA (United Nations Relief and Works Agency), a UN body specifically created to assist Palestinian refugees. The living conditions of Palestinian refugees vary considerably, dependent upon the state in which they reside. In Lebanon, for example, refugees are deprived of most basic rights. A key Palestinian demand is the right of return to Israel/Palestine for the refugees; this demand is also enshrined in international law (UN Resolution 194). Palestinians claim refugees should be given options to return to their previous homes, return to a future Palestinian state, be repatriated in the countries where they reside, and/or receive compensation. Israel claims that it did not create and therefore is not responsible for the refugee problem. It argues that their return, after more than sixty years, is not feasible and that it would undermine the Jewish nature of the Israeli state. Israel insists that the refugees should either be repatriated in the countries where they currently reside or return to a future Palestinian state. In addition, Israel highlights the case of the hundreds of thousands of Jewish refugees from Arab states whom it absorbed. This issue is concerned not only with the aspirations of millions of refugees, but also with the future of Israel. The right of return for the Palestinian refugees is seen by Israel as a demographic threat to its survival as a Jewish state.

In 1967 the June war, also known as the Six Day war, between Israel and its Arab neighbours changed the dynamics of the conflict. The war brought about an Israeli victory and the occupation of territories three and a half times its own size, among them the West Bank, including East Jerusalem, and the Gaza Strip. At the heart of the current conflict is the future of the West Bank and the Gaza Strip – referred to as the Occupied Territories – their population, the settlements Israel established there, and the fate of the Palestinian refugees. Whether the Occupied Territories should be classified as Palestinian is a hotly-debated issue; however, by and large the international community recognises them as such, and in many cases they are referred to as the Occupied Palestinian Territories.

In 1988 the Palestinian Liberation Organization (PLO) – an umbrella organisation representing Palestinian nationalist groups headed by Yasser Arafat – agreed to a two-state solution. This came as a consequence of the first Palestinian popular uprising – known as the first *Intifada* (shaking off) – against Israel's occupation. Until that moment neither Israel nor the PLO had shown any real interest in finding a bilateral negotiated settlement to the conflict. The PLO maintained its desire to destroy Israel and liberate all of Palestine through violent means; Israel, though stating its desire for peace, continued to build settlements in the territories and to deprive Palestinians of basic rights, leading many to believe its real intent was the de facto annexation of the territories and the creation of a greater Israel.

Land and borders

In 1993 Israel and the PLO reached a series of agreements known as the Oslo Accords. These accords brought about mutual recognition and saw Israel cede parts of the Occupied Territories to the PLO. Under the accords a Palestinian Authority (PA) was established through democratic elections and given limited sovereignty over the main Palestinian population centres (known as areas A). The rest of the territories were designated either as areas B (joint control) or areas C, which comprise over 60% of the land and are under full Israeli control. Israel places restrictions on Palestinian movement throughout areas B and C in accordance with its security concerns. This severely restricts Palestinian freedom of movement. Some Palestinian groups, most notably Hamas (the Islamic Resistance Movement), have refused to accept the Oslo Accords, viewing them as Palestinian capitulation and a de facto acceptance of the ongoing Israeli occupation. The main conflict issues, such as Israeli settlements, Jerusalem, future borders and water resources, were left for final status negotiations and were not dealt with in the accords, which were designated as temporary, and were to last for only a few years. However, the sides have been unable to reach an agreement over the final status of the territories.

Water security: Due to the scarcity of water sources, water security is an important issue in the conflict and in the Middle East region in general. The issue of water security has been integral to Israel's relations with the Palestinians as well as with neighbouring states; for example, Israel's unresolved conflict with Syria and Lebanon is based, to some extent, on access to water sources. Water sources in Israel and the West Bank are controlled by Israel and are not shared equally with Palestinians; Israeli settlers receive a far higher allocation of water for agriculture and private consumption than do Palestinians. Israel also prevents Palestinians from drilling independently for water in the areas it controls in the West Bank. Additionally, Israel uses and controls water from the River Jordan which is the eastern boundary of the West Bank.

In the various rounds of negotiations held since 1993, the issue of land and future borders became paramount. Palestinians demand the establishment of an independent Palestinian state, alongside the state of Israel, in the West Bank and the Gaza Strip with East Jerusalem as its capital. In other words, Palestinians demand a full Israeli withdrawal to the ceasefire lines of 1967 (known as the Green Line). Palestinians argue that by accepting a two-state solution they are relinquishing their rights to 78% of historical Palestine, which they see as a great sacrifice on their part.

Israel has exhibited some willingness to negotiate but its proposals have fallen short of the minimum Palestinian demands. Israel has made clear its refusal to withdraw to the Green Line, claiming that such a move would leave it with indefensible borders. Nonetheless, Israel has demonstrated its readiness to withdraw from some areas; for example, Israel dismantled its settlements and unilaterally withdrew from the Gaza Strip in 2005. However, it claims that subsequent attacks by Palestinian armed groups, principally rocket attacks by Hamas, have shown that further withdrawals are a recipe for renewed violence. Israel contends that the conflict is not about land but about the Palestinian refusal to recognise Israel's right to exist as a Jewish state in its historical homeland. It points to its withdrawal from the Gaza Strip as proof of its willingness to make painful concessions and pursue peace. Additionally, Israel demands that any future withdrawals would have to take into account its security concerns and the Jewish settlements it has established in the West Bank.

Palestinians argue that Israel has demonstrated little willingness to withdraw from the territories. The establishment of settlements, the appropriation of lands, the building of a separation wall, and the continued blockade of the Gaza Strip are given as examples of Israel's intransigence and desire to control Palestinian lives and further the occupation.

The Separation Wall: A series of barriers, including an eight-metre wall, has been constructed by Israel, ostensibly to follow the Green Line. Israel claims this is a temporary provision to stop the infiltration of terrorists. Israel points to the fact that attacks against it have significantly decreased since the construction of the wall began. The Palestinians accuse Israel of using the wall to unilaterally annex Palestinian land. They point to the fact that the wall is twice the length of the Green Line and that it snakes around most of Israel's settlements. This has resulted in the creation of a seam area of more than 10% of Palestinian land between the Green Line and the wall. Additionally, the wall has, in some cases, physically divided Palestinian communities and separated villages from their farmlands.

It is clear that any solution proposed would need to take into account factors that can sometimes be contradictory: the settlements created by Israel, the viability and contiguity of the Palestinian state, water sources, the administration of holy sites, the fate of Jerusalem, and Israeli and Palestinian security concerns.

Impact of religion

Even though the conflict is not based on religion, religion has been an integral part of it. Moreover, because of the religious significance of Israel/Palestine, the conflict is an important issue for religious communities around the world; Israel/Palestine is recognised by Christians, Muslims and Jews as the Holy Land. Religion, though not the source of the conflict, has played a crucial part in sustaining and exacerbating it. Religious groups on both sides cite Biblical or Koranic verses in support of exclusion and violence. Religious tension and competition, specifically linking religion with nationalism, have hindered a peaceful resolution. Israeli settler groups have used the Old Testament to justify their actions in the Occupied Territories. Hamas, and other Islamic groups, have used religion to justify their refusal to recognise Israel's right to exist and their attacks on Israeli civilians.

Since Israel's creation, there has been an ongoing debate on the place of religion within the Jewish state. Religion has been a feature of Zionism to varying degrees. Jews view themselves as a nation and a religious community, and Israel is the only country in the world with a Jewish majority (Israel's population is around eight million, a quarter of whom are non-Jewish). In addition, a significant proportion of Israelis define themselves as religious. After the 1967 war and the conquest of the Occupied Territories, and in particular the West Bank and East Jerusalem, religion came to play a more central role in Israeli public and political life. The war led to renewed calls among some Israelis for the annexation of the territories and the creation of a greater Israel. However, Israel has opposed annexation, and the idea of a one-state solution, as the inclusion of millions of non-Jews would threaten its Jewish identity and majority. According to Judaism the land of Israel/Palestine (*Eretz Israel*) was promised by God to the patriarch Abraham and his descendants. This promise is at the heart of the Old Testament and Israel's claim to the land. Jewish fundamentalist groups (many of whom live in settlements in the West Bank and East Jerusalem) are unwilling to compromise over a land they believe to be rightfully theirs.

In recent years religion has also come to play an important role in Palestinian political life. The main opposition to the PLO and the Oslo Accords has been Hamas. It views the Holy Land (*al-Ard al-Muqaddasa*) as part of an endowment given to Muslims by God, and giving away parts of it is therefore not permissible.

Hamas or the Islamic Resistance Movement is an Islamic political and military movement that was established in 1987 during the first *Intifada*. In 2006 Hamas won the Palestinian parliamentarian election, resulting in a short armed conflict with the PLO and the fragmentation of Palestinian politics. Hamas is currently in control of the Gaza Strip while the PLO is in control of the West Bank. Hamas is viewed by Israel as an obstacle for peace because of its refusal to recognise Israel's right to exist and its actions, which Israel deems as terrorism. However, in recent years Hamas leaders have expressed more moderate views, going so far as to suggest a two-state solution under certain conditions.

Israel/Palestine contains sites holy to Islam and Judaism, leading to competing religious claims. The most important of these sites is the Temple Mount in Jerusalem. Both sides demand full sovereignty over the site in any future agreement. The Temple Mount complex, located in East Jerusalem, contains the Wailing Wall (*Hakotel Hama'aravi*) – the holiest site for Jews – believed to be part of the ancient Jewish temple built by King Solomon to house the Ark of the Covenant. Jews believe that the temple was built on top of the Foundation Stone – the cornerstone from which creation began. For nineteen years, from 1948 to 1967, while under Jordanian rule, Jews were barred from praying at the Wailing Wall. Israel is therefore reluctant to relinquish control over the site.

Muslims believe the same site, which they call *al-Haram al-Sharif* (the Noble Sanctuary), to be the point from which Mohammed ascended the heavens. The *al-Aqsa* (the farthest) mosque, built on the Temple Mount, was Islam's first *Qibla* (direction of prayer) before Mecca. Jerusalem is the third holiest city for Muslims after Mecca and Medina.

In addition to Jerusalem, there are many other important religious sites, most of which are in the West Bank, such as the Tomb of Joseph, the Tomb of Rachel, and the Tomb of the Patriarchs. The latter is situated in the Palestinian city of Hebron (*al-Khalil*) and is believed to contain the burial site of the three patriarchs (Abraham, Isaac and Jacob).

The Holy Land also contains the most sacred sites to Christianity. These include the Church of the Holy Sepulchre in East Jerusalem (the site of the crucifixion), the Church of the Nativity in Bethlehem (Christ's birth site) and the Basilica of the Annunciation in Nazareth.

Jerusalem

The city of Jerusalem is a microcosm of the conflict; it encapsulates some of the security, religious, legal and demographic issues facing Israelis and Palestinians. Jerusalem serves as Israel's capital, but Palestinians claim the eastern part of the city as their future capital. In 2000, at Camp David, final status negotiations between Israeli Prime Minister Ehud Barak and Palestinian President Arafat collapsed, leading to a renewed cycle of violence (the Second *Intifada*), partly over the issue of Jerusalem and the sovereignty of the Temple Mount. The Second *Intifada* resulted in the death of over five thousand Palestinians and over a thousand Israelis; a majority of casualties on both sides were non-combatants.

Under the UN partition plan (Resolution 181) Jerusalem was to become an international city. However, after the 1948 war the city was divided with East Jerusalem, including the Old City and the main religious sites, controlled by Jordan, and West Jerusalem becoming Israel's capital. During the 1967 war Israel conquered and subsequently annexed East Jerusalem, declaring the unified city as its eternal capital. This decision has never been recognised by the international community. The conflict over Jerusalem has led many to argue that because of Israel's ongoing policies, a two-state solution is unachievable. Basing its actions on security, religious and demographic considerations, Israel has, through the construction of settlements, security barriers, land appropriation, house demolitions, and the establishment of natural and archaeological parks, sought to transform the urban space of the city.

Since unifying the city Israel has pursued several aims, among them: acquiring international legitimacy for its actions; creating a Jewish demographic majority in the eastern part of the city; promoting policies that will make the eastern part of the city Israeli; promoting a unified Jerusalem as a modern, successful city; and encircling East Jerusalem with Jewish settlements. By and large Israel has failed to fully achieve any of these aims. The international community has unanimously rejected Israel's actions; Jerusalem is the only capital city in the world with no foreign embassies, which are situated mostly in Tel Aviv. Despite Israel's efforts, Palestinians still constitute a majority of the population in East Jerusalem and are a sizeable minority of the city's inhabitants (slightly under a third). They have mostly rejected the opportunity to become Israeli citizens and have tied their future to the future Palestinian state. Jerusalem, in terms of its socio-economic indicators, has not been a success story. The city has high levels of unemployment and poverty, especially among Palestinians. Conditions for Palestinians living in East Jerusalem are very different from those of Jews in West Jerusalem. The status of most Palestinians in the city is further complicated by their not being citizens of the state of Israel. In short, despite Israel's efforts, the city, though technically united, has remained divided.

Jewish settlements in the Occupied Territories

Since 1967 Israel has constructed Jewish settlements in the West Bank. These settlements are considered illegal under international law and are prohibited by the Geneva Convention; a number of settlements are even illegal under Israeli law. In many circumstances, private Palestinian land has been appropriated for the construction of Israeli settlements. However, the settlers, as well as many Israelis, consider the West Bank to be part of the ancient land of Israel. They therefore view the settlements as legal and as integral parts of the state. Nonetheless, the issue of the settlements is controversial in Israel; some Israelis, in particular those supporting the peace movement, have campaigned against the settlements. The overwhelming majority of settlements and settlers are located near the Green Line. There are more than half a million Jewish settlers in the West Bank and East Jerusalem (2012). The Jewish settlements created in and around East Jerusalem have been characterised by Palestinians as major obstacles for resolving the conflict. Israel has made it clear that these settlements are part of the urban space of Jerusalem and has refused to negotiate over them. The Palestinians accuse Israel of trying to encircle East Jerusalem with settlements, thus severing it from the West Bank.

Security and terrorism

In negotiations with the Palestinians, Israel has demanded specific security provisions, which include, among other things, the demilitarisation of the future Palestinian state and continued control over strategic areas, such as the Jordan River Valley. Israel has questioned whether peace with the Palestinians would indeed provide it with security. It takes into account the fragmented nature of Palestinian politics and the actions of Palestinian groups, principally Hamas, which Israel categorises as terrorism. Palestinians retort that they are the party in need of security provisions as Israel is the more powerful side and has one of the most advanced armies in the world. They also point out that Israel has used the excuse of security provisions to further its occupation, for example the Separation Wall. Both sides accuse each other of breaking international law, targeting civilians, and using violence to achieve political aims.

There is a big difference in the way each side defines the issue of security and characterises the use of violence. For Israel, security is defined in terms of personal security, freedom from Palestinian violence, and the protection of the state's Jewish majority and identity. On the other side, Palestinians associate security with freedom of movement, economic development and sovereignty.

Israel has repeatedly accused Palestinian groups, in particular Hamas, of being terrorist organisations. It points to the refusal of these groups to recognise Israel's right to exist and their calls for its destruction through violent means. Israel typically defines Palestinian violence as terrorism, but very rarely applies the same standards to actions taken by Israeli settlers: these are typically referred to as *price tagging*. Actions taken by Hamas and other Palestinian groups against Israel have included the targeting of civilians through the use of suicide bombing and indiscriminate rocket attacks.

Palestinian groups have used a wide range of terms, from martyrdom operations to resistance, to refer to the use of attacks directed at Israeli civilians. Hamas has defended its tactics, claiming they are justified in light of Israel's continued occupation and oppression, and has contextualised them as acts of legitimate resistance. Hamas has advocated the use of these methods (suicide bombing and rocket attacks) as necessary due to its weaker military position and Israel's attacks on Palestinian civilians. It is important to note, however, that Hamas has moderated its stance in recent years.

Conclusion

This chapter has looked at the Israeli–Palestinian conflict, providing a brief history of the conflict and examining some of the main issues, which have been linked to some of the key concepts discussed in the core chapters. For Palestinians, this conflict is about their expulsion and dispossession, as well as their continued subjugation and the denial of their rights. They therefore discuss the conflict in terms of historic injustice, as well as their rights to self-determination and resistance to occupation. For Israelis, the conflict is about recognising their right to live in a Jewish state in their historic homeland, free from external threat, and it is therefore framed in relation to personal security and Jewish history.

At its core the Israeli–Palestinian conflict is about land; initially a struggle over the entire land of Israel/Palestine, the current conflict has focused on the Occupied Territories, namely the West Bank – including East Jerusalem – and the Gaza Strip.

Recommended reading

Caplan, N. *The Israel–Palestine Conflict: Contested Histories (Contesting the Past),* Chichester: Wiley-Blackwell, 2009.

Harms, G. and Ferry, T.M. *The Palestine–Israel Conflict: A Basic Introduction,* 3rd Edition, London: Pluto Press, 2012.

Farsoun, S.K. *Palestine and the Palestinians: A Social and Political History,* Boulder: Westview Press, 2006.

Shindler, C. *A History of Modern Israel,* Cambridge: Cambridge University Press, 2008.

31 Human, national and environmental security in Latin America

Bolivia and Brazil

Lloyd Pettiford and Neil Hughes

Box 31.1: Bolivia and Brazil: two different case studies

- Two very different case studies, Bolivia and Brazil, exemplify both difference and similarity in Latin America.
- The role of colonialism and the exploitation of natural resources is key to understanding either country, but this has meant quite different paths despite a long common border.
- Bolivia's long history of disappointment and optimism has recently been in a positive phase under the left-leaning populism of Evo Morales.
- Key issues in Bolivia are the rights of the indigenous majority, the use of natural resources and the role of the coca leaf.
- Brazil has different issues regarding ethnicity, and entered the twenty-first century as an economic powerhouse.
- Key issues for Brazil most often revolve around contradictions which have arisen on its road to development.

Introduction

When we were asked to write a case study about security in Latin America we thought instantly of Bolivia and Brazil. Although at first glance these countries are very different, they share similarities that cut across their differences. Beginning with the differences, these are not just confined to their relative contribution to the history of the Beautiful Game – Brazil is widely seen as the world's greatest footballing nation, while Bolivia ranks rather lower in the pantheon. In terms of language, Brazil is, for the most part, Portuguese-speaking while Bolivians speak Spanish or indigenous languages. Bolivia is landlocked while Brazil has the longest coastline of any Latin American country. Brazil's population is near two hundred million with less than 0.5% being designated 'indigenous'; there are around ten million Bolivians, with perhaps 60% indigenous. The overall size of economy figures are more extreme even than football rankings, with Brazil a global powerhouse (one of the BRICs – massive emerging economies in the post-Cold War period along with Russia, India and China) while Bolivia's economy is relatively small and peripheral in many senses.

Yet in other respects the two countries do demonstrate similarities, particularly socio-economically where high levels of poverty and inequality continue to blight both nations. Beyond this there are broader similarities of history (colonial rule and then independence in the 1820s), Iberian cultural heritage, the influence of the military and dictatorships in politics, and more recently the coming to power of populist, left-leaning, charismatic politicians in 'Lula' and 'Evo'. However, similarities are more apparent at the general and over-arching scale, but are less easy to find in the detail. So in looking at security in Latin America, it is worth acknowledging at the outset that history, culture, politics and economic models may well give us some broad conclusions, but we must similarly acknowledge that Chile/Ecuador, Argentina/Peru (or any other pairing) may well throw up quite different security challenges which would need to be investigated on their own merits.

Being rich in natural resources has often been a curse in Latin America and throughout the global South, as the history of the Congo DR and much of Africa demonstrates. Having *nothing* to exploit is rare, but has usually been a blessing, especially when time and technology have subsequently revealed 'revenue earners' as has notably been the case with Brazil's energy sector. However, apparent mineral and other wealth has given a reason for external interest, invasion/occupation and expropriation, fighting/militarisation, and for the exploitation of local populations to extract maximum surplus value. As ever, a few have got very rich; for others a hell-on-Earth is created, with the Cerro Rico (now hollowed of all its silver) outside Potosi in Bolivia being a very good example.

Once countries or regions are incorporated in external markets in this way, the following question is often posed: 'what is worse than being exploited by foreign multinationals and the global economy?' The answer, of course, is: '**not** being exploited by foreign multinationals and the global economy'. Those people/ countries wishing to extricate themselves from exploitative patterns, at either the individual or the national level, risk great dangers. The precarious security offered by capitalism is not easy to replace with a different type of security given the vested interests opposed to this.

Human Security *and* autonomy are difficult to achieve. The experience of North Korea does not suggest a model to follow with a population which will surely be insecure whatever the future brings (war, reunification, changing economic system or more of the same – see separate chapter for elucidation). Cuba's high UNDP human development index (HDI) scores may suggest more reason for optimism, but that is not an unproblematic story and it certainly raises different sorts of security concerns, not least for dissenters of whatever stripe. This capitalist exploitation and the difficulty of autonomy is the context for attempts to empower indigenous peoples who have been downtrodden for centuries, and to control natural resources in Bolivia under Evo Morales. It is also the context for more or less leftist administrations in Brazil, Venezuela, Ecuador and Nicaragua. Breaking out of historical patterns and attempting to stand up to the US in its own backyard creates myriad dilemmas and significant security paradoxes. These are examined in more detail below.

Bolivia

Bolivia did not enter the twenty-first century as a happy and prosperous society, but as one with a five-hundred-year history of disappointment and very occasional optimism. If that optimism has flared again intermittently in the new millennium it must still be set against a backdrop of mineral wealth combining with greed and leading to a pattern of externally fuelled exploitation, prejudice and inequality. Bolivia is not close to the United States, but it is close enough that it has been required to follow a familiar Latin American pattern of exploitation where the United States makes the world safe for capitalism.

Notwithstanding this history, things change, and although they are still a factor as the 2009 events in Honduras testify, US-trained militaries now loom less large in the countries constituting America's backyard (following the Monroe Doctrine of 1823, this is a huge area covering Latin America and the Caribbean). Accordingly, spaces have emerged for voices arguing for land reform and more equity. While such voices are certainly still effectively crushed at times (most notably in Colombia), in Brazil, Venezuela and Nicaragua (for instance) critical voices of resistance have been and are heard. This does not always lead to huge changes, but it can certainly lead to significant ones, and Bolivia (where Evo Morales became the country's first indigenous president) is perhaps at the top of the list.

Morales has faced significant structural and historical challenges such that nothing short of a miracle would have resolved Bolivia's problems in such a short space of time. However, in terms of security it is clear that Morales' leadership has a number of significant elements: a reorientation of Bolivia away from the United States and towards greater integration with countries in the region that share Bolivia's anti-imperialist stance; seeking to replace short-term economic gain with a sense of local control, particularly of resources; a re-emphasis on local culture and the importance of indigenous peoples, particularly regarding the cultural and historical importance of the coca leaf; a sense of empowerment in the communities that swept him to power, particularly the self-reliant, indigenous neighbourhood communities of El Alto (the city overlooking, and now out-numbering, the capital La Paz, which it brought to a standstill in the 'gas [petrol] wars' of 2003); and a greater emphasis on social welfare and environmental matters (understood broadly to include issues such as water privatisation), especially since Bolivia can be considered to have contributed little to global environment problems while at the same time being particularly threatened by them. Possibly most remarkable of all, under Morales' leadership, Bolivia has joined the space age, launching its first-ever satellite at the end of 2013. Named after the indigenous leader of a revolt against Spanish colonial rule in the eighteenth century, the Tupac Katari satellite is expected to bring about a revolution in digital telecommunications, with particular benefits for people in rural areas due to improved mobile telephone services and access to the internet and digital television.

Morales' experience has been one of working with and organising indigenous groups, including in Cochabamba against water privatisation, but also on a national scale. The rise of Morales, his political movement/party (MAS) and the emergence of indigenous voices calling for justice and security across a range of issues is one of the defining characteristics of the Bolivian security complex. In Brazil, on the other hand, indigenous communities (and their voices) are small, and as a vast economy/country Brazil is ever more inserted in the global economy, fuelling both growth and a high level of extraction/exploitation of its natural resource base. This demonstrates the need for more nuanced and specific analyses of 'security' issues even in an area previously dismissed as a homogeneous backyard full of military dictators buttressed by the human rights abuses of its security forces. This mini-chapter now moves to look at some specific security issues affecting Bolivia, which – as will be seen – cover a range of themes.

Threats to the regime

The Morales regime enjoys considerable support from Quechua- and Aymara-speaking indigenous peoples, the poor in general, working class communities and sections of the Bolivian middle class. Geographically, the main locus of support can be found in the Andean highlands and in the coca-growing regions of the Bolivian lowlands such as Chapare and the Yungas. One region which has proven less amenable to Morales' rule is Santa Cruz in the east, which might as well be another world. So much advice about going to Bolivia is about coping with altitude sickness, but if you arrive in Santa Cruz de la Sierra (capital of Santa Cruz) you will not need such advice. However, if you go to La Paz first, expect more than just extra oxygen in your lungs. Expect fewer indigenous faces, and a brasher, often racist culture. The differences between prosperous Santa Cruz and cities in the highlands such as sprawling El Alto are pronounced, and ultimately Bolivia is likely to feel less and less like one country and more like two.

The tensions between the two regions are palpable and have come to the surface on more than one occasion since Morales came to power. Conflict, as is so often the case in the developing world, centres on natural resources – Santa Cruz is the location of Bolivia's largest oil and natural gas fields. While Morales has sought to harness these resources to achieve national economic and social development, this has been resisted by the Santa Cruz oligarchy with support from transnational business interests. In an effort to maintain their grip on power in the region, the oligarchy has called for secession from the Bolivian state, organised armed attacks against Morales' supporters in the region, and plotted a coup attempt with anti-regime elements within the armed forces and support from the US Embassy. Although ultimately unsuccessful, these initiatives are evidence of the lingering presence of the types of domestic threat to national security that have shaped Latin America's destiny since independence.

Climate, environment and natural resources

Climate threatens Human Security in a number ways. As in Brazil, Bolivia's location in the tropics means that its population is exposed to the types of diseases that have done so much to threaten health security in tropical countries across the world. The main danger comes from mosquito-borne diseases such as malaria, dengue and yellow fever. In 2009, for example, Bolivia suffered the worst outbreak of dengue fever in its history in which more than thirty thousand people were infected and at least eighteen people died.

Melting glaciers threaten the water supply to the twin cities of La Paz and El Alto, while floods and droughts are playing havoc with local agriculture. In this context, Bolivia has emerged as a significant moral voice in debates about global climate change, also setting up the first Ministry of Sustainable Development in the early 1990s. As many in the North continue to be in apparent denial of the consequences experienced in countries like Bolivia, Bolivia itself has sought to link environmental security and responsibility through the notion of a 'climate debt' owed by North to South. However, thus far this is an idea with considerable moral force but little political muscle; Morales' commitment to 'Pachamama' (mother earth) while also relying on extractive industries to develop the economy may demonstrate some of the contradictions of power, but it also lessens some of the moral traction available. The development imperative has tarnished Morales' environmental credentials in other ways. His decision to build a highway through the Bolivian Amazon caused outrage among the Tipnis indigenous people, who claim land rights over the region. The existential threat this posed to their community, not to mention the impact on the environment, led the Tipnis people to declare themselves in 'peaceful resistance' to Morales and his government.

Coca and indigenous people

Take the coca leaf. Chop it. Crush it. Without pretending we understand the full process, you can end up with a white narcotic powder which is very valuable to some, particularly in richer countries. This possibility can allow guerrilla forces to fund their activities (as in Colombia and previously in Peru). It can allow some producers and distributors to get very rich and others to make a living. In the vagueness of global markets, cocaine (as a high value product) has often been seen as a good bet to produce. Consuming countries, on the other hand, have seen such drug production as a threat. Eschewing scientific evidence that treatment of addicts has more effect than punishment or interdiction of supply, the US has frequently taken its fight against drugs to the poor peasant producers, which has possibly been politically easier than attacking its own well-heeled snorters, even if less effective. Here is a route whereby the US DEA presumes to interfere in the affairs of another country, and where considerable insecurity is caused.

Alternatively, take the coca leaf. Chew it. It will help stave off hunger pangs if you are a peasant suffering from food insecurity. Put it in hot water; it will help you with altitude sickness. (Neither of these processes is more addictive or 'heightening' than smoking a cigarette or drinking a cup of tea.) Take bundles of it to market; sell it, trade it, buy food. Revere it; develop ceremonies and aspects of culture which involve its use. In reality, in Bolivia, coca is a low value, tradable commodity which has significant cultural significance to the indigenous population. However, the US has projected onto this an 'understanding' of coca production which develops out of the greed and stupidity of some of its own populace, and which has caused considerable hardship. For sure, export production began because of the possibility of turning leaves into lots of money, but this is not where Bolivia started. Much of Morales' efforts in this area have been around legitimising small-scale production for local markets – or taking Bolivia back to where it came from. The Morales regime has also sought to develop a market in coca-based products such as tea and breakfast cereals, but without great success.

Access to the sea and national security

Bolivia's loss to Chile of its outlet to the Pacific Ocean in the War of the Pacific at the end of the nineteenth century (1879–83) constitutes the main source of interstate tension. The conflict is used to justify the maintenance of the Bolivian navy with a presence not at sea, but on the world's highest navigable lake – Lake Titicaca. Bolivian national outrage is rekindled every year on the Day of the Sea (March 23) when parades and other events take place to commemorate its loss. At the time of writing tensions between the two countries are on the rise following the Morales government's 2013 decision to sue Chile at the International Court of Justice for restoration of its sovereign sea access to the Pacific Ocean.

Brazil

While Bolivia's large indigenous population has survived despite brutality and in conditions where even breathing itself is difficult (at high altitudes), the indigenous element to ethnicity has largely 'disappeared' in Brazil, where the indigenous population are a small number among a large number in a vast country. Brazilian politicians have made much of the 'melting pot' idea in dealing with ethnicity, but in a country which did not formally abolish slavery until after the United States, and in which gradations of colour make a big difference (Barack Obama, for instance, is not considered 'black' in Brazil), this would certainly be an exaggeration and there is most definitely an *ethnic* dimension to huge social inequality and therefore aspects of Human Security. What is more, modern slavery exists to a significant level.

Notwithstanding these comments, at a macro-level Brazil would appear to be an extremely secure country in terms of military threat, economic profile, energy development and increasing world role. After looking at these below, we can see why the notion of 'Human Security' is so vital for a country like Brazil if we are to fully understand it. As one small illustration, inequality can be exemplified by the fact that in a country experiencing sustained resource-led growth, sales of luxury goods are outstripping growth by as much as three times.

Economics

Brazil has developed into a dynamic, export-led economy which actually improved its credit rating during the global economic downturn. As part of a virtuous circle, this should now help to ease a traditional lack of domestic credit and encourage further growth. The economy is now more stable, diversified and resilient than ever before, and unlike some countries the political costs of adapting to a globalised economy have already been paid. Additionally, the workforce has become better educated and Brazil operates with varied trading partners.

Overall, Brazil's economy is still hampered (and sometimes greased) by corruption, but in macro-terms it has put the lid on inflation and been able to harness some of its great potential. As seen below, it has also had a certain amount of good fortune in how certain aspects of the economy around energy have panned out. As a result, Brazil is seeing rising incomes and a gradual diffusion of wealth, even in the context of staggering inequalities. If its sheer size and complicated patchwork of politics mean it retains significant challenges to maintain economic momentum, it nonetheless has significant human and other resources which should help maintain its trajectory. If 'order and progress' (enshrined on the Brazilian flag) are not unproblematic, they both seem on the increase over time in the economic sphere.

Energy

The curse of natural resources was noted above, but it seems that Brazil has managed to get rich in the right things at the right time. For instance, sugar cane (one of its original staples) became a key ingredient in ethanol fuel, which Brazil turned to following the global oil-price shocks of the 1970s. This was part of enabling Brazil to become self-sufficient in oil and natural gas; in time (thanks to offshore discoveries) Brazil will become an exporting country, although unlike neighbouring Venezuela, the size of oil reserves is not enough to significantly distort the economy.

Ethanol works well due to the existence of dual-fuel engines (petrol/ethanol/mixed) and a developed local car industry. Hydro-electric power is also important with significant further capacity available. Various plants have been identified as suitable for bio-diesel, and wind and solar generation have obvious potential in such a vast, sunny country, but they have yet to be significantly exploited. Brazil also has significant deposits of uranium. In other words, Brazil has a splendid mix of energy supplies, many coming on stream at just the right time; using coal while waiting for hydro-electric and offshore oil developments, as well as sugar cane production being pushed into the Amazon, do raise some environmental concerns (of which more later), but Brazil is very well placed to meet its energy security needs in the future.

Military/sovereignty

Historically, interstate relations have been most tense with neighbours to the south over control of the strategically important Rio Paraná, with tensions between Brazil and Paraguay over this issue deteriorating into armed conflict towards the end of the nineteenth century. Since the so-called War of the Triple Alliance (1864–70), conflict between Brazil and its Southern Cone neighbours have diminished. A key factor in the thawing of relations has been a process of regional cooperation and integration that culminated in 1991 when Argentina, Brazil, Paraguay and Uruguay signed the Treaty of Asunción. This paved the way for the setting up of the Common Market of the South, or MERCOSUR as it is more commonly known.

The absence of traditional security worries means that Brazil has increasingly faced outwards and sought to establish a global role. It has also meant that the military is always looking for a mission; except when it is actually governing as a dictatorship (as in the period from 1964 to 1985) this means an internal focus, or more recently arguing for needing increased capacity to 'guard' offshore oil reserves. As a whole, Brazil seems often to be seeking international approval, being irritated by perceptions of insufficient respect and/or resenting insinuations that the Amazon is anything other than a resource for the exclusive use and control of Brazil.

It is almost as if, shorn of any real traditional security issues, Brazil is determined to create some psychologically as would befit the trappings of a significant power. So although the fate of the Amazon is clearly of concern to the world, Brazil seems to resent suggestions that it is patrimony of humanity, or that it needs help there – this despite not exercising effective sovereignty (through provision of basic services and law enforcement) across large swathes of territory. Only China and the US (and perhaps Indonesia) currently put more CO_2 into the atmosphere, and three-quarters of this comes from cutting down trees.

However Brazilians feel about it, it is this internal lack of sovereignty which has more security implications than traditional external threats. Particularly in the realm of Human Security, slave labour often accompanies activities in the Amazon such as pig-iron production. Confronted with budgetary constraints, Brazil finds it difficult to combat slavery and also to protect the rights of indigenous peoples (of whom there are a significant number, despite being low in percentage terms). If you add to this the uncontrolled interface between poverty and deforestation, and Brazil's fear of seeing its sovereignty weakened, there is often a scenario in which outside help would be very useful, but it is rejected as interference. Policy effectiveness and Human Security is weakened, as the perception of national security wins out.

Conclusion

A love of football (albeit with different levels of success), an Iberian heritage, historically resource-intensive dependent economies and a common border; these two countries share similarities. However, to analyse their security challenges would need much more than this summary, and even this brief description of two Latin American countries makes clear that an area with some superficial similarities for the traveller nevertheless contains myriad security challenges. In responding to these challenges, it is not easy to assess the role of national character, although fatalism has understandably dominated for the indigenous peoples of Bolivia given their downtrodden status. On the other hand, Brazil has sought to propagate a myth of non-racism, and overall it is a society imbued with a sense of optimism encapsulated in the saying: 'everything will be alright in the end; and if everything is not alright, it is only because we have not reached the end yet'. So if differences abound, is there any sense in the notion of Latin American security? The answer we think is yes, and it can be captured in the following bullet points, which might then be analysed in the context of the continent as a whole:

- Traditional/military security: Interstate conflict is on the wane as a result of closer regional cooperation and integration. However, the lack of traditional external threats, leaves militaries looking for a role, especially as their historical 'internal/anti-Communist' Cold War role diminishes.
- Hegemon to the North: The US remains a factor in Latin American security through funding for Latin American armed forces and support for opposition groups. As its support for the coup attempt in Bolivia shows, the US has operated through proxies such as the secessionist movement in Santa Cruz in countries where it has seen its interests to be best served by regime change.
- Domestic threats: The most significant existential threats to national security still come from domestic sources.
- Psychological security: Despite ostensibly left-leaning governments in recent years (the Workers Party/Lula in Brazil and Movement Towards Socialism/Evo in Bolivia), policy has actually been quite different, with Brazil drawing increasingly close to the US. This notwithstanding, how to develop the relationship with the US – given its historical dominance over and interest in the region – is a crucial aspect of practical and psychological security across Latin America.
- Sovereignty and economics: Economic security and sovereignty are closely linked in Latin America around the issue of resources and control of destiny. This is linked to the above point about psychological security, Latin America's incorporation within the global economy and its reliance (or otherwise) on the United States.
- Environmental security: Issues around Brazilian sovereignty and the Amazon obviously loom large here, particularly in discussions about 'tipping points' whereby processes of sea-level rise and global warming become self-sustaining due to an insufficient level of carbon sinks. However, balancing acts around the environment and development apply across the continent, and conceal implicit and explicit bargains and contradictions. Evo Morales wears the cloak of Pachamama even as fossil fuels form part of his development strategy. Friends of the Earth in Chile suggested to one of the authors in 2002 that Chile's impressive regional record constituted a rush to exploit as much as possible environmentally as quickly as possible, so as to then be rich enough to exploit other environments while protecting its own (i.e. joining the rich club while there was still time).
- Human Security: The Cold War and the US obsession with Communism in the region led to military involvement in Latin American politics, widespread human

rights abuses and an either/or approach to politics, such that you were either subject to an authoritarian business-first regime or occasionally a threatened revolution. Few countries managed to avoid this fate (Costa Rica may be an exception). The legacy is seen in high levels of inequality and social injustice, but at least the argument now is more often in terms of a more business-orientated or social democratically orientated approach to incorporation into the global economy.

In summary, then, and while arguing for nuanced analyses of Latin American security by country, the following might well apply to the whole region, or at least we suggest it is worth considering as a yardstick for analysis. Traditional approaches to security do not tend to tell us a great deal about security in Latin America, although how the military re-orientates itself within society in the post-Cold War era is of interest in many places. As politics becomes freer and fairer (as the US/Cold War influence diminishes) the key aspects of security are how to exploit sovereign resources for the national good in a way which allows successful integration into the global economy, takes account of the environment and at the same time recognises the social/human legacy of historical inequality.

Recommended reading

Dangl, B. *The Price of Fire: Resource Wars and Social Movements in Bolivia*, Edinburgh: AK Press, 2007.

Dangl, B. *Dancing With Dynamite: Social Movements and States in Latin America*, Edinburgh: AK Press, 2010.

Rohter, L. *Brazil on the Rise: The Story of a Country Transformed*, Basingstoke: Palgrave Macmillan, 2012.

Tavares, R. *Security in South America: The Role of States and Regional Organisations*, London: Eurospan, 2014.

Ungar, M. *Policing Democracy: Overcoming Obstacles to Citizen Security in Latin America*, Baltimore: John Hopkins University Press, 2011.

32 Korea opportunities

Human, environmental and national security in the ROK and the DPRK

Lloyd Pettiford and Felix Abt

Box 32.1: Objectives

- This chapter starts from, and acknowledges, the fact that the DPRK is a country we really understand little about, but about which statespeople and analysts feel able to make startling generalisations.
- It examines the roles of stereotyping and rhetoric in creating a situation where progress is torturously slow and where blame is a common tactic.
- In this context, the actual threat posed by the DPRK is analysed.
- This allows security in the Koreas to be reframed in a way far from the sensationalised tropes churned out by US media outlets.
- Our conclusions are based on what might be the best way for Western countries to engage with a society which has been stubbornly robust despite repeated assertions that it is on the point of collapse.

Introduction: rhetoric and reality

This short piece does not seek to summarise the 'wealth' of conventional opinion one can easily find these days on Kim Jong Un's North Korea, and the security situation both within that country and on the Korean peninsula more generally. Nor does it seek an analysis of the legacy of the Kim family. Such opinion is often 'knee-jerk' (and in some respects wholly justifiable) anger aimed at a fundamentally flawed and incomprehensible society. Rather, what we attempt to offer here is a more nuanced, forward-focused account (in part based on the 'participant observation' of Felix Abt). The knee-jerk anti-DPRK response might be to decry any attempt to 'understand' or engage with North Korea given its human rights record, military (including nuclear) build-up, posturing and aggressive manner and so on, *none of which* are denied here. However, we will argue in favour of the need to empathise with its people (all of its people), and suggest that limited good has emerged from mild and/or virulent condemnation of the conditions in which its most piteous victims 'live'. As a consequence, the underlying message is one of hope for a country (the Democratic People's Republic of Korea, aka North Korea or the DPRK) and people whose wealth of untapped human and other resources is enormous. The attempt here is to look beyond the human rights abuses, inefficiency, nepotism and 'craziness' – after all, these also exist elsewhere – and look at what might really be the future of the Korean peninsula and security in all its guises, as well as explaining why it is currently so often on a knife-edge.

I offered a friend an opinion on a recent 'nuclear missile scare' involving the DPRK; he had asked for my thoughts, and although I acknowledged that I was not an expert, I had recently read about a dozen books on the subject, including Felix Abt's excellent eyewitness reflections entitled *A Capitalist in North Korea*. For what it was worth, I suggested that both Koreas engaged in, and were subject to, a dialogue of the deaf and high levels of stereotypical assumptions, and that while North Korea had been blown off track, so to speak, it was easy to see how it had got there. The friend quickly felt free to 'put me right', and (on the basis it seemed, of a couple of five-minute CNN pieces) quickly repeated to me the stereotypes of the above-mentioned human rights abuses, inefficiency, nepotism and 'craziness'. For a country about which we know so little, people seem remarkably free to claim expertise; here, what we attempt is to take an oblique look at the issues to offer a slightly different perspective on what security does and might mean for a future Korea – or, as now, Koreas. It is easy to get angry with North Korea, but as Mike Gifford (the current British ambassador to the DPRK) argues, the real challenge and way forward is to persuade Pyongyang to interact with the outside world. He quotes the UK Deputy Prime Minister Nick Clegg in this context: '*Open societies choose democracy and freedom at home, engagement and responsibility abroad.*'

Identifying some Korean stereotypes

So, before looking into the security issues surrounding the Korean peninsula, it is perhaps worthwhile to look at some of the assumptions and stereotypes that do the rounds in this regard and ask about their validity and *relevance*. In the West the DPRK is perceived as a foolish anachronism whose crazed leaders lord it over starving, duped automatons. Life is hell for (almost) *all* North Koreans, who exist in a giant prison camp. The DPRK is also one of the major threats to world peace through its nuclear ambitions, and is responsible for a whole range of international crime, from counterfeit currency through kidnappings and assassination. This caricature, as with caricatures generally, is not without some resemblance to reality, but it is often a huge exaggeration of capability too. One effect of Western paranoia is to allow the DPRK to play a mean game of poker with a very weak hand (Cumings, 2005). *Many* countries have starving populations, unscrupulous power-mad political elites who deceive the people and uncomfortable, and unjust incarceration systems. Similarly, crime is transnational (frequently associated with supplying the demands of wealth/opulence/decadence), and even defenders of all things Western would not deny that good countries do bad things; one loses count of the CIA assassination attempts against Fidel Castro, while the abducting of Western citizens, flying them to secret prisons in a non-democratic country where they were subject to torture, is certainly going to be considered controversial and undermining of democracy, even *if* trying to rid the world of Fidel was not. Such episodes trample on international law in the process. DPRK propaganda is, of course, not slow to point out the 'record' in many respects of the United States and the strongly ethnic dimension to the inequality of income, incarceration and life chances in that country.

Stereotypically, on the other hand, the Republic of Korea (ROK, aka South Korea) is to Western audiences the capitalist success story which says to the North 'this is what you could have won'. Such arguments tend to disregard that for a number of years after separation the DPRK tended to outperform the ROK in some respects, and that ultimate ROK economic gains came not in Utopian fashion, but at the cost of fairly brutal anti-labour policies with an authoritarian feel even to democracy. Pro-ROK arguments also tend to forget that most defectors to the South from North do not express regret at being from the North, they fail to criticise the leadership consistently, and they often struggle to integrate into South Korean society. Their inability (insecurity?) in this last regard is likely to be for a number of reasons related to skills, upbringing and consequent 'world view', but the uber-capitalist pressures of South Korea (which begin with relentless high-pressure schooling) do in any case result in the highest national suicide rate in the world; again a fact which the DPRK is not slow to point out.

While external perceptions can be faulted in a number of regards, DPRK stereotyping of the South has been equally relentless and patently idiotic, although justified/justifiable in terms of national security. The propaganda machine has found it difficult to sustain the more ridiculous claims in an information age, but they paint a picture of the endless toil and suffering of an oppressed population, held in check by a bourgeois elite and their evil Yankee backers, yearning to join with their brothers in the DPRK's socialist paradise. However, for all the pressures of 'getting on' in South Korea and the authoritarian feel of democracy there, most people dropped behind the Rawlsian 'veil of justice' would be relieved to fall south of the thirty-eighth parallel in Korea; suicide rates in the DPRK may be low simply because people understand that no form of escape (including deliberately taking one's own life) will be tolerated, and that one's surviving family may well be the people who get punished for such an act of disloyalty.

The DPRK stereotyping of the ROK's woes compared to its own status as a workers' paradise and a bastion of socialism can seem comical, although it is far from certain that a majority of its citizens are even partially aware of this. The socialist showpiece idea can be maintained by set-piece and grandiose projects, and Pyongyang, if not beautiful, is certainly striking in places, at least superficially. However, much of the DPRK is not like this, and in the absence of Soviet-era support, much of its infrastructure is idle and rusting, some of its people are malnourished and under-employed, and its propaganda about South Korea, the United States and even Canada is all the more absurd for this. Nonetheless, our own stereotypes also need examining: for example, the starving population, a common stereotype in the West, has been refuted by Hazel Smith who studied food security in North Korea and came to the conclusion that 'many people remain malnourished even though malnourishment is lower than in other Asian countries'. Yes, there was a period of severe famine, but at other times the public distribution system has worked well and/or people have made the most of small plots of land around their houses. Talking about stereotypes, we can safely say that the worst prejudices stick most. For example, the rights group Liberty in North Korea claims that '24 million people are living under the most ruthless system of political oppression ever assembled by humankind'.[1] That figure would have to be halved at least if we believe the North Korea expert B.R. Myers, who says that 'there are plenty of worse countries for women to live in'.[2]

The economic inequalities between North and South now number many times more than the differences there were between East and West Germany. Although notions of cultural supremacy and a desire for reunification are still paid lip service, and predictions of Northern collapse come and go without being fulfilled, the situation is now one in which Southerners worry about the economic impact of reunification as much as they welcome it for other (security) reasons. In the North, elites know that their power depends on the survival of the DPRK and it is unlikely ever to extend to the South, nor to survive a major change in the form of social organisation, except if very slow and planned – which is not something that history anywhere suggests is very feasible.[3] *Ordinary* lives in North Korea are not about starvation, even if they are about deprivation, especially of some basic freedoms – see Barbara Demick for absolute stereotyping on this issue (Demick, 2009) – but ordinary people may not be aware of what the outside is like and how 'odd' their society looks; they are – in the main – almost certainly not sufficiently 'skilled' to prosper in a world with values and expectations very different from those with which they have grown up. In this sense, DPRK citizens are a long way from Human Security; not only is it not provided very well by their current regime, they would also be highly vulnerable in any Korean civil war and they are unprepared for the most common socio-economic system on the planet (capitalism), should that emerge in their country in a way which is effectively a Southern take-over and land grab.

Given the 'axis of evil' status of North Korea and the 'shock-horror' stories which abound when talking of the DPRK (a BBC *Panorama* programme by Sweeney is one of the most crude examples of this tendency), this chapter now moves through three phases as follows. First, it tries to describe some of the objective threats that the DPRK represents. This is not non-existent. With a population of twenty-four million, North Korea nonetheless has the fourth largest standing army in the world, even if its quality is debatable. Second, it reflects upon this 'threat' and the stereotyping above to draw some conclusions on how the 'West', broadly defined, should try to engage the DPRK, and in the process suggests that much current 'finger-pointing diplomacy' is ineffective. Third and finally, we draw conclusions about the prospects for Korean security in all its guises, arguing among other things that while many people crave DPRK collapse, it may be a case of being careful what you wish for, given that an uncontrolled or violent collapse may not just lead to Korean insecurity, but may impact more broadly in a range of areas from economic contagion to the proliferation of nuclear materials and devices, even if not nuclear weapons itself (which seems unlikely). However, even in this last regard we ought not to be complacent, since North Korean criticism of events in Eastern Europe in 1989 was not just that a 'superior' form of social organisation had been overthrown, but that for the most part its leaders had allowed this *without firing a shot*.

The threat of North Korea

The significance of all these starkly divergent caricatures and assumptions is that they make it very difficult to get a genuine sense of the real security issues facing the peninsula. Is it possible to even talk to 'evil'? Exaggeration is rife. For all the demonising of North Korea, it does seem that nearby Seoul is not living each and every day as if a DPRK attack were imminent, and this possibly gives a sense of how unlikely it is. This analogy may not work for all parts of the world, but how many of us have felt our blood run cold upon encountering a large and scary-looking house spider? Even when somebody says 'it's probably more scared of you than you are of it', that often doesn't prevent an attempt to eradicate the poor creature with the sole of a shoe. The perceived threat is psychological. The actual threat runs in the opposite direction; whatever the validity of its political system, the fact that South Korea and its US ally pose a genuine existential (nuclear) threat to the DPRK is rarely recognised in all the moral panic around nuclear weapons.

The above notwithstanding, there are those who would put forward the one-sided argument that here is a state that fails to play by the rules, and therefore security needs to be approached with absolute caution. Here is a state whose leaders have made decisions leading to staggering inequality and famine; a state that retro-engineers weapons and sells them on dubiously in search of hard currency; a secretive state which force-feeds its own people ridiculous lies and propaganda and which wastes disproportionate resources on its armed forces and weaponry (most of it not advanced, but in the case of nuclear technology worryingly so). In fact – they will say – the DPRK is a state where economic security is rare and environmental security is threatened by desperate attempts to boost production – goats denuding hillsides being only the start. Human Security – such analyses will conclude – is not provided in North Korea. However, the DPRK is neither a helpless 'spider' nor a ravenous environment wrecker (with reforestation programmes in place to counteract the goats!).

The question really is, ultimately, how different are North Koreans? The answer is – not very. People seek emotional and physical security and tell stories about themselves which glorify their place in the world and which attack enemies old and new. Similarly, DPRK politics are not so very different, in that people seek power and privilege and are often prepared to sacrifice significant moral principles in order to maintain these. Entrenched power does not roll over and accept punishment, but defends and justifies itself tooth and nail. Given these similarities to political (bureaucratic) behaviour elsewhere, the next key question concerns the best way to engage this society and its leaders. One doubts whether it is constant, negative pressure and punishment. Backing the DPRK 'rat' into a corner may actually seem very silly, given that it is a heavily-armed rat in which the esprit de corps of the armed forces may be less than uniform but nevertheless it is likely to lead to at least initial resistance in any conflict. After all, it is doubtful that the Red Army were all 'good Communist comrades' at Stalingrad (and many will have fought for lack of choice), but one cannot doubt the ferocious defence of the 'Motherland' in which they engaged, for whatever patriotic, coercive or political reasons.

So one *can* tell the story of security in Korea as concerning efforts to control North Korea. Peninsular security in this sense is conventionally described as being all about keeping DPRK military ambitions (not to mention lunatic leaders) in check through bilateral and multilateral diplomacy as well as sanctions, and about isolating the regime. In this story, North Korea is hell-bent on oppressing its own people, maintaining elite privilege and developing dangerous weaponry. In such accounts, Korean security is therefore about keeping the lunatics in check until the Kims have their so-called 'Ceaucescu moment' when the masses finally shout 'liar' and the whole house of cards comes tumbling down. In this story, the best ways to destabilise the house of cards are to prevent it importing things, to ensure that it doesn't improve, and to keep applying pressure and ostracising the DPRK as much as possible. The only problem with this argument is that Kim-control seems surprisingly robust, citizen-expressed devotion is still clear, and the DPRK seems to get nearer to having the feared weapons, rather than further away. The definition of madness is doing the same thing and expecting a different result, but that seems to be Western policy towards North Korea these days. So who is mad?

A different take on Korean security dilemmas

However, the argument made by us is that moral indignation is rarely a solid basis for security or policy in international relations. A Western policy of 'push, push, push' may simply lead to recurring security *crises* rather than security itself; after all, it is difficult to become a reformed character if you are being strangled, when the tendency is to fight back with all you have, whatever your position of weakness. It is argued here (with 'on the spot' experience from one of the authors adding credence) that the subterfuge of investment and ideas is really the only way to approach security. Ultimately, the DPRK knows it must lose any military conflict beyond the level of a skirmish, but it may well resist while it has the strength; to have lost strength through the force of ideas is the only way to prevent such an outcome. To do so allows the possibility of greater Human Security for the population, while at the same time meaning that elites do not have to choose to line themselves up against a wall for shooting – a choice they are, let's face it, unlikely to take.

Accordingly, engagement is the only way out for the last spot on Earth still stuck in a Cold War that ended for the rest of the world almost a quarter of a century ago, and technically still in a Hot War that was merely interrupted with an armistice sixty years ago. The US-sponsored policy of throttling and cornering North Korea has not lead to the intended overthrow of the regime but to more and longer sufferings of ordinary North Koreans, and it has induced the country to try to arm itself with nuclear weapons. If Saddam Hussein and Muammar al-Gaddafi had possessed nuclear bombs, they would still be in power, North Korean elites argue. Indeed, strangulating policies may have led to quite absurd consequences not intended by the instigators. Formidable legitimate sources of income have effectively been blocked, which has put pressure on North Korea to substitute them with less legitimate ones.

One good example is as follows: North Korea's gold deposits are estimated at two thousand metric tons by South Korea's governmental Korea Resources Corporation. However, North Korea cannot benefit from these enormous assets because gold cyanidation, the required metallurgical technique for extracting gold, has not been feasible because sodium cyanide is a banned so-called dual-use product. (That is, it is not only used for civilian purposes like gold extraction, pesticides and plastics production; it can also be used to make the nerve gas sarin.) Indeed, sanctions now include a ban on the DPRK buying or selling gold anyway. The ban on countless such dual-use products, or anything that is used for both civilian and military purposes, hurts first and foremost the civilian economy and the population.

For example, these products include chemicals needed for the processing of food items and of pharmaceuticals, as they can also be used in chemical weapons. To name one example: Chinese authorities confiscated reagents at Beijing airport that were required for the laboratory of the pharmaceutical factory Felix Abt was running, reagents which were necessary to detect contaminations in the production environment and the pharmaceuticals. While the country's elite can afford imported pharmaceuticals, sanctions deprive the local population of efficacious and safe, domestically made medication.

Around the world, most motorbikes and cars are made of aluminium alloy. However, that compound is banned since it can also be used in ballistic missiles and gas centrifuges. It is only because most North Korean manufacturers continue to use technologies and materials from the 1960s that this element of the sanctions has not taken a heavier toll.

Other punitive measures such as the financial sanctions cutting North Korean banks off from the international banking system push legitimate businesses underground and force them to use unconventional payment methods such as cash couriers. Western embargoes do not really target illegal activities, but they do hurt legitimate businesses, forcing them into illicit practices. Real criminals could use black market tricks on which sanctions have little effect.

Financial and other sanctions discourage legitimate foreign investment and as a consequence hamper the spread of responsible capitalism. They also constitute a setback to the emerging entrepreneurial middle class of traders and manufacturers struggling to find foreign sellers and buyers willing to deal with them under such dissuasive circumstances. It is important to note that the informal economy keeps most North Koreans afloat and creates new job opportunities, constituting the only way out of hardship for many. Thus sanctions are weakening such beneficial market forces (which also constitute the most important change agents in North Korean society) and are exacerbating food shortages in particular, resulting in increased dependence on foreign aid instead.

Engagement rather than foreign-imposed isolation will lead to change and a better security environment. The more interaction there is between foreigners and North Koreans, the more pressure is being built up to bring about reforms and changes. Foreigners teaching in North Korea or foreign companies building businesses in North Korea are change agents because they bring fresh ideas that challenge existing concepts, but North Koreans travelling and studying abroad become catalysts for change too. Of the first four students that the Soviet Union allowed to study in the West in the fifties, two became leading advocates of Perestroika and Glasnost. Experts believe that one of them, Yakovlev, who became a secretary of the Communist Party Central Committee and Gorbachev's closest ally, was the real architect of those breath taking changes, not Gorbachev. Interestingly, these four students studied in the United States. This would not have been possible if the US and the Soviet Union had not had normal diplomatic relations. Unlike with the Soviet Union, the US has repeatedly rejected North Korea's suggestion to normalise relations and set up embassies in the two countries. If the US wants to see a North Korean Yakovlev one day, it should hurry and change its policies.

In December 2013 the US Secretary of State John Kerry called North Korea's leader Kim Jong-Un the 'new Saddam Hussein'.[4] At the same time the International Crisis Group noted that 'Beijing sees denuclearisation as a long-term goal to be achieved by alleviating Pyongyang's insecurity, for which it considers Washington principally responsible'.[5] Unfortunately, old failed policies and conflicting interests between world powers do not bode well for future reforms in North Korea, or for a détente and security on the Korean peninsula and beyond.

Conclusion

This chapter has attempted to eschew the normal arguments and stereotypes about the DPRK. Yes, the DPRK presents a military threat in the sense that it has a big military. Yes, the world may not be safer if people who do not think like us develop 'nukes'. And yes, some people in North Korea may be suffering as much as other incarcerated people across the world, from Equatorial Guinea and Saudi Arabia to Colombia and the United States. But really, analysing six-party talks and various bilateral relations does not seem to us to be the way to promote genuine human, economic and environmental security throughout Korea. Simply knowing about and protesting against human rights abuses will not of itself begin to change society in ways which will stop such abuses happening, even if this can have value as something that initially raises awareness of a society which is conspicuously low-profile (aka 'secretive').

To conclude, rarely do people feel so free to pass so many general comments about a society about which they know so little. Indeed, the co-authors of this chapter 'met' when one of them played this role in a Twitter discussion with the other, who had lived in Pyongyang for many years and also travelled in other parts of the country. To say that North Korea has an unfortunate recent history and that too many of its people are denied what would be considered a tolerable existence is one thing; we would not dispute this in many ways. However, at the same time, most people would dispute that the best way to deal with a naughty child is simply to repeatedly beat them and sit them on the naughty step. The opportunities for security on the Korean peninsula will remain elusive in so many ways, and the ROK/DPRK relationship will remain tense, until more effort is made to engage the country genuinely and even to recognise its own security fears. This doesn't mean bribes. It doesn't mean encouraging despotism – and as Abt's own experiences make clear, it certainly won't be easy. But it does mean having the vision to go beyond godless, axis of evil stereotyping. North Korea has never given in to pressure, always stubbornly hardening its stance instead, so as the latest human rights report (from the UN) leads to tighter sanctions and even fewer possibilities for legitimate business, we can legitimately ask whose security is affected and who will suffer as a result?

Notes

1 Hazel Smith: http://www.nknews.org/2013/10/what-was-the-biggest-change-in-north-korea-over-the-past-5-years/
2 http://www.newrepublic.com/article/115948/br-myers-purge-kim-jong-uns-uncle
3 To note: peaceful German reunification was made possible because of West German chancellor Willy Brandt's Ostpolitik (comparable to Kim Dae-jung's Sunshine Policy in Korea). Brandt and Kim were close friends. This engaged the Eastern part (e.g. with travel in both directions, trade and business etc.) to the point that the well informed East German population massively demanded ('Wir sind das Volk!') German reunification and its leaders had no other choice (apart from a massive bloodshed which they may not have survived) but to give in.
4 http://nypost.com/2013/12/15/kim-jong-un-is-the-new-saddam-hessein-john-kerry/
5 http://www.crisisgroup.org/en/regions/asia/north-east-asia/china/254-fire-on-the-city-gate-why-china-keeps-north-korea-close.aspx)

Recommended reading

Abt, F. *A Capitalist in North Korea: My Seven Years in the Hermit Kingdom*, North Clarendon, VT: Tuttle Publishing, 2014.
Cumings, B. *Korea's Place in the Sun: A Modern History*, (Updated Edition), London: W.W. Norton & Co., 2005.
Lankov, A. *The Real North Korea: Life and Politics in the Failed Stalinist Utopia*, Oxford: Oxford University Press, 2013.
Myers, B.R. *The Cleanest Race: How North Koreans See Themselves and Why It Matters*, Brooklyn, NY: Melville House Publishing, 2010.
Demick, B. *Nothing to Envy: Ordinary Lives in North Korea*, New York: Spiegel & Grau, 2009.
Oberdorfer, D. and Carlin, R. *The Two Koreas: A Contemporary History*, New York: Basic Books, 2013.

33 Space and security

Ian Shields

Box 33.1: Two conflicting views on the militarisation of outer space

The exploration and use of outer space ... shall be for peaceful purposes and shall be carried out for the benefit and in the interest of all countries, irrespective of their degree of economic or scientific development. ... [The] prevention of an arms race in outer space would avert a grave danger for international peace and security.

'Prevention of an arms race in outer space',
United Nations General Assembly Resolution, A/RES/55/32, January 2001

It's politically sensitive, but it's going to happen. Some people don't want to hear this, and it sure isn't in vogue, but – absolutely – we're going to fight in space. We're going to fight from space and we're going to fight into space. That's why the US has development programs in directed energy and hit-to-kill mechanisms. We will engage terrestrial targets someday – ships, airplanes, land targets – from space.

Commander-in-Chief of US Space Command, Joseph W. Ashy,
Aviation Week and Space Technology, 9 August, 1996,
quoted from *Master of Space* by Karl Grossman, *Progressive Magazine*, January 2000

Introduction

Just as our understanding of power has evolved in the last seventy years from the superpower rivalry of the Cold War to newer forms of power (or perhaps the re-emergence of older forms), so mankind's use of space has evolved. The initial forays into space were arguably solely about prestige and competition between the US and the USSR, but the potential military advantage that both sides from the outset recognised was the use of space for communications and monitoring. Once the initial nationalistic fervour had passed, the rivalry settled into a pattern that has striking parallels with the earthbound military competition. However, the advantages that space offered, particularly in terms of communications and monitoring, were from the outset recognised beyond the narrow confines of the militaries, and just as terrestrial military developments rapidly transferred to the commercial sector, so it was also with space. Being able to communicate across oceans via a satellite link rather than relying on expensive and inefficient undersea cables was one early and obvious advantage; likewise the application of satellite imagery for everything from oil exploration (being able to survey vast areas of desert for changes in rock formations that might indicate where to conduct detailed surveys) to weather forecasting (being able to track the eye of a hurricane) soon found non-military applications. Just as the outcome of the Cold War was, to an extent, decided by technological advances and budgets, so the US came to dominate the Space Race.

However, as with the striking parallels between the Space Race and the military rivalries between the superpowers, there are equally notable reflections of wider economic activity on Earth with what was happening in orbit. Commercial operators, initially from the US but soon also from other nations, sought to gain financial advantage and an entire industry developed based around satellite construction, launch and operation, with companies offering everything from imagery (from across the electro-magnetic spectrum – from radar to beyond the ultra-violet) to bandwidth for broadcast. The rivalry between these companies is as fierce as it is in any other sector, such as automobile manufacturers for example, and it is again noteworthy how many nations have felt it is in their national, and commercial, self-interest to have a space presence: countries as diverse as Algeria and India operate satellites or more. In this respect, space mirrors economic activity and rivalry between both state and non-state actors on Earth, and reflects wider security concerns. While economic globalisation has bound individual countries and regions ever closer, a (largely unnoticed) growing reliance on space has both enabled this globalisation and characterised it. While orbit slots are allocated (and there is considerable competition for the most useful slots), space is defined by the geography of orbit physics and mathematics, not by human-drawn lines on maps. In an era when soft power counts for as much as, if not more than, hard power, space as an enabler of global economic activity, as a mechanism for shrinking the world and deepening the inter-connectedness and interdependence of individual nations, plays a largely unremarked role in our daily lives, to the extent that a 'day without space' would be hard to imagine. But first, back to the hard power roots and uses of space.

Space and hard power

The early 'scramble for space' in many ways epitomises the East–West rivalries of the Cold War. It is far from clear that the early forays into space were undertaken as part of a clear road-map for military advantage, although the need to use space as the apogee stage of intercontinental ballistic missiles was recognised early, not least when the work of former Nazi Germany scientists was exploited by both Washington and Moscow. However, the advantages for each side in the superpower rivalry were rapidly recognised; the very invulnerability that space-based systems – be they spy satellites, communication satellites or dreamt-of and feared weapon systems – made the domination of space an imperative for national security. The shock that the US suffered from the launch of Sputnik was far more profound than national pride – visions of 'death rays' and all-seeing satellites swept the nation, and these shocks were further compounded by the first manned Soviet flight into space. Recognising the needs, both sides sought to gain maximum advantage and the technological battle for more efficient launch vehicles, longer-lasting satellites, more secure communications and better observation – spying – systems soon spawned a new, high-technology industry. Prestige continued to play a part – the Apollo series of manned flights to the moon were at least as much to do with vanity as with any scientific or military advantage, but hard-nosed military advantage rapidly dominated thinking on both sides.

From the outset, the race for space replicated the earthbound rivalry. The initial use of space for communication and observation became increasingly important as the nuclear arms race intensified. For example, as first-strike gave way to second-strike, the need to watch constantly for land- and later sea-launched missiles called for ever more sophisticated, capable and reliable satellites that could, via a web of relay satellites, communicate launch detection near-instantaneously to enable a second-strike launch. However, early thoughts on basing nuclear weapons in space were soon discounted as the difficulties of maintaining the systems in the extremely hostile environment of space (see below), concerns over the reliability of launch vehicles (the thought of a nuclear-armed rocket exploding on lift-off was not an attractive scenario) and the difficulties of targeting (only over the Equator is geostationary orbit possible, so in the mid-latitudes of the US and the USSR it was simply not possible to hold a weapon constantly over a target) all made the option unattractive compared with manned aircraft and later intercontinental ballistic missiles. However, there was one far more practical issue that emerged at the beginning of the 1960s: the Electro-Magnetic Pulse (EMP). Among other effects, a nuclear explosion releases an intense pulse of energy that extends across the entire electro-magnetic spectrum, and in space there is no atmosphere to attenuate its effects. A series of exo-atmospheric tests in the very late 1950s and early 1960s soon persuaded both sides that while such a blast would wipe out the opponent's satellites, such was the increasing reliance by both sides on space-based platforms and the impossibility of sufficiently proofing satellites against an EMP that they were faced with a zero-sum game. Realism won the day, and both sides ceased exo-atmospheric testing and moved, in 1967, to sign the Outer Space Treaty (OST) that banned the positioning of nuclear warheads in space, as well as banning any claim on extra-terrestrial bodies by individual nations. Despite the intense rivalries of the Cold War the OST held, and significantly it remains the only specific treaty governing the uses of space; all attempts to update it since then have foundered on national self-interest.

Nevertheless, the use of space rapidly expanded throughout the remainder of the Cold War and again replicated the technological arms race taking place on Earth. Ever more capable spy satellites were developed; in the early days they used black and white 'wet film' that then had to be ejected from the satellite in cartridges to be processed on Earth, but the limitations both of processing and of seeing through clouds soon demanded better solutions. Developments in electronic image-gathering (which led directly to the development of today's ubiquitous digital camera, to be found in every smartphone) and the use of infra-red, ultra-violet and radar allowed different imagery that overcame the limitations of cloud and night. Rapid advances in communication technology allowed satellites to talk to satellites, enabling near-real time and increasingly global communication coverage. America's growing dominance was evident not just in the Apollo programme, the advent of the International Space Station and the Shuttle programmes, but particularly with the development of the proposed Strategic Defence Initiative (SDI) – the incorrectly-named Star Wars programme.

Early work on high-powered lasers in the upper atmosphere had suggested that a series of space-based lasers (laser energy, like all forms of light, is less attenuated with a thinner atmosphere and would be hardly impacted at all by the extremely thin atmosphere at orbit altitudes) offered the possibility of destroying the target guidance systems of inter continental ballistic missiles during their brief foray into space at the apogee of their ballistic trajectories. Visions of a series of satellites providing either direct laser fire or relay possibilities spawned drawings, inspired in part by the triumph of the George Lucas film franchise of the time, offering the possibility of defeating any first-strike capability. The implications for deterrence theory were significant and although the technology was never proven (and, indeed, may never have been viable), it played its part in the 1980s arms race that brought the Soviet Union to the negotiating table at Reykjavik and beyond. In its way, the very threat of the SDI contributed to bringing a peaceful conclusion to the Cold War.

However, the Space Race was far from over, and the militaries of the Western powers were on the threshold of another, arguably more significant, technological breakthrough: the digitisation and networking of the Battle Space. Advances in digital technology and the advent of the internet to allow shared working and to share information (the internet was, of course, originally a US military research project) that had occurred in both the military and, increasingly in the late 1980s and early 1990s, the civilian sphere, generated what is referred to today as a Revolution in Military Affairs (RMA). The ability to capture large quantities of data, especially imagery, and share this information with multiple users in real time had a profound impact on military capabilities. The 'what is on the other side of the hill' question which lay at the heart of all military intelligence was not only close to being answered, but the resulting picture could now be shared widely: no longer was there any need to copy and distribute a photograph, because sharing real-time still and moving images was becoming a reality. Data in all forms – troop disposition (friendly and enemy), targeting information, updates on logistics – every piece of information that an army needed could now be digitised and shared. The impact was not only to increase knowledge but to share 'situational awareness', giving a tremendous advantage to the technologically-advanced, networked, digitised forces of the early 1990s. The advantage was most starkly shown in the 1993 Gulf War when the digitised and networked forces led by the US routed the analogue-era forces of Saddam Hussein. The lessons were not lost on others, and in particular the People's Liberation Army of China analysed the American advantage carefully and concluded that space represented both the single most significant enabler of this new form of warfare, and also – significantly – a potential single point of failure: space both enabled this new style of fighting, but it was also an absolute prerequisite. Two immediate changes occurred in Chinese military thinking: a crash modernisation process to embrace the principles of digitisation and of networking, but also the need for a space capability, both to guarantee their own satellites and – if necessary – to deny their opponents. Meanwhile, the reliance is increasing: nearly every weapons system currently being procured across the developed world above the scope of small arms will be reliant on space, while every contingency plan for military operations or responses to crises worldwide (including natural disasters) will be reliant on space, even if only for communications, surveillance and navigation. What is perhaps most worrying is that this reliance is rarely questioned, or alternative options considered within military planning.

For the situation today is already acute. For the military (and for other users of hard power, such as the CIA), space has become unique due to both the ubiquitous reliance on it, and the lack of attention that so many users of hard power give to the degree of their reliance. Conflicts today are fought by the major powers at a distance: the US in Afghanistan is perhaps the most telling example of what could be described as either defence in depth or an eight-thousand-mile pre-emptive action. Without space such military (and military-style) operations would be simply impossible: from the all-encompassing Global Positioning System (GPS) that not only provides straightforward navigation for troops, ships and aircraft but also gives timing signals (required to synchronise secure radios that employ a frequency-hopping approach) and target guidance for 'smart' weapons, through to the myriad of communication and surveillance satellites that enable today's fourth-generation warfare. Unmanned air vehicles – or drones, to use the popular vocabulary – operating over Afghanistan are usually controlled from a continent away; pilots sitting in an air-conditioned building in the desert outside Las Vegas, Nevada watching everyday life – and sometimes ending it – can only undertake such missions (now considered routine) thanks to their guaranteed access to, and freedom of use of, space. Contemporary warfare, in all its guises, simply could not be undertaken without this assured access and freedom of use, which suggests that if space were to become a contested arena in old-fashioned, hard power terms, the effects would be potentially catastrophic. However, there is an immediate conundrum in this idea: can one deny one's opponent access to space without damaging one's own ability to use the same resource? Before exploring this issue, it is worth stressing that it is not only the military now reliant on space – it is all of us.

Space and non-military uses

If the military has slipped largely into both a reliance on space and an assumption that access will not be denied, at least some within the military are aware of the threats and the need for alternatives. However, within the non-military field the same reliance has gone both unnoticed and unconsidered. Our everyday lives are reliant on space to an astonishing degree. Consider first, weather forecasting: the days of the 'weather ships' operating in the Atlantic gathering weather data and reporting back to forecasters in North America and Europe have long passed. Today, aircraft criss-crossing the globe automatically pass snap-shots of their position, the outside air temperature and the wind (via satellite, of course) to the world's meteorological offices, and this data is vital to understanding what is happening in the upper atmosphere and therefore for forecasting. However, there is an even greater reliance on visual images, those wide-angle shots of clouds moving across the globe that we have all become used to, and which we take for granted on the television news weather forecasts. Without space, weather forecasting would be hardly possible, and would offer a massively reduced degree of accuracy. This is important not just for the obvious uses for pleasure and recreation as well as for sailors and airmen, but also for so much of the economy in developed nations. All the major supermarket chains use these forecasts to fine-tune their ordering: it is mid-summer and a heatwave is forecast, therefore buy in extra salad leaves and ice cream. It is going to be a cold and wet week; stock up on root vegetables and comfort food.

With the food giants all working on very narrow margins but large volumes, such data is vital – and its accuracy is reliant (albeit indirectly) on space. However, the second consideration is more obvious, and applies not just to the food sector (although theirs is the most telling example). This concerns the issue of just-in-time logistics. In the West the average local supermarket will have, at best, five days' worth of stock – and then only the non-perishables, the tins of baked beans and so on. Beyond that, and for all fresh food (meat, vegetables, fish, dairy), daily deliveries are required – which are tracked by satellite, delivered by trucks that use (if not rely on) GPS, transporting orders that will often have been placed overseas and hence in all probability will have relied on satellites for communication. This leads to the third example: the reliance on satellites for telecommunications. Today we blithely expect to be able to make crystal-clear telephone calls around the globe with none of the echoes or annoying time delays that characterised calls utilising undersea cables. It is cheaper in many instances for European companies to use a call centre in the Indian sub-continent because the differential in wages more than offsets the telecommunications costs – and it is all but impossible to tell from the quality of the telephone line whether the call is coming 50, 500 or 5,000 kilometres. Every aspect of the economies of developed nations (and increasingly developing nations too; it is almost a requirement now to have 'your own' satellites, even if not the ability to launch them) that relies on satellite telecommunications – such as the trader on the stock market floor arguing down the telephone with a trader on another floor half a world away. For travellers, the ability to drop into an internet café while on holiday to check their emails, or to speak to friends and family back at home via programmes such as Skype, is taken for granted. That is if they bother with an internet café at all, since they will expect wireless broadband in their hotel – or they may simply switch on their pocket-sized smartphone.

Likewise, the world has become accustomed to satellite broadcasting of television, be it the live feeds on the news channels, live broadcasting of sports events, or simple wide-area, cheap broadcasts. One of the most striking examples of this assumption that satellite broadcast is not only readily available but almost a basic necessity of life was the pictures of the slightly better-established refugee camps along the Syrian border, showing the profusion of satellite television dishes on the tents. The human misery was palpable – these people had been forced from their homes and their country by violence – but they had re-established their links to their favoured broadcaster. However, it is the fourth example that best demonstrates the ubiquity of space-derived systems in the everyday life of the average European, North American and, increasingly, anyone: the impact of GPS.

The most obvious incursion of GPS into everyday life is satellite navigation – the 'Sally Sat-Nag' in your car telling you to turn around because you have ignored 'her' instructions and are now lost. However, GPS has also largely replaced all other forms of long-range navigation aids, and commercial shipping and aviation rely on it to a worrying degree, as do those who sail and fly for pleasure. Lose GPS and much of the shipping and aviation which enable trade in our globalised world will struggle at best, if not cease to function entirely. Our reliance on GPS stretches well beyond its most obvious use, though. The increasingly ubiquitous smartphone comes with a built-in GPS receiver which not only offers a navigation function, but also constantly updates the phone's (and therefore your) position – which is then re-broadcast via the radio masts that connect the telephone to the wider world. This information has commercial value; at present it is limited to broad, pattern of life re-sale value (i.e. general trends by age group and gender), but if your favourite retailer was allowed to know when you were close to one of their stores they could send you a tempting offer. Subject to legal constraints, this same information is now available to the police and the intelligence services, enabling them to track individuals. Go back one step further, though, and we realise that all mobile telephones are reliant on GPS to operate. GPS works by measuring time differentials. The importance of this is that all GPS satellites broadcast an incredibly accurate (in the order of ten nano-seconds), stable, worldwide and free timing signal. Among many other uses, this timing signal is used by the BBC when it broadcasts the pips in its radio transmissions counting down to the top of the hour, by traders in, for example, the City of London to time-stamp when they place orders or deposit money to gain interest (the sums concerned mean that the difference in a few seconds is potentially worth a great deal of money), and by mobile telephone companies to ensure that all their radio masts are synchronised to avoid mutual interference.

Going beyond GPS, there are already far more commercial satellites in use than military, although their functions are broadly similar: communication and surveillance. Be it telecommunications, satellite television broadcasts or enabling us to use our mobile telephones and internet on a commercial airliner, satellites act as the bearers of data. Indeed, in the case of the commercial airliner, they are in constant contact with their home base, sending data transmissions with updates on engine performance to allow the anticipatory, preventative maintenance vital to allow modern aircraft to operate at the intensity that they do and hence turn a profit. In terms of surveillance, commercial satellite companies offer imagery for sale across the entire electro-magnetic spectrum, with uses as varied as monitoring the size and health of the Amazon rainforest, watching for oil pollution from ships illegally cleaning their fuel tanks in the deep ocean, and helping geologists look for likely sites to drill for oil and rare earths. The commercial uses of space comprises a list that is only going to continue to grow.

In the future, the commercial possibilities are even more exciting. Assuming that launch costs can be driven down and an alternative way to escape Earth's gravity field other than expensive, dangerous, single-use rockets powered by hydrocarbons can be developed (and there is plenty of work ongoing), this will allow a cheaper and more accessible route into space. Then, activities such as mining metal-rich asteroids become commercially viable, which may address the issue of limited sources of certain rare-earth minerals. Some bio-technological research and production would operate better under low or near-zero gravity conditions, and if we developed a way of transmitting electricity from vast, orbiting photo-voltaic space stations we could go a long way to reducing carbon footprints. The moon may offer further possibilities for exploitation (such as mining for tritium, a hydrogen isotope vital for nuclear fusion that again could help with electricity production, or as a low-gravity production facility), while space tourism has yet to be developed beyond the most minor of scales. The possibilities are endless, exciting and – as technology improves and commercial realities driven by the supply–demand equation become favourable – achievable. All of this would, of course, make space even more important for security, and not just at the level of the nation-state, and it will create more pressure to refine space law. At present there is little in the way of laws governing the use of space: the only extant treaty is the (very dated) 1967 Outer Space Treaty which hardly goes beyond outlawing placing nuclear weapons in orbit, or exploding them beyond the atmosphere (exo-atmospheric detonations) and does not allow countries to 'claim' any bodies such as the moon, asteroids or other planets as national territory. All attempts to update this Treaty have so far failed, although nations do abide by the International Telecommunications Union's allocation of orbit slots, vital to maintain order in increasingly congested orbits (space may be vast, but useable, useful and easily accessible orbits are limited). As we become more reliant on space, the need for a stronger legal regime is likely to become more pressing.

So space is not just important for hard power uses, and it is becoming ever more so, but what is the nature of the threats that may deny any particular country or company the ability to use space?

Space and threats

From the outset it should be acknowledged that space is, in itself, an extremely hostile environment. The obvious lack of oxygen has direct implications for all oxygen-reliant life forms, including mankind. However, equally difficult is the fact that hydrocarbons will not burn without oxygen, requiring satellites and space stations to carry stocks of both fuel and oxygen to act as the propellants they need in order to manoeuvre so they can remain within their allocated orbit slot (even in orbit there are still some atmosphere and gravitational effects that require minor uses of thrust to correct the effects of friction). Cleary, any satellite can only carry limited stocks of fuel and oxygen, and practically they cannot be re-fuelled once they have been launched. However, more fundamentally damaging is the effect of the solar environment: extremes of temperature as satellites pass in and out of Earth's shadow, solar radiation (extremely hazardous to humans without the special protection built into space suits and space stations), solar flares, asteroids and even dust all combine to make this a challenging operating environment. Satellites orbit Earth at very high speeds, so even minuscule dust particles have a cumulative effect as repeated, albeit very minor, impacts slowly destroy satellites. This, combined with finite fuel reserves, means that satellites only have a limited life-span, and at the end of their working life they must either be made to descend back into Earth's atmosphere and – hopefully – burn-up on re-entry (although this is not practical for very large objects such as space stations and may create issues with toxic on-board materials or fuel), or else moved out to a redundant orbit and 'parked'.

But space, or at least the most useful orbits, is becoming very crowded and also contaminated with debris: everything from a Hasselblad camera dropped decades ago by an astronaut, along with assorted tools, to pieces of old satellites. Even flecks of paint can be damaging, and for that reason the now-retired US Space Shuttle would fly backwards in orbit so that the large, metal engines (not required for re-entry as the craft glided to earth) would protect the cockpit and its vulnerable human cargo. The effects of space debris are potentially catastrophic, as the hit movie *Gravity* demonstrated, with the potential to create a chain reaction as satellites collide with other satellites and exponentially increase the problem. The worst example to date of creating additional space debris was the Chinese anti-satellite test of 11 January 2007, when China destroyed one of its own redundant weather satellites with a head-on kinetic kill. The FY-1C polar orbit satellite created the largest-recorded amount of debris, with more than 2,300 pieces of debris of golf-ball size or greater, and an estimated 150,000 particles in total. There was nothing illegal about this test, which underlines the need for a better legal regime; meanwhile the debris has made that orbit unusable for decades to come, it is slowly spreading into adjacent orbits, and the impact on all users has been significant – including, of course, on the Chinese themselves.

That said, satellites are surprisingly resilient once in orbit: while naturally occurring and man-made debris is a threat which, together with solar radiation and solar flares, limits the life of satellites, damaging or destroying an orbiting satellite requires considerable technical ability since the potential target is travelling extremely fast, is a small object in relation to the vastness of space, and is following a three-dimensional path. An attack in the style of the Chinese satellite incident requires detailed knowledge of the path of the target, an assumption that it will not manoeuvre to avoid the collision, and the ability to launch a rocket of one's own from a suitable launch position on Earth – which itself is spinning as it travels on its own orbit. There are other methods of attacking the satellites themselves: the effective lack of an atmosphere makes space-based lasers far more effective, and they could be employed to damage or blind a satellite, while the electro-magnetic pulse created when a nuclear weapon is detonated has a devastating impact if the detonation is exo-atmospheric, as both the United States and the Soviet Union discovered in (now banned) tests between 1958 and 1962. However, these pulses could not be controlled, doing as much damage to each nation's own satellites as to their opponent's. This again raises the issue of whether the degradation of one's own ability to use space would be too badly compromised in trying to deny that use to another.

There are alternative approaches available to interfere with space capabilities, including attacking the (limited and vulnerable) ground launch sites and control stations with conventional tactics, or attempting to gain control of a satellite by interfering with the radio-link sending it directions from Earth – literally a cyberspace attack. While such signals are encrypted, there have been attempts made to take over a satellite, and if this were to be used to ram another satellite (difficult though that would be) the space debris issue would re-emerge. However, even if this option was not used, the requirements for other satellites to be manoeuvred to avoid the rogue device would use up their limited on-board fuel reserves more quickly.

Summarising the threats issue, space is intrinsically hostile and it is noteworthy that other than the Apollo moon programme, mankind has not ventured far beyond low-Earth orbit (altitudes between 160 kilometres/99 miles and 2,000 kilometres/1,200 miles – far less than the distance many of us fly across Earth for a holiday). However, damaging satellites deliberately is not easy, and any attempts must be weighed against the impact that this would have on one's own ability to use space, and the limitations on one's own reliance. In the final analysis, what is required is assured access to space. Therefore, what steps are required to maintain the continuity of service that increasingly enables both commercial and military operations across the entire world?

Conclusion

We are all reliant on space, a reliance that is both increasing and very largely unnoticed. Useable orbits, which are remarkably few in number, are becoming increasingly crowded, which may lead to them becoming contested, and yet the legal regime that governs the uses of space is limited and badly outdated, with all significant attempts to update and improve it foundering on the altar of national self-interest. Denying one's opponents access to space or to their own space capability is extremely difficult, and too many of the options would result in unacceptable levels of damage to one's own capabilities, leading to an impasse. Today's thinking is directed more towards guaranteed access, with work underway to develop the capability to replace damaged satellites or launch new ones to address new needs at very short notice, but without tying up vast sums of capital or keeping outdated satellites sitting on a shelf to cover 'what if' eventualities. In large part this requirement for a degree of redundancy and responsiveness is being addressed by satellites becoming much smaller and cheaper (which also reduces launch costs significantly). However, the trend for increasing reliance on space shows no signs of abating, and it is worth asking the question: 'what would a day without space be like?'

Recommended reading

Dolman, E.C. *Astropolitik: Classic Geopolitics in the Space Age,* London: Frank Cass, 2002.

https://www.gov.uk/government/uploads/system/uploads/attachment_data/file/33691/SpacePrimerFinalWebVersion.pdf

McDougall, W.A. *The Heavens and the Earth: A Political History of the Space Age,* Baltimore: John Hopkins University Press, 1985.

Shaw, M. *International Law* (5th Ed.), Cambridge: Cambridge University Press, 2002.

34 Conclusion

Where to next?

Shahin Malik

Box 34.1: A discipline at war with itself

The discipline of Security Studies is not at peace with itself. Deep divisions exist along its corridors, heightened by variations among theorists whose primary concern is often the concept of Security itself. From the very outset academics within the field have debated its origins, its concepts, and what the best way to study in/security may be. This leads to a number of questions, namely: where do these schisms leave us, what should we be concerned with when approaching global security issues, and given the divisions, can there be a viable future for Security Studies?

Writing a conclusion for a book such as this is not an easy task, especially since it has included so many different chapters. As we highlighted at the outset in Chapter 1, we had three overarching goals – to frame the intellectual debates within the field of Security Studies, to provide an overview of the contemporary security environment, and finally to highlight the real world security dynamics of a number of important global regions through a variety of case studies. This has largely been achieved in the various sections of the book, with each of the chapters covering a theme deemed relevant to some component of the discipline. The first section dealt with a variety of theories which have played a significant role in the development of the discipline as well as contributing to debates regarding the meaning of 'security'. These theories also provided opinions regarding the choice of referent object.

Broadly falling into two categories – traditional and critical – each theory has contributed its own perspective on the nature of security, how to achieve it and for whom. Realism has dominated the field since the end of the Second World War, claiming that its view of the international system is the most accurate. It has championed the state as the most important actor whose security is paramount, linked to an insistence that the discipline of Security Studies should remain narrowly focused purely on military threats. For Realists, the international system is characterised by anarchy, where the greatest threats are to states from other states, and safeguarding the state requires that power – especially military power – be sought as an end in itself. This first section then presented a number of additional chapters which introduced the reader to a variety of approaches which criticise the narrow and 'overly militaristic' stance of the traditional approaches. This subfield has been labelled Critical Security Studies, and as the various chapters demonstrated, it is very broad. Opinions range from that expressed by Ken Booth, who sees the emancipation of the individual as key to achieving Security, to Robert Cox, who has sought to distinguish his Critical Theory from traditional approaches by refusing to accept the underlying nature of the international system and insisting on questioning whether the system is fundamentally fair or not. This criticism is particularly levelled against Realists and Liberals who fail to consider the emancipatory potential of existing international structures and merely seek to work alongside those structures. Other critical approaches such as Feminism have also been covered, and in Chapter 4 we showed how this particular approach criticises traditional theories such as Realism for representing a limited masculinist view of the international system in which it is only the opinions of soldiers, diplomats and politicians that are considered. Given that most of these actors are men, Feminists argue that traditional approaches only consider the opinions of half the world's population and in doing so they marginalise weaker groups in society, of which women are one. This section also presented the views expressed by a relatively new area of research, that of Human Security, popularised by the United Nations in the mid-1990s. Although this subfield remains weak conceptually – especially since there is no consensus regarding definitions – it is now in a position to challenge the narrowness advocated by traditional approaches.

Given the immense influence of the traditional military core of Security Studies, Section 2 covered a wide variety of topics that highlighted the premise that military force remains a central component of Security in the new millennium. The most obvious place to begin, therefore, was to reflect on the definitions and nature of both war and peace in Chapter 7. Some of these issues were elaborated upon in Chapter 8, which looked at the rising international concern with failed states. This particular chapter highlighted some key research into the phenomenon, introducing work by academics such as Mary Kaldor, who has, in her New Wars thesis, highlighted the important connections between globalisation and the inability of many states to deal with the forces released by it. Furthermore, the chapter analysed the changing nature of warfare, contending that inter-state conflicts have declined markedly and have instead been replaced by a large number of intra-state wars in which non-state actors play a significant role. Chapters 9 and 10 dealt with the two related yet distinct areas of weapons of mass destruction (specifically nuclear weapons) and the arms trade respectively. In Chapter 9 we looked at the types of nuclear weapons that have been developed, along with their delivery systems. We also analysed the possibility that, given the immense destructive potential of nuclear weapons, they might in certain circumstances actually contribute to stability between two enemies. It is in this light that the chapter considers the famous debate between Kenneth Waltz and Scott Sagan, where both academics highlight opposing arguments. The chapter also considered the ways in which the international community has been expressing its opposition to further proliferation, referring to the spectre of a nuclear Iran and the dangers posed by North Korea as well as highlighting the nightmare scenario of non-state actors acquiring this technology. Chapter 10 made the important point that the international community has rightly remained preoccupied with the dangers posed by nuclear weapons proliferation, but it also contended that no nuclear weapon has been used since the Second World War, whereas smaller conventional weapons have been responsible for the deaths of tens of millions of people around the globe. Small arms and light weapons have become the weapons of choice for many of the intra-state conflicts being fought around the globe, and consequently this chapter analysed their nature and impact.

Chapters 11 and 12 were linked by virtue of the fact that in recent years terrorism has been of a markedly religious character. The attacks of 11 September 2001 were carried out by Islamist extremists, and this act ushered in an era in which religion began to play an increasingly potent role in world politics, since most (though not all) terrorist attacks since that fateful day have been carried out by al-Qaeda itself or by groups affiliated to it. Chapter 11 considered the implications of this, as well as taking a broader view of the phenomenon by analysing other aspects such as definitions, the role of intelligence in tackling terrorism, and the impact of globalisation. Chapter 12 then examined the connections between religion and international conflict in greater detail, beginning with an analysis of Samuel Huntington's influential 'Clash of Civilisations' thesis in which inter-religious clashes took on a prominent role. The chapter then dealt with a number of issues including how certain theories of Security Studies view the issue of religion, coming to the conclusion that the main ones (Realism, Liberalism and Marxism) struggled to explain the phenomenon. The chapter then moved on to a detailed investigation of whether or not Huntington's thesis can stand up to scrutiny, raising a number of factors that showed its shortcomings.

The final two chapters in Section 2, on Intelligence and Security (Chapter 13) and the Private Military Sector (Chapter 14), further highlight the premise that military force remains an important, ever-present and enduring feature of the international system. Chapter 13 investigated the nature and importance of intelligence to state security, whereas in Chapter 14 we highlighted the inexorable rise of the private security and military sector. The chapter demonstrated how this industry has grown in the post-Cold War era, particularly in response to the increasing number of intra-state wars being fought in various regions of the world. These chapters have their basis in the ideas presented earlier in Chapter 2 where we dealt with the military/state-centric core of the discipline – as embodied within the traditionalist approaches of Realism and Liberalism.

Section 3 forms an important part of the book; it is here that we highlight the non-military components of security. Many of the examples and topics presented here resonate with the relatively recent arrival of Critical Security Studies within the discipline. Security Studies had its roots in the years after the Second World War, and its ultimate goal was to protect the state from external (and internal) threats. However, it was this core aim that failed to impress those of a more critical nature. Many, such as Ken Booth, Robert Cox and Anne Tickner, began to question whether Realism could ever successfully account for the insecurity experienced by vulnerable groups of humans the world over. Critical Theorists went so far as to point out that it was often states themselves that threatened the individual. Consequently, the Critical field began to debate with the traditionalists regarding what the ultimate referent object was to be – the state or the human. It is with this in mind that Section 3 covers topics such as *health, food* and *environmental* security, while at the same time highlighting how *natural disasters* can seriously diminish the security not only of states but also, importantly, of humans.

The three chapters in Section 4 highlight the role that institutions, both global and regional, play as security-enhancing structures. Chapter 20 looks at the history of the United Nations, the way it has been organised and the legal provisions within the Charter that establish it as the main authority tasked with maintaining international peace and security. The analysis also extends to a consideration of its role in peace operations in the post-Cold War era, during which time the international community has faced unprecedented problems, with a huge increase in the number of civil conflicts being fought around the globe. The changing nature of conflicts in the post-Cold War era has led to a succession of new mechanisms in the UN's arsenal for dealing with these numerous conflicts. These new instruments have been placed under the general heading of Second Generation Peacekeeping, which includes the traditional forms as practiced during the Cold War, but also, importantly, newer, more forceful methods of Peace Enforcement. Consequently, the chapter considers these contemporary processes (such as the Responsibility to Protect) by analysing not only their definitions, but also their application to various crises. Attention then shifts in Chapter 21 to a consideration of the role played by NATO in enhancing the security of its member states. Here we present an analysis of the reasons behind alliance formation, before considering the historical ethos and the contemporary functions of the security institution. Of particular concern in this chapter was whether NATO had successfully found a role for itself in the post-Cold War era now that the reasons for its original establishment had ended with the demise of the Soviet Union. Chapter 22 on Regional Institutions extends the analysis to a review of the general growth of regional IGOs that have within their remit a security dimension. In addition to NATO, the analysis therefore considers Europe-wide alliances (CSCE and the WEU), Nuclear Weapons Free Zones and alliances of former Soviet Republics, as well as global agreements such as the Kimberley Process – a UN-based scheme introduced in 2003, with the aim of slowing and stopping the trade in 'blood diamonds'. The chapter's attention then shifts to a consideration of IGOs outside the European context, including Africa, the Middle East and the Americas. It ends with an analysis of whether this form of regionalism is adequate as a route to achieve regional and global security.

Finally, in Section 5 we have presented a number of case studies. While many of the textbooks on Security Studies use examples to strengthen conceptual and theoretical features of the discipline, none of those we reviewed prior to writing this book bring together a large number of detailed case studies in one volume. In our long-standing experience as lecturers, we always encounter students who, while recognising the importance of the conceptual and theoretical basis of the discipline, often struggle to make connections at the practical level. In the case studies section, our intention is to build upon some of the concepts and ideas highlighted in the earlier core chapters by relating them to key contemporary concerns. We believe that the practical examples given in these case studies will enable students to gain further understanding of the concepts discussed. Therefore, these shorter chapters consider a wide range of issues ranging from the objectives of great powers in the post-Cold War era to an analysis of the security dynamics of various regions, as well as a number of Human Security concerns.

The wide variety of topics

An obvious conclusion after reading this book is that the discipline of Security Studies is concerned with a very wide range of topics, and it is in this variation that the central characteristics of this discipline can be found. Indeed, we have successfully shown that the discipline is broad and its success is dependent upon an ability to use the theoretical tools available to explain and understand security dynamics in the international system. It is not for us to influence students of International Relations and Security Studies as to which of these theoretical opinions to adopt. As I write this conclusion, we must remain mindful of the wars in Syria, the protracted brutal civil conflict in Iraq, ongoing Islamist insurgency in Pakistan, the continuing development and testing of nuclear weapons on the Korean peninsula and on the Indian subcontinent, and most recently a Russian invasion of Crimea which has resulted in the outbreak of civil war in Ukraine. One overarching observation based on these events (and events elsewhere) is that force continues to be a central feature of Security Studies. Indeed, there is ample evidence today to support the view that traditional views of security remain at the core of the discipline.

And yet Ken Booth has reminded us that 'Issues such as the growth of complex interdependence, the erosion of sovereignty, advances in communications, the declining utility of [inter-state] war, environmental degradation, huge population growth and so on mean that there is vastly growing scope for non-state actors to play a role in the international system' (Booth, 1991: 314). Since his seminal article, *Security and Emancipation*, published in 1991, academics of a 'critical' persuasion have sought to broaden the discipline, and as a result the practical as well as the theoretical boundaries of the discipline have expanded considerably. Events since 9/11 may persuade us that force still has utility; indeed, there are no grounds to dispute this conclusion. However, at the same time poverty continues to reign across vast swathes of the world, the environment continues to be degraded, scientists continue to warn us of impending and dangerous flu epidemics, crime has moved from its intra-state form to a transnational form facilitated by globalisation, and often natural disasters are so violent that they kill more people than wars. Students must ask themselves whether traditional approaches can deal successfully with such issues. This debate between academics regarding the future of the discipline began in the late 1990s, and to say that it has been resolved today is too simplistic. Our claim is that academics remain as far as ever from reaching a consensus regarding both the definition of security and the nature of the threats that face humans. This inevitably means that the future of the discipline is going to remain dominated by debates between exponents of various intellectual positions, each vying for space within the corridors of universities, and all seeking to provide explanations of events and processes in the international system.

Finally, I am reminded of a couple of points raised by two highly influential academics within the field. Soon after the end of the Cold War a prominent Realist, Stephen Walt, reacted against the issue-driven widening that was taking place within the discipline of Security Studies. He pleaded for Security Studies to remain confined, arguing that Security Studies was essentially about the phenomena of war and that it had to be defined as 'the study of the threat, use and control of military force'. He further claimed that broadening the agenda beyond the strictly military domain ran:

> the risk of expanding Security Studies excessively [and that] by this logic, issues such as pollution, disease, child abuse, or economic recessions could all be viewed as threats to security. Defining the field in this way would destroy its intellectual coherence and make it more difficult to devise solutions to any of the important problems.
>
> (Walt, 1991: 227)

Today Stephen Walt remains a staunch advocate of the Realist core of the discipline, but as many chapters in this book have demonstrated, adhering to an exclusively traditionalist standpoint has become increasingly untenable as we proceed through the first two decades of the new millennium. Realism now has to compete with other approaches for a seat at the Security Studies table, given that the expansion of the discipline is now irreversible.

My final quote comes from another academic – Lawrence Freedman – which I find particularly apt given the nature of our objectives in this book. In 2002 he reminded us that 'Marx once wrote that people make their own history but not in the circumstances of their own choosing', before going on to argue that a discipline such as Security Studies should aid in any grasp of 'how individuals go about making history and in doing so reshaping the circumstances they face' (Freedman, 2002: 341). To quote from him:

> … we have not yet succeeded in banishing armed force from human affairs, we will still have to face many extreme situations [such as] the events of 11 September 2001: an attack inspired in one of the most remote and poor points of the world directed against one of the wealthiest. The attack was instigated using the most ancient of military technologies – the knife – in order to turn the most modern civilian aviation technologies against the West.
>
> (Freedman, 2002: 341)

In other words, in light of the increasingly complex circumstances which surround us in the twenty-first century, Security Studies has to provide convincing answers and explanations in the face of such events if it is to flourish as a discipline.

Recommended reading

Booth, K. 'Security and emancipation', *Review of International Studies*, vol.17, 1991.

Baylis, J., Wirtz, J., Cohen, E. and Gray, C.S. (eds), *Strategy in the Contemporary World: An Introduction to Strategic Studies*. Oxford: Oxford University Press, 2002.

Browning, C.S. and McDonald, M. 'The Future of Critical Security Studies: Ethics and the Politics of Security', *European Journal of International Relations*, vol. 19, no. 2, 2011.

Morgan, P.M. *International Security: Problems and Solutions*, Washington: CQ Press, 2006.

Kolodziej, E.A. *Security and International Relations*, Cambridge: Cambridge University Press, 2005.

Glossary

7/7 the accepted shorthand to denote the attack on London's transport network by home-grown Islamic terrorists on 7th July 2005.

9/11 the accepted shorthand to denote the al-Qaeda-led attacks on the United States of America on 11 September 2001.

alliance the coming together of at least two states with the goal of furthering their security needs, be they military, economic, or other.

al-Qaeda translated as 'The Base', al-Qaeda is a network of extremist Muslim groups which seeks to expel Western influence from the Muslim world, often using violence to achieve its aims.

anarchy the defining manner in which the international system is ordered. It simply refers to the absence of central worldwide government.

arms control cooperation between actors (primarily states) that leads to a reduction in the likelihood of military action.

arms trade the importing and exporting of conventional weapons.

authoritarian non-democratic.

balance-of-power theory a distribution and opposition of forces among nations such that no single nation is strong enough to assert its will or dominate the others within the system.

bilateral involving two parties.

bipolar dominated by two sides.

Boko Haram usually translated as 'Western education is a sin', this is a violent, Islamic extremist group in Nigeria opposed to Western influence in the region.

ceasefire a suspension of armed conflict following an agreement between the conflicting parties.

civil war armed conflict within a state fought for the purpose of control of the state's resources and territory.

codify write down in law.

collective goods problem a problem that can only be solved with a collective response since on an individual basis there is an incentive not to act.

collective security a security arrangement in which members treat a threat to the security of one as a threat to all; all members are thus expected to unite in confronting threats.

conflict depicts the confrontation between one or more actors aspiring to incompatible objectives.

constructivism   claims that events in international relations have their basis in 'social process' rather than being the inevitable consequences of fixed and rigid human nature or other natural laws.

conventional weapons   weapons other than Weapons of Mass Destruction (WMDs).

Critical Theory   a theoretical approach developed by the 'Frankfurt School' of thinkers who stressed that all knowledge is historical and therefore subjective. Consequently all claims to objective knowledge are illusory.

cyberwarfare   the use of computer technology to attack the infrastructure or defence capabilities of another state, such as banks, utility companies, and defence communications.

defoliant   chemical used to strip leaves from trees and plants.

disarmament   the gradual or comprehensive reduction of military arsenals and forces.

eastern bloc   the USSR's seven East European satellite states during the Cold War: East Germany, Poland, Hungary, Czechoslovakia, Hungary, Romania and Bulgaria.

emerging markets   states successfully undergoing economic development.

empirical   based on factual evidence and observation (such as data).

epidemic   localised disease outbreak above the norm.

epidemiological   related to the study of disease.

epistemic community   transnational group of experts on a given subject.

epistemic consensus   broad agreement among an epistemic community.

epistemology   how you come know something. The theory of establishing knowledge.

ethnocentricism   the tendency to consider one's own nationality as more significant or superior to others.

failed state   a state that has lost its monopoly on the legitimate use of force and control of its own territory.

Feminism   an approach that has historically drawn on a wide variety of analytical instruments in order to theorise about women's oppression and liberation.

First World   collective term for the states of the developed, capitalist world during the Cold War.

fission bomb   most commonly called an atom bomb, a fission weapon explodes when one type of atom is split, releasing energy. The two elements that can be split to create an explosion are uranium-235 and plutonium.

force   usually associated with military weapons, this refers to the threat or actual use of coercion between actors (usually states) but also non-state actors.

fossil fuels   fuels produced from fossilised organic material (e.g. oil, coal and natural gas).

fusion bomb   most commonly called a hydrogen bomb, it involves an explosion caused by fusing two atoms of hydrogen, releasing energy in the process.

gender   the social differences between the sexes that have been gained through experience, learning and within cultural, religious, political and other contexts.

global North   the world's developed and most wealthy states (which are principally in the northern hemisphere).

global South   the Less Developed Countries (which are principally in the southern hemisphere).

globalisation   a phenomenon entailing increasing global interconnectedness, in spheres including politics, economics and culture.

gross domestic product (GDP)   the sum total from all economic activity in a given country.

hard power the military power of a state. This can also include its economic power, for example when applying tough sanctions against another state.

hegemony the exercise, usually by a single state, of international dominance and leadership, particularly in economic relations.

herbicides chemicals used to kill pest plants.

Human Security a term first coined by the United Nations in the mid-1990s which referred to the protection of all humans from being threatened, regardless of the origin of threats (freedom from fear and freedom from want).

humanitarian intervention the threat or use of force to prevent or halt widespread suffering and violations of human rights, without the consent of the host state in which they are undertaken.

hypothesis a conjectured causal relationship between two phenomena.

idealism term applied to statesmen and academics of the 1920s and 1930s who advocated greater levels of international cooperation, epitomised by the creation of the League of Nations.

improvised explosive device normally used by terrorists in countries such as Afghanistan and Iraq, IEDs are homemade bombs used to target military vehicles or personnel.

integration the process whereby states merge some of their economic and political responsibilities into a wider political unit.

intelligence a form of information that enables policymakers to make decisions. It is almost always secret in nature.

intelligence cycle the process by which intelligence is requested by policymakers or operational commanders, and is then collected, analysed, and passed on to the consumers of that intelligence.

interdependence the condition of interconnectedness between actors in international politics which makes them reliant on each other.

inter-governmental organisation (IGO) an international organisation comprising government representatives of more than one country.

international non-governmental organisation (INGO) an international organisation comprised of private individuals rather than government representatives.

international regime system of rules and policy-making procedures, either formal or informal, which influence the behaviour of actors in a particular international issue.

internecine conflict destructive for all sides.

inter-state war conflict between two or more states.

intra-state war *see* civil war.

Iron Curtain term applied to the tight border established by the USSR during the Cold War to isolate its allies in Eastern Europe from Western Europe.

Liberalism a philosophical tradition that emphasises the ability of human reason to create a world of peace and harmony.

Marxism a school of thought inspired by the writings of Karl Marx, who identified the cause of war as class conflict, especially conflict between and within the capitalist class.

multilateral involving more than two states.

mutipolar a world with a number of major powers, which can be state or non-state.

mutually assured destruction the idea that if one side launched a nuclear weapons first strike against the other, enough weapons would survive for the other to retaliate with a second strike. The resulting casualties on both sides would be so great, stretching at least into the tens of millions, that it would deter either state from considering an attack.

national missile defense   a system of surface to air anti-ballistic missiles designed to shoot down any incoming missiles fired at the US from rogue states.

nationalisation   process of taking parts of a country's economy under state control.

negative peace   the absence of direct violence – violence perpetrated directly against people.

neo-imperialism   the economic domination of one state by another without there being formal imperial control.

Neorealism   a recent version of Realism specified by Kenneth Waltz which highlights the structure of the international system when seeking to explain the behaviour of states.

New Wars thesis   a theory that contemporary wars are qualitatively different to those of the past, in terms of who fights them and for what ends.

Non-Proliferation Treaty   this was designed to limit the spread of nuclear weapons. It was open for signature in 1968, and allows states to develop civil nuclear power but not nuclear weapons.

non-state actor   an organisation with international political significance other than a state. A generic term for both INGOs and IGOs.

normative   moral-based.

ontological   enquiry into 'what there is' (ontology).

overpopulation   condition whereby a given state has a population in excess of its capacity to support them to an optimal level.

pandemic   widespread international outbreak of disease.

paradigm   a set of core assumptions shared by a group of theories and approaches.

peacebuilding   efforts to put in place structures and mechanisms that will create durable peace.

peacekeeping   an activity aimed at preserving the peace, usually initiated after an armed conflict has ended.

power   the material resources that a state has access to.

positive peace   entails overcoming not only direct forms of violence, but also structural violence (arising from the inequalities that result from social structures) and cultural violence (which results from a society's beliefs and values).

private military and security companies (PMSCs)   private businesses that provide a mix of military and security services.

rationality   the assumption that actors in the international system will seek to attain their highest preferences at the least cost.

Realism   a philosophical tradition that sees international politics as a perpetual struggle for power and resources in a world of scarcity.

realpolitik   amoral, self-serving political practice by states.

referent object   in security, the entity which is intended to be protected (for example, the state or an individual person).

regime   *see* international regime.

renewable resources   natural resources which are inexhaustible, such as wind power.

Responsibility to Protect (R2P)   a doctrine that argues that states have a responsibility to protect their citizens from severe human rights abuses – if they do not, the rest of the international community must take up the responsibility instead.

security community a group of states enjoying such good and close relations that they form a community in which war is unthinkable.

small arms and light weapons (SALW) weapons that can be used by a single person.

social construct something which can be defined only in the subjective terms of the participants rather than by objective, empirical analysis.

social movement broad group of people seeking political change through mass activism.

soft power political influence through cultural factors (rather than military or economic power).

sovereignty status of legal autonomy enjoyed by states so that the government has exclusive authority within its borders and enjoys the rights of membership of the international community.

spillover the tendency for political integration in one area to provide the momentum for integration to occur in other, related areas.

state the main unit/actor in the international system.

state-centricism analysis which is biased towards the roles and motivations of states over other actors in international relations.

statist focused on the state.

strategic nuclear weapons weapons which target an enemy's homeland, such as intercontinental ballistic missiles.

structural adjustment the package of conditions accompanying a loan given to a state, such as by the IMF. Such conditions typically entail monetarily conservative measures such as public spending cuts.

Stuxnet a computer virus used to target Iran's nuclear programme, most likely developed by Israel and the US.

superpower a term applied to the US and the USSR during the Cold War because of their dominance of international relations, which superseded that of the *great powers* in earlier eras.

supranational political authority over the state.

sustainable peace long-term, lasting peace.

symbiotic a relationship where two things co-exist for their mutual benefit.

tactical nuclear weapons these are designed to be used in a battlefield situation.

terrorism the threat or use of violence by non-state actors intended to achieve a goal, most often political. Targets are normally non-combatants.

theory a hypothesised pattern of behaviour for individuals, groups, states, and/or the international system.

total war war in which civilians are targeted as well as military and state targets.

transnational linking societies in different countries.

unilateral one (state) alone.

unipolar a world in which one state or power dominates. The dominant power may also be called a hegemon.

unmanned combat air vehicles remotely controlled drones which are often used for surveillance or targeting suspected terrorists.

utilitarian driven by the aim of maximising the utility of something. Term most used in International Relations in situations where governments cooperate to reap mutual material gains.

utopianism *see* idealism.

war organised violence between two or more political units.

weapons of mass destruction   a category of weapons which includes atomic explosive weapons, radioactive material weapons, lethal chemical and biological weapons, and any weapons which have characteristics comparable in destructive effects.

widened security   national security concerns not restricted to military defence.

Bibliography

2011 National Counterterrorism Report on Terrorism, available at www.nctc.gov/docs/2011_NCTC_Annual_Report_Final.pdf (Accessed 31.1.2013).

Abrahamsen, R. and Williams, M.C. *Security Beyond the State: Private Security in International Politics,* Cambridge: Cambridge University Press, 2010.

Abt, F. *A Capitalist in North Korea: My Seven Years in the Hermit Kingdom,* North Clarendon, VT: Tuttle Publishing, 2014.

African Leadership Forum, 'The Kampala Document: Towards a Conference on Security, Stability, Development and Cooperation in Africa', www.africaaction.org/african-initiatives/kampall.htm, 1991 (Accessed 23.7.2003).

Ahmed, A. and Forst, B. (eds) *After Terror: Promoting Dialogue Among Civilizations,* London: Polity, 2005.

Aldrich, R., Andrew, C. and Wark, W. (eds) *Secret Intelligence: A Reader,* London: Routledge, 2008.

Ali, S. Interview by J. Gettlem, *New York Times,* 30 September 2008.

Alison, M. 'Women as Agents of Political Violence: Gendering Security', *Security Dialogue,* vol. 35, no. 4, 2004, 447–463.

Allison, R., Light, M. and White, S. *Putin's Russia and the Enlarged Europe,* Blackwell: London, 2006.

Almond, G., Appleby, R.S. and Sivan, E. *Strong Religion: The Rise of Fundamentalisms Around the World,* Chicago and London: University of Chicago Press, 2003.

Amies, N. 'Alliance of Civilizations: Intercultural Peace Forum or Talking Shop?', *Deutsche Welle,* 28 May 2010. Available at: www.dw.de/dw/article/0,,5610155,00.html (Accessed 15.3.2012).

Ammann, A. and Nogueira, S. 'Governments as Facilitators or Obstacles in the HIV epidemic', *British Medical Journal,* 324, 26 January 2002, 184–185.

Anderson, S. and Sloan, S. *Historical Dictionary of Terrorism,* London: Scarecrow Press, 2002.

Annan, K. 'Press Release: Secretary-General Reflects On "Intervention" In Thirty-Fifth Annual Ditchley Foundation Lecture', www.un.org/News/Press/docs/1998/19980626.sgsm6613.html, 26 June 1998 (Accessed 28.6.2014).

Annan, K. *We the Peoples: The Role of the United Nations in the Twenty-first Century,* www.un.org/en/ga/search/view_doc.asp?symbol=A/54/2000, 2000 (Accessed 28.6.2014).

Anseeuw, W., Wily, L., Cotula, L. and Taylor, M. 'Land Rights and the Rush for Land. Findings of the Global Pressures on Land Research Project', Rome: International Land Coalition, 2011.

Armesto, F. *Ideas That Changed the World,* London: Dorling Kindersley, 2003.

Arnold, M. and Merrick, P. 'Development for Disaster Reduction – the Role of the World Bank', *Australian Journal of Emergency Management,* vol. 16, no. 4, Summer 2001.

Ashdown, P. *Humanitarian Emergency Response Review,* UK Department for International Development, www.dfid.gov.uk/emergency-response-review, 2011 (Accessed 20.9.2011).

Ashley, R. 'Living on Borderlines: Man, Post Structuralism, and War', in J. Der Derian and M.J. Shapiro (eds), *International/Intertextual Relations: Postmodern Readings of World Politics,* Lexington, Mass.: Lexington Books, 1989.

Ashley, R. 'The Poverty of Neorealism' in *Neorealism and its Critics*, Edited by Robert Keohane, New York, Columbia University Press, 1986, 255–300.

Axworthy, L. 'Human Security and Global Governance: Putting People First', *Global Governance*, 7, 2001.

Ayson, R. 'Selective Non-proliferation or Universal Regimes?', *Australian Journal of International Affairs*, vol. 59, no. 4, 2005.

Baev, P. 'Russian Policy in the Arctic: A Reality Check', in D. Trenin and P. Baev (eds), *The Arctic. A View From Moscow*, Washington: Carnegie Endowment for International Peace, 2010.

Bailes, A. and Cottey, A. 'Regional Security Cooperation in the Early 21ˢᵗ Century', in SIPRI, *SIPRI Yearbook 2006: Armaments, Disarmament and International Security*, Stockholm International Peace Research Institute, 2006.

Bajpai, K. 'Human Security: Concept and Measurement', *Kroc Institute Occasional Paper (Number 19)*, Notre Dame, Indiana: University of Notre Dame, 2000.

Baker, R. *Capitalism's Achilles Heel*, Hoboken, NJ: Wiley and Sons, 2005.

Ban Ki-Moon, Closing Remarks, Madrid High Level Meeting on Food Security for all, 26–27 January 2009.

Bankoff, G. 'Rendering the World Unsafe: "Vulnerability" as Western Discourse', *Disasters*, vol. 25, no. 1, 2001, 19–35.

Baylis, J., Wirtz, J., Cohen, E. and Gray, C.S. (eds), *Strategy in the Contemporary World: An Introduction to Strategic Studies*, Oxford: Oxford University Press, 2002.

BBC, *Pulse of Africa*, World Service, 2004, http://news.bbc.co.uk/1/shared/spl/hi/pop_ups/04/africa_the_pulse_of_africa/html/1.stm (Accessed 12.6.2005).

BBC, 'Corruption Costs $1.6tn, UN Says', http://news.bbc.co.uk/1/hi/business/8350239.stm, 2009 (Accessed 21.10.09).

BBC, 'Mexican Drug-Related Violence', www.bbc.co.uk/news/world-latin-america-10681249, 2011 (Accessed 8.10.2011).

Becker, J. *Hungry Ghosts: Mao's Secret Famine*, New York: Free Press, 2000.

Beckett, M. Speech at the UN Security Council, 16 April, *UK Foreign and Commonwealth Office Press Release*, 2007.

Bellamy, A.J. *Global Politics and the Responsibility to Protect: From Words to Deeds*, London: Routledge, 2011.

Bellamy, A.J., Williams, P. and Griffin, S. *Understanding Peacekeeping*, 2nd ed., Cambridge: Polity Press, 2010.

Bellamy, I., 'Towards a Theory of International Security', *Political Studies*, vol. 29, no. 1, 1981, 100–105.

Benatar, S.R., Daar, A.S. and Singer, P.A. 'Global Health Ethics: the Rationale for Mutual Caring', *International Affairs*, vol. 79, no. 1, 2003, 107–138.

Bendavid, E. and Bhattacharya, J. 'The President's Emergency Plan for AIDS Relief in Africa: An Evaluation of Outcomes', *Annals of Internal Medicine*, vol. 150, no. 10, 2009, 688–695.

Bergen, P. *The Longest War: Inside the Enduring Conflict between America and Al- Qaeda since 9/11*, New York: Free Press, 2011.

Betts, R. 'Analysis, War, and Decision: Why Intelligence Failures are Inevitable', *World Politics*, vol. 31, no. 2, 1978, 61–89.

Bigo, Didier, 'International Political Sociology' in *Security Studies: An Introduction*, 2nd Edition, Edited by Paul D. Williams, London, Routledge, 2013, 120–133.

Bloom, M. *Bombshell: The Many Faces of Women Terrorists*, London: Hurst, 2011.

Bolivia, *Law of Mother Earth*, Law 071, 2011.

Bolopian, P. 'After Libya, the Question: To Protect or Depose?', *LA Times*, 25 August 2011.

Booth, K. 'Security and Emancipation', *Review of International Studies*, vol. 17, no. 4, 1991, 313–326.

Booth, K. (ed.) *Critical Security Studies and World Politics*, Boulder, CO: Lynne Rienner, 2005.

Booth, K. *Theory of World Security*, Cambridge: Cambridge University Press, 2007.

Booth, K. and Dunne, T. *Terror in Our Time*, Abingdon: Routledge, 2012.

Borgerson, S. 'Arctic Meltdown', *Foreign Affairs*, vol. 7, no. 2, 2008, 63–77.

Boutros-Ghali, B. *Agenda for Peace*, New York: United Nations, 1992.

Brachman, Z. 'Watching the Watchers: Al-Qaeda's Bold New Strategy', *Foreign Policy*, November 2010.

Brauch, H.G. 'Desertification. A New Security Challenge for the Mediterranean', in W.G. Kepner, J.L. Rubio, D.A. Mouat and F. Pedrazzini (eds), *Desertification in the Mediterranean Region*, Dordrecht: Springer, 2003.

Britton, N. 'A New Emergency Management for the New Millennium?', *Australian Journal of Emergency Management*, vol. 16, no. 4, Summer 2001, 44–54.

Brown, H. 'New Nuclear Realities', *The Washington Quarterly*, Winter 2007–8, 7–22.

Brown, O. and McLeman, R. 'A Recurring Anarchy? The Emergence of Climate Change as a Threat to International Peace and Security', *Conflict, Security & Development*, vol. 9, no. 3, 2009, 289–305.

Browning, C.S. and McDonald, M. 'The Future of Critical Security Studies: Ethics and the Politics of Security', *European Journal of International Relations*, vol. 19, no. 2, 2011.

Brownmiller, S. *Against Our Will: Men, Women and Rape*, New York: Fawcett Books, 1993.

Brzezinski, Z. 'Moving Toward a Reconciliation of Civilizations', *China Daily*, 15 January, 2009a.

Brzezinski, Z. 'What Next for NATO?', *Foreign Affairs*, September/October 2009b.

Bull, H. *The Anarchical Society: A Study of Order in World Politics*, London: MacMillan, 1977.

Bull, H. *The Anarchical Society: A Study of Order in World Politics*, 4th ed., New York: Columbia University Press, 2012.

Bullock, J. and Adel, D. *Water Wars: Coming Conflicts in the Middle East*, London: St. Edmundsbury Press, 1993.

Bundy, M. *Danger and Survival*, New York: Vintage Books, 1988.

Bush, G.W. 'Address to Joint Session of Congress and the American People', 20 September 2001, http://georgewbush-whitehouse.archives.gov/news/releases/2001/09/20010920-8.html (Accessed 2.7.2011).

Bush, G.W. *State of the Union Speech*, 29 January 2002, available at http://georgewbush-whitehouse.archives.gov/news/releases/2002/01/20020129-11.html (Accessed 2.7.2011).

Bush, G.W. *State of the Union Speech*, 20 January 2004, available at http://georgewbush-whitehouse.archives.gov/stateoftheunion/2004/ (Accessed 1.7.2011).

Buzan, B. *People, States and Fear: An Agenda for International Security Studies in the Post-Cold War Era*, 2nd edition, London: Harvester Wheatsheaf, 1991.

Buzan, B. and Hansen, L. *The Evolution of International Security Studies*, Cambridge: Cambridge University Press, 2009.

Buzan, B., Waever, O. and de Wilde, J. *Security: A New Framework for Analysis*, Boulder: Lynne Rienner Publishers, 1998.

Byers, M. *Who Owns the Arctic? Understanding Sovereignty Disputes in the North*, Vancouver: Douglas and McIntyre, 2010.

Byers, M. 'Cooling Things Down: the Legalization of Arctic Security', paper presented at conference entitled *Carnegie Council's Programme on U.S. Global Engagement: a Two-Year Retrospective*, Carnegie Council for Ethics in International Affairs, US, June 1–3, 2011.

Byman, D. 'Terrorism after the Revolutions', *Foreign Affairs*, vol. 90, no. 3, May/June 2011, 48–54.

Campaign Against Arms Trade, 'SIPRI assessment of UK arms export subsidies', www.caat.org.uk/resources/publications/economics/subsidies-sipri-2011.pdf, 2011 (Accessed 28.6.2014).

Canada, *Foreign Affairs Agenda 2003*, Ottawa, 2002.

Canadian Peace Alliance, 'Transformation Moment: A Canadian Vision of Common Security', *Report of the Citizens' Inquiry into Peace and Security*, March 1992.

Cants, W. 'Al-Qaeda's Challenge', *Foreign Affairs*, September/October 2011.

Caplan, N. *The Israel–Palestine Conflict: Contested Histories (Contesting the Past)* Chichester: Wiley-Blackwell, 2009.

Caprioli, M. 'Democracy and Human Rights versus Women's Security: A Contradiction?', *Security Dialogue*, vol. 35, no. 4, September 2004, 411–428.

Carlile, A. 'The Definition of Terrorism', *Report by Independent Reviewer of Terrorism Legislation*, presented to Parliament March 2007, London: UK Government.

Carnegie Council, www.carnegiecouncil.org/resources/articles_papers_reports/0102.html (Accessed 19.11.11).

Carpenter, T. *NATO Enters the Twenty-First Century*, London: Frank Cass, 2000.

Carr, J. *Inside Cyber Warfare: Mapping the Cyber Underworld*, 2nd Edition, Sebastopol, CA: O'Reilly Media, 2011.

Carter, J. *US President State of the Union Address*, 23 January, Washington DC,, 1980.

Casanova, J. *Public Religions in the Modern World*, Chicago and London: University of Chicago Press, 1994.

Castello-Cortes, I. and Feldman, M. *Guinness Book of World Records 1997*, London: Guinness, 1996.

Chandler, D. *From Kosovo to Kabul and Beyond: Human Rights and International Intervention*, London: Pluto Press, 2006.

Chassy, P. and Amey, S.H. 'Bad Business: Billions of Taxpayer Dollars Wasted on Hiring Contractors', Project on Government Oversight, http://pogoarchives.org/m/co/igf/bad-business-report-only-2011.pdf, 2011 (Accessed 28.6.2014).

Chatham House, 'European Defence and Security 2012: Commitments, Capabilities and Cash', Conference Summary', Rapporteur: Benoît Gomis. www.chathamhouse.org/sites/default/files/public/Research/International%20Security/0112confsummary.pdf (Accessed 10.1.2014).

Chen, L. and Wilson, M. 'The Role of the Traveler in Emerging Infections and Magnitude of Travel', *Med Clin North America*, vol. 92, no. 6, 2008, 1409–1432.

Chomsky, N. 'Drain the Swamp and There Will Be No More Mosquitoes', *The Guardian*, 9 September, 2002.

Chomsky, N. *Failed States: The Abuse of Power and the Assault on Democracy*, New York: Metropolitan Books/Henry Holt, 2006.

Chomsky, N. and Otero, C.P. *Radical Priorities*, New York: AK Press, 2003.

Clausewitz, C. von, *On War*, rev. ed., ed. and trans. M. Howard and P. Paret, Princeton, NJ: University Press, [1832] 1984.

Clinton, H. *Foreign Policy Address at the Council on Foreign Relations*, 15 July 2009, available at www.state.gov/secretary/rm/2009a/july/126071.htm (Accessed 19.7.2011).

Clutterbuck, L. 'Terrorists Have to Be Lucky Once; Targets, Every Time', at www.rand.org/commentary/2008/11/30/DNA.html, 2012 (Accessed 12.12.2012).

Coch, N. *Geohazards. Natural and Human*, Englewood Cliffs, US: Prentice Hall, 1995.

Cockburn, C. 'Militarism and War', in L.J. Shepherd (ed.), *Gender Matters in Global Politics: A Feminist Introduction to International Relations*, London: Routledge, 2010, 105–115.

CoE, *European Sourcebook on Crime and Criminal Justice*, PC-S-ST (99)8 DEF: Strasbourg: Council of Europe, 1999.

Cogan, C. 'Hunters not Gatherers: Intelligence in the Twenty-first Century', *Intelligence and National Security*, vol. 19, no. 2, 2004, 304–321.

Cohen, A. 'Russia's Race for the Arctic', *Heartland Eurasian Review of Geopolitics*, vol. 2, no. 36, 2008, 28–36.

Cohn, C., Kinsella, H. and Gibbings, S. 'Women, Peace and Security Resolution 1325', *International Feminist Journal of Politics*, vol. 6, no. 1, June 2010, 130–140.

Comfort, L., Wisner, B., Cutter, S., Pulwarty, R., Hewitt, K., Oliver-Smith, A., Weiner, J., Fordham, M., Peacock, W. and Krimgeld, F. 'Re-framing Disaster Policy: The Global Evolution of Vulnerable Communities', *Environmental Hazards*, vol. 1, 1999, 39–44.

Commission on Human Security (CHS), *Human Security Now: Final Report*, New York: CHS, 2003.

Conca, K. and Dabelko, G. (eds) *Environmental Peacemaking*, Washington DC: Woodrow Wilson Press, 2002.

Contest: The United Kingdom's Strategy for Countering Terrorism, July 2011, London: HMSO.

Coonan, C. 'Beijing Orders its Industries to Cut Emissions', *Independent*, 17 June 2013, 33.

Coppola, D. *Introduction to International Disaster Management* (2nd ed.), Oxford: Butterworth-Heinemann, 2011.

Cottey, A. *Security in 21st Century Europe*, New York: Palgrave Macmillan, 2013.

Country Reports on Terrorism, 2013, United States Department of State Publication, Bureau of Counterterrorism, Released April 2014, US State Department, www.state.gov/documents/organization/225886.pdf (Accessed 18.5.2014).

Cox, R. 'Social Forces, States and World Orders: Beyond International Relations Theory', *Millennium: Journal of International Studies*, vol. 10, no. 2, 1981, 126–155.

Cox, R. *Approaches to World Order*, Cambridge: Cambridge University Press, 1995.

Craft, C. and Smaldone, J.P. 'The Arms Trade and the Incidence of Political Violence in Sub-Saharan Africa, 1967–97', *Journal of Peace Research*, vol. 39, no. 6, 2002, 693–710.

Craig, S.L. *Chinese Perceptions of Traditional and Non-traditional Security Threats*, www.StrategicStudiesInstitute.army.mil/, March 2007 (Accessed 14.7.2014).

Cramer, C. 'Does Inequality Cause Conflict?', *Journal of International Development*, vol. 15, no. 4, 2003, 397–412.

CRED, *International Disaster Database*, Centre for Research on the Epidemiology of Disasters: Brussels, www.emdat.be/, 2011 (Accessed 20.9.2011).

Cumings, B. *Korea's Place in the Sun: A Modern History*, (Updated Edition), London: W.W. Norton and Co., 2005.

Dalby, S. 'Security and Ecology in the Age of Globalization', *The Environmental Change and Security Project Report*, vol. 8, Summer 2002, 95–108.

Dalby, S. *Security and Environmental Change*, Cambridge: Polity, 2009.

Dallaire, R. *Shake Hands with the Devil*, Toronto: Random House Canada, 2003.

Dangl, B. *The Price of Fire: Resource Wars and Social Movements in Bolivia*, Edinburgh: AK Press, 2007.

Dangl, B. *Dancing With Dynamite: Social Movements and States in Latin America*, Edinburgh: AK Press, 2010.

Darby, J. and MacGinty, R. (eds) *Contemporary Peacemaking: Conflict, Peace Processes and Post-War Reconstruction*, 2nd ed., Basingstoke: Palgrave Macmillan, 2008.

Davies, P. 'Intelligence Culture and Intelligence Failure in Britain and the United States', *Cambridge Review of International Affairs*, vol. 17, no. 3, 2004, 496–520.

Davis, M. *Late Victorian Holocausts: El Nino Famines and the Making of the Third World*, London and New York: Verso, 2001.

De Wilde, J. 'Environmental Security Deconstructed' in H. Brauch (ed.), *Globalization and Environmental Challenges* (vol. 3), Berlin: Springer, 2008, 595–602.

Demick, B. *Nothing to Envy: Ordinary Lives in North Korea*, New York: Spiegel and Grau, 2009.

Detraz, N. *International Security and Gender*, Cambridge: Polity Press, 2012.

Deudney, D. 'The Case Against Linking Environmental Degradation and Security', *Millennium*, vol. 19, no. 3, 1990, 46–76.

Deutsch, K.W., Burrell, S.A., Kann, R.A., Lee, M. Jr., Lichterman, M., Lindgren, R., Loewenheim, F.L. and van Wagenen, R.W. *Political Community and the North Atlantic Area*, Princeton: Princeton University Press, 1957.

Diehl, P.F. (ed.) *The Politics of Global Governance: International Organizations in an Interdependent World*, London: Lynne Rienner Publishers, 2005.

Ditmer, J., Moisio, S., Ingram, A. and Dodds, K. 'Have You Heard the One About the Disappearing Ice? Recasting Arctic Geopolitics', *Political Geography*, vol. 30, no. 4, 2011, 202–214.

Dodds, K. 'Flag Planting and Finger Pointing: The Law of the Sea, the Arctic and the Political Geographies of the Outer Continental Shelf', *Political Geography*, vol. 29, 2010, 63–73.

Dolan, C. *In War we Trust: the Bush Doctrine and the Pursuit of Just War*, Aldershot: Ashgate, 2005.

Dolman, E.C. *Astropolitik: Classic Geopolitics in the Space Age*, London: Frank Cass, 2002.

Dorrington, R., Bradshaw, D. and Budlender, D. 'HIV/AIDS Profile in the Provinces of South Africa – Indicators for 2002', Centre for Actuarial Research, University of Cape Town, 2002.

Doyle, M. *Liberal Peace: Selected Essays*, New York: Routledge, 2012.

Dreze, J. and Sen, A. *Hunger and Public Action*, Oxford: Clarendon, 1991.

Drozdiak, W. 'The Brussels Wall: Tearing Down the EU-NATO Barrier', *Foreign Affairs*, May/June, vol. 89, no. 3, 2010, 7–12.

Duffield, J. 'NATO's Functions After the Cold War', *Political Science Quarterly*, vol. 109, Winter 1994/5, 763–787.

Duffield, J. *World Power Forsaken: Political Culture, International Institutions, and German Security Policy After Unification*, Stanford, CA: Stanford University Press, 1998.

Duffy, R. *The Road to Nunavut: the Progress of the Eastern Arctic Inuit since the Second World War*, Montreal: McGill-Queen's University Press, 1988.

Dunne, T. 'The Social Construction of International Society', *European Journal of International Relations*, vol. 1, no. 3, 1995, 367–389.

Dupont, A. and Pearman, G. *Heating up the Planet: Climate Change and Security*, Lowry Institute Papers 12, Sydney: Lowry Institute, 2006.

Duyvesteyn, I. and Angstrom, J. (eds) *Rethinking the Nature of War*, London: Routledge, 2004.

Dyer, H. 'Environmental Security and International Relations: The Case for Enclosure', *Review of International Studies*, vol. 27, 2001, 441–450.

Economist The, 'Economic Focus. A Voice for the Poor', May 4: 93, 2002a.

Economist The, 'Mother Nature's Biological Warfare', August 10: 42, 2002b.

Economist The, 'Ploughing On', 1 July 2010.

Ecuador, 'Rights for Nature', *Constitution*, adopted 28 September 2008.

Edwards, A. and Gill P. (eds) *Transnational Organized Crime: Perspectives on Global Security*, London and New York: Routledge, 2006.

Ehrlich, P. *The Population Bomb*, New York: Balantine, 1968.

Elbe, S. *Security and Global Health: Toward the Medicalization of Insecurity*, Cambridge: Polity Press, 2010.

Elshtain, J.B. 'Woman, the State, and War', *International Relations*, vol. 23, no. 2, 2009, 289–303.

Emerson, M. *Post-Mortem on Europe's First War of the 21st Century. CEPS Policy Brief No. 167*, 27 August 2008.

Emmerson, C. *The Future History of the Arctic*, London: The Bodley Head, 2010.

Enloe, C. *Bananas, Beaches and Bases: Making Feminist Sense of International Politics*, London: Rivers Oram Press, 1989.

Europol, 2012 http://www.europol.eu.int/index.asp?page=ataglance&language= (Accessed 19.6.2012).

Executive Office of the President United States, *National Strategy for Countering Terrorism*, Washington DC: Government Printing Office, 2003.

Falk, R. *This Endangered Planet*, New York: Random House, 1971.

FAO, 'FAO: What It Is – What It Does', www.fao.org/UNFAO/e/wmain-e.htm, 2002 (Accessed 5.4.2002).

FAO, *Women and the Right to Food: International Law and State Practice*. Rome: Food and Agricultural Organization, 2008.

FAO, 'Forestry', Rome: Food and Agricultural Organization, www.fao.org/forestry/30515/en/, 2011a (Accessed 23.6.2013).

FAO, 'Review of the State of World Marine Fishing Resources', FAO Fisheries and Aquaculture Technical Paper 569. Rome: FAO, 2011b.

FAO/WHO, 'Final Report of the International Conference on Nutrition', Rome, 5–11 December 1992.

Farah, D. and Braun, S. *Merchant of Death: Money, Guns, Planes, and the Man Who Makes War Possible*, Hoboken, NJ: John Wiley and Sons, 2007.

Farrall, L. 'How Al-Qaeda Works', *Foreign Affairs*, vol. 90, no. 2, March/April 2011, 128–138.

Farsoun, S.K. *Palestine and the Palestinians: A Social and Political History*, Boulder: Westview Press, 2006.

Failed State Index, *Fund for Peace*, http://ffp.statesindex.org/rankings-2013-sortable, 2013 (Accessed 7.3.2014).

Feinstein, A. *The Shadow World: Inside the Global Arms Trade*, London: Hamish Hamilton, 2011.

Ferguson, N. *Civilization: The West and the Rest*, London: Penguin, 2011.

Ferris, E. and Petz, D. (eds) *A Year of Living Dangerously. A Review of Natural Disasters in 2010*, London: Brookings Institute, 2011.

Ferris, J. 'Netcentric Warfare, C4ISR and Information Operations', in L.V. Scott and P.D. Jackson (eds), *Understanding Intelligence in the 21st Century*, London: Routledge, 2004, 54–77.

FFP (2013) *The Failed States Index 2013*, http://ffp.statesindex.org/rankings-2013-sortable (Accessed 28.6.2014).

Fidler, D. *International Law and Infectious Diseases*, Oxford: Clarendon Press, 1999.

Finland, *Finnish Security and Defense Policy 2004*, Helsinki: Prime Minister's Office, 2004.

Floyd, R. *Security and the Environment. Securitisation Theory and US Environmental Security Policy*, Cambridge: Cambridge University Press, 2010.

Floyd, R. and Mathew, R. *Environmental Security. Approaches and Issues,* London and New York: Routledge, 2013.

FoE, *Overconsumption? Our Use of the World's Natural Resources*, Vienna: Friends of the Earth Austria, 2009.

Foucault, M. *Discipline and Punish: The Birth of the Prison*, London: Penguin Books, first translation 1978.

Freedman, L. 'Conclusion: The Future of Strategic Studies', in J. Baylis, J. Wirtz, E. Cohen and C. Gray (eds), *Strategy in the Contemporary World: An Introduction to Strategic Studies*, Oxford: Oxford University Press, 2002, 328–342.

Freedman, L. *The Evolution of Nuclear Strategy*, 3rd ed., London: Palgrave Macmillan, 2003.

Freedman, L. 'War in Iraq: Selling the Threat', *Survival*, vol. 46, no. 2, 2004, 7–49.

Friborg, J. and Melbye, M. 'Cancer Patterns in Inuit Populations', *The Lancet Oncology*, vol. 9, no. 9, 2008, 892–900.

Froese, R. and Quaas, M. 'Rio+20 and the Reform of the Common Fisheries Policy in Europe', *Marine Policy*, vol. 39, 2003, 53–55.

Fukuyama, F. *The End of History and the Last Man*, New York: Free Press, 1992.

Fund for Peace, 'Fragile States Index 2014', http://ffp.statesindex.org/rankings-2014, 2014 (Accessed 28.6.2014).

Gaddis, J.L. *Strategies of Containment: A Critical Appraisal of Post-war American National Security Policy*, revised edition, Oxford: Oxford University Press, 2005.

Galeotti, M. 'Cold Calling. Competition Heats Up for Arctic Resources', *Jane's Intelligence Review*, October 2008, 8–15.

Galtung, J. 'An Editorial', *Journal of Peace Research*, vol. 1, no. 1, 1964, 1–4.

Galtung, J. 'Violence, Peace and Peace Research', *Journal of Peace Research*, vol. 6, no. 3, 1969, 167–191.

Galtung, J. 'Three Approaches to Peace: Peacekeeping, Peacemaking, and Peacebuilding', in J. Galtung (ed.) *Peace, War and Defense: Essays in Peace Research*, Vol. II, Copenhagen: Christian Ejlers, 1976, 282–304.

Galtung, J. 'Cultural Violence', *Journal of Peace Research*, vol. 27, no. 3, 1990, 291–305.

Garrett, L. 'The Challenge of Global Health', *Foreign Affairs*, vol. 86, no. 1, 2007, 14–38.

Gartzke, E. 'Globalization, Economic Development, and Territorial Conflict', in M. Kahlera and B. Walter (eds) *Territoriality and Conflict in an Era of Globalization*, Cambridge: Cambridge University Press, 2006, 156–186.

Gartzke, E. 'The Capitalist Peace', *American Journal of Political Science*, vol. 51, no. 1, 2007, 166–191.

Gaubutz, K.T. 'Democratic States and Commitment in International Relations', *International Organization*, vol. 50, no. 1, 1996, 109–150.

Gause, F.G. III 'Can Democracy Stop Terrorism?', *Foreign Affairs*, vol. 84, no. 5, September/October 2005, 62–76.

Gay, N. and Edmunds, W. 'Developed Countries Should Pay for Hepatitis B Vaccine in Developing Countries', *British Medical Journal*, vol. 316, 1998, 1457.

Gélinas, J. *Juggernaut Politics: Understanding Predatory Globalization*, London: Zed Books, 2003.

Gibson, I. 'Human Security Post 9-11: Gender Perspectives and Security Exclusion', *Ritsumeikan Annual Review of International Studies*, vol. 3, 2004, 157–175.

Githens, M., Norris, P. and Lovenduski, J. *Different Roles, Different Voices*, New York: Harper Collins, 1994.

Gladwell, M. and Shirky, C. 'From Innovation to Revolution', *Foreign Affairs*, vol. 90, no. 2, March/April 2011, 153–154.

Gleditsch, N., Wallensteen, P., Eriksson, M., Sollenberg, M. and Strand, H. 'Armed Conflict 1946–2001: A New Dataset', *Journal of Peace Research*, vol. 39, no. 5, 2002, 615–637.

Glenny, M. *McMafia: Crime Without Frontiers*, London: The Bodley Head, 2008.

Glenny, M. *Dark Markets: Cyberthieves, Cybercops and You*, London: The Bodley Head, 2011.

Global Policy Forum 'Changing Patterns in the Use of the Veto in the Security Council', www.globalpolicy.org/images/pdfs/Changing_Patterns_in_the_Use_of_the_Veto_as_of_August_2012.pdf, 2012 (Accessed 28.6.2014).

Godson, R. and Williams, P. 'Strengthening Cooperation against Transsovereign Crime', in M. Cusimano (ed.) *Beyond Sovereignty: Issues for a Global Agenda*, Boston: St. Martins, 2000.

Goklany, I. *Death and Death Rates Due to Extreme Weather Events*, London: International Policy Press, 2007.

Goldammer, J. 'Wildfire', in J. Ingleton (ed.) *Natural Disaster Management. A Presentation to Commemorate the International Decade for Natural Disaster Reduction (IDNDR)*, Leicester: Tudor Rose: 1999, 67–69.

Goldstein, J.S. 'Think Again: War', *Foreign Policy*, September/October, 2011, 1–9.

Gorbachev, M. 'Speech at the Ceremonial Meeting on the Occasion of the Presentation of the Order of Lenin and the Gold Star to the City of Murmansk', *Murmansk*, 1 October 1987.

Gore, A. UN Security Council Opening Session, 10 January 2000.

Gottlieb, S. 'Syria and the Demise of the Responsibility to Protect', *National Interest*, http://nationalinterest.org/commentary/syria-the-demise-the-responsibility-protect-9360, 5 November 2013 (Accessed 28.6.2014).

Grant, S. *Polar Imperative: A History of Arctic Sovereignty in North America*, Vancover: Douglas and McIntyre, 2010.

Green, J. *Risk and Misfortune. The Social Construction of Accidents*, London: UCL Press, 1997.

Grein, T.W., Kamara, K.B., Rodier, G., Plant, A.J., Bovier, P., Ryan, M.J., Ohyma, T. and Heymann, D.L. 'Rumors of Diseases in the Global Village: Outbreak Verification', *Emerging Infectious Diseases*, vol. 16, no. 2, March/April, 2000, 97–102.

Grice, A. 'Cameron: We were wrong to call Mandela a terrorist', *The Independent*, 28 August, at www.independent.co.uk/news/uk/politics/cameron-we-were-wrong-to-call-mandela-a-terrorist-413684.html, 2006 (Accessed 12.11.2012).

Grygier, P. *A Long Way from Home: The Tuberculosis Epidemic Among the Inuit*, Quebec: McGill-Queens University Press, 1994.

Guardian, 'US Embassy Cables: Saudi King Urges US Strike on Iran', *Guardian*, 28 November 2010.

Guerin, O. 'US Drone War in Pakistan Prompts Fear and Anger', 12 October, at www.bbc.co.uk/news/world-asia-19842410, 2012 (Accessed 17.10.2012).

Haass, R. 'The Age of Nonpolarity', *Foreign Affairs*, vol. 87, no. 3, May/June 2008, 44–56.

Hagerdorn, J. 'The Global Impact of Gangs', *Journal of Contemporary Criminal Justice*, vol. 21, no. 2, 2005, 153–169.

Hagerty, D.T. 'South Asia's Big Bangs: Causes, Consequences and Prospects', *Australian Journal of International Relations*, vol. 53, no. 1, 1999, 19–22.

Haken, J. *Global Financial Integrity, Transnational Crime in the Developing World*, Washington DC: GFI, 2011.

Halliday, F. *The Middle East in International Relations: Power, Politics and Ideology*, Cambridge: Cambridge University Press, 2005.

Hammond, P. 'Review Article: Making War and Peace', *Contemporary Politics*, vol. 9, no. 1, March 2003, 83–90.

Hanson, M. 'The Future of the NPT', *Australian Journal of International Affairs*, vol. 59, no. 3, 2005.

Hardin, G. 'Lifeboat Ethics: The Case Against Helping the Poor', in W. Aitken and H. LaFollette (eds) *World Hunger and Morality*, New Jersey: Prentice Hall, 1995.

Harms, G. and Ferry, T.M. *The Palestine–Israel Conflict: A Basic Introduction*, 3rd Edition, London: Pluto Press, 2012.

Haynes, J. 'Al-Qaeda: Ideology and Action', *Critical Review of International Social and Political Philosophy*, vol. 8, no. 2, 2005a, 177–191.

Haynes, J. 'Review Article: Religion and International Relations After "9/11"', *Democratization*, vol. 12, no. 3, 2005b, 398–413.

Haynes, J. 'Religion and Democracy: The Case of the AKP in Turkey', in J. Fox (ed.), *Religion, Politics, Society, & the State*, Oxford: Oxford University Press, 2012, 73–88.

Haynes, J. *An Introduction to International Relations and Religion*, 2nd ed., London: Pearson, 2013.

Held, D., McGrew, A., Goldblatt, D. and Perraton, J. *Global Transformations: Politics, Economics and Culture*, Cambridge: Polity, 1998.

Henderson, E. 'Disturbing the Peace: African Warfare, Political Inversion and the Universality of the Democratic Peace Thesis', *British Journal of Political Science*, vol. 39, no. 1, 2008, 25–58.

Hendricks, K. 'African Vultures: The New Prevalence of Interstate War in Africa', *Amsterdam Social Science*, vol. 4, no. 1, 2012, 49–66.

Henrikson, A. 'The United Nations and Regional Organizations: "King Links" of a "Global Chain"', *Duke Journal of Comparative and International Law*, vol. 7, no. 35, 1996, 35–70.

Herman, M. *Intelligence Power in Peace and War*, Cambridge: Cambridge University Press, 1996.

Herman, M. *Intelligence Service in the Information Age*, London: Frank Cass, 2001.

Herz, J. 'Idealist Internationalism and the Security Dilemma', *World Politics*, vol. 2, no. 2, 1950, 171–201.

Heymann, D. 'The Fall and Rise of Infectious Diseases', *Georgetown Journal of International Affairs*, vol. 2, no. 2, Summer/Fall, 2001, 7–14.

Hicks, J. 'DDT – Friend or Foe?', *Pesticide News, Journal of the Pesticides Trust*, 17 September 1992.

Hill, C. and Smith, M. *International Relations and the EU*, Oxford: Oxford University Press, 2005.

Hirst, P. *War and Power in the 21st Century*, Cambridge: Polity Press, 2001.

Hirst, P., Thompson, G. and Bromley, S. *Globalization in Question*, 3rd ed., Cambridge: Polity Press, 2009.

Hoffman, B. *Inside Terrorism*, Revised edition, New York: Columbia University Press, 2006.

Hoffman, B. *Inside Terrorism*, New York: Columbia University Press, 2008.

Hoffman, S. 'The High and the Mighty: Bush's National Security Strategy and the New American Hubris', *American Prospect*, vol. 13, no. 28, 2003, http://prospect.org/article/high-and-mighty (Accessed 31.10.2014).

Holland, M. and Doidge, M. *Development Policy in the European Union*, New York: Palgrave Macmillan, 2012.

Homer-Dixon, T. 'Environmental Scarcities and Violent Conflict: Evidence from Cases', *International Security*, vol. 19, no. 1, 1994, 5–40.

Hoogensen, G. and Stuvøy, K. 'Gender, Resistance and Human Security', *Security Dialogue*, vol. 37, no. 2, 2006, 207–228.

Hopf, T. 'The Promise of Constructivism in International Relations Theory', *International Security*, vol. 23, no. 1, Summer 1998, 171–200.

Hopkins, N. 'War on al-Qaida Drawing to a Close, says Obama', *The Guardian*, 1 December 2012.

Hough, P. *International Politics of the Arctic: Coming in From the Cold*, London and New York: Routledge, 2013.

Hough, P. *Understanding Global Security* (3rd ed.), London: Routledge, 2013.

Hough, P. *Environmental Security. An Introduction*, London and New York: Routledge, 2014.

Hsiang, S., Meng, K. and Cane, M. 'Civil Conflicts are Associated with Global Climate', *Nature*, vol. 476, 2011, 438–441.

Hudson, H. 'A Feminist Reading of Security in Africa', http://www.issafrica.org/Pubs/Monographs/No20/Hudson.html, 1998 (Accessed 28.10.2014).

Hudson, H. 'Doing Security as Though Humans Matter: A Feminist Perspective on Gender and the Politics of Human Security', *Security Dialogue*, vol. 36, no. 2, 2005, 155–174.

Hudson, V.M., Caprioli, M., Ballif-Spanvill, B., McDermott, R. and Emmett, C.F. 'The Heart of the Matter: The Security of Women and the Security of States', *International Security*, vol. 33, no. 3, Winter 2008/09, 7–45.

Human Security Centre (2005) *Human Security Report*, http://www.humansecurityreport.info/component/option,com_frontpage/Itemid,1/ (Accessed 13.7.2012).

Hunt, K. 'The War on Terrorism', in L.J. Shepherd (ed.) *Gender Matters in World Politics: A Feminist Introduction to International Relations*, London: Routledge, 2010, 116–126.

Huntington, S. *The Third Wave: Democratization in the Late Twentieth Century*, Norman: University of Oklahoma Press, 1991.

Huntington, S. 'The Clash of Civilisations?' *Foreign Affairs*, vol. 72, no. 3, 1993, 22–49.

Huntington, S. *The Clash of Civilizations and the Remaking of World Order*. New York: Free Press, 1996.

Huntington, S. 'The Lonely Superpower', *Foreign Affairs*, vol. 78, no. 2, March/April 1999, 35–49.

Hughes, B.B., Kuhn, R., Peterson, C.M., Rothman, D.S. and Solorzano, J.R. *Improving Global Health (Patterns of Potential Human Progress)*, Oxford: Oxford University Press, 2010.

Hungary, Resolution No. 94/1998. (XII.29) of the Hungarian National Assembly on 'The Basic Principles of the Security and Defence Policy of the Republic of Hungary', 1998.

Hurrell, A. 'There are no rules (George W. Bush): International order after September 11', *International Relations*, vol. 16. no. 2, 2002, 185–204.

IAEA, *Convention on Nuclear Safety*, 2012. http://www-ns.iaea.org/conventions/nuclear-safety.asp (Accessed 13.6.2012)

ICIDI, *North-South: The Report of the International Commission on International Development Issues*, London: Pan Books, 1980.

ICISS (International Commission on Intervention and State Sovereignty), *The Responsibility to Protect*, http://responsibilitytoprotect.org/ICISS%20Report.pdf, 2001 (Accessed 28.6.2014).

Ikenberry, G.J. *American Foreign Policy: Theoretical Essays*, 6th Edition, Boston: Wadsworth, 2011a.

Ikenberry, G.J. 'The Future of the Liberal World Order: Internationalism After America', *Foreign Affairs*, vol. 90, no. 3, May/June, 2011b, 56–68.

ILO/WHO, *World Day for Safety and Health at Work: A Background Paper*, Geneva: International Labour Organization, 2005.

Ilulissat, *The Ilulissat Declaration*, Governments of Denmark, Norway, Russia, US and Canada, 28 May, http://arctic-council.org/filearchive/Ilulissat-declaration.pdf, 2008 (Accessed 12.5.2011).

IMF, 'Sub-Saharan Africa. Keeping the Pace', *World Economic and Financial Surveys*, New York, IMF, 2013.

IMO, 'Piracy: Orchestrating the Response', background paper www.imo.org/About/Events/WorldMaritimeDay/2011/background/Pages/default.aspx, 2011 (Accessed 4.10.2013).

INCB, 'Report of the International Narcotics Control Board for 2001' E/INCB/2002/1, New York: International Narcotics Control Board, 2002.

Ingleton, J. (ed.) *Natural Disaster Management. A Presentation to Commemorate the International Decade for Natural Disaster Reduction (IDNDR)*, Leicester: Tudor Rose, 1999.

The Institute for Economics and Peace, *Global Terrorism Index*, at www.visionofhumanity.org (Accessed 10.12.2012).

Intergovernmental Panel on Climate Change, *Fourth Assessment Report Climate Change International Affairs*, vol. 79, no. 1, 2007, 107–138.

Interpol, 'An Overview. Foreword', www.interpol.int/Public/ICPO/Overview.pdf, 2002 (Accessed 4.8.2005).

Interpol, 'An Overview', http://www.interpol.int/, 2012 (Accessed 14.3.2012).

Jacobs, G. and Aeron-Thomas, A. 'A Review of Global Road Accident Fatalities', TRL Report 44, Transport Research Laboratory, Crawthorne, UK. www.transport-links.org/transport_links/filearea/publications/1_771_Pa3568.pdf, 2000 (Accessed 15.9.2011).

Jackson, R., Murphy, E. and Poynting, S. (eds) *Contemporary State Terrorism: Theory and Cases*, London: Routledge, 2010.

Jacques, M. *When China Rules the World: The End of the Western World and the Birth of a New Global Order*, 2nd Edition, London: Penguin, 2012.

Jeggle, T. 'The Goals and Aims of the Decade', in J. Ingleton, *Natural Disaster Management. A Presentation to Commemorate the International Decade for Natural Disaster Reduction (IDNDR)*, Leicester : Tudor Rose, 1999.

Jentleson, B. *American Foreign Policy: The Dynamics of Choice in the 21st Century*, 5th Edition, New York: W.W. Norton, 2014.

Jervis, R. *Perception and Misperception in International Politics*, Princeton, NJ: Princeton University Press, 1976.

Jervis, R. 'Reports, Politics, and Intelligence Failures: The case of Iraq', *Journal of Strategic Studies*, vol. 29, no. 1, 2006, 3–52.

Joffe, J. 'The Default Power: The False Prophecy of America's Decline', *Foreign Affairs*, vol. 88, no. 5, September/October 2009, 21–35.

Jett, D. *Why Peacekeeping Fails*, Basingstoke: Palgrave, 2000.

Johnson, C. *Blowback: The Costs and Consequences of American Empire*, New York: Henry Holt, 2000.

Johnson, L. (ed.) *Handbook of Intelligence Studies*, London: Routledge, 2009.

Juergensmeyer, M. *The New Cold War? Religious Nationalism Confronts the Secular State*, Berkeley: University of California Press, 1993.

Jung, D. (ed.) *Shadow Globalization, Ethnic Conflicts and New Wars: A Political Economy of Intra-state War*, London: Routledge, 2002.

Kaldor, M. *New and Old Wars: Organised Violence in a Global Era*, 1st ed., Cambridge: Polity Press, 1999.

Kaldor, M. 'Wanted: Global Politics', *The Nation*, vol. 273, no. 14, 5 November 2001, 15–18.

Kaldor, M. *New and Old Wars: Organized Violence in a Global Era*, 2nd ed., Oxford: Polity Press, 2006.

Kaldor, M. *New and Old Wars: Organized Violence in a Global Era*, 3rd ed., Cambridge: Polity Press, 2012.

Kaldor, M. 'In Defence of New Wars', *Stability: International Journal of Security and Development*, vol. 2, no. 4, 2013, 1–16.

Kant, I. *Perpetual Peace*, trans. L.W. Black, Indianapolis: Bobbs-Merrill, [1795] 1957.

Kaplan, L.S. *NATO Divided, NATO United: The Evolution of an Alliance*, Westport, CT: Praeger, 2004.

Kaplan, R. 'The Coming Anarchy', *The Atlantic Monthly*, 273, 1994, 44–76.

Katzenstein, P. (ed.) *The Culture of National Security: Norms and Identity in World Politics*, New York: Columbia University Press, 1996.

Kegley Jr., C.W. 'The Neoidealist Moment in International Studies? Realist Myths and the New International Realities', *International Studies Quarterly*, vol. 37, no. 2, June 1993, 131–146.

Kendall, R.E. 'Responding to Transnational Crime', *Transnational Crime*, 1998, 269–275.

Kennan, G. 'Morality and Foreign Policy', *Foreign Affairs*, vol. 64, 1985, 205–218.

Keohane, R. *After Hegemony: Cooperation and Discord in the World Political Economy*, Princeton, NJ: Princeton University Press, 1984.

Keohane, R.O. 'Beyond Dichotomy: Conversations between International Relations and Feminist Theory', *International Studies Quarterly*, vol. 42, no. 1, March 1998, 193–198.

Keohane, R.O. and Nye, J.S. *Power and Interdependence: World Politics in Transition* (3rd ed.), New York: Longman, 2001.

Ker-Lindsay, J. 'Greek-Turkish Rapprochement: The Impact of Disaster Diplomacy?', *Cambridge Review of International Affairs*, vol. XIV, no. 1, Autumn-Winter 2000, special section, *Disaster Diplomacy*, eds. I. Kelman and T. Koukis, 214–294.

Kimberley, www.kimberleyprocess.com/en/about, 2013 (Accessed 2.11.2013).

Kissinger, G., Herold, M. and De Sy, V. *Drivers of Deforestation and Forest Degradation. A Synthesis Report for REDD+ Policymakers*, 2012.

Kissinger, H., Schulz, G.P., Perry, W.J. and Nunn, S. 'A World Free of Nuclear Weapons', *Wall Street Journal*, 4 January 2007 at http://online.wsj.com/news/articles/SB116787515251566636 (Accessed 5.4.2014).

Köchler, H. 'Resolution 1973 and the Intervention in Libya. Are they Legal?' *Silvia Cattori Political Writings*, www.silviacattori.net/article1645.html, 2011 (Accessed 13.11.2013).

Koizumi, J. *Comments by Mr. Junichirō Koizumi at the International Symposium on Human Security*, Tokyo, 15 December 2001.

Kolodziej, E.A. *Security and International Relations*, Cambridge: Cambridge University Press, 2005.

Krahmann, E. *States, Citizens and the Privatisation of Security*, Cambridge: Cambridge University Press, 2010.

Kraska, P. 'Researching the Police-Military Blur: Lessons Learned', *Police Forum*, vol. 14, no. 3, 2005, 1–14.

Krasner, S. *International Regimes*, Ithaca and London: Cornell, 1983.

Krastev, I. 'Russia's Post-Orange Empire', Opendemocracy.net, 20 October 2005 www.opendemocracy. net (Accessed 23.10.2009).

Krause, K. and Williams, M. *Critical Security Studies: Concepts and Cases*, London: Routledge, 1997.

Krauthammer, C. 'The Unipolar Moment', *Foreign Affairs*, vol. 70, no. 1, 1990/91, 23–33.

Krauthammer, C. 'The Unipolar Moment Revisited', *The National Interest*, vol. 70, no. 1, Winter 2002–03, 22–33.

Kristensen, H. and Norris, R. 'Global Nuclear Weapons inventories, 1945–2013, *Bulletin of Atomic Scientists*, vol. 69, 2013, 75.

Krummel, E. 'The Circumpolar Inuit Health Summit: A Summary', *International Journal of Circumpolar Health*, vol. 68, no. 5, 2009, 509–518.

Kupchan, C. 'NATO's Final Frontier', *Foreign Affairs*, vol. 89, no. 3, May/June 2010, 100–112.

Kupchan, C. *No One's World: The West, the Rising Rest and the Coming Global Turn*, New York: Oxford University Press, 2012.

Lacina, B. and Gleditsch, N.P. 'Monitoring Trends in Global Combat: A New Dataset of Battle Deaths', *European Journal of Population*, vol. 21, no. 2–3, 2005, 145–166.

Langer, J., 'Stuxnet's Secret Twin', at www.foreignpolicy.com/articles/2013/11/19/stuxnets_ secret_twin_iran_nukes_cyber_attack, 2013 (Accessed 22.2.2014).

Lankov, A. *The Real North Korea: Life and Politics in the Failed Stalinist Utopia*, Oxford: Oxford University Press, 2013.

Larsen, J.A. and Wirtz, J.J. (eds) *Arms Control and Cooperative Security*, Boulder, CO: Lynne Rienner Publishers, 2009.

Laurance, J. 'Climate Change Blamed for Legionnaire's Disease Outbreak', *The Independent*, 18 October 2006.

Laurance, J. 'Deadly Animal Diseases Poised to Infect Humans', *The Independent*, 4 January 2010.

Laurelle, M. *Russian Eurasianism: An Ideology of Empire*, Baltimore, MD: John Hopkins University Press, 2008.

Law, A.K. and Stohl, A. 'Arctic Air Pollution: Origins and Impacts', *Science*, vol. 315, 2007, 1537–1940.

Layne, C. 'Kant or Cant: The Myth of the Democratic Peace', *International Security*, vol. 19, no. 2, Fall 1994, 5–49.

Leaver, R. 'The Failing NPT: the Case for Institutional Reform', *Australian Journal of International Affairs*, vol. 59, no. 4, 2005, 417–424.

Leffler, M. 'Bush's Foreign Policy', *Foreign Policy*, vol. 144, 2004, 22–28.

Lenin, V.I. *Imperialism: The Highest Stage of Capitalism*, Moscow: Progress Publishers, [1917] 1966.

Levy, J.S. and Thompson, W.R. *Causes of War*, Oxford: Blackwell, 2010.

Lim, S. *et al.*, 'A comparative risk assessment of burden of disease and injury attributable to 67 risk factors and risk factor clusters in 21 regions, 1990–2010: A systematic analysis for the Global Burden of Disease Study 2010,' *Lancet*, vol. 380, 2012, 2224–2260.

Linz, J. and Stepan, A. *Problems of Democratic Transition and Consolidation. Southern Europe, South America, and Post-Communist Europe*, Baltimore and London: John Hopkins University Press, 1996.

Livingston, I. and O'Hanlon, M. 'Afghanistan Index – Also Including Selected Data on Pakistan', Brookings Institution, 13 December, 2012, www.brookings.edu/~/media/programs/foreign%20policy/afghanistan%20index/index20121213.pdf (Accessed 14.12.2012).

Lizza, R. 'The Consequentialist: How the Arab Spring Remade Obama's Foreign Policy', *The New Yorker,* 2 May 2011, available at www.newyorker.com/reporting/2011/05/02/110502fa_fact_lizza (Accessed 15.7.2011).

Lopez, M. 'The Politics of Lands at Risk in a Philippine Frontier', in P.D. Little and M.M. Horowitz (eds) *Lands at Risk,* Boulder, US: Westview Press, 1987.

Loretti, A. 'The Health Sector in Disaster Reduction and Emergency Management', keynote address for the session: 'Managing and Preparing for Disasters', *International Public Health Congress,* Health 21 in Action, Istanbul, 8–12 October 2000.

Lovenduski, J. 'Introduction', in M. Githens, P. Norris and J. Lovenduski (eds), *Different Roles, Different Voices,* New York: HarperCollins, 1994 ix–xvi.

Lowenthal, M. *Intelligence: From Secrets to Policy,* 5th edn., Washington DC: Congressional Quarterly, 2012.

Lynn-Jones, S.M. 'Realism and Security Studies', in C.A. Snyder (ed.), *Contemporary Security and Strategy,* New York: Routledge, 1999.

Lyon, D. *Surveillance Studies: An Overview,* Oxford: Polity, 2007.

MacFarlane, S. and Foong Khong, Y. *Human Security and the UN. A Critical History,* Bloomington, US: Indiana University Press, 2006.

MacKay, P. *Question Period,* August 2, CTV, 2007.

MacQueen, N. *Peacekeeping and the International System,* Abingdon: Routledge, 2006.

Machiavelli, N. *The Prince,* Chichester: Capstone, [1532] 2010.

Madsen, F. *Transnational Organized Crime (Global Institutions),* Abingdon: Routledge, 2009.

Makarychev, A. 'Russian Policy after Colour Revolutions', *PONARS Eurasia Policy Memo No. 4,* March, 2008.

Malthus, T. *An Essay on the Principle of Population,* London: J. Johnson, 1798.

Marshall, M. *Conflict Trends in Africa 1946–2004,* Report for UK Government, London, Department for International Development, 2006.

Masala, C. *Den Blick nach Süden? Die NATO im Mittelmeerraum (1990-2003). Fallstudie zur Anpassung militärischer Allianzen an neue sicherheitspolitische Rahmenbedingungen,* Baden-Baden: Nomos, 2003.

Mathers, C. and Loncur, D. 'Projections of Global Mortality and Burden of Disease from 2002 to 2030', *PLoS Medicine,* vol. 3, no. 11, 2006, 2011–2030.

Mathew, R.A., Barnett, J., McDonald, B. and O'Brien, K.L. (eds) *Global Environmental Change and Human Security,* Boston: MIT Press, 2010.

Mathews, J. 'Redefining Security', *Foreign Affairs,* vol. 68, no. 2, 1989, 162–177.

Mathews, J. 'Power Shift', *Foreign Affairs,* vol. 76, no. 1, 1997, 50–66.

Matin, N. and Taher, M. 'Disaster Mitigation in Bangladesh: Country Case Study of NGO Activities', Report for Research Project NGO National Disaster Mitigation and Preparedness Projects: An Assessment of the Way Forward, ESCOR Award no. R7231, 2000.

Matthew, R. and Zalidi, A. 'People, Scarcity and Violence in Pakistan', in R.A. Matthew, M. Halle and J. Switzer (eds) *Conserving the Peace: Resources, Livelihoods and Scarcity,* Geneva: International Institute for Sustainable Development, 2002, 57–98.

Mazza, P. 'The Invisible Hand: Is Global Warming Driving El Nino?', *Sierra Magazine,* vol. 83, May/June, 1998.

McDougall, W.A. *The Heavens and the Earth: A Political History of the Space Age,* Baltimore: John Hopkins University Press, 1985.

McEwen, F. and Stephenson, G. *The Use and Significance of Pesticides in the Environment,* New York: Wiley, 1979.

McMichael, A., Campbell-Lendrum, D. and Kovats, S. 'Global Climate Change', in M.J. Ezzati, A. Lopez, A. Rodgers and C. Murray (eds), *Comparative Quantification of Health Risks: Global and Regional Burden of Disease Due to Selected Major Risk Factors*, Geneva: World Health Organization, 2004.

McMillan, S.M. 'Interdependence and Conflict', *Mershon International Studies Review*, vol. 41, no. 1, 1997.

McMurray, C. and Smith, R. *Diseases of Globalization. Socioeconomic Transition and Health*, London: Earthscan, 2001.

McNeill, W. *Plague and Peoples*, Toronto: Doubleday, 1989.

Mearsheimer, J. 'Back to the Future: Instability in Europe after the Cold War', *International Security*, vol. 15, no. 4, 1990, 5–56.

Mearsheimer, J. 'The Case for a Ukrainian Nuclear Deterrent', *Foreign Affairs*, vol. 72, no. 3, Summer 1993, 50–66.

Mearsheimer, J. 'The False Promise of International Institutions', *International Security*, vol. 19, no. 3, 1994/1995, 5–49.

Mearsheimer, J. *The Tragedy of Great Power Politics*, New York: Norton, 2001.

Mearsheimer, J. 'E.H. Carr vs. Idealism: The Battle Rages On', *International Relations*, vol. 19, no. 2, June 2005, 139–152.

Mearsheimer, J. 'Structural Realism', in T. Dunne, M. Kurki, and S. Smith (eds), *International Relations Theories: Discipline and Diversity*, Oxford: Oxford University Press, 2006.

Mearsheimer, J.J. and Walt, S.M. 'An Unnecessary War', *Foreign Policy*, no. 134, January/ February, 2003, 50–59.

Medvedev, D. Speech. Berlin. 5 June 2008 at www.ln.mid.ru/brp_4.nsf/0/C080DC2FF8D 93629C3257460003496C4 (Accessed 14.6.2013).

Milner, H. 'The Assumption of Anarchy in International Relations: A Critique', in D.A. Baldwin (ed.), *Neorealism and Neoliberalism: The Contemporary Debate*, New York: Columbia University Press, 1993.

Ministry of Foreign Affairs of Japan, Human Security, www.mofa.go.jp/policy/human_secu/ sympo0112_pm.html (Accessed 17.2.2014).

Minteh, B. and Perry, A. 'Terrorism in West Africa – Boko Haram's Evolution, Strategy and Affiliations', paper presented at the Mid-West Political Science Association's 71st Annual Conference, Palmer House Hotel, Chicago, Illinois, USA, 2013.

Mitchell, D. *A Note on Rising Food Prices*. Policy Research Working Paper 4682, Washington DC: World Bank Development Prospects Group, 2008.

Modelski, G. 'The Study of Alliances: A Review', *Journal of Conflict Resolution*, vol. 7, no. 4, 1963, 769–776.

Møller, S. *Press Release after Ilulissat Declaration*, 28 May 2008, Ilulissat, Greenland.

Monk School of Global Affairs (MSGA), *Rethinking the Top of the World: Arctic Security Public Opinion Survey*, University of Toronto, 2011.

Moore, M. 'Arming the Embargoed: A Supply-Side Understanding of Arms Embargo Violations', *Journal of Conflict Resolution*, vol. 54, no. 4, 2010, 593–615.

Morgan, P. *International Security: Problems and Solutions*, Washington: CQ Press, 2006.

Muldoon, James P. (ed.) *The New Dynamics of Multilateralism: Diplomacy, International Organizations and Global Governance*, Boulder: Westview Press, 2011.

Münkler, H. *New Wars*, trans. P. Camiller, Cambridge: Polity Press, 2005.

Mychajlyszyn, N. and Shaw, T. *Twisting Arms and Flexing Muscles: Humanitarian Intervention and Peacebuilding in Perspective*, Aldershot: Ashgate, 2005.

Myers, B.R. *The Cleanest Race: How North Koreans See Themselves and Why It Matters*, Brooklyn, NY: Melville House Publishing, 2010.

Nakajima, H. 'Global Disease Threats and Foreign Policy', *Brown Journal of World Affairs*, vol. 4, no. 1, 1997, 319–332.

National Intelligence Council (NIC), 'The Global Infectious Disease Threat and its Implications for the United States', NIE 99-17D, Washington DC: National Intelligence Council, 2000, http://www.cia.gov/cia/publications/nie/report/nie99-17d.html (Accessed 8.2.2002).

National Intelligence Council (NIC), 'Mapping the Global Future', December 2004, available at www.foia.cia.gov/2020/2020/pdf (Accessed 1.6.2011).

National Intelligence Council (NIC), 'Global Trends 2025: A World Transformed', November 2008, available at www.dni.gov/nic/PDF_2025/_2025_Global_Trends_Final_Report.pdf (Accessed 1.6.2011).

National Intelligence Council (NIC), 'Global Trends 2030: Alternative Worlds', 2012, available at www.dni.gov/index.php/about/organization/national-intelligence-council-global-trends (Accessed 1.12.2012).

National Security Strategy, 2002 at http://georgewbush-whitehouse.archives.gov/nsc/nss/2002/index.html (Accessed 2.7.2011).

National Security Strategy, 2006 at http://georgewbush-whitehouse.archives.gov/nsc/nss/2006/ (Accessed 2.7.2006).

National Security Strategy 2010 at www.whitehouse.gov/sites/default/files/rss.viewer/national_security_strategy.pdf (Accessed 1.7.2011).

NATO *Environmental Security,* http://www.nato.int/cps/en/natolive/topics_49216.htm 2013 (Accessed 18.10.2013).

Netherlands, *Policy Agenda 2006*, Ministry of Foreign Affairs, Netherlands

Neumann, I. 'Russia as a Great Power: 1805–2007', *Journal of International Relations and Development,* vol. 11, 2008, 128–151.

Neumann, P. 'Negotiating with Terrorists', *Foreign Affairs,* vol. 86, no. 1, January/February 2007, 128–138.

Newman, G. (ed.) *Global Report on Crime and Justice,* United Nations Office for Drug Control and Crime Prevention, New York: Oxford University Press, 2002.

Newton, A. 'The "Talking Cure": Intelligence, Counter-terrorism, Doctrine and Social Movements', *Intelligence and National Security,* vol. 26, no. 1, 2011, 120–131.

Noble, R. 'Interpol's Way: Thinking Beyond Boundaries and Acting Across Borders through Member Countries' Police Services', Secretary General of Interpol speech delivered at Tufts University, Boston, 1 March 2003.

Norris, P. and Inglehart, R. *Sacred and Secular. Religion and Politics Worldwide,* Cambridge: Cambridge University Press, 2004.

Nossel, S. 'Smart Power', *Foreign Affairs,* vol. 83, no. 2, March/April 2004, 131–142.

Nunavut, *Nunavut's Health System. A Report Delivered as Part of Inuit Obligations Under Article 32 of the Nunavut Land Claims Agreement 1993,* Iquailut: Nunavut Tunngavik, 2008.

Nuruzzaman, M. 'Beyond Realist Theories: "Neo-Conservative Realism" and the American Invasion of Iraq', *International Studies Perspectives,* vol. 7, no. 3, 2006, 239–253.

Nye, J. *Bound to Lead. The Changing Nature of American Power,* New York: Basic Books, 1990.

Nye, J. *Soft Power: The Means to Success in World Politics,* New York: Free Press, 2004.

Nye, J. *Understanding International Conflicts: an Introduction to Theory and History,* 6th Edition, New York: Pearson Longman, 2007.

Nye, J. 'The Future of American Power: Dominance and Decline in Perspective', *Foreign Affairs,* November/December, vol. 89, no. 6, 2010, 2–12.

Nye, J. *The Future of Power,* New York: Public Affairs, 2011.

Nye, J. and Lynn-Jones, S.M. 'International Security Studies: A Report of a Conference on the State of the Field', *International Security,* vol. 12, no. 4, 1988, 5–27.

Obama, B. 'A New Strategy for a New World', Washington DC, 15 July 2008 at http://my.barackobama.com/page/content/newstrategy (Accessed 1.7.2011).

Obama, B. 'Inaugural Address', 21 January 2009, www.whitehouse.gov/the-press-office/president-barack-obamas-inaugural-address (Accessed 1.7.2011).

Obama, B. 'Remarks by President Barack Obama', speech at Hradcany Square, Prague, Czech Republic, 5 April, 2009b, www.whitehouse.gov/the_press_office/Remarks-By-President-Barack-Obama-In-Prague-As-Delivered (Accessed 5.4.2014).

Obama, B. 'Remarks by the President in Address to the Nation on the Way Forward in Afghanistan and Pakistan', 1 December, 2009c, at www.whitehouse.gov/the-press-office/remarks-president-address-nation-way-forward-afghanistan-and-pakistan (Accessed 10.7.2011).

Obama, B. 'Remarks by the President in the Defense Strategic Review', 5 January 2012, www.whitehouse.gov/the-press-office/2012/01/05/remarks-president-defense-strategic-review (Accessed 7.2.2012).

Obama, B. 'Remarks by the President at the United States Military Academy Commencement Ceremony, 28 May 2014, available at http://www.whitehouse.gov/the-press-office/2014/05/28/remarks-president-west-point-academy-commencement-ceremony (Accessed 4.11.2014).

Oberdorfer, D. and Carlin, R. *The Two Koreas: A Contemporary History*, New York: Basic Books, 2013.

Ohmae, K. *The End of the Nation State*, London: HarperCollins, 2008.

Omand, D. *Securing the State*, London: Hurst and Company, 2010.

Ong, R. *China's Security Interests in the 21st Century*, London and New York: Routledge, 2007.

O'Rourke, K.H. and Williamson, J.G. 'When Did Globalisation Begin?', *European Review of Economic History*, vol. 6, no. 1, 2002, 23–50.

Ortiz, C. *Private Armed Forces and Global Security: A Guide to the Issues*, Santa Barbara, CA: Praeger, 2010.

Osborn, F. *Our Plundered Planet*. New York: Grosset and Dunlap, 1948.

Osgood, R. *Alliances and American Foreign Policy*, Baltimore, MD: Johns Hopkins University Press, 1968.

Østensen, A.G. 'UN Use of Private Military and Security Companies: Practices and Policies', Geneva Centre for the Democratic Control of Armed Forces, www.dcaf.ch/content/download/45662/678940/file/SSR_PAPER3.pdf, 2011 (Accessed 28.6.2014).

Oxfam, *Cut the Cost. Patent Injustice: How World Trade Rules Threaten the Health of Poor People*, Oxford: Oxfam, 2002.

Oxfam, 'Campaigning for a Bulletproof Arms Trade Treaty', www.oxfam.org.uk/get-involved/campaign-with-us/our-campaigns/rights-in-crisis/arms-trade-treaty, 2012 (Accessed 5.7.2012).

Paarlberg, R. *Food Politics: What Everyone Needs to Know*, Oxford: Oxford University Press, 2013.

Paddock, W. and Paddock, P. *Famine 1975*, London: Weidenfield and Nicolson, 1967.

Palme, O. *Common Security. A Programme for Disarmament*, London: Pan Books, 1982.

Pant, H. (ed.) *Handbook of Nuclear Proliferation*, New York: Routledge, 2012.

Paris, R. 'Human Security: Paradigm Shift or Hot Air?', *International Security*, vol. 26, no. 2, Autumn 2001, 87–102.

Peng Er, Lam, 'Japan's Human Security Role in Southeast Asia', *Contemporary Southeast Asia*, vol. 28, no. 1, April 2006, 141–159.

Petito, F. 'The Global Political Discourse of Dialogue among Civilizations: Mohammad Khatami and Vaclav Havel', *Global Change, Peace & Security*, vol. 19, no. 2, 2007, 103–125.

Petito, F. 'Dialogue of Civilizations as an Alternative Model for World Order', in M. Michalis and F. Petito (eds.) *Civilizational Dialogue and World Order: The Other Politics of Cultures, Religions and Civilizations in International Relations*, New York: Palgrave, 2009, 47–67.

Petito, F. and Hatzopoulos, P. *Religion in International Relations. The Return from Exile*, New York: Palgrave, 2003.

Pew Research Global Attitudes Project (2011) 'Muslim-Western Tensions Persist', available at www.pewglobal.org/2011/07/21/muslim-western-tensions-persist (Accessed 20.4.2014).

Pew Research Centre, 'Drone Strikes Widely Opposed: Global Opinion of Obama Slips, International Policies Faulted', 13 June 2012, at www.pewglobal.org/2012/06/13/global-opinion-of-obama-slips-international-policies-faulted/ (Accessed 12.11.2012).

Phillips, A. *Feminism and Politics*, Oxford: Oxford University Press, 1998.

Pickup, G. 'Desertification and Climate Change: The Australian Perspective', *Climate Research*, vol. 11, 1998, 51–63.

Pierre, A.J. (ed.) *Cascade of Arms: Managing Conventional Weapons Proliferation*, Cambridge, Mass.: World Peace Foundation, 1997.

Pillar, P. 'Think Again: Intelligence', *Foreign Policy*, January/February, 2012.

Pingeot, L. *Dangerous Partnership: Private Military and Security Companies and the UN*, Global Policy Forum, www.globalpolicy.org/images/pdfs/GPF_Dangerous_Partnership_Full_report.pdf, 2012 (Accessed 28.6.2014).

Pinker, S. *The Better Angels of Our Nature: Why Violence Has Declined*, New York: Viking, 2011.

Pirages, D. and Runci, P. 'Ecological Interdependence and the Spread of Infectious Disease', in M. Cusimano (ed.) *Beyond Sovereignty: Issues for a Global Agenda*, New York: St Martin, 2000, 177–193.

Prescott, E. 'SARS. A Warning', *Survival*, vol. 45, issue 3, 2003, 207–226.

Preston, S. 'The Changing Relationship between Mortality and Level of Economic Development', *Population Studies*, vol. 29, no. 2, 1975, 231–248.

Prezelj, I. 'Challenges in Conceptualizing and Providing Human Security', *HUMSEC Journal*, Issue 2, 2008. www.humsec.eu/cms/index.php?id=327 (Accessed 18.2.2014).

Price, R. and Reus-Smit, C. 'Dangerous Liaisons? Critical International Theory and Constructivism', *European Journal of International Relations*, vol. 4, no. 3, 1998, 259–294.

Price-Smith, A. *The Health of Nations: Infectious Diseases, Environmental Change, and Their Effects on National Security and Development*, Cambridge, MA: MIT Press, 2001.

Prins, G. and Stamp, R. *Top Guns and Toxic Whales: The Environment and Global Security*, London: Earthscan, 1991.

PRIO, *Data on Armed Conflict*, www.prio.no/Data/Armed-Conflict/?id=348 2014 (Accessed 12.2.2014).

Putin, V. *Speech*. 43rd Munich Security Conference, 10 February 2007, www.securityconference.de/konferenzen/rede.php?sprache_en&id_179 (Accessed 12.6.2013).

Putin, V. Speech at the International Forum, '*The Arctic. Territory of Dialogue*', 23 September. http://premier.gov.ru/eng/events/news/12304/, 2010 (Accessed 3.10.2011).

Putin, V. Speech, *Russia Today*, 17.04.2014.

Rapoport, D. 'The Four Waves of Modern Terrorism', in A. Cronin and J. Ludes (eds) *Attacking Terrorism*, Washington, DC: Georgetown University Press, 2004, 46–73.

Rasmussen, A.F. 'NATO After Libya', *Foreign Affairs*, vol. 90, no. 4, July/August 2011, 2–6.

Rasmussen, M. 'Reflexive Security: NATO and International Risk Society', *Millennium Journal of International Studies*, vol. 30, no. 2, 2001, 285–309.

Rid, T. 'Think Again: Cyberwar', *Foreign Policy*, March/April 2012, 80–84.

Risse-Kappen, T. 'Collective Identity in a Democratic Community: The case of NATO', in P. Katzenstein (ed.) *The Culture of National Security: Norms and Identity in World Politics*, New York and Chichester: Columbia University Press, 1996, 357–399.

Roberts, A. 'Lives and Statistics: Are 90% of War Victims Civilians?', *Survival*, vol. 52, no. 3, 2010, 115–136.

Rohter, L. *Brazil on the Rise: The Story of a Country Transformed*, Basingstoke: Palgrave Macmillan, 2012.

Rose, R. and Shiratori, R. (eds) *The Welfare State East and West*, New York: Oxford University Press, 1986.

Rostow, W. *The Stages of Economic Growth*, Cambridge: Cambridge University Press, 1960.

Rotberg, R. (ed.) *When States Fail: Causes and Consequences*, Princeton, NJ: Princeton University Press, 2004.

Rothkopf, D.J. 'Inside the Committee That Runs the World', *Foreign Policy*, vol. 147, 2005, 30–40.

Rothschild, E. 'What is Security', *Daedalus*, vol. 124, no. 3, 1995, 53–98.

Ruggie, J. *Constructing the World Polity: Essays on International Institutionalism*, London: Routledge, 1998.

Russett, B. 'An Empirical Typology of International Military Alliances', *Midwest Journal of Political Science*, vol. 15, 1971, 262–289.

Russett, B.M. and Oneal, J.R. *Triangulating Peace: Democracy, Interdependence, and International Organizations*, New York: W.W. Norton and Company, 2001.

Russia, *Environmental Security of Russia*, issue 2, the Security Council of the Russian Federation, Moscow, 13 October 1994.

Russia, *The Foreign Policy Concept of the Russian Federation*, Moscow: Ministry of Foreign Affairs, 12 February 2013.

Russian Government, *Fundamentals of Russian State Policy in the Arctic up to 2020 and Beyond*, Moscow, 2009.

Sagan, S. and Waltz, K. *The Spread of Nuclear Weapons: A Debate Renewed* (2nd ed.), New York: Norton, 2002.

Sagan, S.D. 'The Perils of Proliferation: Organisation Theory, Deterrence Theory, and the Spread of Nuclear Weapons', *International Security*, Spring, vol. 4, 1994, 66–107.

Saikal, A. 'The Iran Nuclear Dispute', *Australian Journal of International Affairs*, vol. 60, no. 2, 2006, 193–199.

Sakwa, R. 'New Cold War or Twenty Years Crisis? Russia and International Relations', *International Affairs*, vol. 84, no. 2, 2008, 241–267.

Sanchez, S., Swaminathan, M.S., Dobie, P. and Yuksel, N. *Halving Hunger. It Can be Done*, UN Millennium Project Task Force on Hunger, London: Earthscan, 2005.

Sarkees, M.R. 'The COW Typology of War: Defining and Categorizing War', www.correlatesofwar. org/COW2%20Data/WarData_NEW/COW%20Website%20-%20Typology%20of%20war. pdf, 2010 (Accessed 28.6.2014).

Scahill, J. *Blackwater: The Rise of the World's Most Powerful Mercenary Army*, New York: Nation Books, 2007.

Schlosser, E. *Command and Control: Nuclear Weapons, the Damascus Accident, and the Illusion of Safety*, London: Penguin Press, 2013.

Schmid, A. and Jongman, A. *Political Terrorism: A New Guide to Actors, Authors, Concepts, Databases, Theories and Literature*, New Brunswick, NJ: Transaction Press, 2005.

Schwartz, M. and Church, J. 'Department of Defense's Use of Contractors to Support Military Operations: Background, Analysis, and Issues for Congress', Congressional Research Service, www.fas.org/sgp/crs/natsec/R43074.pdf, 2013 (Accessed 28.6.2014).

Scot, L. 'Secret Intelligence, Covert Action and Clandestine Diplomacy', *Intelligence and National Security*, vol. 19, no. 2, 2004, 322–334.

Seale, P., Shellenberger, S. and Spence, J. 'Alcohol Problems in Alaska Natives: Lessons from the Inuit', *American Indian and Alaska Native Mental Health Research: The Journal of the National Center*, vol. 13, no. 1, 2006, 1–31.

Sen, A. 'Democracy as a Universal Value', *Journal of Democracy*, vol. 10, no. 3, 1999, 3–17.

Shafer, J. 'Live and Let Live: State Secrets in the Snowden Era', *Foreign Affairs*, vol. 93, no. 2, 2014, 136–142.

Shah, P.Z. 'My Drone War', *Foreign Policy*, March/April, 2012, 56–62.

Shankar Jha, P. *The Twilight of the Nation State: Globalisation, Chaos and War*, London: Pluto Press, 2006.

Sharma, S. 'Assessing Diet and Lifestyle in the Canadian Arctic Inuit and Inuvialuit to Inform a Nutrition and Physical Activity Intervention Programme', *Journal of Human Nutrition and Dietetics*, vol. 23, special supplement, 7 September 2010, 5–17.

Shaw, M. *International Law* (5th Ed.), Cambridge: Cambridge University Press, 2002.

Shepherd, L.J. (ed.) *Gender Matters in Global Politics: A Feminist Introduction to International Relations*, London: Routledge, 2010.

Shepherd, L.J. 'The State of Feminist Security Studies: Continuing the Conversation', *International Studies Perspectives*, vol. 14, 2013, 436–439.

Sheptycki, J. 'Global Law Enforcement: A Protection Racket', in A. Edwards and P. Gill (eds) *Transnational Organized Crime: Perspectives on Global Security*, London and New York: Routledge, 2003, 42–58.

Shindler, C. *A History of Modern Israel*, Cambridge: Cambridge University Press, 2008.

Shlapentokh, V. 'Perceptions of a Threat to the Regime as a Major Factor of Russian Foreign Policy', *Johnson's Russia List*, 2007, available at http:www.cdi.org/Russia/Johnson (Accessed 13.5.2013).

Shlapentokh, V., Woods, J. and Shiraev, E. (eds) *America. Sovereign Defender or Cowboy Nation?* Aldershot, UK and Burlington, VT: Ashgate, 2005.

Shulsky, A. (revised by Schmitt, G.) *Silent Warfare: Understanding the World of Intelligence*, 3rd ed., Washington DC: Brassey's, 2002.

Shupe, A. 'The Stubborn Persistence of Religion in the Global Arena', in E. Sahliyeh (ed.) *Religious Resurgence and Politics in the Contemporary World*, Albany: State University of New York Press, 1990, 17–26.

Simon, S. and Martini, J. 'Terrorism: Denying Al-Qaeda Its Popular Support', *The Washington Quarterly*, vol. 28, no. 1, Winter 2004–05, 131–145.

Singer, P. *Corporate Warriors: The Rise of the Privatized Military Industry*, Ithaca, NY: Cornell University Press, 2003.

Sjoberg, L. (ed.) *Gender and International Security*, London: Routledge, 2010.

Sledge, M. 'The Toll of 5 Years of Drone Strikes: 2,400 Dead', *Huffington Post*, www.huffingtonpost.com/2014/01/23/obama-drone-program-anniversary_n_4654825.html, 23 January 2014 (Accessed 28.6.2014).

Small Arms Survey 2002: Counting the Human Cost, Oxford: Oxford University Press, 2002.

Small Arms Survey 2007: Guns and the City, Geneva: SAS, 2007.

Small Arms Survey, 'Weapons and Markets', www.smallarmssurvey.org/weapons-and-markets.html, 2014 (Accessed 28.6.2014).

Smith, B. 'Poison Pen', www.nrapublications.org/index.php/16708/poison-pen/, 2013 (Accessed 28.6.2014).

Smith, D.E. *Religion and Political Development*, Boston, MA: Little Brown, 1970.

Smith, K. *Environmental Hazards. Assessing Risk and Reducing Disaster*, London and New York: Routledge, 2001.

Smith, K. and Petley, D. *Environmental Hazards. Assessing Risk and Reducing Disaster*, 5th edn, London and New York: Routledge, 2009.

Smith, S. 'The End of the Unipolar Moment? September 11th and the Future of World Order', *International Relations*, vol. 16, no. 2, 2002, 171–183.

Smith, S. 'The Contested Concept of Security', in K. Booth (ed.), *Critical Security Studies and World Politics*, Boulder, CO: Lynne Rienner, 2005.

Sobek, D. *The Causes of War*, Cambridge: Polity Press, 2009.

Soderbaum, F. 'Introduction: Theories of New Regionalism', in F. Soderbaum and T. Shaw (eds) *Theories of New Regionalism. A Palgrave Reader*, London: Palgrave, 2003.

Sokolski, H. and Ludes, J. *Twenty-First Century Weapons Proliferation: Are We Ready?* London: Frank Cass, 2001.

Sopoanga, S. 'Statement by Tuvalu', Johannesburg: World Summit on Sustainable Development, 2 September 2002.

Sprout, H. and Sprout, M. *Toward a Politics of the Planet Earth*, New York: Van Nostrand Reinhold, 1971.

Stark, H. 'Mossad's Miracle Weapon: Stuxnet Virus Opens a New Era of Cyber War', *Speigel On Line*, 8 August 2011, www.speigel.de/international/world/mossad-s-miracle-weapon-stuxnet-virus-opens-new-era-of-cyber-war-a-778912-druck.html (Accessed 1.5.2014).

Starr, J. 'Water Wars', *Foreign Policy*, vol. 82, Spring 1991, 17–36.

Steans, J. *Gender and International Relations*, Cambridge: Polity, 2013.

Stepan, A. 'Religion, Democracy, and the "Twin Tolerations"', *Journal of Democracy*, vol. 11, no. 4, 2000, 37–57.

Stern, J. *The Ultimate Terrorists*, Cambridge, MA: Harvard University Press, 1999.

Stern, J. 'Mind Over Martyr: How to Deradicalize Islamic Extremists', *Foreign Affairs*, January/February, 2010, 95–108.

Stern, N. *The Economics of Climate Change – the Stern Review*, Cambridge: Cambridge University Press, 2006.

Stiglitz, J. *Globalization and its Discontents*, New York and London: Norton, 2002.

Stiglitz, J. *Making Globalization Work*, London: Allen Lane, 2006.

Stockholm International Peace Research Institute (SIPRI), *SIPRI Yearbook 2012: Armaments, Disarmament and International Security*, Oxford: Oxford University Press, 2012.

Stohl, R. and Grillot, S. *The International Arms Trade*, Cambridge: Polity Press, 2009.

Store, J. and Lavrov, S. *Joint Communique*, Globe and Mail, 2010.

Strauss, S, 'Wars do end! Changing Patterns of Political Violence in sub-Saharan Africa', *African Affairs*, March 2012, 1–23.

Strindberg, A. and Wärn, M. *Islamism. Religion, Radicalism and Resistance*, Cambridge: Polity, 2011.

Sukhdev, P. *Economics of Ecosystems and Biodiversity-TEEB*, Germany: Helmholz Association, 2008.

Svetlichnaja, J. and Heartfield, J. 'Sovereign Democracy: Dictatorship over Capitalism in Contemporary Russia', *Radical Philosophy*, vol. 159, Jan/Feb 2010, 38–43.

Swiss Re, 'Natural and man-made catastrophes in 2011', Sigma study 2/2012, 2012.

Sylvester, C. 'Tensions in Feminist Security Studies', *Security Dialogue*, vol. 41, 2010, 607.

Synder, G. *Alliance Politics*, Ithaca, NY: Cornell University Press, 1997.

Takala, J. *Introductory Report: Decent Work, Safe Work*, XVI World Congress on Safety and Health at Work, Vienna, 27 May 2002.

Talmadge, C. 'Deterring a Nuclear 9/11', *The Washington Quarterly*, Spring 2007, 21–34.

Tatham, C. and McCleary, R. 'Just Cause? The 1989 US Invasion of Panama', in R. McCleary (ed.) *Seeking Justice. Ethics and International Affairs*, Boulder, CO and Oxford: Westview Press, 1992.

Tavares, R. *Security in South America: The Role of States and Regional Organisations*, London: Eurospan, 2014.

Tenenbaum, D. 'POPs in Polar Bears: Organochlorines Affect Bone Density', *Environmental Health Perspectives*, vol. 112, no. 17, 2004, A1011.

Theis,W.J. *Why NATO Endures*, Cambridge: Cambridge University Press, 2009.

Thomas, S. *The Global Transformation of Religion and the Transformation of International Relations. The Struggle for the Soul of the Twenty-First Century*, New York and Basingstoke: Palgrave Macmillan, 2005.

Thompson, W.S. 'The Communist International System', *Orbis*, vol. 20, no. 4, 1977, 841–856.

Tickner, J.A. *Gender in International Relations: Feminist Perspectives in Achieving Global Security*, New York: Columbia University Press, 1992.

Tickner, J.A. 'Feminist Responses to International Security Studies', *Peace Review: A Journal of Social Justice*, vol. 16, no. 1, 2004, 43–48.

Transparency International, *Government Defence Anti-Corruption Index 2013*, http://government. defenceindex.org/sites/default/files/documents/GI-main-report.pdf, 2013 (Accessed 28.6.2014).

Trenberth, K. 'El Nino and Global Warming', *Journal of Marine Education*, vol. 15, no. 2, 1998, 12–18.

Trenin, D. *The End of Eurasia: Russia on the Border between Geopolitics and Globalization*, Washington DC: Brooking International Press, 2002.

Trenin, D. 'Russia Leaves the West', *Foreign Affairs*, vol. 85, no. 4, July/August 2006, 87–96.

True, J. *The Political Economy of Violence Against Women*, Oxford: Oxford University Press, 2012.

Tsygankov, A. 'Mastering Space in Eurasia: Russia's Geopolitical Thinking after the Soviet break-up', *Communist and Post Communist Studies*, vol. 36, 2003, 101–127.

Tsygankov, A. 'Finding a Civilizational Idea: "West", "Eurasia", and "Euro-East" in Russian Foreign Policy', *Geopolitics*, vol. 12, no. 3, 2007, 375–399.

UK FCO, 'Cyber Crime', *Global Issues*, www.fco.gov.uk/en/global-issues/cyber-space/, 2011 (Accessed 25.6.2011).

Ullman, R. 'Redefining Security', *International Security*, vol. 8, no. 1, Summer, 1983, 129–153.

UN, www.unifem.org/gender_issues/violence_against_women/facts_figures.html, nd (Accessed 20.4.2014).

UN, 'Secretary-General Salutes International Workshop on Human Security in Mongolia', two-day Session in Ulaanbaatar, May 8–10, 2000. Press Release SG/SM/7382.

UN, *United Nations Convention Against Transnational Organized Crime* www.unodc.org/unodc/en/treaties/CTOC/, 2000.

UN, *A More Secure World. Our Shared Responsibility,* United Nations Secretary-General's High-Level Panel on Threats, Challenges, and Change, New York, 2004.

UN, *Small Arms Review. International Small Arms Survey,* 2006.

UN, 'A New Global Partnership: Eradicate Poverty and Transform Societies Through Sustainable Development', *Report of the UN High Level Panel of Eminent Persons on the Post 2015 Development Agenda,* New York: United Nations, 2013.

UN, 'Peacekeeping', www.un.org/en/peacekeeping/operations/, 2014 (Accessed 28.6.2014).

UNAIDS, *World AIDS Day Report. How to Get to Zero Faster, Smarter, Better,* Geneva, UNAIDS, 2011.

UNDP *Human Development Report. People's Participation,* Oxford: Oxford University Press, 1993.

UNDP, *Human Development Report 1994,* Oxford: Oxford University Press, 1994.

UNDP, *Human Development Report. Globalization with a Human Face,* Oxford: Oxford University Press, 1999.

UNDP, *Humanity Divided: Confronting Inequality in Developing Countries,* www.undp.org/content/undp/en/home/librarypage/poverty-reduction/humanity-divided--confronting-inequality-in-developing-countries.html, 2014 (Accessed 28.6.2014).

UN Economic Commission for Africa (UNECA), *Assessing Progress in Africa Towards the Millennium Development Goals 2013. Food Security in Africa: Issues, Challenges and Lessons,* Geneva: UN, 2013.

UNEP, *GEO 3: Global Environmental Outlook,* http://geo.unep-wcmc.org/geo3/ 2002 (Accessed 3.10.2002).

UNEP (2012) South Sudan Joins Montreal Protocol, http://www.unep.org/Documents. Multilingual/Default.asp?DocumentID=2666&ArticleID=9010&l=en (Accessed 12.5.2013).

UN General Assembly, 'In Larger Freedom: Towards Development, Security and Human Rights For All', *Report of the Secretary-General,* A/59/2005, 21 March 2005.

UN General Assembly, 'Resolution 60/1. 2005 World Summit Outcome', www.unrol.org/files/2005%20World%20Summit%20Outcome.pdf, 2005 (Accessed 28.6.2014).

UNGA and UNSC, *A Regional-Global Security Partnership: Challenges and Opportunities,* Report of the Secretary-General, 28 July 28 A/61/204–S/2006/590, 2006.

UN-Habitat, *The Challenge of Slums. Global Report on Human Settlements,* London: Earthscan, 2003.

UN High-Level Panel on Threats, Challenges and Change, *A More Secure World: Our Shared Responsibility,* www.un.org/en/peacebuilding/pdf/historical/hlp_more_secure_world.pdf, 2004 (Accessed 28.6.2014).

UN Security Council, 'Resolution 1973', http://daccess-dds-ny.un.org/doc/UNDOC/GEN/N11/268/39/PDF/N1126839.pdf, 2011 (Accessed 28.6.2014).

Ungar, M. *Policing Democracy: Overcoming Obstacles to Citizen Security in Latin America,* Baltimore: John Hopkins University Press, 2011.

United States Geological Society *Survey of Undiscovered Oil and Gas in the Arctic,* 2008.

University of North Dakota *Volcano World* http://volcano.und.nodak.edu/vwdocs/volc_images/southeast_asia/indonesia/tambora.html (Accessed 3.10.2002).

UNODC, *World Drug Report,* Vienna: UN Office for Drugs and Crime, 2005.

UNODC, *World Drug Report,* Vienna: UN Office for Drugs and Crime, 2007.

UNODC, *The Globalization of Crime. A Transnational Organized Crime Threat Assessment,* Vienna: UN Office for Drugs and Crime, 2010.

UNODC, *Global Study on Homicide. Trends, Context Data,* Vienna: UN Office for Drugs and Crime, 2011a.

UNODC, *Overview of Global and Regional Drug Trends and Patterns,* Vienna: UN Office for Drugs and Crime, 2011b.

United Nations Security Council, Resolution 1308, 17 July 2000, S/RES 1308.

UNSC, Letter dated 5 April 2007 from the Permanent Representative of the United Kingdom of Great Britain and Northern Ireland to the United Nations, addressed to the President of the Security Council, 5 April S/2007/186, 2007.

Uppsala/PRIO, *Armed Conflict Dataset*, www.prio.no/Data/Armed-Conflict/UCDP-PRIO/2010 (Accessed 3.6.2013).

Upton, M. 'Global Health Trumps the Nation-State', *World Policy Journal*, Fall, 2004, 73–78.

US, *Trafficking in Persons Report*, Washington DC: State Department, 2011.

US Government, *Homeland Security Directive on Arctic Regional Policy*, 2009.

USA, *National Security Strategy Document*, Washington DC, 1994.

Usher, M. with Callaghan, T.V., Gilchrist, G., Heal, B., Juday, G.P., Leong, H., Muir, M.A.K. and Prestrud, P. 'Human Impacts on the Biodiversity of the Arctic', *Encyclopedia of the Earth*, 2010, http://www.eoearth.org/article/Human_impacts_on_the_biodiversity_of_the_Arctic (Accessed 15.12.10).

Uvin, P. *The International Organization of Hunger*, London and New York: Kegan Paul, 1994.

Valentino, B. 'The True Cost of Humanitarian Intervention', *Foreign Affairs*, November/December, 2011, 60–73.

van Creveld, M. *The Transformation of War: The Most Radical Reinterpretation of Armed Conflict Since Clausewitz*, New York: Free Press, 1991.

Vinokurov, E. and Libman, A. *Eurasian Integration: Challenges of Transcontinental Regionalism*, Basingstoke: Palgrave Macmillan, 2012.

Wadley, J.D. 'Gendering the State', in L. Sjoberg (ed.) *Gender and International Security*, London: Routledge, 2010, 39.

Waever, O. 'Securitization and Desecuritization', in Lipschutz, R. (ed.) *On Security*, New York: Columbia University Press, 1998, 46–86.

Wallander, C. and Keohane, R. *Imperfect Unions: Security Institutions over Time and Space*, Oxford: Oxford University Press, 1999.

Wallander, C. 'Institutional Assets and Adaptability: NATO after the Cold War', *International Organization*, vol. 54, no. 4, 2000, 705–735.

Walt, S.M. *The Origins of Alliances*, New York: Cornell University Press, 1987.

Walt, S.M. 'The Renaissance of Security Studies', *International Studies Quarterly*, vol. 35, no. 2, June, 1991, 211–239.

Walt, S.M. 'Why Alliances Endure or Collapse', *Survival*, vol. 39, no. 1, 1997, 156–179.

Walt, S. 'The Ties that Fray: Why Europe and America are Drifting Apart', *The National Interest*, no. 54, Winter 1998–1999, available at http://nationalinterest.org/article/the-ties-that-fray-why-europe-and-america-are-drifting-apart-900 (Accessed 29.10.2014).

Walt, S.M. 'Delusion Points: Don't Fall for the Nostalgia – George W. Bush's Foreign Policy Really was that Bad', *Foreign Policy*, 8 November 2010, at www.foreign policy.com/articles/2010/11/08/delusion_points (Accessed on 8.7.2011).

Waltz, K. *Man, the State and War*, New York: Columbia University Press, 1959.

Waltz, K. *Theory of International Politics*, Reading, MA: Addison-Wesley, 1979.

Waltz, K. 'The Emerging International Structure of International Politics', *International Security*, vol. 18, no. 2, 1993, 44–79.

Waltz, K. 'Globalization and American Power', *National Interest*, vol. 59, 2000, 46–57.

Waltz, K. 'Structural Realism After the Cold War', *International Security*, vol. 25, no. 1, Summer 2000, 5–41.

Waltz, K. *Man, the State, and War: A Theoretical Analysis*, rev. ed., New York: Columbia University Press, 2001.

Waltz, K. 'Why Iran Should Get the Bomb. Nuclear Balancing Would Mean Stability', *Foreign Affairs*, vol. 91, no. 4, July/August, 2012, 2–5.

Warner, M. 'Wanted: A Definition of Intelligence', *Studies in Intelligence*, vol. 46, no. 3, 2002, 15–23.

WCO, 'About Us', www.wcoomd.org/home_about_us.htm, 2006 (Accessed 22.11.2006).

Weber, M. *From Max Weber*, trans. and ed. H.H. Gerth and C. Wright Mills, London: Routledge and Kegan Paul, [1921] 1991.

Weber, M. *Gesammelte Aufsatze zur Wissenschaftslehre*, Tubingen: Mohr, 1997.

Weigel, G. *Witness to Hope: The Biography of Pope John Paul II, 1920–2005*, New York: HarperCollins, 2005.

Weigel, G. *Faith, Reason, and the War Against Jihadism: A Call to Action*, New York: Doubleday, 2007.

Weiss, T.G. and Daws, S. (eds) *The Oxford Handbook on the United Nations*, Oxford: Oxford University Press, 2007.

Weiss, T.G, Forsythe, D.P., Coate, R.A. and Pease, K.-K. *The United Nations and Changing World Politics*, 6th ed., Boulder, CO: Westview Press, 2010.

Weitsman, P. *Dangerous Alliances: Proponents of Peace and Weapons of War*, Redwood City, CA: Stanford University Press, 2004.

Wendt, A. 'Anarchy Is What States Make of It: The Social Construction of Power Politics', *International Organization*, vol. 46, no. 2, Spring 1992, 391–425.

Wendt, A. 'Constructing International Politics', *International Security*, vol. 20, no. 1, Summer 1995, 71–81.

WER, *World Ecology Report: Desertification, its Effects on Land and People*, vol. 21, no. 1, 2009.

Wesley, M. 'It's Time to Scrap the NPT', *Australian Journal of International Affairs*, vol. 59, no. 3, September 2005, 283–299.

Western, J. and Goldstein, J. 'Humanitarian Intervention comes of Age', *Foreign Affairs*, November/December, 2011, 48–59.

WFP, 'Hunger', wwwwfp.org/hunger/stats, 2009 (Accessed 28.6.2009).

White, P. 'TB Once Again Stalking the Arctic', *Globe and Mail*, 12 December 2010.

Whiteneck, D. 'Deterring Terrorists: Thoughts on a Framework', *The Washington Quarterly*, Summer 2005, 187–199.

Whittow, J. *The Penguin Dictionary of Physical Geography*, London: Penguin, 1984.

WHO, *World Health Report*. Part 1, 'Health and Development in the Twentieth Century', Geneva: WHO, 1999.

WHO, *World Report on Road Traffic Injury Prevention*, Geneva: World Health Organization, 2004.

WHO, *Global Burden of Disease 2008*, Geneva: World Health Organization, 2009.

WHO, *The Burden of Health Care Associate Infections Worldwide*, Geneva: World Health Organization, 2010.

WHO, *Global Burden of Disease 2008*, Geneva: World Health Organization, 2011.

WHO, *10 Facts on Malaria*, www.who.int/features/factfiles/malaria/en/, 2013 (Accessed 11.2.2014).

Wilkinson, C. 'The Copenhagen School on Tour in Kyrgyzstan: Is Securitization Theory Useable Outside Europe?', *Security Dialogue*, vol. 38, no. 1, 2007, 5–25.

Wilkinson, P. *Terrorism versus Democracy: The Liberal State Response*, 2nd ed., Abingdon: Routledge, 2006.

Williams, M. 'What is the National Interest? The Neoconservative Challenge in I.R. Theory', *European Journal of International Relations*, vol. 11, no. 3, 2005, 307–337.

Williams, P. 'Transnational Criminal Networks', in J. Arquilla and D. Ronfeldt (eds), *Networks and Netwars: the Future of Terror, Crime and Militancy*, Santa Monica, CA: RAND, 2001, 61–97.

Williams, P. 'Strategy for a New World: Combating Terrorism and Transboundary Crime' in J. Baylis, J. Wirtz, E. Cohen and C.S. Gray (eds) *Strategy in the Contemporary World*, 2nd ed., Oxford: Oxford University Press, 2006, 192–208.

Williams, P. and Woesner, P. 'Gangs Go Nuclear', *World Today*, 7–9 December 2000.

Wilson, N. and Thomson, G. 'Deaths from International Terrorism compared with Road Crash Deaths in OECD Countries', *Injury Prevention*, vol. 11, 2005, 332–333.

Wisner, B. 'Disasters. What the United Nations and its World Can Do', *United Nations Chronicle (online edition)* XXXVIII, 4. www.un.org/Pubs/chronicle/2000/issue4/0400p6.htm2000 (Accessed 13.8.2002).

Woodhouse, T. and Ramsbotham, O. *Humanitarian Intervention in Contemporary Conflict: A Reconceptualization*, Cambridge: Polity, 1996.

Woodhouse, T. and Ramsbotham, O. (eds) *Peacekeeping and Conflict Resolution*, London: Frank Cass, 2000.

Woods, M. 'Reflections on Nuclear Optimism: Waltz, Burke and Proliferation', *Review of International Studies*, vol. 28, 2002, 163–189.

Woodward, B. *Bush at War: Inside the Bush White House*, London: Simon and Schuster, 2002.

Woollacott, M. 'Keeping our Faith in Belief', *The Guardian*, 23 December, 1995.

World Bank, *World Development Report 1993: Investing in Health*, New York: Oxford University Press, 1993.

World Bank, *World Development Report: Investing in Health*, Washington DC, 1993.

World Bank, 'The Sunken Billions', *World Bank Publications*, Washington DC: 2009.

World Bank, *Conflict, Security and Development. World Development Report 2011*, http://wdr2011.worldbank.org/fulltext 2011 (Accessed 4.1.2012).

World Bank, *GDP per capita ppp*, http://data.worldbank.org/indicator/NY.GDP.PCAP.PP.CD 2013 (Accessed 3.11.2013).

World Economic Forum, *The Global Gender Gap Report 2013*, www3.weforum.org/docs/WEF_GenderGap_Report_2013.pdf (Accessed 15.7.2014).

World Food Programme, *Mission Statement*, Rome: WFP, 2002a.

World Food Programme, *WFP in 2000: A Quick Glance*, Rome: WFP www.wfp.org/aboutwfp/facts/2000.html, 2002b (Accessed 5.4.2002).

World Food Programme, *WFP Management Plan 2012-14*, Rome: WFP, 2011.

World Health Organization, *Global and Regional Estimates of Violence Against Women: Prevalence and Health Effects of Intimate Partner Violence and non-partner Sexual Violence*, Geneva: WHO, 2013.

Young, O. 'The Future of the Arctic: Cauldron of Conflict or Zone of Peace? (Review Article)', *International Affairs*, vol. 87, no. 1, 2011, 185–193.

Youngs, G. 'Feminist International Relations: A Contradiction in Terms? Or: Why Women and Gender are Essential to Understanding the World we Live in', *International Affairs*, vol. 80, no. 1, 2004, 75–87.

Zakaria, F. *The Post-America World*, New York: W.W. Norton and Company, 2009.

Index